Oxford Archaeological Guides
General Editor: Barry Cunliffe

The Holy Land

Jerome Murphy-O'Connor is Professor of New Testament at the École Biblique et Archéologique Française, Jerusalem, and author of *Paul: A Critical Life* (1996).

Barry Cunliffe is Professor of European Archaeology at the University of Oxford. The author of over forty books, including *The Oxford Illustrated Prehistory of Europe* and *The Ancient Celts*, he has served as President of the Council for British Archaeology and the Society of Antiquaries, and is currently a member of the Ancient Monuments Board of English Heritage.

'Always respectful, yet never gullible or preachy, Father Murphy-O'Connor's *The Holy Land* is by far the best popular guide to its subject ever written. Every entry bears the indelible mark of having been written by someone who knows the place it describes, and has seen it with an expert intelligence and an open mind. In short, it's that rare thing, an excellent, up-to-date, well-written guide book.'
JOHN ROMER

'a brilliant accomplishment, packed with authentative information . . . the one book you must bring with you when you visit Israel.'
WALTER ZANGER

Oxford Archaeological Guides

The Holy Land

An Oxford Archaeological Guide
from Earliest Times to 1700

Jerome Murphy-O'Connor, OP
École Biblique et Archéologique Française, Jerusalem

FOURTH EDITION
Revised and expanded

OXFORD
UNIVERSITY PRESS

OXFORD

UNIVERSITY PRESS

Great Clarendon Street, Oxford OX2 6DP

Oxford New York

Athens Auckland Bangkok Bogotá Buenos Aires Calcutta
Cape Town Chennai Dar es Salaam Delhi Florence Hong Kong Istanbul
Karachi Kuala Lumpur Madrid Melbourne Mexico City Mumbai
Nairobi Paris São Paulo Singapore Taipei Tokyo Toronto Warsaw
and associated companies in Berlin Ibadan

Oxford is a trade mark of Oxford University Press

© Jerome Murphy-O'Connor, OP,
1980, 1986, 1992, 1998

First published 1980
Second edition 1986
Third edition, revised and expanded 1992
Fourth edition, revised and published as an Oxford Archaeological Guide 1998

British Library Cataloguing in Publication Data
Data available

Library of Congress Cataloging in Publication Data
Murphy-O'Connor, J. (Jerome), 1935–
The Holy Land: an Oxford archaeological guide: from earliest
times to 1700 / Jerome Murphy-O'Connor. — 4th edn., rev. and expanded.
p. cm. — (Oxford archaeological guides)
Includes bibliographical references and index.
1. Palestine—Antiquities—Guidebooks. 2. Palestine—Guidebooks.
3. Excavations (Archaeology)—Palestine—Guidebooks. I. Title II. Series.
DS111.M88 1998   915.69404'54—dc21   97–11120
ISBN 0-19-288013-6

5 7 9 10 8 6 4

Designed by First Edition, London
Typeset by Best-set Typesetter Ltd., Hong Kong
Printed in Spain by Book Print

Series Editor's Foreword

Travelling for pleasure, whether for curiosity, nostalgia, religious conviction, or simply to satisfy an inherent need to learn, has been an essential part of the human condition for centuries. Chaucer's 'Wife of Bath' ranged wide, visiting Jerusalem three times as well as Santiago de Compostela, Rome, Cologne, and Boulogne. Her motivation, like that of so many medieval travellers, was primarily to visit holy places. Later, as the Grand Tour took a hold in the eighteenth century, piety was replaced by the need felt by the élite to educate its young, to compensate for the disgracefully inadequate training offered at that time by Oxford and Cambridge. The levelling effect of the Napoleonic Wars changed all that and in the age of the steamship and the railway mass tourism was born when Mr Thomas Cook first offered 'A Great Circular Tour of the Continent'.

There have been guidebooks as long as there have been travellers. Though not intended as such, the *Histories* of Herodotus would have been an indispensable companion to a wandering Greek. Centuries later Pausanias' guide to the monuments of Greece was widely used by travelling Romans intent on discovering the roots of their civilization. In the eighteenth century travel books took on a more practical form offering a torrent of useful advice, from dealing with recalcitrant foreign innkeepers to taking a plentiful supply of oil of lavender to ward off bedbugs. But it was the incomparable 'Baedekers' that gave enlightenment and reassurance to the increasing tide of enquiring tourists who flooded the Continent in the latter part of the nineteenth century. The battered but much-treasured red volumes may still sometimes be seen in use today, pored over on sites by those nostalgic for the gentle art of travel.

The needs and expectations of the enquiring traveller change rapidly and it would be impossible to meet them all within the compass of single volumes. With this in mind, the Oxford Archaeological Guides have been created to satisfy a particular and growing interest. Each volume provides lively and informed descriptions of a wide selection of archaeological sites chosen to display the cultural heritage of the country in question. Plans, designed to match the text, make it easy to grasp the full extent of the site while focusing on its essential aspects. The emphasis is, necessarily, on seeing, understanding, and above all enjoying the particular place. But archaeological sites are the creation of history and can only be fully appreciated against the *longue durée* of human achievement. To provide this, each book begins with a wide-ranging historical overview introducing the changing cultures of the country and the landscapes which formed them. Thus, while the Guides are primarily intended for the traveller they can be read with equal value at home.

Barry Cunliffe

Preface to Fourth Edition

This guidebook was OUP's first venture into this particular literary form. It has now become the flagship of a series of archaeological guides with a common format. The need to have all the illustrations redrawn in order to bring them into line with those of the other volumes opened the door to a significant improvement in the figures, and to a thorough revision of the text. The number of entirely new entries (six) is less than in the third edition, but one of them deals with 'Roman Roads'. I describe portions of six roads constructed by the Roman legions which are accessible and have easily recognizable features. They serve as the framework to integrate notes on a host of minor sites in their immediate vicinity. Nearly fifty other entries have been completely or partially rewritten in the light of more up-to-date information.

The really significant difference in this edition is the appearance of over seventy boxes, for which the credit is due to George Miller, my editor at OUP. These have permitted me to expand the guide as a mini-anthology of ancient texts. Not only do such documents illustrate the sort of material on which our historical knowledge is based, but their vividness and immediacy give a new dimension to the sites.

Once again I must express my gratitude to my colleague Marcel Beaudry for advice and assistance. I am also indebted to Bettina Muscheidt, Geoffrey Haley, Simon and Dilly Erskine Crum, and Per and Elizabeth Eklund, who made sure that I got to all the sites which I needed to check, and to Jean Michel de Tarragon for the photographs from the collection of the École Biblique.

I rededicate the guidebook to all the members past and present of the Sunday Group, which has just celebrated its Silver Jubilee. Of the founders only Val Vester and I remain in Jerusalem, but the wonderful qualities of those with whom we first sought out little-known sites in the desert remain constant in those who have taken their places.

Jerome Murphy-O'Connor, OP

Jerusalem,
May 1997

Contents

Part 2: A–Z Guide to the Land

Note

★★ Outstanding sites (see p. xix)
★ Highly recommended sites

The letter and number following a title are a grid reference to the 'Israel Touring Map' (see p. xviii)

List of Maps

Introduction

Scope of this Guide

The most useful guide-book caters to a specific interest. This guide focuses on the historical sites of the Holy Land and is designed to help the visitor find and appreciate the visible remains.

The history of the Holy Land is so long and so much archaeological work has been done that to attempt complete coverage would be self-defeating. A guide-book is not intended to be an encyclopaedia; it is a practical aid. A selection has to be made and three criteria have determined which sites (of many thousands) should be included: antiquity, accessibility, and intelligibility.

'Antiquity' covers everything from the beginning of human history in the Holy Land to AD 1700. The only justification for this limit is a legal definition: nothing created after 1700 is classified as an antiquity.

'Accessibility' normally means that one can drive to the entrance. Places at some distance from a tarmac road have been included if the site has a unique feature and if the walk to it is in itself interesting. To acquire the 'feel' of the Holy Land one should walk as much as possible. Some sites that would otherwise merit inclusion have been omitted because physical or political obstacles make access unusually difficult if not impossible.

'Intelligibility' is perhaps the most difficult criterion. In the context of this guide it means the presence of a coherent complex of remains; there must be something significant to *see*, and 'significant' is interpreted with the average seriously interested visitor in mind. Certain sites which have made very important contributions to our understanding of the history of the area have been omitted, either because they have been eroded to nothing or because they are such complicated mixtures of apparently unrelated elements that only a professional archaeologist could draw profit from visiting them.

How to use the Guide

The guide is divided into two parts, the City of Jerusalem and the Land, each being organized on different principles.

The City of Jerusalem

In this part the sites are grouped in areas (see the table of Contents) because Jerusalem and its vicinity will most naturally be explored in this way. Each section is accompanied by a detailed sketch-map showing the precise location of each site described. Where appropriate, the visit to particular sites is preceded by a general historical survey of the area in which they are found.

Two maps published by the Survey of Israel will be found useful. 'Jerusalem' (1 : 14,000) covers the entire urban area, and the larger-scale 'Jerusalem: The Old City' (1 : 2,500) shows every street in the walled city. They are available at virtually all bookshops and bookstands in addition to the offices of the Survey of Israel (1 Heshin St., Jerusalem; 1 Lincoln St., Tel Aviv; 28 Yafo Road, Haifa; Merkaz HaNegev Building 22, Beer Sheva). The map on p. 8 shows in outline that part of Jerusalem covered by the guide, marking only the main areas (as listed in the Contents) and a few other focal points to help visitors get their bearings.

To facilitate travel in Greater Jerusalem the Egged Bus Company publishes a map (available at its offices and in bookshops) with all the bus routes superimposed on the street-plan.

The Land

In this part sites scattered throughout the Holy Land are listed alphabetic-ally, to obviate the need for frequent reference to an index. A letter and a number appear in round brackets after the name of each site. These refer to the grid on the 'Israel Touring Map' (1 : 250,000). Published by the Survey of Israel and updated every two years, this map is extremely accur-ate and clear; with it one can find the way to any site. Those who intend to be a little more adventurous in their exploration are advised to buy the English overprint edition of the Israel 1 : 100,000 map; it comes in 23 sheets sold separately or as a neatly boxed set. Before buying these maps check the revision date in the bottom right-hand corner.

The spelling of place-names follows that of the 'Israel Touring Map'; this will sometimes differ from the version found on signposts or in other publications; e.g. *c* instead of *k*, *z* instead of *s*, *v* instead of *b*, or vice versa. As a general rule, if the names *sound* the same when read aloud, presume identity. The reason for such differences is that the English version is always a transliteration from Hebrew, Arabic, or Greek, and not all the various official bodies follow the same principles.

Types of entries

There are four categories of entries in the second part:

(1) *Entries on General Areas.* A general presentation of certain areas (e.g. Jericho, Golan, Sea of Galilee, Negev) has the double advantage of directing attention to interesting sites which might be ignored and of showing them as representative of different stages in the historical development of the area.

(2) *Entries on Individual Sites.* In each case a summary of the history of the site is followed by information for a detailed visit.

(3) *Entries on Specific Subjects.* Such entries (e.g. Crusades, Desert

Monasteries) provide the general information on a particular social phenomenon and direct the visitor to sites where it has left traces.

(4) *Entries on Social Groups.* These provide a survey of the history of particular groups (e.g. Essenes, Nabataeans, Philistines, Samaritans) which appear frequently in the presentation of a number of sites.

Starred sites

Exceptionally important and interesting sites have been awarded star points. Those sites which have two stars are unmissable, and those with one star are highly recommended.

Cross-references

Names in small capitals in the text indicate that more information is given under that entry or that it refers to a comparable feature.

Bibliography

Works on the history and the archaeology of the Holy Land are legion. The following selection is limited to primary sources which have an immediacy and impact that commentaries lack.

Archaeological sites

Over a hundred years' work on 367 sites has been conveniently summarized in the *New Encyclopaedia of Archaeological Excavations in the Holy Land* (4 vols.; Jerusalem: Israel Exploration Society, 1993) edited by E. Stern. Most of the articles are written by the archaeologists who dug the respective sites, and good photographs, plans, and bibliographies are included. This authoritative work is the source for the dates given in this guide.

Old Testament Period

The basic text is, of course, the Bible whose religious message is set in a well-defined historical and geographical context. Frequent references to the Old Testament have been provided because, when read on the site, they often provide the human dimension which brings the ruins to life.

Extra-biblical texts are equally illuminating. Rulers of the great states adjoining Palestine, whose armies marched through the country century after century, left detailed records of their battles and conquests. Petty kings of city states wrote to their overlords. Merchants noted their dealings. Schoolboys copied exercises. These documents have been published in *The Ancient Near East: An Anthology of Texts and Pictures* ed. J. B. Pritchard (Princeton University Press, 1958; reissued in two paperback volumes, 1975). Excellent indices make it easy to find the texts and pictures relevant to a particular site.

Josephus

Detailed information on places and people of the New Testament period is provided by the Jewish historian Flavius Josephus (AD 37–100). Born Joseph ben Matthias, he was made governor of Galilee at the beginning of the First Revolt (AD 66) but as soon as possible turned traitor and sided with the Romans. As an imperial pensioner he wrote four books: his auto-biography, an attack on anti-Semitism, and two historical works, *The Antiquities of the Jews* and *The Jewish War*. The former is dull and long-drawn-out because it covers the whole period from Creation to the outbreak of hostilities against Rome in AD 66. *The Jewish War*, though sometimes inaccurate and written with a clear pro-Roman bias, is always interesting because it concentrates on a much more limited period, 170 BC to AD 75. I have given references to it wherever possible. Available in a Penguin Classics translation, it is an intriguing guide to any Herodian monument and the best to certain sites (e.g. Masada); a detailed index ensures that it can be used for this purpose.

References to Josephus are given to book and paragraph. Thus *War* 5: 24 means paragraph 24 in Book 5 of *The Jewish War*. In the Penguin edition this system of reference appears in the inner top corner of each page.

Byzantine Pilgrims

The adoption of Christianity as the official religion of the Empire in the early C4 AD brought about the first tourist boom in the history of the Holy Land. Pilgrims came in increasing numbers until the Arab Conquest in the C7 created obstacles which eventually deterred all but the most persistent. Many of these visitors wrote accounts of their tour of the country and described the buildings they visited. These narratives have been presented by J. Wilkinson in two books which do not overlap, *Egeria's Travels to the Holy Land* (rev. edn., Warminster: Aris & Phillips; Jerusalem: Ariel, 1981) and *Jerusalem Pilgrims before the Crusades* (Jerusalem: Ariel, 1977); the translations of Byzantine authors in this guide are taken from these two volumes. The translator has made the narratives intelligible by providing numerous maps and plans, and the Gazetteer appended to *Jerusalem Pilgrims* condenses (and critically evaluates) all the Byzantine information regarding each site under its name.

Islamic Period

From the publication of Ibn Khurdadbih's *Book of Roads and Kingdoms* in AD 864, Arab authors wrote voluminously on the geography and history of the Holy Land, and often with great insight. Muqaddasi (C10), for example, described Jerusalem as 'a golden basin full of scorpions'. Twenty-four of these texts have been collected by Guy Le Strange, *Palestine under the Moslems: A Description of Syria and the Holy Land from A.D. 650 to*

1500 translated from the Works of the Mediaeval Arab Geographers (London: Watt for the Palestine Exploration Fund, 1890; repr. Beirut: Khayats, 1965). Basically the same ground is covered by A.-S. Marmardji, OP, who, however, cast his net a little more widely; his *Textes Géographiques Arabes sur la Palestine* (Paris: Gabalda, 1951) contains the accounts of thirty-one authors ranging from the C9 to the C18, which are arranged according to sites.

Medieval Period

In the Middle Ages the Holy Land again became a magnet for pilgrims, and was seen by eyes as diverse as those of abbots from Iceland and Russia, a king from Norway, and a Muslim from Sicily commissioned by a Norman. Their impressions have been collected and translated by J. Wilkinson with J. Hill and W. F. Ryan in *Jerusalem Pilgrimage 1099–1185* (London: Hakluyt Society, 1988). None of these accounts, however, are as detailed or as personal as the narratives of two other visitors, one a Spanish Jew, the other a German Dominican friar. Both ostensibly came on pilgrimage but they were men with a sharp eye for the unusual and possessed the ingenuity to satisfy their curiosity.

Benjamin of Tudela passed through the Holy Land in the course of a long journey throughout the Middle East between 1166 and 1171. His account has been translated by M. N. Adler, *The Itinerary of Benjamin of Tudela* (London: Oxford University Press, 1907). Friar Felix Fabri made two pilgrimages to the Holy Land, the first in 1480, the second three years later when he also managed to get to Mount Sinai. He wrote more than 1,500 pages about his experiences because he was in truth nine parts observant tourist to one part pious pilgrim. This mass of material has been condensed with grace and wit by H. F. M. Prescott in two books, *Jerusalem Journey* (London: Eyre and Spottiswoode, 1954), which appeared in the USA as *Friar Felix at Large* (New Haven: Yale University Press, 1960), and *Once to Sinai* (London: Eyre and Spottiswoode, 1957; New York: Macmillan, 1958).

Selections from the above-mentioned works, and from many others, are collected in a wonderful anthology by F. E. Peters, *Jerusalem: The Holy City in the Eyes of Chroniclers, Visitors, Pilgrims, and Prophets from the Days of Abraham to the Beginnings of Modern Times* (Princeton: Princeton University Press, 1985).

Modern Period

From the beginning of the C18 a new spirit begins to permeate writings about the Holy Land; the natural curiosity of the traveller gives way to critical inquiry, and scientific publications proliferate. For Jerusalem some order and control has been introduced by J. D. Purvis, *Jerusalem: The Holy City: A Bibliography* (Metuchen: American Theological Library Association; London: Scarecrow Press, i, 1988; ii, 1991).

The classic F.-M. Abel, *Géographie de la Palestine* (Paris: Gabalda, 1933 and 1938) is still valuable for its physical description of the country and the identification of ancient sites. More recent work is incorporated in Y. Karmon, *Israel: A Regional Geography* (London, 1971), and Y. Aharoni, *The Land of the Bible: A Historical Geography* (rev. edn., London: Burns & Oates; Philadelphia: Fortress, 1979). The latter collaborated with M. Avi-Yonah to produce *The Macmillan Bible Atlas* (rev. edn., London and New York, 1972) which illustrates the topography of all major biblical events. Accurate mapping, however, is to be found only in the *Student Map Manual: Historical Geography of the Bible Lands* (Jerusalem, 1979).

Practical Advice

Travel and lodging

Most countries have Israel Government Tourist Offices, normally located in the capital city or financial centre, and all major towns in Israel have Tourist Information Offices. These will supply up-to-date information regarding all modes of travel to and within the country as well as the location and prices of hotels, youth hostels, and camping sites. In the United Kingdom the address is 18 Great Marlborough St., London W1V 1AF (tel.: 0171–434–3651); in the USA, 800 Second Avenue, New York, NY 10017 (tel.: 212–499–5650), with additional offices in Chicago, Atlanta, Houston, Miami Beach, and Los Angeles; in Canada, 180 Bloor St. West, Toronto, Ont. M5S 2V6 (tel.: 416–964–3784).

Tourist Information Offices in Jerusalem are at 24 Ha-Melekh George (tel.: 02–675–4811); 34 Yaffo Road (02–628–2295). The Christian Information Centre in Jerusalem (tel.: 02–627–2692) is located inside Jaffa Gate facing the east entrance of the CITADEL; open: 8.30 a.m.–1 p.m.; closed Sunday.

Opening hours

Opening hours have been given for each site wherever possible, but these should be used with caution because local conditions may impose unforeseeable modifications. Religious feasts may mean that the site closes early or is not open at all. Sites under Jewish control close one hour earlier on Fridays and two hours earlier on the eve of major feasts and do not open at all on Yom Kippur. Admission to Christian sites is normally restricted on Sunday mornings and to Muslim sites on Fridays and at the times of prayer on other days. Some sites stay open longer in summer (April–September).

National Parks

Many of the sites treated in this book are in National Parks. They are marked by an asterisk (*). The entrance fee includes an explanatory leaflet with a detailed plan. For visitors who wish to visit a number of sites in a region it is more economical to get a card which permits access to all parks in a 14-day period (beginning on the date of the first entry) from the National Parks Authority (4 Rav Aluf Maklef Street, HaKirya, 61070 Tel Aviv; tel.: 03–695–2281; fax: 03–696–7634) or at certain sites.

Dress

Once pavement is left behind the ground is rough and stony; rubber soles (the thicker the better) are strongly recommended. Climatic conditions can vary considerably within a relatively small area; one can freeze in Jerusalem (750 m above sea-level) and swelter in Jericho (400 m below sea-level) only thirty minutes later. It is advisable to dress in layers that can be shed and replaced at will. Winter (December–March) in the hill country is usually cold and wet; a warm windcheater is essential. Some religious sites do not permit entry to those in shorts or sleeveless tops.

Desert areas

When visiting sites in desert areas basic safety precautions should be observed. Always take at least one canteen of water per person. Always tell someone where you are going and at what time you expect to return. Never go alone; always take an experienced companion. All the important trails in Galilee in the Judaean Desert, and in the hills north-west of Elat are marked with colours (between two white stripes) corresponding to those on special maps issued by the Society for the Protection of Nature in Israel (4 Hashfela St., Tel Aviv), but they can still be difficult to follow and you should not set out without a guide who knows the area. These maps are only in Hebrew on the scale of 1 : 50,000. The Society for the Protection of Nature also organizes desert hiking and driving trips; a brochure is available on request.

Export of antiquities

No object manufactured before 1700 can be taken out of Israel unless a written export permit has been obtained from the Department of Antiquities and Museums which is located in the Rockefeller Museum, Jerusalem: telephone 02–628–2251 for an appointment. Fakes greatly outnumber genuine articles in the antique shops and it is risky to buy without expert independent advice.

Acknowledgements

All that I know of the Holy Land rests on what I learned from two of my professors who later became colleagues and friends: Fr. Pierre Benoit, OP, introduced me to the City and the late François Lemoine, OP, to the Land. It is a pleasure to be able to acknowledge publicly all that I learned from them. I must also thank Fr. Benoit for his ready response to innumerable questions during the writing of this guide.

One's knowledge of history and archaeology tends to remain vague and ill-defined without the opportunity to communicate it. Hence, I am also conscious of a debt to three groups whose eager questions over a period of ten years have stimulated research and discovery: the United Nations Truce Supervision Organization, the students of the École Biblique et Archéologique Française, and the members of the Sunday Group. All deserve my gratitude but none more than the Sunday Group to whose members I dedicate this guide. They are friends of many different nationalities whose duties have now taken them to other parts of the world, but when they lived in the Holy Land their energy and enthusiasm for out-of-the-way places brought me to sites that I probably would never have explored otherwise.

Other friends have also made essential contributions and to them I express my deep gratitude: to John Wilkinson for suggesting my name when Oxford University Press recognized the need for a guide such as this; to Peter Janson-Smith my editor at OUP; to Alice Sancey who expended such care and patience on the drawings; to Étienne Nodet for his translations from modern Hebrew; to Rachel Lepeer for many photocopies; to Dominic Baldwin for classifying all my drafts; to Jim Poston, Michael Stark, and Michael Burgoyne for their advice and assistance; and finally to my brethren at the École Biblique who freed me from other duties so that the guide might be finished in a reasonable time.

Jerome Murphy-O'Connor, OP

Jerusalem,
March 1980

A Brief Historical Outline

Human history in Palestine extends over half a million years, and is more complicated than that of other regions because Palestine is a narrow land bridge between the vast land masses of Africa and Asia; peoples from north and south have moved back and forth across it continuously. The purpose of this outline is to highlight the salient features of the major historical periods.

The Stone Age 1,400,000–4500 BC

The oldest part of a human skeleton found in Palestine is dated to about 1.4 million years ago. People would then have lived by the shores of rivers and lakes which were numerous because the area received much more rain than it does today. Here pluvial and dry periods corresponded to the glacial and inter-glacial periods in Europe. Large animals abounded in the savannah-type landscape, and as the technique of making flint tools improved the hunters could move further from sources of this basic raw material in search of game. By the end of the Stone Age a good artisan could get 6 m of cutting edge from the kilo of flint that at the beginning produced only 10 cm of cutting edge.

Evidence of fire first appears about 200,000 BC, but the major revolution occurred between 10,000 and 8000 BC when the economy shifted from food-gathering to food-producing. The domestication of animals and the production of grain permitted nomads to settle, and this forced them to develop new skills and a new type of social organization: villages replaced camps, and pottery took the place of stone vessels.

The Copper and Bronze Ages 4500–1200 BC

The first settlements were near springs because the recession of the ice cap resulted in a much drier climate in Palestine. Trade in a new raw material, copper, lessened the isolation of the villages and fostered the spread of culture and ideas. Villages blessed with a strategic location on a trade route grew to fortified towns. Urban life facilitated the development of specialized skills; the potter's wheel was introduced and copper was combined with tin to produce a much harder metal, bronze. Evolution progressed much more quickly in the great river valleys of the Nile and Tigris–Euphrates. Empires grew up in Egypt and Mesopotamia while Palestine remained a mosaic of city-states.

Energetic pharaohs assumed control of the coastal plain of Palestine and had held it for several hundred years by the time (c.1800 BC) a group of nomads arrived from Mesopotamia led by Abraham. His tribe ranged freely in the mountains until famine forced them to migrate to the great granary of Egypt. The Israelites remained there until Moses led the Exodus *c*.1250 BC. While Joshua was carving out territory in the hill country, the Sea Peoples, repulsed by Egypt, installed themselves in the coastal plain, Philistia.

The Iron Age 1200–586 BC

The Philistines and the Canaanites had developed the use of iron and their chariotry controlled the plain and the wide valleys that penetrated into the mountains. The pressure they exercised eventually forced the Israelites to abandon their loose tribal system in favour of a centralized monarchy. The success of the first king, Saul, was limited, but David (1004–965 BC) made the new system work; he conquered a new capital, Jerusalem, and made it an effective political centre by installing there the Ark of the Covenant, the religious symbol to which all Jews gave allegiance.

Solomon (965–928 BC) consolidated the victories of his father but the price demanded—tight bureaucratic control and heavy taxes—proved too much for his people. On his death the northern portion of his realm seceded and became the kingdom of Israel in which bloody uprisings became the normal means of succession to the throne. In both Israel and the southern kingdom of Judah prophets cried out for purity of faith and condemned blatant social injustices.

In the C8 BC a reborn Assyria swept out across the Fertile Crescent subduing the Aramaean kingdoms of Syria which had frequently threatened the two Israelite states. Their turn was soon to come. After dismembering Israel in 721 BC, the Assyrians laid Judah under tribute and made themselves masters of Lower Egypt. As Assyria gradually weakened Babylon grew strong and by 600 BC controlled all Mesopotamia. Jerusalem fell in 586 BC and the people of Judah suffered the traumatic experience of the Exile.

The Persian Period 538–332 BC

The Jews were permitted to return to their homeland (538 BC) by Cyrus, king of Persia, whose army had taken Babylon the year before. Syria and Palestine became but one remote province of an empire that covered the whole of the Middle East. The Jews had to suffer the hostility of the Samaritans until a Jewish governor, Nehemiah, was appointed in the middle of the C5 BC. His political manœuvres achieved a quasi-independence, and the morale of the people was strengthened by the religious reform of Ezra.

The Hellenistic Period 332–63 BC

Alexander the Great brought the Persian Empire to an end in 331 BC, having campaigned in Palestine the previous year. After his death in 323 BC his generals carved up his short-lived empire: Ptolemy acquired

Egypt and Palestine while Syria and Babylon fell to the lot of Seleucus. Palestine became the battleground of these two dynasties, but the Ptolemies held it until 200 BC when it passed into the hands of the Seleucids.

Since the Exile the High Priest had been obliged to assume many of the functions previously discharged by the king. In order to guarantee their dominance the Seleucids had to control this office. Their nominees displaced the traditional Sadokite dynasty, but the extent of foreign influence, particularly in so far as it touched religion, eventually sparked off a revolt led by the three Maccabean brothers in 167 BC. What began as a struggle for religious freedom soon became a successful fight for political independence. The bloodline of the Maccabees evolved into the Hasmonean dynasty which extended Jewish dominance to the whole of Palestine, the Golan, and the east bank of the Jordan, almost the extent of the empire of David and Solomon.

The Roman Period 63 BC–AD 324

A strong Jewish state served the interests of Rome as a buffer against the Parthians, but when internecine struggles paralysed the Hasmoneans the Romans had to step in and take control in 63 BC. They preferred, however, to have a client state and when a strong Romanophile ruler emerged in the person of Herod the Great (37–4 BC) they gave him autonomy and, where possible, added new territories to his domain. Herod's sons lacked the qualities of their father, forcing the Romans to resume direct control in AD 6. Political authority was vested in a Procurator who resided in Caesarea.

The ministry of Jesus of Nazareth (AD 28–30), destined to have such tremendous consequences for the world, was at the time but one factor in an intense religious and political ferment which, under Roman mismanagement, exploded into the First Revolt in AD 66. In reprisal Titus and Vespasian laid waste the land. The destruction of the Temple in AD 70 precipitated a major shift within Judaism; sacrificial worship was no longer possible and the old priestly aristocracy ceded their primacy to legalists convinced that a scattered community could only be held together by obedience to a common law.

Jerusalem, however, remained central. When the emperor Hadrian proposed so many benefactions that for Jews it risked becoming a pagan city, the Second Revolt (AD 132–5) erupted. It was led by Bar Kokhba whom some considered to be the Messiah. With difficulty the Romans prevailed and Aelia Capitolina was built on the levelled ruins of Jerusalem. Excluded from Jerusalem and even Judaea, Jews began to move north, founding villages and building synagogues in Galilee and the Golan. Palestine became a backwater which the Romans did not disturb as long as taxes were paid.

The Byzantine Period AD 324–640

The shift from the Roman to the Byzantine Period does not imply a cultural change. The capital of the empire was simply transferred from Rome to the Greek city of Byzantium which was renamed Constantinople (AD 300). The political significance of this move was less important to Palestine than the decision of the emperor Constantine (AD 274–337) to legalize Christianity and to foster its development (AD 313). His consecration of the sites associated with Christ's birth, death-resurrection, and ascension, by the erection of great churches awakened interest in the Holy Places. Pilgrims flocked to the Holy Land, stimulating development in all spheres; churches sprang up everywhere and monasteries made the desert a city. Jerusalem grew again to the size it had been under Herod the Great.

Palestine, though rife with theological controversy, was troubled by serious violence only twice during these centuries, the Samaritan revolt in AD 529 and the Persian invasion in AD 614. Both were short-lived but proved extremely destructive.

The Early Arab Period AD 640–1099

Divided by internal intrigues and exhausted by the struggle against Persia, the Byzantine Empire could offer no resistance to the highly motivated cavalry who swept out of the Arabian desert inflamed by the new faith preached by Muhammad (AD 570–632). For Palestine the end came at the battle of the Yarmuk on 20 August 636. Two years later, after the conquest of Persia, the second caliph (successor of the Prophet) Omar (AD 634–44) accepted the surrender of Jerusalem.

Recognized as a Holy City because sacred to the two religions of the Book (Judaism and Christianity) regarded as the predecessors of Islam, Jerusalem became a centre of Muslim pilgrimage. It was protected and embellished by successive dynasties—Umayyad (661–750), Abbasid (750–974), and Fatimid (975–1171)—until 1009 when the mad caliph Hakim unleashed a savage persecution of Christians and many churches were destroyed.

Organized groups of pilgrims came regularly from Europe until the capture of Jerusalem by the Seljuk Turks in 1071. These refused to co-operate and the frustrated religious fervour of Europe expressed itself in overwhelming assent when Pope Urban II, in 1095, called for a crusade to liberate the Holy Places.

The Crusader Period AD 1099–1291

The scale of the enterprise meant that, once set in motion, it could not be halted, even though the Fatimids had retaken Jerusalem at the beginning of 1099. The Crusaders occupied the Holy City on 15 July 1099. Their first act was to massacre all the Muslim inhabitants. From such unthinking fanaticism was born the inflexibility of Islam. The memory of the massacre forever stood in the way of a permanent *modus vivendi*.

The first king, Baldwin I (1100–18), gave the new realm a solid territorial base. The feudal system which the Crusaders brought with them furnished an effective administration. Palestine was never so efficiently governed on the local level and full use was made of the alms which flowed from Europe. Castles, abbeys, and manor houses were surrounded by fertile fields.

Decisively defeated by Saladin at the Horns of Hattin in 1187, the Crusaders recovered parts of their former territories through treaties in the first part of the C13, but the castles and the fortifications of Jerusalem had been torn down. In 1250 the Bahri Mamluks of Cairo toppled the Ayyubid dynasty of Saladin and began a series of campaigns which culminated in the capture of the Crusader stronghold, Acre (Akko), in 1291.

The Mamluk Period AD 1250–1517

A continuous internal struggle for power in Egypt and the need to defend Syria against the Mongol hordes gave the Mamluks little leisure to occupy themselves with Palestine. Once again it became a backwater; the great currents of power ran elsewhere. Jerusalem became a political limbo to which out-of-favour emirs were banished. As a Holy City it continued to attract scholars and pilgrims. In order to serve the needs of Christian pilgrims the Franciscans returned to Jerusalem in 1335.

The Ottoman Period AD 1517–1918

The Ottoman Turks took Constantinople in 1453, and Egypt fell to them in 1517. The first two sultans were vigorously effective administrators. Suliman the Magnificent (1520–66) rebuilt the walls of Jerusalem. Then followed a series of incompetents whose minimal energy had to be concentrated on trying to keep in order the independent-minded Egyptian pashas. Palestine was left to fend for itself under the capricious authority of pashas whose only concern was to meet their tax quota and to have a little over for themselves. Lack of effective control promoted a sense of insecurity which expressed itself in apathy and a decline in population.

The Jews were the one community to grow during this period. Refugees from persecution in Europe and Russia found fragile stability in Palestine where outbursts of anti-Semitism occurred infrequently.

The Modern Period AD 1918–

The Turks sided with Germany in the First World War, and the victors dismembered their empire, Britain being given a mandate to govern Palestine in the name of the League of Nations. Able administration gave the country a modern infrastructure which facilitated rapid development.

Increased Jewish immigration led to racial strife which grew in intensity to the point where the British could no longer control the situation. They turned the problem over to the United Nations which, in 1947, recommended that Palestine be partitioned between Arab and Jew. Jewish acceptance was nullified by a flat rejection on the part of the Arabs. War broke out when the British withdrew on 14 May 1948. An armistice was accepted on 18 July 1948 leaving Jordan in possession of the West Bank and the Old City of Jerusalem and the new state of Israel in control of the western part of Jerusalem and the rest of the country. Israel was victorious in the war which erupted in June 1967 and since then has occupied the whole area between the River Jordan and the Mediterranean Sea.

Significant remains from the above periods are visible at the following sites:

Stone Age. Amud Caves, Carmel Caves, En Avdat, Ramat Hanadiv (Kebara Cave), Tel es-Sultan, Wadi Khareitun.

Copper Age. En Gedi.

Bronze Age. Aphek, Arad, Dor, Gezer, Hazor, Megiddo, Rujm el-Hiri, Tel Balata, Tel el-Farah.

Iron Age. Beer Sheva, Gezer, Hazor, Jerusalem (City of David; Jewish Quarter; Kidron Valley), Jib, Lakhish, Megiddo, Rosh Zayit, Shiloh, Tel Dan, Tel el-Farah, Timna.

Hellenistic Period. Bet Guvrin, Jerusalem (Citadel; City of David; St Anne's), Lakhish, Samaria, Tel er-Ras.

Roman Period. Ashqelon, Bet Shean, Bet Shearim, Bethar, Caesarea, Dor, En Farah, En Yael, Gamla, Hazan, Hazeva, Hebron, Herodion, Jerusalem (Citadel; Damascus Gate; Dominus Flevit; Ecce Homo Arch; St Anne's; Temple Mount; tombs in the New City), Khirbet Mird, Kypros, Maale Aqrabim, Mamre, Mamshit, Masada, Qasrin, Qumran, Ramat Hanediv, Roman Roads, Samaria, Sepphoris, Shivta, Solomon's Pools, Susita, Tel es-Samrat, Tulul Abu al-Alaiq.

Byzantine Period. Arbel, Ashqelon, Avdat, Bet Alpha, Bethlehem, Bet Shean, Caesarea, Capernaum, Chorozain, Dor, En el-Mamoudiyeh, En Farah, Eshtemoa, Gush Halav, Hammat Gader, Hammat Tiberias, Heptapegon, Jerusalem (Bethany; Dominus Flevit; Holy Sepulchre; Nea; St Anne's; St John the Baptist; Western Wall excavations), Khan el-Ahmar, Khirbet ed-Deir, Khirbet Mird, Khirbet Shema, Khirbet Suseya, Kursi, Latrun, Maon, Mar Saba, Mamshit, Meron, Meroth, Monasteries of St George and St Martyrius, Mount Gerizim, Mount Tabor, Nizzana, Qasrin, Ramat Hanediv, Shepherd's Fields, Shivta, Susita.

Early Arab Period. Khirbet al-Mafjar, Jerusalem (Dome of the Rock; Western Wall excavations), Ramla.

Crusader Period. Abu Ghosh, Akko, Ashqelon, Banyas, Belvoir, Caesarea,

En Afeq, En Hemed, Hebron, Hunin, Jerusalem (Bethany; Cathedral of St James; Holy Sepulchre; St Anne's, Virgin's Tomb), Latrun, Montfort, Nabi Samwil, Nimrud, Qubeiba, Samaria, Yehiam.

Mamluk Period. Jerusalem (Citadel; Haram esh-Sharif; Muslim Quarter), Nabi Musa.

Ottoman Period. Akko, Arbel, Jerusalem (Walls and Gates), Tiberias.

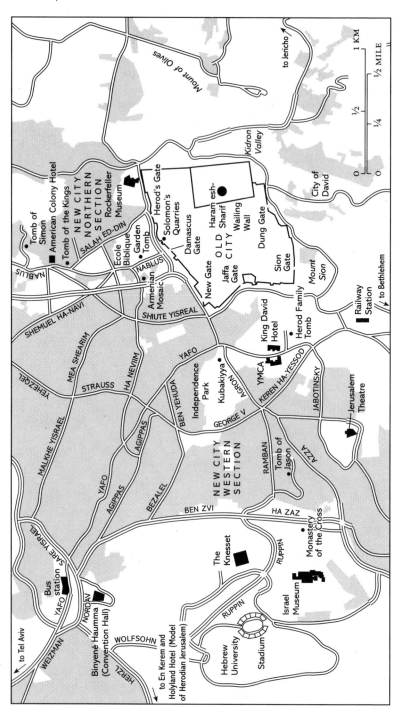

▲ **Map 1.** Jerusalem

Part 1

The City of Jerusalem

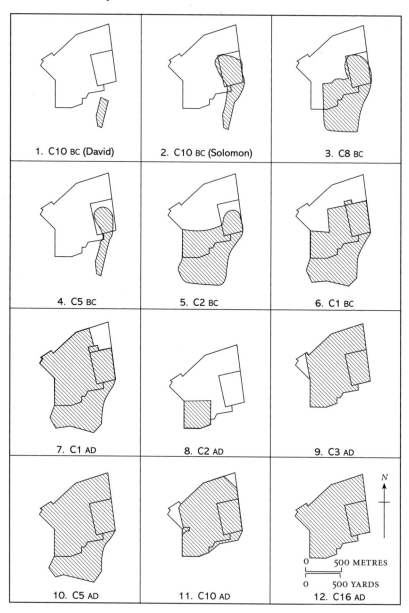

1. C10 BC (David)
2. C10 BC (Solomon)
3. C8 BC
4. C5 BC
5. C2 BC
6. C1 BC
7. C1 AD
8. C2 AD
9. C3 AD
10. C5 AD
11. C10 AD
12. C16 AD

N

0   500 METRES
0   500 YARDS

▲ **Fig. 1.** Jerusalem. The shaded areas overlaid on the present walled city represent the size of the city at different periods.

Walls and Gates

The walls of the Old City enclose without dominating, limit but do not define. The impression of strength is an illusion; the city is not a fortress and its walls are not a barrier but a veil. The visitor is drawn forward, challenged, and finally embraced. The city inspires passion, and the expansion and contraction of its walls (Fig. 1) show how it has struggled to accommodate the expectations it has aroused.

The city of David [**1**] was a small settlement on the eastern hill, close to the only spring and defended on two sides by deep valleys. By bringing the Ark of the Covenant within its walls, David made it the symbol of a religious ideal which transcended the petty jealousies of the twelve tribes of Israel. To underline this dimension his son Solomon (965–928 BC) built the first temple to enshrine the Ark. He had to extend the city, and the valleys gave him no choice but to move northwards along the ridge [**2**].

In subsequent centuries suffering caused the city first to expand and then to contract. The Assyrian invasion of the north in the latter part of the C8 BC sent refugees flooding towards Jerusalem. Failing to find space, many built outside the city wall to the west. They had to be protected when Sennacherib menaced the city in 701 BC, and a new wall was built to enclose the western hill [**3**], quadrupling the size of the city. This was the city devastated by the Babylonians in 586 BC. After its inhabitants returned from exile some 50 years later they were refused authority to rebuild the walls; it was accorded to Nehemiah (445–443 BC) but a greatly reduced population forced him to revert to a line which encompassed less than the city of Solomon [**4**].

Only after the Maccabean revolt in the first part of the C2 BC had restored Jewish independence did the city grow again. Under powerful Hasmonean kings, such as John Hyrcanus (134–104 BC) and Alexander Jannaeus (103–76 BC), it spread first to the west [**5**] and then to the north [**6**]. It was destined to grow further to the north, but the lines of the eastern and western walls have remained constant ever since.

Herod (37–4 BC), surprisingly, does not appear to have touched the walls; he concentrated his attention on buildings within the city. One of these, the Temple, naturally affected the eastern wall; it was replaced by one side of his great platform. According to Josephus (*War* 5: 147–55), Herod Agrippa I (AD 37–44) laid the foundations of a new north wall which was completed only during the First Revolt (AD 66–70), but his directions are so vague and the archaeological evidence so ambiguous that the exact trace of this famous 'Third Wall' continues to exercise scholars. It is most probable, however, that it followed the line of the present north wall [**7**]. After his victory in AD 70 Titus ordered the walls of Jerusalem to be razed, 'leaving only the loftiest of the towers, Phasael, Hippicus, and Mariamne, and the portion of the wall enclosing the city on the west; the latter as an encampment for the garrison that was to remain and the towers to indicate to posterity the nature of the city and the strong defences which had yet yielded to Roman prowess' (*War* 7: 1-2). The destruction begun by Titus was completed by Hadrian in AD 135. In his new city, Aelia Capitolina, only the camp of the Tenth Legion was walled [**8**]. A wall became necessary only when the Legion left at the end of the C3. The area it enclosed [**9**] was very close to that of the present Old City whose street plan (such as it is) is conditioned by the layout of Aelia; the main arteries are still the same.

The small city, deadened by the absence of Jews, who were forbidden to enter it, received a new lease of life when Christianity received the public support of the emperor in 313. The places made holy by contact with Jesus drew pilgrims from all over the known world. The city was forced to expand: in the C5 the empress Eudokia confirmed this development by walling in the Christian Mount Sion and the original city of David [**10**]. Jerusalem submitted peacefully to the caliph Omar in 637, but it never became as central to Islam as it was to Judaism and Christianity. Pilgrimage continued, but the stable population decreased steadily, so that when the Fatimid caliph el-Aziz (975–96) felt that the Byzantine emperor John Zimisces was threatening the city in 975 he abandoned the area included by Eudokia, retaining only the northern portion of the Byzantine city [**11**].

The city thus acquired the dimensions that it has today [**12**], but a whole series of walls was built and torn down before the Ottoman sultan Suliman the Magnificent (1520–66) erected the present rampart. He began in the north in 1537 and continued down the east and west sides. The south wall was completed only in 1540, apparently because there was a dispute as to whether Mount Sion should be included. The authorities objected to the expense involved in extending the wall for the sake of one building, the Cenacle, and tried to get the Franciscans to bear the cost. They had no money, and so were left outside. Suliman's anger—he had the architects executed—shows that he intended his wall to honour and protect all the places of popular veneration. The depredations of modern urban development reveal more clearly every day that no one ever gave Jerusalem a finer gift.

Visit (Fig. 2). It is possible to walk round most of the Old City on top of the rampart. Not only is it the best way to appreciate its negligible defensive value, but it provides a unique perspective on the life of the city. The walk is protected by railings and provided with explanatory displays. Women, however, are advised not to go alone. The access points (open: 9 a.m.–4 p.m.; Fridays 2 p.m.) are at Damascus Gate, Jaffa Gate, and the

▲ **Fig. 2.** Jerusalem. The gates and quarters of the Old City.

Citadel; descent only is permitted at St Stephen's Gate, Herod's Gate, New Gate, Sion Gate, and just west of Dung Gate.

Suliman the Magnificent set six gates in his wall, and it is obvious that all were designed by the same hand; a straight or slightly curved joggled lintel, above which is an Arabic inscription, is set slightly inside a higher broken arch. Only Herod's Gate, Damascus Gate, Jaffa Gate, and Sion Gate retain their original L-shaped entry. Such entrances worked well as long as all goods were carried on pack animals, but once wheeled traffic developed modifications became inevitable. During the British Mandate St Stephen's Gate and Herod's Gate became direct entrances. The Dung Gate was originally only a postern, but was widened after the Second World War. Suliman gave all six gates official names, but in fact the names vary according to language and religious community.

Herod's Gate and its Vicinity

The official name of this gate is Bab ez-Zahr, 'the Flowered Gate'. It got its present name only in the C16 or C17 because pilgrims believed a Mamluk house inside, near the Franciscan Monastery of the Flagellation, to be the palace of Herod Antipas. The original entrance is in the east face of the tower. It was at this point that the Crusaders first established a bridgehead on the walls at noon on 15 July 1099.

Just beside the west face of the first tower going towards Damascus Gate the channel of an **aqueduct** is marked by a series of irregular covering slabs. Pottery embedded in the plaster of the last repair shows it to have been in use until the late C3 or early C4. The ditch in which the present road runs must therefore be subsequent to this date, because it cuts the aqueduct. This suggests that the earliest wall on the present line at this point must be dated to the last years of Aelia Capitolina.

Slightly further west the wall makes a curve inward and follows the rim of an **ancient quarry** which extended across the road into what is now the bus station; for details see SOLOMON'S QUARRIES (p. 142). The small walled section in the centre at ground level enshrines part of a sloping glacis of uncertain date. The wall of Herod Agrippa I (AD 41–4) linking Damascus Gate with the East Gate in the ECCE HOMO CONVENT (p. 33), must have turned south on the highest point to the west now occupied by the Spafford Hospital.

Damascus Gate

This is the most elaborate of the city gates, and is the finest example of Ottoman architecture in the region; it is the only one to have been excavated.

Medieval Jerusalem

'The city has seven gates, of which six are firmly locked every night until after dawn. But the seventh [the Golden Gate] is blocked with a wall, and only on the Day of Palms and at the Exaltation of the Holy Cross is it opened. Even though the city is oblong, it has five angles, of which one goes inward. Underfoot nearly all its streets are made with closely lodged large stones, and up above there are many with stone roofs, and everywhere among these there are windows arranged to let in light. The houses have carefully made walls stretching up to a considerable height, but their roofs are not raised up in our manner with beams, but are a flat shape, and of equal height. The rain which falls on them is led into cisterns, and they use no other water, because they have none.' (Theoderic (C12), *The Holy Places*, 11; trans. J. Wilkinson)

The first gate on this site was founded by Herod Agrippa I (AD 41–4). Rebuilt by Hadrian in AD 135 as the free-standing monumental entrance

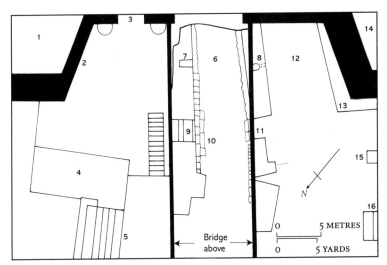

▲ **Fig. 3.** Excavations at Damascus Gate (after Hennessy). 1. Tower;
2. Moulding; 3. Pedestrian entrance; 4. Medieval tower; 5. Medieval steps;
6. Crusader Road; 7 and 8. Troughs; 9. Entrance; 10. Tenth Legion mark;
11. Chapel entrance; 12. Chapel of St Abraham; 13. Medieval revetment;
14. Tower; 15. Undated wall; 16. Modern access to site.

to Aelia Capitolina, it gave on to a semicircular plaza from which ran the
two principal roads of the city corresponding to the present Tariq el-Wad
and Suq Khan ez-Zeit. This arched gate, with a pedestrian entrance on
either side (similar to that at the ECCE HOMO, p. 33) was integrated into a
wall following the line of the present north wall only at the end of the C3;
it remained in use at least until the C5. By the C8 debris had blocked the
two side entrances and Umayyads sank a cistern in front of each. The
central entrance must have been raised. Certainly the medieval gate was
on a higher level and 20 m outside the present entrance. This gate opened
to the east between two towers and the roadway ran west for some 15 m
before turning south, roughly on the axis of the present bridge.

Visit (Fig. 3). The rough modern steps [**16**] lead down, past a wall [**15**]
of uncertain date to the Crusader chapel of St Abraham [**12**]. The lavabo
[**8**] just beside the emplacement of the altar communicates with the water
trough reached from the road outside [**6**]. The heavy masonry revetment
[**13**] is medieval. It does not go completely round the tower [**14**], and
excavations against the west face revealed the same moulding which is
visible at the base of the east tower [**2**]. The mid-C12 chapel rests on an
Umayyad cistern.

The kerbstones of the medieval roadway [**6**] are clearly visible in the
café beneath the modern bridge, whose extent is marked by the heavy

lines in Fig. 3. Opposite the entrance to the chapel of St Abraham [**11**] a flight of steps [**9**] led up to another building; one stone [**10**] bears the mark of the Tenth Legion Fretensis. The two water troughs [**7** and **8**] could be closed by hinged doors. The present paved area with a seat [**4**] reveals the emplacement and size of the south tower of the medieval gate; one hinge stone remains in place and its height above the line of stones [**5**] means that the entrance must have been stepped.

The iron steps lead down to what was once an Umayyad cistern: its collapse and clearance permits appreciation of the magnificent work-manship of Herod Agrippa's tower [**2**] and pedestrian gate [**3**]; the arch and capping-stone date, however, from the Hadrianic restoration in the C2 AD. Hadrian also reconstructed the tower, which underwent internal modifications in the Byzantine and Early Arab periods.

The tower is open 9 a.m.–5 p.m. (Fridays 3 p.m.). Inside the visitor has two options: (a) to visit the guardroom and climb the stairs to the rampart walk, or (b) to explore the Hadrianic plaza. The great paving stones of the plaza resemble those in the ECCE HOMO CONVENT (p. 33) even to the engraved gaming board; the striations were to facilitate horse traffic on the slight slope. In the Middle Ages houses encroached on the plaza.

The exhibition of maps of Jerusalem from the C7 to the C16 repays attention. A unique feature is the holograph representing what is thought to have been the central feature of the plaza, a tall column supporting a statue of Hadrian. The representation of such a column in the C6 Madaba Map is no proof that one existed there four centuries earlier. The Arabic name of the gate is Bab el-Amud, 'the Gate of the Column', but since all the Ottoman gates take their names from things outside them, it is possible that the point of reference is the huge column drums just inside the entrance to ST STEPHEN'S CHURCH (p. 139) on Nablus Road some 200 m to the north. These imply a Roman commemorative column almost 14 m high, and are unlikely to have been moved far from their original position. A head of Hadrian and an inscription were found not far away.

New Gate and its Vicinity

This gate was not in Suliman's plan, as its form clearly indicates. It was opened only in 1887 by the Ottoman sultan Abdul Hamid II to facilitate access to the Old City from the new suburbs developing to the north outside the city wall.

Just west of the gate there is a little park in an inset of the wall. In it one can see the base of a **great tower** projecting out beneath Suliman's wall. It is known by the Arabs as Qasr Jalud, 'Goliath's Castle', because of a legend (attested in the C11 AD) that David killed the Philistine a bow-shot away; in Crusader maps it is identified as Tancred's Tower. It is in fact a C11 tower (35 × 35 m) constructed of blocks dating from the Herodian period. It stands 3 m inside the **Fatimid forewall**, which was protected by a ditch 19 m wide. A portion of the ditch was left unquarried in order to carry an **aqueduct** that passed beneath the wall. The two channels coming from the north join on the bridge; heavy slabs still cover the eastern channel.

If one moves around the north-west corner to a point where Jaffa Gate becomes visible the footpath roughly marks the line of the Fatimid forewall, of which a segment is visible just outside Jaffa Gate.

Jaffa Gate to the South-West Corner

Arabs still call Jaffa Gate by its official name, Bab el-Khalil, 'the Gate of the Friend', the reference being to HEBRON which takes its Arabic name from Abraham, 'the Friend of God' (Isa. 41: 8). The wall between the L-shaped gate and the CITADEL (p. 22) was torn down and the moat filled by the Ottoman sultan Abdul Hamid II in 1898 in order to permit Kaiser Wilhelm II and his suite to ride into the city along the route followed by the present motor road. According to legend, the two graves behind the wrought-iron fence just inside the gate to the left are those of the architects executed by Suliman the Magnificent for leaving MOUNT SION (p. 103) outside the walls. In fact they belong to a peaceful burger and his wife.

The two mounted figures on the saluting platform outside the Citadel represent very accurately the equipment of Crusader and Muslim cavalry during the period of the Latin Kingdom (1099–1187). A surcoat protected chain mail from the sun, and the need to save weight dictated a smaller shield than the shoulder-to-heel version common in Europe.

From Jaffa Gate to the south-west corner (Fig. 4) the area outside the wall has been well excavated; it is a privileged spot in which to appreciate the vicissitudes of the wall from the C2 BC to the C16 AD.

The C16 Turkish wall is built on the line of the late C2 BC Hasmonean wall, which is visible as a slight projection at the base of the present tower [**2**] and in the corner [**3**], where it blocks a door in a tower of the early

▼ **Fig. 4.** Jaffa Gate to the south-west corner (after Broshi). 1. Herodian wall; 2 and 3. Hasmonean wall; 4. Tower; 5. Baulk; 6. Herodian wall; 7. Herodian tower; 8. City gate; 9. Turkish tower; 10. Medieval tower.

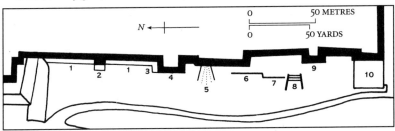

C2 BC. Herod the Great (37–4 BC) built a wall [**1**] with a tower [**2**] immediately outside the Hasmonean wall, both to protect the foundations and to buttress the wall against the pressure of the fill inside on which he built his palace. The three metal grilles mark the entrances to C8 BC tombs which were cleared when the Hasmonean wall was built

The face of the next tower [**4**] offers a panorama of the history of the wall. The stonework between the rock bulges is Herodian; above it is a medieval tower which slopes in to become the present Turkish tower. On either side the Herodian wall lies outside the elements of the Hasmonean wall projecting beneath the actual rampart. One baulk [**5**] was left to show the ground level before the excavations.

The Herodian wall [**6**] continues to become a tower [**7**] which flanked a gate [**8**] of the C1 AD; a corresponding tower was excavated on the other side but is no longer visible. In the trench just in front of the tower [**7**] were found the remains of a C7 BC house. It was in this sector that the Romans, after a month of desperate effort, finally broke through into the Upper City (*War* 6: 374–99) in late September AD 70.

The next tower [**9**] is entirely Turkish, as is its companion on the corner [**10**]. The latter pales into insignificance beside the well-preserved base of a gigantic medieval tower on the same site; it was thrown down with the rest of the city's fortifications in 1219 by el-Melek el-Mouadzam (1218–27), the Ayyubid sultan of Damascus and nephew of Saladin, only seven years after he had repaired them. He had insufficient troops to garrison the city and refused to hand the Crusaders a well-fortified site should they advance on Jerusalem.

Sion Gate to Dung Gate

Sion Gate owes its name to the fact that it is the exit to MOUNT SION (p. 103). In Arabic it is known as Bab Nabi Daud, 'the Gate of the Prophet David', because his tomb is located, according to legend, on Mount Sion. Its pockmarked outer face bears mute testimony to the fierce fighting in 1948 for the JEWISH QUARTER (p. 68).

Extensive excavations on both sides of the wall between Sion Gate and Dung Gate (Fig. 5) have brought to light interesting remains of virtually all periods in the city's history. Those outside the wall are beautifully presented; all the important elements have explanatory signs and are readily accessible from the path running beside the wall.

Inside the wall. The great square tower (23 × 23 m) with a central pillar [**1**] is an **Ayyubid tower** built in 1212 and destroyed only five years later, when it seemed clear that the Crusaders would return; part of it projects outside the present wall [**5**]. Running east is a C11 **Fatimid wall** with a city gate [**2**]. The large building [**3**] just below the interior road is medieval. The **four-columned hall** is particularly impressive. The outer

▲ **Sion Gate.** The original 1540 gate before being damaged in the fierce fighting of 1948.

ends of the vaults were supported by stylized Corinthian capitals resting on elbow-shaped consoles embedded in the wall. In the Mamluk period the hall served some craft necessitating great quantities of water. The eastern part of this building served as a bath-house.

The abortive amphitheatre [**4**] built in the corner of the present wall covers an enormous **cistern** dated to AD 549 by an inscription that reads, 'This is the work which our most pious emperor Flavius Justinian carried out with munificence, under the care and devotion of the most holy

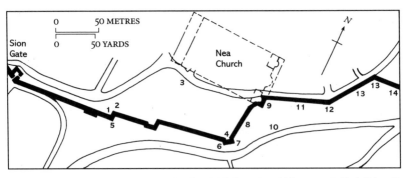

▲ **Fig. 5.** Excavations along the South Wall. 1. Ayyubid tower; 2. Fatimid wall;
3. Crusader building; 4. Byzantine cistern; 5. Ayyubid tower; 6 and 7.
Herodian aqueduct; 8. Byzantine hostel; 9. Corner of the Nea; 10. Herodian
house; 11. Aqueduct channel; 12. Medieval tower; 13. Ritual baths;
14. Medieval tower.

Constantine, priest and superior, in the thirteenth year of the indiction.'
From another source we know that this Constantine was the monastic
superior of the Nea, the 'New Church' built by Justinian in 543, and
depicted in the Madaba Map ([**1**] in Fig. 28). The great height of the
cistern was not a function of the volume of water required, but was
dictated by the need to level the space just south of this church, one of
the most splendid in the empire; its eastern wall is profiled in stones
in the tarmac road and the south lateral apse is tucked into the corner
of the Turkish wall. The corresponding south-east corner projects
outside the rampart [**9**]. The north lateral apse is visible in the JEWISH
QUARTER (p. 68).

Outside the wall. About 15 cm of the Ayyubid tower [**5**] projects outside
the wall just beside the path. Part of the C1 BC lower **aqueduct** bringing
water from SOLOMON'S POOLS near Bethlehem is visible [**6**] near the tower
Burj el-Kibrit [**7**]. The signs of frequent repair are obvious. The ceramic
pipe was placed in the channel during the early Ottoman period. The
aqueduct can also be picked up again in the deep narrow channel with
capstones [**11**] running under the wall to the Temple area. This section
also contains part of a house [**10**] destroyed by the Romans in AD 70, but
the most significant remains are on a higher level right under the wall [**8**];
they represent a **hospice** associated with the Nea Church. The massive
blocks in the five courses of the **corner of the Nea** [**9**] projecting out
beneath the present wall are highly suggestive of the grandeur of the
edifice, and indicate that Procopius of Caesarea should be taken fairly
seriously when he tells us that to transport the stones for the Nea 'they
made special wagons the size of the stones, put a stone in each, and had it
drawn up by 40 oxen'.

The rock surface running towards Dung Gate has been cut to create a great number of baths and cisterns, which formed part of the basements of **dwelling houses** of the Herodian period. East of the medieval tower [**12**] are two **ritual baths** [**13**]. Beside Dung Gate is another medieval tower [**14**] in whose western face is the **Tanners' Postern Gate**, so called because the cattle market just inside furnished hides to pungent tanneries nearby. This tower rests on a paved **Byzantine street** going down to the POOL OF SILOAM (p. 114). It continues to the north beneath the city wall.

The Arabic name of the next gate is Bab el-Magharbeh, 'the Gate of the Moors', because Muslim immigrants from North Africa settled in that part of the city in the C16. Jews called it the Dung Gate after a gate in the south wall of Nehemiah (Neh. 2: 13). The pointed gadroon arch above the modern (1985) lintel shows that the original gate was only a postern. In 1953 the Jordanians widened it in order to get motor vehicles to the CITADEL. For nearly 20 years (1948–67) Jaffa Gate was sealed by a *de facto* frontier. For the area east of Dung Gate see the section EXCAVATIONS AT THE WESTERN WALL PLAZA (p. 96).

St Stephen's Gate

Suliman called the east gate of the city Bab el-Ghor, 'the Jordan Gate', but this name never took root. An earlier gate on roughly the same spot was called St Stephen's Gate, and this was the name that remained among the Christian communities. According to Byzantine pilgrims, however, the C6 gate of this name was in the north wall (today Damascus Gate). The shift illustrates the tendency of places in Jerusalem to move to suit the convenience of visitors. After the fall of the Latin Kingdom (1187), Christian pilgrims were not permitted near the north wall, militarily the weakest point of the city. They had to leave the city by the east gate to visit the Mount of Olives and Jericho and returned via the Dung Gate. The local guides simply moved to the Kidron Valley certain holy places, notably the church of St Stephen, which in reality were north of the city, and business went on as before.

The current Hebrew name, 'the Lion's Gate', is derived from the heraldic emblems of the Mamluk sultan Baybars (1260–77), which Suliman's architects set on either side of the gate. According to local legend they represent the lions who were prepared to eat Suliman's father, the first Ottoman sultan Selim I (1512–20) if he carried through his plan to level Jerusalem. The original back wall of the gate, which created an L-shaped entrance, was removed under the British Mandate in order to enable vehicles to reach the Austrian Hospital.

For the series of sealed gates, the Golden Gate, the Triple Gate, and the Double Gate, see the sections HARAM ESH-SHARIF (p. 80) and EXCAVATIONS AT THE WESTERN WALL PLAZA (p. 96).

The Citadel   ★★

The west side of the Old City is dominated by the minaret and towers of the Citadel, which has been its bastion since the time of Herod the Great (37–4 BC). The instinct of artists, who have used it to symbolize Jerusalem girt about with walls, has been validated by archaeologists; it encapsulates the history of the city.

Israelite settlement in this area is attested as early as the C7 BC, but it was definitively brought within the city walls only in the late C2 BC, when the Hasmonean dynasty reached the apogee of its power under John Hyrcanus (134–104 BC). The Hasmonean wall is mentioned by Josephus in his description of the three towers which Herod erected in memory of his friend Hippicus, his brother Phasael, and his wife Mariamne: 'while such were the proportions of these three towers, they seemed far larger owing to their site. For the old wall in which they stood was itself built upon a lofty hill, and above the hill rose as it were a crest 30 cubits higher still' (*War* 5: 173). 'Adjoining and on the inner side of these towers, which lay to the north of it,' he continues, 'was the king's palace, wondrous beyond words' (*War* 5: 176). Excavations in the Armenian garden have shown that the palace reached almost to the present south wall.

When the Romans assumed direct control in Palestine in AD 6 the Procurator, who lived in CAESAREA, used the palace as his Jerusalem residence. It was the praetorium in which Pontius Pilate judged Jesus (John 18: 28–19: 16). A similar murderous farce was played out on the same spot under another Procurator: 'Florus took up his quarters at the palace, and on the next day had his tribunal set before it and sat upon it . . . The soldiers caught many of the quiet people, and brought them before Florus, whom he first scourged and then crucified' (*War* 2: 301–8). Such brutality was one of the causes of the First Revolt, and in September AD 66 Jewish revolutionaries attacked and burnt the palace (*War* 2: 430–40). The Roman general Titus, after his victory four years later, preserved the gigantic towers as a monument to the valour of his troops, whom he garrisoned in the area of the old palace (*War* 7: 1–2), it remained the camp of the Tenth Legion Fretensis for over 200 years.

Considering the western hill to be Mount Sion, the Byzantines inevitably identified the site with the palace of David. The remains of the great tower became known as David's Tower; in the C19 this name moved to the minaret in the south-west corner. It is not clear when the fortress was first rebuilt, but one certainly existed in the C8. The Fatimid defenders were permitted to march out with honour when the Crusaders took the city in July 1099. In 1128 it became the residence of the Crusader kings of Jerusalem, who extended it to the west. From those battlements, on an October day in 1187, Saladin watched two lines of Christians leave the defeated city, one going to slavery, the other (who could afford the ransom) to freedom. In the following century, as the Crusaders struggled to maintain a toe-hold in Palestine, the Citadel was rebuilt and torn down more than once. Only when the Crusaders had

▼ **Fig. 6.** The Citadel (after Heva). 1. North-west tower; 2. Entrance to 1873 model; 3. Byzantine wall; 4. Undated wall; 5. Phasael tower; 6. Byzantine wall; 7. Outer entrance; 8. Bridge; 9. Mosque; 10. Inner entrance; 11. Hexagonal room; 12. Herodian tower; 13. Hasmonean tower; 14. Hasmonean wall; 15. Podium grid; 16. Medieval wall; 17. Byzantine wall; 18. Byzantine cistern; 19. Early Islamic entrance; 20. Hasmonean tower; 21. Herodian tower; 22. C1 AD tower; 23. Early Islamic tower; 24. Postern gate; 25. Mosque; 26. Entrance to medieval hall; 27. Minaret; 28. Entrance to rampart walk; 29. South-east tower; 30. Rock steps; 31. Water channel; 32. East tower.

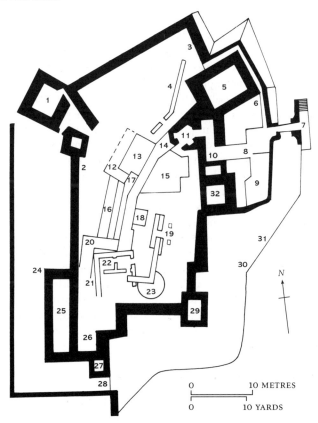

clearly abandoned all hope of return did the Mamluk sultan al-Nasir Muhammad (1309–40) give the central portion of the fortress its present form in 1310. He retained the Crusader outer line, but levelled the old city wall which had divided the interior into two wards. In the C16 the Ottoman sultan Suliman the Magnificent contributed the monumental entrance and added the platform for cannon along the western wall.

Visit (Fig. 6). Open: Sunday–Thursday 10 a.m.–4 p.m. (winter); 9 a.m.–5 p.m. (summer); closes 2 p.m. on Friday, Saturday, and eves of Jewish holy days. The entrance [**7**] is on the east side of the complex, i.e. facing Christchurch within the Old City. From 1 April to 31 October there is a Sound and Light show in English in the courtyard at 9.30 p.m. on Monday and Wednesday and at 9 p.m. on Saturday. To check time and performances in languages other than English telephone 02–627–4111. A warm jacket is recommended even in summer. Use the Jaffa Gate entrance.

The Museum

The archaeological remains in the courtyard are all of different periods. Hence, it is better to begin with the museum scattered throughout the various rooms of the complex. Its models, plans, and exhibits go a long way towards disentangling the multitude of threads which make up the complicated web of Jerusalem's history. From the entrance [**10**] go up the stairs to the right and on the roof turn left into a large room in the tower [**5**], where an animated film provides an evocative introduction to the history of the city. Then cross the roof of the hexagonal room to the east tower [**32**]. The upper exhibition room records the history of Jerusalem to the Babylonian exile, whereas the one beneath it brings the story up to the destruction of the city by the Romans in AD 70.

Continue on the lower level to the base of the south-east tower [**29**] whose exhibits reflect the splendour of Jerusalem during the late Roman and Byzantine periods (C2–C7 AD). The Early Islamic, Crusader and Ayyubid periods (C7–C13) are dealt with in what used to be a mosque [**25**]. The story ends (on the same level) in the north-west tower [**1**] whose exhibits evoke the Mamluk, Ottoman, and British periods in the history of Jerusalem. In what used to be a huge cistern beneath this tower is displayed the 1 : 500 zinc model of Jerusalem built by the Hungarian Stefan Illes for display at the World Fair in Vienna in 1873; the entrance is via a flight of stairs outside [**2**].

The Building and the Excavations

Since the archaeological remains in the courtyard are all of different periods, it is advisable to begin with a series of bird's-eye views from the towers. Only from a height is it possible to grasp the shapes of the various units and to appreciate their interrelationship.

The East Entrance. A series of inscriptions over the ornamental gate [**7**], in the open-air mosque [**9**], and on the north side of the bridge [**8**], date their construction to the C16. They are contemporary with Suliman the Magnificent's restoration of the city walls. A glance at the tower [**5**] reveals two building phases; the small stones of the top, erected by the C14 Mamluks, who built for show, stand in vivid contrast to the great blocks of the base erected by Herod the Great, who built for eternity. The base is solid all the way through, and if this tower is correctly identified with Phasael it was much larger than the Pharus, the great lighthouse of Alexandria, which was one of the seven wonders of the world (*War* 5: 166–9).

A flight of steps beside the remains of a Byzantine wall [**6**] permits one to pass under the bridge [**8**] and out into **the moat**. The area south of the bridge in the C8 BC was a quarry. The date of the wall cannot be determined. Further on is a flight of steps [**30**] with a rock-cut, plastered water channel [**31**]. Coins in the plaster used to level the rock surface date the installation to the Hasmonean period; its function then and subsequently in Herod's palace is unknown.

The **main entrance** [**10**] is Crusader but was restored by the Mamluks in the C14; it is L-shaped in order to force attackers to slow their momentum. The stone benches of the guardroom are original, as are the slits for the portcullis just in front of the iron-plated C16 doors. There is an entrance to the courtyard from the C14 hexagonal room [**11**], but it is better to climb the outer stairs to the upper level first.

Upper Level. A cut near the top of the stairs shows clearly that the Mamluk construction is merely juxtaposed to the Herodian tower [**5**]. The top of the tower offers a splendid panorama of the Old City. The two domes (one larger than the other) to the left in the middle distance are those of the HOLY SEPULCHRE (p. 45). The great hole directly in line with them is the POOL OF THE PATRIARCH'S BATH (p. 61), known to Josephus as Amygdalon (*War* 5: 468). To the right one looks down on to Christchurch, the first Anglican church built in the Holy Land (1849). Further to the south are the domes of the ARMENIAN QUARTER (p. 62).

The minaret [**27**] was erected by Muhammad Pasha in 1655. An inscription over the *minbar* (pulpit) of the **mosque** [**25**] testifies to repairs effected by Suliman the Magnificent to the original Mamluk mosque built above a Crusader hall. There is a fine view from the roof of the mosque. Inside the city wall to the south are the buildings erected in the mid-C19 as the Kishla ('winter barracks') for Turkish troops. This was the area occupied by the palace of Herod the Great (*War* 5: 176–81). The remains at the external base of the wall (p. 17) are clearly visible. The dried-up reservoir in the Hinnom Valley, now called **Birket es-Sultan**, was once the Serpent's Pool (*War* 5: 108); it took its name from the serpentine wanderings of the lower aqueduct from SOLOMON'S POOLS, which can be traced on both sides. The long one-storey building below the windmill is Mishkenoth Shaananim, erected by Moses Montefiore in 1857 (p. 136).

From the north-west tower [1] one can look down on **Jaffa Gate**. The space between it and the base of the tower was once part of the medieval moat; it was filled in 1898. This is also the best spot from which to view the archaeological remains in the courtyard; it is recommended to read the following notes before descending to examine the details.

Courtyard. The **Hasmonean wall** of the late C2 BC is represented by the sweeping curve [14], whose thickness would have suggested that it was a city wall even without the two projecting **towers** [13 and 20]. This is the First Wall described by Josephus (*War* 5: 142–5); to the south it appears beneath the present west wall (p. 17), while its extension to the east has been traced in the JEWISH QUARTER (p. 71). Dwellings were built against its inner face [15], one of the entrances is still visible.

When Herod the Great decided to build his **palace** in this area in the last quarter of the C1 BC, his major contribution was to insert the great tower [5] into the line of the earlier wall; the other two towers mentioned by Josephus must have been sited further east. Herod also decided to raise the ground level inside the wall in order to create an artificial platform that would make his structures even more imposing. To this end he laid a grid of walls intersecting at right angles over the Hasmonean dwellings [15]; their function was to hold the fill firmly in position. As a further precaution against lateral pressure, he extended the tower [13] outwards, creating a much bigger bastion [12], and thickened the wall [14] between the two towers [12 and 5]. Curiously, he did not extend the larger tower [20]. Instead he reduced its width from 18.5 to 14.5 m, but kept the same orientation [21]. Even though history records no destruction, this tower had to be rebuilt early in the C1 AD. The new tower [22] was given a slightly different orientation and was built into the wall [14], the north and east walls and the room dividers are of the C1 AD, but the west wall was reconstructed in the Byzantine period. A thick destruction layer was found in the eastern room, mute testimony to the attack by Jewish rebels in September AD 66. 'They dug a mine from a great distance under one of the towers and made it totter, and having done that, they set fire to what would burn and left it; when the foundations had burnt the tower suddenly collapsed' (*War* 2: 435).

The excavations brought to light sporadic but unambiguous evidence of the 200-year Roman presence on this site; the remains were too insignificant to be worth preserving. At the beginning of the **Byzantine period**, the early C4 AD, a new wall [3] was built northwards from the

Herodian tower [5], several stepped courses are visible beneath the present wall. It would have followed the ridge to a point just east of New Gate (p. 16), and then turned east on the line of the present north wall to enclose Aelia Capitolina for the first time. The Byzantines also strengthened the Hasmonean-Herodian wall [14] by adding to its outer face [17], and resurrected the late-Herodian tower [22] by reconstructing its western wall. They are also responsible for the cistern [18] dug against the inner face of the Herodian wall.

The first significant change in the disposition of the site occurred after the **Arab occupation** in 638. Sometime in the C7 or C8 a round tower [23] was erected to strengthen the corner of a new wall running west and north. Since the entrance [19] was on the east, it seems reasonable to assume that this fortress was bounded on the west by the old wall [14] and incorporated both the Byzantine tower [22] and the Herodian tower [5]. It is evident near the entrance [19] that the early Islamic wall was strengthened on both faces. This is the fortress that held out against the Crusaders until the evening of 15 July 1099 when the rest of the city had been taken.

The Muslim fortress was too small to serve the needs of a royal court, forcing the **Crusaders** to build a much larger citadel. They retained the Herodian tower [5], a tribute to its enduring strength: it appears on the royal seal of the Kingdom of Jerusalem between the DOME OF THE ROCK (p. 85) and the HOLY SEPULCHRE (p. 45). There are traces of C12 workmanship at the base of the present circuit of walls and towers, and the size is compatible with the number of citizens who took refuge there when Saladin threatened in 1177. The old external wall [14] was perfectly positioned to divide the enclosed area into two wards. Should it have been buried, however, the same role could be assigned to the massive medieval wall [16]. Crusader remains are visible in the vaulted chamber beneath the mosque [25]; it is reached by two medieval tunnels, one from a postern gate [24], now closed, the other from the courtyard [26]. The two square pillar bases [19] are also Crusader.

From the point of view of construction technique and fortification style the actual walls and towers and the upper portion of the Herodian tower could be either Ayyubid or **Mamluk**. For historical reasons, and because of an inscription that once adorned the east entrance [10], they are assigned to the Mamluk sultan al-Nasir Muhammad in 1310. The south-east tower [29] with its adjoining walls is entirely his work, and the line he established for the west wall is apparently some metres inside the Crusader wall on that side.

The rough wall of small stones [4] is so far a mystery. Its level would suggest a date in the Herodian period, but it is not strong enough to be a built escarpment defending the base of the wall, and it is too close to a strongly defended tower to be part of the Roman circumvallation wall.

The Muslim Quarter

The Muslim Quarter covers 31 hectares in the north-eastern sector of the Old City (Fig. 2). The dilapidated buildings huddle wearily together and only the domes bubbling up everywhere suggest the intensity of life within. The population is estimated at 14,000. Although within the city walls since AD 40 the quarter has little to show for its long history; what it does have can be shown with pride. There are striking Roman and Crusader remains (Fig. 7) along the street inside ST STEPHEN'S GATE (p. 21), and marvellous Mamluk façades in the warren of little streets beside the HARAM ESH-SHARIF.

St Anne's   ★★

Crusader Jerusalem is seen at its best in the simple strength of St Anne's (AD 1140), certainly the loveliest church in the city. According to Byzantine tradition, the crypt enshrines the home of the Virgin Mary and her parents Joachim and Anne. Next to it are the ruins of miraculous medicinal baths where clients of the god Serapis (Asclepius) gathered in hope of healing; Jesus there cured one, a man ill for 38 years (John 5: 1–13).

In the C8 BC a dam was built here across a shallow valley to capture run-off rain-water. It became known as 'the upper pool' (2 Kings 18: 17; Isa 7: 3). There was a vertical shaft in the centre of the dam with sluice gates at various heights. Thus controlled, water flowed south in a rock-cut

▼ **Fig. 7.** Jerusalem. The area immediately inside St Stephen's Gate. Letters locate Mamluk buildings.

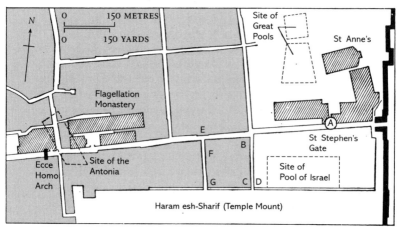

Healing Gods need Help

'For all temples there shall be chosen the most healthy sites with suitable springs in those places where shrines are to be set up, and especially for Asclepius and Salus, and generally for those gods by whose medical power sick persons are manifestly healed. For when sick persons are moved from a pestilent to a healthy place and the water supply is from wholesome fountains, they will more quickly recover. So will it happen that the divinity (from the nature of the site) will gain a greater and higher reputation and authority.' (Vitruvius (C1), *On Architecture*, i. 2, 7; trans. F. Granger)

channel to the City of David. The high priest Simon added a second pool on the south side of the dam about 200 BC (Sir. 50: 3), transforming the channel into a tunnel.

Sometime in the next century a number of natural caves east of the pools were adapted to serve as small baths; their function can only have been religious or medicinal, and at this time the two were inseparable: health was a gift of the gods. The site was then outside the walled city and the founders were probably soldiers from the pagan garrison of the Antonia fortress (p. 32). The twin pools were taken out of commission when Herod the Great (37–4 BC) dug the Pool of Israel closer to his new temple, but they continued to fill with water during the winter rains.

John begins his account of Jesus' miracle with the words, 'Now at the Sheep Gate in Jerusalem is a pool with five porches, its name in Hebrew is Bethesda' (5: 2). The name may mean 'House of Mercy', a very appropriate designation for a healing sanctuary. After AD 135 when Jerusalem was paganized into Aelia Capitolina the sanctuary expanded into a temple; votive offerings of the C2 and C3 AD in gratitude for cures show that it was dedicated to Serapis (Asclepius). In Hadrian's grid-plan (reflected in today's streets, Fig. 7) a street ran across the dike dividing the ancient pools to terminate in front of the temple.

Origen (*c.* AD 231) was the first to relate the five porches mentioned in the gospel to the shape of the double pool 'four around the edges and another across the middle'. The hypothesis is an obvious one; it is doubtful that he actually saw anything. By the middle of the C5 AD a church commemorating the miracle had been built; its west end projected out over the dike dividing the pools. The name of the Virgin Mary appears for the first time in the next century; it may have been the title of a second church.

How a church might have survived the destructive edict of the Fatimid sultan Hakim in 1009 is a mystery, but one certainly existed at the very beginning of the Crusader occupation. In 1104 Baldwin I committed his repudiated wife, the Armenian princess Arda, to the care of the community of Benedictine nuns who served it, and endowed the convent royally. They first erected a small chapel in the middle of the large Byzantine church: a stairway down to a corner of the northern pool permitted pilgrims to venerate the miracle of John 5. Sometime between 1131 and 1138 the convent church was replaced by the beautiful Romanesque church of St Anne. Soon too small for the growing community, which included members of the royal family, the church was enlarged by moving the façade out 7 m. Note the difference between the two piers just inside the entrance and the other four.

On 25 July 1192 Saladin transformed the church into a Muslim theo-logical school; his inscription is still above the door. Other rulers were not so careful; they did not destroy but neither did they protect and by the C18 the church was roof-deep in refuse. It recovered its former glory only when the Ottoman Turks presented it to France in 1856 as a gesture of gratitude for aid in the Crimean War.

Visit. Open: 8 a.m.–noon and 2–5 p.m. (winter), 2–6 p.m. (summer); closed Sunday. Entrance at A in Fig. 7. The museum containing the more important objects found in the excavations is not open to visitors, but those really interested should ask the guardian.

The location of the medieval cloister is preserved by the garden around the bust of Cardinal Lavigerie, founder of the White Fathers to whose charge the church is entrusted. Around are various objects brought to light by the excavations. A narrow stairway protected by a railing permits a view of the plastered south-east corner of the southern pool (200 BC); it is 13 m deep.

▼ **Fig. 8.** St Anne's Church. Excavated area (after Duprez). 1. Piers supporting wall of C5 church; 2. Modern steps; 3. Columns of C5 church; 4. Healing baths; 5. Vaulted rooms; 6. Healing bath.

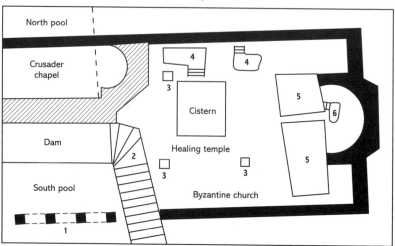

The church deserves silent contemplation. The change of masonry in the north wall betrays the medieval extension. The crypt is older than the church; the foundations of the pillars interfere with the original shape of the caves which once formed part of the sanctuary of Serapis; only one section is open to the public.

Before visiting the excavations examine carefully the plan affixed to the railings; it is the only way to grasp the relationships of the various elements which come from several different periods. The monoapsidal Byzantine church was built directly above the healing sanctuary. The centre of the west end of the church rested on the dam dividing the two pools; one side was supported by a series of huge arches [1] founded on the bottom of the pool while the other rested on a cistern of the C2 AD built into the south-east corner of the northern pool; a perspective drawing opposite the shop at the street entrance facilitates visualization. It is possible to enter the cistern by stairs beneath the ruined apse of the Crusader chapel.

Note in particular the section in the centre furthest from the apse of the medieval chapel. This was the most important part of the C2–C4 healing temple of Serapis/Asclepius. The curvature of the low walls shows that two rooms [5] were vaulted; from one, three steps lead down to a small cave cut in the rock [6]; a rectangular shallow depression at one end is the bath. Other similar baths are easily detected [4]. After bathing, the client of Serapis slept in a darkened vaulted room; drug-induced dreams provided the basis of the priest's diagnosis. The apse of the C5 Byzantine church was sited directly over this area, both to commemorate the miracle and to obliterate a pagan temple.

Minor Monuments

From St Anne's the road runs uphill into the Old City. In the little street (Tariq Bab Hitta) to the left after the first covered section are three dilapidated Mamluk buildings (see p. 36). First on the right is the C14 **Ribat al-Maridini** ([**B**] in Fig. 7) and at the far end on the left is the slightly earlier **Madrasa Karimiyya** [**D**]. Opposite the latter is **the tomb of al-Malik al-Awhad** (d. 1299) [**C**], a great-great-nephew of Saladin. The entrance is noteworthy. Reused Crusader columns accentuate the outer corners. In the hub of the cloister vault above is a design based on the fleur-de-lis; its purpose is more likely to be decorative than heraldic.

The huge smooth flagstones in the street were recovered during the laying of a sewer; they date at least from the Byzantine period but may possibly be earlier. The large rough stones on the north side of the beginning of the next covered section of the street are the base of the now-vanished minaret of the **Muazzamiyya Madrasa** (1274) [**E**]. A rather dark street on the south (Tariq Bab al-Atm) contains the beautiful red and cream façade of the **Sallamiyya Madrasa** (1338) [**F**] with the three

A Pious Foundation

'In the name of God the Merciful, the Compassionate. The construction of this blessed khanqah, called the House of the Pious, was ordered by the servant needful of God Almighty, the servant of God, son of the servant of the Lord, son of the servant of the Creator, Sanjar al-Dawadari al-Salihi. He made it a waqf, in his desire for the countenance of God Almighty, in favour of 30 persons from the community of Sufis and novices, Arab and non-Arab, 20 of whom shall be unmarried and 10 married, to dwell there without leaving, not in summer, winter, spring, nor autumn, except on specific business; and to give hospitality to those Sufis and novices who visit, for a period of 10 days. It was endowed with the village of Bir Nabala in the district of Jerusalem, and the village of Hajla in the district of Jericho, and an oven and mill, and the apartment above them, in Jerusalem, and a house, a soap factory, 6 shops, and a paper mill in Nablus, and 3 orchards, 3 shops and 4 mills in Beisan. . . .' (Founding inscription (C13); trans. M. Burgoyne)

grilled windows of its assembly hall and the recessed main entrance. The founder was a merchant from Iraq, who served the Mamluk sultan al-Nasir Muhammad both as an importer of *mamluks* (cf. p. 36) and as a peace negotiator with the Mongols.

On the same side of the street but closer to the gate of the Haram esh-Sharif is the **Dawadariyya Khanqah** (1295) [**G**]. It was founded as a residence for contemplative Sufis by the Amir who commanded the siege artillery at the battle of AKKO in 1291 (see box). Unfortunately the vaulting of the street leaves barely enough light to see the extraordinary quality of the vaulting of the entrance. Note that the voussoirs of the pointed arch are joggled not in one plane but in two, and try to work out why the central impost stays in place!

Antonia Fortress

At the crest of the hill a wide flight of steps on the left (south) side of the road leads up to the Umariyya Boys' School, which is accessible out of school hours at the whim of the caretaker. This rocky crag was the site of the Antonia, the great fortress built by Herod the Great (probably between 37 and 35 BC) and named in honour of his patron, Mark Antony; it both protected and controlled the Temple (*War* 5: 238–47). The arrest of St Paul was typical of the responsibilities of its Roman garrison (Acts 21: 27–23: 35).

Occupied by the rebels in AD 66, it became the focal point of Titus' attempt to penetrate the final defences of Jerusalem. Having smashed through two walls further north (*War* 5: 302, 331), he dedicated the Fifth and Twelfth Legions to the subjection of the Antonia (*War* 5: 466). After two months of bitter fighting the fortress fell on 24 July 70. It was razed to the ground on the orders of Titus (*War* 6: 93,149); all that remains is a portion of its 4 m-thick south wall.

After entering the school go diagonally left and up to the large recess whose two windows offer a magnificent view of the HARAM ESH-SHARIF (for the outside, cf. p. 83). These windows and part of the recess are cut into the wall of the Antonia whose inner limit is marked by the point in the walls where the recess widens slightly. In its present form the structure dates from 1315–20, when it served as the south chamber of **Jawiliyya Madrasa**. The founder had a distinguished career both as soldier and scholar, but his blazon on the façade of the recess—a circle enclosing two parallel lines and a dot—does not clearly indicate what his court office was (cf. p. 37). Mamluk and Ottoman governors of Jerusalem used the recess as their seat of judgement. In 1835 the complex was rebuilt as a barracks for Ottoman troops, and became a school in 1924.

Monastery of the Flagellation

Across the road from the Umariyya School is the Franciscan Monastery of the Flagellation, an eminent school of biblical and archaeological studies: open 8 a.m.–noon; 2–5 p.m. (winter) to 6 p.m. (summer). A museum displays finds from the excavations at NAZARETH, CAPERNAUM, and DOMINUS FLEVIT, and has a fine collection of coins. Open: Monday–Saturday 9–11.30 a.m.; Sunday by appointment for small groups (tel.: 02–628–0271).

In popular piety the Antonia was assumed to be the residence of Pontius Pilate, and so the immediate vicinity abounds with memories of the passion of Christ (John 18: 28–19: 16). The chapel on the right on entering the courtyard is the **Chapel of the Flagellation** of Jesus which was completely rebuilt in 1929 on medieval foundations. At the other end of the court is the **Chapel of the Condemnation** of Jesus; the early C20 building (again a medieval site) covers part of the pavement of the C2 AD eastern forum of Aelia Capitolina. A more extensive portion is to be seen next door at the Ecce Homo. The striations on certain slabs were to give beasts of burden a grip on stones which polish easily through use.

Ecce Homo

To reach the Antonia fortress in AD 70 the Romans had to build a ramp across a rock-cut pool (hatched outline in Fig. 7) called Struthion (*War* 5: 467), which also protected a city gate erected by Herod Agrippa I (AD 41–4). The central bay is now the Ecce Homo Arch. After the Roman victory in AD 70 the wall running to the north and the gate were torn down, but the debris of the superstructure protected the lower part of the gate. When Hadrian replanned Jerusalem in AD 135 he created a forum here. The three-bayed gate, now a monument to a Roman triumph, stood in the middle of a great paved area covering the Struthion Pool. Part of this pavement is visible in the Chapel of the Condemnation in the Franciscan monastery of the Flagellation (see above), but the most extensive remains are displayed in the Convent of the Sisters of Sion.

Visit. Open: 8.30 a.m.–12.30 p.m. and 2–5 p.m. (to 4.30 p.m. in winter); closed Sundays. The chapel is not open to tourists, but the essential is visible from the vestibule some 20 m downhill west of the arch. The similarity between the northern side arch of the city gate and that beneath the Damascus Gate (p. 14) is obvious. The springing of the central bay continues through the wall and across the road outside. It supports a small room.

The entrance to the rest of the complex is just round the corner of the side street (Aqabat er-Rahbat) east of the arch. After going through the information area one descends into the **Struthion (sparrow) Pool**. Despite its impressive dimensions, less than half the pool is visible. The arches on the left cut the pool in two, and its length has been shortened at both ends. From behind the modern wall at the far end a channel runs towards the HARAM ESH-SHARIF and can be reached from the WESTERN WALL TUNNEL (p. 98). The magnificent vaulting was constructed to support the C2 AD Hadrianic pavement above. The pool is filled by rain-water collected from the roofs of the convent.

After passing through three rooms devoted to a small museum, a wooden bridge crosses a portion of a channel that once brought water to the pool from the valley in which DAMASCUS GATE lies (p. 14). The beautiful **pavement** of large smooth stones was once thought to be the Pavement (*lithostrothon*; John 19: 13) on which Pilate judged Jesus, and so was identified with the place where Pilate said, 'Behold the man' (in Latin, *Ecce Homo*, John 19: 5), but it is now certain that the pavement cannot date from the C1 AD. The condemnation of Jesus took place at the CITADEL (p. 22). Note in particular the well-cut gutters that carried rain-water from the forum to the Struthion Pool below. A railed area protects marks on the pavement which have been identified as the King Game. This was a dice game in which the player to first land on the crown was the winner. It was presumably to be found wherever off-duty soldiers congregated, and were it to have been played by Pilate's guard, it might well have suggested the form that their mockery of Jesus took. 'They plaited a crown of thorns, and put it on his head, and arrayed him in a purple robe. They came up to him saying, "Hail, King of the Jews!" ' (John 19: 2–3).

Via Dolorosa

The first two stations of the Way of the Cross are located in the immediate vicinity of the Ecce Homo arch. These and seven other stations are indicated by numbers 1–9 in Fig. 10; the other five are within the Holy Sepulchre.

The Via Dolorosa is defined by faith, not by history. On the night of Holy Thursday Byzantine pilgrims used to go in procession from the Eleona church on the top of the Mount of Olives (p. 125) to Calvary. After a stop at GETHSEMANE (p. 128), they entered the city by the present St Stephen's Gate, and followed approximately the present route, but there were no further devotional halts along the way. By the C8 a number of stops had become customary but the route was completely different: from Gethsemane it went round the city on the south to the house of Caiphas on Mount Sion, then to the Praetorium of Pilate at St Sophia somewhere near the Temple, and finally to the Holy Sepulchre. In the Middle Ages the picture becomes much more complicated as the Latin Christians were divided into two camps. One group located the Praetorium and the palace of the high priest on Mount Sion; the other placed both north of the Temple; in consequence, they followed completely different routes to the Holy Sepulchre. The basis of the conflict was simple: one group possessed churches on the western hill, the other on the eastern.

In the C14 the Franciscans organized a devotional walk to follow the steps of Jesus in Jerusalem; a number of the present stations figured on this itinerary, but the starting-point was the Holy Sepulchre. This remained the standard route for nearly two centuries, and impressed itself firmly on the imagination of European pilgrims. A number of these pilgrims (starting in the early C15) created symbolic representations of the events of the Passion in their home countries in order to foster the devotion of those who could not make the pilgrimage. Inevitably, they followed the order of events in the gospels; independently, religious permanently resident in Jerusalem had begun to do the same but, whereas the Jerusalem tradition had only eight stations (the last being the present Seventh Station), the European tradition had fourteen stations. Since pilgrims expected to find in Jerusalem what they were accustomed to else-where, the European tradition gradually prevailed. The Jerusalem Way of the Cross was extended to include stations within the Holy Sepulchre. The actual route was fixed in the C18, but a number of the stations (nos. 1, 4, 5, 8) were given their present location only in the C19.

The present Way of the Cross has little chance of corresponding to historical reality; it is more probable that Pilate condemned Jesus to death on the other side of the city at the CITADEL (p. 22), the 'high point', *Gabbatha*, according to John 19: 13. This was the palace of Herod where Pilate normally resided when he came up from Caesarea to ensure control during the great Jewish feasts (Philo, *Delegation to Gaius*, 38). According to the gospels, the trial took place on a platform (Matt. 27: 19) in the open (Luke 23: 4, John 18: 28). Such a structure existed at the palace in AD 66, as we know from what Josephus says of one of Pilate's successors: 'Florus lodged at the palace, and on the following day had a platform placed in front of the building and took his seat; the chief priests, the nobles, and the most eminent citizens then presented themselves before the tribunal' (*War* 2: 301); as in the case of Jesus, the affair ended in crucifixions.

If, as seems likely, Jesus was brought through the city on his way to execution, the approximate route would have been east on David Street, north on the Triple Suk (bottom left in Fig. 10), and then west to Golgotha.

Mamluk Buildings   ★

The depth and rather steep sides of the Tyropoeon Valley inhibited the Crusaders from building close to the walls of the Temple; the west wall could be seen from a distance. It was only with the advent of the Mamluks (1250–1517) that the area began to fill with buildings. On huge substructures they erected religious colleges and pilgrim hospices in such numbers that the whole sector west and north of the Haram glowed with clean-cut stone—red, white, and black—whose austere decoration still preserves its dignity. The nature of these buildings is surprising when one remembers that the Mamluks were all forced converts to Islam (see box). Some streets have changed very little, but they lie off the beaten track and few venture in. Those with the courage to explore will discover a little-known facet of Jerusalem's rich history.

Much is known about these buildings from a British architectural survey, and from inscriptions still in place which give the name of the

The Mamluks

The Arabic word *mamluk* means 'owned', and the term was applied to boys, bought in the slave-markets of the steppes north of the Black Sea, who were then trained to be professional soldiers as mounted archers. Those who emerged from the regiments into leadership roles bought slaves for themselves in order to have retainers who had no relationship to any other family or political faction; they could then have no conflict of loyalties. Fostered by the Ayyubid dynasty of Saladin, these military mandarins eventually turned on their master, and in 1250 assumed violent control of a state whose focal points were Cairo and Damascus. Once in power they continued the recruitment policy for the reasons behind it remained valid. The first phase of their history was dominated by Qipchaq Turks of the Bahri regiment (1250–1390); they were supplanted by Circassians of the Burji regiment (1390–1517). For over 250 years the Mamluks held the northeast frontier of the Levant against the Mongols. Finally they were defeated by the Janissaries of the Ottoman Turks in battles near Aleppo (1516) and Cairo (1517).

 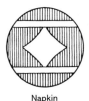 

◀ **Fig. 9.** Mamluk blazons.

Polo Sticks	Napkin	Cup
(Bearer of the	(Master of the Robes)	(Cup-Bearer)
Polo Stick)		

founder, the date of construction, and the function of the building. As befitted their warrior caste, the Mamluks were conscious of the importance of badges of distinction. Thus the founding inscriptions of their buildings are often enhanced by blazons symbolizing their office at court (Fig. 9). The emblem of the cup, for example, is found on all the buildings erected by Tankiz, the great Viceroy of Syria. So many Mamluk sultans were assassinated that the position of Cup-Bearer implied superlative loyalty.

Most of the buildings are now tenements and are not open to the public; a glance through an open doorway is generally the most one can hope for. Fortunately the most interesting part of a Mamluk building is the ornate façade which normally has but one door highlighted by a much larger recess; the combination offers welcome shade and protection. The conscious use of shadow and silhouette brings out the detail of the embellishment of the door recess, and alternating courses of red, cream, and occasionally black stone give interest to a broad expanse of masonry. The intricate complexity of the ornamentation is a challenge to adequate appreciation. Detailed explanation is no substitute for the discerning eye delighting in discovery.

For convenience the buildings are grouped by streets rather than by date; the initial letter gives the location on the map in Fig. 10. All the fountains in the area are due to the munificence of the Ottomans in the C16.

Aqabat et-Takiya

[**A**] *Serai es-Sitt Tunshuq.* The Lady Tunshuq was a Mongol or Turkish slave forced to live abroad when the Kurdish dynasty of her husband or protector began to crumble under the onslaughts of Tamerlane at the end of the C14. She managed to bring with her enough money to erect this palace in which she lived until her death in July 1398. In 1552 it was incorporated into a larger complex known as the *Imaret of Khasseki Sultan* [**C**], which was built and endowed by Roxelana, the favourite wife of Suliman the Magnificent. In addition to a soup kitchen for the poor, it contained a convent for Sufi mystics, and a caravanserai. The Ottoman governor of Jerusalem in the C19 used part of the edifice as his residence. Subsequently it was transformed into an orphanage.

The building is unusual in having three doors; in order to vary the effect all are framed in different ways. Note the inlaid panel above the left door (now blocked), the intricate joggling of the lintel and circular decoration of the centre door, and the fine dressing of the masonry. The extension to the east (left) is obviously of a different period; no colour stones are used and the construction of the lintel is different.

[**B**] *Turbat es-Sitt Tunshuq*. Six years before her death the Lady Tunshuq prepared her domed tomb immediately across the street from the palace. In addition to the stone mosaic panel (which differs subtly from its sister across the road), note the voussoirs of black, white, and red stones.

[**D**] *Ribat Bayram Jawish*. This building is the last notable Muslim contribution to the architecture of Jerusalem. The emir Bayram endowed it as a hospice for pilgrims to the Haram in 1540, but the style suggests that it was created by craftsmen trained in the Mamluk period. It is at present a thriving school whose name, *er-Rasasiyya*, derives from the fact that the courses are bonded by lead plates. This unusual and highly expensive feature was designed to produce a crisp visual distinction between the courses, thus achieving an effect similar to the black lines on an architectural drawing. Note the effect of a single course of black basalt, the shell vault behind the slightly pointed arch, and the joggled relieving lintel.

Tariq Bab en-Nazir (Tariq Bab el-Habs)

This street is one of the main routes to the Haram esh-Sharif, and like all the others leading to the Haram it takes its name from the gate at the end. Since this gate has two names—Gate of the Inspector or Gate of the Prison—so has the street. The names derive from the founder and subsequent use of one of the buildings.

[**E**] *Ribat Ala ed-Din el-Basir* (1267). The founder of this pilgrim hospice was a Mamluk emir famous for his wisdom and holiness. When he became blind he settled in Jerusalem and was appointed Inspector of the Two Harams (Jerusalem and Hebron); his judgement was so respected that, despite his affliction, he was known as *el-Basir*, 'the Clear-sighted'. The Ottomans used his hospice as a prison for criminals serving long sentences, this explains the strong barred gate and the minute cells in the courtyard. It needs little imagination to justify the name 'Prison of Blood'.

This is the earliest Mamluk building in Jerusalem, no coloured stones are used. Note the chamfering of the left pier, the carved panel over the door, and the bossed stones above the pointed arch.

[**F**] *Ribat Mansuri* (1282). The construction of this hospice, ordered by the sultan al-Mansur Qalawun (1279–90), was probably supervised by the emir Ala ed-Din whose own hospice is just across the road. Under the Ottomans it served first as a barracks and then as a prison, the small cells may still be seen in the courtyard.

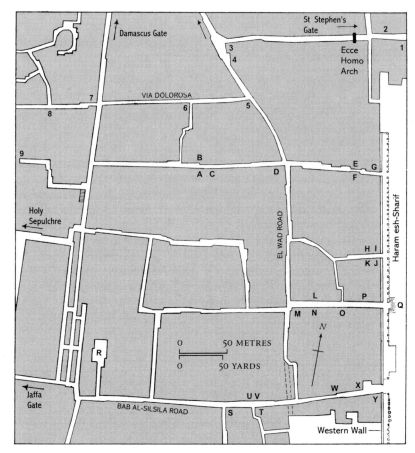

▲ **Fig. 10.** Muslim Quarter of Jerusalem. Locations of Stations of the Cross (numbers) and Mamluk buildings (letters).

The projecting entrance narrows the street at this point. The deep vestibule is paved with striated stone slabs reminiscent of those belonging to the forum of Hadrian (AD 135) preserved in ECCE HOMO (p. 33). The basic structure of the entrance is similar to that of [**E**] but an evolution is perceptible; coloured stones appear in the wide pointed arch and in the relieving lintel above the door, but as yet there is no joggling.

[**G**] *Madrasa Manjakiyya* (1361). Continually caught off balance in the power struggles of the emirs, the founder, Sayf al-Din Manjak (d. 1375), bounced in and out of prison before ending up in glory with complete authority throughout the state. The columned entrance, beside the original recessed door to the left, was constructed in 1923 when the building was refurbished as offices for the Department of Awqaf (Islamic Endowments).

Tariq Bab el-Hadid

As seen from the main thoroughfare, Tariq el-Wad, this is a curved uninviting street on the east side which disappears into an ominous looking tunnel leading to the Iron Gate of the Haram. The tunnel is in fact very short and opens into a quiet street lined on both sides with fine Mamluk buildings of the C13–C15.

[**H**] *Madrasa Jawhariyya* (1440). The founder of this college was an Abyssinian eunuch; most eunuchs were given names of precious stones or substances, and Jawhar means 'jewel'. After being given his freedom, his energy and talent won him the offices of Treasurer and Superintendent of the Royal Harem in Cairo.

The one noteworthy feature of this building is the founder's concern to be in direct contact with the Haram; in order to achieve this he had to extend his structure above the one-storey Ribat Kurt next door.

Note the continuity of the courses above the moulding of Ribat Kurt, and the circular ornamentation above the windows.

[**I**] *Ribat Kurt al-Mansuri* (1293). The modesty of this single-storey hospice with its diminutive entrance is unusual. Sayf ed-Din Kurt was chief chamberlain of the court in Cairo before being named governor of Tripoli (Lebanon) in 1299. In December of that year he died when leading a charge against the Tartars at Homs. Here entrance is easy but unfortunately recent constructions hardly make it worthwhile.

[**J**] *Madrasa Arghuniyya* (1358). Arghun el-Kamili was hardly thirty when he died an exile in Jerusalem only some five months before his college was completed. He served as Master of the Robes (note the blazon on the inscription above the door, Fig. 9) and had been governor of Damascus and twice governor of Aleppo before being caught on the wrong side in the perpetual Mamluk power struggle for the throne. After imprisonment in Alexandria he was banished to Jerusalem, and we are fortunate that his frustrated talent sought expression in architecture.

The original height of the building is indicated by the bold moulding which returns on the right to exclude the entrance to the Madrasa Khatuniyya built four years earlier (1354). Note in particular the entire course of joggling and the elaborate inlay over the openings on either side of the portal.

[**K**] *Madrasa Muzhiriyya* (1480). When he erected this college Abu Bakr Muhammad ihn Muzhir had been secretary of the Chancery of Egypt for eight years. He was stricken by fever in Nablus in 1488 trying to raise troops for an expedition against the Ottoman sultan of Rum (Constantinople) and died the same year.

In order to bring his college into direct contact with the Haram he extended the upper floor over the Madrasa Arghuniyya. Note the trefoil arch over eight courses of imprecise stalactites, the cream and black joggling above the lintel, and the decoration of the windows.

Suq el-Qattanin

Cleared and restored in 1974, this shopping arcade is considered the finest in the region. The name, which is not the original, means Market of the Cotton Merchants, and it was built in order to provide revenue from rents to support charitable works.

A glance along the shop-fronts reveals two periods of construction: the fifteen bays nearest the entrance from Tariq el-Wad have a simple arch, whereas the fifteen at the end near the Haram have a heavy lintel. The join near the centre is marked by pendentives coming together around a beautiful stalactite oculus. The western part [L] is a rebuilt version of a Crusader market which originally stood alone, and may have been damaged by an earthquake; at a later stage the market was extended to the east [P] to join the Haram. The shops have living or storage space above; the entrances to these rooms are from corridors along the outer walls of the complex.

Three inscriptions mention the emir Tankiz. One is on the bands of brass affixed to the great doors of Bab el-Oattanin [Q], the second is on the lintel above these doors, and the third is on the lintel of the entrance to Khan Tankiz [N]. This caravanserai is entered through a double bay located on the south side after the seventh shop from the Tariq el-Wad. The first two inscriptions provide the date 1336.

The blazon on the **Khan Tankiz** lintel shows that Tankiz held the office of Cup-Bearer (Fig. 9). Having accumulated a vast fortune during his 28 years as governor of Damascus and viceroy of Syria (1312–40), he spent much of it in beautifying Jerusalem. When his loyalty became suspect, he was removed from office and executed in Alexandria in 1340.

It seems likely that Tankiz took over the old western section of the market and incorporated it into a new building project crowned by the magnificent Bab el-Oattanin. In this case he would also be responsible for the **two baths**, Hammam el-Ayn [M] and Hammam el-Shifa [O]. The former, which is being restored, is entered from the Tariq el-Wad and is a classic Mamluk bath. The latter has a vaulted entrance porch in bays 18–20 (counting from the west) and the structure is not at right angles to the market. It sits above a 26 m-deep well, which probably served an earlier structure.

Tariq Bab es-Silsila

The Street of the Gate of the Chain is the main east–west artery in the Old City and the principal route to the Haram esh-Sharif (see box).

Variety in a Medieval Street

'This is the great street, which begins at the gate of the Haram known as the Gate of the Chain and goes to the Gate of the Prayer Niche [i.e. Jaffa Gate]. The street is divided into various segments, each of which has its own proper name,' which Mujir al-Din then lists starting from the Haram: the Goldsmith's Bazaar, the Straw Bazaar, the Bazaar of the Bleachers, the Charcoal Bazaar, the Bazaar of the Cooks, the Street of the Warehouse, the Bazaar of the Silk Merchants, and the Street of the Place of the Cereals. 'Taken all together these sections constitute David Street, so called because King David had an underground passage under it that led from the gate of the Haram called the Gate of the Chain to the Citadel, known in ancient times as the Prayer Niche of David, and the place where he lived. This passage still exists and can be inspected.' (Mujir al-Din (C15), *History of Jerusalem*, 289; trans. F. E. Peters)

[R] *Khan es-Sultan* (1386). The name derives from an inscription mentioning Barquq, the first of the Circassian Mamluk sultans (1382–99), but it is clear that his contribution was merely to expand and restore a Crusader merchant inn. Here goods from afar were brought for storage and distribution to local retailers. To the left just outside the main entrance and behind the shops on Tariq Bab al-Silsila is a little street of medieval shops. Unfortunately the archways at either end have been built up to create doorways. The main hall of the inn had store-rooms at ground level. Animals were housed in a stable reached by a passage half-way along the left (west) wall. Above the fine corbelled cornice on either side a walkway gave access to rooms where the merchants lodged. The Mamluks expanded the premises by the addition of an open courtyard surrounded by the same arrangement of store-rooms below and living quarters above. Modifications were made in the Ottoman period.

[S] *Madrasa/Turba Tashtimuriyya* (1382). The emir Tashtimur exercised a number of important functions in Egypt and Syria before becoming a victim of the chronic Mamluk power struggle for control of the empire. In 1382 he retired to Jerusalem where he immediately began to build his tomb: his state of mind is admirably expressed by Shakespeare: 'If a man do not erect in this age his own tomb ere he dies, he shall live no longer in monument than the bell rings and the widow weeps' (*Much Ado About Nothing*, v, ii). He was laid to rest there two years later (1384); his son Ibrahim was buried beside him in 1393. A passage beside the tomb leads to a magnificent cruciform college.

The façade contains three elements, the high door, the two windows of the tomb, and an elegant balcony. Note the intricate joggling surrounding the inscription above the tomb windows and the fleur-de-lis interlock at the end of the inscription; Tashtimur's blazon was the pen-box of a Secretary of State.

[T] *Turba Barka Khan* (Khalidi Library). A glance at the façade of this building suggests a complicated history. The Romanesque decoration above the window on the right (near the corner of Aqabat Abu Madyan which leads to the Western Wall) originally surmounted the entrance to the mausoleum of Barka Khan, a curious figure to have a monument in Jerusalem. He was commander of the Khwarizmians, a ferocious Tartar tribe who swept as far south as Gaza in 1244.

Two years later, while still very young, he died drunk in battle near Homs. His head was taken in triumph to Aleppo. Sultan Baybars (1260–77), however, married Barka Khan's daughter, with the result that her two brothers prospered greatly. One of them, Badr al-Din Muhammad Bey, built his father's tomb some time between 1264 and 1280, Given the career of his father, there is a certain poignancy in the Koranic verses he had inscribed on the mausoleum: 'Pure we came from nothing and impure we have become; tranquil we came into this world and anguished we have become.'

Some time after 1280 a series of vaulted structures was added on the east; hence the arches still evident in the façade. In 1390 these were blocked up and the present door and window inserted by one Muhammad ibn Ahmad. He also built a room above: the supports of a balcony project at the top of the wall. In 1900 the original tomb was converted into the reading room of the Khalidi Library housing 12,000 books and manuscripts.

Note in particular the double lintel of the centre window, and the intricate centre-piece (containing the word 'Allah') of the joggled lintel. The blazon at each end of the lintel inscription has no parallel in Mamluk heraldry and may be the personal emblem of Barka Khan.

[U] *Turba Kilaniyya* (1352). The fine proportions of the monochrome façade show how disciplined austerity can be used to effect. Behind each set of double windows is a tomb-chamber, an unusual feature that has a very human explanation. The emir Kilani left 100,000 dirhems to his nephew to build a tomb in Jerusalem and convey his body there for burial; at his uncle's expense the nephew added a tomb-chamber for himself!

Note the restrained moulding framing both the entire building and the two sets of windows. The course above the lintel of the blocked windows is undercut in a decorative profile to achieve the same effect as a relieving arch. The next course is set back to form a long panel with decorated terminals.

[V] *Turba/Madrasa Taziyya* (1362). Having begun his career as a cupbearer at the court of Sultan al-Nazir Muhammad (note the blazon, Fig. 9), Taz rose to become governor of Aleppo when Arghun el-Kamili (see [J]) was recalled in 1354. He suffered the same fate four years later, and was imprisoned in Kerak and Alexandria, where he was blinded, before being exiled to Jerusalem. The poverty of his tomb suggests that he had few resources! Even his hopes were unfulfilled. He died in Damascus in 1362, and was buried there.

[**W**] *Turba Turkan Khatun* (1352). All that is known about the Lady Turkan is that she was from the eastern borders of the Islamic world. The names of her father and grandfather given in the inscription are found among members of the family of the Khans of the Golden Horde. The façade is striking in its simple elegance, the arabesques in its grey stone are the most subtle in Jerusalem. Note the use of the blunt star first introduced as architectural decoration by the Mamluks.

[**X**] *Turba Sadiyya* (1311). This tomb of Saad al-Din Masud is noteworthy for the fine stalactite corbelling, the earliest of its kind in Jerusalem, and for the mosaic of coloured marble over the door.

[**Y**] *Madrasa Tankiziyya* (1328). The open square in front of Bab al-Silsila permits full appreciation of the magnificent entrance to the college erected by the emir Tankiz whose career is described apropos of Suq el-Qattanin (p. 41). The big inscription is punctuated by three cup blazons (Fig. 9). Note in particular the stalactites and the moulding of the semi-dome above.

The street and college rest on Wilson's Arch, a huge bridge (named after its discoverer) built to span the Tyropoeon valley: it can be visited from the Western Wall area (p. 98). Part of the C1 AD street that crossed the original Herodian bridge is visible in the excavated area before the gate. The fountain was a gift of Suliman the Magnificent in the mid-C16 AD. It reuses older elements. The trough was originally a Roman sarcophagus; the rest is Crusader.

The street terminates at the main entrance to the HARAM ESH-SHARIF (p. 80). The left bay (north) is Bab al-Sakina, 'the Gate of the Dwelling', and the right Bab al-Silsila, 'the Gate of the Chain'. The huge arch below indicates that a principal gate of Herod's temple was located here, but no trace of it remains. When the site was brought back into use in the C8 AD the Umayyads constructed a roundheaded gateway. By the C11 it was decorated with mosaics. No wonder the Crusaders considered it the Beautiful Gate (Acts 3: 2)! Sometime before 1198 the Ayyubids inserted the joggled lintels, and erected the two domed bays using Crusader materials.

The Christian Quarter

The Christian Quarter covers an area of 18.2 hectares in the north-west section of the Old City (Fig. 2); its population is estimated at 4,500. Just as the Mamluks clustered their buildings around the HARAM ESH-SHARIF, Christians erected their institutions as close as possible to the Holy Sepulchre (A in Fig. 11). The area is quieter (more clerics, less children) and more affluent than the MUSLIM QUARTER, because for several generations Christians had the benefit of a better educational system operated by Europeans. Most of the shops are now in the hands of Muslims who bought from emigrating Christian Arabs.

The Holy Sepulchre [A]   ★

One expects the central shrine of Christendom to stand out in majestic isolation, but anonymous buildings cling to it like barnacles. One looks for numinous light, but it is dark and cramped. One hopes for peace, but the ear is assailed by a cacophony of warring chants. One desires holiness, only to encounter a jealous possessiveness: the six groups of occupants—Latin Catholics, Greek Orthodox, Armenians, Syrians, Copts, Ethiopians—watch one another suspiciously for any infringement of rights. The frailty of humanity is nowhere more apparent than here; it epitomizes the human condition. The empty who come to be filled will leave desolate; those who permit the church to question them may begin to understand why hundreds of thousands thought it worthwhile to risk death or slavery in order to pray here.

Is this the place where Christ died and was buried? Very probably, Yes. At the beginning of the C1 AD the site was a disused quarry outside the city walls ([6] in Fig. 1). Tombs similar to those found elsewhere and dated to the C1 BC and the C1 AD had been cut into the vertical west wall left by the quarrymen. These latter had also cut around a bank of inferior cracked stone and left it jutting out from the east wall. These facts are the meagre contribution of archaeology, but at the least they show that the site is compatible with the topographical data supplied by the gospels. Jesus was crucified on a rock eminence reminiscent of a skull outside the city (John 19: 17), and there was a grave nearby (John 19: 41–2). Windblown earth and seeds watered by winter rains would have created the covering of green in the quarry that John dignifies by the term 'garden'.

The positive argument for the authenticity of the site is the tradition of the Jerusalem community, which held liturgical celebrations at the site until AD 66. Even when the area was brought within the walls in AD 41–3 it was not built over. The memory of the site remained, and was probably reinforced by bitterness when Hadrian in 135 filled in the quarry to provide a level base for his Capitoline temple, which was flanked by a shrine honouring Aphrodite. The value of the Jerusalem tradition must

▼ **The Main Entrance of the Holy Sepulchre.** Carved rosettes in a hoodmould surmount the early C12 gadrooned arch. The late C12 Tuscan lintel (now in the Rockefeller Museum) shows scenes from the life of Christ. A mosaic once decorated the triangular tympanum.

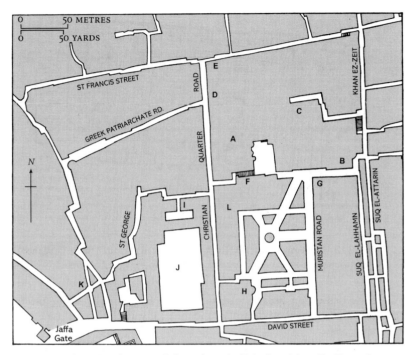

▲ **Fig. 11.** Christian Quarter of Jerusalem. A. Holy Sepulchre; B. Alexander Hospice; C. Deir es-Sultan; D. Crusader entrance to Holy Sepulchre; E. Khanqah Salahiyya; F. Mosque of Omar; G. Church of the Redeemer; H. Church of St John; I. Coptic Khan; J. Pool of the Patriarch's Bath; K. Roman column; L. Site of Crusader hospital.

have been scrutinized very carefully when in the early C4 the emperor Constantine decided to build a church commemorating the Resurrection. Acceptance of the tradition involved a double expense: substantial buildings had to be torn down, and a new one put in their place. And just to the south was the open space of Hadrian's forum! The suggestion must have been made that the church be built there, but the insistence of the community that the tomb was under Hadrian's temple prevailed, and, as the eyewitness Eusebius, bishop of Caesarea, tells us, 'At once the work was carried out, and, as layer after layer of the subsoil came into view, the venerable and most holy memorial of the Saviour's resurrection, beyond all our hopes, came into view' (*Life of Constantine* 3: 28).

Constantine's church, started in 326, was dedicated in 335. It comprised four elements (Fig. 12): [**1**] an atrium, which reused part of Hadrian's temenos wall, at the head of the steps from the main street; [**2**] a covered absidal basilica; [**3**] an open courtyard with the block of stone venerated as Golgotha in the south-east corner; [**4**] the tomb in a circular edifice. The work on this last element was not quite finished at the time

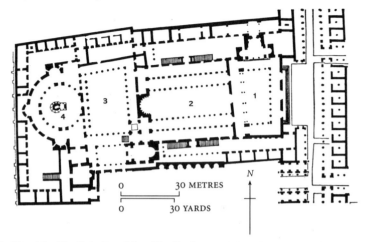

▲ **Fig. 12.** The Holy Sepulchre. The C4 Constantinian church (after Couäsnon).
1. Atrium; 2. Basilica; 3. Courtyard; 4. Rotunda.

of the dedication because of the immense labour involved in cutting away the cliff in order to isolate the tomb; it was completed sometime before 384.

The reconstruction of the patriarch Modestus, after the building had been set on fire by the Persians in 614, made no significant changes. When the caliph Omar came to sign the treaty of capitulation in 638, which

An Eyewitness Describes Constantine's Holy Sepulchre

'First of all (since it was the principal feature) Constantine adorned the holy Cave, where the bright angel once announced good news of a new birth for all, revealed through the Saviour. This principal feature the munificent Emperor adorned with choice columns and much ornament, sparing no art to make it beautiful. He passed on to a vast area open to the sky. The Emperor paved it with polished stone, and surrounded it with long colonnades on three sides. To the side opposite the cave (on the east) was attached a basilical church, a masterpiece. It was enormously lofty, and of generous proportions. The inner surfaces of the building were finished with polychrome marble panels, and the outer surface of the walls was veneered with polished stones which gave them a superb finish quite equal to marble. The outer covering of the roof was lead, a reliable protection against winter rain. The inside was carved and coffered, making a pattern of connected coffers which stretched over the whole basilica like a great sea. It was all brightly gilded, and made the whole church shine and sparkle.'
(Eusebius (C4), *Life of Constantine* 3: 34–6; trans. J. Wilkinson)

transferred Jerusalem from Christian to Muslim control, he refused the patriarch's invitation to pray in the Holy Sepulchre, saying, 'If I had prayed in the church it would have been lost to you, for the Believers would have taken it saying: Omar prayed here.' Such generosity had unfortunate consequences; had the church become a mosque it would not have been touched by the Fatimid caliph Hakim in 1009. His destruction was systematic; wrecking crews knocked the courses from the walls and attacked the rock tomb of Christ with picks and hammers, stopping only when the debris covered what remained.

The poor community of Jerusalem could not afford repairs. It was not until the reign of Constantine Monomachus that the Imperial Treasury provided a subsidy for reconstruction (1042–8). It was not adequate for complete repairs, however, and a great part of the original edifice had to be abandoned (Fig. 13). The atrium and the basilica ([1] and [2] in Fig. 12) were lost for ever; only the courtyard and the rotunda remained. The latter was developed into a church by the insertion of a large apse into the façade. This was the church to which the Crusaders

▼ **Fig. 13.** The Holy Sepulchre. The church as restored by Constantine Monomachus in the C11 (after Couäsnon).

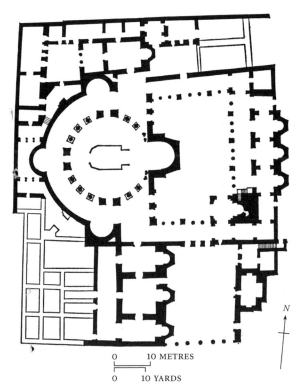

N

| 0 | 10 METRES |
| 0 | 10 YARDS |

came with tears of piety to sing their *Te Deum* after capturing the city on 15 July 1099.

The Crusaders were slow to modify the church. They first (1114) erected the monastery of the canons where the Constantinian basilica used to be, having first excavated the Crypt of St Helena. Then in 1119 they completely replaced the replica of Christ's tomb. The coronation in the rotunda of Fulk of Anjou and Melisende, daughter of Baldwin II, on 14 September 1131 emphasized the need for a radical transformation of the church. The solution adopted was to cover the Constantinian court-yard with a Romanesque church (dedicated in 1149) which communicated with the rotunda by the great arched opening left after the demolition of the C11 apse. Around 1170 a bell tower was added.

In subsequent centuries the church suffered desecration and destruction more than once. Inept repairs were no less damaging. A fire in 1808 and an earthquake in 1927 did extensive damage, but it took until 1959 for the three major communities (Latins, Greeks, and Armenians) to come to agreement on a major repair programme. The guiding principle was that only elements incapable of fulfilling their structural function were to be replaced; this explains the rather surprising juxtaposition of old and new stones. Local masons were trained to trim stone in the style of the C11 for the rotunda, and in that of the C12 for the church.

Visit (Fig. 14). Open: 4 a.m.–7 p.m. (winter); to 8 p.m. (summer); when Summer Time is in force 5 a.m.–9 p.m.; no shorts or sleeveless garments permitted. The Christian Information Centre inside Jaffa Gate provides lists of the time of the services of the various communities.

The three chapels [**1–3**] to the left of the entrance court [**4**] were added in the C11 and belong to the Greek Orthodox. Facing them are the entrances to Coptic, Armenian, and Greek Orthodox monasteries. The last (furthest from the entrance to the church) covers a huge vaulted cistern of the C2 AD. The two and a half upper storeys of the Crusader bell-tower had become so dilapidated that they had to be removed in 1719. That the tower was an afterthought is evident from the way it destroys the symmetry of the medieval façade; the run of the moulding above the windows shows that the tower blocks a small window which balanced the one on the far side. The upper cornice reuses C2 AD Roman stones and served as the model for the C12 cornice below the windows.

The so-called **Chapel of the Franks** [**6**] was built by the Crusaders to provide a ceremonial entrance to Calvary [**7–8**]. It was closed sometime after the fall of Jerusalem in 1187, when the southern half of the main entrance to the church [**5**] was also walled up; the Muslims were determined to exercise tight control over Christian use of the edifice. The original carved Crusader lintels were removed to the Rockefeller Museum for safety after the earthquake of 1927. The wooden cover just in front of

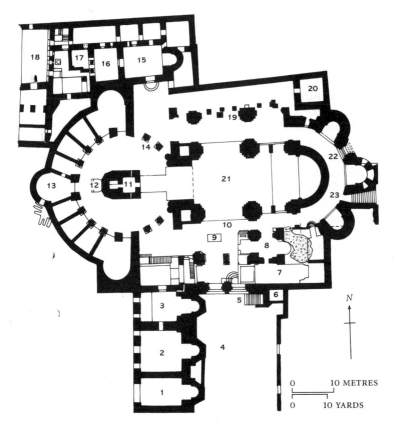

▲ **Fig. 14.** The Holy Sepulchre. The C12 church (after Corbo). 1–3. C11 chapels; 4. Courtyard; 5. Steps; 6. Chapel of the Franks; 7. Latin Calvary; 8. Greek Calvary (above); Chapel of Adam (below); 9. Stone of Anointing; 10. Greek wall; 11. Tomb of Christ; 12. Coptic chapel; 13. C1 tomb; 14. Tapering columns; 15. Chapel of St Mary Magdalene; 16. Franciscan choir; 17. C11 atrium; 18. C7 room; 19. Byzantine and Crusader columns and piers; 20. Prison of Christ; 21. Greek Orthodox Catholicon; 22. Entrance to medieval monastery; 23. Entrance to the Crypt of St Helena.

the blocked door hides the tombstone of an English knight, Philip d'Aubigny (d. 1236).

The present stairway to **Calvary** is necessarily later than the blocking of the door [**5**]. The floor above is on a level with the top of the rocky outcrop on which Christ was crucified, and is divided into two chapels whose variety of decoration is evocative of other differences between the Eastern and Western churches. The mosaics in the Latin chapel [**7**] are modern, save for the medallion of the Ascension on the ceiling, which is C12. The window was created by blocking the Crusader entrance; from it one can look down into the Chapel of the Franks [**6**]. Cardinal Ferdinand de Medici presented the bronze altar in 1588; it was made in Florence. The rock of Calvary is visible all round the Greek altar [**8**] beneath which a round hole permits one to touch the rock below.

The area directly beneath the Greek Orthodox chapel is called the **Chapel of Adam,** because of the tradition that Christ died where Adam had been buried. The two piers and the apse they flank are of the C11. Behind the window is the crack in the poor quality rock, which is why the quarrymen left this section untouched. The other two piers are medieval; at their feet were the tombs of the first two Crusader rulers, Godfroy de Bouillon and Baldwin I, which were removed by the Greeks in 1809.

The **Stone of Unction** [**9**], commemorating the anointing of Jesus before burial (John 19: 38–40), appeared first in the C12; the present one dates from 1810. The wall behind [**10**] has no structural function, and blocks a fine view across the church. When the fire of 1808 cracked the great arch above, a wall was erected to support it, and the Greeks hung icons on it. The recent restoration of the arch made the wall unnecessary, but the Greeks now had nowhere to hang their icons, and built a new one just for this purpose! It covers the graves of four Crusader kings.

Originally, the **rotunda** was also much more spacious, for the circle outside the columns was designed as an open ambulatory; the space is now taken up by meaningless store-rooms. The outer walls of the rotunda, for 11 m above ground, are C4. The C11 piers and columns, cracked in the fire of 1808, have all been restored, two [**14**] exactly as they were found. Note that one has a rim around the top and the other around the bottom, and that the taper of the latter is continued in the former. They were originally one great column, which graced either the Capitoline temple of Hadrian or the C4 Holy Sepulchre; it was cut in half and reused in the C11 restoration of the building.

The **tomb monument** [**11**], indulgently described as a 'hideous kiosk', dates only from the C19, the fire of 1808 having damaged the last of a series of replicas which replaced the tomb destroyed by Hakim in 1009. It bears little resemblance to the original, whose form (Fig. 15) has been reconstructed by J. Wilkinson on the basis of representations of the C4 tomb embossed on pilgrim flasks of the C6 and on a pre-C10 stone model of the tomb found in Narbonne. The polygonal part was the original rock decorated by columns, a canopied masonry structure adorned the entrance.

According to a report made during the reconstruction of 1809, traces of the original limestone structure of the tomb were visible only on the north and south sides. In consequence, the piece of granite unveiled so solicitously by the guardian of the little Coptic shrine [**12**] cannot be authentic; it must belong to one of the edifices that have succeeded each other on this site since the Middle Ages.

The C4 outer wall of the rotunda and the central exedra are visible in

▲ Fig. 15. J. Wilkinson's reconstruction of the C4 Tomb of Christ.

the **Syrian chapel** [13]. A dark hole in the wall leads to a Jewish burial chamber; such *kokhim* graves are typical of the C1 BC and the C1 AD, and these could not have been dug after the quarry was incorporated into the city in AD 41–3. Their relationship to the tomb of Christ is best explained by postulating a catacomb (see Fig. 34 for an example). Constantine's engineers would have cut away all save the outermost chamber, in which the body of Christ had been laid in haste (John 19: 41–2), and this portion of the innermost one.

In the C4 the area north of the rotunda was part of the Patriarchate; buildings one-room deep surrounded an L-shaped courtyard, and all the east–west walls at ground level are Constantinian. In the C11 the courtyard was transformed into the **chapel of St Mary Magdalene** (John 20: 11–16) [15] with its narthex [16] from which one passed via a two-column entrance into a small atrium [17]. The atrium was reduced to virtually nothing in the C12 when the Crusaders erected a stairway leading to what is now Christian Quarter Road; its monumental entrance, whose decoration is identical with that of the main door of the Holy Sepulchre, is still partially visible ([**D**] in Fig. 11) from the street. The stairway passes over a fine chamber [18] whose west and north walls are cut out of the rock; the unusual vaulted ceiling is the work of Modestus in the early C7, but the arched doorway is probably C11.

The curious arrangement of **two lines of very different pillars** [19] is due to the C12 architect's concern to preserve what remained of the C11 colonnade on the north side of the Byzantine courtyard in front of the rotunda (see Fig. 13). He therefore placed his weight-bearing pillars immediately inside the slender Byzantine columns with their basket capitals. The outer wall at this point is C4, as is the small room

▲ **Holy Sepulchre.** Kokhim tombs of the early first century in the Syrian Chapel.

[20], which is identified as the **Prison of Christ** on the basis of a C8 legend that Christ and the two thieves were held there while the crosses were being prepared.

The simple dignity of the **Crusader church** [21]—transitional between Romanesque and Gothic—is unfortunately marred by the lack of taste displayed in the modern decorations of the Greek Orthodox, whose Catholicon it now is. The upper gallery, unusual in churches of this period, was inspired by the corresponding gallery in the rotunda.

The masonry on both sides of the ambulatory around the apse is Crusader. One doorway [**22**] originally gave access to the monastic cloister built on the ruins of the Constantinian basilica ([2] in Fig. 12). The other [23] is the entrance to the **Crypt of St Helena**. On the walls on either side of the steps note the multitude of crosses carved by pilgrims. The crypt, now in the possession of the Armenians, was opened only in the C12, but its north and south walls (left and right when facing the altar) are the foundations of the nave of the C4 basilica. The stairs on the right lead down to an area reputed to be the cistern in which St Helena is supposed to have discovered the True Cross.

In fact it is part of a quarry which extends to the north behind the altar into the **Chapel of St Vartan**. In order to reach the prized *meleke* limestone the quarrymen of the C8–C6 BC tunnelled beneath the overburden of inferior stone (see SOLOMON'S QUARRIES, p. 142). When Hadrian chose this site for his Capitoline temple, three walls were built to support the roof of the cave. While one of the stones was lying on the surface a visitor from abroad drew a picture of the ship in which he had travelled, and scrawled the words best read as DD M NOMINUS 'the gift of Marcus Nominus'. Subsequently the quarry was filled in again to support the floor of the C4 basilica above.

Hidden Parts of the Constantinian Holy Sepulchre

The church of the C4 was much bigger than the present one, and very interesting traces of it are to be found hidden in other buildings in the immediate vicinity. The capital letters locate them in Fig. 11.

The Russian Mission in Exile [B]

Open: 9 a.m.–1 p.m.; 3–5 p.m; closed Sunday. The presence of ruins, which had already been identified as elements of the original Holy Sepulchre, led to the acquisition of the site by Russia in 1859. The 1882 excavations and the edifice protecting the remains were funded by the Grand Duke Serge Alexandrovitch, whence the popular name 'Alexander Hospice'. The most significant remains (Fig. 16) illustrate the relationship between the C4 atrium ([1] in Fig. 12) and the street outside.

When first discovered, the column [1] was backed by a brick and stone wall equal to that on the other side [2–3]. This pitiable imitation of a triumphal arch was all that the desperately poor Christians of Jerusalem could offer the emperor Constantine Monomachus in gratitude for his restoration of the Holy Sepulchre (1042–8). The remains of an earlier commemorative arch on the same spot probably inspired the gesture. Once the C11 material [2] is removed, it becomes possible to reconstruct (inset) the northern bay of a Roman triple arch erected by the emperor Hadrian when he founded Aelia Capitolina in AD 135. It stood near the eastern edge of his forum [4]: some of the flagstones are very ancient but they are unlikely to go back to the C2.

The heavy wall [9 and 16], which reuses some Herodian blocks, is

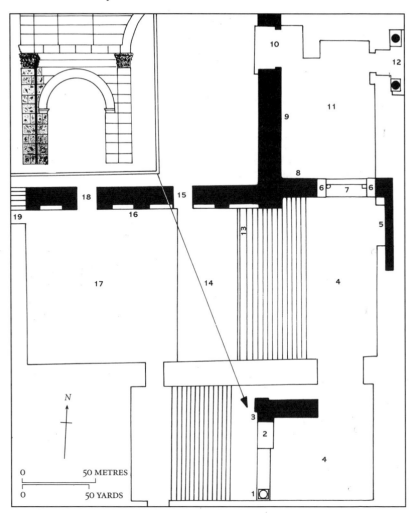

▲ **Fig. 16.** The Russian Mission Excavations. 1. Column; 2. C11 construction;
3. Pier of C2 AD arch; 4. C2 AD forum; 5. C4 AD wall; 6. Blocks; 7. Gate;
8–9. Wall pierced to hold marble slabs; 10. C4 AD door; 11. C2 AD sidewalk;
12. C2 AD colonnade; 13. Ancient slabs; 14. Sanctuary; 15. Door; 16. C2 AD
wall. 17. Modern church; 18. Door; 19. Medieval door.

part of the wall erected by Hadrian around his Capitoline temple (p. 46);
it is very doubtful if any of the doors existed at this period. Outside
was a pavement [**11**] flanked by the columns [**12**] of the *cardo maximus*
or main street. Since it is unlikely that the pavement terminated at a meaningless gate [**7**], there may have been an arch at this point in the
C2 AD.

In the C4 Constantine's engineers cut a door [10] in the wall: its secondary character is underlined by the quality of the jambs and the absence of an engaged sill. The groove in one of the protruding blocks of the foundation course was to receive a marble slab. Similar slabs were attached to the outer face of the wall [8 and 9] by pins whose holes are still visible. The gate [7], whose sill is conserved in a glass case because popular piety takes it to be the way by which Christ left the city on his way to execution, was probably constructed at this period, together with the wall [5] which would have enclosed a space to the south of the Holy Sepulchre. Inside there would have been a flight of steps whose top row is signalled by the line of ancient slabs [13] partly hidden by the screen cutting off the sanctuary of the modern chapel [14]. Only on the assumption of a pavement running along the south side of the Holy Sepulchre do the doors [15 and 18] become intelligible. Sometime later the gate [7] was taken out of commission, and the space enlarged by cutting back the walls [5 and 8] and inserting two blocks [6].

The drafted margins of the lower course of the wall [16] are visible just above the floor of the modern chapel [17]. The door [18] leads to a small museum in which artefacts found in the excavations are very inadequately displayed. The arched entrance [19] is evidently medieval and led to the monastic cloister that is now the Ethiopian Monastery.

Ethiopian Monastery [C]

At the end of the passage reached by the stairs that start at a shop called 'Zelatimo's Sweets' (which contains the now inaccessible main door of the Constantinian atrium) on the Suq Khan es-Zeit, a small door opens into a cluster of mud huts. These poor dwellings, ironically called Deir es-Sultan, are occupied by Ethiopian religious forced from their building by the Copts. Silent and inward-looking, the immense dignity of the tall, slender men generates the atmosphere of contemplation so desperately lacking in the Holy Sepulchre. They live among the ruins of a medieval cloister, which the Crusaders erected in the space once occupied by Constantine's great basilica ([2] in Fig. 12). The cupola in the middle of the courtyard admits light to the Crypt of St Helena below. A door in the south-west corner of the courtyard permits access to the courtyard of the Holy Sepulchre via Ethiopian and Coptic chapels. On the northern side of the courtyard is the Coptic Patriarchate, which is built over a vast cistern of uncertain date.

Two Mosques [E and F]

North of the Holy Sepulchre is the Khanqah Salahiyya [E], a convent of Sufi mystics founded by Saladin between 1187 and 1189 on the site of the palace of the Crusader patriarch of Jerusalem. During the restoration of 1417 a minaret was erected beside the entrance.

Directly across from the main entrance of the Holy Sepulchre is the so-called Mosque of Omar [**F**]. In popular tradition it commemorates the caliph's prayer at the entrance of the basilica in February 638 (cf. p. 49). In the C7, however, the entrance was on the east. The present entrance was inaugurated only in the C11, but it would have been the only one known to Saladin's son, Afdal Ali, when he built the mosque in 1193 in the corner of the great hospital of the Knights of St John. The base of the minaret contains much Crusader masonry (some possibly *in situ*). According to Mujir al-Din, the minaret was given its present form sometime before 1465, possibly after the earthquake of 1458.

The tops of the two minarets are identical in structure, and in the quality of the light stone, which contrasts with the darker lower sections of both. This hint that they were intended to be a pair is reinforced by the observation that, despite a significant difference in ground level, a line joining their summits is absolutely horizontal. A. Walls has further shown that the mid-point of a line drawn between the minarets falls approximately at the entrance of the tomb of Christ in the Holy Sepulchre. There can be no doubt that this arrangement was intentional. The Mamluks may have desired to 'nullify' the Holy Sepulchre, which is the only site associated with Christ that Muslims do not accept.

The Mauristan

This name is given to the square area south of the Holy Sepulchre, one corner being marked by the newest church in the Old City, the Lutheran Church of the Redeemer [**G**], and the other, diagonally opposite, by the oldest intact church in Jerusalem, the Church of St John [**H**]. Mauristan is a Persian word meaning 'hospital or hospice', and recalls a tradition going back to the friendship between Charlemagne and the caliph Harun-al-Rashid (of *One Thousand and One Nights* fame) at the beginning of the C9.

In 870 Bernard the Monk wrote of his visit to Jerusalem: 'we stayed in the hospice of the Most Glorious Emperor Charles. All who come to Jerusalem for reasons of devotion and speak the Roman language [i.e. Latin] are given hospitality there. Beside it there is a church in honour of St Mary, and thanks to the Emperor it has a splendid library.' Damaged, if not destroyed, by the caliph Hakim in 1009, these edifices were restored some 50 years later by a group who had a particular interest in this part of the city, the merchants of Amalfi.

These traders combined piety and profit by erecting three churches with their attendant hospitals or hospices. St Mary of the Latins (*c*.1070) was for male pilgrims, St Mary Minor for women (*c*.1080), and St John (*c*.1070) for the poor. Overall charge was confided to Benedictine monks and nuns. All traces of St Mary Minor, which by the middle of the C12 was known as St Mary Major, were destroyed when the Greeks built the

The Hospital of St John of Jerusalem

'Next to the Church of the Holy Sepulchre, on the opposite side towards the south, is a beautiful church erected in honour of Saint John Baptist. The hospital is next to it, in which in various houses a great crowd of sick people is collected, some of them women and some men. They are cared for, and every day fed at vast expense. The total of persons at the time when I was present I learned from the servitors talking about it, and it was 2,000 sick persons. Between day and night there were sometimes more than 50 corpses carried out, but again and again there were new people admitted.' (John of Würzburg (C12), 159; trans. J. Wilkinson)

market in front of the Church of the Redeemer in 1901; the hospice would have been on the site of the present fountain.

On the evening of 15 July 1099 the warden of St John took in a number of knights wounded in the assault on the city. Some stayed on to serve at his side, and ten years later committed themselves to serving the sick and protecting pilgrims as the Knights of St John of the Hospital. In a short time they became the military order of the Hospitallers, but they kept the little church of St John unchanged to remind them of their origins in the midst of great power and wealth. They built their immense hospital or hospice in the area between the church of St John and the Holy Sepulchre ([**L**] in Fig. 11).

After the fall of Jerusalem in October 1187 Saladin permitted ten Hospitallers to remain for a year to nurse those still in the hospital. When he returned to Jerusalem in 1192, he took over the hospital and endowed it so that it might continue to function as a hospice (*bimarestan*) for the sick. As late as the C15 the edifice was capable of receiving 400 pilgrims, even though it was falling into decay. The end came in the C16 when the masons of Suliman the Magnificent used the massive ruins as a quarry of dressed stones to rebuild the walls of Jerusalem.

Church of the Redeemer [G]

The gallery at the top of the tower (open: 9 a.m.–1 p.m., 1.30–5 p.m.; closed Sunday) offers a magnificent bird's-eye view of the whole area. This alone makes the 178-step climb worthwhile. More specifically, from this vantage point it is possible to correlate visually the scattered remains of the Constantinian Holy Sepulchre.

The present church, erected in 1898, preserves the outline of the C11 church of St Mary of the Latins. In keeping with the custom of Benedictine churches of this period, the main entrance was in the north wall; the medieval porch has been conserved with its decoration of the symbols of the months (see Fig. 53). Muslim iconoclasts damaged the figures which begin with January at bottom left; the most recognizable figure is the thresher representing August. An entrance in the western façade was opened only in the early C13 when the church was transformed into a mosque and the adjoining hospice into a Muslim law school.

The modern Lutheran hospice located immediately south of the church has as its centre-piece the medieval cloister, which was in great part rebuilt by the Arabs in the C13 or C14. It can no longer be entered from the church; one must go out into the street and around to the main door of the hospice. Just inside, the link between the two levels of the cloister is established by a staircase with a beautifully proportioned double window of the mid-C13. This had originally been part of a loggia and staircase inserted in the south wall of the church by the Arabs to link the mosque with the law school, and was transferred to this point at the beginning of this century.

By prior arrangement with the Probst (tel.: 627–6111) it is possible to visit the excavations beneath the church; entrance is from the cloister. The bottom of the deep trench reveals the typical cuttings of a quarry, evidently the same as that beneath the Holy Sepulchre (p. 45). The 1.6 m-wide wall is founded on small stones set directly on soft earth, and is incapable of bearing any great weight. It was built sometime after AD 68, and its function is a matter of guesswork; it may have been the foundation of a small building on Hadrian's C2 forum. The portion of mosaic interspersed with pieces of marble near the entrance is medieval.

▼ **Fig. 17.** The C5 church of St John the Baptist.

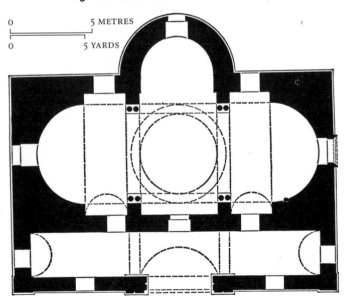

Church of St John the Baptist [H]

The silver dome of this, the oldest church in Jerusalem, is visible from the fountain in the middle of the Mauristan. It can also be reached from Christian Quarter Road, where it is clearly signposted; the flight of steps conforms to the slope descending to the Tyropoeon Valley and gives access to the courtyard of a modern Greek Orthodox monastery whose priest (when present) will open the church.

The present façade with its two small bell-towers is a modern addition to the C11 church of the merchants of Amalfi, which became the cradle of the Knights Hospitallers. As foundations they used the walls of a much earlier church, built about the middle of the C5 and restored by John the Almoner, Patriarch of Alexandria, after its destruction by the Persians in 614. Some alterations were made in order to ensure the stability of the superstructure, but it is still possible to detect the original plan (Fig. 17). It was composed of three apses and a long narthex.

The tradition that this was the house of Zebedee, father of the apostles James and John, is first attested in the C14, and must have arisen through a confusion between John the Evangelist and John the Baptist.

Pool of the Patriarch's Bath [J]

This great reservoir is entirely surrounded by buildings, and is accessible only through the Coptic Khan [I]. Once a typical caravanserai, the buildings around the courtyard are now used as workshops; when approached properly the owners will sometimes permit visitors to peer through the back windows overlooking the pool. It may be seen from a distance from the top of the north-east tower in the CITADEL ([5] in Fig. 7) and from the roof of the Petra Hotel facing the Citadel. At present the dry pool is used as a rubbish dump by the dwellings which surround it on all sides, but a much needed restoration project is on the drawing-board.

Since the pool has never been investigated by archaeologists factual information is sparse. It is thought to date from the Herodian period when it was fed by an aqueduct (visible outside Jaffa Gate) coming from Mamilla Pool in what is now Independence Park in the new city. It may have begun life as a quarry from which stones were cut for the pre-Herodian Second Wall which bordered it some distance to the east.

Josephus mentions it in order to locate one of the points where the Romans attempted to break through the rampart in June AD 70. He gives it the name Amygdalon, 'almond tree' (War 5: 468), which is probably a deformation of the Hebrew migdal, 'tower', the point of reference being the renowned towers of Herod's palace nearby (p. 22). In the Middle Ages the pool supplied water to baths located near the palace of the Crusader patriarch, whence its present name.

Roman Column [K]

A circle at the intersection of four covered streets is lit by a lamp stand-ing on a column with a Latin inscription, which reads, 'M(arco) Iunio Maximo leg(ato) Aug(ustorum) Leg(ionis) X Fr(etensis) Antoninianae— C. Dom(itius) Serg(ius) str(ator) eius'.

The inscription honours Marcus Iunius Maximus, Legate of the Augusts (i.e. the emperor Septimius Severus and his eldest son Caracalla), which implies that he was the governor of the province of Judaea, and Legate of the Tenth Legion Fretensis. It was erected *c*. AD 200 by one of his aides, C. Domitius Sergius Honoratus. After participating in the capture of Jerusalem in AD 70, the Tenth Legion was based in the city for over 200 years, occupying the area that is now the Armenian Quarter.

The Armenian Quarter

This quarter (Fig. 2) takes its name from its central feature, the great compound of the Armenian Monastery, which is in fact a city in miniature with its own schools, library, seminary, and residential quarters, all arranged around the Cathedral of St James. Much of the area was once covered by the palace of Herod the Great (p. 22).

Armenia was the first nation to adopt Christianity as its official reli-gion at the very beginning of the C4. Shortly thereafter Armenian pilgrims began to come to Jerusalem, and by the middle of the following century their church was strongly represented in the Holy Land. A C7 document lists seventy monasteries in Jerusalem; only the magnificent mosaic floor of one remains (p. 141).

The disappearance of the kingdom of Armenia at the end of the C4 inaugurated a period of persecution and exile which culminated in the systematic massacre of almost two million Armenians by successive Turkish administrations in the first part of the C20. As an exiled people their unity is founded on their language and culture, both of which are rooted in their church; two great saints of the early C5, Isaac and Mesrob, are credited with the creation of a national identity which has survived centuries of dispersion.

A restored Armenian kingdom in Cilicia (1080–1375) had very close relations with the Latin Kingdom; intermarriage was frequent, and the beauty and intelligence of Armenian women won for a number the dignity of Queen of Jerusalem. After the fall of Jerusalem in 1187 Saladin expelled all Christians save the Armenians, whose prerogatives and

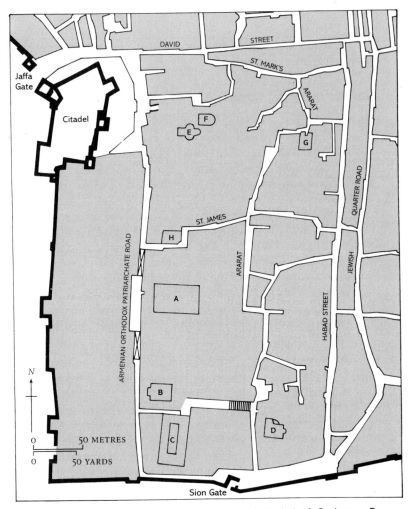

▲ **Fig. 18.** Armenian Quarter of Jerusalem. A. Cathedral of St James; B. Library; C. Mardigian Museum; D. Convent of the Olive Tree; E. Christchurch; F. St James the Cut-Up; G. St Mark; H. St Thomas.

possessions he guaranteed. The prosperity they enjoyed was gradually eroded through increased taxation in the C15, and for several years (1717–21) Gregory, the Armenian patriarch of Jerusalem, begged at the door of the church of the Holy Mother of God in Istanbul in order to pay off the debts of his community; he became known as the Chainbearer on account of the iron chain he wore around his neck. It is to his sacrifice that the Cathedral of St James owes much of its present splendour. After the Turkish massacres what were designed as temporary lodging for pilgrims within the monastery became the permanent residence of refugees.

The letters following the headings in what follows refer to the locations in Fig. 18.

Cathedral of St James [A]   ★

In sharp contrast to the sombre weariness of the HOLY SEPULCHRE, this church mirrors the life and vigour of a colourful and unified people. On the tessellated floor magnificent carpets glow softly in the reflected light of the innumerable lamps that hang in the air like stars. Fact and legend are juxtaposed as casually as are artistic creations of different talents and periods.

The first sanctuary on this site was an oratory dedicated to St Menas, an Egyptian martyr, by the patrician lady Bassa, who came to Jerusalem with the empress Eudokia in 444: she settled nearby as superior of a convent of women. What remains of the restoration that followed destruction by the Persians in 614, and the Georgian developments in the C11, have been absorbed into the present edifice constructed by the Armenians between 1142 and 1165 during the Crusader occupation of Jerusalem. The pattern of narrow aisles flanking a wide nave surmounted by a dome supported by six crossing ribs imitates that of the C10 church at Haghbat in Armenia.

Visit (Fig. 19). Open: Monday–Friday 6–7 a.m.; 3–3.30 p.m.; Saturday–Sunday 6–9.30 a.m.

Behind the modern fountain in the main entrance to the compound is a Mamluk inscription [1] of 1432 granting the Armenians tax-free status. The small courtyard contains two Armenian inscriptions, one [2] dated 1192 and the other [4] 1310. More significant are the **khatchkars**, crosses carved in relief and donated by pilgrims. In several instances four small crosses are set within the arms of a larger one, this is the so-called Jerusalem Cross, but the oldest examples come from Armenia and are dated to the C9–C10. Those preserved in the wall [3] of the part of the medieval monastery above the entrance passage date from the C12.

The **porch** [5] was added by Gregory the Chainbearer in the C18 in order to give dignity to what had previously been only a secondary entrance. The pierced brass grilles on the windows are worthy of note, as are the lengths of wood and brass that were hammered to summon the faithful to worship in the periods when Christians were forbidden the use of bells.

The small door [6] behind the secondary episcopal throne gives access to a stepped passage in the thickness of the wall, which leads to two upper oratories. There is a similar secret passage in the south wall leading to chapels above the two lateral apses; an inlaid panel [16] set amid the

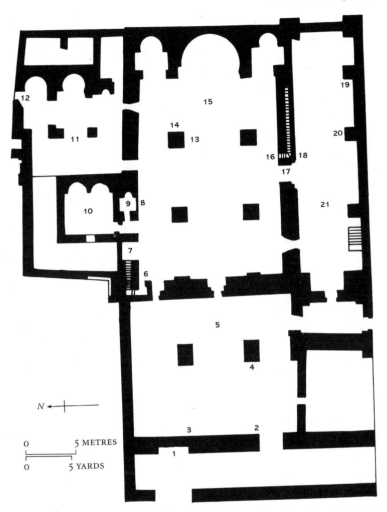

▲ **Fig. 19.** Armenian Cathedral of St James. 1. Mamluk inscription; 2. Armenian inscription; 3. Khatchkars; 4. Armenian inscription; 5. Porch; 6. Secondary episcopal throne; 7. Chapel of St Macarius; 8. Painting; 9. Chapel of St James the Less; 10. Chapel of St Menas; 11. Chapel of St Stephen; 12. Baptismal font; 13. Patriarchal throne; 14. Grave of St James the Less; 15. *Opus sectile* floor; 16. Inlaid panel; 17. Entrance; 18. Pictorial tiles; 19. Holy stones; 20. Pictorial tiles. 21. Etchmiadzin chapel.

painted tiles about 1.2 m above floor-level hides the magnificently carved wooden door, dated 1371.

The beautiful **wooden doors** of the chapels of St Macarius [**7**] and of St James the Apostle [**9**] are inlaid with tortoiseshell and mother-of-pearl; they date from the C18. The same type of workmanship appears in the **patriarchal throne** of St James the Less [**13**], the brother of the Lord and first bishop of Jerusalem; it was made in 1656. This throne is used but once a year or when a new patriarch is installed; on normal occasions he uses the chair set beside it and within the wrought-iron fence of 1796.

The C5 **chapel of St Menas** [**10**] is the oldest part of the edifice, but unfortunately it is open to visitors only once a year. The C10–C11 **chapel of St Stephen** [**11**] serves as both sacristy and baptistery. Hanging above the baptismal font set into the wall [**12**] is the iron chain worn by Gregory the Chainbearer during his years of misery; it is somewhat lighter than one might have expected.

A low iron grille [**14**] encloses the reputed grave of St James the Less. It is set into the *opus sectile* floor [**15**] created in 1651 by an artist from Van. The dedicatory inscription in the top centre of the carved marble panels which decorate the **front of the altar platform** indicates that they were carved in 1730. The Armenian liturgy does not involve an iconostasis, but at times during the service the altar is screened by a curtain; some of these are of great antiquity and beauty, as are the embroidered altar frontals.

The original cruciform piers supporting the C13 dome were squared in the C18 to take Kutahya tile decoration, but the capitals are medieval. The paintings of rather uneven quality that cover the walls hide frescos; the mid-C15 one that can be viewed if the sacristan can be persuaded to move the curtain [**8**] suggests that the decision to cover them may have been a wise one.

The **chapel of Etchmiadzin** [**21**] was the narthex of the medieval church. The decoration of the door [**17**] with cushioned gadroons, which are reminiscent of the façade of the HOLY SEPULCHRE, shows it to have been the principal entrance. The pilasters in the south wall were originally free-standing pillars, but the arches were walled up in 1666 by the patriarch Eliezer, who also gave the chapel its name. It is said that he aspired to be Catholicos, i.e. supreme spiritual leader of the Armenians; this office is as closely tied to the city of Etchmiadzin in the Republic of Armenia as the papacy is to Rome, and in order to get round this difficulty he created his own Etchmiadzin in Jerusalem! To increase the sanctity of the chapel he constructed an altar in which are stacked one above the other stones from Mount Sinai, Mount Tabor, and the place of Jesus' baptism in the Jordan [**19**].

The furniture of the chapel (iron screen, throne, altar-piece, and marble relief slabs) dates from the C18. The most noteworthy features, however, are the vivid **pictorial tiles** [**18** and **20**]. The two vertical series were applied by the monk Elia between 1727 and 1737, while the horizontal sets were installed at different periods, some as late as the Second World War. All come from Kutahya in Turkey, and most were made by Christer Thoros. Some were originally intended to decorate the Holy Sepulchre in

1718, while others were donated by individual pilgrims. Depicted are scenes from the Old and New Testaments and the lives of the saints.

Mardigian Museum [C]

Open: 10 a.m.–5 p.m.; closed Sunday. The normal entrance is from Armenian Orthodox Patriarchate Road.

The area between the cathedral and the museum is taken up by several of the courtyards around which live the 2,000 inhabitants (mostly lay) of the compound. There is also the Gulbenkian Library [**B**], built in 1929; it is open 3.30–6 p.m. Monday–Friday. The periodical room with its collection of 350 newspapers and magazines in Armenian attests in the most graphic way possible the vitality of an ancient culture.

The museum is housed in a building erected in 1843 as a seminary; the two levels of single rooms shaded by galleries looked on to a long narrow courtyard. The ground floor is devoted to the history of the Armenian people from their origins to the genocide, while in the first storey are displayed archaeological finds made in the compound and gifts offered to the monastery by pilgrims.

Convent of the Olive Tree [D]

One feature alone makes a visit to the little chapel of Deir el-Zeitouneh worthwhile. Built into its outer wall is a relic that immediately arouses suspicion but which no one can ever prove false; it is one of the stones that would have cried out had the disciples not praised God (Luke 19: 40).

At the bottom of the steps east of the museum a low door in the far wall gives access to a courtyard. The entrance to the chapel is on the right, but straight ahead in a walled corner is a rather young olive tree which, according to a C15 tradition, marks the spot where Jesus was tied during the scourging (Mark 15: 15). A step away, built into the north-east corner of the chapel, is the famous stone; it has a well-cut margin and there is a shallow cavity in the very rough boss. Another legend claims that the cavity was made by Jesus' elbow as his body jerked at the pain of the first lash.

The chapel, built about 1300, is a fine example of classical Armenian architecture, but the unusually large narthex has not been satisfactorily explained. The northern end projects beyond the chapel and has its own apse; it is identified as the Chapel of the Flagellation. The recess in the north wall of the chapel is called the Prison of Christ. Two of the many *khatchkars* (pilgrim crosses) mention restorations carried out in the chapel in 1362 and 1371. An oblique passage to the right of the apse leads to the small oratory of St Hripsimé where there is a beautifully carved wooden door that is dated to 1649 by its inscription.

Only in the late C14 was the chapel identified as the house of the high priest Annas, the father-in-law of Caiaphas (John 18: 13), and this was the starting point of the other pious legends.

Medieval Chapels

Scattered throughout the quarter are three small one-apse churches dating from the Middle Ages. They are of no special historical or architectural interest, and only one still functions as a church.

[F] *St James the Cut-Up*. Located just behind Christ Church [E], the first Anglican church built in the Holy Land (1849), is a little mosque whose name, Yaqubieh, still preserves its medieval dedication to St James of Persia, who was martyred in 422 by being cut into small pieces.

[H] *St Thomas*. Possession of this ruin has long been a bone of contention between Muslims and Armenians.

[G] *St Mark*. Open: 8 a.m.–4 p.m. (winter) to 5 p.m. (summer); closed Sunday. This church is the centre of the Syrian Orthodox community, one of the most interesting of the Eastern churches, and one in which Syriac is still a living language. Its most prized possession is a painting on leather of the Virgin and Child attributed to St Luke, a tradition which Raphael immortalized in a famous picture showing Mary and Jesus posing for the evangelist. The painting is in fact very old, but does not antedate the Byzantine period. There was a church on this site in the C4.

The little building is the focus of an extraordinary number of traditions. It is supposed to cover the house of Mary, the mother of St Mark, to which Peter went when an angel released him from prison (Acts 12: 12). A stone font against the south wall is reputed to be the one in which the Virgin Mary was baptized. Above hangs the famous painting. The Last Supper was eaten here, and it was here that the Spirit descended at Pentecost. All these legends give a sense of identity and pride to one of the smallest Christian communities in Jerusalem.

The Jewish Quarter

Located in the south-east sector of the city (Fig. 2) the Jewish Quarter was badly damaged in the siege laid to it by the Arabs from December 1947 to May 1948; after the surrender there was looting and wanton destruction. The consequences of this tragedy could not then be foreseen, but they proved to be very fortunate. The restoration, which began immediately

after the conquest of the Old City in 1967, was preceded by an archaeological survey. Even if the archaeologists did not always prevail against the
developers, they managed to bring to light remains from all the major
periods of Jerusalem's history. Most of the discoveries are on display
beneath the new buildings, whose fine clean stone highlights the extraordinary variety of courtyards, which make the area an entrancing one to
stroll through. A wheelchair-accessible touring route has been prepared.

Virtually every intersection has signs to all the places of interest.
Those of specifically archaeological interest are identified by capital letters

▼ **Fig. 20.** Jewish Quarter of Jerusalem. A. Views of ancient walls; B. Crusader
shopfronts; C. Crusader market; D. Cardo Maximus; E. Information Office; F.
Restored Cardo Maximus; G. Cardo Maximus; H. C8 BC wall and Cardo
Maximus; J. C7 BC tower; K. C8 BC wall; L. Burnt House; M. Crusader 'Bazaar';
N. Church of St Mary; O. German hospital; P. Wohl Archaeological Museum; Q.
The column; R. Apse of the Nea; S. Sephardi synagogues; T. Hurva; U. CI
paving; V. Access to roofs.

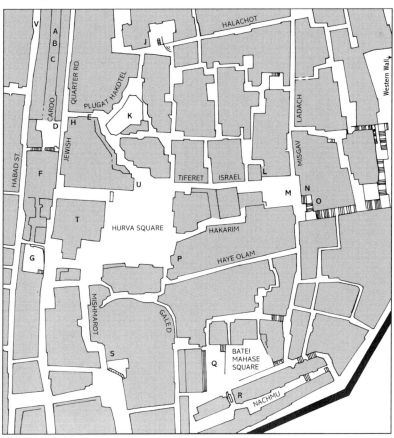

in the text and in Fig. 20. The Western Wall area will be treated in the section on EXCAVATIONS AT THE WESTERN WALL PLAZA (p. 96).

Israelite and Hasmonean Walls

The only remains that are not immediately intelligible to the visitor are sections of the north walls of Old Testament Jerusalem. Not enough was unearthed to give a clear pattern, and even less is now exposed to view. There are five 'windows', one very big, two ridiculously small; most are separated by buildings so that the eye cannot travel from one to the other. Fig. 21 brings these scattered elements together. The letters [**A**, **J**, and **K**] denote the 'windows'; their location on the street plan is given by the same letters in Fig. 20. Fig. 21 distinguishes between what is still visible within the 'window', what was found but is no longer to be seen (a continuous line), and what has been suggested by the excavators as a possible reconstruction (a broken line). [**J**] is open 9 a.m.–5 p.m. daily.

The First Israelite Wall [**H** and **K**]. This great 7 m-wide wall is securely dated to the late C8 BC; it can only be the 'Broad Wall' of Neh. 3: 8. In [**K**] it is clear that C8 BC houses were demolished in order to make way for the wall. The function of the wall, therefore, was to enclose a built-up area

▼ **Fig. 21.** Jewish Quarter. Israelite and Hasmonean Walls (after Avigad). A1. C2 BC wall; A2. C7 and C2 BC walls; A3. C7 BC wall; J. C7 BC tower; K. C8 BC wall.

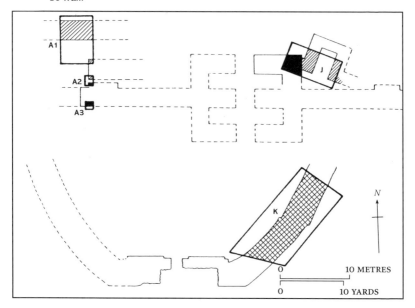

outside the previous city wall ([**2**] in Fig. 1). This must have been the *Mishneh*, 'the Second (Quarter)', mentioned in 2 Kgs. 22: 14; the unplanned extension of the city of Solomon and David can only have been caused by the flood of refugees from Samaria after the Assyrian invasion in 722 BC. They had to be protected when Sennacherib of Assyria menaced Jerusalem in 701 BC (2 Kgs. 18: 13–19: 37), and the archaeological data fit perfectly with the words of the prophet Isaiah to king Hezekiah, 'You counted the houses of Jerusalem, and you broke down the houses to fortify the wall' (Isa. 22: 10).

The visible remains are only the foundation of the 8 m-high wall; the exposed part would have been built of dressed stones. The peculiar curve was apparently dictated by the lie of the land; it had to skirt on the south a tributary of the transversal valley that runs from Jaffa Gate to the Tyropoeon Valley, and which provided a natural ditch to protect the wall. It is not at all certain if there was a gate in the centre.

The Second Israelite Wall [**A** and **J**]. This wall, dated with some plausibility to the C7 BC, is reconstructed from two elements, what might be the corner of a projecting tower ([**A2** and **A3**]; the outline in red in the modern street should be carefully observed) and what could be a segment of a two-bay gate [**J**]. Should this latter hypothesis be correct, it is tempting to identify it with the Middle Gate, which is mentioned by Jeremiah (39: 3) as the meeting place of the Babylonian generals after the forcing of the north wall in June or July 586 BC. Israelite and Babylonian arrowheads were found just outside the gate [**J**] amidst signs of a great conflagration, mute witness to a desperate battle for the wall.

In order to understand the layout of [**J**] it is important to remember that you are standing on the north wall of the Hasmonean tower and looking inwards. The sheet of plastic representing a wheeled vehicle with a large spear directed towards the C7 gate illustrates how the Babylonians breached the wall. It is based on the relief from Nineveh showing Sennacherib's siege of LAKHISH (Fig. 84). Soldiers protected by the roofed mobile wagon manipulated the spear to pick out the small stones used to level up the courses, and then went to work to edge out the large stones, eventually causing the structure to collapse.

The Hasmonean Wall [**A** and **J**]. The two elements dated to the C2 BC are not at all as easy to correlate as those of the Second Israelite Wall. The suggestion that the western and eastern segments of a city wall overlapped in [**A1**] to create a gate would, to say the least, produce a rather unusual configuration. Moreover, there is no trace of a link with the Israelite two-bay gate in [**J**], which the suggested line demands. It is unfortunate that buildings were erected before this important point could be clarified, because a gate at this point could only be the Gennath Gate, mentioned by Josephus as the starting-point of the Second Wall running to the north (*War* 5: 146).

If one goes down the stairs in [**A1**] it is clear that the two segments of the wall do not join; the section on the right is profiled in black on the modern street, and is seen to be contiguous to the Israelite tower in [**A2**] whose other side appears in [**A3**]. A similar junction is evident in [**J**]. The Hasmoneans simply juxtaposed their tower to the ruined C7 gate, thus giving some substance to Josephus' attribution of the First Wall to David, Solomon, and their successors (*War* 5: 142–4). In its final form, however, the First Wall was apparently begun by Jonathan Maccabaeus (1 Macc. 10: 10–11) and finished by his brother Simon (1 Macc. 13: 10), i.e. between 160 and 134 BC.

Model of Iron Age Jerusalem

At the corner of Shonei Halachot and Plugat HaKotel, just across from [**J**], the Rachel Yanait Ben-Zvi Centre displays a model of Jerusalem in the First Temple Period. Unlike the MODEL OF HERODIAN JERUSALEM (p. 143) which attempts a complete reconstruction of the C1 city, this 6.5 by 4.5 m model merely superimposes the known archaeological remains of the C8–C6 BC on to what is known or surmised about the bedrock of the city. Not only does this permit one to grasp in a single view widely dispersed elements, but it highlights how much the topography has changed through the filling up of valleys and the smoothing of crests.

The model may be viewed only with a guided tour. These are conducted at 12 noon, 12.30, 4 and 4.30 p.m. on Sunday to Thursday inclusive. Groups of twenty-five or more can arrange tours between 9 a.m. and 5 p.m. on the same days (tel.: 02–628–6288).

Crusader Market

In the C12 AD the Crusaders transformed what had been the Byzantine Cardo Maximus into a long covered shopping area. At [**B**], opposite the excavated area [**A**], there is a line of four shop-fronts, one of which has been rehabilitated. The construction of the façade of the three to the left is worthy of note; the voussoirs over the entrance are cut as if for an arch, and this effect is heightened by the curving recess, but the bottom is a straight line. These three were an independent development some yards outside the original entrance of the market. At a later stage someone inserted the fourth shop which, by following the façade line of the other three, obscured an ornamental pillar of the market entrance. All the vaulting is original, but one can be sure that the medieval shops offered much less in terms of luxury items.

Just at the end of the covered section, the Cardo on which the market was built is evident on the left [**D**] in the shape of two columns, which mark the edge of the eastern sidewalk and several cracked flagstones of the street. The three metal grilles cover the channel that drained water from the street; there was one on each side.

The Information Office [**E**] is located in the open court; open: 10 a.m.–4.30 p.m. except Saturday. It is housed in a Crusader edifice, whose semicircular basin with a drain dates the circular one in the court-yard. Guided walking tours of the area begin here.

Cardo Maximus   ★

Two large areas [**F** and **G**] permit full appreciation of this most impressive street, which was the main north–south artery of Byzantine Jerusalem. The street is 12.5 m wide with a slight rise in the centre: rain-water drained to either side. It was bordered by pavements each 5 m wide: the technique used to cover them is demonstrated by a partial restoration in [**F**]. The eastern side of the street can be seen on the other side of Jewish Quarter Road in [**H**], where a line of shops fronts on to the pavement. The shops on the west side of the street are best preserved in [**G**]: they were partly hewn out of the rock ascending from the Tyropoeon Valley to the Citadel, and partly built of cut stone, as the one to have survived intact shows.

It is certain that the Cardo in this area does not antedate the Byzantine period; it is not a refurbishment of the Cardo of Aelia Capitolina. The Roman Cardo, whose beginning is visible beneath DAMASCUS GATE (p. 14) came only as far as the junction of David Street and Street of the Chain. From AD 70 to the end of the C3 the whole area now occupied by the ARMENIAN QUARTER and the western part of the Jewish Quarter (see Fig. 18) was the camp of the Tenth Legion Fretensis and would not have been incorporated in the city plan of Aelia Capitolina. This area became truly part of the city only in the Byzantine period, and the Cardo could have been built anytime from the C4 on. The pottery found beneath the street and that found under the Nea Church (p. 77) are contemporary, however, so both are assigned to the reign of Justinian (527–65). According to the Madaba Map the Nea was on the east side of the Cardo (Fig. 28): the gate in the wall beside it, known as the 'Nea Gate', must lie beside the Ayyubid tower in the present south wall (p. 18).

The Burnt House [L]

Open: 9 a.m.–5 p.m.; Fridays to 1 p.m.; closed Saturday. Fifteen-minute English language sound-and-light show: 9.30, 11.30, 1.30, and 3.30.

A month after the destruction of the Temple and the Lower City in early September AD 70, the Romans stormed into the Upper City: 'when they went in numbers into the lanes of the city, with their swords drawn, they slew without mercy those whom they overtook, and set fire to the houses whither the Jews had fled, and burnt every soul in them' (*War* 6: 403). This was one of those houses. The latest coin found among the charred debris on the floor was dated AD 69; an unused spear stood in one corner.

The visible remains (an entrance corridor, four rooms, a kitchen, and a bath) were identified by the equipment they contained as belonging to the basement of a much larger establishment which could not be excavated. A stone weight inscribed with the words 'Belonging to Bar Kathros' gave the name of the owner. He was a scion of the high priestly family mentioned in the folk-song, 'Woe is me because of the House of Kathros, woe is me because of their pens. Woe is me because of the House of Ishmael, son of Phiabi, woe is me because of their fists. For they are High Priests, and their sons are treasurers, and their sons-in-law are trustees, and their servants beat the people with staves' (Babylonian Talmud, *Pesahim*, 57: 1).

Herodian Houses [P]   ★★

On the south side of Ha-Karaim Road where it opens on to Hurvah Square is the Wohl Archaeological Museum. Open: 9 a.m.–5 p.m.; Friday 9 a.m.–1 p.m.; closed Saturday. In addition to artefacts found in the excavation, models, and plans, it contains the remains of the ground floors of six houses of the Herodian period. Each was built around a central courtyard, and was two, if not three, storeys high. The characteristic feature is the number of baths, ritual and otherwise. Rain was the only source of water: it was conserved in cisterns.

Only the bathing area of the **Western House** is preserved. In the centre is a small vestibule with a mosaic floor. In the bottom left-hand corner of the design is a type of elongated perfume bottle which became obsolete in the C1 AD. The floor, therefore, should be dated in the previous century. To the left is a mosaic-floored room with a bathtub. Here one washed thoroughly before crossing the vestibule to the stepped ritual bath. To the right at the top of the steps is a foot bath. The central pillar supported the foot as water was poured over it

Continue along the corridor to the auditorium where the maps repay careful examination. The plan of Herodian Jerusalem as Jesus knew it is particularly instructive. After the auditorium the corridor divides into two walkways. The one on the left leads to the **peristyle courtyard,** most of which is unexcavated. It is the only one known in Jerusalem. Note the attractive tiled floor, which has been restored from the few elements found.

The walkway on the right permits close inspection of the **Middle Block**, which contained two separate houses. One room in the first house has been destroyed by a Byzantine drainage channel. Just to the east is a spacious room with a maze mosaic floor. When discovered it was covered by burnt wood, mute testimony to the destruction wrought by the Romans in AD 70. A coin beneath the ashes was dated to AD 67. Beneath

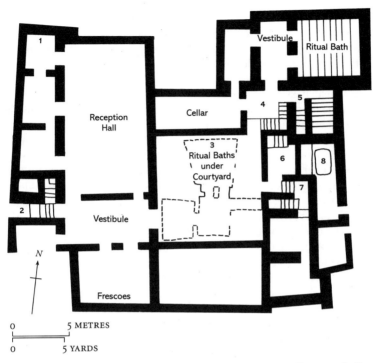

▲ **Fig. 22.** Herodian Mansion (after Avigad). 1. C2 BC pool; 2. Entrance; 3. Cutaway steps; 4. Service courtyard; 5. Ritual bath; 6. Bathroom; 7. Stairs to basement; 8. Pool.

the limestone serving table are two large lathe-turned stone jars. A stone tray with pierced ledge handles carries a set of small bowls. Stone was used so frequently because it could not become ritually unclean. The family or guests ate from the low circular tables around which they reclined on couches. The house next door is remarkable only for a small bathroom with a mosaic floor. There are a number of stepped ritual baths.

The next building is the most complete, and its intelligibility is enhanced by the model in the central courtyard. The edifice covers 600 m² which certainly justifies its title of the **Palatial Mansion** (Fig. 22). The number of its ritual baths has led to the hypothesis that it was the dwelling of a high priest.

Steps [**2**] lead down to a vestibule on whose mosaic floor are the remains of the burnt cypress ceiling, which collapsed when the Romans fired the building in AD 70. Beneath the floor was found a coin of year 3 of the reign of Herod the Great, i.e. 37 BC. The fire also marked the room to the south in which there are large frescos. Unfortunately, the supports of the modern building above destroy the proportions of the magnificent reception hall, which is a perfect golden rectangle (1 : 1.614). Its stucco ornamentation of bossed ashlars and broad panels is overlaid on painted plaster, a change presumably dictated by a shift in fashion. Pottery found in the stepped pool under the floor of the corner room [1] shows that there was a building on this site in the C2 BC. Whether it was the Hasmonean palace is an open question.

At the far side of the central courtyard is a beautiful little bathroom [6]; one undressed in the room with the mosaic floor and bench and immersed oneself in the small stepped pool. Beside it steps [7] lead down to a rock-hewn corridor roofed with slabs. It provided access to two vaulted ritual baths. Their entrances were blocked in the Byzantine or Early Arab periods to create cisterns. Traces on the wall of the two-door pool [3] show that steps were cut away to increase the capacity. Originally it would have been a ritual bath with an entrance and an exit, exactly similar to the pool in the north-west corner, whose two doors open on to a vestibule. Access to this area was via a staircase leading to a service courtyard [4] with a cistern. On one side was a vaulted cellar and on the other side two ritual baths; the smaller one [5] must have been for purifying vessels which had become unclean. The functions of other rooms in this wing of the mansion, e.g. the room with the pool [8], are unclear. Indispensable facilities such as a kitchen and toilets must lie outside the excavation area.

The design of the **Southern Building** appears to be identical with that of the Mansion, rooms around a central courtyard with a basement below. It has been left as it was found in order to highlight the pedagogic value of restoration. The pierced stone basins were for washing feet before entering a ritual bath.

St Mary's of the Germans [N]

The centre of this C12 complex was a triapsidal church, which is entered through its original portal from Misgav Ladach Street. It was flanked on the north by a hospice for pilgrims, but nothing remains of this structure. On the south are the remains of the hospital [O], whose entrance is on the

---

An Uncharitable Judgement

'On the way down the same street, which goes to the gate by which one reaches the Temple, and on the right, is a cross street with a long portico. In this street is a hospital with a church, which has been newly built in honour of Saint Mary, and is called the House of the Germans. Few if any people of another tongue have anything good to say about it.' (John of Würzburg (C12), 161; trans. J. Wilkinson)

steps leading down to the WESTERN WALL PLAZA (p. 96). The partially restored vaulting originally supported an upper floor, there are other vaulted areas below.

French was, literally, the lingua franca of the Latin Kingdom. In about 1140, when it was perceived that this caused difficulties for poor pilgrims who spoke only German, the Knights of the Hospital of St John assigned German members of the order to set up a centre here for their fellow-countrymen. The quasi-autonomy this group enjoyed ceased with the fall of Jerusalem in 1187, but in AKKO in 1190 it stimulated the formation of an independent military order, the Teutonic Knights, who made their headquarters at MONTFORT. They returned to serve this hospital when a treaty permitted a brief Crusader reoccupation of Jerusalem (1229–44).

The Column [Q]

The fine space of Batei Mahase Square is dominated by the arches of Rothschild House (1871) in front of which stand columnar elements. The Roman numeral VIIII (= 9) is scratched into the drum of the Ionic capital, while the triangular Greek letter *delta* (= 4) is incised on the Attic base lying to the north. The former indicates that it must have been the top element of a column 10 m high. The latter shows that the base was the fourth in a row. Both must date from the Roman period. They were not found here, and the monumental structure(s) to which they belonged is still a matter of guesswork.

Apse of the Nea Church [R]

From the column cross the square diagonally (south-east) to the corner of a house with the sign 'Beit Hashoeva Street'. Go down the steps on the right and turn left under the arch on Nachamu Street. After a flight of seven steps, take another double flight down. Facing one at the bottom is the green metal-latticed entrance to the Nea apse (open: 9 a.m.–5 p.m. daily).

Inside one can see the north lateral apse of the Nea, the 'New Church' built by the emperor Justinian in 543. The thickness of the wall surrounding the apse is sufficient indication of the great size which made the edifice celebrated. Plans show the relation of the church to the CARDO MAXIMUS (p. 73) and indicates the location of the south lateral apse. To reach this latter point continue down Nachamu Street and out under the arch to the right. Walking up the road beside the rampart watch the surface of the road; at one point the tarmac gives way to a band of rough limestone paving. This marks the width of the east wall of the Nea, and the apse can be seen in the corner made by a double turn of the rampart. For this area see SION GATE TO DUNG GATE (p. 18).

The Four Synagogues [S]

Open: 9 a.m.–4 p.m.; Fridays 1 p.m.; closed Saturday. This complex, reached from a small sunken courtyard, was the spiritual centre of Sephardi Jews from the C17. Refugees expelled from Spain (1492) and Portugal (1497) settled in the Ottoman empire, and began to migrate to Palestine when it came under Ottoman control in 1516. Very quickly they became the dominant group in the Jewish community, and retained that position until the influx of Ashkenazi Jews in the mid-C19.

The **Prophet Elijah Synagogue** began life as a study hall in 1625 and was converted into a synagogue in 1702. It owes its name to the legend that he appeared on the eve of Yom Kippur to become the tenth adult male required to form a *minyan* (a quorum necessary for synagogue prayer). The **Yohannan Ben Zakkai Synagogue** was originally called El Kahal Grande, 'the Great Congregation', and was built about 1610. Its courtyard, now the **Central Synagogue**, originally served as the women's section: its present shape dates to the mid-C18. The construction of the **Istambuli Synagogue** was finished in 1857. All four synagogues were thoroughly looted in 1948, but not destroyed. They have been restored, using furniture that survived the wreckage of Italian synagogues during the Second World War.

Hurva and Ramban Synagogues [T]

The **Ramban Synagogue** enshrines the name of Rabbi Moshe Ben Nachman (Nachmanides), a celebrated scholar of the Middle Ages who settled in Jerusalem in 1267. He found only two Jews in the city, both dyers, and dedicated himself to the establishment of a Jewish community. His synagogue, originally located on Mount Sion, moved to this site about 1400, and made use of the ruins of a Crusader church, possibly St Peter in Chains. It had to be rebuilt after a destruction at the end of the C15, and in 1523 it was noted as the only Jewish place of

---

An Appeal to Return

'You, God-fearers, must therefore come to Jerusalem, dwell there and become its guardians until the rebuilding of Jerusalem. . . . One should not say, "How can I go up to Jerusalem for fear of bandits and robbers or for fear of not being able to learn a livelihood in Jerusalem?" . . . Are there not nations beside Israel who come from the four corners of the earth to Jerusalem every year to be in awe of the Lord? Why is it that you, our brethren of Israel, do not do as the other nations of the world do and come and pray?' (Daniel al-Kumisi (C9); trans. F. E. Peters)

worship in Jerusalem. Between 1599 and 1967 Jews were forbidden to worship here.

Outside the Ramban Synagogue is the **minaret of Jami Sidi Umar**, the only minaret in the Jewish Quarter. According to Mujir al-Din it stood above a mosque located on the south side of a synagogue, and was rebuilt in 1397.

In response to an age-old imperative (see box) the first group of organized Ashkenazi immigrants to Jerusalem arrived in 1700. They settled in a courtyard north of the Ramban Synagogue, but when their leader died they fell into disarray. Soon they were deep in debt, and Muslims took control of the courtyard when they could not pay. As the edifice deteriorated it became known as '**the Ruin**' (*Hurva*). It was restored to the Ashkenazi community by Ibrahim Pasha in 1838; a great synagogue was completed some 20 years later only to be destroyed in 1948; it is commemorated by a slender arch 13 m high.

The Paved Street [U]

In the north-west corner of Hurva Synagogue Square a series of great ancient slabs appears among the modern paving. The undressed surfaces are very rough, and they probably served as the foundation for a layer of smoother flagstones, which would have been the visible surface of a street going east to the Temple. This street was laid over houses erected in the Herodian period, and its construction may have been part of a social relief project undertaken in AD 62–4 when 18,000 men were thrown out of work by the completion of the Temple. Herod Agrippa II employed them to pave the city with the white stone (*Antiquities* 20: 219–22).

The Roofs of the Market

At the very north end of the Jewish Quarter, where St Mark's Road joins Habad Street, a metal ladder permits access to roof level. It is possible to go north for some distance over the Triple Suk (bottom left-hand corner in Fig. 10), a Roman street built-over to create a Crusader market. There is nothing of archaeological interest, but the view is unique, and sometimes it is simply good to be above all the bustle below.

Haram esh-Sharif (Temple Mount)

The jewel of Jerusalem architecture, the Dome of the Rock, graces a vast esplanade whose quiet spaciousness is the antithesis of the congested bustle of the surrounding narrow streets. Muslims call it 'The Noble Sanctuary'. No name could be more appropriate.

The site had a long history as a holy place before the day in AD 638 when Omar, Commander of the Faithful, took possession of the city. A little eminence north of the City of David caught the winnowing wind. David bought the threshing-floor there from Arauna to erect an altar (2 Sam. 24: 18–25). About 960 BC, in order to provide a more fitting shrine for the Ark of the Covenant, Solomon erected the first temple on the spot; his palace to the south linked it to the city of his father (1 Kgs. 5: 5–8). No trace has ever been found of this temple which Zorobabel rebuilt *c.*520 BC after its destruction by the Babylonians in 587 BC. However, both John (10: 23) and Luke (Acts 3: 11; 5: 12) identify the eastern cloister of Herod's temple as Solomon's Portico. This C1 usage is explained by Josephus (*Antiquities* 20: 220–1; *War* 5: 185), who may well be correct because the base of the east wall is certainly pre-Herodian.

In 169 BC Antiochus IV of Syria sacked the temple (1 Macc. 1: 20–4; 4: 38). After the first Maccabean victories it was not only cleansed but extensively rebuilt (1 Macc. 4: 57–60; 12: 37), probably in the form of the 250 m-square complex described in the tractate 'Middoth' in the *Mishnah*. If the

▼ **Haram esh-Sharif in 1900.** The Dome of the Chain is to the left of the Dome of the Rock with the el-Aqsa mosque in the background.

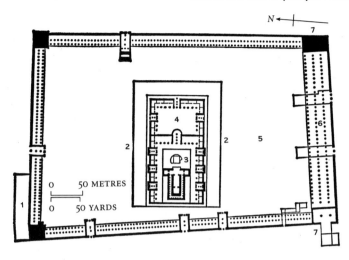

▲ **Fig. 23.** Reconstruction of the Temple built by Herod the Great. 1. Antonia fortress; 2. Barrier; 3. Court of the priests; 4. Court of the women; 5. Court of the gentiles; 6. Royal portico; 7. Stairs to the Lower City.

great ashlars at the foot of the steps at the north-west corner of the present platform are taken to mark the north-west corner of the Maccabean temple it is exactly 250 m to Solomon's Portico, and 250 m south of that point is the inexplicable 'bend' at the base of the east wall noticed by Warren in one of his underground tunnels. In order to explain the clearly visible 'seam' 41.20 m south of the 'bend', it has been suggested that, after Simon Maccabaeus had razed the Syrian citadel, he extended the square temple area to the south in order to deny any future enemy such a prime site (1 Macc. 13: 52). Subsequently, Herod the Great (37–4 BC) would have extended the temple on all sides save the east.

Josephus offers a comprehensive account of the building of the last temple (*Antiquities* 15: 380–425; *War* 5: 184–247). Herod's grandiose project so frightened the Jews that he had to promise that he would have all the materials ready before touching a stone of the old edifice. In order to obtain a flat surface he surrounded the crest of the hill with immense retaining walls on the west, south, and east; fill and arched supports brought the surface up to the required level. The strength of this platform has enabled it to withstand all the vicissitudes of history, so the dimensions of the present esplanade are Herodian. All Herod's buildings have disappeared; any which might have survived the destruction wrought by Titus (AD 70) having been swept away by Hadrian (AD 135). Information provided by Josephus enables us to reconstruct them (Fig. 23).

Covered galleries ran along all four sides, the Royal Stoa [6] being twice as wide as the others; ramps from the doors at the base of the south wall passed beneath it to emerge in the courtyard [5]. There were also monumental staircases at either end [7]. The Antonia fortress [1] and a huge reservoir adjoined the north wall. A fence almost 2 m high [2] separated the specifically religious area from the rest: at each of the 13 gates a notice in Latin or Greek proclaimed: 'No Gentile to enter the fence and barrier around the Temple. Anyone caught is answerable to himself for the ensuing death'; this is the wall of partition mentioned by Paul in Eph. 2: 14. Such intolerance was to be continued by Christians and Muslims. The Temple proper was on the west side; the altar of sacrifice stood in the Court of the Priests [3]; at the other side of the Beautiful Gate was the Court of the Women [4]. The rock now enshrined in the Dome of the Rock must have been the foundation of the Holy of Holies (the innermost part of the temple building).

Amid the ruins of AD 70, the emperor Antoninus Pius (138–61) erected two statues on the platform. Jews were forbidden entry save for one day in the year when they were permitted to come to anoint 'a pierced rock' (Bordeaux pilgrim, AD 333). The emperor Julian the Apostate (361–3) encouraged them to rebuild the temple, but work was immediately stopped by his successor. In general, Byzantine Christians avoided the area as a place accursed (Mark 13: 2); but some grew cucumbers there and others took its cut stones for their own purposes. The attitude of Jews remained constant (see box).

Many legends surround the caliph Omar's visit to receive the surrender of the city in 638, but two points are consistently emphasized, his interest in the Temple area and his erection of a mosque. According to Arculf (670) this was a crude affair of beams laid on the broken columns of the Royal Stoa. Umayyad caliphs gave the esplanade its first great mosques, the Dome of the Rock (691) and el-Aksa (705–15), but they also denied all access to the Haram to non-believers. This prohibition lasted until the arrival of the Crusaders in 1099 and, because of the loss of con-

The Sanctity of the Temple

'Even though the Sanctuary is today in ruins because of our iniquities, we are obliged to reverence it in the same manner as when it was standing. One should not enter save where it was permissible; nor should anyone sit down in the Court or act irreverently while facing the East Gate; for it is said, "You shall keep My sabbaths and reverence My sanctuary" [Lev. 19: 30]. Now just as we are obliged to keep the Sabbath for all time to come, so must we reverence the Sanctuary for all time to come; for even though it is in ruins, its sanctity endures.' (Maimonides (C12), *The Book of Temple Service*, 28–30; trans. M. Lewittes)

tinuity, medieval Christians had to invent their own identifications of what they found in the Haram.

The el-Aksa mosque, thought to be the 'Temple of Solomon', served as the residence of the king of Jerusalem until 1131 when he handed it over to an order of soldier-monks founded ten years earlier; from the location of their new headquarters they became known as the Templars. The Dome of the Rock, identified as the 'Temple of the Lord', became a church (dedicated 1141), but to restore its original form Saladin (1187) had only to remove the altar. He also removed the Templar cloister west of el-Aksa, and a monastery north of the Dome of the Rock. A few small edicules were added in this period, but the Haram was given its present form in the C14–C15 by the Mamluks who are responsible for most of the buildings along the north and west walls. The Haram Wall was renewed by Suliman the Magnificent in the C16.

Visit (Fig. 24). One may leave the Haram by any gate but non-Muslims must enter by one of the following: Bab en-Nazir, Bab el-Qattanin, Bab al-Silsila, or Moors' Gate. Entrance to the Haram is free, but tickets for the Dome of the Rock, the el-Aksa mosque, and the Islamic Museum should be bought at the ticket offices near Bab el-Qattanin and Moors' Gate. Open: 8–11.30 a.m.;12.30–2 p.m.; during Ramadan 7.30–10 a.m.; closed Fridays. The mosques are closed during prayer hours, which vary slightly with the season, roughly between 11 and noon and again between 2 and 3 p.m. Shoes, bags, and cameras have to be left outside the mosques.

Along the North Wall

In its present form the architecture of the north wall is essentially Mamluk (cf. p. 36). The three gates (starting from the west) are Bab al-Atm/Bab Faysal, which was once a triple Umayyad gate identical with that in the south wall of the Haram (cf. p. 102), Bab Hitta, and Bab al-Asbat. The interesting remains are in the north-west corner between the Ghawanima Minaret (1298) and Bab al-Atm, and we go from left to right.

A vertical **rock scarp** supports the Umariyya School. The five windows (3 large, 2 small) in red and cream courses belong to the Jawiliyya Madrasa. The coloured Mamluk stones are cemented to the great wall of the Antonia fortress (Josephus, *War* 5: 238–47), which is visible within Umariyya School (cf. p. 32). In the rock scarp below the school are two sets of sockets [**1**]. The lower trapezoid shaped sockets (3 m above ground level) were cut sometime between the C7 and C10 AD to hold the vaulting springers of a portico. Six metres above them is a series of sockets 0.48 m square, which held the massive roof beams of a majestic portico, whose columns were 9 m high. This can only be the one built by Herod the Great which, according to Josephus, was 15 m wide (*War* 5: 190). The importance of this observation is that, when taken in conjunction with the Antonia wall and the (inaccessible) Herodian corner block which lies 4 m north of the Ghawanima Minaret, it is now certain that the present dimensions of the temple mount are those established by Herod the Great.

▼ **Fig. 24.** The Haram esh-Sharif (Temple Mount). 1. Portico sockets; 2. Isardiyya; 3. Almalikiyya; 4. Pavilion of sultan Mahmud II; 5. C2 BC ashlars; 6. Bab el-Matara; 7. West qanatir; 8. Ashrafiyya; 9. Qubba Nahwiyya; 10; Pulpit of Burhan ed-Din; 11. Entrance to the Double Gate; 12. Double Gate; 13. Triple Gate; 14. Single Gate; 15. Entrance to Solomon's Stables.

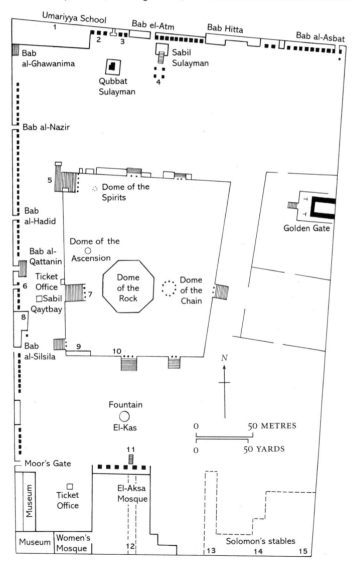

The triple-domed **Isardiyya Madrasa/Khanqah** [**2**] projects out from the scarp. Just to its left, beneath the new portion of the Umariyya School, is a blocked door of the C15 Subaybiyya Madrasa. Note the blazons at each end of the lintel; a cup charged with a napkin stands above another cup (cf. p. 37). The Isardiyya was constructed sometime before 1345. The central semicircular projection is the *mihrab* of the assembly hall. Separating this room from the rest of the building to the north is the 4 m-thick wall of the Antonia fortress.

Next to the Isardiyya is the **Almalikiyya Madrasa** (1340) [**3**]. The façade is framed by two buttresses. The central grilled window is surmounted by an oculus and flanked by two smaller windows. Between the two supporting arches is an inscription with the blazon of the *Jukandar*. The founder, although at one time Viceroy of Egypt, had been Bearer of the Polo-stick. The archways stretching along to the east were originally a covered portico built in the C13–C15. Unfortunately many have now been walled up as rooms.

Three free-standing monuments deserve mention. The octagonal **Qubbat Sulayman** (C12–C13) is built over a little rock outcrop which has been a magnet for legends. Solomon, we are told, prayed there when the temple was completed (1 Kings 8: 22–54). There Jesus sat as he instructed the doctors of the Law (Luke 2: 46–7). Just inside Bab al-Atm is the **Sabil al-Sultan Sulayman,** a fountain donated by the second Ottoman ruler Suliman the Magnificent in 1537. The utility of this contribution to the Haram contrasts with the futility of its immediate neighbour to the south, a meaningless square structure [**4**] erected by Sultan Mahmud (1817–19), which symbolizes the decline of the Ottoman dynasty.

Dome of the Rock ★★

The Dome of the Rock, begun in AD 688 and finished in 691, is the first major sanctuary built by Islam. It is also the only one to have survived essentially intact.

The extraordinary impression produced by this building is in part due to the mathematical rhythm of its proportions (Fig. 25). All the critical dimensions are related to the centre circle circumscribing the rock. The plan has its closest parallel in the Mausoleum of Diocletian (AD 303) in Split, Croatia, but the same principles were used in the construction of Byzantine churches in Italy, Syria, and Palestine. In none of these, however, do we find the integration of plan and elevation that is evident here.

According to current Arab tradition, the purpose of the Umayyad caliph Abd al-Malik in building the Dome of the Rock was to commemorate Muhammad's Ascension into heaven after his night journey to Jerusalem (Sura XVII), but were this in fact the case there would have been

The Dome of the Rock

'The outside of the dome is completely covered with gilded brass plates, while the whole of the building proper—floor, walls, and drum, inside and out—is decorated with marble and mosaics . . . At dawn, when the light of the sun first strikes the dome and the drum catches the rays, then is this edifice a marvellous sight to behold, and one such than in all of Islam I have not seen the equal; neither have I heard tell of anything built in pagan times that could rival in grace this Dome of the Rock.' (Mukaddasi (C10), *Description of Syria*, 46; trans. G. Le Strange)

no need to erect the later Dome of the Ascension (*Qubbat el-Miraj*) nearby! Abd al-Malik's purpose was more complex and subtle. By erecting a beautiful building he intended to instil a sense of pride in Muslims over-awed by the majestic churches of Christendom, tours of which were organized by the clever Byzantines for simple desert Arabs who tended to equate splendour and power. In addition Abd al-Malik intended to make a symbolic statement to both Jews and Christians, the two religions that Islam considered its imperfect predecessors. His building spoke to Jews by its location, to Christians by its interior decoration.

In addition to the memory of its association with the Temple, Jewish legend had endowed the rock with a complex mythology centring round the figures of Abraham and Isaac. By building above it, Abd al-Malik appropriated the rock and its Abrahamic resonances for Islam. The message to Jews was that their faith had been superseded.

The message to Christians was no less clear. The diadems and breast-plates represented in the mosaic decoration are the imperial jewels of Byzantine rulers or the ornaments worn by Christ, the Virgin and saints in Byzantine religious art. These symbols of holiness and power are in the sanctuary of an alien faith, like the Persian crowns, because they are the spoils of the victor. Lest the hint be missed it is formally underlined in the founding inscription, part of which reads, 'O you People of the Book, overstep not bounds in your religion, and of God speak only the truth. The Messiah, Jesus, son of Mary, is only an apostle of God, and his Word which he conveyed unto Mary, and a Spirit proceeding from him. Believe therefore in God and his apostles, and say not Three. It will be better for you. God is only one God. Far be it from his glory that he should have a son.' An invitation to abandon belief in the Trinity and in the divine Sonship of Christ could hardly be put more clearly.

Visit. According to a visitor of the C14, 'Externally the building is covered up to a height of 7 cubits [= 3 m] with white veined marble, and above 7 cubits up to the gutters with mosaics depicting various forms of vegeta-

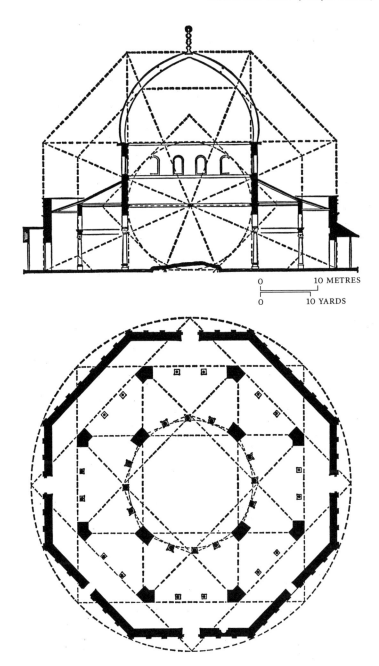

0   10 METRES

0   10 YARDS

▲ **Fig. 25.** Dome of the Rock. Mathematical rhythm of structural proportions in plan and elevation (after Creswell and Wilkinson).

tion.' Such **mosaics** must have suffered severely from their exposure to Jerusalem winters. They were repaired in the Mamluk period, and in 1545 Suliman the Magnificent decided to solve the problem permanently by replacing them with tiles. In the process he created the parapet wall with its intricate inscription by filling up the thirteen small arches which originally crowned each façade. The inscription around the drum is part of the sura of the Night Journey of Muhammad (XVII), but it does not antedate the C16. The tiling was completely replaced in the last major restoration (1956–62). The only other significant external alteration concerns the four entrances; all the porches have been modified in one way or another.

The mosaics of the interior immediately evoke an exotic garden; some would say Paradise. The artists were Syrian Christians but Muslim law forbade the representation of living beings; hence the profusion of vegetation both realistic and stylized. There is also jewellery in abundance. Damage to the dome meant that the mosaics of the drum needed restoration at least six times, but experts agree that the original designs were retained. All the other mosaics needed only light repairs.

Two points of **mosaic technique** are worth noting. The gold cubes of the background in the drum are tilted forward 30 degrees, and so appear brighter than the winged motifs which they overwhelm. The contrary is found on the inner face of the inner octagon; the cubes of the background are vertical but those of the motifs are tilted forward. The result is that the motifs stand out much more clearly, and it is precisely in this register that the significant jewels appear. As a rule of thumb, crowns curve upwards while breastplates and necklaces curve downwards. Note in particular the Persian crown (feathers gathered at the base and curving inward) facing the east entrance and a second one (with two unequal floating ribbons) across from the west entrance. These prove that the Byzantine trained artists were not merely repeating their conventional repertoire. The caliph Omar had conquered Persia in 637, and the mosaics symbolize the crowns he sent to hang in Mecca.

The **founding inscription** is a single line of Kufic script running along the top of both sides of the inner octagon, 240 m in all! It gives credit for the construction of the building to the Abbasid caliph al-Mamun in the year 72 of the Hegeira. However, 72H = AD 691 and al-Mamun reigned from 813 to 833! This maladroit effort to claim credit for the achievement of a member of the previous dynasty is of a piece with the claim of the Abbasid historian Yaqubi (c. AD 874) that Abd al-Malik built the Dome of the Rock in order to replace the Kabah at Mecca as the place of pilgrimage. He was trying to discredit the caliph by accusing him of heresy, the pilgrimage to Mecca being one of the foundations of the faith of Islam.

The **columns** supporting the inner octagon and those in the centre circle are all of different sizes; the crosses on some show them to have been borrowed from churches. None of the **windows** antedates the reconstruction of the exterior by Suliman the Magnificent in 1552; the light coming through the pieces of coloured glass set in carved plaster has already been filtered by panes of green glass set inside the pierced tiles of the exterior. The **carved ceilings** on either side of the inner octagon were not part of the original design; they first appeared in the C14 and have been renewed since; the Mamluk star is the dominant motif.

The **wooden screen** around the rock was given by the Ayyubid sultan al-Aziz in 1198. The Crusaders protected the rock from pilgrims greedy for relics by erecting a magnificent wrought-iron screen between columns of the circle. It remained in position until 1960 and is now on display in the Islamic Museum.

The high **reliquary** beside the rock contains a hair of Muhammad's beard; it dates from the Ottoman period. Muslims call the cavity beneath the rock Bir el-Arwah, 'the Well of Souls'; the voices of the dead mingle with the falling waters of the still lower rivers of paradise as they drop into eternity. In days gone by those who prayed here, after having walked round the rock, were given a certificate entitling them to admission to paradise; it was to be buried with them. It is one of many legends (see box).

The Cavern in the Rock

'They say that on the night of his Ascension into Heaven the Prophet, peace and blessing be upon him, prayed first at the Dome of the Rock, laying his hand upon the Rock. As he went out, the Rock, to do him honour, rose up, but he laid his hand on it to keep it in its place and firmly fixed it there. But by reason of this rising up, it is even to this present day partly detached from the ground beneath.' (Nasir-i Khusraw (C11), *Diary of a Journey through Syria and Palestine*, 49–50; trans. G. Le Strange)

The small flat *mihrab* (slab showing the direction of Mecca) in the cave belongs to the original building, and is the oldest preserved in the Islamic world. The hole in the ceiling of the cave is that seen by the Bordeaux pilgrim (AD 333).

Dome of the Chain

The Dome of the Chain is simply a small dome supported on 17 columns all of which can be seen from any point. The earliest description (AD 903) gives it twenty columns, showing that its original form has been radically modified, probably by the Mamluk sultan Baybars in the C13.

The immediate reaction is to wonder why such a building exists. One answer is that it was the model for the Dome of the Rock (whose contemporary it in fact is), but this does not stand up to any critical comparison between the two edifices, it is a legend that appears for the first time at the end of the C15. Another answer, based on parallels in other great Islamic sanctuaries, is that it was the Treasury of the Haram. This may well be correct, but is impossible to verify. It owes its name to the legend that Solomon hung a chain from the roof; those who swore falsely while holding it were struck by lightning. Such legends would tend to confirm the hypothesis that it was a treasury, superstitious fear of the place being its best protection. Another theory highlights the fact that the Dome stands at the approximate centre of the Haram area and concludes that its function was to mark the 'omphalos' (navel) of the Haram, which may also have been the navel of the world.

The Platform of the Dome of the Rock

Each of the eight stairways leading to the platform of the Dome of the Rock is surmounted by a graceful arcade or *Qanatir*, but they are known popularly in Arabic as *mawazin*, 'scales', because of the belief that on the Last Day the scales of judgement will be suspended there to weigh human hearts against truth. They were not all built at the same time. Two are dated to the C10 and the last was added in the C15.

The **north-west qanatir** is of particular interest because its stairway is the only one not at right angles to the platform. The steps are aligned on the lowest, which is in fact a line of large bossed ashlars [**5**], probably the outer wall of the Hasmonean temple (see p. 80). Inside the arcade on the platform stand the eight marble columns of the **Qubbat el-Arwah** 'the Dome of the Winds/Spirits' (C16?). Almost due south is an uninteresting square school building (1700) and then the octagonal **Qubbat al-Miraj** 'the Dome of the Ascension of Muhammad' (1200), which reuses Crusader material. The mere existence of this structure shows that the original purpose of the Dome of the Rock was not to commemorate the Ascension of Muhammad.

The **west qanatir** [**7**] opposite the west door of the Dome of the Rock is the oldest, being dated to 951 by the builder's signature. The building in the south-west corner of the platform [**9**] is the **Qubba Nahwiyya** 'the Dome of Literature' (1208); note the marble columns flanking the door.

Beside the south qanatir (C10?) is the stepped **pulpit of the judge Burhan ed-Din** [**10**] erected in 1388 reusing Byzantine and Crusader elements. It is especially associated with prayer for rain.

Fountain of Sultan Qaytbay   ★★

After the Dome of the Rock, the most beautiful edifice in the Haram is the *sabil* (a public fountain founded as a charitable act pleasing to God)

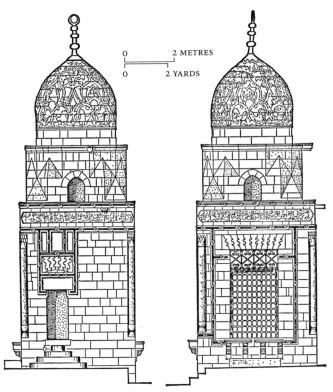

0 | 2 METRES
0 | 2 YARDS

▲ **Fig. 26.** Fountain of Sultan Qaytbay. East (left) and south (right) elevations (after Burgoyne).

donated by Circassian sultan Qaytbay in 1482. Located on the lower level near the ticket office, it is often ignored because the attention of the visitor is dominated by the vivid colouring of the nearby Dome of the Rock, but it is a superb example of Mamluk decorative architecture (Fig. 26). The interior is executed with the same care. Both repay close examination.

The ornate inscription running round all four sides provides three items of historical interest in addition to quotations from the Koran: the existence of an earlier Mamluk domed building, the name and date of the existing *sabil,* and mention of a restoration in 1883. Apart from the inscription, the restoration made no significant changes, except in the window lintels. The original star-pattern strapwork is preserved inside, but the joggled external lintel, typically Mamluk in form, is the work of an Ottoman sultan Abdul Hamid II!

The building was erected by Egyptian craftsmen under the direction of a Christian master builder, and the unique form of the fountain is due to the fact that, being experts in funerary architecture, they gave a simple fountain the prominence normally reserved for tombs. The relief decoration of the dome, found elsewhere only in Cairo, is achieved by cutting back the stone blocks.

The well-shaft inside explains the eccentric position of the door; from it water was poured into troughs beneath each window; cups chained to a bronze ring fitted into the two holes in the window sill.

Madrasa Ashrafiyya

Just beside the Sabil Qaytbay a building projects into the Haram area interrupting the covered porch [**8**]. When new (1482) this theological college had the reputation of being 'the third Jewel of the Haram' (Mujir al-Din); the square porch on the south gives a very clear idea of its former glory. Note particularly the red and white fan ceiling with the Mamluk star in the centre, and the very intricate black and white joggling of the relieving lintel.

It was built, on the orders of the sultan Qaytbay (one of whose names was al-Ashraf), by the same team of Egyptian craftsmen who constructed the fountain. Visiting Jerusalem in 1475, he was disappointed at the college which he had inherited and royally endowed, so he ordered it to be torn down and a new one built. The upper floor collapsed in the earthquake of 1545, but it is known from Mujir al-Din that it had a magnificent triple window resting on a low parapet wall (whose base is still visible). A faint hint of the lost magnificence may be gleaned from the double-arched loggia of the adjoining Madrasa Uthmaniyya above Bab el-Mathara.

Bab el-Mathara

Just north of Madrasa Ashrafiyya an unpretentious gate [**6**], euphemistic-ally called the Ablutions Gate, gives access to what are probably the oldest public latrines in the world still in use. They were built in 1193, shortly after the Crusaders lost Jerusalem, by Saladin's brother Malik Adil Abu Bakr.

Immediately outside the gate, at the head of the passage leading to the latrines, are two fine Mamluk buildings. The **Madrasa Uthmaniyya** on the left (south) was built by an Asiatic princess, Isfahanshah, in 1437; the college is called by her family name which shows her to have been related to the Ottoman dynasty. On the other side of the passage is the **Ribat Zamani**, a pilgrim hospice erected in 1476 by one of the close advisers of the sultan Qaytbay; note in particular the very intricate centre joggle over the window.

Bab el-Qattanin

This ornate gate, built by the emir Tankiz in 1336, was but one of his many contributions to the beautification of Jerusalem; see the note on Suq el-Qattanin in the section MAMLUK BUILDINGS (p. 41).

He is also responsible for the covered porch stretching out on both sides of the gate. The architectural unity of this portion of the west portico is evident, and shows that other parts were added and/or rebuilt at different periods.

Golden Gate

The Golden Gate is the focus of many traditions, but there is little certitude regarding its origins. According to the *Mishnah* (Middoth 1: 3) the Shushan Gate of the Temple was on its eastern side, and was used for the ceremony of the red heifer (Num. 19: 1–10). Traces of an arch indicating an older gate have been found beneath the present structure. This may be what the Piacenza pilgrim saw in AD 570; he noted that the north gate of Jerusalem was 'next to the Gate Beautiful which was part of the Temple, and its threshold and entablature are still in position there'. It is significant that he does not relate it to Peter's cure of the lame man at the Gate Beautiful (Acts 3: 1–10), because it has been suggested that the empress Eudokia built the present edifice in the mid-C5 to commemorate the miracle.

Lack of Christian interest in the site is confirmed by the note of Theodosius (before 518) that on Palm Sunday Jesus entered Jerusalem by the Gate of Benjamin (today: St Stephen's Gate/Lions Gate). If any, it was this latter gate which Modestus restored in order to receive the emperor Heraclius in 631 when he returned the True Cross taken by the Persians in 614. The Byzantines considered the Jewish temple a place accursed, and treated it as a quarry and a dump. It contained no Christian holy places and was not crossed by any road.

Both architectural style and historical probability argue that the present structure was built by the Umayyad caliph Abd al-Malik (685–705) as part of his rehabilitation of what had been the Jewish temple. Its elaborate decoration parallels that of the Double Gate, and sets these two apart from the other five gates. Few if any Muslims would have used the Golden Gate, and it was probably blocked sometime in the C8 when access to the Haram was denied to all unbelievers. It was perhaps this which gave rise to the legend (first mentioned about 830) that, when the emperor Heraclius appeared in his magnificent robes 'suddenly the stones of the gate descended and closed together to make a solid wall'; when he humbled himself the gate opened again.

This story gained tremendous popularity in the Middle Ages, when the Crusaders unblocked the gate twice a year, on Palm Sunday and on the feast of the Exaltation of the Cross. The present Western name also took firm root at this period, although attested in the C7; the Greek *horaia*, 'beautiful', was confused with the Latin *aurea* 'golden' because of the similarity in sound.

After the departure of the Crusaders the gate served no practical purpose in the life of the city and remained closed. Various theological explanations flourished among Jews, Christians, and Muslims. The latter call one part the Gate of Mercy and the other the Gate of Penance; through these the just will enter with their final Judge.

El-Aksa Mosque

The name el-Aksa first applied to the whole Haram area, and dates from the time (C10 AD?) when it was firmly accepted that Jerusalem was the *masjid el-aksa*, 'the furthermost sanctuary', whither Muhammad was transported on his famous Night Journey. Its use was eventually restricted to the great prayer mosque.

The first impression on entering is of a forest of glacial marble columns (donated by Mussolini) and a garish painted ceiling (a gift of King Farouk); they belong to the last restoration (1938–42). Virtually nothing (except perhaps the general proportions) remains of the first mosque built by the caliph al-Walid (AD 709–15), and twice destroyed by earthquakes in the first 60 years of its existence. As restored by the caliph al-Mahdi in 780 it had fifteen aisles, but these were reduced to the present seven when the caliph az-Zahir rebuilt it after the earthquake of 1033.

The oldest visible element in the mosque is the **mosaic** decoration of the drum supporting the dome and of the façade of the arch dominating the centre aisle; an inscription dates these mosaics to 1035. The artistic quality is clearly inferior to those in the Dome of the Rock, but there are certain similarities in the motifs; it is suggested that the Byzantine master craftsman was instructed to copy an earlier Umayyad mosaic.

After the capture of Jerusalem in 1099 the mosque became first the royal residence and then the headquarters of the Templars. They left their mark on the building by adding the three central bays of the porch (restored 1217). Saladin contributed the decoration of the *mihrab* in 1187 and a magnificent carved wood pulpit that unfortunately was destroyed in the fire of 1969 (started by an insane Christian tourist who believed that the Messiah would not come until abominations had been cleared from the Temple Mount). Saladin tore down the Templar constructions west of the mosque with the exception of the refectory of the knights along the south wall of the Haram, which is now divided between the Women's Mosque and the Islamic Museum.

Mamluk sultans restored both sides of the mosque and added two bays to either side of the Crusader porch (1345–50). Their work is visible only on the west side of the interior, because the nave and east side were torn down and rebuilt in 1938–42.

Just outside the main entrance a flight of 16 steps leads down to a green door [**11**]. This is the entrance to an underground area which for centuries took the overflow from the mosque above on great feasts. It is not normally open to visitors, but those with sufficient charm and persistence can sometimes prevail on the officials of the Supreme Muslim Council (whose offices are at [**G**] in Fig. 10) to send someone with the key. Inside, a long vaulted passage leads to the blocked-up **Double Gate** [**12**]; it was by a ramp such as this that visitors entered Herod's temple from the south. The vestibule just inside the Double Gate is characterized by a single column supporting two pairs of domes. This column and the two others beside the steps belonged to the original Herodian entrance. Other elements, particularly the structure of the domes, have close parallels in the Golden Gate and must be dated to a reconstruction in the early C7 AD. Still later the monolithic lintels of the doors cracked and were shored up by marble columns at either side; these repairs must be related to the building of the mosque above (C8 AD) or to one of its early reconstructions.

Solomon's Stables

This great underground area has nothing to do with Solomon. The lower courses of the outer walls are Herodian, and the twelve rows of pillars support the esplanade. Since the hill sloped steeply to the south, substructures were necessary to create a flat surface above. This fact explains why el-Aksa has suffered so much from earthquakes; this end of the Haram shakes much more than the bedrock on which the Dome of the Rock is built. The entrance is in the south-east corner of the esplanade [**15**]. To gain admittance, follow the same procedure as noted above for the underground part of el-Aksa.

Archaeologists have never investigated this area thoroughly and, in consequence, precise information is lacking. Many blocks in the pillars are of Herodian cut; they may have stood continuously or may have been relaid during the repair work undertaken in the C8 and C12 AD. The beginning of a **great arch** in one of the walls belonged to the pre-Herodian temple: it probably supported one of the terraces stepping down to the City of David. At one time it was possible to go through to the far end to see the interior of the **Triple Gate** [**13**], but this is now blocked off; nothing now remains but it must have been substantially identical with the Double Gate described above, and served the same purpose in Herod's temple.

The size of the underground area excited the wonder of medieval visitors. John of Würzburg claimed that 'it could take more than 2,000 horses, or 1,500 camels', whereas Theodoric estimated the capacity as '10,000 horses with their grooms'. The Templars used this area to stable their specially bred war-horses which were remarkable for their size and power. The holes in the pillars to which they were tied can still be seen. The **Single Gate** [**14**] was introduced at this stage. The shell decoration of a

Roman building which is shown at the bottom of the entrance steps was identified by medieval piety as the cradle of Jesus.

Islamic Museum

Open: 8–11.30 a.m.; 12.30–2 p.m.; 7.30–10 a.m. during Ramadan; closed Friday. The entrance and the domed bay inside date only to 1871, but the hall at a lower level was built as a mosque for the Moroccan community by Saladin's son, al-Malik al Afdal in 1194. The exhibits are not systematic and merely represent the more remarkable gifts made to the Haram.

The door at the far end is the entrance to the Templar refectory (1160) in which are conserved parts of the Dome of the Rock and the el-Aksa Mosque removed during repairs to these edifices. Particular attention should be paid to the wrought-iron Crusader screen of French workmanship, which stood between the columns of the inner circle of the Dome of the Rock until 1960; to the copper-plated doors donated to the Dome of the Rock by the sultan Qaytbay in 1467; and to the C7 cypress roof-beams of the el-Aqsa, which were removed in 1948.

Excavations at the Western Wall Plaza

The excavations around the Haram esh-Sharif (Fig. 27) can be divided into three sections: the Western Wall [**A**], the area around the south-west corner of the Haram inside the city wall [**B**], and the area outside the Double and Triple Gates [**C**]. The ticket office for the two latter sites is located just inside Dung Gate.

One of the routes leading to the plaza is particularly worthy of note. It is the continuation of Tariq el-Wad, which enters the plaza through a tunnel in the north-west corner. The northern arch was erected sometime between the C8 and the C11 to support an earlier arch of uncertain date which had started to collapse. These were part of a bridge structure that carried the predecessors of the present Street of the Chain across the Tyropoeon Valley to the Temple Mount.

The Western Wall [A]

For centuries this section was called the Wailing Wall; Jews from the adjoining JEWISH QUARTER came there to pray and to lament the destruction of the Temple. Houses came to within 4 m of the wall, but after 1967 they, and a number of Ayyubid and Mamluk mosques, were razed to create the present plaza and the name was changed to something less evocative of a sad past.

The great stones of the lower part of the wall have drafted margins in the characteristic Herodian style. They formed part of the retaining wall built by Herod the Great in 20 BC to support the esplanade of the Temple. Originally such stones went all the way to the top, which had pilasters at regular intervals; evidence from the excavations is confirmed by the intact Herodian wall of the Tomb of the Patriarchs at HEBRON. The part projecting above the esplanade was pushed outwards in the Roman destruction of the Temple in AD 70. It was restored by the Umayyads in the C7 (large almost square stones without margins), and again after the great earthquake of 1033 (much smaller stones).

The southern extremity of the women's section of the Western Wall is marred by a small iron staircase. Behind it is a stone two-courses high with a notched top-left corner. This is the visible portion of the 7 m-long

▼ **Fig. 27.** Excavations at Western Wall Plaza. 1. Entrance to underground area; 2. Wilson's arch; 3. Barclay's gate; 4. Stairs to Upper City; 5. C1 AD street; 6. Pier of Robinson's arch; 7. Arches of Herodian ramp; 8. South-west corner; 9. Entrance to Umayyad hostel; 10. Entrance to Umayyad palace; 11. City wall; 12. Medieval tower; 13. Byzantine house; 14. Gate; 15. Herodian basements; 16. Ritual baths; 17. Law court; 18. Byzantine house; 19. The seam; 20. Springers of arch; 21. Umayyad building; 22. Palace of Helena of Adiabene; 23. Byzantine houses.

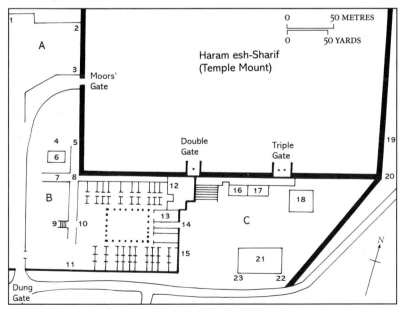

lintel of a gate of Herod's temple, now known as Barclay's Gate after its 19th-century discoverer [**3**]. The gate measured almost 9 m from lintel to sill, and is a clear indication of how much the ground level outside has risen since the days of Herod.

Western Wall Tunnel   ★★

Wilson's Arch [**2**], named for the celebrated 19th-century explorer of Jerusalem, is part of a series (already encountered in the Tariq el-Wad entrance) which carried the road from the Upper City to the Temple. Religious Jews have access from the prayer area, but tourists must enter by the entrance in the middle of the buildings which form the northern limit of the plaza [**1**]. Visits must be booked in advance: phone 02–627–1333. Open: Sunday–Thursday, 8.30 a.m.–3.30 p.m.; Friday 8.30 a.m.–12 noon; closed Saturday and Jewish holy days. The exit is beneath the stairs leading to the Umariyya Boys' School (p. 32).

A right turn inside the entrance brings one into a **vaulted corridor**, the 'secret passage' mentioned by Mujir al-Din (p. 42). The arches on the left carried the aqueduct from SOLOMON'S POOLS in the Herodian period. The original causeway was destroyed by Jews defending the Temple against the Romans in AD 70. These ruins served as the foundations for Umayyad reconstruction of the aqueduct in the C7. They were again repaired by the Crusaders. The impression of heterogeneity is entirely justified!

At one point a low window on the right permits a glimpse at a lower level of what Charles Warren called the **Masonic Hall** in the mistaken belief that it was the meeting-place of Solomon's masons. Sections of the finely constructed Herodian walls are preserved to a height of some 6 m. The column in the middle of the room was inserted to support a damaged roof in the Umayyad period.

The pier of **Wilson's Arch** is Herodian, but the arch in its present form is certainly Umayyad (C7–C8 AD). Its Herodian predecessor was destroyed by the Zealots during the First Revolt in order to isolate the Temple and make it more difficult to attack. The debris raised the actual pavement well above the level of the Herodian street below. Warren dug **two shafts** which betray the steepness of the slope of the Tyropoeon Valley; The one at the western side of the arch is 12.5 m deep, whereas the one along the face of the Temple wall reaches bedrock at 17.5 m. Fourteen courses of Herodian stones are visible. The Herodian street was some 7 m above bedrock.

From Wilson's arch a tunnel has been dug along the face of the Temple wall to the north. It begins in a great **cruciform chamber**. Stones of many periods were used by the Mamluks to create high substructures in the Tyropoeon Valley which brought the ground-floors of their houses (p. 37) to the same level as that of the interior of the Haram esh-Sharif. The lowest levels were filled, while upper levels served as basements or cisterns (note the white cistern hole in the roof). Such substructures are found the length of the wall, diminishing in height as the floor of the Tyropoeon Valley mounts to the north. Beneath the entrance stairs another door leads to the Masonic Hall. The first chamber on the right (with the concrete wall) contains a stepped street of the Herodian period, similar to that on the north side of the pier of Robinson's Arch (cf. p. 101).

The bridge in the first part of the tunnel obscures the view of what has been called the **'master course'**. Its four 3.5 m-high stones measure 13, 12, 8, and 2 m. Their thickness is estimated at 4 m. The great weight of such stones was designed to serve as a counterforce to a massive vault inside, which has been revealed by modern scanning technology. The regularly spaced holes were made in the C2 AD to hold pegs to which was affixed the plastered wall of a cistern.

Some yards further on a large section of concrete dash (opposite a staircase) marks the location of an entrance to Herod's Temple (**Warren's Gate**) similar to Barclay's Gate. The original threshold, a single stone, has been preserved, but the arch dates from a C11 reconstruction. Inside is a cistern (27 × 5 m and 10.5 m deep), which occupies the site of a pre-Crusader synagogue known as the Cave. It was the nearest Jews could get to the hiding place of the Ark of the Covenant (see box).

The Hiding Place of the Ark of the Covenant

'There was a stone in the Holy of Holies, at its western wall, upon which the Ark rested. In front of it stood the jar of manna and the staff of Aaron. When Solomon built the Temple, knowing that it was destined to be destroyed, he built underneath, in deep and winding tunnels, a place in which to hide the Ark. It was King Josiah who commanded the Ark be hidden in the place which Solomon had prepared.' (Maimonides (C12), *The Book of Temple Service*, 17; trans. M. Lewittes)

The tunnel widens to expose a **highly polished stone** standing on the **Herodian street**, which has risen with the slope of the Tyropoeon Valley At this point Herod cut away half a Hasmonean cistern whose centre pier and two steps are visible in the Temple wall. The stone served as a balustrade of the pool; its polish betrays the activity of generations of idlers.

The paving of the **chamber with two columns** a little further on is that of the Herodian street. The slabs are laid to the edge of the rock still being quarried, and two paving-stones (found *in situ*) are ready to be placed. Apparently the work was never finished, perhaps because of the death of Herod in 4 BC. Notice how the rock is trimmed to give the impression of drafted Herodian masonry.

The next chamber on the left shows how blocks were quarried; wedges driven into the trench cut on three sides broke a slab free. At this point the Temple wall moves out 2 m to the west in order to lessen the labour of cutting away the side of the hill on which the Antonia fortress was built (p. 32).

At the bottom of a flight of stairs a half-trimmed block is visible. At the top of the stairs is a foundation trench of the Herodian Temple. From it a left turn leads into a **Hasmonean water channel** still roofed with its original slabs. These show that it was cut down from the surface; it is not a tunnel. The increasing height reveals a hill to the north. It brought water to the Temple from the Struthion pool. Only a small portion of one half of the great cistern is visible; the rest can be seen beneath the ECCE HOMO (p. 33). The sloping rock escarpment supported the Antonia fortress.

The South-West Corner [B]   ★

The excavations are open 8 a.m.–5.30 p.m. every day except Saturday. The entrance is just inside Dung Gate.

When this area was brought within the city in the late C8 BC ([**3**] in Fig. 1) earlier tombs were cleared and became baths and cisterns for the houses built above. In the Herodian period some of the space was cleared to permit the construction of a great pier, which linked an arch coming from a high-level Temple entrance to a huge stairway descending towards the City of David. The Byzantines built baths and houses, but these were later buried beneath three vast edifices of the Umayyad period (C8 AD). The northernmost of these buildings [**4**] has been completely demolished in order to reveal the Herodian levels.

The walls of the two other Umayyad structures are preserved to a considerable height and create a passage leading to a staircase [**8**] just at the south-west corner of the Temple. In the middle of the trench to the

The Guarantee of the Caliph Omar

'Omar came to the region of Damascus, then he went to the Holy House [Jerusalem], took it without a struggle, and sent the inhabitants the following written message, "In the name of God, the Compassionate, the Merciful. This is a writing of Omar ibn al-Khattab to the inhabitants of the Holy House. You are guaranteed your life, your goods, and your churches, which will be neither occupied nor destroyed, as long as you do not initiate anything blameworthy." He had it confirmed by witnesses.' (Yaqubi (C9), *History* 2: 167; trans. F. E. Peters)

west is a wall [**7**] of the Herodian period with the beginning of an arch on either side. Since the one on the right (north) side is higher than that on the left, it can only have been the pier of a ramp. Prior to this discovery it was thought that **Robinson's Arch** (whose beginning is visible half-way up the Temple wall) was part of a bridge to the upper city. It is now clear that the exit from the Royal Stoa ([**6**] in Fig. 23) crossed the arch and then turned south on the pier from which it descended on a great staircase.

The size and quality of the blocks in the **corner of the Temple** contribute to its immense strength, which is reinforced by the method of construction; three or four great blocks are laid in parallel on one side of the corner and the same number of stones in parallel in the courses above and below on the other side of the corner. The horizontal cuts were made in the Umayyad period to carry water pipes to the adjoining buildings.

The **Hebrew inscription** on the wall is a quotation from Isa. 66: 14: 'You shall see, and your heart shall rejoice; your bones shall flourish like the grass.' It was probably cut during the brief reign of the emperor Julian the Apostate (361–3), who permitted Jews to restore the Temple. Miracles ensured that the project was never completed.

The great slabs at the bottom of the steps belong to the C1 AD street. They look too unworn to be the original Herodian stones, and probably date to the street-paring project of Agrippa II in AD 62–4, when he had to find employment for the 18,000 men thrown out of work when the Temple was completed.

Facing the street are four **little shops** set into the base of the pier [**6**], on which Robinson's Arch landed. There are two **flights of steps** [**4**] of the same period on the north side of the pier. One gave access to chambers within the tower, the other, supported on a series of vaults, ascended to the upper city.

After their conquest of Jerusalem in AD 70, when the Temple was the innermost fortress, the Romans determined that it could never be used as such again. They systematically destroyed the outer wall of the Temple by levering stones to the ground outside. Here the impact cracked parts of the street. The archaeologists have left a jumble of these stones exactly as they were found, to illustrate this dramatic moment.

Just inside the gate [**9**] of the southern Umayyad hospice are the remains of a flight of steps which led to the central courtyard. Directly opposite is the paved entrance [**10**] to the **Umayyad palace**, which has been extensively restored. In the north-east corner metal steps give access to the **medieval tower** [**12**], which was probably built by the Crusaders and then transformed by Saladin in 1191 and later by the Mamluks at the end of the C15. From the top the plan of the palace is perfectly evident. The C16 city wall [**11**] is built on top of the east and south walls of the palace; inside, long rectangular rooms surround a courtyard. One may go as far as Dung Gate on the rampart walk but there is no exit at the far end.

To the left of the restored eastern entrance [**14**] to the palace a metal circular staircase [13] leads down to a **Byzantine house,** whose mosaic floors are original, but whose wooden roofs and wall plaster have been restored. From the northern portion of the house one passes through an Umayyad drain to the southern portion, from which more metal steps go down to a magnificent Herodian cistern. Exit through the original rock-cut entrance; this passes under the city wall and brings one into an area [15] in which Byzantine remains are once again superimposed on Herodian cellars and cisterns.

Outside the Double and Triple Gates [C]   ★★

The differences between C8 Umayyad and C16 Ottoman construction is clear on both sides of the gate [14]. In the lower Umayyad portion are embedded two pieces of a huge white stone lintel. The garlanded cross indicates that it belonged to a Christian edifice; it may have crowned the main entrance of the Nea, the great church built by Justinian in 543 (p. 77).

The wide flight of steps leading up to the **Double Gate** is Herodian: the restored elements are rougher than the ancient stones still in place. Most of the Double Gate, the western Hulda (= Mole) Gate of Herod's Temple, is hidden by the medieval tower [12], and only a small portion of the eastern part is still visible. The great lintel and relieving arch may be Herodian, but the ornate curved cornice is Umayyad. In this section the upper portion of the wall has been rebuilt many times. In the third course above the cornice is part of an upside-down Roman inscription. It is a dedication to Antoninus, the emperor Hadrian's adopted son who succeeded him in AD 138, and it may have been attached to the plinth of one of the two statues set up in the ruined Temple at the beginning of Aelia Capitolina. For the interior of the Double Gate see EL-AKSA MOSQUE (p. 94).

Immediately to the east of the steps there is a cut-back in the pavement. Below are a series of Jewish ritual baths [16], and a number of rock-cut rooms [17]. They were surmounted by two buildings, a bath-house where Jews could purify themselves before entering the Temple, and a law court, if this is the edifice mentioned in the *Mishnah* (Sanhedrin, 11: 2).

In its present form the **Triple Gate** is Umayyad, but the moulded western jamb of the Herodian eastern Hulda Gate is still visible. It was blocked in the C11. All that survives of the original monumental staircase is part of the supporting arch cut in bedrock. A portion of the original pavement can be seen in front of the central bay of the gate. Further to the east is the **Single Gate,** which was cut by the Templars as a postern and sealed by Saladin in 1187. Beneath the Single Gate the wall of the Temple retains traces of the arches supporting an Herodian street.

From the pavement in front of the Triple Gate one looks out over a large **Byzantine edifice** [18] which stretches as far as the railed restored roof. The building, which is mistakenly identified as a monastery, is entered from a winding, narrow Byzantine street descending to the south with a sewage channel beneath. Construction on three levels adapts the house to the slope; all the stairs are original. Romantics think in terms of the palace of the empress Eudokia.

Following the Byzantine street down one comes out on to a wide wall with a metal railing. It makes an angle to enclose a series of masonry piers [**21**]. These, together with the wall, represent the foundations of a great **Umayyad building** of the C8. The much smaller walls running at a different angle beneath them are dated to the Iron Age.

From the wall one looks down on to two building complexes that are partly buried by the modern road. The one on the left [**22**] is dated to the Iron Age, and is variously interpreted as a building or as an inner city gate. The walls of the complex on the right [**23**] are at a higher level and oriented differently: they represent **Byzantine houses** and courtyards, and the furthest to the west is well preserved.

Some 30 m north of the south-east corner a **seam** [**19**] is visible; the Herodian blocks of the southern part of the Temple are carefully aligned with an older wall, whose batter indicates a corner. This is probably the Hasmonean extension covering the site of the Syrian Akra, the fortress that played such a critical role in the Maccabean wars (1 Macc. 4: 41; 10: 9; 11: 20–44; 13: 49–52). The Herodian section of the wall contains the springing of an arch similar to Robinson's Arch on the western side. There must have been a monumental staircase on this side of the Temple also. The Herodian city wall, therefore, must have run some 30–50 m east of the corner.

The smooth well-cut stones in the **city wall** now running parallel to the road from the corner [**20**] are dated to the mid-C5, when the empress Eudokia enclosed the City of David and Mount Sion within the city ([**10**] in Fig. 1). There are a number of towers and the trace is marked on the tarmac road in front of the UNRWA building. Beneath this wall remains of a C8 BC city wall have been discovered. A much cruder wall is built over the wall of Eudokia, but on a slightly different line. This may be a late Byzantine or early Islamic restoration, for it remained in use until the C11 ([**11**] in Fig. 1).

Mount Sion

Today Mount Sion designates the part of the western hill projecting out beyond the south wall of the Old City in the area of Sion Gate; it is bordered on the west and south by the Hinnom Valley and on the east by

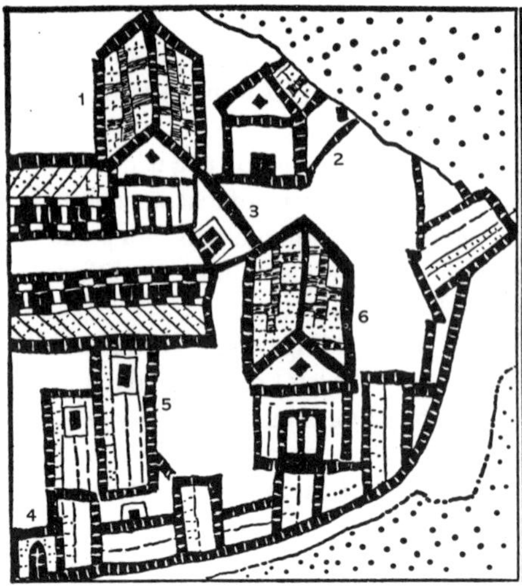

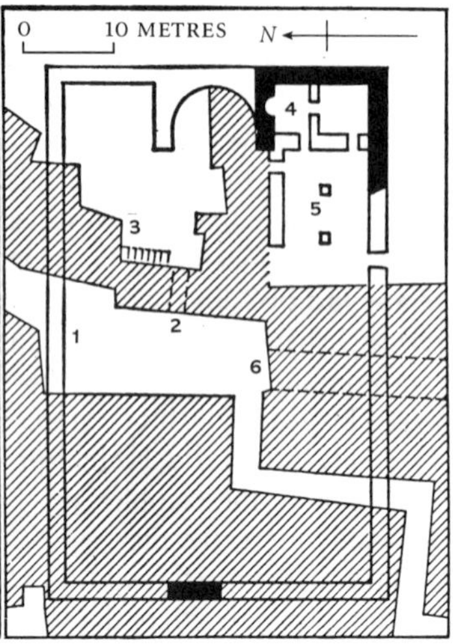

▲ **Fig. 28.** *(left)* The southern part of Jerusalem in the mosaic map on the floor of a church in Madaba (Jordan). 1. Nea church; 2. Siloam church; 3. Gate in C3 AD wall; 4. Jaffa gate; 5. Tower of David; 6. Sion church.

Fig. 29. *(right)* Reconstruction of the Church of Mount Sion (after Wilkinson). The solid black indicates the remains of ancient walls. 1. Alley; 2–3. Entrance to the Cenacle; 4. Tomb of David; 5. Cenacle (above); 6. Covered passageway.

the Tyropoeon Valley. In the Old Testament period Sion was the eastern hill, David 'captured the stronghold of Sion, and it is now known as the City of David' (2 Sam. 5: 7). The name changed in the C4 AD, presumably on the basis of such passages as Mic. 3: 12: 'Sion shall be ploughed as a field, Jerusalem shall become a heap of ruins, and the Mountain of the Lord [i.e. the Temple Mount] a wooded hill.' The prophet intended to say the same thing in three different ways but Christians, such as the Bordeaux pilgrim (333) who quotes the text, took it as a description of the two hills on which Jerusalem is built; if the eastern hill was the Temple Mount, Sion had to be the western hill.

This area was first brought inside the city walls in the C2 BC. The present south wall probably represents the southern limit of the Legion camp (AD 135), Titus having dismantled the earlier walls in AD 70. The empress Eudokia rebuilt the ancient walls surrounding Mount Sion between 444 and 460. Her walls survived until 975 when the caliph el-Aziz had them torn down because they enclosed an area too great to defend effectively. Saladin extended the Crusader wall to include the Tomb of David.

The C6 AD Madaba map (Fig. 28) gives a surprisingly detailed picture of Mount Sion as it was in the Byzantine period. From the city gate [**4**] the wall turns past the Tower of David [**5**] to the south, enclosing the church of Sion [**6**] and the church of Siloam [**2**]. The colonnaded street, the CARDO MAXIMUS (p. 73) passes in front of the church of New St Mary, the Nea [**1**], and terminates at a gate [**3**] in the old wall of Aelia Capitolina.

The Cenacle and the Tomb of David ★

Both these monuments are located in the same building (Fig. 29); it has a minaret and small cupola and stands in the shadow of the great round church of the Dormition (built 1900). To reach the **Cenacle** from the little alley [**1**] outside Sion Gate, enter the doorway [**2**] and, after climbing the stairs [**3**], pass through a room and across the roof to the vaulted chamber above [**5**]; open 8 a.m.–5 p.m.; Friday to 1 p.m. To reach the **Tomb of David** [**4**], enter the passageway [**6**] and keep bearing left until just before the **cloistered courtyard** of the C14 Franciscan monastery; open Sunday–Thursday 8 a.m.–5 p.m.

David, of course, was buried in his city on the eastern hill (1 Kgs. 2: 10). In the Byzantine period, however, he and James, the Jewish and Christian founders of Jerusalem, were the focus of a liturgical celebration in the Church of Mount Sion. Eventually this gave rise to the popular belief that the two were buried on Mount Sion. David's tomb was located here and that of James in the Armenian Cathedral (p. 64). The Franciscans built a monastery here in 1335 when they returned to assume the guardianship of the holy places. In the C15 the legend of treasures buried with the king (*Antiquities*, 16: 179–82) gripped the imagination of fanatical Muslims who made it their objective to gain control of the site.

Franciscans Expelled by Imperial Decree

'By the receipt of this august and imperial sign, know that by the request addressed to our Sublime Porte we have been made aware that near to the noble city of Jerusalem there is the tomb of the Prophet David . . . and that the convent and church of Mount Sion, possessed and inhabited by the religious Franks, are next to the tomb. The latter, in making the processions required by their false beliefs, cross the earth which covers the tomb of the Prophet David—may peace be upon him. It is neither just nor appropriate that this most noble place remain in the hands of the infidels and that, in obedience to their impious customs, their feet foul the places sanctified by the prophets who have a right to our complete veneration. We order, then, upon receipt of this august order, that you expel from the church and the convent immediately and without delay the religious and all those who reside there.' (Suliman the Magnificent on 18 March 1523 to the Governor of Damascus; trans. F. E. Peters)

They succeeded in 1524 (see box), but in turn they lost out to religious Jews in 1948.

Beneath the present floor of the Tomb of David [4] are Crusader, Byzantine, and Roman floors, so the foundations of the building go back at least to the C2 AD. It is not impossible that it should have been the **'little church of God'** mentioned by Epiphanius of Salamis (315–403) as having been in existence on Mount Sion in AD 130. Danger and difficulty of access exclude Christian invention of a new holy place in the C2 AD. If they continued to frequent the site, it must have been of great importance in the previous century. At that stage this was an affluent quarter and a wealthy follower of Jesus may have turned his house into a place of assembly (Acts 2: 44–5).

The C4 reconstruction was first known as 'the Upper Church of the Apostles', and then in the C5 as 'Sion, Mother of all the Churches'. Since it is impossible that the niche behind the Crusader cenotaph could have belonged to a synagogue, as some claim, it is best to see it as a receptacle in the exterior wall of an inscribed apse. The stones were blackened and cracked by the fires which consumed the church of Sion in 614 and again in 965. The building owes its present form to the reconstruction by the Franciscans in 1335. The arches of the upper room are typical Lusignan or Cypriote Gothic.

The tradition concerning this building as the site of the Last Supper is unreliable. It is first attested in the early C5 AD and appears to be a derivation from the better supported tradition which located on Mount Sion the descent of the Spirit on the apostles at Pentecost (Cyril of Jerusalem, before 348). This latter event took place in an **upper room** (Acts 1: 13; 2: 1), and it was natural to assume it to be the same one in which Jesus ate his last meal with his disciples (Mark 14: 15).

The reconstruction of this church, known as the 'Mother of all the Churches', in Fig. 29 (following Wilkinson) is based on very slight evidence. In addition to two small sections of ancient masonry (solid black) we have only a sketch by Arculf (670) and C9 and medieval estimates of the dimensions. Already in ruins and outside the walls when the Crusaders arrived, it was one of the stations on the penitential procession which preceded the final assault in July 1099. Restored, it became one of the glories of Jerusalem, but from the mid-C13 the ruins were exploited as a quarry.

Hermitage

To the west of the little cloister a covered passage leads out through a garden to an empty area. On the left a crude modern structure covers a series of cisterns which in the Byzantine period were transformed into a hermitage with a chapel.

The Essene Gate

Josephus, in his description of C1 AD Jerusalem, mentions a Gate of the Essenes (*War* 5: 145) in such a way as to suggest that it was in the south-west corner of the city. Excavations have brought to light a gate in the lower southern part of the Protestant Cemetery on Mount Sion. Entrance is through the Institute for Holy Land Studies, Jerusalem University College, which holds the key to the cemetery in which is buried Sir W. M. Flinders Petrie, the father of ceramic typology and stratigraphic excavation. The authorization of the Dean of St George's Cathedral (02-628-3261) is required in order to obtain the use of the key.

The visible threshold with its sockets is from the Byzantine period. Beneath it are two other sills. The lowest is securely dated to the C1. No precise date (within the limits determined by the other two) can be assigned to the intermediate sill. It has been suggested that the first gate gave access to an Essene Quarter which, during the reign of Herod the Great (37–4 BC), was populated by refugees forced out of QUMRAN by the partisans of Antigonos.

Saint Peter in Gallicantu

A modern church dominates the eastern slope of Mount Sion, St Peter at the Crowing of the Cock (open: 8.30–11.45 a.m., 2–5 p.m.; closed Sundays). It enshrines most interesting rock-cut structures, cellars, cisterns, stables, dating to the Herodian period (37 BC–AD 70). Beside it runs the ancient stepped way from the top of the hill to Siloam; from the belvedere uphill from the church there is a magnificent view of the CITY OF DAVID (p. 108), and of the three valleys which shaped Jerusalem. Where the Hinnom Valley joins the others note the Greek Orthodox monastery of St Onuphrius, an Egyptian hermit famous for the length of his beard which was his only garment! To its right is the ruin of a vaulted medieval charnel house near a series of *kokhim* graves cut into the low cliff. This is the traditional site of ACELDAMA (p. 119).

Some Christians venerate the site as the house of the high priest Caiaphas to which Jesus was taken after his arrest (Mark 14: 53) and where Peter denied him (Mark 14: 66–72). Enough traces have been found to demonstrate the existence of a monastic church of the C6 which a very late document (*c.*675) identifies as the place where Peter went after his betrayal; 'he went out and wept bitterly' (Matt. 26: 75). The same text places Jesus' confrontation with Caiaphas, and Peter's denial, in the immediate vicinity of the church of Sion. It is much more likely that the house of the high priest was at the top of the hill; luxurious houses of the Herodian period have been found in the Armenian property (just beside the Dormition Abbey) where another house of Caiaphas is exhibited.

The City of David and the Kidron Valley

The oldest part of Jerusalem lies on the Ophel Ridge running south from the Haram esh-Sharif (Temple Mount) ([**1**] in Fig. 1). It is a long triangle created by the Tyropoeon Valley on the west and the Kidron Valley on the east; these are marked by the two converging roads in Fig. 30. In order to get a clear impression of the whole area, go to the Maison d'Abraham on the south end of the Mount of Olives ([**9**] in Fig. 35).

Though mentioned in Egyptian texts of the C20 BC, the little Jebusite city on the ridge was too insignificant to attract Joshua's murderous attention during the Conquest. Although technically part of Benjamin, it was not occupied; its population was a mixture of Amorites and Hittites (Ezek. 16: 3). In fact, therefore, it did not belong to any tribe and in 997 BC, when David needed a capital independent of the tribal structure, he took it (2 Sam. 5: 6–9; 1 Chr. 11: 4–7). By bringing the Ark of the Covenant, the religious symbol which united the Twelve Tribes, into the city (2 Sam. 6), he made Jerusalem the effective centre of his people; politics and religion have been inextricably mixed in the history of Jerusalem ever since. Inevitably the seat of power moved as the city grew to the north and then to the west, but the Ophel Ridge was within the city walls during the Herodian and Byzantine periods.

The Acropolis ★

Two footpaths give access to the site. A new path begins where the Byzantine wall (p. 104) is marked on the road south of the Haram. The other is on the left side of the first empty lot on the left going down the Tyropoeon Valley road from the parking-lot outside Dung Gate. Open: 9 a.m.–5 p.m; to 1 p.m. Friday; closed Saturday.

The large excavation displays remains which encapsulate the history of Jerusalem from just before the time of David to its capture by the Babylonians in 586 BC (Fig. 31). The hatched walls [**4, 13, 14**], which run north–south and east–west, date from the C13 BC. They were designed to hold fill on the steep slope and thus to create two large terraces on which the buildings of the **Jebusite acropolis** were erected. Sometime in the C10 BC, presumably after David had taken the city, the stepped glacis [**5, 15, 16**] was constructed, both in order to strengthen the defences and to provide a solid base for the **palace** that David erected on the summit. The two openings [**10**] are too small to be postern gates, and may have served for drainage.

About the middle of the C7 BC houses were built into and over the glacis. The west side of the four-room **'House of Ahiel'** [8] was dug into the glacis while its east side was supported on fill laid over the glacis [15, 16] and retained by a wall [17]. The archaeologists have left only the west side with the two monoliths which supported the roof; the outside stairway [7] presumably turned to the right and provided access to the flat

▼ **Fig. 30.** The City of David.

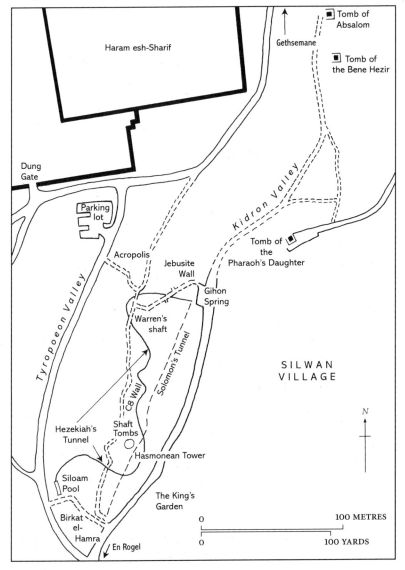

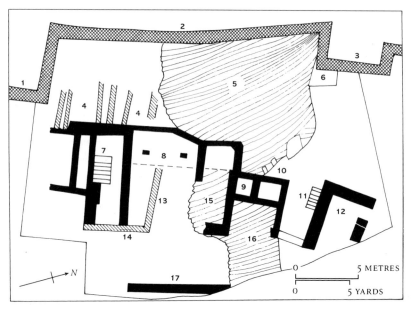

▲ **Fig. 31.** The Acropolis of Sion in the City of David. 1–3. C2 BC wall and towers; 4. C13 BC wall; 5. Glacis; 6. Modern reinforcement; 7. Stairs; 8. House of Ahiel; 9. Toilet; 10. Small openings; 11. Stairs; 12. Burnt room; 13–14. C13 BC walls. 15–16. Glacis. 17. Foundation of House of Ahiel.

roof. In one corner of the small room [**9**] a stone with a hole in it was placed above a cesspit over 2 m deep; it can only have been the toilet. The signs of the destruction of this house were not as evident as those in the **Burnt Room** [**12**], which also had an outside stairway [**11**]. The arrowheads found on the floor amid the carbonized wood of the ceiling mutely attest the fierce resistance of the Jews and its ultimate failure. Nabuzaradan, the Babylonian general, 'burnt the Temple, the royal palace, and all the houses of Jerusalem' (2 Kgs. 25: 9).

The **wall built by Nehemiah** in the C5 BC (Neh. 3: 1–32) must have run along the crest. Only a minority of the Jews deported to Babylon had returned to Jerusalem, and he did not have the men to defend the line of the old wall further down the slope. No traces of Nehemiah's wall have been found, but it must lie under the wall [**2**] and towers [**1 and 3**] erected by the Hasmoneans in the latter part of the C2 BC. The masonry [**6**] supporting the corner of the northern tower is modern.

Warren's Shaft ★★

Leaving the Acropolis go down the hill; turn left at the junction (the right-hand path goes to the ROYAL TOMBS and the POOL OF SILOAM) and take the first set of steps to the right. Open: 9 a.m.–5 p.m.; Friday to 1 p.m.; closed Saturday.

Named after its English discoverer, this is a rock-cut sloping tunnel leading to a vertical shaft through which a bucket could be dropped by rope into a pool fed by the GIHON SPRING (p. 112). The horizontal crack above the shaft is the frontier between the porous *meleke* limestone above and the impermeable *mizzi ahmar* dolomite below. Rain-water percolating through the limestone flowed along the surface of the dolomite to create the horizontal tunnel, which continues above the shaft to exit on the slope outside. A fissure in the dolomite attracted water downwards creating a sink-hole, which is more than 40,000 years old. These natural features were skilfully enlarged by the Jebusites in order to provide secure access to water when under siege. The entrance to the tunnel was well within the C18–C6 city wall further down the hill. Either the horizontal tunnel or the vertical shaft could be the *sinnor* 'water-shaft' by which Joab gained entrance to the city for David (2 Sam. 5: 8; 1 Chr. 11: 6).

The inverted-V entrance, opposite the dead-end sink-hole marked in black at the top of the metal stairs, is probably contemporary with the construction of the glacis associated with the C2 BC wall higher up. A cave-in sometime during the Herodian period is the best explanation of the barrel vaulting, because this type of roof does not appear before the C1 BC.

The Jebusite Wall

Continue down the steps from Warren's Shaft to a hole on the left. On the far side the size of the blocks of the two ancient walls at the bottom clearly distinguish them from the stepped retaining walls of much smaller stones built on top of them by the archaeologists.

The Jebusite wall of the C18 BC is the lowest, and is constructed of very big untrimmed stones. It runs the width of the trench. The dog-leg line suggests a tower. A gate at this point was required to give access in peace-time to the Gihon Spring just outside. To find the wall so far down the side of the hill was a surprise. Even if the inhabitants were not numerous, it was imperative that the city wall should enclose the area containing the entrance to WARREN'S SHAFT.

David retained this wall, and it remained in use until the C8 BC when another wall was built just inside it. This later wall is in the centre and its rough construction marks it off from the modern retaining walls; it served until the Babylonian invasion of 586 BC. In order to visualize what the terraced city might have looked like in the time of David, look across the valley at the village of Silwan. Since the palace must have been on the crest it would have been very easy for the king to have seen Bathsheba bathing on the roof of her house (2 Sam. 11: 2)!

Gihon Spring and Hezekiah's Tunnel   ★

The reason why the Jebusites settled on the low Ophel Ridge was the presence of a perennial spring in the Kidron Valley. It is first called Gihon in the dramatic account of the rush to get Solomon anointed king before his older half-brother Adonijah could usurp the title (1 Kgs. 1: 33). The name means 'gushing', and once described the siphonic action of the spring, which periodically increased its flow. This phenomenon appears to have ceased in recent years. The slow continuous flow of between 40 and 100 cubic metres per day could support a population of about 2,500.

In order to ensure a better water supply for his expanding city Solomon (965–928 BC) drove a tunnel along the bottom of the hill, part of which can be seen in the excavation beside the road below the Hasmonean tower. The side of the tunnel was pierced at intervals, permitting surplus water to be used to irrigate the fields in the bottom of the Kidron Valley, then known as the King's Garden (2 Kgs. 25: 4). The tunnel terminated in a great pool at the end of the Tyropoeon Valley, today called Birket el-Hamra and planted with fig trees; the cut through the tip of the Ophel Ridge is visible on both sides.

The stability of Solomon's reign meant that this tunnel was no risk, but later it became a liability. Realizing that Sennacherib's advance was the preliminary to an attack on Jerusalem, 'Hezekiah [727–698 BC] and his officers and champions decided to cut off the water supply from the springs situated outside the city. A great many people were gathered and they stopped all the springs and the brook that flowed through the land [the Solomonic tunnel with its sluices], saying, Why should the kings of Assyria come and find much water?' (2 Chr. 32: 2–4). Having thus camouflaged the source of the city's water supply, Hezekiah 'constructed the pool and the tunnel to bring water into the city' (2 Kgs. 20: 20); 'he directed the waters of Gihon down to the west side of the city of David' (2 Chr. 32: 30). We know exactly how he did it because of a Hebrew inscription (see box) placed by the proud engineer some 10 m inside the tunnel near the pool of Siloam. Had the king ordered the inscription it would have contained his name and been in a much more prominent position! The authenticity of the inscription (now in the Istanbul Museum) is guaranteed by the archaic script and spelling.

A straight line linking the Gihon Spring to the Pool of Siloam is only 323 m. The actual tunnel is in the shape of a huge S, and measures 538 m. The sinuous course suggests that the workmen were following a natural crack in the rock through which water trickled. It alone explains, not only how the two teams met, but how they were able to breathe despite the oxygen-eating oil lamps at the work-face.

It is possible to walk through the tunnel starting at the Gihon spring (open: 8.30 a.m.–3 p.m.; Friday to 1 p.m.; closed Saturday). A flashlight

The Siloam Inscription

'Behold the tunnel. This is the story of its cutting. While the miners swung their picks, one towards the other, and when there remained only 3 cubits to cut, the voices of one calling his fellow was heard—for there was a resonance in the rock coming from both north and south. So the day they broke through the miners struck, one against the other, pick against pick, and the water flowed from the spring towards the pool, 1200 cubits. The height of the rock above the head of the miners was 100 cubits.' (trans. E. Puech)

is indispensable. Footwear should be worn. The passage is narrow and low in parts, but perfectly safe, and it is impossible to get lost! Apart from two deeper parts near the beginning and the end, the water is normally about hip high. The steps to the water level at Gihon are medieval, the ground in the valley having risen some 12 m due to debris falling down the slopes.

Some 20 m into the tunnel, at a point where it makes a right-angled bend to the left, a chest-high wall blocks another channel; this leads to the vertical Jebusite shaft discovered by Warren (cf. p. 110). The rough natural roof of the tunnel at both ends betrays the original crack. In the middle the ceiling was too low and the miners had to raise it. The false starts in this region defy explanation. Where the miners met is clear because the join is 10 cm off-centre, and the direction of the pick marks on the wall changes. Once the roof starts to rise the pool of Siloam is close. The inscription was found 10 m before the end of the tunnel on the left-hand wall.

The Iron Age Wall

The C8 wall just inside the Jebusite Wall (p. 111) continues to the south and almost 100 m is visible beneath the vertical excavated scarp. The thick wall has salients, exactly as in the citadel at ARAD. The remains inside are those of the residential quarter built up in the following two centuries. It is from little homes such as these that the inhabitants of Jerusalem were dragged off to exile in Babylon in 586 BC.

Shaft Tombs

From the southern end of the Iron Age Wall it is possible to climb up to another large excavated area in which there are two large shafts, which some have identified as the tombs of the kings of Judah.

The irregular shaping of the rock shows that it was worked as a **quarry**. To extract stones a narrow trench was cut around three sides of the block and wedges were then driven in to break it free. All the stages of the process can be seen at different points throughout the area. Since the 3.5 m-wide wall running north–south at the edge of the eastern scarp is built on a half-extracted block, the quarry must be earlier than the wall, which defended the city from the mid-C2 BC to the destruction of Jerusalem by the Romans in AD 70. The city wall is unusual in that it is not all of one piece; the addition of another wall on its outer side doubled the width of the original wall, which at one stage may have been the edge of a terrace.

The quarry destroyed a number of cisterns and half-demolished two great **shafts** running into the hill. Their location suggested that they were the tombs in which David (1 Kgs. 2: 10) and his successors were buried. The workmanship, however, is crude and careless, far inferior to that of the TOMBS IN THE KIDRON VALLEY (p. 117). Since it is unlikely that the graves of nobles were superior to those of their rulers, the hypothesis of a royal necropolis is questionable, even though this means that no date or function can be assigned to the shafts.

There is another tomb just below the edge of the scarp. From this point one can look down on the foundations of a **round tower** dated to the C2 BC. Jesus mentions a tower at Siloam which fell killing eighteen people (Luke 13: 4). The water channel built by Solomon (see above) is between the tower and the road; three windows are visible. The long wall running from the scarp to just north of the tower was the southern limit of a series of terraces stepping down the hill outside the city wall.

Pool of Siloam

The location of the pool is indicated by a small minaret at the tip of the Ophel Ridge. The original form of the pool has been lost for ever. It is likely that Herod introduced alterations during his vast building programme in Jerusalem, but these can hardly have survived the sack of

The Church at Siloam

'You descend by many steps to Siloam, and above Siloam is a hanging basilica beneath which the water of Siloam rises. Siloam has two basins constructed of marble, which are separated from each other by a screen. Men wash in one and women in the other to gain a blessing. In these waters many miracles take place, and lepers are cleansed. In front of the court is a large man-made pool and people are continually washing there; for at regular intervals the spring sends a great deal of water into the basins, which goes on down the valley of Gethsemane (which they also call Jehoshaphat) as far as the River Jordan.' (Piacenza Pilgrim (C6) 25; trans. J. Wilkinson)

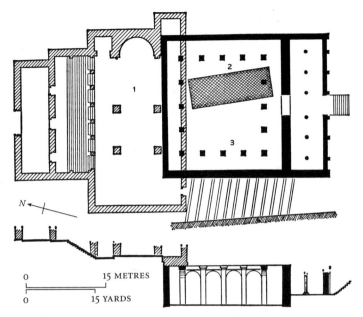

▲ **Fig. 32.** The C5 church at pool of Siloam (after Vincent). 1. Restoration of Byzantine church; 2. Present rectangular pool; 3. Restoration of C2 AD pool.

the City of David by the Romans, who 'burnt the whole place as far as Siloam' (*War* 6: 363).

The Bordeaux pilgrim's description (333) of the **pool** as having four porches probably refers to Hadrian's reconstruction in AD 135; it has been confirmed archaeologically [**3**]. Christians were attracted to the pool because of its association with Jesus' miraculous cure of the man born blind (John 9), but the first **church** there was built by the empress Eudokia *c.*450. Excavations have borne out the description of the C6 Piacenza pilgrim (see box), in which it is clear, however, that the relationship of the pool to Gihon had long been forgotten; the existence of the tunnel was unknown. Josephus in fact always speaks of Siloam as a spring (*War* 5: 145).

The church was destroyed by the Persians in 614, but the tradition of the curative powers of the waters, mentioned by Byzantine pilgrims, continued among the Arabs; the colonnade around the pool is mentioned in the Middle Ages. What happened thereafter is a mystery. Possibly debris from higher up the valley washed down into the pool and was sporadically cleared to the sides by Silwan villagers who needed the water; drawings and descriptions of early C19 travellers show the pool to have acquired its present form [**2**] by that period. The mosque was built in the 1890s.

The rock at the point where the path reaches the Kidron Valley road is pierced by a **tunnel** which in its first stage carried the water from Solomon's tunnel (p. 112) to the pool created by damming the Tyropoeon Valley, and now called Birket el-Hamra. In the C7 the floor of the tunnel segment was lowered to carry the overflow from the Pool of Siloam to the gardens in the Kidron Valley. The sloping wall at the top of the escarpment is Byzantine; its function is unknown.

The vegetation in the valley bottom attests the life-giving power of the present flow. It must always have been so, and this makes it the obvious place to locate the **King's Garden** (2 Kgs. 25: 4). Further down the valley, just beyond the junction with the Hinnom Valley, is the modern pumping station of **Bir Ayyub**. The water is drawn from a 38 m-deep well, part of whose stone lining may be Roman. The site is identified with the en-Rogel of 1 Kgs. 1: 9, where Adonijah, the half-brother of Solomon, tried to have himself anointed king.

Tombs in the Valleys

The prophets speculated on where God would finally judge the world. Joel declared for a valley called Jehoshaphat (3: 2, 12), whereas Zechariah opted for the Mount of Olives (14: 4). The Bordeaux pilgrim (333 AD) recorded the obvious harmonizing solution as a well-established identification; the Kidron Valley is the Valley of Jehoshaphat (= 'Yahweh judges'). Hence the cemeteries of all faiths which line its slopes. Those interred there hope to be first in line and to benefit by the charity of an unjaded Messiah. There were tombs in the valley, however, long before either prophet wrote.

▼ **Fig. 33.** *(left)* The 'Tomb of Absalom' (after Vincent).
Fig. 34. *(right)* The Tomb of the Bene Hezir (after Vincent).

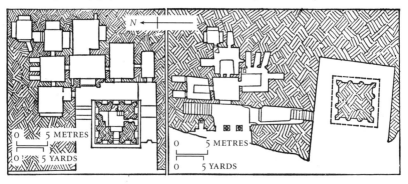

A number are structures of unusual interest. Inevitably they have been given popular names which have changed over the centuries and which, in most cases, have little to do with reality. Three free-standing rock monuments catch the eye from the modern road running round the south-east corner of the Haram esh-Sharif (Temple Mount), the 'Tomb of Absalom', the 'Tomb of Zachariah', and the 'Tomb of the Pharaoh's Daughter'.

It is no longer possible to drive down into the Kidron Valley from the Jericho road, but pedestrians can walk from near GETHSEMANE (p. 128). It is also possible to walk up from the GIHON SPRING (p. 112).

Tomb of Absalom

The bottle-shaped top of the 'Tomb of Absalom' (Fig. 33) has always attracted unusual names. Local Arabs call it *Tantour Firaoun* 'the Pharaoh's Hat', which echoes the medieval 'the Pharaoh's House'. The association with Absalom, the son of David, was first made by Benjamin of Tudela (1170) on the basis of 2 Sam. 18: 18, 'Absalom in his lifetime set up for himself a pillar that is in the King's Valley'. The monument is dated to the latter part of the C1 BC. It is rock up to the cornice; the top is masonry. It in fact contains a tomb, but the position of the door (above the cornice on the south side) shows that the tomb had been cut in the cliff before the decision to free the monolith was taken. The structure was designed to serve as a funerary monument or *nephesh* for the eight-chambered catacomb cut in the cliff behind; the entrance is surmounted by a fine pediment.

Tomb of Zachariah

Some 50 m further south the pyramid-roofed 'Tomb of Zachariah' serves as the funerary monument of another catacomb (Fig. 34). In the pilgrim literature it is associated with a number of Jewish and Christian (notably St James) saints, but a Hebrew inscription on the architrave above the two Doric columns identifies it as belonging to the priestly family of the Bene Hezir (1 Chr. 24: 15). Certainly earlier than its neighbour, the complex is dated to the second half of the C2 BC.

Tombs in Silwan

The village of Silwan is built on and in a cemetery of the Iron Age. A series of square openings in the middle of the cliff below the houses are the entrances to **tombs with gabled ceilings**. They were cut by high officials in the mid-C9 BC when Jerusalem was under Phoenician influence (2 Kgs. 8: 16–1: 20). Swept from office by the rising led by the priest Jehoiada, they came to less dignified ends than they had planned. The tombs were never used.

▲ **Tomb Complex of the Bene Hezir.** To the left of the pyramid-roofed *nefesh* ('memorial') a passage leads into the catacomb lighted by the two-columned Doric façade.

Their existence, however, inspired later Jewish officials to prepare tombs for themselves in the same area, but of a very different type. The most visible example is the Monolith of Silwan, which is popularly known as **'The Tomb of Pharaoh's Daughter'** because De Saulcy romantically identified it as a temple erected by Solomon for his Egyptian wife (1 Kgs. 3: 1). It sits in a walled area on the very edge of a small escarpment at the north end of the village. At first sight it looks like one of the small houses of Silwan, but it has no windows. The arch beneath it was added in the C19 to facilitate access by widening the space in front. When the adjoining rock was cut away in the C8 BC, the free-standing rock cube was surmounted by a pyramid like that of the 'Tomb of Zachariah'. The pyramid was carved into blocks in later quarrying operations, which did much damage to the cemetery. Other changes were effected by the hermit who made it his home in the Byzantine or Crusader period; in enlarging the entrance he cut through an ancient Hebrew inscription, two letters of which are visible near the upper left-hand corner.

Three other tombs of the same type have been found in Silwan, but the temper of the inhabitants makes a visit ill-advised. Mention, however, must be made of one tomb. Its 8 m façade with a recessed entrance and crude window, lies flush with the main street, and once carried two inscriptions in ancient Hebrew, which were cut out in the C19 AD and are now in the British Museum. The longer one reads 'This is [the sepulchre of . . .] yahu who is over the house. There is no silver and no gold here but [his bones] and the bones of his slave-wife with him. Cursed be the man who will open this.' It is identified as the **tomb of Shebna**, one of the officials sent by king Hezekiah to negotiate with the Assyrians in 701 BC (2 Kgs. 18: 18; Isa. 36: 3; 22: 15–25).

Aceldama

The lower southern side of the Hinnom Valley is dominated by a monastery (1874) dedicated to St Onuphrius, an Egyptian hermit famous for the length of his beard which was his only garment! According to a C13 source his cave was in the vicinity. If so, it was certainly a tomb, like those of so many other hermits in the vicinity.

For Byzantine Christians, however, the real association of the site was with the tragic figure of Judas. Eusebius identified it as the erstwhile Potter's Field, which became Aceldama, the 'Field of Blood', where Judas committed suicide (Acts 1: 18–19), and which was bought by the chief priests as a burial place for strangers (Matt. 27: 3–9). It is uncertain whether Eusebius was inspired by anything more than an erudite fusion of the Hebrew and Greek versions of Jer. 19: 1–6. The former speaks of a Pottery Gate opening on to the Hinnom Valley, while the latter mentions a common grave in the same area.

Pilgrims who died in the MAURISTAN were interred here in the C9. In 1143 the title of the Benedictines passed to the Hospitallers, who had to bury an average of fifty a day (see p. 59). To provide individual graves for so many was out of the question so they constructed a **charnel house** by putting a vault over an old quarry in which there were Jewish or Byzantine graves. The massive central pier and an arch survive in the ruins west of the monastery.

There are two remarkable Jewish tombs in the monastery, both of the Herodian period if not earlier. One, known as the **Refuge of the Apostles** (Mark 14: 50), has been transformed into a chapel. The magnificent Roman Doric frieze that surmounted the square entrance is perfectly preserved. Vertical lines separate eight squares each decorated differently. It has both arched burial niches (*arcosolia*) and burial cavities (*kokhim*). The same combination occurs in the second tomb, whose **distyle in antis** façade is even more elaborate. From the courtyard of the monastery one passes between two columns (the arches are modern) and through a decorated door into a square room surmounted by a smooth dome. There are two pairs of burial benches to right and left. Straight ahead two doors lead to rooms with *arcosolia*.

There are further tombs between the monastery and the Kidron Valley road. The most significant, but unfortunately not the best preserved, is roughly in the middle of the area. A pair of benched apses at right angles flank a large opening surmounted by the remains of a scallop shell decorative element. Originally it gave dignity to the middle entrance to an anteroom, from which a single door opened into a square room with a deeply carved domed ceiling in which 32 petals radiate out from a whorl rosette. Acanthus leaves fill the four corners The closest parallels to such decoration are the four Herodian domes inside the Double Gate. The apse cut into the eastern wall betrays the presence of a Byzantine hermit.

This tomb had a masonry superstructure, and may well be the **monument of Annas the high priest**, which is mentioned by Josephus in precisely this area in his description of the Roman siege wall constructed by Titus in AD 70 (*War* 5: 506). Annas (AD 6–15) is mentioned in the trial of Jesus because he was the father-in-law of Caiaphas (John 18: 13). Five of his sons became high priests, one of whom murdered James the brother of Jesus (*Antiquities* 20: 198–200).

There are at least six other tombs in the immediate vicinity. Paradoxically the one with the best preserved entrance—its elegant square moulding is intact—has the least interesting interior. It is more important to recognize that all the tombs in this area belonged to very wealthy Jewish families, a number of them from the Diaspora. It is most improbable that anyone in the C1 AD would have thought of locating a common grave for strangers among such neighbours.

Hell

The Valley of Hinnom (Josh. 15: 8) in Hebrew is *Ge Hinnom*, which was transliterated into Greek as *Gehenna*. In the C1 AD and subsequently both Christians ('Gehenna of fire', Matt. 5: 22) and Jews ('Gehenna, the pit of destruction', *Mishnah*, Aboth 5: 19) use it as the name of the place of eternal punishment. How and why did a beautiful sunlit valley give its name to Hell?

Symbolic values were most important. The bottom of the Hinnom Valley is the lowest point of the city, the antithesis of the Temple Mount. If the latter evoked the Mountain of the Lord (Isa. 2: 3), the former symbolized Sheol, the underworld (Amos 9: 2), the kingdom of Death (Hab. 2: 5), the universal grave to which all individual tombs gave entrance. The end of the valley was also the beginning of the desert, which was both the continuation of the primeval chaos and the home of the demons, in particular Azazel (Lev. 16: 10).

The heinous crimes committed in the Hinnom Valley were also a

The Accursed Valley

'I looked and turned to another part of the earth and saw there a deep valley with burning fire. And they brought the kings and the mighty and began to cast them into this deep valley. And my eyes saw how they made these their instruments, iron chains of immeasurable weight. And I asked the angel of peace who went with me, saying, "For whom are these chains being prepared?" And he said to me, "These are being prepared for the hosts of Azazel, so that they may take them and cast them into the abyss of complete condemnation."' (1 *Enoch* 54: 1–5; trans. R. H. Charles)

factor. It was the place of the Topheth ('the Burner'), where children were burnt alive in sacrifice to the god Moloch (2 Kgs. 23: 10). Isaiah prophesied that Moloch—and by implication his adherents—would be burnt there (30: 33; 33: 14), a theme repeated by Jeremiah (7: 31–3). 'The furnace of Gehenna shall be made manifest, and over against it the Paradise of delight' (4 *Ezra* 7: 36). The association of the Hinnom with punishing fire was greatly dramatized in later Jewish writings (see box).

The Mount of Olives

From Jerusalem the view to the east is blocked by the Mount of Olives (Fig. 35) rising some 100 m above the city. A road [1] runs along the top of the ridge, at various points there are magnificent views over the Old City and out across the Judaean desert to the Jordan Valley and the mountains of Moab.

In the time of David (1004–965 BC), who escaped that way when confronted by Absalom's treachery, there was a Jewish sanctuary (Nob?) on the summit (2 Sam. 15: 30–2). In the next generation other sanctuaries appeared; Solomon built temples for the gods of his foreign wives on the southern spur (2 Kgs. 23: 13) near the present Maison d'Abraham [9], from whose wall there is a dominant view encompassing the whole of the CITY OF DAVID (p. 108). After the establishment of the Temple in Jerusalem the ritual of the Red Heifer (Num. 19: 1–10) was celebrated on the Mount of Olives; leaving the Temple by the East Gate, the procession led by the High Priest crossed the Kidron Valley on a special causeway and climbed to the summit where the animal was sacrificed (*Mishnah*, tractate 'Parah').

Jesus' familiarity with the Mount of Olives stemmed from the fact that, when in the Jerusalem area, he stayed with his friends at Bethany (Luke 10: 38; Mark 11: 11). At pilgrimage time the population of Jerusalem tripled. The cost of lodging within the city became exorbitant and the poor had to make arrangements in the surrounding villages. Thus each day he walked over the hill to the city and returned at nightfall (Luke 21: 37). The lie of the land permits only one route if the traveller wants to avoid climbing in and out of wadis: from Gethsemane straight up the hill to et-Tur and along the ridge to Bethphage (roughly the modern road), then along another ridge to Bethany. One evening, seated on the slope opposite the Temple, Jesus spoke to his disciples of the future of the city (Mark 13: 3) whose lack of faith had driven him to tears (Luke 19: 37, 41–4). At the bottom of the

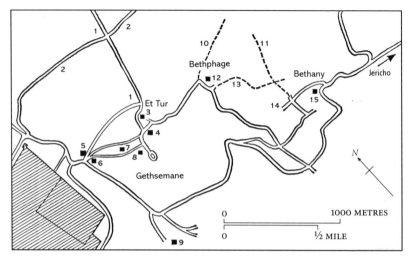

▲ **Fig. 35.** The Mount of Olives. 1–2. Modern roads; 3. Mosque of the
Ascension; 4. Pater Noster Church; 5. Tomb of the Virgin; 6. Church of All
Nations; 7. Dominus Flevit; 8. Tombs of the Prophets; 9. Maison d'Abraham;
10. Ancient road; 11. Ancient road; 12. Bethphage; 13. Ancient road; 14. C1
AD Bethany; 15. Tomb of Lazarus.

slope is the garden of Gethsemane where he was arrested a few days later
(Mark 14: 26–52). Luke locates the Ascension on the Mount of Olives
(Acts 1: 6–12).

As the Roman legions gathered for the siege of Jerusalem in AD 70,
the Tenth Legion came up the east side of the Mount of Olives and
camped in the vicinity of the crossroads in the shallow saddle (the junction of [1] and [2]). The Roman road [2] coming over the saddle and
down into the city may have been constructed at this period, but a date in
the early C2 AD is perhaps more likely. Titus was camped with the Twelfth
and Fifteenth Legions on the northern extremity of the ridge at a spot
called Scopus (the area today occupied by the Hebrew University and the
Second World War military cemetery), so named because it permits
'the first sight of the city and the grand pile of the temple gleaming afar'
(*War* 5: 67–70).

Christians flocked to the Mount of Olives in the Byzantine period
both because of its associations with Jesus and because of the splendid
view of the holy places in the city. By the C6, according to eye-witnesses,
there were twenty-four churches on the mount surrounded by monasteries containing vast numbers of monks and nuns.

The concentration of **cemeteries** (Christian, Jewish, and Muslim) on
the south-western end of the Mount of Olives and on the other side of the
Kidron valley beneath the Temple walls is due to the belief that the Kidron

The Lament of Jesus over Jerusalem

'As Jesus drew near and came in sight of the city, he shed tears over it, and said, "If you had only recognized on this day the way to peace! But in fact it is hidden from your eyes! Yes, a time is coming when your enemies will raise fortifications all round you, when they will encircle you and hem you in on every side. They will dash you and the children inside your walls to the ground. They will leave not a stone upon a stone, because you did not recognize the moment of your visitation." '
(Luke 19: 41–4)

is the valley of Jehoshaphat where humanity will assemble to be judged by God (see TOMBS IN THE VALLEYS).

Visit. Since the slope is steep, it is best to take a bus or taxi to the esplanade in front of the Seven Arches Hotel, from which there is a splendid panorama of the Old City, and to walk down. It is easy to get another bus or taxi at Gethsemane. Alternatively one may walk to Bethphage and on to Bethany. It is dangerous for women to go alone.

Russian Ascension Church

The slender square tower of a convent of Russian nuns dominates the skyline of the Mount of Olives. The complex on the edge of et-Tur was built between 1870 and 1887, and the purpose of the tower was to permit pilgrims incapable of the walk to the Jordan to at least see the holy river. The excavation of the foundations brought to light two beautiful Armenian mosaics of the Byzantine period, which originally belonged to funerary chapels.

Visit. Open: Tuesday and Thursday 9 a.m.–noon. The archaeological museum of the convent was built to enshrine the incomplete C5 AD Artavan mosaic. It owes its name to the dedicatory inscription along its border: 'This is the tomb of the blessed Susannah, mother of Artavan'. A lamb is represented in the centre. Distributed around him are a pearl, clusters of grapes, a citron, and three living creatures, a hen, a Nile duck, and a fish. These latter appear tridimensional because of the way the plane closest to the spectator is highlighted.

The second mosaic is slightly later and not quite of the same quality. It adorns the floor of the **Chapel of the Head of St John the Baptist**. An inscription identifies it as 'The monument of the Lord Jacob, made at his request'. Alternating squares and circles contain pheasants, flamingos, ibises, doves, ducks, parrots, pearl hens, and one lonely fish. In the central horizontal row a dog barks at a frightened lamb. The symbolism is obscure.

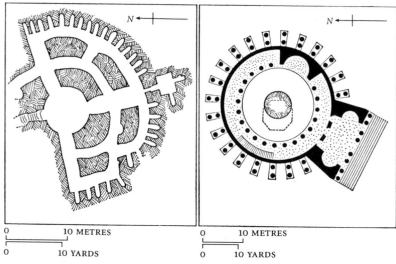

0   10 METRES   0   10 METRES

0   10 YARDS   0   10 YARDS

▲ **Fig. 36.** *(left)* The Tombs of the Prophets on the Mount of Olives.
Fig. 37. *(right)* J. Wilkinson's reconstruction of the C4 Church of the Ascension.

Mosque of the Ascension

Luke is the only evangelist to mention the Ascension of Jesus. At the end of his gospel he says, 'He led them out as far as towards Bethany, and lifting up his hands he blessed them. And it came to pass that as he blessed them, he parted from them and was carried up into heaven' (Luke 24: 50–2). Reading the whole of ch. 24 one has the impression that the event occurred on Easter Sunday; the place is not precisely located. According to Luke's second work, the Acts of the Apostles, the Ascension (1: 9) took place forty days after the Resurrection (1: 3), somewhere on the Mount of Olives, a Sabbath day's journey (= 2,000 paces) from the city (1: 12). The inconsistency of the two accounts is real, but Luke could accept it because he was aware that he was not recording an historical event; from his point of view the Ascension was much more a literary way of drawing a line between the terrestrial mission of Jesus and that of the apostles, which began with the descent of the Holy Spirit at Pentecost (Acts 2: 1–4).

In the pre-Constantinian period Jerusalem Christians venerated the Ascension in a cave on the Mount of Olives, probably because it was safer to congregate in a hidden place. When Egeria participated in the liturgical celebration of the Ascension in 384 it took place on the nearby open hillock. Poimenia, a member of the imperial family, built the first church on the site ([**3**] in Fig. 35) before 392; the proposed reconstruction (Fig. 37) is based on the descriptions of Byzantine pilgrims, a drawing by Arculf (670), and archaeological investigations.

' Nothing visible remains of this church whose centre was open to the sky. In the Crusader reconstruction an octagon replaced the original circular shape, and the shrine was surrounded by a fortified monastery. In the Middle Ages great veneration was accorded to the mark of Jesus' feet in the stone floor of the edicule; in the Byzantine period the footprints were 'plainly and clearly impressed in the dust' which pilgrims were permitted to take away (Arculf)! Saladin conveyed the site by deed to two of his followers in 1198 and it has remained in Muslim possession ever since. The Muslim restoration of 1200 preserved much of the Crusader edicule but added a roof and a *mihrab*; though not mentioned in the Koran, Muslims believe that Jesus ascended into heaven.

Visit. If the door is not open, ring the bell. From the entrance it is immediately evident that the much repaired medieval octagon surround-wall has been truncated on the east. From the hooks set into this wall the various Christian communities stretch awnings to provide a temporary roof for the celebration of the feast of the Ascension.

At the corners of the octagonal shrine note the reused Crusader capitals, and in particular the two with bird-headed winged quadrupeds. Inside the edicule a small rectangle surrounds the mark of Jesus' right foot; the section bearing the imprint of the left foot was taken to the el-Aksa mosque in the Middle Ages. To its left is another stone in which holes have been bored; at one time they may have held a protective grating. The eccentric position of the supposed footprint highlights the secondary character of the edifice. The dominating minaret and its adjoining mosque date from 1620.

Church of the Pater Noster

The apocryphal *Acts of John* (C3 AD) attests the existence of a particular cave on the Mount of Olives associated with the teaching of Jesus (ch. 97). According to Eusebius (260–340), Constantine's building programme in Palestine focused on the three caves linked to the key mysteries of the faith, the birth cave in Bethlehem, the rock-cut tomb near Golgotha, and the cave on the Mount of Olives with which the Ascension was also linked. The church built over this cave ([**4**] in Fig. 35), under the direction of Queen Helena, was seen by the Bordeaux pilgrim in 333. Egeria (384) is the first to record what became the common name, 'Eleona' (Jerusalemites attached an Aramaic *a* to the Greek *elaion*, meaning 'of olives'). After the site for the commemoration of the Ascension had been moved further up the hill, the cave was exclusively associated with the teaching of Jesus on the ultimate conflict of good and evil (Matt. 24: 1–26: 2—the gospel Egeria heard read in the cave on Tuesday of Holy Week).

Despite the destruction of the church by the Persians in 614, the memory of Jesus' teaching remained, but there was a significant shift in its content. It tended to become the place where he taught the disciples the Our Father; the basis being a sophisticated harmonization of Luke 10: 38–11: 4 with Mark 11: 12–25. This was the dominant tradition when the Crusaders constructed an oratory in the ruins (1106). In 1102 a pilgrim heard a story of a marble plaque with the Lord's Prayer inscribed in Hebrew; another saw one in Greek placed beneath the altar (1170); an inscribed Latin version was found in the excavations.

This tradition has been revived in the decoration of the cloister erected after the Byzantine foundations were brought to light in 1910; tiled panels give the Lord's Prayer in sixty-two languages.

Visit. Open: 8.30–noon and 3–5 p.m.; closed Sunday. After passing through the iron gate go left and then immediately right, into the area once occupied by the Byzantine basilica. The **half-reconstructed church** gives a good idea of the C4 building whose raised sanctuary covered the cave. It has the same dimensions, and the garden outside the three doors outlines the area of the atrium.

The **cave** acquired its present shape under the chisels of the C4 builders. There were two entrances, one opposite the other; the cutting near the apse may have been the original entrance. In preparing the cave the builders broke through into a C1 AD *kokhim* tomb. They blocked the hole with masonry which has now been removed; the tomb can be entered via the steps at the end opposite the apse. It seems unlikely that the venerated cave was originally a tomb; had the builders cut away *kokhim* graves it would have been much wider.

Leaving the church by a door in the south wall one can go either right or left. The former leads to an area paved with mosaic and identified as a **baptistery**; the latter brings one into the **cloister** (1868) with different versions of the Lord's Prayer. Exit via the first door on the right (in the middle of the east wall). The tomb is that of the Princesse de la Tour d'Auvergne who bought the property in 1857 and built the adjoining convent of contemplative Carmelite sisters in 1872.

The little road to the right on leaving the property leads to Bethphage and Bethany. The road to Gethsemane begins at a flight of steps midway between the Pater Noster and the Seven Arches Hotel.

Tombs of the Prophets

Open: Monday to Friday 9 a.m.–3.30 p.m.; bring a flashlight. The sign at the entrance ([8] in Fig. 35) claims that this catacomb contains the tombs of the prophets Haggai, Zechariah, and Malachi who lived in the C6–C5 BC. This medieval Jewish tradition is contradicted by the form of the graves; *kokhim* shafts came into use only in the C1 BC. The catacomb was part of the pre-AD 135 Jewish cemetery on the Mount of Olives. The only unusual feature is the fan shape (Fig. 36), which suggests an economical commercial development.

Dominus Flevit

Further down the hill on the right is the entrance to the tear-shaped church called Dominus Flevit ([**7**] in Fig. 35). Open: 8 a.m.–noon; 2.30–5 p.m.; toilets.

Medieval pilgrims were the first to designate a rock on the Mount of Olives as the place where Jesus wept over Jerusalem (Luke 19: 41). When the Muslims denied access to Christians, the Franciscans (in 1881) built a small chapel just on the other side of the centre track. In 1954 excavations in the southern part of their property brought to light a monastery of the C5 AD and an immense cemetery, first used *c.*1600–1300 BC and again later in two main periods, 100 BC–AD 135 and AD 200–400.

Visit. The **cemetery** has been covered in again but examples of the two types of tombs have been left visible. The first two on the right (counting from the entrance gate) are typical *kokhim* graves of the period 100 BC–AD 135, the dead were buried in oven-shaped shafts and later their bones were collected in beautifully made stone boxes (ossuaries) in order to make room for others. Such burials ceased here in 135 when Hadrian forbade Jerusalem to Jews; BET SHEARIM was adopted as an alternative. The XP (chi-rho) sign on one ossuary does not mean that the person was a Christian, it is attested as an abbreviation for 'sealed'.

The third tomb is quite different, the bodies were laid in arched niches (*arcosolia*); it is dated in the C3–C4 AD. The fourth tomb is of the earlier period; two fine sarcophagi are displayed. So little remained of the 'Jebusite' (pre-Israelite inhabitants of the town on the Ophel Ridge) tomb that nothing could be preserved; it was located in the area now occupied by the toilets.

The new **church** (1955) reproduces the outline of the late C7 chapel whose apse is preserved to a considerable height; the emplacement of the altar and that of the chancel screen are still visible. The fragmentary inscription mentions neither the dedication nor the function of the monastery to which the chapel belonged. After the death of the founder the adjoining sacristy was transformed into a funerary chapel with a well-preserved mosaic floor whose inscription reads, 'Simeon, friend of Christ, made and decorated this oratory and offered it to Christ our Lord in expiation of his sins and for the repose of his brothers, the hygumenos Georgios and the friend of Christ Dometios.' The present open space was the monastic courtyard. The monastery was abandoned towards the end of the C8.

At least from the C7 to the arrival of the Crusaders the liturgical procession from the Eleona (p. 125) on Holy Thursday night commemorated here the prayer of Christ in agony. According to Luke 22: 41 it was 'a stone's-throw' from Gethsemane where he was arrested. The same tradition is apparently attested by Egeria for the late C4. That there was a Byzantine monastery on the site is confirmed by the date of the mosaic-floored wine tank in the corner of the courtyard and other (no longer visible) elements.

The Church of St Mary Magdalene

Open: Tuesday and Thursday 10–11.30 a.m. This typically Russian church was built by the Czar Alexander III in 1888. To the left of the path just inside the street entrance there are three steps cut in the rock. Steps going up from Gethsemane are mentioned in the *Commemoratorium* (AD 808), but these certainly antedate the C1 AD.

Gethsemane ★★

Having eaten the Paschal meal somewhere in the city (Luke 22: 10), Jesus 'went forth with his disciples across the Kidron Valley, where there was a garden' (John 18: 1) on the Mount of Olives called Gethsemane (Mark 14: 26, 32). The place was known to Judas, 'for Jesus often met there with his disciples' (John 18: 2), perhaps to take a rest (while reflecting on the experiences of the day) before starting the climb up the steep steps *en route* to Bethany. Jesus knew his life to be in danger (John 11: 8, 16); he suspected Judas of treachery (Mark 14: 17–21). On his way up the Kidron Valley he could not have avoided seeing the tombs (p. 117) in the bright moonlight. Awareness of the imminence of death struck him with great force; he had to stop and be alone for a moment because a decision had to be made. His enemies would come from the city, but ten minutes' fast walking would bring him to the top of the Mount of Olives with the open desert before him. Escape would be easy; he could postpone the inevitable. Only in prayer could he find the answer to the agonizing question of whether to stand or retreat.

The Church of All Nations

This church ([**6**] in Fig. 35), built in 1924, is located on the traditional site of the garden in which Jesus collapsed. No one can be sure of the exact spot at which he prayed, but this limited area was certainly close to the natural route leading from the Temple to the summit of the Mount of Olives and the ridge leading to Bethany.

The present edifice (shaded area, Fig. 38) is the latest in a series of three churches. It covers 'the elegant church' (Egeria) built between AD 379 and 384 (solid black line) on the site where the pre-Constantinian Jerusalem community commemorated the prayer of Christ. Willibald, in 724–5, is the last pilgrim to mention this church; it was destroyed by an

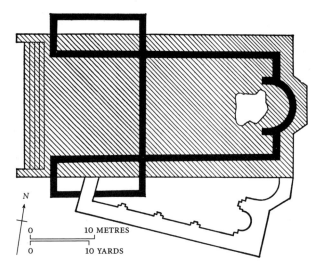

▲ **Fig. 38.** Superimposed churches at Gethsemane (after Wilkinson): C4 (solid black), C12 (white), C20 (shaded).

earthquake some twenty years later. The Crusaders first built an oratory in the ruins which they later (*c.*1170) replaced by a church (double line); they gave it a slightly different orientation in order to have a piece of rock in each apse—a rather material interpretation of the triple prayer of Christ. The fate of this building is unknown; still functioning in 1323, it was abandoned in 1345.

Visit. Open: 8 a.m.–noon; 2.30–5 p.m. (winter); to 6 p.m. (summer). The olive trees in the garden, though extremely ancient, are unlikely to have been in existence in the time of Christ; the wooded slopes of the Mount of Olives must have been a prime source for the vast quantities of timber required for the cooking fires of three legions, and for their siege equipment in AD 70 (*War* 5: 264).

The rock in the nave was also the central feature of the C4 church whose outline and columns are traced in black marble on the floor; glass panels protect sections of the Byzantine mosaic floor. Part of the present south wall near the apse is solid rock. This was the centre-piece of the Crusader church; on the top (about eye level) note a levelled surface and a cut hole suggesting the emplacement of an altar. The reconstructed trace of the Crusader edifice can be seen outside the south wall. Leave the church by the main door and turn left.

The Tomb of the Virgin

The domed structure on the bend of the main road is reputed to be the tomb of Mujir al-Din (1456–1522), a famed Arab scholar whose history of

The Burial of Mary

'The Holy Spirit said to the disciples, "Take up the Lady Mary this morning and go forth from Jerusalem on the road that goes out to the head
of the valley on this side of the Mount of Olives, where there are caves,
a large outer cave, another within it, and a small inner cave with a
raised bench on the east side. Go in and place the Blessed One on that
bench, and minister about her until I shall speak to you." ' (*Transitus
Mariae*, trans. A. Lewis Smith)

Jerusalem remains invaluable. On either side steps lead down to the courtyard in front of the Tomb of the Virgin ([**5**] in Fig. 35).

The New Testament says nothing about the death of Mary. Her death
on Mount Sion and burial in a cavern in the valley of Jehoshaphat is first
mentioned in the *Transitus Mariae*, an anonymous work whose substance
may be as early as the C2–C3 AD. Ephesus claimed the honour in 431, but
in 451 the eloquence of the Patriarch Juvenal persuaded the emperor
Marcian that Jerusalem had the better case. The existence of a church is
attested by writers of the late C6. If the Persians destroyed it in 614 it was
rebuilt, because Arculf (670) thus describes what he saw: 'It is a church
built at two levels, and the lower part, which is beneath a stone vault, has a
remarkable round shape. At the east end there is an altar, on the right of
which is the empty rock tomb in which for a time Mary remained
entombed. . . . The upper church of Saint Mary is also round.' The
Crusaders found only the ruins left by the destructive passage of the
caliph Hakim in 1009, but by 1130 the Benedictines had rebuilt the double
church; in 1178 Theodoric noted that there were as many steps down to
the crypt as there were up to the church. In 1187 Saladin destroyed the
superstructure and used the stones to repair the city wall, but removed
only the decoration of the crypt.

Visit (Fig. 39). Open: 6–11.30 a.m. and 2.30–5 p.m. The façade and the
monumental stairway are early C12. On the right [**1**] is the tomb of Queen
Melisande (d. 1161), the daughter and wife of Crusader kings of
Jerusalem; other members of the family of Baldwin II were buried in the
niche opposite [**2**]. An arch protruding above the modern door [**3**]
betrays the Byzantine entrance; there was another on the far side of the
apse [**4**]. About the middle of the steps the architectural style changes; the
pointed arches giving way to round vaults.

The crypt [**5**] is Byzantine, in part constructed (solid black) and in
part cut out of the rock. The rising passage [**6**] disturbs the cruciform
symmetry of the Byzantine crypt; it is in fact a much older entrance to an
underground cemetery—there are good parallels further up the hill in the
DOMINUS FLEVIT and in the TOMBS OF THE PROPHETS. A grille high in the

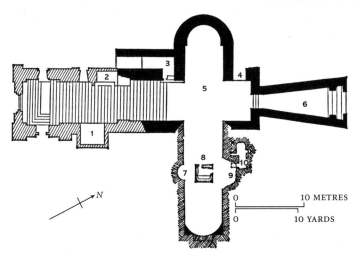

▲ **Fig. 39.** The Tomb of the Virgin at Gethsemane (after Bagatti). 1. Tomb of Queen Melisande; 2. Family tomb of Baldwin II; 3–4. Byzantine entrances; 5. Byzantine Crypt; 6. Original entrance to cemetery; 7. Mihrab; 8. Tomb of the Virgin; 9. Niche; 10. C1 AD tomb.

side of the niche [**9**] covers part of a tomb [**10**] whose type is compatible with a C1 AD date. Its entrance disappeared when the rock was cut away to isolate another tomb [**8**] which tradition considers to be that of the Virgin Mary. Glass plates reveal the living rock on three sides; the rock bench, on which the body was laid, has suffered from the piety of pilgrims. Originally there was only one entrance; the lintel over the secondary door facing the niche [**9**] is medieval. The idea of isolating the tomb in the middle of the crypt was suggested by the Holy Sepulchre where, a century earlier, Constantine's engineers had cut away the rock around the tomb of Christ in order to bring it within the church.

The curved *mihrab* [**7**] gives the direction of Mecca; the site is holy to Muslims because, according to Mujir al-Din, Muhammad saw a light over the tomb of his 'sister Mary' on his night journey to Jerusalem (see DOME OF THE ROCK, p. 85).

The Cave of Gethsemane

From the facade of the Virgin's Tomb a narrow passage leads to a cave which Byzantine Christians regarded as the place where the disciples rested while Jesus prayed a stone's-throw away (Luke 22: 41); it was there that Judas saluted him with the traitor's kiss.

Visit. Open: 8.30 a.m.–noon; 2.30–5 p.m. The original opening of the cave was between the entrance steps and the first altar on the left. On the right side of the altar at the far end is a hole in the wall. It is just at the right height to hold one end of a wooden beam which, when weighted at the other end, pressed crushed olives piled in loosely woven baskets. Gethsemane means 'oil press'. The stars on the ceiling were painted during the C12 AD. The paving dates only from 1957. Just inside the door to the right is a water cistern, traces of Byzantine mosaics at two different levels, and a gutter. Their original function and relationships are obscure.

Bethphage

Bethphage is mentioned in the Gospels as the starting-place of Jesus' triumphal entrance into Jerusalem amid waving palms, but the texts are not as clear as one would wish. According to Mark, Jesus was in the vicinity of 'Bethphage and Bethany, at the Mount of Olives' when he sent the disciples into the village opposite to fetch the ass (11: 1–2), but for Matthew, Jesus had entered Bethphage before sending the disciples on their mission (21: 1–2). Inevitably, the location of Bethphage is uncertain. Everything depends on the route that Jesus took coming from Jericho. The ancient road lay in the long wadi Umm esh-Shid continuing due east from [2] in Fig. 35; once one got to the back of the Mount of Olives there were different options, the best two of which are numbered [10] and [11] in Fig. 35. Bethphage could have been on the ridge between the two. The present site ([12] in Fig. 35) has a reasonable chance of being in the vicinity; the chapel is the starting-point for the Palm Sunday procession.

Visit. Open: 8–11.30 a.m.; 2–4.30 p.m. (winter); to 5 p.m. (summer). Ring the bell for admission. From the courtyard it is obvious that the lower part of the church walls is older than the rest. The present church was built in 1883 on the ruins of a medieval church which enshrined a stone that the Crusaders regarded as the mounting-stone of Christ, forgetting that a Palestinian donkey was in no way comparable to their huge battle-chargers. The medieval paintings on the stone are beautiful, and have not been damaged by the 1950 restoration. One records the meeting of Lazarus's sisters with Jesus (John 11: 20–30). In 384 Egeria noted, 'About half a mile before you get to the Lazarium [= Bethany] from Jerusalem there is a church by the road. It is the spot where Lazarus's sister Mary met the Lord.' The original purpose of the stone is unknown.

It is sometimes possible to get permission to go behind the church into the Franciscan property. Numerous cisterns, tombs (one closed by a rolling stone), and a mosaic-paved wine press witness to continued occupation from the C2 BC to the C8 AD.

To walk to Bethany from Bethphage go left on leaving the church and follow the path beside the high wall of the monastery ([13] in Fig. 35). Some 50 yards after the wall swings away to follow the side of a small wadi, the path divides: take the rougher track to the right and the churches of Bethany soon come into sight.

For those who prefer to drive, it is best to go down the hill to the right, straight through the crossroads and turn left on the main Jericho road; it is possible to go left at the crossroads but the road is very narrow and steep.

Bethany

Bethany was the village in which Jesus' friends Martha, Mary, and Lazarus lived. From its cemetery he raised Lazarus from the dead (John 11). There is no problem about its identification. A village ([15] in Fig. 35) on the main Jericho road fits the distance from Jerusalem given in John 11: 18, and its Arabic name el-Azariyeh preserves the Greek *Lazarion*, 'the place of Lazarus', by which it was known to Eusebius (330) and all subsequent Byzantine and medieval pilgrims.

The present village is built round the tomb of Lazarus as the result of a development parallel to that which occurred in HEBRON. In the C1 AD the area was a cemetery; tombs of this period have been found a short distance north of the church. The village of (Bet) Ananiah inhabited by Benjaminites after the Exile (Neh. 11: 32) was located further up the hill ([14] in Fig. 35). The site is not accessible to visitors; excavations prove it to have been occupied from the C6 BC to the C14 AD.

Jerome records the existence of a church in 390. After its destruction by an earthquake, a second one was built in the C6. It had the same width as its predecessor, but the apse was moved 13 m further east. The extra space was necessary because Egeria (384), who knew the first church, says, 'so many people have collected that they fill not only the Lazarium itself, but all the fields around'. From the courtyard to the west of both these churches a rock-cut passage gave access to the tomb of Lazarus.

Money poured into the site between 1138 and 1144 when Queen Melisande transformed it into a convent of Benedictine sisters for her younger sister Iveta, who became abbess in 1157. The piers and north wall of a Byzantine church were strengthened to take a stone roof. It remained the focal point for pilgrims. The conventual church of the sisters was built directly over the tomb. Its triapsidal east end was supported by barrel vaults, the largest of which later became the mosque. A square cloister lay along its south side.

By the end of the C14 both churches were in ruins, and the original entrance to the tomb had been turned into a mosque. The Muslims also venerated the raising of Lazarus and at first permitted Christians to continue their liturgical visits. When this became progressively more difficult the Franciscans cut the present entrance to the tomb between 1566 and 1575. They erected the new church and the adjoining monastery in 1954. The Greek Orthodox church (begun in 1965) on the other side of the tomb incorporates part of the north wall of the medieval Benedictine chapel.

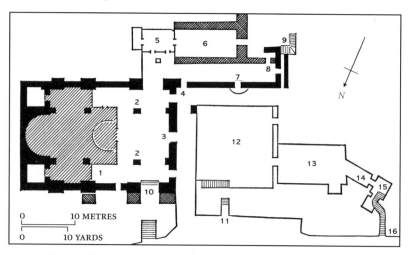

▲ **Fig. 40.** Superimposed churches at Bethany (after Saller): C5 (solid black), C12 (cross hatching), C20 (shaded area). 1. Masonry of C4 church; 2. Piers of C5 church; 3. Façade of C5 church; 4. Corner of C5 atrium; 5. Toilets; 6. Crusader monastery; 8. Door; 9. Stairs. 10. Modern entrance; 11. Mosque entrance; 12. Mosque courtyard; 13. Mosque; 14. C4 entrance to tomb of Lazarus; 15. Tomb of Lazarus; 16. Modern entrance to the tomb of Lazarus.

Visit (Fig. 40). Open: 8–11.25 a.m.; 2–5 p.m. (winter); to 6 p.m. (summer). Toilets.

Just inside the entrance of the modern (1955) cruciform church (shaded) trapdoors on both sides expose the masonry of the apse of the C4 church. The mosaic beneath the grille is that of the C6 church (solid black lines) whose apse is outlined in white marble on both sides of the main altar.

In the courtyard one can see part of the masonry of the C4 church [**1**] whose mosaic floor once covered the entire area; the preserved portions are now covered by metal plates; those nearest the C6 façade [**3**] with its three doors shows how this wall cuts across the original design. On the side of the centre pillars [**2**] fragments of mosaic about 30 cm above ground level belong to the floor of the C6 church; a few centimetres above them another fragment of mosaic betrays the floor laid during the Crusader restoration in the C12. Just outside the C6 south door [**4**] is a pillar of the atrium, and two medieval graves; the mosaic floor is C4–C5 and can be seen again at the door [**7**] which connected the atrium with a long room on its south side.

Beside the pilgrims' dining room [**5**] is a room of the medieval monastery [**6**] containing a mill and oil press. Immediately inside the small door [**8**] one can see the turn of the C6 wall. The staircase [**9**] leads to the extensive upper section of the Crusader monastery.

When climbing the stairway [**10**] to the street note the medieval reinforcement (cross hatching) of the C6 church wall. From the entrance [**11**] of the **Mosque el-Ozir** one can look down into the courtyard [**12**] of the C4 and C6 churches. When the guardian is in good humour one can sometimes gain access to the mosque [**13**] where the original entrance to the tomb [**14**] is clearly visible; the odd angle at which this passage meets the mosque suggests that it antedated the construction of the Byzantine atrium. Since the hill slopes to the south the original entrance to the tomb must have been on that side.

Today the **tomb of Lazarus** [**15**] is entered from the street by a flight of very uneven steps [**16**] which enters the antechamber through the north wall. The outline of the earlier entrance is clear in the east wall. At one time the floor level of the two chambers may have been the same; rotten limestone falling from the unusually high ceiling could have raised the level of the antechamber; the floor of the passage [**14**] is two steps above the level of the mosque. Falls may have occurred when the Crusaders constructed their church directly above; to strengthen the tomb they introduced the masonry which still obscures the original rock except for a few holes in the inner chamber.

Walking up the street from the present entrance [**16**] one passes the new Greek Orthodox church before coming to a four-way crossroads. To the left are the ruins of a Crusader tower in which the Benedictine sisters could take refuge in case of a Muslim attack. Its walls are 4 m thick and enclose a cistern. The track to the right leads to BETHPHAGE. The path winds up between the houses. At the top one can look down into a shallow wadi which carried the ancient road from Bethany to Jericho; keep left along the high wall of the Franciscan property to get to Bethphage.

New City

New suburbs were first built outside the walled city in 1860. The impetus to expand did not come from within the Old City. Three centuries of Ottoman rule had reduced its inhabitants to a state of torpid misery. Arbitrary taxation penalized any initiative, and foul cisterns, the only source of drinking water, meant that 50 per cent of the small population suffered from endemic malaria; the rubbish of centuries clogged the streets.

The authorities of Czarist Russia, responsible for 12,000 pilgrims each year, were not prepared to permit them to live in such dangerous and unsanitary conditions, and built a series of great hostels on a hill outside the north-west corner of the Old City. Its centre-piece, a many-domed church near Jaffa Road, is still a Jerusalem landmark, but the defensive wall has disappeared. Such protection was necessary because the Turkish authorities were neither capable nor willing to provide protection outside the walled city; they had only 120 troops in Palestine and these were themselves no more than licensed brigands; to recruit new members they simply shanghaied peasants.

Encouraged by the Russian initiative, an English philanthropist, Sir Moses Montefiore, went ahead with his project to house residents of the Jewish Quarter west of the city at Mishkenoth Shaananim ('Abode of Tranquillity'); its symbol is the windmill which he had erected in 1857 to grind flour for the city.

The success of these two efforts had its impact on inhabitants of the walled city only in 1869 when, attracted by the commercial opportunities offered by the presence of so many Russian pilgrims, seven Jewish families moved out to the area near the present Sion Square.

As the century progressed Christian and Jewish immigration consolidated these gains. Jewish immigrants concentrated in the north-western and western sectors. German Christians founded a farming village in the south-west, the Refaim Valley, while American and European Christians spearheaded expansion north of the Old City. The architecture of all these developments still betrays the concern for security. Housing areas were so designed that the backs of contiguous houses formed a wall and gates at the end of streets could be locked; institutions were surrounded by forbidding walls.

This situation changed only in 1918 when Palestine came under the Mandatory Government. The great contribution of the British was the provision of an efficient police force; security permitted free expansion, but ripening tensions between Jews and Arabs fostered the development of homogeneous neighbourhoods. The population of Jerusalem grew continuously under British administration, increasing 162 per cent between 1922 (62,700) and 1946 (164,000). The contribution of Jews and Arabs to this growth was almost equal.

The bitter fighting which followed the departure of the British and the creation of the State of Israel resulted in the partition of Jerusalem. Arabs retained possession of the Old City, whose Jewish population had decreased steadily during the British Mandate, and the area along the ridge to the north. Fortunately subsequent growth in this sector was slow because lack of planning permitted linear development along the Nablus road. Growth in the western sector was intense because of the need to absorb Jewish immigrants from Europe and Arab countries; the population increased from 82,900 in 1948 to 197,750 in 1967.

No development outside the walled city was ever intended to consecrate a site of historical or archaeological interest, but scattered throughout the urban area are a number of sites which reflect the history of Jerusalem. Most are in fact tombs, some of them unusually interesting.

The two sketch maps (Figs. 41 and 43), which locate sites in the northern and western sectors, should be used in conjunction with a detailed map of the city; the best is 'Jerusalem' (1 : 14,000) produced by the Survey of Israel.

New City: Northern Section

One salient feature of the landscape immediately to the north of the Old City is the amount of open space now filled by a major road. This was the No-Man's Land during the twenty years when the city was divided between Jordanians and Israelis (Fig. 41). A tall slender sun-dial on the road divider marks the site of the famous **'Mandelbaum Gate'**. No gate ever existed here. Between 1948 and 1967 it was the only point where visitors could cross from one side of the city to the other.

By the C1 AD the low hills surrounding Jerusalem on the north and east had become a vast cemetery. A great number of tombs have been discovered and many excavated, one containing the body of a young man crucified by the prefect Varus in AD 6. It is possible to mention only those of exceptional interest. Capital letters refer to the locations in Fig. 41.

Sanhedrin Tombs [A]

Located in a garden at the end of Sanhedrin Street, the cave containing these tombs is notable for its magnificent carved pediment, the finest in

▼ **Fig. 41.** New City. Northern Section. A. Sanhedrin tombs; B. Tomb of Simon the Just; C. Tombs of the Kings; D. St Stephen's church; E. Garden Tomb; F. Armenian mosaic; G. Solomon's Quarries; H. Rockefeller Museum; J. Benshoot Museum.

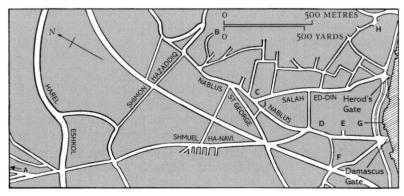

Jerusalem. Pomegranates and other fruits are scattered among the stylized acanthus leaves; the workmanship is typically C1 AD. Open 9 a.m.–sunset.

The entrance to the tomb chamber has a smaller pediment. The great chamber immediately inside is unique in that it has two rows of shaft graves (*kokhim*) one above the other; *arcosolia* group those of the upper level in pairs. There are two other chambers on the same level, and others below reached by stairs.

The number of burials that the tomb can accommodate is responsible for its popular name; it approximates to the membership (70) of the Jewish Sanhedrin.

Tomb of Simon the Just [B]

Popularly identified as the tomb of the high priest Simon (Sir. 50: 1–21) who said, 'By three things is the world sustained: by the Law, by the Temple-service, and by deeds of loving-kindness' (*Mishnah*, Aboth 1: 2), this tomb in fact belongs to the Roman matron Julia Sabine, as an inscription proves.

Its interest lies less in its architectural style, which is negligible, than in the fact that it illustrates an ancient Jewish custom; it is a place of pilgrimage for Oriental Jews who offer prayers of petition. The custom of praying at the graves of revered religious leaders is attested for the C1 AD by a work called *The Lives of the Prophets*. The disciples of Jesus did the same; texts such as Mark 16: 6 take on their full meaning when spoken during prayer services at his tomb. It is not surprising, therefore, that the location of the tomb of Christ should have been indelibly fixed in the memories of Jerusalem Christians.

Tomb of Queen Helena of Adiabene [C] ★

The majestic façade of this tomb complex convinced the first archaeologist to explore it that the graves belonged to the kings of Judah, whence the popular name Tombs of the Kings. His intuition regarding royal origin was correct, but the founder was a queen of Adiabene in northern Mesopotamia, about whom Josephus tells us much (*Antiquities* 20: 17–96).

Early in the C1 AD Helena, dowager queen of Adiabene, and her son Izates, were converted to Judaism by proselytizing Jewish merchants. She arrived in Jerusalem on pilgrimage during the great famine (Acts 11: 27–30) which occurred between AD 46 and 48, and immediately set about procuring food from as far away as Egypt and Cyprus. Deciding to stay in Jerusalem, she built a palace in the Lower City (*War* 5: 253) where she lived for some 20 years. The death of king Izates brought her back to Adiabene in 64–5, but she did not outlive him long; 'Monobazus [another son] sent her bones, as well as those of Izates, his brother, to Jerusalem, and

The Tomb of Helena

'The Jews have the grave of a local woman called Helen in the city of Jerusalem, a city which the Roman king destroyed to its foundations. They have contrived to make the door of the tomb, which is stone like all the rest of it, so that it opens only on a certain day of the year; at that moment the machinery opens the door on its own, holds it open for a little while, and then closes it up again. At the time you can get in like that, but if you tried to open it at any other time it would never open—you would have to break it down first.' (Pausanias (C2), *Guide to Greece* 8: 16. 5; trans. P. Levi)

gave order that they should be buried at the pyramids which their mother had erected; they were three in number, and distant more than three furlongs from the city of Jerusalem' (*Antiquities* 20: 95).

Robbers looted the tomb but they did not find the sarcophagus of the queen; it bore her Aramaic name 'Saddan' and is now in the Louvre. Her suite decided not to place the sarcophagus in the main chamber designed for it; the First Revolt was on the point of exploding and the risk would have been too great. They had to knock off the corners of the sarcophagus lid in order to get it into one of the lower chambers, and disguised the entrance so well that it escaped casual notice. The ingenuity displayed in the construction of the tomb gave it a legendary reputation as far away as Greece (see box).

Visit (Fig. 42). Open: 8.30–5 p.m. Bring a flashlight. The vast courtyard originated as a quarry producing beautiful *meleke* stone; the staircase developed from the ramp up which blocks were hauled. Winter rains cascading down the steps are caught in two gutters which direct the water into channels in the side which terminate in cisterns at the landing level. Both outside [1] and inside the vestibule [2] are basins which were used for purifications for the dead. The cuts around the small entrance closed by a rolling stone [3] were to take heavy slabs designed to hide the entrance completely. From the antechamber [4] doors lead into three burial chambers [5,6,8]; note the unusual double shaft-graves (*kokhim*) with ossuaries at the side or far end. Further development was planned, but these chambers [9, 10] were never finished. The chamber containing queen Helena's sarcophagus was entered by a secret stairway below the floor of a *kokh* grave [7].

St Stephen's Church [D]

A squat tower and a high gable roof set back from the high wall fronting Nablus Road marks the site of a church built by the patriarch Juvenal to

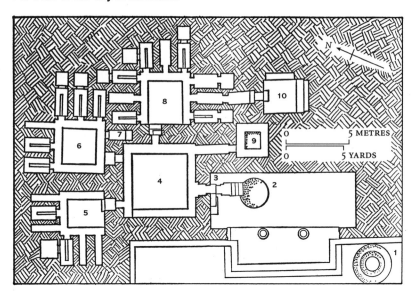

▲ **Fig. 42.** Tomb of Queen Helena of Adiabene (after Vincent). 1–2. Basins; 3. Entrance; 4. Antechamber; 5–6. Burial chambers; 7. Secret stairway; 8. Burial chamber; 9–10. Unfinished burial chambers.

which Cyril of Alexandria brought the relics of St Stephen, the first Christian martyr (Acts 6: 8–7: 60) in 439. The new basilica (dedicated in 1900) is part of the complex of the École Biblique et Archéologique Française founded in 1890 by French Dominicans as the first graduate school for biblical and archaeological studies in the Holy Land.

Excavations revealed the complete plan of the Byzantine church; it was retained when the new church was built, and the rugs on the floor protect large sections of the original mosaic floor. Nothing remains of the vast complex of buildings, which in 516 served as the meeting place for 10,000 monks, save the cistern system and a number of tombs. These are marked by metal covers in the cloister of the atrium; the pavement around the well is Byzantine. One of the tombs was closed by a stone door, the other by a rolling stone. Standing in a niche beside the former is the tombstone which originally sealed the flight of steps, the inscription reads, 'Tomb of the deacon Nonnus Onesimus of the Holy Resurrection of Christ and of this monastery'.

The monastery was destroyed by the Persians in 614, but a small chapel was built before 638 by the patriarch Sophronius. It survived until 1113, when it was damaged by a Fatamid raid from ASHQELON. The Benedictines of the Mauristan restored it, but in the late summer of 1187 the Crusaders tore down the chapel in order to deny Saladin a staging point so close to a city gate. The Hospitallers, however, refused to demolish the nearby stables. This turned out to be providential, because in 1192 they were developed into a hospice for Christian pilgrims, whom the Ayyubids did not permit to live within the walled city.

Garden Tomb [E]

This tomb in a quiet garden is venerated by many as the tomb of Christ: it conforms to the expectations of simple piety and it is outside the walled city. It is much easier to pray here than in the Holy Sepulchre. Unfortunately there is no possibility that it is in fact the place where Christ was buried. Open: 8.30 a.m.–noon; 2–5.30 p.m.; closed Sundays.

The first visitor to popularize this site as Golgotha was General Charles Gordon in 1883: he thought he recognized the shape of a skull in the hill behind the tomb. The excavation of the nearby Church of St Stephen, and in particular the discovery of the tombstone of the deacon Nonnus which mentioned the Holy Sepulchre, quickly convinced Protestants desirous of having a Holy Place of their very own that this was the place where the Byzantines located Calvary and the Tomb. Despite the protestations of those best qualified to judge, the Anglican Church committed itself to the identification, and what had been known scornfully as 'Gordon's Tomb' suddenly became the 'Garden Tomb'. Sanity eventually prevailed, and the Anglican Church withdrew its formal support, but in Jerusalem the prudence of reason has little chance against the certitude of piety.

The tomb consists of two chambers, side by side; from the vestibule one has to turn right into the burial chamber. This configuration is typical of tombs of the C9–C7 BC. In tombs hewn out at the time of Jesus the burial chamber was normally behind the vestibule in a straight line, and one would expect each body bench (*arcosolium*) to be set within an arch. Here on the contrary the body benches simply extended from the wall, as in other Iron Age tombs. From a strictly archaeological point of view, therefore, it certainly was not a new tomb in the C1 AD. Moreover, in the Byzantine period the benches were cut down to create rock sarcophagi. Such radical disfigurement of the structure clearly indicates that Christians of the C4–C6 did not believe that this tomb was the burial place of Christ.

The Crusaders lowered the rock surface in front of the tomb in order to ensure that the vaults, which they built against the rock escarpment, should not project above it. They used the site as a stable.

Armenian Mosaic [F]

Perfectly preserved, this mosaic floor is perhaps the most beautiful in the country; still brilliant colours depict many species of birds in the branches of a vine. The caged bird reflects a Neoplatonic vision of the relation between body and soul; the threat of evil is evoked by the eagle above. The peacocks drinking the elixir of eternal life symbolize survival after death. An Armenian inscription at the far end, just where the apse should begin, reads, 'For the memory and salvation of the souls of all Armenians whose names are known to God alone'. When the mosaic floor was laid down in the mid-C6 AD this was a mortuary chapel; many tombs were found in the immediate vicinity.

The building is clearly indicated by a sign identifying the chapel as St Polyeuctos in a cul-de-sac just beside the Jerusalem Student House in Prophet Street. Regretfully it is rarely open.

Solomon's Quarries [G]

So great is the reputation of Solomon that Jerusalem Arabs tend to attribute anything grandiose to him. They may be correct in this case, because the vast cave beneath the city wall was once part of a quarry which extended across the road into what is now the bus station. The blocks for the first temple may have been hewn here (1 Kgs. 5: 15–17). It is equally possible, however, that the quarry was exploited by Herod the Great (37–4 BC).

The great cavern was rediscovered accidentally in 1854 after having been concealed by the Ottomans in the C16, but it was well known in previous centuries. Josephus was probably referring to this spot when he mentions the Royal Caverns (*War* 5: 147) in his description of the wall built by Herod Agrippa I (AD 41–4). It appears in Jewish works from the C3 AD onwards as Zedekiah's Grotto; it was thought to run all the way to Jericho and this provided a neat explanation of how the king managed to evade the encircling Babylonian army in 586 BC (2 Kgs. 25: 4–5; Jer. 52: 7–8). This legend was accepted by the famous Arab geographer al-Muqadassi in 985.

Visit. Open: Sunday–Thursday and Saturday 9 a.m.–4 p.m.; Friday 9 a.m.–2 p.m.; tickets for Saturday must be bought in advance. The entrance is signposted in the garden across from the bus station on Suleiman Street. The cave runs under the city for about 200 m in a general south-easterly direction. There is little to see save the traces of ancient quarry working. Stones were released by cutting a trench around three sides and then driving in wedges to break blocks free. Pieces of wood were wedged in the triangular niches in the walls to support oil-lamps. Note the different types of limestone, in particular the prized *meleke*, the hard white limestone that Herod used so much; the cave probably originated because of a bank of this stone, which is easy to cut but very resistant to erosion.

Museums

There are two museums worth visiting in the northern sector of the new city:

The Rockefeller Museum [**H**]. Established in 1927, this museum is exclusively archaeological. The exhibits, running from the Stone Age to the C18, are arranged chronologically starting in the South Gallery (left of the entrance). Open: Sunday–Thursday 10 a.m.–5 p.m.; Fridays and Saturdays to 2 p.m.; closed on Jewish holy days.

The Benshoof Museum [**J**]. Located in the grounds of St George's Cathedral, this museum is housed in a vast Byzantine cistern. It displays the intact material from graves of the Late Bronze and Early Iron Age periods found at Tel Dothan. Open: Tuesday–Saturday 10 a.m.–1 p.m.; at other times by appointment (tel.: 628–4372).

New City: Western Section

Most of the historical monuments are concentrated in a band running between the Old City and the campus of the Hebrew University at Givat Ram. Capital letters refer to the location in Fig. 43.

Model of Herodian Jerusalem [A] ★★

In the grounds of the Holyland Hotel there is a 1 : 50 scale model of Jerusalem as it was at the beginning of the First Revolt in AD 66. Covering several hundred square metres, it offers a unique opportunity to visualize

▼ **Fig. 43.** New City. Western Section. A. Model of Herodian Jerusalem; B. Monastery of the Cross; C. Israel Museum; D. Jason's Tomb; E. Zawiya Kubakiyya; F. Herod's family tomb.

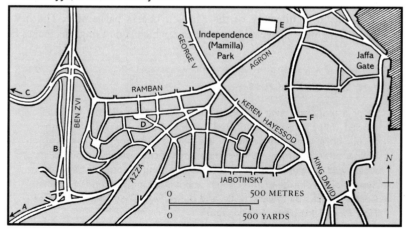

the city of Herod the Great. The hotel lies between Herzog Street and Herzl Avenue; the access road, Uziel Street, is clearly signposted on both. Open: 8 a.m.–10 p.m. (tel.: 643–7777).

The model, based on data supplied by Prof. M. Avi-Yonah, reflects what is known of the C1 AD city both from archaeological excavations and from texts, the New Testament, Josephus, the *Mishnah*, the *Tosephtha*, and the Talmuds. The topographical information provided by the New Testament is incidental, and never detailed. Josephus furnishes many details, but his enthusiasm sometimes led him to exaggerate, and he does not always give a precise location for the buildings he mentions. The information in other Jewish works was recorded after Hadrian had radically changed the appearance of the city in AD 135, and occasionally contradicts what is found in Josephus.

In order to construct the model many arbitrary decisions had to be made, and imagination often supplied what the texts or archaeologist's trowel could not provide. The model, therefore, is a hypothesis, a vision of the city as it might have been, and not all elements carry the same guarantee.

The portrayals of the Temple and of the Palace of Herod are excellent, but the presentation of the northern part of the city is almost certainly wrong. The line assumed by the northernmost wall of the model rests on inadequate archaeological evidence, and all the buildings it encloses are the product of pure imagination. Equally ill-founded are the locations of the theatre and the hippodrome. The latter was probably in the Kidron Valley, and the former was outside the city wall to the south, as at CAESAREA.

Monastery of the Cross [B]

The buttressed walls of the fortified monastery appear alien in a landscape dominated by the graceful silhouette of the Israel Museum and the modernistic architecture of the Knesset, Israel's parliament. The new divided highway, Sederot Hayyim Hazaz, which runs alongside, makes it

The Tree of the Cross

'Over a mountain near to Jerusalem there is a very fertile and well-tended valley, in which is located a noble church. It stands in honour of our Lord Jesus Christ and of his beloved Mother, and there, in a hollow altar, the place is reverenced in which the trunk stood from which was cut the Cross. On it the Saviour hung for our salvation. The Syrians are in charge of this church, and it is strongly defended against Gentile attacks by towers, walls, and bulwarks.' (Theoderic (C12), *The Holy Places* 41; trans. J. Wilkinson) seem even more out of place, a relic of the days when this valley was the vineyard of the Crusader kings of Jerusalem.

The monastery was founded by king Bagrat of Georgia between 1039 and 1056 on the site of a C5 church, and derives its name from the legend that the tree from which the cross of Jesus was made grew here. The Georgians enjoyed excellent relations with the Mamluks because they came from the same part of the world, and though they lost the monastery in 1300 because of the welcome they gave the Tartars (also neighbours) it was restored to them in 1305. Their numbers decreased consistently in succeeding centuries, and eventually they were obliged to sell the monastery to the Greek Orthodox in 1685.

Visit. Open: 10 a.m.–1.30 p.m. (tel.: 679-0961). The access road is a little difficult to find. It begins on Herzog almost at the junction with Hayyim Hazaz.

The fortress-like character of the building underlines its exposed position far outside the city walls. Apart from the narthex the church is the C11 original but various additions were made throughout the centuries to other parts of the complex. The C19 ornate clock tower cannot be considered the most successful. The basic theme of the C17 frescos in the church is the vicissitudes of the tree from which the cross was made. The intermingling of Christian saints, Greek philosophers, and pagan gods is unusual, to say the least. The mosaic floor to the right of the altar is all that remains of the C5 church destroyed by the Persians in 614. Visitors are free to wander through the rest of the complex in order to get some sense of conditions of life in an eastern monastery.

Israel Museum [C]   ★★

Open: 10 a.m.–5 p.m.; Friday to 2 p.m.; Saturday to 4 p.m.; Tuesdays 4–10 p.m. Tickets are valid for multiple visits for one week. No tickets are sold on Saturday or Jewish Holy Days.

Located in Ruppin Street opposite the Knesset building, this museum has exhibits of all facets of Jewish history. In addition to the magnificent displays in the Bronfman Archaeological Museum (guided tour in English at 3 p.m. Monday), there is the Shrine of the Book (whose roof represents the cover of a QUMRAN scroll jar) which houses some of the Dead Sea Scrolls and other manuscripts found in the Judaean desert; open: as the Israel Museum except Tuesday 10 a.m.–10 p.m.; guided tours on Sunday at 1.30 p.m. and on Tuesday at 3 p.m.

Jason's Tomb [D]

A small stone pyramid in a quiet residential road, Alfasi Street, reveals the presence of what is perhaps the most interesting tomb in Jerusalem. Not only is it a beautiful monument, but its history is known in detail.

It was the family tomb of the Sadducean high priestly family of Jason, who was forced out of Jerusalem in 172 BC by Menelaus (2 Macc. 5: 5–10). The rehabilitation of the Sadducees by Alexander Jannaeus (103–76 BC) permitted the restoration of the tomb in order to receive the remains of his grandson, also named Jason, in 81 BC. The drawing in the porch of two warships escorting a transport, and the mention of the coast of Kanopos in an inscription, indicate that this Jason, like certain of his relatives (*Antiquities* 13: 285, 349), served Egypt as a naval commander.

The tomb was pillaged in 37 BC, and destroyed by the earthquake of 31 BC. One final burial took place in the ruined tomb in AD 30, the year in which Jesus was buried elsewhere in the city.

Visit. Open: Monday and Thursday 10 a.m.–1 p.m. The pyramid over the porch (supported by a single central column) has been reconstructed; it is preceded by three courts, the one immediately before the porch being entered by a vaulted gate. The ship drawings and the inscription identifying Jason were all drawn in charcoal on the walls of the porch. Looking in through the protective iron grille, the burial chamber with eight shaft graves (*kokhim*) is through the small opening on the left. When space was needed for later burials the bones were transferred to the charnel chamber, the small opening directly in front.

Zawiya Kubakiyya [E]

In the Muslim cemetery at the eastern end of Independence (Mamilla) Park stands a square one-room building surmounted by a dome. An inscription over the door identifies it as the tomb of the emir Aidughdi Kubaki, buried there in AD 1289. Having started life as a slave in Syria, he rose to be governor of Safed and of Aleppo before falling foul of a new Mamluk sultan, who first imprisoned him and then exiled him to Jerusalem. He was 60 when he died, a very good age for a Mamluk.

Crusader materials are reused; note the elbow columns supporting the porch. The relieving arches above the door and windows are in fact monoliths cut to simulate joggled voussoirs.

The nearby **Mamilla Pool** has a capacity of 30,000 m³. It collected run-off rain-water. Its date is uncertain, but it would have been the easiest source of water for the new quarters on the western hill, when the wall was extended to enclose that area in the C2 BC. It is connected by a channel to the POOL OF THE PATRIARCH'S BATH (p. 61) in the Christian Quarter of the Old City. It may also have received water from the high level aqueduct from SOLOMON'S POOLS.

Herod's Family Tomb [F]

Towards the end of a cul-de-sac, Abba Sikra Street, just south of the King David Hotel, a great round stone signals the entrance to the family tomb of Herod the Great (37–4 BC). A narrow passage leads to four chambers, three square and one rectangular, disposed on each side of a much smaller room; all are beautifully faced with cut stone. Little was found inside because tomb robbers got there before the archaeologists.

The existence of a family tomb in Jerusalem belonging to Herod is attested by Josephus; the king brought his youngest brother there for burial in 5 BC (*War* 1: 581). The tomb may have been cut for the interment of his father Antipater in 43 BC (*War* 1: 228). We know it was located west of the city because Josephus uses the monument as a reference point in his description of the Roman circumvallation wall in AD 70 (*War* 5: 108 and 507), the nearby 'Serpent's Pool' is probably to be identified with the present Birket es-Sultan in the upper part of the Hinnom Valley. Herod himself was buried at the HERODION.

Specialized Museums

Scattered throughout West Jerusalem are a number of museums with specific orientations which fall within the terms of reference of this guide:

The Skirball Museum (13 King David Street) displays finds from the excavations of its host institution, Hebrew Union College, at TEL DAN, GEZER, and Aroer in the Negev. Fortifications, burial customs, and cultic practices are highlighted. Open: 10 a.m.–4 p.m.; Friday and Saturday 10 a.m.–2 p.m.

The Bible Lands Museum (25 Granot Street) is designed to enhance comprehension of the Bible by a chronologically arranged display of artefacts from all the societies in the ancient Near East. Open: 9.30 a.m.– 5 p.m.; Wednesday 1.30 a.m.–9.30 p.m. (winter), 9.30 a.m.–9.30 p.m. (summer); Friday and Saturday 9.30 a.m.–2 p.m. Guided tours in English are available Sunday–Friday at 10 a.m. and on Wednesday at 5.30 p.m.

The L. A. Meyer Memorial Institute for Islamic Art (2 Ha-Palmach Street) traces the development of all aspects of the culture of Islam from the C7 to C19. Open: 10 a.m.–5 p.m.; Tuesday 4–8 p.m.; Friday and Saturday 10 a.m.–2 p.m.

En Kerem

The far western suburbs of Jerusalem now incorporate what was once the village of En Kerem. The site was continuously occupied from about 2000 BC, but all the significant remains are of the Byzantine and medieval periods.

The attractiveness of the site, and the fact that it is equidistant from Jerusalem and Bethlehem probably explain the C6 AD tradition which placed here the home of Zachary and Elizabeth, the encounter between the latter and the Blessed Virgin (Luke 1: 39–56), and the birthplace of John the Baptist. Two churches are mentioned in the C12 when the property apparently belonged to the Augustinian canons who served the Templum Domini (DOME OF THE ROCK). In the post-Crusader period traditions tended to move from one church to the other and back again depending on which was the more accessible at any given time.

Church of St John the Baptist

The earliest church on the site goes back to the C5. The Crusaders took over a C11 church, whose proportions they retained. What modifications they introduced cannot be determined in detail. Used by the Muslims as a byre, the building was recovered by the Franciscans in the second half of the C17.

Visit. A tall thin tower with a small spire marks out the church from the other buildings to the north of the main road in the centre of the village. Open: Sunday 9 a.m.–noon; 2.30–5 p.m.; Monday–Friday 8 a.m.–noon; 2.30–6 p.m.; closed Saturday.

A blocked Byzantine doorway left of the porch indicates a church of approximately the same size as the present one. Built against the southern half of its west wall were two C5 chapels. Normally such secondary chapels are parallel to the long walls, as at KURSI. Their unusual position here is perhaps to be explained as compensation for the rather steep fall of the hill; they distracted the eye from a disproportionate south-west corner.

The apse of the chapel beneath the porch contains two rock-cut tombs, and the Greek inscription in the centre of the diamond-shaped mosaic of the chancel reads, 'Hail martyrs of God!' It is certainly a memorial chapel, but no one knows to whom it was dedicated. Even less is known about the function of the chapel to the south.

Only two features of the present church are worthy of note. The *opus sectile* or Cosmatesque floor decoration beneath the dome is of the C11 or C12. The same design appears in the cave chapel reached by a flight of steps in the north aisle. It may have originated as a silo or cistern (note the circular opening in the ceiling), but the birth of John the Baptist had been firmly fixed there by the early C12.

Church of the Visitation

With its mosaic façade (1955) depicting Mary visiting Elizabeth this church stands out clearly in the direction of the Hadassah Hospital. The approach road is narrow, and it is better to park near the small mosque built over the Spring of the Virgin. The road leads past the cottages and churches of a convent of Russian nuns (1871).

The two-tier church was completely rebuilt in 1946, but care was taken to incorporate all the medieval and Byzantine elements that came to light.

It is identified as the church of the abbey of St John in the Woods, which the Cistercians established in 1169. Subsequently it became an Armenian monastery, but in 1480 Felix Fabri saw only 'broken altars and ruined vaults'.

A pre-Crusader double church is attested by a visitor in 1106, who confirms the localization there of a C2 AD legend in which John the Baptist escaped the massacre of the children of Bethlehem (Matt 2: 16). 'Elizabeth, when she heard that John was sought for, took him and went up into the hill country, and looked around to see where she could hide him, and there was no hiding place. Elizabeth groaned aloud and said, "O mountain of God, receive me, a mother, with my child." For Elizabeth was so afraid she could go no further. Immediately the mountain was rent asunder and received her' (*Protoevangelium of James* 22: 3). In the Middle Ages a development of the tradition made her pass underground to EN EL MAMOUDIYEH near HEBRON.

Visit. Open: Sunday–Friday 8–11.45 a.m.; 2.30–6 p.m.; closed Saturday. The cleft in the rock through which Elizabeth passed is commemorated in the medieval crypt by a barrel-vaulted passage running to an apse which encloses a well-head associated with a late Roman or Byzantine overflow pipe some 70–90 cm below the medieval floor. To the right of the passage is the 'Rock of Concealment'.

A flight of steps within the south wall leads to the upper church, whose western part is built directly over the crypt; the eastern part rests on a rock-cut terrace. Four courses of the medieval apse survive, as do ten courses of the eastern section of the north wall. The original south wall remains to a height of 4 m.

Part 2
The Land

Abu Ghosh (J17)

Abu Ghosh is a village to the north of the Tel Aviv–Jerusalem highway 15 km from the Holy City. In the early C19 AD it was the encampment of a brigand chief powerful enough to defy the Turkish authorities but not sufficiently ambitious to pose a serious threat to their rule. As a result they permitted him to levy tribute on travellers, and his name replaced the traditional name of the village, Qaryet el-Enab, which is simply the Arabic version of Qiryat Yearim.

Qiryat Yearim is mentioned frequently in the Old Testament as a mountain village on the border between the territories of the tribes of Judah and Benjamin. What makes it unique is that it was the resting place of the Ark of the Covenant for the twenty years between its restoration by the Philistines (1 Sam. 6: 21–7: 2) and its removal to Jerusalem by David (2 Sam. 6). The village of this period is located on the height of Deir el-Azhar, today crowned by the great statue of the Virgin and Child. The modern sanctuary of Notre-Dame de l'Arche d'Alliance is built on the ruins of a C5 AD church, sections of whose mosaic floor are still visible.

It is not clear when the village moved down the hill to the valley. It can only have happened during a period when strong control assured peace, and when there was sufficient traffic on the road to make the move worthwhile. Thus it may have happened as early as the C2 AD when a detachment of the Tenth Legion was stationed there and built a reservoir over the spring. This reservoir was incorporated into an Arab caravanserai in the mid-C9 AD when the road formed part of the Byzantine road system renewed by the Umayyad caliphs; two milestones of Abd el-Malik (685–705), the builder of the Dome of the Rock, were found in the vicinity of Abu Ghosh.

The Byzantine tradition which located the Emmaus where the Risen Christ made himself known to two disciples (Luke 24: 13–35) at LATRUN was known to the Crusaders. They rejected it as a mistake, however, because their Latin Bibles gave the distance of Emmaus from Jerusalem as only 60 stadia (11.5 km). The choice of Qaryet el-Enab as Emmaus may have been influenced by the existence of the caravanserai. It was a perfect place for travellers to rest, and it was easy for medieval pilgrims to imagine the meal that Jesus shared with his disciples. The identification was firmly established by 1140 when the church was built by the Hospitallers.

After the defeat of the Latin Kingdom at the Battle of the HORNS OF HATTIN in 1187 Qaryet el-Enab lost all its importance, principally because travellers took another route to Jerusalem. One consequence of this change was the transfer of the dignity of Emmaus to QUBEIBA.

When the Mamluks restored the caravanserai between 1350 and 1400 they left the church intact, contenting themselves with adding a mosque.

Visit. The **Crusader church** is the largest building in the village. From the Jerusalem side it is hidden by trees but the minaret of the nearby mosque is clearly visible. Ring the bell in the top left-hand corner of the door for admission. Open: 8.30–11 a.m., 2.30–5.30 p.m.; feast-days: 8.30–9.30 a.m., 2.30–4.30 p.m.; closed Sunday and Thursday.

The plan is virtually identical with that of another Hospitaller church, st mary of the germans in Jerusalem (p. 76), its exact contemporary. The peeling frescos of the two eastern bays give the building a slightly tragic air, but they are precious relics of the short period when Eastern and Western churches were in harmony (bethlehem). Though the inscriptions are in Latin, the style of the paintings is Byzantine, and can be attributed to the early dynamic phase of the Comnenian style (c.1170). The half dome of the central apse depicts the Risen Lord. Christ appears between Mary and John the Baptist in the north apse, while in the south apse Abraham, Isaac, and Jacob receive the souls of the elect. On the north wall is the Dormition of the Virgin (left), and a mounted soldier saint with two other figures (right above the doorway). The same vague theme is repeated in the first bay of the south wall with the Crucifixion to its right in the second bay.

The crypt is entirely medieval save for the outer walls which are those of the Roman reservoir; beside the entrance in the north wall is an inscription reading 'Vexillatio leg[ionis] X Fre[tensis]'. The two original stairways leading into the reservoir still exist on either side of the medieval staircase at the west end of the church. In order to take the reservoir out of service the medieval engineers lowered the level of the spring and cut a new channel which can be seen through the grating on the steps between the two pillars. The low altar over the spring is out of alignment with the crypt; it is oriented due east and the Crusaders probably intended this to correct the slightly false orientation of the church.

On the far side of the Benedictine monastery (1906) are the remains of the **caravanserai**. An open court was entered from the north. Originally two reservoirs limited it on the east. The southern pool was transformed into a large vaulted chamber in the C12; facing the entrance was a bread oven.

Akko (Acre) (H5) ★★

The Crusades account for only about one twentieth of the long history of the walled port of Akko, but the imprint of their passage is more enduring than that of any other occupant. Beneath a thin veneer of modernity, often no more than a coat of whitewash, it is still a medieval city. The logic of the

Crusaders' planning commanded respect, while the strength of their constructions made other options unviable.

Egyptian execration texts from about 1800 BC are the first to mention Akko. The oldest city is Tel el-Fukhar, just east of the railway line on route 85. Its location on a river at the junction of the Way of the Sea and another trade route reaching into Syria made it one of the area's principal coastal cities. Its strategic importance, both military and commercial, became progressively more evident and in the C4 BC it assumed the primacy that Tyre and Sidon had once enjoyed. The Hellenistic character of the city became more pronounced after the visit of Alexander the Great in 332 BC; in Greek its name was transformed into Akê.

In the struggle for power, which followed the death of Alexander in 323 BC, Akko came under Egyptian control, and Ptolemy II (285–46) changed its name to Ptolemais, which it retained until the Arab conquest in AD 636. In 63 BC Pompey gave the city its independence. For nearly 300 years it counted its years from the visit of Julius Caesar in 47 BC.

As CAESAREA, founded by Herod the Great in 10 BC, developed, the importance of Akko decreased. Christianity quickly won adherents among the foreign population; Paul spent a day there during his third voyage (Acts 21: 7) and its first known bishop was Clarus (190). By the time of the Arab conquest in 636 the artificial harbour of Caesarea had become badly silted up, and Akko regained its position as the premier port of Palestine. Development of the port facilities by Ibn Tulun (870–92) (see box) made it inevitable that Akko should become the main link between the Latin Kingdom and Europe after its conquest by Baldwin I in 1104 with the aid of the Genoese fleet.

The medieval development of the city was determined by the maritime powers of Europe, the city-states of Genoa, Pisa, Venice, and Amalfi; recruits, pilgrims, and supplies travelled in their ships. Each nation governed and maintained its own self-sufficient quarter. The military orders of the Temple and the Hospital also had their own territories and they provided facilities for pilgrims on landing and departure, and guaranteed the security of the route to Jerusalem. Such divisions did not matter as long as the Latin Kingdom remained secure, but they contained the seed of the city's destruction.

Akko surrendered to Saladin without a battle in 1187. The Crusader presence in the Holy Land was reduced to Tyre, but reinforcements arrived in 1191 under Richard the Lion-Heart of England and Philip of France. These enabled the Crusaders to pursue the siege and still hold off Saladin's counter-attacks; for a year he had pinned the army of Tyre against the walls of the city. Victory came quickly and the city became the Latin Kingdom for just 100 years. The space within the original wall (just inside the present wall) soon proved to be insufficient and new walls were built enclosing an area three times as great as the walled city of today.

The Construction of the Harbour

'In those days none knew how the foundations of a building could be laid in the sea. Then someone mentioned to Ibn Tulun the name of my grandfather, Abu Bakr, the architect. So Ibn Tulun wrote to his Lieutenant in Jerusalem commanding that he should dispatch my grandfather to him. And on his arrival they laid the affair before him. "The matter is easy," said my grandfather, "let them bring such sycamore beams as be large and strong." These beams he set to float on the surface of the water, as a prolongation of the town walls seawards, and he bound them one to another, while toward the west he left the opening for a mighty gateway. And upon these beams he raised a structure with stones and cement. After every five courses he strengthened the same by setting in great columns. At length the beams became so weighted that they began to sink down; but this was little by little, and finally they rested on the sand. Then they ceased building for a whole year, that the construction might consolidate itself, after which, returning, they began again to build.' (Mukaddasi (C10), *Description of Syria* 162; trans. G. Le Strange)

These were the days of Akko's glory, but for every Francis of Assisi who came on pilgrimage, or Marco Polo who used it as a staging point for his great journey to the Orient, there were three merchants. As Akko emerged as the centre of east–west trade, the merchant colonies began to interfere more and more in politics. Since the king was the source of the privileges on which profits depended, disputes over the succession became progressively more bitter, eventually erupting into open war between the fortified quarters. Venice and Genoa fought sea battles in sight of the city when it was threatened by the Mongols in 1259, and by the Mamluks of Egypt in 1265.

The arrival of Henry II of Cyprus in 1285 established his claim to the crown. His concern for the common good brought about a concerted effort to improve the defences, but it was already too late. The Mamluks had committed themselves to the conquest of Akko. The attack began in April 1291 with the defenders outnumbered ten to one. They held out for two months, time for some of the population of between 30,000 and 40,000 to escape to Cyprus, but the end was inevitable.

Akko lay in ruins for the next 450 years until a local Arab sheikh, Daher el-Omar, exploited the weakness of the central Ottoman administration to create a virtually independent fiefdom in Galilee. He encouraged trade and developed Akko as the port for Syrian exports from 1749 until his assassination in 1775. His place was taken by the Albanian soldier of fortune Ahmed Pasha, known as el-Jazzar, 'the Butcher', because of his cruelty. He continued the restoration of the town and its fortifications.

With the aid of a British fleet he successfully defended the city against Napoleon in 1799; the siege lasted sixty days. Napoleon was moving north after his conquest of Egypt in order to open a route to India; his failure here forced him to retreat to Egypt and changed the course of history.

In 1832 Ibrahim Pasha with an Egyptian army took Akko from the Turks, he ruled Palestine and Syria from the city until 1840 when British intervention forced him to retire to Egypt. The walls, damaged by the bombardment, were repaired and Akko resumed its place as the principal port for exporting grain from the southern Golan.

Visit (Fig. 44). Three roads permit cars to enter the walled city: Rehov Ha-Hagana [**A**] with parking near the lighthouse at the southern tip; Rehov Weizmann [**B**] and Rehov Jonathan Ha-Hashmonai [**C**] with parking near the tall minaret of the Mosque of el-Jazzar [**6**].

The present **broad wall** [**1**] with its ditch and counterscarp was built by Ahmed Pasha el-Jazzar after Napoleon's retreat in 1799. He also refaced the whole of the sea-wall, in part with stones from the Crusader castle at Atlit. Only two of the gates are original, the Land Gate [**7**] and the Sea Gate [**12**] which is now part of the Abu Christo café [**13**].

Parts of the C12 **Crusader wall** [**2**] can be seen on both sides of Rehov Weizmann; these were probably incorporated into the C18 wall of Daher el-Omar. The C13 Crusader wall is now covered by the new city; on the east it reached the sea in the vicinity of the high-rise Palm Beach Hotel. One medieval mole extended from the Sea Gate [**12**] to the Tower of Flies [**14**] on which there used to be a lighthouse; the other reached out from a point about halfway between the Land Gate [**7**] and the Palm Beach Hotel; in 1172 a pilgrim counted over eighty ships in the port.

The **great mosque** [**6**] was erected by el-Jazzar in 1781. The columns creating the porch around the courtyard were looted from CAESAREA; the rooms were intended for students and pilgrims. Below are large vaults, the basement of the Crusader church of St John.

This area was in fact the **quarter of the Knights of the Hospital** whose ruined building was resurrected by Muslim rulers of the C18–C19 as their citadel [**3**]; it is inaccessible except for what is now a large underground area, the street level in this part of the city being 7–8 m above the Crusader level. The entrance [**5**] is just across from the mosque [**6**]; open: 8.30 a.m.–6.30 p.m.; Friday to 2.30 p.m.; Saturday 9 a.m.–6 p.m. Toilets.

The hall containing the ticket office is Turkish (the ticket is valid also for the Turkish bath). The C18 Burj el-Khazne dominates the open courtyard; it marks the site of the north-east tower of the Hospitaller fortress. A large Turkish gate gives access to the **Knight's Halls**. Only three are open to the public, but seven exist, corresponding to the nationalities represented in the Hospitallers (Auvergne, England, France, Germany, Italy, Provence, and Spain). Abutting what was then the city wall, they perhaps served as barracks. The present vaulting is Turkish.

▲ **Fig. 44.** Street plan of the walled city of Akko (Acre). 1. C19 wall; 2. Crusader wall; 3. Hospitaller fortress; 4. Turkish bath; 5. Entrance to Hospitaller fortress; 6. Mosque of el-Jazzar; 7. Land Gate; 8. Khan esh-Shawarda; 9. Khan el-Franji; 10. Gate of Genoese quarter; 11. Khan el-Umdan; 12. Sea Gate; 13. Abu Christo café; 14. Tower of Flies; 15. St John's church; 16. Site of Templar fortress; 17. Khan esh-Shuna; 18. Junction of Templar, Genoese, and Pisan quarters; 19. Medieval square; 20. Medieval square; 21. St George's church; 22. Rectangular quarter; 23. Museum of Heroism.

The many-piered, partially excavated room, which faced the barracks across a narrow street, has been variously identified as the dormitory of the soldier-monks and as the administrative centre of the complex. The

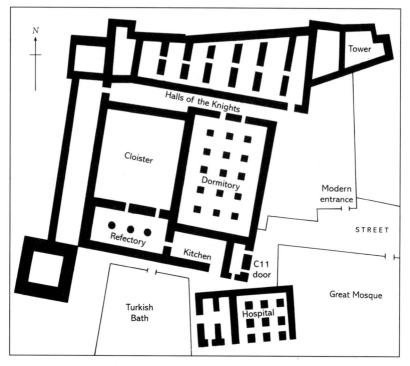

N

Tower

Halls of the Knights

Cloister

Dormitory

Modern entrance

STREET

Refectory

Kitchen

C11 door

Great Mosque

Turkish Bath

Hospital

▲ **Fig. 45.** The fortress of the Knights Hospitallers (after Goldmann).

steep descent penetrates into the south-east corner of the open monastic cloister before entering the refectory of the knights.

The **refectory** was planned in Romanesque style, but the heraldic fleur-de-lis in the north and south-east corners suggest that the present Gothic fan ceiling was due to the influence of Louis VII of France, who was in Akko in 1148. The change in plan is evident in the composite character of the rib consoles in the south wall.

A pit (dug by the archaeologists) in the centre of the hall gives access to an **underground passage** which the Crusaders discovered in building the refectory, and which they maintained and improved because of its secrecy value. Their entrance was from a shaft in the street outside in front of the Turkish bath. From it they constructed a high flat-roofed tunnel to join two portions of the low tunnel with a pitched roof dating from the C6–C2 BC, and which may originally have been a sewer. Neither end has yet been excavated.

The archaeologists have provided a convenient exit from the tunnel via a flight of wooden steps leading to the western entrance of what was probably the **hospital** of the knights. The architecture suggests that a C11 Fatimid building (possibly a caravanserai) was restored by the

Hospitallers. The northern entrance to the second storey is a magnificent C11 doorway, which can be reached only by going round the building outside.

The **Turkish bath** [4] was built by el-Jazzar and is an excellent example of its type. According to written records there was a bath in this area in the Crusader period. The dome a little to the west crowns the guest-house of the Sheadliyeh, a C19 North African Islamic sect. It is sited on the ruins of the south-west tower of the Hospitaller complex.

Khan esh-Shawarda [8] dates only from the time of Daher el-Omar or el-Jazzar. Like the other *khans* (inns) it served the great camel caravans which brought the grain of the southern Golan to the ships. The tower in its south-east corner is the only C13 tower still standing; note the mason's marks (crosses, triangles, letters) on the bossed stones.

Khan el-Faranj [9] owes its name, 'Inn of the Franks', to the French merchants who established themselves there in 1516. In the C13 it was the centre of the Venetian quarter and Crusader materials are recognizable in the foundations and columns of the present building. At the north-east corner is the C18 church of the Franciscans.

A square clock-tower erected by the Ottoman sultan Abdul Hamid II in 1906 stands over the entrance to the picturesque **Khan el-Umdan** [11], 'Inn of the Columns', restored by el-Jazzar. This was the inn of the Genoese quarter which fronted on to a large empty square (reaching as far as Khan el-Faranj [9]) used for loading and unloading from the port. The Genoese quarter was the oldest and biggest merchant commune and enjoyed special privileges because the Genoese fleet played a crucial role in Baldwin I's capture of Akko in 1104. It ran due north through the centre of the city from the gate [10] which once opened directly on to the main port square. The street level in this sector is the same as that of the Crusader period and the alley running towards the church of St George [21] has Crusader buildings on both sides.

There are two exits from the Khan el-Umdan [11]. The one in the south-west corner leads into the heart of the **Pisan quarter**: all the buildings on both sides are Crusader. The café Abu Christo [13] is on the site of the Pisan port; the Sea Gate [12] and its wall are medieval.

The street parallel to the tip of the peninsula leads into the **Templar Quarter**. The Franciscan church of St John [15] built in 1737 rests on vaults corresponding to the position of the Crusader church of St Andrew. According to medieval maps the fortress of the knights, famed for its beauty and strength, must have stood where the sea has eroded into the town [16]. It was undermined by the Mamluks in 1291 and its stones later used for other buildings; not a trace remains.

Directly opposite the south-west exit from Khan el-Umdan [11] is **Khan esh-Shuna**, once the Inn of the Pisans [17]. Follow the street which borders it on the north to the four-way cross [18] which was the junction of several quarters, Pisan on the south, Templar on the west,

Genoese on the north; a strong Templar tower controlled this critical point. The street to the right (north) has interesting Crusader residences on the left; it leads to a square [**19**] which follows Crusader building lines. Such open spaces were a feature of the C12–C13 city but buildings have encroached on many of the others.

The square [**20**] also preserves its medieval dimensions, and was the junction of several quarters. The street leading to the C17 Greek Orthodox church of St George [**21**] was the fortified gate of the Genoese quarter.

The little street behind the Bahai Temple cuts through the middle of the **Rectangular quarter** whose two long strips [**22**] make it the best-defined of all the medieval units. The street to the right (east) was a neutral street dividing this quarter from the Genoese. The inner street is Crusader on both sides, but the houses on the left (west) are worth close examination for they have been well preserved on the ground floor. The street has a sharp turn at both ends; otherwise attackers would have had a clear field of fire. Some houses were deliberately set forward to provide enfilading fire; this occurs regularly at intervals of about 50 m. The same mode of defence was used in the small central square where the well of the quarter and a public building were probably located. The white house on the south-west corner of the Rectangular quarter facing the sea was the home for six years of Baha'u'llah, the founder of the Bahais (see MOUNT CARMEL: HAIFA).

Amud Caves (Mearat Amira) (M5)

The plain of Ginnosar is divided into three by two wadis, Nahal Zalmon and Nahal Amud, which terminate in the SEA OF GALILEE. Nahal Amud contains three easily accessible prehistoric caves (Fig. 107). At the north end of the plain of Ginnosar take the turn-off signposted 'Huqoq'; from there on route 8077 it is 2.6 km to the bridge, where there is a parking-lot. The **Amud Cave** is located 1 km north of the bridge on the left (west) side of the wadi, near the spring, and beside the natural limestone pillar (in Arabic 'amud') which gives the wadi its name. Care must be exercised in winter and spring when rain to the west may suddenly flood the wadi. To reach the other two caves pass under the bridge going towards the lake. Both are located on the left (north) bank, the **Zuttiyeh Cave** is about 400 m from the bridge, and the **Emireh Cave**, a further kilometre.

The oldest traces of human occupation appeared in the Zuttiyeh Cave, notably the skull fragment of an archaic *Homo sapiens* (the earliest stage in the development of modern human beings), who lived a quarter of a million years ago. Both the other caves were occupied during the Middle

Palaeolithic period (120,000–45,000 BC). The Amud Cave produced the almost complete skeleton of an adult Neanderthal male from the very end of that period. He had been buried lying on his left side with his knees drawn up; he was 1.8 m tall and about 25 years old. Nearby were fragments of the bones of another adult male and of five children, whose ages range from 6 months to 8 years.

Aphek (Antipatris) (G14)

The jagged outline of a C16 Turkish fort at the top of a green slope marks the site of a town as old as trade between Egypt and Mesopotamia. It lies at the source of the River Yarkon (whence the name of the nearby township Rosh ha-Ain = the head of the spring); the foothills of the Judaean mountains begin 3 km to the east. The great trade route, the Way of the Sea, had to pass through this gap which shade and water made an attractive resting-place. Today a beautiful park offers the same sense of ease that weary traders of the past experienced.

A walled city stood here *c.*3000 BC; its name is mentioned in Egyptian texts of the C19 and C15 BC. Joshua took the city from the Canaanites (Josh. 12: 18) whose ruler had a monumental palace on the summit of the mound. In the C12 BC with the advent of the PHILISTINES, or even earlier, the Israelites were forced to move back to the hills and the city marked the northern border of Philistia. Here the Philistines assembled for two great battles against Israel a century later. In the first, when the Israelites gathered at Eben-ezer (= Izbet Sartah?), the Philistines captured the Ark of the Covenant (1 Sam. 4: 1–11) and drove through to SHILOH. In the second they slaughtered Saul and Jonathan at Mount Gilboa and hung their bodies on the walls of BET SHEAN (1 Sam. 29–31). Thereafter the Aphek is not mentioned in the Bible, but Assyrian and Babylonian texts show it to have been an important stronghold in the C7.

In the Hellenistic period (332–37 BC) the city was known as Pegae (= the springs); Herod the Great (37–4 BC) changed the name again to commemorate his father, 'choosing a site in the loveliest plain in his kingdom with an abundance of rivers and trees, and naming it Antipatris' (*War* 1: 417). After the foundation of CAESAREA the city lay on the route between the principal port and Jerusalem; from being a staging point on the north–south route it had become a major crossroads. Paul spent the night there on his way under guard from Jerusalem to Caesarea (Acts 23: 23–35). The early southern battles of the First Revolt (AD 66–70) were fought in this area (*War* 2: 513–55). Antipatris paid the price, and did not recover until the late C2 AD. Faltering development came to an end when the earthquake of 363 AD levelled the city.

To the Crusaders of the C12 the tel was known as 'Le Toron aux fontaines sourdes' (= the tower of the silent springs); they had a fortress, Mirabel (Migdal Aphek), on the first slopes of the hills to the east. An edict of the Ottoman sultan in 1571 ordered the reconstruction of the ruined Mamluk fort; it was allowed to fall into decay some two centuries later.

Visit. The **Turkish fort** is clearly visible to the left (north) of the road from Petah Tiqwa to Rosh ha-Ain. The turn-off is signposted 'Aphek'. Each of the parking lots has an entrance to the park.

Just inside the angled gate of the fort a significant portion of a **Canaanite monumental building** (1550–1200 BC) has been exposed. The one immediately recognizable element is a flight of six steps leading from a paved court into a tower with a U-shaped chamber; east of the court, and perpendicular to it, is a 4 m-wide passage, probably a street. This complex was burnt after a vicious battle; arrowheads were found driven into the walls. The destruction date (c.1200 BC) would fit with the campaign of Joshua, but internecine warfare was endemic among the Canaanite city-states.

The south-eastern tower of the fort lies above an **Herodian street** which continues to the south. Many of the flagstones, laid in a herringbone pattern, are still in place and the camber is obvious. There were raised pavements on both sides. The excavated areas to the south are so badly overgrown as to make a visit impossible.

From a number of points on the site the Crusader castle of **Mirabel** (Migdal Aphek) can be seen at the edge of the hills to the south-east. It appears as a stark, brooding block of buildings. To its left at a slightly higher level is the domed tomb (*weli*) of a Muslim saint flanked by a tree. To reach the castle, about which virtually nothing is known in detail, take the obvious dirt road from the point where route 444 turns south at a sharp angle. Today the fortress has been absorbed into the sprawling mass of Sheikh Sadiq, but Crusader elements are easy discernible, particularly in the north-west tower. The walls of the keep are 2 m thick; the Greek inscription over the entrance is in secondary use.

The view to the west from the *weli* offers one of the best opportunities of understanding **the rivalry between the Philistines and the Israelites**. From barren spurs such as this, at the very edge of the Judaean foothills, Israelites of the period of the Judges (1200–1050 BC) gazed enviously at the well-watered plain below controlled by the Philistines. The Israelites could make sporadic raids into the plain, as Joshua did at Aphek (Josh. 12: 18), but they could not hold it against the chariotry of the Canaanites and Philistines. Only in the hill country had the Israelites some degree of security; the rough terrain rendered the chariots impotent.

One of the little forward Israelite settlements may still be seen to the north of Rosh ha-Ain at **Izbet Sarta**, which is on the little wooded hill to the right of the Trans-Samaria Highway (route 5/505) at 2.7 km east of the Qesem Junction. The site is plausibly identified with Ebenezer. From here the word went out (*c*.1050 BC) that the Philistines were massing at Aphek, and it was here that the Israelites assembled to meet them. Things went badly on the first day, and the Ark of the Covenant was brought from Shiloh. Disaster struck the next day; the Philistines captured the Ark and routed the Israelite army (1 Sam. 4: 1–11). The only intelligible remains are those of a large four-roomed house (now restored) of the C12 BC. It was built in the open centre of the settlement previously occupied only by round silos, in one of which the oldest known copy of the Proto-Canaanite alphabet was found scratched on a potsherd.

Artefacts from the excavation of Aphek are displayed in the archaeological pavilion of the **Yad Lebanim Museum** (30 Arlozorov Street, Petah Tikva). Open: Monday–Friday 4.30–7.30 p.m.; Saturday 10 a.m.– 1 p.m.; closed Sunday.

Arbel (M6)

The southern end of the fertile plain of Ginnosar is dominated by the sheer cliffs below the C2 BC village of Arbel (Fig. 107). The caves with which they are honeycombed recall dramatic moments in Jewish history.

In 161 BC the Syrian general Baccides slaughtered partisans of the Maccabees who had sought refuge in the caves (1 Macc. 9: 2). The best-documented and most dramatic episode occurred in 38 BC when Herod the Great moved against the supporters of his rival Antigonus who had holed up in the caves now linked by hewn stairways (see box). It has been suggested that the wall at the top of the cliff on the other side of the valley is what remains of the camp from which Herod supervised the siege.

Despite such a gory warning Josephus fortified the caves as a storage base when he prepared Galilee to receive the assault of the Romans in AD 66. On one of the occasions when his authority was challenged, he held a meeting in the village at the top of the cliffs (*Life* 311). Continuity of Jewish occupation up to the C8 at least is attested by a synagogue. Great rabbis earned their living processing flax. The Teutonic knights had a small fort near the C13 village. The caves were again fortified by Fakhr-a-Din II (1591–1635), of the DRUZE Maan dynasty, whence the local Arab name Qalaat Ibn Maan 'the fortress of the son of Maan'.

Visit. Access to the site is through Moshav Arbel. The first or second road on the left in the settlement leads to the ancient village. To reach the caves

Fishing for Men

'The king, whose men were unable either to climb up from below or creep upon them from above because of the steepness of the hill, had cribs built and lowered these upon them with iron chains as they were suspended by a machine from the summit of the hill. The cribs were filled with armed men holding great grappling hooks, with which they were supposed to draw toward them any of the brigands who opposed them, and kill them by hurling them to the ground. . . . One of the soldiers in irritation at the delay caused by the brigands who dared not come out, girded on his sword, and holding on with both hands to the chain from which the crib was suspended, lowered himself to the entrance of a cave. And when he was opposite an entrance, he first drove back with javelins most of those who were standing there, and then with his grappling hook drew his opponents toward him and pushed them over the precipice.' (Josephus, *Antiquities* 14: 423–6)

drive to the highest point of the cliff from which there is a magnificent view over the plain of Ginnosar and the northern end of the Sea of Galilee. Walk back along the cliff edge towards the village following the red trail-markers. The descent to the caves is signposted.

Village and Synagogue

The village built of grim basalt is typical of other agricultural settlements in the region. It was known for its linen products. The all-important water supply was a deep spring well south-east of the ruins. Projecting stones created a staircase which permitted descent to the water level. There are two large reservoirs, and an oil press. Architectural elements suggest that the village had two public buildings, both probably synagogues, because the 10 hectares of ruins suggest a population of around 2,500.

One is certainly a synagogue. It was constructed in the C4 AD, and the U-shaped arrangement of columns suggests that it was orientated towards Jerusalem by its southern façade. It had stepped benches along the walls. Unusually, the main entrance was in the east wall. The threshold, jambs, and lintel are cut from a single block! Outside was a large paved courtyard. How and when it was destroyed is not clear, but it had to be rebuilt completely in the C6. The main entrance was moved to the north wall, and an apse for the scrolls of the Law was constructed in the south wall above the platform (*bema*) which had a marble screen. This edifice survived until the C8 when it was again destroyed, most probably by the earthquake of 747. A flight of steps cut into the cliff connected the village with Nahal Arbel (Wadi Hammam).

The Caves

A survey found that 100 caves, divided into eight groups, showed signs of human occupation from the C2 BC; there were cisterns and ritual baths. These were transformed when integrated into the fortress of Fakhr-a-Din. The building followed the line of the cliff face and had double walls built to the full height of the 30 m façade. The stepped entrance is flanked by two round towers. From the large natural cave inside stairs lead to the upper levels of natural and artificial caves. The water supply of the fortress was assured by a channel cut in the face of the cliff which brought water from the spring which flowed through a pipe into a cistern.

East of Qalaat Ibn Maan near the beginning of the main trail leading down to the bottom of the valley is another fortress hewn in the rock as a gigantic hall some 75 m long, 14 m wide, and 10 m high. The outer side was walled to the ceiling.

Ashqelon* (C19)

From the promontory of MOUNT CARMEL the coast descends to the southwest in a smooth line unbroken by any natural harbour. Sand dunes line the pitiless lee shore. Only the presence of drinking water can explain the choice of any particular spot as the site of a city. Ashqelon has no spring, but it is sited above an underground river, which from antiquity was exploited by wells. Inevitably, therefore, it became an important staging point on the great trade route linking Egypt and Mesopotamia, the Way of the Sea, which continued north through APHEK, MEGIDDO, and HAZOR. Today it is a beautiful National Park combining the pleasures of archaeology and the beach.

By 2000 BC Ashqelon was a city of some 61 hectares housing a population of 15,000. In subsequent centuries its name appears regularly in Egyptian texts. It is found on the Stele of Merneptah (1230 BC), the only Egyptian text to mention Israel during the Exodus (see box). Not long afterwards it was taken by the PHILISTINES, becoming one of the five city-states into which their territory was divided (Josh. 13: 3; 1 Sam. 6: 4). The city lost its independence in the C8 BC, being first controlled by the Assyrians, and then in turn by Egypt and Babylon. The city was systematically destroyed by Nebuchadnezzar in November 604. It rose from the ashes some eighty years later. Under the Persians it belonged to Tyre, but in the C2 BC, when the Jews, having consolidated their position in the mountains, began to eye the fair cities of the plain, Ashqelon put itself under the protection of Rome. Thereafter it flourished as a free city.

The grape was domesticated about 3000 BC, and, from the beginning

The Victory Hymn of Merneptah (C13 BC)

'The princes are prostrate, saying "Mercy!"
   Not one raises his head among the Nine Bows.
Desolation is for Tehenu; Hatti is pacified;
   Plundered is Canaan with every evil;
Carried off is Ashqelon; seized upon is Gezer;
   Yanoam is made as that which does not exist;
Israel is laid waste, his seed is not;
   Hurru is become a widow for Egypt!
All lands together, they are pacified;
   Everyone who was restless, he has been bound
By the king of Upper and Lower Egypt.'

(trans. J. A. Wilson)

of recorded history, wine was always an important source of Ashqelon's prosperity. Large-scale production is attested in the Iron Age, and continued to increase until the advent of Islam. In the C4 to C7 AD Ashqelon wine was exported as far as Germany. Valued for its taste, it was also an essential ingredient in medical prescriptions for the eyes and stomach. In the C1 AD Ashqelon exported a local onion that became a favourite around the Mediterranean; it took its name (*Caepa ascalonia*) from the city, and the last four syllables resonate in the modern 'scallion'.

According to Josephus, Herod the Great (37–4 BC) endowed Ashqelon with 'baths, magnificent fountains, and colonnaded quadrangles, remarkable for both scale and craftsmanship' (*War* 1: 422). After Herod's death his palace there was given to his sister Salome by imperial decree (*War* 2: 98). Herod's munificence may have been motivated by the fact that his grandfather had been hierodoulos of the temple of Apollo in Ashqelon. The loyalty of the city to Rome during the First Revolt (AD 66–70) won for it new privileges which it used to the utmost during the six centuries of peace which followed. It became ever more prosperous and powerful, a centre of learning and religion. An Egyptian visitor reported spending 600 drachma in visiting the temple, the golden basilica, the theatre and the odeum. A fragment of the C6 Madaba Map shows a great colonnaded street inside the massive east gate.

In AD 636 Ashqelon surrendered to the caliph Omar, and suffered badly in a last paroxysm of Byzantine martial energy. Rebuilt by Abd el-Malik in 685, it grew again to a beautiful city lauded by the Arab chroniclers (see box). The etymology of its name was given as *Arus ash-Sham* 'the Bride of Syria' (Yakut).

Secure on its high walls, with the gates selfishly shut, the inhabitants saw the Frankish charge which destroyed the Muslim army of Egypt in August 1099. Ashqelon remained a Fatimid base until after a seven-month

Tenth Century Ashqelon

'Askalân on the sea is a fine city, and strongly garrisoned. Fruit is here in plenty, especially that of the sycomore tree, of which all are free to eat. The great mosque stands in the market of the clothes-merchants, and is paved throughout with marble. The city is spacious, opulent, healthy, and well fortified. The silkworms of this place are renowned, its wares are excellent, and life there is pleasant. Also its markets are thronged, and its garrison alert. Only its harbour is unsafe, its waters brackish, and the sand-fly, called Dalam, is most hurtful.' (Mukaddasi (C10), *Description of Syria*, 174; trans. G. Le Strange)

siege the Crusaders finally took it on 19 August 1153. They did not hold it long. Immediately after the Battle of Hattin in 1187 Saladin laid siege to Ashqelon; a Christian fleet could put new forces ashore there. His prisoner, the king of Jerusalem, persuaded the garrison to surrender.

In September 1191, when Richard the Lion-Heart looked like reconquering the Holy Land, Saladin ordered the fortifications of Ashqelon to be torn down. This was the beginning of a pattern to be repeated several times in the next 200 years. Richard could see the flames from his camp at Jaffa, but his desire to march at once was overruled by the war council. The Crusader army finally reached Ashqelon several months later, and in the first four months of 1192 rebuilt the walls. The defortification agreed with Saladin the following September was repaired by Richard of Cornwall in early 1241. It survived a bare seven years. The destruction initiated by the Mamluk sultan Baybars in 1247 was made total in 1270. This time the damage was mortal. Ashqelon never rose again.

Visit (Fig. 46). Open: 8 a.m.–4 p.m. (winter) to 5 p.m. (summer). The plan shows the main roads in the park; the arrows indicate one-way traffic. To reach the archaeological park from the coastal highway (route 4), turn west at Ashqelon Junction and drive straight through the new city for some 5 km to the first T-junction and there turn left. The park offers shady picnic areas, toilets, and snacks.

The northern part of the majestic **city wall** (broken line), which protected Ashqelon since the beginning of its history, is just inside the park entrance [**6**], which coincides with the Crusader Jaffa Gate [**1**]. The massive earthworks run in an arc for 2.4 km, which enclosed an area of 61 hectares with an estimated population of 15,000.

The first dirt road to the right permits a view of part of a **stone glacis** supporting a ruined wall [**3**]. Constructed by the Fatimids of Egypt in the C10 AD, it was built on and over the **great rampart** dating from the Middle Bronze Age (2000–1500 BC). It was rebuilt four times in that period alone. What appear to be mud-brick steps originally held a smooth

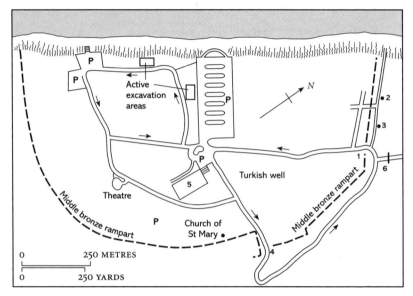

▲ **Fig. 46.** The ancient city of Ashqelon. 1. Jaffa Gate; 2. Middle Bronze Gate; 3. Fatimid Wall; 4. Jerusalem Gate; 5. Basilica; 6. Park entrance.

covering of plaster. This made the 40 degree slope impossible to climb. The great thickness of the base of the triangular rampart, however, was designed to deter attackers from attempting to tunnel beneath it.

At the time of writing **the gate** which pierced the wall at the top of the slope is under protective covering [**2**]. Made of sun-dried bricks, it is an arch 3.5 m high covering a passageway 2.4 m wide. Erected between 1900–1750 BC, this fragile treasure is paralleled only by the gate of the same period at TEL DAN. A dirt road passing over the rampart enables the visitor to appreciate the fortifications from within the city.

From the parking-lot by the café the lines of standing columns mark the site of a **basilica** [**5**], which is dated to the first decade of the C3 AD. Part of the 8.3 m-high granite columns, which were imported from Egypt, remains buried, but the original floor level has been preserved in a small section at the far (southern) end where the semicircular tiered **City Council Chamber** was located. Elements from different parts of the excavation are there collected. The reliefs representing Egyptian Isis with the infant Horus and two Winged Victories, one standing on a globe borne by Atlas, may have decorated the façade of the Council Chamber; all are dated *c.* AD 200. The edifice was destroyed by fire or earthquake in the C4. The Council Chamber area was rebuilt in the C5 as a theatre, the floor of the chamber becoming the orchestra. In the C7 the Muslims demolished the theatre in order to make it part of a mosque extending the length of the quadrangle.

Leaving the car in the parking-lot near the café, walk towards what the Crusaders called the Greater Gate or the **Jerusalem Gate**; it is the exit from the park [**4**]. On the left is a **restored Turkish well**. The horizontal wheel, turned by an animal, activated the vertical wheel which caused an unending series of small wooden buckets to descend and ascend into the well. On reaching the rampart go to the right (south) in the unpaved parking-lot for some 50 m. A fence protects a little church. Four columns still stand, and the single apse flanked by two niches is notched into the rampart. It is identified as the **church of St Mary the Green**, which served Greek-speaking Christians from 400 to 1191, apart from a short interruption in the C10 when it was transformed into a mosque. The curious adjective (*viridis*) translates a Greek term (*chlôros*) that can express every colour between green and yellow. It may refer to the hue of the building material or to the Virgin as the patroness of crops.

At this point it is recommended to climb the rampart and walk along the summit to the south. All the visible stonework is of the C10 AD. Just above the church is a **semicircular tower** reinforced by granite columns at regular intervals.

The circular depression (now fenced) excited the wonder of both Christians and Muslims. In the pre-Crusader period they identified it as the '**Well of Abraham**'. It is in fact the impression of a Roman theatre, whose carved seats were recycled for service elsewhere. About half have been restored, and the site functions as an open-air auditorium.

The road to the southern parking-lot passes two active excavation areas. What is visible changes from season to season, and thus makes description here impossible. The excavation nearest the sea was the site of an extraordinary **dog cemetery**. For some fifty years in the C5 BC at least 700 dogs of all ages, who died of natural causes, were buried here. In all probability they were sacred animals that participated in the rituals of a Phoenician healing temple. The presence of dogs in this socio-religious context must have been inspired by the observation that canine sores healed after being licked by their possessor. In consequence, dogs' tongues were considered to have medicinal properties!

The rampart can be traced all the way round the site to the southern Sea Gate; on this section the sand which has invaded the city underlines the presence of the desert to the south. The two great bastions in the south-west corner, the Tower of the Virgins and the Tower of Blood, have collapsed on to the beach. Parts of the **sea wall** are visible at the base of the cliffs, the granite columns used for bonding protrude dramatically from the eroded wall just north of the bastions. Some have thought that the columns in the water were part of a Crusader mole, as at CAESAREA, but it is more likely that they have simply fallen from the wall. The different strata in the cliff face proclaim the long and complicated history of the city.

Nothing remains of **the harbour**. Both Saladin and Baybars filled it in order to make it unusable. As early as the C11 the Muslims realized that they could not rival the naval might of Europe, and so directed their efforts to ensuring that the Crusaders could find no safe haven on the coast of Palestine.

Avdat (Horvot Avedat)* (E28)   ★

The kibbutzim in the Negev command admiration for the courage and skill that have made the desert bloom, but their achievement pales beside that of the NABATAEANS who created great cities in the same harsh environment. Avdat is the most impressive of these desert cities. The silhouette of the large buildings on the acropolis dominates the plain around the canyon of EN AVDAT with its prehistoric remains. The site is 65 km south of Beer Sheva on the Mizpe Ramon road to Elath (route 40).

Coins and pottery betray the existence of a town here in the C2 BC, and attest contacts with Egypt, Greece, and Asia Minor. At this time Avdat was already one of the key points on the trade route linking Petra with the Mediterranean coast. The town died when the Nabataeans lost control of the port of Gaza about 100 BC. It came to life again in the C1 AD when the death of Herod the Great in 4 BC gave them easy access to the Mediterranean. The revival of Avdat received a further stimulus when the deified king Obodas II (30–9 BC) was buried there, and the town became known as Oboda (which in Arabic became Abdah, and in Hebrew Avdat). His son, Aretas IV (9 BC–AD 40), created a flat area on the acropolis by building great retaining walls, and erected a temple in the north-west corner.

The shift of the trade route from Arabia to the Nile Valley meant that life became progressively more difficult for Avdat. To support itself the city turned increasingly to agriculture; the evidence for its continued existence in the reign of Rabel II (AD 70–106) comes principally from agricultural installations in the valleys to the south and west (see box).

The decline of Avdat was intensified in the C2 AD when nomads from the south began to move into the cultivated areas where Nabataean installations provided water. These bedouin were responsible for the rock-drawings in the vicinity. When the growing insolence of the nomads made travel dangerous, the Romans, who had annexed the Negev in AD 106, were forced to intervene, and ex-soldiers were settled at Avdat. In return for land grants they patrolled the roads, and provided a reserve force for emergencies.

Fortifications were also erected on the acropolis. The names in inscriptions of the C3 show the population to have been the usual eastern Mediterranean mixture of races. There were temples to Zeus, Obodas, and

Desert Agriculture

Aerial surveys show that the whole area (202,340 hectares) between MAMSHIT and SHIVTA, including barren slopes, was put to the service of agriculture. The oldest system is also the simplest: low terrace walls were built across the bed of shallow wadis to hold direct rainfall and to ensure some ponding in case of floods. The Byzantine and especially the Umayyads significantly increased the efficiency of this method by systematic control of the catchment area.

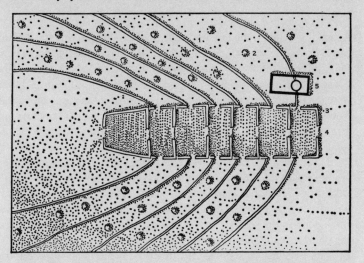

▲ Fig. 47. Schematic drawing to illustrate desert farming techniques. 1. Channel; 2. Pile of stones; 3. Wall; 4. Water overflow; 5. Farmhouse.

The key to desert agriculture is run-off, i.e. surplus rain which is not absorbed into the soil. The Negev gets mostly light rain (3–10 mm at a time: rarely more than 20 mm in any one day) but the loess soil quickly forms an impermeable crust when dampened and run-off always develops. The inhabitants divided the catchment area into sections by building low walls [1] at an angle across the sloping side of the wadi. This not only divided the run-off into manageable quantities, but the 15 cm walls served as conduits which directed the run-off into specific fields. They also increased the run-off from light rains by as much as 20–40 per cent by collecting the stones on the slopes into heaps [2]. The net result, since the ratio of catchment area to cultivated area averages 20 : 1, was that each field received water equivalent to a rainfall of 300–500 mm per year (the average in the mountains round Jerusalem) even though the average in the Negev is only 100 mm per year.

The cultivated area in the centre of a shallow wadi was walled [3] to ensure even ponding, and was divided into fields by terrace walls projecting some 40 cm above soil level. In the middle of each was a drop structure [4] which permitted surplus water to pass to the field below. Many of these units had their own farmhouse, each equipped with an internal underground cistern [5] served by its own catchment conduit. A catchment area of a fifth of a hectare would be more than adequate to create the 20 cubic metres of drinking water per year necessary for a family of six plus a donkey, a couple of camels, and a small flock of sheep and goats. A farm of this type has been restored at SHIVTA.

Aphrodite. Though the city was badly damaged by an earthquake in the early C5 AD, the transition from the Late Roman to the Byzantine period took place without any interruption in occupation. It seems likely, however, that there was an influx of new inhabitants, because churches were soon built. The population in the Byzantine period is estimated at 2,000 to 3,000. This figure is based on the 350–400 dwelling units arranged on terraces on the slope between the acropolis and the main road.

These dwellings are unique in that a cave cut in the rock forms an integral unit with the house in front. The caves were used as store-rooms or workshops, and some were certainly wine-cellars. Grapes were cultivated in addition to barley, wheat, and lentils. A complex system of channels and small dams in the fields below the city extracted the maximum value from the slight annual rainfall and the night dews.

The Persians sacked the city in AD 620; the excavators found the acropolis area covered by a thick layer of ashes. Any hope of restoration was ended by the arrival of the Arabs some years later.

Visit. Open: Sunday–Thursday and Saturday 8 a.m.–4 p.m., Fridays to 3 p.m. Restaurant and toilets. The circuit of the remains involves a rather strenuous climb. This can be avoided by making each of the three parking-lots a starting point for an excursion. Everything above a black line on the buildings has been reconstructed.

On the same level as the restaurant parking-lot is the best-preserved **Byzantine bath-house** in the country. It is built on the classic Roman pattern which the Byzantines passed on to the Arabs (KHIRBET EL-MAFJAR). Water came from a 60 m-deep well. The door of the frigidarium with its large pool (4.4 × 4.1 × 1.35 m), and that of the apodyterium (dressing-room) open on to the courtyard. The second door in the apodyterium gives access to the tepidarium, and then to the double caldarium, each heated by its own external furnace.

The intermediate parking-lot is is in the middle of the residential units laid out on terraces in the Byzantine period. One of these **cave-house combinations** has been reconstructed. Note in particular the square lavatory and the method of roofing. A passage connects the house with the multi-chambered purpose-cut cave behind. Handles were carved in the ceiling to facilitate hanging vegetables. The two rows of hollows in a rock-cut bench were to hold jars of wine upright. Grain was stored in rock-cut bins. Two other caves of the same type have been cleared further up the slope: one has four capitals carved from the rock. The graffiti in all these caves suggest that they served as places of refuge during and after the Persian invasion.

To the right of the road to the upper parking-lot the first sign indicates **burial caves**. The most important is a big square chamber containing twenty-two burial places cut into the rock on three sides; note in each the slots to hold the slabs covering the body interred below. At one time thought to be the tomb of Obodas, this complex is now dated to the middle of the C3 AD. A second sign points to a **Roman villa** of the C2–C3 AD. It is constructed around a courtyard built over a cistern. The observation point just outside offers an instructive view of the site. On the far side of the valley are the **Rammaliya cisterns**. These are typical of the effort made by the Nabataeans to make water available throughout the desert.

Once at the upper parking-lot it is best to go first to the top of the reconstructed C3 **tower** (an inscription above the lintel dates it to AD 294). From there, facing the acropolis, one can see the Byzantine wine press (left), the residential quarter of the C3 (below and in front), and the Nabataean pottery workshop (right).

The **wine press** has a square treading area into which grapes were fed from small storage rooms on three sides. On the fourth side is a round pit into which the grape juice flowed via a channel under the treading floor from a central sump. There are three other wine presses elsewhere in the city.

The **pottery workshop** was in use in the C1 AD, and is the only such Nabataean installation known. There were three kilns. Near one is a room with a bench on three sides; this served to dry the pottery made on the wheel supported on the adjacent round pedestal. Embedded in the floor of this area are broken sea-shells, apparently from the Red Sea: they may have been used as temper.

The C1 AD **Nabataean military camp** (visible from the railed viewpoint on the fortress wall) imitates a Roman garrison camp. The double walls strengthened by square towers surround eight long barracks separated by passageways 6 m wide with a pavement on either side. In the Byzantine period this camp was used as a source of ready-made cut stones. The troops patrolled the C1 AD **trade route**, which can be traced to the south-east for some 12 km. The untrimmed kerbstones (which first appear on the ridge 530 m from the camp) show it to be 5 m wide; it was never paved, but all loose stones were carefully cleared. The first milestones appear at 4.7 km from the camp. This was part of the trade

route between Petra and Gaza. Another section can be visited in the
MAKTESH RAMON.

The C4 AD **fortress** is simply a large open space encircled by a heavy
wall with three towers on each side; it could have offered protection to the
inhabitants and their flocks only against hit-and-run bedouin raiders.
The small chapel was built after the Persian invasion.

The ecclesiastical area to the west of the fortress is supported by
Nabataean retaining walls on the north and south; the staircase-tower
leading to the terrace overlooking the slope is also Nabataean, but nothing
remains of their buildings. The **North Church** is a typical example of a C4
monoapsidal church with three doors opening on to a colonnaded atrium
above a cistern. The apse and sanctuary are skewed to the east, presumably to compensate for the false orientation imposed on the church by
the shape of the Nabataean podium. Just outside the atrium is a
cruci-form **baptismal font**. Pillars supported the roof. The **Church of
St Theodore** is dated to the middle of the C5. Its apse abuts a C3 AD
tower. The square rooms on either side housed reliquaries. The circular
block in front of the sanctuary is the base of the pulpit. The tombstones in
the floor date from 514 to 618. The small rooms clustered around the
atrium may have been monastic cells.

Banyas (01)

The present name is a corruption of Paneas, signifying a place sacred to
the god Pan. The Jordan is by far the most important river in the region,
and in antiquity a spring in the large cave was one of its principal sources.
Little wonder, therefore, that it became a place where a nature god was
venerated. Today, because of seismic movements, the water bursts (20 m³
per second) from a crack below the cave.

The Seleucids of Syria defeated the Ptolemies of Egypt here in 200 BC
to assume control of Palestine. The Maccabees and their successors the
Hasmoneans never conquered the district. In 20 BC the emperor Augustus
gave it to Herod the Great, who in gratitude dedicated to his patron a
temple of white marble near the spring. On his death the area passed to his
son Philip, who in 2 BC built here the capital of his territory, naming it
Caesarea. To distinguish it from the coastal CAESAREA, it became known
as Caesarea Philippi, but the name that took root was Caesarea Paneas
(Pliny, *Natural History* 5: 71). According to Josephus, this Philip conducted the first experiment to determine the true source of the Jordan.
He had chaff thrown into the circular volcanic lake Berekhat Ram, and
it appeared at Paneas (*War* 3: 512–13). In fact there is no connection
between the two; an adroit courtier ensured the verification of the
royal hypothesis!

Somewhere in the vicinity of the city Jesus promised Peter that he would be the rock on which the church would be built (Matt. 16: 13–20). Agrippa II further enriched the city and tried to name it after the emperor Nero (AD 54–68) but the new title did not take. The amenities of the city were such that Titus spent a long time here celebrating the capture of Jerusalem in AD 70; 'many of the prisoners perished here, some thrown to wild beasts, others forced to meet each other in full-scale battles' (*War* 7: 24). A continuing Jewish presence is attested in the C2–C3. Christianity was well established by the early C4.

In 1126 Banyas came into the possession of the fanatical sect of the Assassins, who fortified it as their headquarters. Fearing an attack from Damascus they claimed Crusader protection; the price they paid was the city, which Baldwin II confided to Renier Brus. It was taken by the Damascenes in 1129, but in 1139 the ruler of Banyas sided with Zengi, atabeg of Mosul and Aleppo, who was viewed as a dire threat by Damascus. This gave Crusaders and Damascenes common cause, and a combined Christian-Muslim army took Banyas in 1140. The city became a place where Franks and Muslim nobles gathered for conversation and sport.

This idyllic situation changed when Zengi's son, Nur ed-Din, made himself master of all Syria in 1154. The strategic importance of Banyas increased enormously. It was the most advanced position of the Latin Kingdom, and controlled the route from Damascus to the coast. In May–June 1157 Nur ed-Din rampaged through the town, burning houses, and throwing down the walls, but he failed to take the fortress and retired when Crusader reinforcements arrived. Baldwin III brought masons and carpenters from all over the kingdom to ensure that repairs were completed in the shortest possible time. It was to no avail, because when Nur ed-Din tried again in October 1164 he was successful. The Ayyubid sultan al-Muazzam systematically demolished the fortifications in 1219. Thus Banyas could offer little resistance to the Mongol cavalry in 1260. In short order, however, the latter were driven out by the Mamluks, who restored the fortifications. Subsequently, however, there was no public building, and it was only a village of some 200 inhabitants when the Israelis took it from the Syrians in 1967.

Visit (Fig. 48). Open: Sunday–Saturday 8 a.m.–5 p.m. The by-pass that leaves and returns to the Qiryat Shemona–Golan road (route 99) divides the site into two parts, the sanctuary of Pan by the spring and the Roman/Crusader town. The hiking trail to NIMRUD (1151) begins at the parking-lot.

The Sanctuary of Pan

The excavated area to the left of the entrance to the parking-lot (snacks and toilets) is not very intelligible. Public buildings of the C1–C4 AD

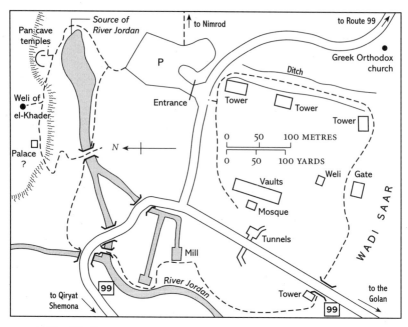

▲ **Fig. 48.** Banyas.

underlie a Crusader fortification, which was replaced by a Mamluk building.

The building to the left above the cave is the *weli* (tomb of a Muslim saint) of el-Khader (St George), sacred to Muslims and Druze.

Before seismic movements changed the terrain the spring burst forth within the **great cave**. It was the innermost sanctuary of the **temple** dedicated to Augustus by Herod the Great. The pattern of alternating semicircular and rectangular niches in the wall to the left has a precise parallel in the sunken garden in Herod's winter palace in Jericho (TULUL ABU EL-ALAIQ). Coins minted by his son Philip show the façade as a pediment supported by four columns.

East of this temple is an **open-air shrine** (18 × 15 m) of uncertain date on a high rocky projection; a cave and three niches were cut in the scarp. The inscription in the *tabula ansata* beneath the niche above the cave reads, 'The priest Victor, son of Lysimachos, dedicated this goddess to the god Pan, lover of Echo'. The same name appears in the left *tabula ansata* of the second niche to the right, 'For Pan and the nymphs, Victor son of Lysimachos with his children dedicated a likeness in stone of Hermes, child of Maia, son of Zeus, having vowed it; the year 150'. Thus this sanctuary can be dated to the middle of the C2 AD.

Still further east (20 m from the temple to Augustus) are the foundations of an **unidentified C2 AD temple**. A porch (11 × 4.15 m) projected out from a 13 m-long hall perpendicular to the scarp. The façade dominated the eastern source. Along the east wall is another **open-air shrine** consisting of a long narrow court (16.5 × 4.3 m) approached by steps and facing a niche cut in the rock. None of these sanctuaries appear to have survived the C4 AD.

West of the spring a natural terrace some 15 m above the water, and directly below the *weli*, was artificially levelled to receive a building. Some speculate that it may have been Philip's **palace**. The site is worthy of it, but the evidence is very slight, merely a wall constructed in *opus reticulatum* (square bricks laid at 45 degrees to create a net effect), which is visible as one descends the path to the bridge. The same building technique appears at Herod's winter palace in Jericho.

The Town

The medieval town made full use of the defensive advantages of the Wadi Hermon and the Wadi Saar for its western and southern boundaries. In the Roman and Byzantine periods, however, the city was twice as large, extending some 750 m beyond these limits to the west, and 500 m to the south.

A modern house perched high on a massive **Crusader tower** dominates the approach from the parking-lot. It was the north-east corner of the medieval city. Nothing else remains of the northern fortifications of the medieval town. A wall parallel to the modern road can be safely assumed. It would have been protected by a **dry ditch**, as the equally vulnerable east wall in fact is; it is 17.3 m wide. **Three towers** strengthened the wall on this side. That in the south-east corner was the biggest and strongest. From it the south wall ran some 35 m to a **gate-tower**, all of whose elements including the bridge outside are integral to its original plan. In the lintel below the arch facing the wadi is an Arab inscription dated 1227, and a chamber on the east side of the 4.5 m-wide bridge was built as a mosque. This suggests that the fortifications in their present shape are Mamluk (1250–1517). A collapsed modern bridge obscures the south-west tower. The west wall of the working water-activated **flour mill** belongs to the medieval curtain wall. The north-west tower, which is partly obscured by the ruins of a modern house, guarded the 9 m-wide medieval bridge spanning the Wadi Hermon some 22 m to the north.

The **twelve parallel vaults** (7.6 m deep, 6.6 m high and 5 m wide) within the medieval fortifications are identified as warehouses associated with the market of the C1 town. The vaulting supported paving, but we shall never know what function it might have served. The ground outside gradually rose, necessitating a change in the floor level. The monumental structure became the east wall of the Crusader inner fortifications. In its courtyard the Mamluks built a **mosque** with an apse in the south wall.

The *weli* with the large Mount Tabor oak commemorates Sheik Sidi Ibrahim, who in the Ottoman period was controller of weights and measures in Banyas.

West of the vaults ongoing excavations have brought to light an ancient **tunnel** complex of extraordinary workmanship. One tunnel angles from the south-east into a square chamber, from which another runs beneath the modern road before angling to the south-west. At this point, because of the slope, the channel breaks into the open and is no longer vaulted. At the time of writing its date and function are unclear.

Baram (Kefar Baram)* (L3)

There are enough architectural elements lying around the sites of CAPERNAUM and CHOROZAIN to give a reasonable idea of what these synagogues looked like. This effort is unnecessary at Kefar Baram because the magnificent façade has been preserved virtually undamaged up to the cornice.

The site (open: 8 a.m.–4 p.m.; Fridays to 3 p.m.) is just over 2 km from the Israel-Lebanon border and 1 km south of the village of Dovev; it is not to be confused with the settlement of Baram. The rolling hills of Upper Galilee are a perfect setting for the serene dignity of the synagogue which should be on the itinerary of anyone visiting the MERON area.

▼ **Baram.** The façade of the C4 synagogue.

The plan of the synagogue is identical with that of its sisters at Capernaum and Chorozain. The three entrances face south and there are rows of columns parallel to the other three walls, the floor is paved with stone slabs. The only difference is that here a porch is built along the length of the façade, one column with the architrave connecting it to the building remaining in place. A broken architrave showing the beginning of a curve suggests that the porch was surmounted by a triangular pediment with an arch in its centre. A Hebrew inscription on the sill of the eastern window in the façade reads, 'Built by Elazar, son of Yudan'.

Rabbi Moses Basula, who visited the site in 1522, ascribes the synagogue to Simeon bar Yohai, one of the five disciples of Rabbi Akiva who survived the massacre which followed the failure of the Second Revolt in AD 135, but a date in the C3 AD is more likely.

The buildings in the vicinity of the synagogue belong to a Christian village abandoned in 1948.

Belvoir (Kokhav Hayarden)* (M8)   ★

As its name indicates ('Fair View'), the view from this Crusader fortress is spectacular. From its location on the edge of the western scarp 500 m above the Jordan Valley one can see the hills of Samaria (south-west), the perfect breast shape of Mount Tabor (north-west), north over the Sea of Galilee and the Golan to the snows of Mount Hermon, and north-east the deep slash of the Yarmuk Valley which is the border between Syria and Jordan.

The Velos family of Tiberias began to farm this area in the reign of Fulk of Anjou (1131–42). In 1168 they sold the property for 1,400 gold bezants to the Knights of the Hospital, who built the castle. The fortress is a perfect example of a concentric castle. In the last days of the Latin Kingdom the loyalty of auxiliaries and mercenaries could not be taken for granted, and in planning a castle it became important to guard against treachery. An inner line of defence, therefore, was reserved to the hardcore loyalists. This, of course, was bad psychology. Mercenaries were tempted to go over to the enemy, and knights to retreat to the central keep.

The fortress came under attack from Saladin during his two campaigns in the Beisan Valley in 1182–3, but had little difficulty holding out against what was no more than a diversionary tactic. On 1 July 1187 the impotent defenders saw his 12,000 mounted archers stream down the north edge of the Yarmuk on their way to victory at the HORNS OF HATTIN. Thereafter they were under siege. It lasted until January 1189 when sappers brought down the barbican protecting the switchback entrance ramp. The writing was now on the wall, and the defenders sued for terms.

Saladin permitted them to march out to Tyre. His troops tore down the gates, but the castle was systematically destroyed only in the early C13 when there was reason to fear that the Crusaders would return. They did regain possession of Belvoir in 1241, by treaty not by arms, but their stay was too short to permit reconstruction.

Visit. The steep and rather narrow access road (route 717) is signposted on the Jordan Valley road (route 90). The road coming from the west should not be attempted. Open: 8 a.m.–4 p.m., Fridays to 3 p.m. A plan of the castle is available at the ticket office.

The **moat** is 20 m wide and 12 m deep. It was not dug merely as a defensive measure. It provided stone for the construction of the fortress. Other blocks came from an abandoned Jewish village some 700 m to the south-east. When crossing what used to be the drawbridge note the **sally-ports** at the base of the towers. Once inside, an imaginative effort is necessary to appreciate the fortress. On all sides the space between the outer wall and that immediately inside was vaulted, providing space for barracks, stables, and storage, and a broad platform for troops at the top of the wall. The doors of this structure opened on to a **courtyard**, in whose eastern arm is a **cistern** with a capacity of 650 m³. The garrison had to rely entirely on rain for drinking and washing. The gate in the south-east corner was part of the **principal entrance**. From there it is easy to appreciate the switchback road to the outer gate protected by the great multi-storey barbican.

The **four-towered keep** stands in the centre of the courtyard. In it vaulted buildings (partly preserved) surround a second courtyard in which was another cistern with a capacity of 100 m³. Its angled **entrance tower** was on the west in order to force attackers, who had broken through the outer gate, to circle the keep, and thereby to expose them to the defenders' fire. The keep has a small postern door in the eastern wall. Just inside to the south is the **kitchen**, and beyond it the monastic **dining-room** running the length of the south wall. The chapel appears to have been on the second floor above the entrance.

Bet Alpha* (M9)   ★★

A C6 AD synagogue celebrated for the colour and vigour of its mosaic floor. Open: 8 a.m.–4 p.m.; Fridays to 3 p.m.

Only fragments of walls remain but they show that there was an open courtyard with two doors leading into the vestibule from which three doors gave on to a basilical hall. The apse, which orients the building towards Jerusalem, housed the Ark of the Law and the community safe (a hole in the floor covered with stone slabs). Just inside the entrance to the central aisle are two inscriptions: one, in Greek, mentions the two crafts-men who laid the mosaic floor, Marianos and his son Hanina, the other, in Aramaic, says that the floor was laid during the reign of the emperor Justin. The inscription is mutilated just at the point where the exact date was given, but there were only two Justins; the first reigned from 518 to 527, and the second from 565 to 578. Since Justin II was notorious for his persecution of Jews, it is assumed that the inscription refers to Justin I. The inscriptions are flanked by a lion and a bull. These have a long history in the ancient Near East as symbols of forces locked in combat, but they were also complementary as the symbols of the god Hadad and his consort Atargatis. Were they intended to remind Jews of the world they would re-enter on leaving the synagogue?

The world evoked by the three panels of the mosaic floor (Fig. 49, Hebrew lettering omitted) was very different. In the first, Abraham's readi-ness to sacrifice a willing Isaac symbolizes absolute submission to the Divine will (Gen. 22: 1–19). The donkey driver with his whip stands by as his helper prepares to take off the saddle. The ram tethered to a bush and the bound hands of a small, fearful Isaac (apparently suspended from his father's fingertips) are details not found in the Bible; they show that the artists had been listening to the Aramaic paraphrase which made the Hebrew Bible intelligible to the average Jew. The whole scene is dominated by the hand of God and the words 'Do not lay (your hand upon the boy)'. The radiant dark cloud, from which the hand emerges, underlines the paradox of religious truth, a theme reinforced by the contrast between the neatly ordered stylized palm trees of heaven and the rather haphazard vegetation scattered round the feet of the human figures.

The centre panel elaborates the theme of heaven in a quite different way, drawing on the symbolism of the pagan world. It is described facing the apse. The busts of winged women represent the four seasons (anti-clockwise from the top left-hand corner): *Nisan*, Spring; *Tammuz*, Summer; *Tishri*, Autumn; and *Tebeth*, Winter. In the hub of the zodiac wheel Helios, the sun god, drives his four-horse chariot across a sky studded with moon and stars. The twelve signs start at 3 o'clock and run anti-clockwise: *Taleh*, Aries (ram); *Shor*, Taurus (bull); *Teomin*, Gemini (twins); *Sartan*, Cancer (crab); *Aryeh*, Leo (lion), *Betulah*, Virgo (virgin); *Meoznayim*, Libra (scales); *Aqrab*, Scorpio (scorpion); *Kashat*, Sagittarius (archer); *Gedi*, Capricornus (goat); *Deli*, Aquarius (water carrier); and *Dagim*, Pisces (fish). The twisted cord border underlines the unity of the wheel, but if the intention was to divide the twelve signs into groups of three someone slipped!

This arrangement of the solar chariot, zodiac wheel, and personified seasons is taken directly from paganism, and reflects the Graeco-Roman assimilation of Babylonian astrology. The influence of classical sources is much more evident in the zodiac floor of the C4 AD synagogue found at

HAMMAT TIBERIAS. Such pagan beliefs naturally created problems for the rabbis, but the very human desire to look into the future was too strong, and they were forced to find ways to make the zodiac acceptable. The

▲ **Fig. 49.** Bet Alpha. Mosaic floor of C6 synagogue.

frequency of the number twelve in the Bible (tribes, shewbread, jewelled dress of high priest, etc.) furnished an obvious link with received tradition. Such juxtaposition of the sacred and the profane (found also in the synagogue floors at Naaran and Hammat Tiberias) is much less effective than the solution adopted here where the zodiac is bracketed by two specifically religious panels which reduce it to a purely decorative role. Nowhere else is the zodiac associated with the sacrifice of Isaac whose message implicitly condemns the futility of star-gazing; it is God who guides the course of human life.

The open curtains framing the upper panel invite the believer to enter the realm of mystery by contemplating the symbols which are the traces of God's presence in history, the Temple and the Law. The Temple in Jerusalem is suggested by the double *menorah*, the two square incense shovels, the two *shofars* (ram's-horn trumpets), and the *lulab* (bundle of branches) plus *ethrog* (citrus fruit). These souvenirs of a ritual which no longer existed—the Romans had destroyed the Temple in AD 70—are relegated to a secondary position by being disposed around the central element, the shrine of the Law. Pilasters support its heavily inlaid doors; a lamp hangs from the apex of the stepped gable adorned with a shell motif. The richness of decoration symbolizes the honour accorded the Law, the focal point of Jewish life. It seems precarious to assign any symbolic value to the five animals.

Bet Guvrin* (G19) ★★

South of the modern kibbutz of Bet Guvrin is Tel Maresha. From the Bible we know that Rehoboam (928–911 BC) fortified the city as a storehouse and armoury (2 Chr. 11: 8–11). It could not resist Sennacherib in 701 BC (Mic. 1: 15). After the Exile (586–538 BC) Maresha became part of Idumaea. The Ptolemies established a colony of Sidonians in the city in the C3 BC and, according to Zenon, an Egyptian official who visited Palestine in 259 BC, it was a centre of the slave trade with Egypt. Under Seleucid control (from 193 BC) the city lost its importance, and inscriptions show the colonists merging with the local population.

Conquest by John Hyrcanus (134–104 BC) forced the inhabitants to become Jews under threat of exile (*Antiquities* 13: 257). The name of the place to which Herod the Great went on his way to MASADA in 40 BC is textually uncertain; some scholars suggest that we should read Marisa (= Maresha), which may even have been his birthplace, and this would explain why the Parthians destroyed the city (*War* 1: 263–70).

Thereafter the role of Maresha passed to the nearby village of Bet Guvrin which grew into a city to which the emperor Septimius Severus gave the *ius italicum* and the name Eleutheropolis in AD 200. He endowed the city with a huge tract of land stretching from EN GEDI almost to the Mediterranean coast. The prosperity of the city at this period is underlined by an oval amphitheatre. The quality of life of the Byzantine city is well illustrated by the elaborate mosaic floor of a C4 villa above which was found the equally beautiful floor of a C6 chapel; both are now in the Israel Museum, Jerusalem.

The site was settled by Crusaders very early in the C12, no doubt because of the fertility of the area but also because they identified it as BEER SHEVA! The settlement was vulnerable to raids by the Egyptian garrison of ASHQELON, and eventually it and ten neighbouring villages were handed over to the Hospitallers. Their castle was built in 1136 as one of a series ordered by Fulk of Anjou (1131–43) in order to blockade Ashqelon; the tactic succeeded only when the capture of Gaza in 1150 closed the circle. The fall of Ashqelon in 1153 reduced the strategic value of Bet Guvrin, but the importance of the crossroads guaranteed the fortress continuing significance even in the post-Crusader period, when an important Arab village grew up around it.

Visit (Fig. 50). The Qiryat Gat–Bet Shemesh road (route 35) runs east–west through the site. To visit the ruins north of the road simply park on the verge at the sign reading 'Gas 300 m'. To reach the better-developed part of the site south of the road (the underground areas) take the

▼ **Fig. 50.** Bet Guvrin. 1. Fortress; 2. Crusader church; 3. Park entrance; 4. Burial caves; 5. Cistern; 6. Columbarium; 7. Bath; 8. Oil factory; 9. House; 10. Houses; 11. Tomb of Apollophanes; 12. Tomb of the musicians; 13. North-west tower; 14. Bell caves and columbarium.

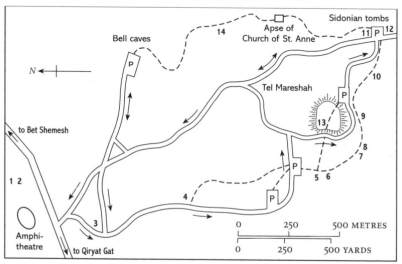

turn-off opposite the gas station. Open: Sunday–Thursday and Saturday 8 a.m.–4 p.m; Friday to 1 p.m.

The Underground Areas

The area around Maresha is honeycombed with hundreds of underground chambers; the hard surface stone (*nari*) provided a solid roof while the soft chalk below was very easy to work. Paradoxically it was less trouble to excavate than to build, an advantage which the citizens exploited from the C2 BC to the C7 AD. In times of danger they went underground, as at HAZAN. It is possible to visit all the sights by foot, but distances are considerable, and it is best to make sorties from the various parking-lots. The hatched line in Fig. 50 indicates marked paths; the arrows show one-way roads.

Two **burial caves** [4] of the C3–C2 BC lie to the left of the road before the first parking-lot with its picnic area. From the next parking-lot (toilets) a path leads to a series of typical installations. A bannistered staircase enabled drawers to descend to the water level in a deep **cistern** [5] of the C4–C3 BC. Subsequently niches were cut in the walls for pigeons, which were raised for food and fertilizer. Nearby is a much more spectacular example of such a **columbarium** [6]. Its elaborate double cruciform shape and decorative moulding, however, suggest that the original intention might have been different. The channels leading into the **bath cave** [7] were so arranged as to prevent those pouring the water from seeing the bathers. The equipment of a C3–C2 BC **oil factory** [8] has been reconstructed. Olives were first crushed in the mill, and then placed in rush bags to be squeezed slowly by the beam press. Adding stones progressively increased the pressure. Olive oil was fundamental to the lifestyle of these people. It was a skin moisturizer that could be eaten as a condiment, in addition to being used for cooking and illumination.

The rooms arranged around the central courtyard of a C3–C2 BC **house** [9] in a slight hollow have been partially reconstructed (unplastered brick). Extensive as the house is, it pales into insignificance with what is below, three huge **cisterns** whose stairs spiral down the walls. They were fed by run-off from the roofs and courtyard. Continue up the slope to a set of similar houses [10], beneath which are an amazing series of cisterns, store-rooms, oil presses, and columbaria. The present passage from one end to the other is artificial.

From this point it is best to climb the tel and follow the path cutting diagonally across the top. It brings you through the C3–C2 BC city of Maresha. The plan is well known from excavations at the beginning of the century, but today only the **north-west tower** [13] is visible. The tower rests on a 3.5 m wall of the Iron Age.

The Sidonian Tombs

From the north-east corner of a tree-filled parking-lot it is only a few steps to the bush-framed entrance to the **Tomb of Apollophanes** [11]. Excavated at the end of the C3 BC as the family tomb of Apollophanes, who headed the Sidonian colony for thirty-three years, it remained in use until the C1 BC. The rock chambers with their 41 gable-shaped coffin places are intact, but in 1993 the figures were completely repainted on metal sheets applied to the rock. The crowing **cock** above a small altar had the capacity to frighten demons. The three-headed **dog** on the right jamb is Cerberus, guardian of the entrance to the underworld. Above his head are messages scrawled by lovers separated by an arranged marriage:

WOMAN: I can neither suffer aught for you, nor give you pleasure. I lie with another loving you dearly.

MAN: But by Aphrodite, I rejoice greatly at one thing, your cloak lies as security [i.e. she might return to claim it].

WOMAN: But I run away and leave you complete freedom; do what you will.

CYNICAL OBSERVER: Do not rap the wall for it breeds disturbance; it lies in nods through the doors [i.e. the lovers should not advertise but should be content with nods in public].

Below the garlands the animal frieze begins on the same side as the inscription. A **trumpeter** summons the hunt. A **hunter** drives his lance at a she-leopard, which is already wounded in the breast by a dart and is under attack from behind by a dog. The ruff of the next animal suggests a lion but the inscription identifies it as a **panther**. One or two animals were destroyed when two *loculi* were combined into one. Blood dribbles from the mouth of a **bull** brought to its knees by a huge snake. A popeyed **giraffe** (of whom the artist had heard but certainly never seen) calmly stares down a **boar**, which has been flicked on the rump by the tail of a mythical **griffin**, whose attentions are not well received by a rather nervous **oryx**. Another tree separates this group from a **rhinoceros** and an **elephant** with a negroid keeper. He and the other human figures were defaced by religious Arabs when the tomb was first opened.

The gabled recess gives access to three sarcophagus chambers, evidently intended for the chief members of the family. The designs on each side are basically symmetrical. A bright red **eagle** swinging on a garland represents the phoenix reborn from the ritual fire in the sacred basin supported by a lion-footed tripod on a red podium. The ornate doorway of the burial chamber of Apollophanes himself is flanked by classical Greek **amphoras**.

The workmanship of the continuation of the animal frieze is noticeably poorer. It begins with **two fish**, whose bizarre appearance is best explained by the belief that water contains creatures corresponding to those on land; hence an elephant fish with tusks and trunk and a rhinoceros fish! An ibis stands on the back of a **crocodile**, whose jaws open to devour a **hippopotamus**. A snake is torn to pieces by **a wild ass**. The next two animals cannot be identified. The **porcupine**, however, is unmistakable, as is the **lynx**. The gentle bearded face of the **man-lion** carries the hesitant smile of one unsure of a welcome.

The entrance to the **Tomb of the Musicians** [**12**] is at the far side of the parking-lot. The name comes from the painting, near the door of the last burial room, a man blowing a flute and a woman playing a harp. The slope on which they walk suggests that they are descending to the abode of the dead to cheer them up. Though smaller than the Sidonian Tomb, it is of the same type, and was in use in the middle third of the C2 BC.

The Bell Caves

On leaving the parking-lot of the Sidonian tombs turn right and look for the sign for the Bell Caves (toilets); in these vast underground areas the quiet and the play of light are reminiscent of a great cathedral.

The caves are in fact chalk quarries. In this area chalk deposits are covered by an extremely hard crust called *nari*. The quarrymen found it most economical to cut only a circular opening 1 m in diameter in the *nari*. The chalk was then removed in layers 25–30 cm deep, the tool marks are still visible on the walls. In order to retain moisture in the chalk and to diminish the amount of dust, the chalk was extracted in blocks of 5–7 kg. It takes little imagination to envisage the hellish working conditions. The radius was increased as the pit descended, sometimes breaking through the wall of the pit alongside. The absence of any dumps shows the chalk to have been transported elsewhere to create mortar and plaster. There are about 800 of these pits within a 3 km radius round Bet Guvrin; they were worked between the C6 and C10 AD.

The **free-standing apse** on the adjoining hill belongs to the C12 Crusader church of St Anna, whence the Arabic name for Maresha, Tel Sandakhanna.

The Amphitheatre, Fortress, and Moat

Between the entrance to Kibbutz Bet Guvrin and the Delek gas station is a field of ruins whose complexity mirrors the history of the site. The most obvious feature is three crudely restored arches. They cover the north aisle of a triapsidal **Crusader church** [**2**]; the other two aisles disappeared when their stones were robbed for later buildings. Erected sometime after 1153 to meet the needs of an expanding civil population, the north wall of the church is juxtaposed to the south wall of the castle; the joint is obvious in the small sacristy entered from the second bay and in the passage leading from the third bay. The one advantage of the restoration is that it creates a platform from which one can get a bird's-eye view of the area.

With one's back to the road one looks out over a **square fortress** [**1**] with a tower at each corner. The visible elements date from the Mamluk period when the keep of the Crusader fortress was rebuilt; it had been torn down in 1192 when there was danger that the Crusaders might retake Bet Guvrin. Arab structures of the Ottoman period have been juxtaposed to the far and right walls. Between the church and the main road are domestic quarters and store-rooms of the Crusader period.

From the viewpoint one can also look down into the **Roman amphitheatre** outside the enclave to the left. It was constructed in the late C2 AD. The barrel-vaulted double oval ring is almost intact but the 11–14 tiers of seats which it supported have all been robbed out. The seating capacity has been estimated at 5,000. Simeon ben Lakhish, a well-known Jewish gladiator of the C3 AD, may have been among those who fought here. He ended by becoming the intellectual sparring-partner of his brother-in-law, Rabbi Johanan ben Nappaha of TIBERIAS, in the formulation of the Palestinian Talmud. The emperor Arcadius (383–408) forbade gladiatorial displays. The change in function of the amphitheatre is symbolized by the nine columns inserted into the arena at this time. Their precise function is unknown.

Some 10 m due north of the amphitheatre and parallel to the northern side of the fortress is the ashlar-built wall of the **moat** whose far side is now marked by the barbed wire fence of the kibbutz. It can be easily traced to the east as far as the kibbutz entrance road which dips as it passes over it. The southern part of the moat was filled in to create the modern Qiryat Gat–Bet Shemesh road. The east and west parts of the moat can be discerned only with great difficulty.

Bet Shean* (M9)   ★★

The numerous fish-ponds in the Harod Valley give Bet Shean a unique character. In an arid land it is virtually surrounded by water. It contains the best-preserved Roman/Byzantine city in the country and a unique Byzantine mosaic floor.

The tremendous natural advantages of the site make it easy to understand why it has been continuously occupied for nearly 6,000 years; the 80 m-high tel contains fifteen superimposed cities. The fertile land receives a good rainfall and the Harod is a perennial stream. The valley climbs gently to the west from the Jordan, merging imperceptibly with the Jezreel Valley running to the coast. Immeasurably the easiest east–west crossing in the whole country, these valleys have been a trade route from time immemorial, and they are controlled by Bet Shean.

During the first 2,000 years of the settlement on the mound the most crucial cultural change was the substitution of metal for stone tools. In the C15 BC the pharaoh Thutmose III made it an Egyptian administrative centre. The occupation levels for the next 300 years furnished abundant evidence of Egyptian influence; the city was one of the major strongholds from which the pharaohs controlled Palestine. The highest part of the mound was always crowned by a temple. Bet Shean formed part of the territory that fell to the lot of the tribe of Manasseh, but the iron chariots of the Canaanites forbade any attack (Judg. 1: 27). The city fell to another chariot people, the Philistines, in the C11 BC. After the defeat of the Israelites on Mount Gilboa in 1004 BC, they hung the bodies of King Saul and his son Jonathan on the walls of Bet Shean (1 Sam. 31: 10), thus occasioning the famous lament of David, one of the greatest Hebrew poems (see box).

David's Lament over Saul and Jonathan

'Does the splendour of Israel lie dead on your heights? How did the heroes fall? Tell it not in Gath, nor cry it in the streets of Ashqelon, lest the daughters of the Philistines rejoice, lest the daughters of the uncircumcised gloat. You mountains of Gilboa, no dew, no rain fall on you. O treacherous fields where the heroes' shield lies dishonoured! Not greased with oil, the shield of Saul, but with the blood of wounded men, the fat of warriors! The bow of Jonathan never turned back, the sword of Saul never came home unsated! Saul and Jonathan, beloved and handsome, were divided neither in life, nor in death. Swifter than eagles were they, stronger than lions. O daughters of Israel, weep for Saul who gave you scarlet and fine linen to wear, who pinned gold jewellery on your dresses! How heroes fell in the thick of battle! Jonathan, by your dying I too am stricken. I am desolate for you, Jonathan my brother. Very dear you were to me, your love more wonderful to me than the love of women. How the mighty have fallen, and the weapons of war perished!' (2 Sam. 1: 17–27).

The history of the city from the point where it is mentioned (1 Kgs. 4: 12) as a city of Solomon's empire (965–928 BC) remains obscure until we reach the C3 BC when it reappears as Scythopolis. There have been many attempts, none satisfactory, to explain why it was suddenly known as the 'City of the Scythians'. It was probably at this period that the city moved to the foot of the tel. Under Antiochus IV (175–164 BC) the city received the rights of a *polis* and a new name, Nysa. This implies that Dionysos was held in special veneration; it was the name of the place where he was brought up by the nymphs.

Josephus reports that John Hyrcanus (134–104 BC) razed the city to the ground in 107 BC (*Antiquities* 13: 280), but it must have been swiftly rebuilt, because it is listed as a forcibly converted city in the reign of his successor, Alexander Jannaeus (103–76 BC) (*Antiquities* 13: 396). In 63 BC the Roman general Pompey (106–48 BC) made the city part of the

Decapolis, a league of ten cities designed as a source of Graeco-Roman influence in the area. In AD 66 the Jewish inhabitants fought against their compatriots, but were subsequently massacred (*War* 2: 466–8).

The city expanded greatly in the C2 AD when the Sixth Legion Ferrata was based in the area. The social problems this caused became apparent in the following century when Jewish religious leaders tried to slow the movement of Jewish peasants into the city but, as usual, economics prevailed; Scythopolis was on its way to becoming one of the textile centres of the Roman empire. The Edict of Maximum Prices promulgated by the emperor Diocletian (AD 284–305) consistently ranks the linen produce of Scythopolis as first class. Inevitably Christians were also drawn to the city, and their position improved immeasurably when the empire became Christian in the early C4. At the end of that century the city became the capital of the province of Palestina Secunda. The greatest figure the Christian community produced was the C6 historian Cyril of Scythopolis whose biographies of seven Palestinian religious leaders are a mine of accurate detail.

Linen workers began to drift away from Scythopolis in the C6 because state control of the economy had effectively reduced master craftsmen to the status of slaves; the weakness of Byzantine authority made it impossible to enforce the law of AD 374 which imposed a heavy fine on 'those who attempt to harbour Scythopolitan linen workers who are bound to the regular public corvée'. The Arab conquest restored the old Semitic name Beisan but could not halt the city's decline which was hastened by a major earthquake in 749. No attempt was made to rebuild any major structure. From the small Jewish community which survived the presence of the Crusaders came the first Hebrew book on the geography of the Holy Land (1322).

Visit. The town contains three distinct sites (Fig. 51): (1) the tel and the Roman city, which are in a National Park; (2) the Amphitheatre; (3) the Monastery of the Lady Mary.

Tel and Roman-Byzantine City

Open. 8 a.m.–4 p.m.; Fridays to 3 p.m. Toilets and refreshments. The entrance from the main street, Shaul HaMelech, is clearly signposted. Both the tel and the ancient city are still being excavated, and what follows is necessarily approximative.

What has been, and will be, brought to light on the **top of the tel** can be appreciated only by a professional archaeologist. For the average visitor the steep climb is justified by the magnificent overview of the ancient city. Only from this dominant position can one grasp the inter-relationship of the various streets and buildings laid out below (Fig. 52). Since excavation continues around the periphery, only the centre can be dealt with here.

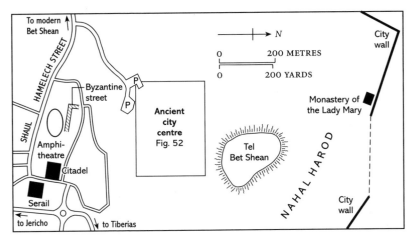

▲ **Fig. 51.** Bet Shean. Roman and Byzantine Remains (after Foerster and Tsafrir).

Even though the upper part of the seating has disappeared, the **theatre** [**29**], built about AD 200, is a striking monument. Designed for dramatic presentations, it had seating for 7,000. The upper tier has completely disappeared. The seats of the middle tier have been robbed out. Those of the lowest tier have survived. A **stairway** [**30**] on the east side gave access to the dignitaries' entrance on the axis of the stage, and to the eight other entrances (*vomitoria*). The theatre remained in use throughout the Byzantine period, but was not rebuilt after the earthquake of 749. At the foot of the steps are a square **Roman temple** [**22**] and a **fountain house** [**23**].

From the back of the theatre one looks out over the stage to a huge **Byzantine bath** covering 0.6 hectares. It is the largest in the country. A colonnaded exercise gallery [**27**] with swimming pools [**26**] surrounds the heated halls [**25**] on three sides. Socializing took place in the unheated rooms on the north [**24**]. All the visible buildings were erected in the C5–C6, but it is most probable that the site was already occupied by a bath in the Roman period. A **monumental entrance** (*propylaeum*) [**28**] gave access to the bath from the main street [**18**].

At the north-east corner of the bathing complex was a Roman **odeon** [**15**], a small theatre used particularly for musical performances. It was partially destroyed by a Byzantine building, one room of which contains a **mosaic floor representing Tyche**, the goddess of good fortune. She wears a turreted crown representing a walled city, and carries a cornucopia. The complexity of the surrounding decoration is striking.

The south-east corner of the bath-house is cut off by a well-preserved C6 **Byzantine street** [**18**]. The road is paved with black basalt slabs laid diagonally. In the centre specially shaped flagstones cover a 2 m-deep

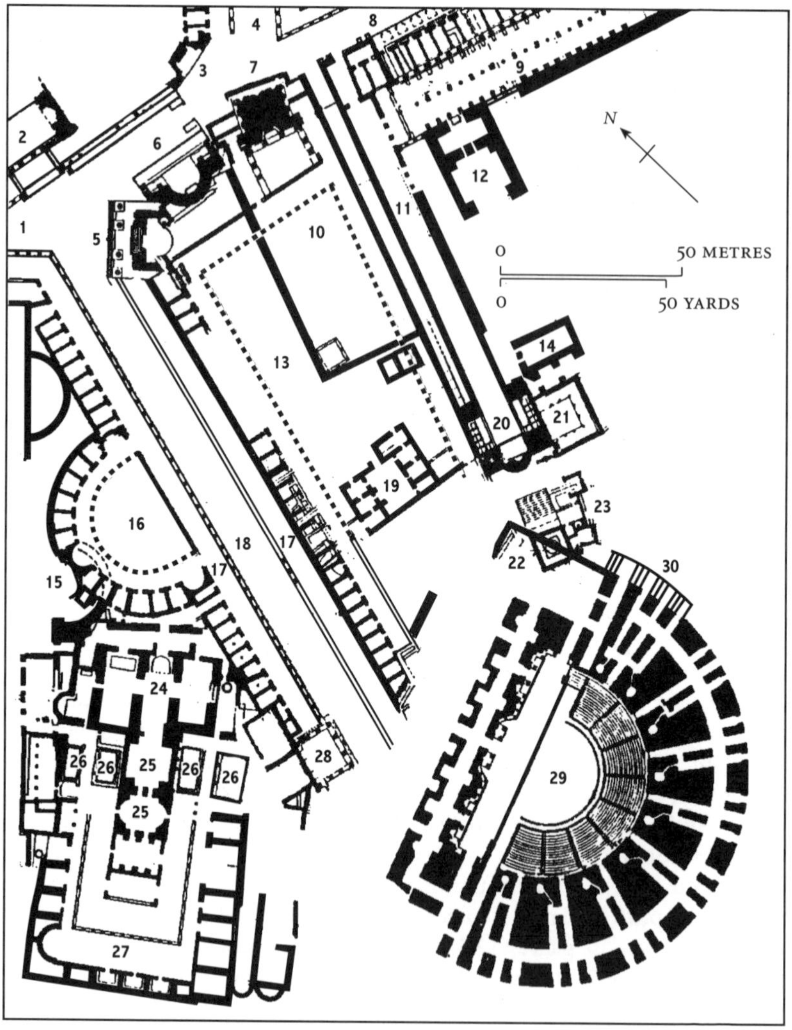

▲ **Fig. 52.** Bet Shean. The Centre of the Roman and Byzantine City (after Foerster and Tsafrir). 1. Byzantine street; 2. Monumental entrance (*propylaeum*); 3. Antonius monument; 4. Byzantine street; 5. Temple of Dionysos; 6. Nymphaeum; 7. Monumental structure; 8. Byzantine street; 9. Roman stoa; 10. Roman basilica; 11. Street. 12. East wing of a public bath; 13. Byzantine market-place; 14. West wing of a public bath; 15. Roman odeon; 16. Byzantine market; 17. Covered sidewalk; 18. Byzantine street (Palladius Street); 19. Artisan's house; 20. *Tetrapylon*; 21. Public services building; 22. Roman temple; 23. Fountain house; 24. Unheated rooms of a public bath; 25. Heated rooms; 26. Swimming-pools; 27. Sports area (*palestra*); 28. Monumental entrance (*propylaeum*) to the public bath; 29. Theatre; 30. Entrance steps.

drain, which is joined by ancillary drains coming from both sides. The 6 m-wide mosaic-floored **sidewalk** [17] is raised almost a metre above street level; an inscription records the last reconstruction by Flavius Palladius, son of the governor, Porphry. Marble-fronted **shops** line the western side. A large semi-circular **market** [16] increased their number. Any distance from the noise of the main street would have been an advantage.

At the base of the tel the street divides to go round it on both sides [1 and 4]. From the street on the left a **monumental entrance** (*propylaeum*) [2] gave dignity to a flight of steps leading to the temple of Zeus Akraios on the summit of the tel. The adjacent plaza was dominated by a large **temple** [5], presumed to have been dedicated to Dionysos, the main god of the city. Four steps lead up to the colonnaded entrance façade. Four 10 m columns rested on 2 m-high plinths and supported a triangular pediment. Inside six more steps lead up to the temple itself, resting on a podium supported by barrel vaults.

Beside the temple to the east is an ornate apsidial structure of basalt faced with limestone [6]. The decoration suggests that it was built in the C2 AD, but an inscription identifies the edifice as a **nymphaeum**, a decorative fountain, and dates it to the C4 AD. Facing it across the street is a **commemorative monument** [3]; according to a very fragmentary inscription it was dedicated to a certain Antonius.

Angled to face the road [4] running down the Amal Valley is a **monumental platform** [7] with rectangular and semicircular niches which originally contained statues; its function at the centre of the city appears to have been purely decorative. When it was erected in the C2 it was backed by a rectangular **basilica** [10] in which the business of the city was done. By the Byzantine period the basilica had fallen into disrepair, and in a programme of urban renewal it was replaced by a large **market** [13]. Shops shaded by a covered sidewalk fronted on to an open space, whose southern end was taken in the Ummayad period as a dwelling [19]. A street [11] separated the Byzantine market from another large public **bath**, only parts of which have been brought to light [12 and 14]. The street terminates in a structure having four massive square piers [20]. In all probability this was a **tetrapylon** covering the intersection of two streets in the Roman period. The Umayyads transformed it into an industrial complex by inserting basins between the piers. They may have served in the preparation of textiles. The adjoining square structure [21] is identified as a public-service building of the Byzantine period; manifestly the street pattern had changed.

The most difficult part of the city centre to understand lies north of this bath; it takes a great imaginative effort to separate the elements belonging to two different periods. In the C2 AD an ornamental stepped **pool** (50 m × 7.5 m) separated the street [8] from a magnificent **stoa** [9], whose tall columns it reflected. Some 300 years later, at the beginning of the C6, after the stoa had collapsed or been demolished, a new street [**8**] flanked by a **row of shops** was built on the site.

The Amphitheatre

The C2 AD Roman amphitheatre lies just to the north of Shaul HaMelech Street. The seating begins 3.2 m above the floor of the arena, indicating that it served for gladiatorial and hunting contests, entertainments likely to interest the soldiers of the Sixth Legion. It is estimated that the eleven to thirteen rows of seats could accommodate approximately 6,000 spectators. By the C5 it no longer functioned as an arena, and the area was developed as a residential quarter. The **paved street** linking it with the city centre contains an inscription dating the paving and the drainage system to AD 522.

Monastery of the Lady Mary

The building is kept locked but the key may be obtained (against deposit of one's passport or identity card) at the museum (open: 8.30 a.m.–

▼ **Fig. 53.** Bet Shean. Calendar mosaic in the Monastery of the Lady Mary. 1. January; 2. February; 3. March; 4. April; 5. May; 6. June; 7. July; 8. August; 9. September; 10. October; 11. November; 12. December.

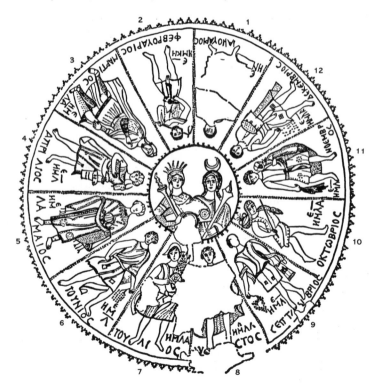

3 p.m.; closed Saturdays). The turn south from the bypass linking the Bet Shean–Afula and Bet Shean–Tiberias roads is not marked; there is a café on the corner, and the debris-strewn road runs beside a row of factories; the asbestos-roofed ruin is at the end on the left.

An inscription in the south-east corner of the chapel identifies the builder as 'the Lady Mary'; the title was used by the wives of high Byzantine officials. A tombstone in the chapel shows the monastery to have been erected shortly before AD 567. It survived the Persian invasion in 614 only to be abandoned not long after; through some miracle the mosaics escaped the attention of vandals. Many of the floors have simple geometric designs; three are of exceptional interest.

The centre-piece of the mosaic in the main hall is a calendar in which the twelve months form a circle around the Sun and Moon. Each month is represented by a man equipped for an occupation typical of the season; at his feet is the Latin name of the month in Greek script with the number of days (Fig. 53): January [1]–effaced; February [2] man with hoe and sapling; March [3]–soldier; April [4]–man carrying goat and basket; May [5]–man bearing flowers in cloak; June [6]–man holding basket of fruit; July [7]–man holding sheaf of corn; August [8]–effaced; September [9]–man with knife and basket for grape harvest; October [10] and November [11]–uncertain; December [12]–man scattering seed.

In the room at the far end of the hall from the entrance a vine trellis is used to create twelve medallions containing (reading left to right and top to bottom): spear-bearer attacking lioness with two cubs; two damaged; negro leading a giraffe; vintager with load of grapes; vintager cutting grapes; dog howling accompaniment to pipe player; treading grapes; man leading pannier-laden donkey; vintager cutting grapes over basket; man thinking about the vintage; damaged. The circular medallions making up the floor of the chapel contain eighty small birds in addition to two large peacocks.

Bet Shearim* (J7)

In the extreme north-west corner of the Jezreel Valley the first low hills create a small valley which houses a unique monument to Jewish culture. Cut into the hillsides are thirty-one catacombs whose architecture and decoration give them an important place in the history of art. The site should not be confused with the new settlement of the same name located 5 km further east. The entrance to the necropolis is from the secondary road (route 722) south-east of Qiryat Tivon, linking the Haifa–Nazareth (route 75) and the Haifa–Megiddo (route 70) roads.

From Josephus (*Life* 118–19) we know that Bet Shearim (in Greek

Besara) was the central village of an agricultural estate belonging to Berenice the great-granddaughter of Herod the Great. It was normal practice for royal estates to become the personal property of a conquering monarch; after the failure of the First Revolt (AD 66–70) this territory would have come into the possession of the Roman emperor. The recognized leader of the Jewish people in the C2 AD was Rabbi Judah ha-Nasi (c.135–217), the compiler of the *Mishnah*. It seems probable that his decision to establish the Sanhedrin at Bet Shearim was motivated by a gift of land there from his friend the emperor Marcus Aurelius Antoninus (161–80). Under this great and tolerant teacher the town expanded considerably; if the Talmud hints that there were two magnificent buildings it can be safely assumed that there were many more. For health reasons Rabbi Judah ha-Nasi lived the last seventeen years of his life in SEPPHORIS but had planned for his burial in Bet Shearim, and was in fact interred there: 'Miracles were wrought on that day. It was evening and all the towns gathered to mourn him, and eighteen synagogues praised him and bore him to Bet Shearim, and the daylight remained until everyone reached his home' (*Ketubot* 12, 35a).

Jews had always desired to be buried on the Mount of Olives where the Messiah was expected to appear, but this became impossible after AD 135 when Hadrian closed the area round Jerusalem to Jews. Bet Shearim became the ideal alternative because of the reverence in which Rabbi Judah ha-Nasi was held, and for a hundred years Jews from throughout Palestine and the Diaspora brought their dead to be interred there. Services to the dead became the main industry of the town, and quarrymen, stonecutters, and sculptors were in continuous employ.

Towards the beginning of the C4 AD the tombs become less ornate, though as numerous as ever. This decline ended in the middle of the century when the town was burnt, presumably when Gallus Caesar in 352 suppressed a Jewish revolt against Byzantine rule. Occupation was sparse in the Byzantine period, and in the Arab period only tomb robbers frequented the ruins. Memory of the great necropolis vanished so completely that in the Middle Ages Jews venerated the tomb of Rabbi Judah ha-Nasi in Sepphoris. The site was rediscovered only in 1936.

Visit. Open. Sunday–Thursday 8 a.m.–6 p.m.; Friday 8 a.m.–1 p.m.; Saturday 8 a.m.–4 p.m. The site is composed of two parts, the town on the crest of the hill, which is outside the park, and the necropolis below.

The Town

The first ruins on the left of the access road are houses. Behind them is the wall of a **synagogue**, most of which is under a garden. It was oriented towards Jerusalem by three doors. The foundation of the synagogue is not precisely dated, but it is certainly prior to the middle of the C4 AD. A hoard of 1,200 coins (all C4 but none later than 351), found in the two-storey building between the synagogue and the present road, provides a date for the destruction level covering the whole area.

About 100 m further on is an **olive press**. Baskets of olives were stacked between two uprights on the circular grooved stone, a heavy horizontal beam let into a notch in the wall acted as a lever to press out the oil which flowed round the circular groove into a plastered basin in the rock floor. At a later stage a monumental gate was inserted between the two-room olive press and a building to the west; note how the doorways on either side had to be modified. The whole complex is dated to the C4 AD.

Almost 200 m from the olive press, and some 25 m up the slope from the point where the road begins to curve sharply is the **basilica**. Designed as a multipurpose public building, it is a simple rectangle divided by two rows of columns, with a raised platform at the end opposite the doors which opened on to a wide court. The quality of the stonework indicates that it was built at a time of great prosperity; hence, in the late C2 or early C3 AD.

The Necropolis

A small **museum** is located in an ancient rock-cut reservoir near the parking-lot. In addition to artefacts and thematic displays, it illustrates the development of the *menorah* in Jewish art. The necropolis contains thirty-one catacombs which vary considerably in design. Unfortunately only one (catacomb 20) is open to the public.

The proportions of the courtyard enhance the triple-arched façade of **catacomb 20**. The three stone doors, which are cut to imitate wood studded with nails, lead into a 50 m-long hall, with rooms on both sides. The plan is irregular with much wasted space. This is the oldest catacomb on the site, and is dated in the lifetime of Rabbi Judah ha-Nasi. Two types of burial were envisaged. Some rooms were intended for sarcophagi placed against the walls or in special recesses. In other rooms single-grave *arcosolia* (arch recessed into wall) were cut, some with niches for bone deposits. In addition to 200 such graves, the catacomb contains 125 sarcophagi whose placement (as space became a problem) was dictated by expediency. Manifestly this was a public cemetery.

All the inscriptions in this catacomb are in Hebrew. There is no doubt that those interred here were Jewish. This makes the decoration all the more surprising. Eros, Aphrodite, Nike, and Amazons are the most explicit borrowings from pagan mythology. Their presence in a centre of religious orthodoxy demonstrates that rabbis of the C3 AD made a distinction between images intended for worship and images intended as simply decorative. They mitigated the absolute character of the Second Commandment by emphasizing the second sentence, 'You shall not bow down before them' (Exod. 20: 4–5; Deut. 5: 8–9).

The plan of the unfinished triple entrance of **catacomb 14** was borrowed from catacomb 20, but the function of this catacomb was quite different. A vast amount of space is devoted to very few burials; it can only have been a family tomb. The only inscriptions mention three rabbis, Shimon, Gamaliel, and Hanina. The first two were sons of Rabbi Judah ha-Nasi, and the third was a close collaborator. It seems likely, therefore, that this was the tomb that the Patriarch had prepared for himself and his family. The built tomb in the back room may be the tomb of the Patriarch himself. The simplicity of the graves here is in vivid contrast to the ornate sarcophagi in catacomb 20; in a family unit all were honoured by the monumental façade.

Both catacombs (14 and 20) are surmounted by **open-air structures** comprising rows of benches and a wall with an apse. These were assembly places where the dead were remembered in prayer and study. The plain square mosaic floor above catacomb 23 (between 20 and 14) without benches probably served the same function.

The great development of the cemetery that followed on the burial there of Rabbi ha-Nasi brought with it commercial rationalization, and all the catacombs cut subsequently conform to a common plan. A certain flexibility was necessary, however, because some clients could afford more than others. Catacomb 12 was designed for the wealthy; it is spacious and well organized, the one-grave *arcosolia* in one hall are carefully segregated from the less expensive multi-grave *arcosolia* in the other hall. Just alongside is catacomb 13 where the intention was obviously to get the maximum number of graves into the minimum space. The area is roughly the same, but whereas catacomb 12 has 56 burial places in two halls on the same level, catacomb 13 has 192 burial places in twelve halls on four levels. No provision was made for sarcophagi in any of the later catacombs; their size and weight (four tons) would have raised costs to an unacceptable level.

Bethlehem (J18) ★★

The town is first mentioned in the C14 BC when the king of Jerusalem wrote to his Egyptian overlord asking for archers to help him recover Bit-Lahmi which had seceded from his jurisdiction (see box), but it really enters history with the figure of David. He was born there (1 Sam. 16) to an Ephrathite family who had lived there for many generations (Ruth 1–4). When the jealousy of Saul forced him to become an outlaw, he led an attack on the PHILISTINES (1 Sam. 23: 5) who, in reprisal, put a garrison in Bethlehem (2 Sam. 23: 14). The only piece of information concerning the character of the town at this period is provided by David's nostalgic cry, 'O that someone would give me water to drink from the well of Bethlehem which is by the gate!' (2 Sam. 23: 15); when three of his followers broke through the Philistines to get it for him, he refused to drink because of the risk they had taken. Even though Bethlehem was a walled city, David decided not to make it his capital, because Saul had greatly diminished his own effectiveness by locating the capital in the territory of the tribe to which he belonged.

An Exasperated Letter from Jerusalem

'To the king, my lord say: Thus Abdu-Heba [king of Jerusalem], thy servant. At the two feet of the king, my lord, seven times and seven times I fall. Behold the deed which Mikilu [king of Gezer] and Shuwardata [king of Hebron] did to the land of the king, my lord! They rushed troops of Gezer, troops of Gath and troops of Keilah; they took the Rubutu, the land of the king went over to the Apiru people. But now even a town of the land of Jerusalem, Bit-Lahmi by name, a town belonging to the king, has gone over to the people of Keilah. Let my king hearken to Abdu-Heba, thy servant, and let him send archers to recover the royal land for the king! But if there are no archers, the land of the king will pass over to the Apiru people.' (*Amarna Letter*, n. 290; trans. W. F. Albright)

David's grandson Rehoboam (928–911 BC) fortified Bethlehem, together with Etam (POOLS OF SOLOMON) and Tekoa, to protect the eastern flank of his kingdom (2 Chr. 11: 6). Two centuries later Bethlehem was an insignificant village, but intimately associated with the Messianic hope, 'You Bethlehem Ephrathah, the least among the clans of Judah, from you shall come forth for me one who is to be ruler in Israel, whose origin is from of old, from ancient days' (Mic. 5: 1). An archaeological survey has shown that the town of this period (C10–C8 BC) was in the area of the Church of the Nativity and that the caves beneath the church were then in use. Presumably the 123 Bethlehemites listed among those who returned from the Exile in the C6 BC (Ezra 2: 21) resettled in their ancient home.

Mary and Joseph were natives of Bethlehem, and only moved to NAZARETH because of the atmosphere of insecurity generated by the Herodian dynasty (Matt. 2). Their long residence in Galilee gave Luke the impression that they had always lived there and he had to find a reason which would place them in Bethlehem at the moment of the birth of Jesus (Luke 2: 1–7). He mistakenly invoked the census of Quirinius, but this took place in AD 6. The Greek underlying the phrase, 'she laid him in a manger because there was no room for them in the inn' (Luke 2: 7) can also be rendered, 'she laid him in a manger because they had no space in the room'. We should envisage an overflowing one-room house. The gospels make no mention of a cave, yet in the C2 AD Justin and the *Protoevangelium of James* speak of the cave in which Jesus was born. Many houses in the area are still built in front of caves, and perhaps we should envisage Joseph (then living with his parents) as taking his wife into such a back area in order to give birth away from the confusion of the living room; the cave part would have been used for stabling and storage.

In AD 395 Jerome wrote, 'From Hadrian's time (135 AD) until the reign of Constantine, for about 180 years . . . Bethlehem, now ours, and the earth's, most sacred spot . . . was overshadowed by a grove of Thammuz, which is Adonis, and in the cave where the infant Messiah once cried, the paramour of Venus was bewailed' (*Epistle* 58); Cyril of Jerusalem, writing before AD 348, also mentions that the area was wooded. Hadrian had expelled Jews from the Bethlehem area, thus giving free rein to the development of pagan cults; Thammuz was beloved by farmers as the personification of the seed which dies and springs to life again. The commemoration of his mythical death in the cave may have been motivated by a desire to interfere with the veneration of Christians. In this case bitterness would have reinforced the memory of the local tradition attested in the C2 by Justin, and in the C3 by Origen and Eusebius. Pre-Constantinian localizations of sacred sites have much greater validity than identifications which first appear in the C4 when the questions of pilgrims stimulated the imaginations of local guides.

The first church was dedicated on 31 May 339. The octagonal apse (Fig. 54) was sited directly above the cave which was entered by stairs passing under the stone chancel screen [1]. In the centre a 4 m-wide hole [2] surrounded by a railing offered a view of the cave. The only visible element of this church are sections of the mosaic pavement. The cave must have undergone certain alterations but these have been so completely absorbed by later modifications that no details are available. Given the slope of the hill, the natural entrance must have been on the north or west.

In 384 Jerome took up residence in Bethlehem, to be joined two years later by Paula and her daughter Eustochium. Together they made Bethlehem a great monastic centre; within this framework Jerome wrote prolifically, his most notable achievement being a new translation of the Old and New Testaments (the Vulgate) which remained the authoritative version of the Bible for Catholics until the C20. One of the caves (Fig. 55) is identified as Jerome's study [1]. This is probably legendary, but the existence of caves adjacent to the main cave [8] is implied by Jerome's assertion that Paula 'was buried beneath the church beside the cave of the Lord'. There he interred Eustochium, and arranged a place for his own burial. A C6 pilgrim noted that his tomb was in a cave.

According to Eutychius of Alexandria (C9), after the Samaritan uprising of AD 529, 'The Emperor Justinian ordered his envoy to pull down the church of Bethlehem, which was a small one, and to build it again of such splendour, size and beauty that none even in the Holy City should surpass it.' He lengthened the church by one bay, added a narthex, and replaced the octagonal apse by a more spacious triapsidal form. This building has remained in use to the present day. The destructive Persians (614) passed

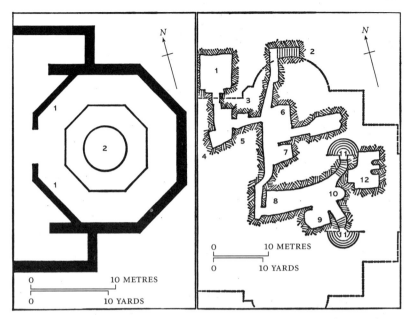

▲ **Fig. 54.** (*left*) Bethlehem. Reconstruction of the C4 apse of the Church of the Nativity (after Bagatti). 1. Chancel screen; 2. Hole.

Fig. 55. (*right*) Bethlehem. Caves beneath the Church of the Nativity. 1. Study of St Jerome; 2. Entrance from Franciscan church; 3. Tomb of Eusebius of Cremona; 4. Tomb of St Jerome; 5. Tombs of Paula and Eustochium; 6. Chapel of the Holy Innocents; 7. Chapel of St Joseph; 8. Cave of the Nativity; 9. Manger altar. 10. Birth altar; 11. Entrances from the basilica; 12. Cistern.

it by because they found the Magi in familiar dress represented in the mosaic on the façade (this was quoted at a C9 synod in Jerusalem to show the utility of images). Muslims prevented the application of Hakim's decree (1009) ordering the destruction of Christian monuments because, since the time of Omar (639), they had been permitted to use the south transept for their devotions.

Tancred's night ride from Latrun on 6 June 1099 secured the church before the Muslims could react. Baldwin I and II were crowned there, and in an extraordinary display of tolerance the Franks and Byzantines co-operated in the restoration of the church between 1165 and 1169. In the north transept is preserved a Greek inscription which reads, 'This work was brought to completion by the monk Ephram, the painter of history and mosaic master craftsman, during the rule of the great emperor Manuel Porphyrogenitus Comnenus, and in the days of Amaury, king of Jerusalem, and in the time of the bishop of Bethlehem, Raoul, in the year 1169, the second of the indication'. All the interior decoration was renewed and the roof replaced.

After the fall of the Latin Kingdom (1187), Ayyubid respect for the holy place preserved the church, but this dynasty was supplanted by the Mamluks in the C13 and they saw it only as a source of revenue and political leverage. Repairs were permitted only infrequently; deterioration was assisted by pillage. Felix Fabri, a C15 pilgrim, describes the interior as 'a barn without hay, an apothecary's without aromatic pots, a library without books'. With the arrival of the Ottoman Turks in 1517 looting became systematic; much of the marble in the HARAM ESH-SHARIF came from Bethlehem. Despite an earthquake in 1834, and a fire in 1869 which destroyed the furnishings of the cave, the church survives; its dignity, though battered, is not tarnished.

Visit (Fig. 56). (Open: 5.30 a.m.–6.30 p.m. (May–October); to 5 p.m. (November–January); to 6 p.m. (February–April).) The **façade**, when viewed from the open paved area [1] which replaced the original atrium in the Middle Ages, is a summary of the church's history. The three C6 entrances are still visible, but the two lateral doors are betrayed only by the tips of the cornice mouldings, one [2] projecting beyond the C19 buttress, the other [4] all but hidden by the Armenian monastery bounding the paved area on the south. The great centre door [3] is clearly outlined, but a broken arch shows how it was reduced by the Crusaders; it was made even smaller in the Mamluk or Turkish period to prevent looters driving carts into the church.

▼ **Fig. 56.** Bethlehem. Church of the Nativity. 1. Buttress; 2. C6 lintel; 3. Entrance; 4. C6 lintel; 5. Narthex; 6. Armenian carving; 7. Entrance to Franciscan cloister; 8. Aisle closure; 9. St Cathal; 10. C4 mosaic floor; 11. St Canute; 12. St Olaf; 13. C4 baptismal font; 14. Entrance to Franciscan church; 15. Entrance to caves; 16. C4 mosaic floor; 17. Entrance to Nativity cave; 18. Greek Orthodox altar.

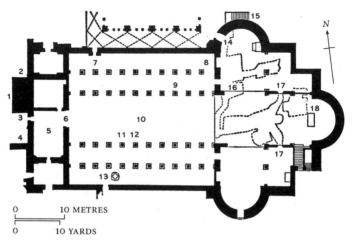

▲ **Main Door of the Nativity Church in Bethlehem.** The battered façade is mute witness to the turbulent history of the edifice. The height of the C6 lintel reveals the size of the original entrance. The blocked arched door is medieval, and the present entrance Mamluk or Ottoman.

The Justinian **narthex** [5] was a long open corridor; the present partitions are of varying date. All but one [6] of the three doors of the church have been blocked up; the carved panels in the upper part of the centre door are all that remain of a splendid wooden door given by two Armenians in 1227. The C4 church had no narthex.

With the exception of the roof and floor, which have been replaced several times, the structure of the body of the church is as it was in the time of Justinian; the closure of the aisles [8] took place in the Middle Ages.

Most of the red limestone **pillars**, quarried near Bethlehem, served in the C4 church whose outer walls are still in use. From 1130 individual Crusaders decorated the upper part of the pillars with paintings of saints whose names appear in Latin and/or Greek. Note particularly Cathal of Ireland [**9**], Canute IV of Denmark (d. 1086) [**11**], and Olaf II Haraldsson of Norway (d. 1030) [**12**]. These two kings played a major role in the Christianization of Scandinavia, whereas Cathal was the patron of the Normans from Sicily.

The octagonal **baptismal font** [**13**] originally stood near the high altar [**18**] of the C6 church; the inscription reads, 'For remembrance, rest, and remission of sins of those whose names the Lord knows'. Archaeologists found an octagonal bed of exactly the same dimensions over a cistern ([**12**] in Fig. 55) which provided the required water. After the Baptistery was moved in the Crusader renovation of the church the cistern became the focus of various legends, it was the well into which the star of the Magi fell, the well where the Magi watered their beasts, and the well to which David's three heroes came!

A small door [**7**] leads to the restored **medieval cloister** in front of the Franciscan church of St Catherine built in 1881. Wooden trap doors [**10**] cover the **mosaic floor** of the C4 church. Similar doors [**16**] protect another mosaic of the same period showing the Constantinian apse to have been octagonal; these are sometimes opened on request.

The remains of **mosaic decoration on the walls of the nave** date from the restoration of 1165–9. Each side had three registers; the detailed description made by the Franciscan Qaresmius in 1628 enables us to complete the missing sections. The lowest depicted the ancestors of Jesus according to Luke 3: 23–38 (north wall) and according to Matt. 1: 1–16 (south wall). The middle register of the north wall contained the key decisions of six provincial councils. The text from the Council of Antioch (AD 272), for example, reads, 'The Holy Synod of Antioch in Syria of 33 bishops took place before the Ecumenical Council of Nicaea against Paul of Samosata who held that Christ was a mere man. The Holy Synod expelled him as a heretic'; the other text (to the left) is from the Council of Sardica (347). The corresponding register on the south wall enshrined the decisions of six ecumenical councils, from left to right the preserved fragments recall the Councils of Nicaea (325), Constantinople (381), Ephesus (431), Chalcedon (451), and Constantinople (680). According to Qaresmius, only one council text was in Latin, that of Nicaea (787) which condemned the iconoclast heresy; by deciding in favour of the legitimacy of images it made the flowering of church art possible. The top register on both sides is composed of a series of angels between the windows. The name of the artist appears at the foot of the third angel from the right on the north wall, 'Basilius Pictor'; it is written with the syllables placed one above the other.

The entire west wall was covered with mosaic; Old Testament

prophets, each holding a text considered to refer to Jesus, sat in the branches of the tree of Jesse. The mosaics of the transepts and choir recorded scenes from the life of Jesus.

A pilgrim in 870 described the present entrances to the **birth cave** [**17**] ([**11**] in Fig. 55); the northern one was used by Arculf in 670 because (subsequent numbers in this paragraph refer to Fig. 55) he encountered the birthplace [**10**] before coming to the site of the manger [**9**]. The main body of the present cave [**8**] certainly existed at this period because traces of an earlier entrance have been found at the west end (now blocked by a door). All the furnishings are subsequent to the fire of 1869.

The passage linking the cave of the Nativity with the **other caves** to the north has not been dated with certitude. Felix Fabri observed it in 1480; then, as now, it was closed to pilgrims. To enter these caves one must leave the church by the small door in the north transept [**14**] and use a medieval entrance [**15**] ([**2**] in Fig. 55 to which subsequent numbers refer). Pottery and pre-Constantinian masonry suggest that these caves were in use in the C1 and C2 AD; they have been significantly modified since and were given their present form in 1964. The various elements are identified as the cell of Jerome [**1**], the tombs of Jerome [**4**], Paula, and Eustochium [**5**], and Eusebius of Cremona, the successor of Jerome as head of the monastic community [**3**], the chapels of the Holy Innocents [**6**] and of St Joseph [**7**]. These identifications have no historical value.

Bethsaida (N5)

Despite Jesus' extensive ministry in Galilee, only three towns/villages are mentioned by name, CAPERNAUM, CHOROZAIN, and Bethsaida (Matt. 11: 21–4). All are criticized for their lack of faith in Jesus, despite the fact that he worked miracles in each. In Bethsaida he restored sight to a blind man (Mark 8: 22–6). The attitude of the town stands in vivid contrast to that of some of its native sons, Peter, Andrew, and Philip (John 1: 44), who gave up all to follow Jesus.

The earliest occupation of the site dates from the first part of the third millennium BC. Then apparently there is a gap until the Iron Age, which is followed by a further break until the site was resettled in the C2 BC. Under the will of Herod the Great the area came into the hands of his son Philip (4 BC–AD 34). He brought in new settlers, raised the village to the rank of a city, and renamed it Julias (*Antiquities* 18: 28). According to Josephus, the Julia in question was the daughter of the emperor Augustus. This, however, is improbable. A much more likely candidate is the mother of the reigning emperor, Tiberius (AD 14–37). Around AD 30 Philip minted coins with the inscription 'Julia Augusta' and the image of Augustus' wife Livia.

Fish and Fishing

Fish is still an important industry on the Sea of Galilee. In antiquity meat was very expensive, except when a surplus came on the market during great feasts when there were many sacrifices. Fish, in consequence, was the main source of protein for the majority. Its price was carefully controlled, and legislation restricted the number of middlemen. Fishmongers were considered only slightly less depraved than money lenders.

Some 200 different species of fish were available in the eastern Mediterranean, but how many of these existed in the Sea of Galilee is unknown. The sea was ringed by little harbours from which boats like that conserved in Kibbutz Ginnosar set forth. It has a length of 9 m, a beam of 2.5 m, and is 1.25 m from keel to rail. It could hold four men (*War* 2: 635) and fishing nets. Two types of nets are attested, the seine net, which is hauled on to the shore (Matt. 13: 47–8), and the trammel net, which is pulled into the boat (Luke 5: 4–7).

Fish did not long stay fresh in the heat of Galilee. To be transported any distance they had to be preserved. The Hebrew and Greek names of a site between Tiberias and Capernaum reveal the two techniques. 'Magdala' comes from 'Migdal Nunnaya', meaning 'Tower of Fish', and evokes a wooden structure in which fish were smoked. 'Taricheae' means a place where fish were pickled. The quality of its product was known as far away as Rome (Strabo, *Geography* 16: 2. 45).

The implication that fishing on the Sea of Galilee was well organized is confirmed by what we are told about Jesus' companions. Peter and Andrew worked in partnership (Luke 5: 7) with James and John, the sons of Zebedee (Luke 5: 10), who had employees (Mark 1: 20). One has the impression that they owned their own boats (Luke 5: 11). They apparently worked under a system whereby fishing rights were farmed out to those who could guarantee a certain supply.

She took the name Julia when she was adopted into the Julian family in AD 14 (Tacitus, *Annals* 1: 8), and died in AD 29. Hence, Philip's interest in Bethsaida must be dated late in his reign. The Hellenistic character of the city is underlined by the fact that Andrew and Philip both have Greek names (with no correspondence in a Semitic language), and both spoke Greek (John 12: 20–2). Herod Philip died here, but it is not clear whether the tomb he had prepared was also in Julias (*Antiquities* 18: 108). The city did not survive the First Revolt (AD 66–70).

Visit. The site is 750 m north of the Bethsaida Junction on the west side of route 888 (Fig. 107). The excavation is still at an early stage, and it is not decided what remains will be conserved.

It seems very likely, however, that one building will survive. It is a 430 m² house of the period C2 BC–AD C1 built around three sides of a paved courtyard (13.5 × 7 m). There are four small rooms on the north, a kitchen with two ovens on the east, and a single large room on the south. Scattered through these rooms were a fishing hook, lead weights for nets, and a curved bronze needle which could be used to make or repair a sail. It is hard to avoid the conclusion that a fishing family owned the house. Peter and Andrew belonged to such a family (Mark 1: 16)!

The distance of Bethsaida from the sea—2 km as the crow flies— might explain why at some point the brothers moved to Capernaum (Mark 1: 21, 29), which is located right on the lake. Much less time would be wasted going back and forwards to their boat. The move to Capernaum also made economic sense. The Jordan river was a border, as we know from the fact that the first village on the other side, Capernaum, had a customs post (Matt. 9: 9) backed up by a small garrison under a centurion. (Matt. 8: 5). Those like Peter and Andrew who came from the territory of Philip had to pay a tax as they crossed the border. Thus it cost them more to have their fish smoked or pickled at Magdala/Taricheae in the territory of Herod Antipas. It was cheaper to become residents of Capernaum.

Caesarea* (G9) ★★

Capital of Palestine for almost 600 years, later a Crusader port, Caesarea was renowned for the splendour of its buildings. Three of its columns are now in Venice, and its most beautiful stones adorn the C18 AD structures of Jezzar Pasha in AKKO. None the less, recent excavations and careful restorations enable the visitor to recapture the highpoints of its colourful history.

The city was founded by Herod the Great (37–4 BC) on the site of an ancient fortified town known as Strato's Tower. Strato is the Greek form of a name borne by three kings of Sidon in the C4 BC, and a century earlier in gratitude for the assistance of the Sidonian fleet in the invasion of Greece, the Persians had granted the coast between DOR and Yafo (Jaffa) to Sidon. The anchorage served traders plying between Phoenicia and Egypt: it is first mentioned by Zenon, an Egyptian official, who landed there for supplies in 259 BC. The town changed hands many times before the emperor Augustus gave it to Herod in 30 BC.

Josephus waxes even more lyrical than usual about the marvels of Herod's constructions (*War* 1: 408–15, *Antiquities* 15: 331–41), being particularly impressed by the size of the port and the ingenuity of the sewer system. He also mentions the grid street pattern, a temple dedicated to Caesar, a palace, a theatre, an amphitheatre—and the fact that all was completed in 12 years (22–10 BC)! After the Romans assumed direct control of Palestine in AD 6 Caesarea became the capital. Presumably the official representative of Rome had his residence there from this time, but the first of whom we are certain is Pontius Pilate (AD 26–36); an inscription bearing his name was found in the ruins of the theatre. Cornelius, a centurion of the Roman garrison, was the first Gentile converted to Christianity by Peter (Acts 10). Paul passed through the port several times on his missionary journeys, and was imprisoned for two years (AD 58–60) in Herod's praetorium until he forced a decision by demanding to be judged by the emperor (Acts 23–6).

Tensions between Jews and Gentiles always ran high in Caesarea; the desecration of the synagogue was one of the contributory causes of the First Revolt (AD 66–70). When Vespasian arrived to put it down, he established his headquarters in the city, and directed operations from there until the legions acclaimed him emperor in AD 69. Thereafter, the city became a Roman colony, though with limited rights. Even though the harbour had been destroyed by the earthquake of AD 130, the prosperity of Caesarea increased continuously, creating an environment which made other developments possible, notably scholarship.

At the beginning of the C3 AD, after the city had been declared levitically clean, Bar Qappara founded a rabbinical School which soon rivalled that of his master, Rabbi Judah ha-Nasi, at SEPPHORIS. A graduate of this school, Yohanan bar Nappaha, founded the great academy at TIBERIAS, but the glory of rabbinical Caesarea is Abbahu, who was active around the beginning of the C4 AD. The anti-Christian polemic which characterized the rabbis of Caesarea was nullified by the irenic brilliance of Origen (185–254). The tradition of scholarship which he inaugurated during his 20-year residence here (231–50) was continued by Pamphilius (d. 309). By adding to the manuscript collection of Origen he created a library second only to that of Alexandria; in 630 it had 30,000 volumes. His pupil Eusebius (260–340), who became bishop of Caesarea in 314, is both the first church historian and the first biblical geographer; without his *Onomasticon* many biblical sites would never have been identified.

The intellectual vitality of Caesarea had virtually disappeared long before the city fell to the Arabs in 640; they crept in through the low-level aqueduct. The port had gone out of use at this stage, but the fertility of the hinterland continued to make it one of the richest cities in the area. None the less there was a continuous decline in populations, and by the C10 the city had contracted to approximately the present walled area. Fatimid fortifications underlie the extant Crusader defences. It had been briefly retaken twice by the Byzantines (685 and 975) before falling to the Crusaders in May 1101. An hexagonal green glass thought to be the Holy Grail formed part of the booty of the Genoese; it is still preserved in the cathedral of San Lorenzo in Genoa. Since the Crusaders relied principally on Akko and Yafo, they rehabilitated only part of the Herodian port.

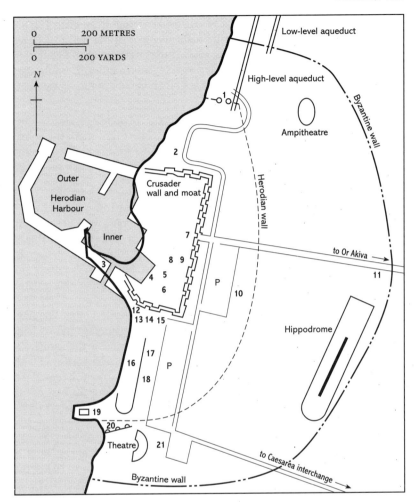

▲ **Fig. 57.** Caesarea (after Ziek and Porat). The Herodian harbour is superimposed on the present coastline. 1. Herodian city gate; 2. Synagogue area; 3. Crusader citadel; 4. Herodian quay; 5. Octagonal church; 6. Great mosque/Crusader cathedral; 7. East gate; 8. Frankish house; 9. Covered Crusader street; 10. Byzantine street and statues; 11. Arch; 12. Entrance to the Crusader city; 13. Byzantine bath; 14. Archive building; 15. Ticket office; 16. Amphitheatre; 17. Vaulted warehouses; 18. Storage buildings; 19. Herod's palace; 20. Byzantine fortress; 21. Pontius Pilate inscription.

Caesarea fell to Saladin in July 1187. He demolished the fortifications in 1191, as did al-Muazzam in 1219. The refortification begun in 1228 was completed by Louis IX of France between March 1251 and May 1252. The defences offered no effective resistance to the Mamluk sultan Baybars in

February 1265. The inhabitants, who had taken refuge in the citadel on the southern breakwater, escaped by night to Akko in the midst of peace negotiations; in reprisal Baybars levelled the city. It lay abandoned until 1878 when the Turks installed Muslim refugees from Bosnia on the site. Their little mosque beside the port is all that remains of the village obliterated in 1948.

Visit. The exit from the Tel Aviv–Haifa highway (route 2) is clearly indicated at the Caesarea interchange. Much smaller signs mark the access road skirting Sedot Yam. The area around the theatre and within the Crusader walls is a national park; a ticket bought in one area should be retained for entrance into the other. Open: 8 a.m.–4 p.m., Fridays 3 p.m.

South of the Crusader City

The theatre is the first monument encountered coming from the highway (Fig. 57). Just inside the entrance [21] is a replica of the **Pontius Pilate inscription**. A suggested restoration reads: 'Pontius Pilate, Prefect of Judaea, made and dedicated the Tiberieum to the Divine Augustus'. Its proximity to the large marble foot is probably accidental, but Pilate's tended to end up in his mouth.

The original **theatre** was built by Herod, the earliest in the country; it would have accommodated about 4,000 spectators. In subsequent centuries some elements were modified and others added; the semicircular platform behind the stage is dated to the C3 AD. The great wall with towers [20] is part of a Byzantine fortress of the C6 AD, which reused the high back of the theatre as part of the defences. It became the base of the provincial governor after Samaritans and Jews burnt his palace in 555. Caesarea's non-Christian hinterland became progressively more aggressive as the Byzantine empire declined.

The use of the theatre for concerts makes a fence imperative. It is unclear whether there will be direct access to the excavations. Hence the rest of the visit is described as beginning from the ticket office [15] near the Archive Building.

The main entrance of the Byzantine **Archive Building** [14] is on the west side of the *Cardo Maximus*, the main street of a Roman city. It gives access to a courtyard around which are disposed eight rooms. The identification of the edifice is based on a series of inscriptions, of which one reads, 'Christ help Ampelios, the keeper of the archives, and Musonius, the financial secretary, and the other archivists of the same depository'.

The **Cardo Maximus** was 5.5 m wide and paved with limestone blocks laid on the diagonal; beneath it is a 3 m-wide vaulted sewer. The columns on either side are spaced about 3 m apart and supported roofs that protected the patterned mosaic pavements, each as wide as the street. In their present form all these elements are Byzantine, but it is extremely probable that the Herodian Cardo followed the same line. Sections of this great street can be traced in a straight line to the south.

The circular and semicircular structures further west [**13**] belong to a **bath-house** of the Byzantine period. At this point one can go right into the Crusader city [**12**] or left along the sea-front.

Lining the sea-front, which served originally as an additional anchorage in fine weather, and then as an improvised harbour in the C2–C3 AD, are four long vaulted **warehouses** [**17**] of the C3 AD. At a later stage the northernmost warehouse was transformed into a **Mithraeum** by the addition of benches along the sides and an altar at the far end. An off-centre light-shaft near the eastern end of the vault permits a ray of sunlight to fall on the altar at noon on 21 June. This Mithraeum must have served the Roman garrison, and is the only one known in Palestine. It probably went out of use in the C4 AD. Smaller storage areas of the Byzantine period run along the south side of these warehouses. These face onto a street that crosses the Cardo Maximus at right angles. On the left just before that intersection is a large public **latrine**.

The area [**18**] between this street and the wooden walkway is made up of six buildings constructed as part of a unified development in the Byzantine period. All are built around courtyards and served for storage. A number of **granaries** are sunk into the ground. **Liquids**, such as wine and oil, were stored in rooms with one or more circular jars sunk into the floor. Any spillage was swept into them for recovery. On the other side of the walkway is a vast **Byzantine bath**.

According to Josephus, 'south of the harbour and set back from the shore Herod built an **amphitheatre** capable of accommodating a large crowd of people, and conveniently located for a view over the sea' (*Antiquities* 15: 341). Once one recognizes the fluidity of Josephus' use of the term 'amphitheatre', this description perfectly fits the stepped structure, whose curved south end and east side are well preserved [**16**]. Its proportions (50 × 290 m) mean that it could have been used for a variety of entertainments from chariot races to running. The podium wall was 1.7 m above the original floor, and above it on the east side were twelve rows of seats. Here in 11 BC Herod celebrated the great games inaugurating the new city (*Antiquities* 16. 138–9). The open land east of the amphitheatre was developed for residential construction in the mid-C1 AD. A portico was laid along the top of the east wall of the amphitheatre, and the shallow valley between it and the next kurkar ridge filled in with debris.

The upgrading of racing facilities by the construction of the large hippodrome in the mid-C2 AD meant that the amphitheatre was no longer needed for equestrian sports. At this stage a curving wall was built across the arena some 130 m from the south end to give the space a shape closer to that of the standard amphitheatre. The complex went out of use in the C3 AD when the true amphitheatre was constructed. In the waste land a lover of beauty created a sunken garden with a covered **absidal hall** and a fountain.

From the theatre area a rocky promontory [**19**] juts out into the sea. Its most distinctive feature is a rectangular **rock-cut pool** (35 × 18 × 2 m) with what appears to be a square statue base in the middle. It was originally the centre–piece of a large two-storey building (83 × 51 m) which can only have been the private wing of **Herod's palace**. It was from here that he oversaw the construction of the harbour and other amenities. Colonnades lined the three sea sides of the pool. At the north-east corner a staircase led up 6 m to the level of the public (administrative) wing of the palace, which was juxtaposed to the amphitheatre. It was built around a large courtyard. The rooms on the south side have been completely destroyed by the action of the sea.

The Herodian Harbour

From land nothing is visible of the great harbour that was the *raison d'être* of Caesarea. Underwater exploration, however, has revealed its dimensions with a rather high degree of precision; they complement the admiring description of Josephus (see box).

Underwater excavations have revealed that the great foundation blocks were in fact wooden forms filled with rubble held together by underwater mortar made of lime combined with *pozzolana*, a volcanic ash from central Italy. Josephus does not mention the inner harbour, whose eastern limit was just in front of the podium of the temple of Augustus and some 80 m inland from the present shore line. Its western limit is marked

---

Herod's Harbour

'Having calculated the relative size of the harbour Herod let down stone blocks into the sea to a depth of 20 fathoms. Most of them were 50 feet long, 9 high, and 10 wide, some even larger. When the submarine foundation was finished, he then laid out the mole above sea-level, 200 feet across. Of this, a 100-foot portion was built out to break the force of the waves, and consequently was called the breakwater. The rest supported the stone wall that encircled the harbour. At intervals along it were great towers, the tallest and most magnificent of which was named Drusion, after the stepson of Caesar. There were numerous vaulted chambers for the reception of those entering the harbour, and the whole curving structure in front of them was a wide promenade for those who disembarked. The entrance channel faced north, for in this region the north wind always brings the clearest skies. At the harbour entrance were colossal statues, three on either side, set up on columns. A massively built tower supported the columns on the port side of boats entering the harbour, whereas those on the starboard side were supported by two upright blocks of stone yoked together and higher than the tower on the other side.' (*War* 1: 411–13)

by a circular tower, now in 1 m of water some 20 m from the bathing beach; it must have anchored a seawall running to the north.

There are two geological fault-lines about 250 m apart running north–south just outside the modern harbour. When the rock between them subsided, probably in the earthquake of AD 130, the whole of the great harbour dropped nearly 6 m. Its moles then would have been just beneath the surface, ready to tear the bottom out of any unwary ship. There are seventeen shipwrecks on the breakwater. At this stage the bay between the breakwater and the promontory [19] was transformed into an improvised harbour. In 502 the emperor Anastasius (491–518) is praised for repair works, 'The city welcomes ships with confidence and she is filled with all necessities' (Procopius of Gaza).

The Crusader City

The Crusader city represents only a fraction of the area occupied by earlier cities; the Herodian city was over three times greater, and the Byzantine city nearly eight times as large (Fig. 57). The population of the last mentioned is estimated at 100,000. Thus the Crusaders would have numbered about 12,000.

The existing **wall and moat** date from the last reconstruction under Louis IX of France (1251–2). In most places only the sloping glacis remains; originally a 10 m wall rose above it. There was a gate in each of the three walls. The principal entrance to the city was the **East Gate** [7], which has been beautifully restored; its roof is one of the very few points from which a panoramic view is possible. Just inside the gate to the left (south) are the arches of a Crusader **covered street** [9] and just off it a **Frankish house** [8] built in the eastern style around a central court.

The excavated area [4] is well signposted. The key element is the podium mentioned by Josephus: 'at the edge of the harbour, upon a podium, was a **temple of Augustus**' (*War* 1: 414). This podium was linked to the quay of the inner harbour [4] by a monumental stairway. In the C2 AD the northern projection was transformed into an elegant **fountain**. A century later vaulted **warehouses** were constructed to fill the space between these projections.

The same podium supported the elegant C6 **octagonal church** [5] and the great mosque of the early Arab period, which later became the **Crusader cathedral** dedicated to St Peter [6]. It appears to have been damaged or demolished by the Ayyubids. The existing apse with the polygonal exterior represents the foundations of a temporary edifice (1228?), behind which the three apses of the C13 church were being constructed. Subsequently this single apse was buried beneath the floor of the new church, which was standing in 1265 when Baybars made it his command post for the siege of the citadel.

The Crusader **citadel** [3] was located on the south breakwater. The much restored central element is now crowned by a restaurant. It was surrounded by four towers. The two on the east are visible on either side of the causeway just beyond the western end of the row of modern shops; the marble and granite columns integrated into the base of these towers made them impossible to sap. Moreover, they fronted on a 20 m-wide sea moat separating the city from the citadel.

East and North of the Crusader City

In the eastern section of the main parking-lot a **Byzantine street** [10] has been brought to light. An inscription at the foot of the steps attributes it to Flavius Strategius, a mayor of the C6. Two columns create a triple entrance to a square paved with marble slabs. The **two statues** are much older (C2–C3 AD) and originally belonged to temples. The white marble statue is unidentified, but the dark porphyry one is considered to represent the emperor Hadrian (AD 117–38) holding a sceptre and orb. The statue was probably commissioned from the one porphyry quarry in the ancient world, in Egypt, during his first visit to Caesarea (AD 130) and dedicated during his second visit three or four years later. The present green granite chair is not the original; the side had to be broken to take the statue.

Immediately north of the Crusader wall, in which there is a ruined gate, is the **synagogue area** [2]. The remains left by the archaeologists do not offer any coherent pattern. A series of superimposed synagogues was built here from the C3 to the C5 AD. Foundations of houses of the Hellenistic period (C4–C2 BC) were found at the lowest level. The massive section of rubble wall in the sea a little to the north was part of the Byzantine fortification system. Between it and the shore 30 m of a 4 m-wide quay have survived, the use of lead dovetail clamps to join the finely cut blocks is typical of Herodian construction, but the structure appears to have been in use from the C3 to the C2 BC.

Just about this point the road crosses a large **city wall** with three towers [1]. The use of all headers in certain courses makes the two round towers parallel to the Hellenistic tower at SAMARIA. This and other factors have led some to date the gate and wall to the Hellenistic period. Others, however, insist that they are Herodian. Certainly the gate fits perfectly into the street grid established south of the Crusader city, which originated with Herod the Great. Such being the case it must have been integrated with the high-level aqueduct, which entered the city here. Inside the gate are two large buildings of uncertain date.

Outside at a higher level is a paved **Byzantine street**, beneath two sewers cross at right angles; note the corresponding tunnel in the city wall, then out of use.

From the top of the rubble heap beside the road it is possible to see an oval depression in the fields to the east. This is plausibly identified as an **amphitheatre**, which must be dated to the late Roman period. Here in 306 the emperor Maximinus had Christians executed before him. Its stones were robbed out when Christianity suppressed such bloody and brutal entertainment. This precarious vantage-point also reveals the aqueducts stretching away to the north. In order to reach them, however, the condition of the road makes it preferable to go past the hippodrome (see below).

A modern arch [**11**] just beside the road is the easiest way to reach the **hippodrome**, which was probably a contribution of the emperor Hadrian in AD 130. Even though it is now under cultivation, the great rectangular space (450 × 90 m) is extremely evocative. The races at Caesarea were world-famous in the C4 AD, and it is easy to imagine the 30,000 cheering spectators. The uncared-for remains are monumental. The square base of the obelisk lies against the east fence, the granite obelisk itself, which must have been brought from Egypt, lies where it fell from the *spina* in the middle of the racecourse. Piled beside it are the bases of the conical turning-points; their upper portions were found in the harbour. Slight irregularities in the terrain, seen in aerial photographs, establish the line of the Byzantine city wall just outside the hippodrome.

Many of the finds made during the excavations are displayed in the **Caesarea Museum/Beit Hanna Sennech** in Kibbutz Sdot Yam located south of the Roman theatre. Open: Sunday–Friday 9 a.m.–noon; Saturday 10 a.m.–noon or by appointment (tel: 06–364367).

The Aqueducts

After the hippodrome on the Or Akiva road, take the first turn left on to Aqueduct road, and then again the first left. The high-level aqueduct bars the parking-lot from the sea. To reach the low-level aqueduct take the sandy path through the bushes at the north-east corner of the parking-lot. Within 10 m you will be walking on top of it. A dirt road beside the low-level aqueduct leads to a luxuriously appointed private **bath-house** belonging to one of the wealthy **villas** built on the high ground to the north-east of the city in the late Byzantine period (between 550 and 640).

The **high-level aqueduct** contains two channels with independent foundations. The eastern side (facing the parking-lot) was built by Herod; note the cornice on both sides. The western side (facing the sea) is an addition made by Hadrian in AD 130. Inscriptions identify work done by the Second, Sixth, and Tenth Legions, who served together in Palestine in the years just prior to the Second Revolt (132–5). The parallel earthenware pipes are probably Byzantine; the Crusaders filled in this channel to create a higher and smaller channel. The arched portion of the aqueduct is 10 km long.

Originally this aqueduct went only as far as the springs at Shuni (cf. p. 392). Hadrian extended it into Nahal Tanninim to springs south-east of Ammiqam in order to increase the volume of water. His engineers used a mixture of tunnelling and construction on the north side of the wadi. The tunnel is 1.10 m high and 0.80 m wide; in places it is 45 m below the surface. Stepped shafts cut at an angle facilitated the evacuation of rock, and subsequent cleaning and ventilation. Five of these shafts can be seen in the chalk cliff between Aviel and Ammiqam; the best access is via Benjamina on route 653, then left to Aviel on route 654, and finally right on route 6533 to Ammiqam. Cross the valley on the blue bridge over the dam, which diverts the river into the concrete channel, and walk west on the road beyond the barrier.

The covered **low-level aqueduct** is dated to the C4 or early C5 and was fed by an artificial lake 5 km north of the city. One dam, 200 m long, blocked the river. The other 1.6 km further north and over a kilometre long kept the lake from spreading too far.

The shorter **dam** is easily accessible and worth a visit. Leave the coastal highway at the Zikhron Yaaqov interchange, and turn south on route 4 at the Fureidis intersection. From Caesarea go through Or Akiva to the T-junction with route 4 and turn left. Follow the signs to Maagan Mikhael. Once across the highway take the first road to the left which skirts the kibbutz and terminates in a small park.

The dam spans both the Nahal Tanninim (Crocodile River—from the reptiles which infested it until the C19 AD) and the Nahal Adah. The base, which is stepped on the west side, is Byzantine, but the superstructure has been repaired time and again in order to serve the mills; the majority are not ancient and one was operating in 1922. The modern bridge openings were cut to drain the once-malarial Kebara marshes.

The rock-cut channel perpendicular to the south end of the dam has four channels running from its north side. The first is straddled by the rock-cut machine area of a C4–C5 AD **flour mill**. The flow of water drove a vertical wheel. On each side gears transformed the horizontal rotation of its axle into vertical rotation of the shaft powering the upper mill-stone. There would have been similar mills on each of the other channels.

Some 40 m south-east of these channels begins the wide (3.5 m) deep cut which fed the low-level aqueduct whose capacity was six times that of the double high-level aqueduct. About 500 m from its inception there is a sluice gate where the cut narrows to 1.7 m. It regulated the flow to the city.

Below the dam the two streams combine, and it is a pleasant walk to follow their 1.5 km course to the sea. The mound at the mouth was **Crocodilopolis** (Tel Tanninim), a short-lived town of the Hellenistic period. Nothing is known of its history. In the C1 BC, according to Strabo, only its name remained (*Geography* 16: 2.27). Remains of a bridge on the north bank show that a road passed here in the Roman period; two Roman milestones found on the beach are now in front of the Gail library in the nature centre of Maagan Mikhael.

A large **reservoir** east of the tel served the farms of the area in the Byzantine period. It was fed by an off-shoot of the low-level aqueduct. Where it crosses a little gully two construction periods can be detected.

First they tried a sealed pipe, on the principle that water equalizes itself in connected vessels. When that did not work satisfactorily, they built a bridge resting on the pipe; only the piers remain.

Caesarea Philippi: *see* BANYAS

Capernaum (N5) ★

Frequently mentioned in the gospels, Capernaum (Fig. 107) was apparently the closest to a permanent base that Jesus had during the Galilean ministry; it is referred to simply as 'his own city' (Matt. 9: 1; Mark 2: 1). Much of the town that he knew has been brought to light again, together with a primitive house-church later transformed into an octagonal building. The most famous synagogue of Galilee has been partially restored.

Though traces of occupation in the C13 BC were discovered, the history of the town begins in the C2 BC. When Herod's kingdom was divided after his death, it fell to the lot of Herod Antipas. As the first town encountered by travellers coming from his brother Philip's territory on the other side of the Jordan, it was equipped with a customs office (Matt. 9: 9) and a small garrison under a centurion. The poverty of the inhabitants can be inferred from the fact that the latter, a Gentile, had to build them a synagogue (Luke 7: 5). At this period the place had little depth and stretched along the lake-front for some 300 m. No unique advantages induced Jesus to settle there; it offered nothing that could not be found in the other lakeside towns. He probably chose it because his first converts, the fishermen Peter and Andrew, lived there (Mark 1: 21, 29). This initial success was not maintained; Jesus' preaching had no more impact here (Luke 10: 23–4) than it had at Nazareth.

None the less, some of his converts either lived or settled down there, because a continuing Christian presence is attested both archaeologically and textually. Writing in 374 Epiphanius says that it was one of the towns in which Jews forbade Gentiles, SAMARITANS, and Christians to live. This might perhaps have been enforceable in the pre-Constantinian period, but for the C4 it is contradicted by rabbinic texts, which imply that relations between the two communities were marked by considerable tension. The steady improvement in the quality of life indicates that anger was contained. Houses became more substantial and the city grew towards the hills. Both communities had their religious centres, as Egeria noted on her visit there between 381 and 384: 'In Capernaum the house of the prince of the apostles has been made into a church, with its original walls still standing. . . . There also is the synagogue where the Lord cured a man possessed by the devil [Mark 1: 23]. The way in is up many stairs, and it is made of dressed stone.' The synagogue was erected in the Byzantine period, and, given the rivalry between the two communities, it is not improbable that its construction inspired the transformation of the house-church. Writing in 570, the Piacenza pilgrim noted that 'the house of St Peter is now a basilica'.

Both of these edifices were destroyed prior to the Arab conquest in the C7. The general history of the period suggests a possible scenario. The Persian invasion of Palestine in 614 gave the Jews the opportunity to avenge the slights to which they had been subjected, and they demolished the church. Fifteen years later the balance swung the other way. In 629 the emperor Heraclius led Byzantine troops into Palestine and under their protection the Christians exacted their revenge by destroying the synagogue.

The remnants of the population, inspired one hopes by mutual shame, founded a new town just to the east. Some of the large houses had two storeys and an extensive sewage system underlay the broad straight streets. The transition to Arab rule (638) was peaceful but the prosperity of the settlement was destroyed by the earthquake of 746. Rebuilt in a much poorer fashion, its decline was progressive until the site was abandoned in the C11. As one might expect, there was renewed interest in the site during the Crusader period, but it was too exposed and too close to a dangerous frontier for any investment to be made in it. In the C13, we are told by Burchard, 'The once renowned town of Capernaum is at present just despicable; it numbers only seven houses of poor fishermen.'

Visit. Open: 8.30 a.m.–4.15 p.m. Toilets. The carved stones belong to the ruined synagogue, and many of the details are of great interest. They convey an idea of the splendour of the edifice, but no consensus has emerged as to how precisely all the elements fit together. There are also mills and presses of various types.

House of St Peter

From the C1 BC to the C4 AD the site (Fig. 58) was occupied by small houses grouped around irregular courtyards [1]. A very good idea of how they looked is provided by Insula II, the only difference being that the buildings here were much poorer. The drystone basalt walls would have supported only a light roof; one automatically thinks of the cure of the paralytic in Mark 2: 1–12. One room in this complex has been singled out since the mid-C1 AD; unlike all the other rooms in the area, its walls were plastered. At the same time there was a shift in the use to which the room was put. Prior to the mid-C1 AD the broken pottery found in the floor revealed normal family use; thereafter only storage jars and lamps were found. Despite our ignorance regarding the contents of the jars, the hint that the room was put to some type of public use is confirmed by the great

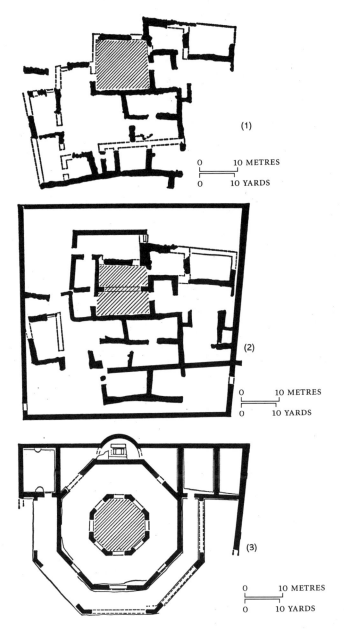

▲ **Fig. 58.** Capernaum. The three stages in the development of the House of St Peter (after Corbo).

number of graffiti scratched in the plaster walls. Some of them mention Jesus as Lord and Christ. Most of the others are too badly preserved to permit a convincing interpretation.

In the C4 this room was the centre-piece of a complex cut off from other sectors of the town by a wall with entrances on the north and south [2]. The room was given a more solid roof, which necessitated the construction of a central arch, and the space was extended by the addition of other rooms on the two sides. There can be little doubt that this was the house-church seen by Egeria. It may have been the work of the converted Jew, Count Joseph of Tiberias, who, according to Epiphanius, obtained from the emperor Constantine the authority to erect churches in Capernaum and other towns of Galilee.

About the middle of the C5 all the buildings within the enclosure were levelled in preparation for the erection of an octagonal church [3]. The central octagon enshrined the venerated room, which was given a mosaic floor. The peacock centre-piece was surrounded by a geometric design with a lotus-flower border identical with that of the Church of the Loaves and Fishes (HEPTAPEGON). The proportionate relationship between the inner octagon and the two outer ones is identical with that of other churches of the same type in Italy and Syria; the closest parallel in this area is the DOME OF THE ROCK in Jerusalem. Shortly after construction had been completed an apse containing a baptistery (?) was added on the east side. This church was put out of commission early in the C7.

Certitude as to the original ownership of this room is, of course, impossible, but the evidence of consistent veneration in the pre-Constantinian period demands an explanation. The most reasonable assumption is the one attested by the Byzantine pilgrims, namely, that it was the house of Peter in which Jesus may have lodged (Matt. 5: 20). Certainly, nothing in the excavations contradicts this identification.

Insula II

This group of basalt buildings is bordered on all four sides by streets. Only five doors provided access from the street, suggesting that the 15 houses grouped around small courtyards might have been occupied by related families, i.e. about 100 persons in all. The basalt stones were neither cut nor shaped, and smaller stones were used to create more or less horizontal courses. Such walls could not take any great weight. This had two consequences. They could not be weakened by windows. They could not carry a second storey. The roofs were made of a network of light branches covered with straw and earth (Mark 2: 1–12). The floors of the rooms and the courtyards were of black basalt cobbles. It would have been very easy for a coin to slip between them (Luke 15: 8). Occupation levels run from C1 to C6 AD. Insula III near the lake reflects the same time-span, but the two other insulae (III and IV) do not begin as early. Presumably they were developed in order to accommodate the increase in population that accompanied the growing prosperity of the town in the early Byzantine period.

Synagogue

The elevated position, the quality of the external decoration, and the brilliance of the white limestone against the surrounding black basalt houses all gave this edifice exceptional status. The three entrances are in the south wall; within, the other walls are paralleled by rows of columns supporting the roof; there was no gallery. A side door in the east wall leads to a courtyard roofed on three sides; it fulfilled many of the functions we encompass under the term 'community centre'.

The dating of this impressive structure has given rise to a lively ongoing debate. The excavators claim that the building was built in several pre-planned stages over a century beginning in the middle of the C4 AD. They rely essentially on coins and pottery sealed beneath the cement floor of the synagogue. Proponents of an earlier date consider these to be due to repairs and restoration, as for example after the earthquake of 363, which is known to have partially destroyed TIBERIAS. They argue that the elaborate external decoration has its closest parallels in regional pagan temples of the C3 and early C4, and that the quality of the masonry does not reflect the decline in workmanship that began in the late C4.

Excavations in the Greek Orthodox Property

From the walkway in front of the synagogue a Greek Orthodox church is visible some 140 m to the east. It marks the site of the post-C7 site of Capernaum. Along the lake-front is a 2 m-wide basalt wall, which can only have been a **quay**. Just in front of the modern house two sections of the wall about 20 m apart turn at right angles and extend about 25 m into the lake, presumably to create a sheltered anchorage for fishing boats. Between the house and the church the remains of a large building consisting of indoor pools came to light, it may have served as a fish market. The clearest stratigraphic sequence came from the area in the western corner of the property; occupation began in the early C7 and terminated in the mid-C11. In this area one can see 2 m-wide straight roads flanked by large, well-constructed plastered buildings; these date to the first half of the C7.

Carmel Caves (Mearot Karmel) (G7)

These are the most accessible prehistoric caves in Israel and reveal the evolution of humanity in the last stages of the Stone Age. They are located just to the east of route 4, the road running parallel to the Tel Aviv–Haifa highway (route 2), about half-way between En Hod and Kerem Mararal. A paved road leads to the parking-lot of the nature reserve facing the caves.

Visit. Open: Sunday–Thursday and Saturday 8 a.m.–4 p.m.; Friday 8 a.m.–1 p.m. The Skhul Cave is located round the corner to the left of the ticket office; the other three caves are to its right and are named (from left to right) el-Wad (or Nahal), Gamal, and Tabun (or Tannur).

The caves are located in a fossilized reef formed about 100 million years ago (Lower Cenomanian). Its core is composed of rudists, conical bivalves between 10 and 30 cm long; they look like ice-cream cones stacked one inside the other, and can be seen in the reserve.

Tabun (Oven) Cave

This is the westernmost and highest cave. The whole front of the cave has been eroded away. The 25 m of deposits reveal that humans lived here more or less continuously between 500,000 and 50,000 BC. When first occupied the sea-level was some 50 m higher than at present. Sand from the narrow coastal plain drifted into the cave. The sea dropped to its present level c.80,000 BC, at the beginning of the last glacial period. The cave was abandoned when the infiltration of water opened the chimney in the innermost part of the cave. The climate at this period became progressively colder. The occupants moved to the el-Wad Cave, and used the chimney as a trap into which forest animals were driven to their death. One skeleton of a woman close to the Neanderthal type was found in the Mousterian level.

Gamal Cave

No remains were found, but it is difficult to think that the cave was not occupied in antiquity. Today it houses an exhibit showing the daily life of cave people in the Mousterian period (100,000–40,000 BC).

el-Wad (Valley) Cave

This cave is 90 m deep. A high entrance area gives access to a long corridor and inner rooms. The main period of occupation was in the period 40,000–20,000 BC, but the most interesting finds come from the Natufian period (11,000–9,000 BC) when the cave was reoccupied as part of a much larger settlement located on the rocky terrace in front of the cave. This was a true village reflecting humanity's transition from hunting and gathering to the domestication of plants and animals. Traces of circular stone dwellings were found. The four carefully cut conical depressions may have been associated with burial rites; almost 100 skeletons were found in the vicinity. They were buried in the foetal position in shallow depressions beneath a pavement of heavy slabs.

Skhul (Kid) Cave

The fourteen skeletons found beneath the floor of the cave were buried between 100,000 and 80,000 BC when the cave was in use. They are all of the Cro-Magnon type, and the great controversy centring on this site is related to the discovery of a Neanderthal type in the Tabun Cave dating from the same Mousterian period. Did the different human types coexist or follow one another? At present it is thought that the two coexisted for a while but that Neanderthal (*Homo erectus*) eventually became extinct leaving the field to Cro-Magnon (*Homo sapiens sapiens*). The latter did not derive from the former, but represented a new human strain which developed in Africa some 200,000 years ago among those who had not followed Neanderthal into Europe.

Chorozain (Korazim)* (N5)

CAPERNAUM with a view is perhaps the most succinct characterization of Chorozain. Both contain synagogues in the midst of an excavated urban area, but sited 3.5 km up the slope and 270 m above the SEA OF GALILEE Chorozain offers a wide perspective over the northern end of the lake (Fig. 107).

A town existed in the C1 AD, together with Capernaum and Bethsaida it was condemned by Jesus for its lack of faith (Matt. 11: 20-4). This site appears to be the one mentioned by Eusebius and Jerome in the C4, but from the C8 Chorozain was identified with KURSI on the far side of the lake. The town expanded considerably as a result of the influx of Jews expelled from Judaea by Hadrian in AD 135, but was a heap of ruins when seen by Eusebius. The reason for the catastrophe is unclear, but life returned to the city in the latter part of the C4, when the synagogue was rebuilt, and continued until the C8. The city covered between 32 and 40 hectares. After the Arab conquest it suffered the fate of so many other Jewish settlements in the area; the site was again occupied in the Middle Ages (C12-C14).

Visit. Open: 8.30 a.m.-4 p.m., Fridays 3 p.m. Follow the signs to Almagor from the Tiberias-Rosh Pinna road (route 90); the parking-lot is on the right just after the sharp bend made by the road in crossing the Nahal Korazim .

Behind the toilets near the entrance are **Byzantine houses**. The first excavated area on the right of the path leading from the entrance is a large public building of the Byzantine period. It contains a **ritual bath** adjoining a large elliptical cistern. The parallel stone slabs are the roof of the steps leading down to the bath. The construction of the roof of the **cistern** is particularly noteworthy. A decorated central pillar supports slabs corbelled out from the sides, thus creating a double arch, which supported the inner ends of a further set of slabs laid at right angles.

The disposition of the ground floor of the partially restored C4 **syna-gogue** is the same as at Capernaum, but the building material is black basalt. The large rock in the north-west corner was left for some reason when the building was notched into the slope. A flight of steps leads up from the open piazza to the three entrances by which the building is oriented to Jerusalem. Two carved gables, now in the courtyard of the Israel Museum, Jerusalem, probably crowned structures within the building on either side of the main door, the Torah niche to the west and the reader's platform with its Chair of Moses to the east. It is unlikely that there was an upper gallery in which women would have been segregated. Juxtaposed to the synagogue on the west is a long hall with two small rooms (one a *geniza*?) at the northern end. When the original steps were blocked by a wall in the C6, a new flight of steps was added on the east.

To the east of the synagogue are two **large buildings**, each about 30 m square. These were constructed in the C4, and underwent repairs in the late C7 or early C8. Each probably housed an extended family. The rooms were entered from a large cobblestone courtyard. The complex nearest the synagogue is made up of small rooms surrounding a core of long rooms. In the adjoining complex fourteen rooms surround its own courtyard. Note the arches and fenestrated wall in the south-east corner; these supported the 2 m basalt slabs of the roof. The repairs made during the early C5 and again in the C7 did not significantly change the original plans.

The best-preserved buildings, on the spur jutting out into the wadi on the west, date to the C12–C13. In those that have been restored, note particularly the roofing technique, which is particularly well adapted to a land rich in stone but poor in long timber. A number of olive presses have survived intact. Olives were spread on mats slightly smaller than the incised circle, and piled one on top of the other. Pressure was brought to bear by means of a screw set between two upright wooden posts, and the oil that dripped into the circular incision flowed into a lower basin.

Church of the Multiplication of the Loaves and Fishes: *see* HEPTAPEGON

Church of the Primacy: *see* HEPTAPEGON

Crusades

The Crusades were a series of military expeditions which established and maintained a European Christian presence in the Holy Land from 1099 to

1291. Groups in fact came annually, but the largest are numbered in a conventional order.

The First Crusade took Jerusalem on 15 July 1099, having forced the north wall near Herod's Gate about noon. Godfrey of Bouillon was elected leader, but Tancred, a Norman from Sicily, made the first territorial gain by conquering Galilee later that year. The foundations of the Latin Kingdom were established by Baldwin I (1100–18) who passed most of the nights of his reign in his battle-tent. He first secured the coast (1101–5), then expanded the northern border to link up with the Principality of Tripoli (1106–10), and finally cut communications between Damascus and Cairo by setting up a line of fortresses on the east side of the Araba, the valley linking the Dead Sea with the Gulf of Aqaba (1115–16).

Reinforcements brought by the Second Crusade in 1147 provided the manpower to hold this territory, but more and more reliance was placed on the permanent standing army constituted by the two great military orders, the Hospitallers (1109) and the Templars (1128). Starting as small groups of dedicated knights, these orders soon became immensely wealthy and powerful organizations furnishing highly trained and disciplined cavalry units.

Castles guarded the major lines of communications, but two groups of fortresses had a special function: one in the north blockaded Tyre (captured 1224), and another in the south blockaded ASHQELON (captured 1153).

Saladin came to power in Egypt in 1170 but he became a serious threat only when he changed his battle tactics. At the beginning he relied on Egyptians whose cavalry, backed up by archers, fought at close quarters; these elements had no answer to the disciplined weight of the Frankish charge. Later Saladin switched to Kurdish mounted archers who never provided a target for the charge, the one tactical weapon of the Crusaders. In reply the Crusaders developed the armoured column which could move through the Kurds guaranteeing a stalemate but never victory.

On 3 July 1187, by slowing the advance of a column comprising the whole army of the Latin Kingdom of Jerusalem, Saladin ensured success next day at the HORNS OF HATTIN; the knights had exhausted their water supplies and could not fight effectively.

A new military order, the Teutonic Knights, came into being during the Third Crusade (1189–92) when a combination of military threat and adroit diplomacy led to a new Latin Kingdom with territory in Galilee and around Jerusalem. A series of treaties in the first half of the C13 gave the Crusaders more land, but then the tide turned as the Mamluks of Egypt began to make forays into Palestine. The Crusaders were first pushed back towards the sea. Then Baybars (1260–77) began his advance up the coast taking city after city in a series of campaigns. Acre (AKKO), the last strongpoint, fell in 1291.

There are extensive Crusader remains throughout the country, but only some are really worth a visit:

Churches: in Jerusalem—HOLY SEPULCHRE, ST ANNE'S, ST MARY OF THE GERMANS; VIRGIN'S TOMB; outside Jerusalem—ABU GHOSH, HEBRON, SAMARIA, QUBEIBA, LATRUN.
Castles: BELVOIR, HUNIN, MONTFORT, NIMRUD.
Towns: AKKO, CAESAREA.
Retirement Home: EN HEMED.
Mill: EN AFEQ.

An excellent map, 'The Crusader Kingdom of Jerusalem (1099–1291)', is published by the Survey of Israel.

Dead Sea (M18–25)

Today the Dead Sea is 411 m below sea-level, which makes it the lowest point on the earth's surface. Fifty thousand years ago it was a much bigger lake, and its surface was 225 m above the present level. Even at the beginning of this century the sea was 12 m higher than it is now. The dropping water-level caused the length of the sea to decrease from 70 km to 50 km in 1976, when the Lynch Straits dried out. The ford linking the Lisan (HaLashon) to the west bank would be passable for the first time since the early C19 were it not for the new canal bringing water to the salt-pans at Sedom.

Such variation is directly related to the amount of rainfall. In recent times the volume of water coming into the Sea has been further reduced by pumping from the SEA OF GALILEE and from the Yarmuk river. There is a plan to dig a canal from the Mediterranean in order to prevent the sea from drying up completely.

The sea has no exit and water is lost only through evaporation, in summer as much as 25 mm in 24 hours. This produces a concentration of all the chlorides (magnesium, sodium, calcium, and potassium) in the water (275 g per litre). It is possible to swim in the sea at EN GEDI and at En Boqeq; a shower is essential immediately afterwards to wash off the salt. Being nearly several times as dense as ordinary sea water, one can sit in it and read a newspaper comfortably. But while it is impossible to sink, water in the lungs is fatal. Enter the water slowly and cautiously. Do not dive or put the head under water.

The commercial exploitation of the Dead Sea, today centred on Sedom, was anticipated by the NABATAEANS and others. As early as the C4 BC they collected bitumen from the surface and sold it to the Egyptians for embalming. This remained an important industry well into Roman times, giving rise to the name the Lake of Asphalt (*War* 4: 476–85). The physical properties of the sea excited the curiosity of eminent minds from the time of Aristotle (384–322 BC). He mentions it, as do Strabo (see box), Pliny the Elder, Tacitus, Pausanias, and Galen; the last two first used the present name in the C2 AD. The sea carried heavy marine traffic in the Byzantine and Crusader periods, but thereafter became the 'Sea of the Devil' and a magnet for all sorts of legends (e.g. no birds could fly over it because of the exhalations), which were exploded only by the first scientific survey accomplished by the US navy in 1848.

A magnificent scenic road (route 90) runs along the west side of the Dead Sea, providing easy access to a number of important sites (Fig. 59). Just south of QUMRAN a green area is created by a number of brackish springs collectively called **En Feshkha** or Enot Zuqim. The ruins of an Essene farm are visible from the main road on the right of the entrance to the bathing area. Some 200 m before the headland of Rosh Zuqim an isolated rock on the west side of the road carries the mark of the Palestine Exploration Fund; in 1900 it was 4 m above the water which lapped its base!

After skirting the headland, the road emerges on to the alluvial fan of the Wadi ed-Nar (Nahal Qidron); this wadi is easily identified because the detergent from the sewers of Jerusalem is still intact as the evil-smelling stream passes beneath the road. A small ruin between the road and the sea is called **Khirbet Mazin**. Though dated to the Roman period, it is unclear whether it had any connection with the ESSENES.

Other ruins occur further south in the area of dense vegetation between **Enot Qane** and **Enot Samar** (En el-Ghuweir and En at-Turaba). Those between the cliffs and the road are of the C8 BC, whereas those just east of the road were occupied from the reign of Herod the Great (37–4 BC) until the middle of the C1 AD. The pottery from this latter

The Lake of Asphalt

'It is deep to the very shore and has water so very heavy that no one can dive in it. In fact any person who walks into it and proceeds no further than up to his navel is immediately raised afloat. It is full of asphalt. The asphalt is blown to the surface at irregular intervals from the midst of the deep, and with it rise bubbles, as though the water were boiling, and the surface of the lake, being convex, presents the appearance of a hill. With the asphalt there arises also much soot, which, though smoky, is imperceptible to the eye. It tarnishes copper and silver and anything that glistens, even gold. When their vessels are becoming tarnished the people who live round the lake know that the asphalt is beginning to rise; and they prepare to collect it by means of rafts made of reed.' (Strabo (C1), *Geography* 16: 2. 42; trans. Jones)

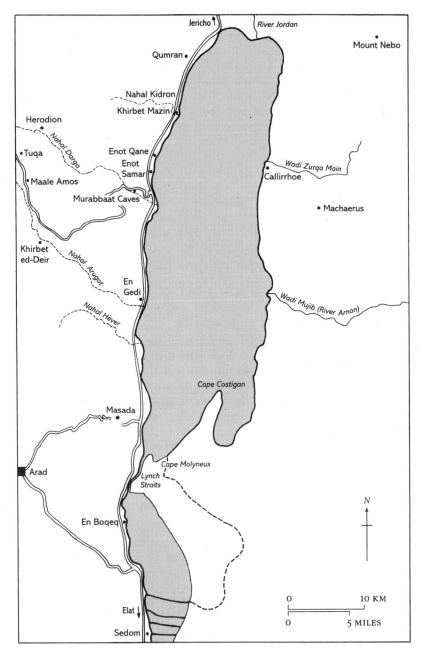

▲ **Fig. 59.** Antiquity sites around the Dead Sea.

building (a large room with a kitchen in the corner) is identical with that of the post-earthquake period at Qumran, and the cemetery some 800 m to the north exhibits precisely the same form of burial as at Qumran. The Essenes may have retreated here when they were forced to abandon Qumran during the reign of Herod the Great, or it might have been another farming outstation like En Feshkha.

The road to the top of the cliffs at **Metzoke Dragot** extends to connect with the road coming south from Tuqa. Beyond the holiday village it is unsealed, and crosses a number of wadis. Special care should be taken during the rainy season (mid-December to early April), and the road should not be attempted except in a car with better than average clearance. About 1.5 km west of the settlement a small white sign near the road marks the beginning of the trail down to the caves in the **Wadi Murabbaat** (Nahal Darga), which yielded manuscripts of the Second Revolt (AD 132–5), including an autographed letter of its leader Simon Ben Kosba (= Bar Kokhba). This dangerous path should be attempted only in the company of someone who knows the desert.

From the parking-lot at the top of the cliffs (turn to the left just before the settlement) there is a splendid view over the Dead Sea. Directly opposite are two important sites. In the northern (left) corner of the vast natural amphitheatre are the celebrated hot springs of **Callirrhoe**, whither went Herod the Great in his last terrible illness (*Antiquities* 16: 171). Just below the skyline a truncated cone slightly whiter than the surrounding hills is the site of **Machaerus**, where, according to Josephus, Herod Antipas put John the Baptist to death (*Antiquities* 18: 116–19); it fell to the Romans some two years before MASADA, whose natural strength it parallels (*War* 7: 163–209).

In addition to its archaeological remains the oasis of EN GEDI offers bathing in the Dead Sea and the magnificent nature reserve in Nahal Arugot. During the Second Revolt (132–5) the Roman camps above the Nahal Hever were supplied through this valley. From the circular Roman

The Stinking Lake

'The Sea of Zoar is also called the Sea of Sodom and Gomorrah, and these last were two of the cities of Lot, which Allah overwhelmed [Gen. 19: 1–29], so that the place of them became the Stinking Lake. It is also known as the Dead Sea, because there is nothing in it that has the breath of life, neither fish nor beast, nor any other creature, of the kinds found in other stagnant and moving waters. The waters are warm and of a disagreeable odour. There ply on the lake small ships which make the voyage of these parts, and carry over corn and various sorts of dates from Zoar to Jericho and the other provinces of the Jordan valley.' (Idrisi, *Geography* 3; trans. G. Le Strange)

fort on the little plateau to the right (north) of the path near the hidden waterfall one can see the marvellous cliff road (**Maale Isiyyim**) built by the Tenth Legion on the far side of the wadi. In order to climb it an experienced guide is essential.

Nahal Hever drains into the Dead Sea about 7 km south of En Gedi. Its vertical cliffs are honeycombed by caves in which followers of Bar Kokhba took refuge; under the eyes of the Romans above they died of thirst and starvation, leaving behind many documents of the C1 and C2 AD. These caves are now totally inaccessible.

The first group of hotels 14 km south of the entrance to Masada marks the site of **En Boqeq**. Its present development as a health spa continues an ancient tradition because in the Herodian period pharmaceutical plants were cultivated here. A well-preserved fortress is clearly visible from the main road just north of the hotels. Built in the second half of the C4 AD, it was staffed by agricultural frontier militia who farmed the area where the hotels are now sited. It served until the Arab conquest in the C7.

At Newe Zohar the road divides. One (route 90) continues south past Mount Sodom to HAZEVA, MAALE AQRABIM, TIMNA, and Elat. The other (route 31) turns west to TEL ARAD. On this latter road two viewpoints permit one to look down into Nahal Zohar. From the first, one can see the pile of stones which is all that remains of an **Israelite fort** of the C8–C6 BC. From the second, one can see a **Byzantine fort** perched on a rock finger. Its history parallels that at En Boqeq. These installations protected the ancient Way of Edom; it is the only route from the Dead Sea to the west which does not involve a cliff climb.

Dead Sea Scrolls: *see* QUMRAN **and** ESSENES

Deir Hajla (M17)

Looking from JERICHO towards the river Jordan the eye is caught by the glint of a silver dome above a square building standing alone in the wilderness. The immediate impression is one of strength and endurance. It is in fact a Greek Orthodox monastery, whose popular name is an echo of the biblical Bet Hogla (Josh. 15: 6; 18: 19, 21). Originally dedicated to Our Lady of Kalamon, it survived into the Crusader period, after which it was abandoned. It was rebuilt in 1588 only to be destroyed around 1734. The present edifice dates only from 1885, but it has inherited the mantle of the famous laura which St Gerasimus founded here in AD 455.

Surprisingly little is known about this personage, despite the fact that he was known as 'the founder and patron of the Jordan wilderness', a title elsewhere accorded only to such pre-eminent monastic figures as Euthymius and Sabas (see MONASTERIES IN THE JUDAEAN DESERT). Already a monk when he came to the Holy Land from Lycia in Asia Minor, he was one of the hermits who followed Euthymius into the desert (451–3) and, under his influence, accepted the Christological definition of the Council of Chalcedon (451).

Prior to Gerasimus, monastic foundations were either monasteries or laurae. His innovation, later copied by the MONASTERY OF ST GEORGE OF KOZIBA, was to combine the two. A monastery (containing church, cells, kitchen, refectory, store-rooms, and staffed by a superior, a priest, and a steward) was surrounded by seventy hermitages, some constructed, others cut into the soft lake deposit of the Wadi en-Nukheil ('Valley of the Little Palm'). Gerasimus died and was interred there in 475. In the C8 there were ten monks, but when John Phocas visited there in 1185 he found among the ruins only a single hermit, who was befriended by two lions living among the dense undergrowth along the Jordan.

Visit. There is easy access from the Jericho bypass road. The foundations of the present edifice, which reuse stones of the original monastery, were laid in the reign of the emperor Manuel I Comnenus (1143–80) by John IX, the patriarch of Jerusalem, according to an inscription. Part of the **medieval mosaic floor** is visible along the northern side of the restored church. The monastery, which is alive with the sound of bird-song, is built around a deep well. This might explain why it is not located on the site of the original monastery which is thought to be some 400 m to the east. The only remains are occasional mosaic tesserae and small mounds of decayed mud-brick.

On the contrary, the **chapel and cells** cut into the chalky rock of the south bank of the Wadi en-Nukheil are fairly well preserved. Follow the security road running due east from the monastery for about a kilometre

---

Initiation into the Monastic Life

'Cyriacus of Corinth made obeisance to the great Euthymius and was clothed by his holy hands in the habit. He was not allowed to stay there because of his youth, but was sent to the Jordan to the sainted Gerasimus; the great Euthymius absolutely forbade having an adolescent in his laura. The sainted Gerasimus accepted him and, noting his youth, told him to stay in the monastery. There he hewed wood, carried water, cooked, and performed every kind of service with zeal. He spent his days in labour and toil, and his nights in prayer to God, adding to his manual work great zeal in the office of psalmody. While serving in the monastery, he mastered the life of hermits, taking bread and water every other day, and abstaining from oil, wine, and mixed drink.' (Cyril of Scythopolis (C6), *Life of Cyriacus* 4–5/224–5; trans. R. M. Price)

until it rises to a rusting tank in a fixed position. To the left (north) is a grove of palm trees. The caves are in the steep cliff-face. Access to the western ledge is from above and should only be attempted by the agile. It is much easier to get down than up again! Two wide ledges with cells at the outer ends are linked by a rock-cut corridor with a chapel carved into one side and a cell into the other. At the entrance to this cell is a plastered cistern fed by a channel bringing run-off rain-water from the plain above.

Some 3.5 km to the south-west of the monastery, in a semicircle around En Abu Mahmud to the east, lie a series of other **hermit caves**, which also belonged to the laura. Fortunately the best preserved (1962/1336) is also the most elaborate. A 15m-long corridor, which terminates in a two-burner stove with an air-vent above, gives access to a chapel, and two cells, each with a bed niche cut into the wall.

Dor (G8)

The natural beauty of the stubby promontory of Dor is enhanced by a unique archaeological feature. Three long boat slips cut into the rock side of the central bay are without parallel on the eastern coast of the Mediterranean. They are the sole visible sign that Dor was once a famous harbour.

The site was certainly occupied in the C15 BC. It is mentioned in an inscription of Rameses II (1304–1237 BC), the pharaoh of the Exodus, and was the scene of an amusing conflict in the C12 BC Egyptian story of Wen-Amon's journey to Byblos. He was robbed by one of his crew and the local ruler, Beder of the Sekels/Sikuli, refused to accept responsibility. The Sekels/Sikuli were one of the Sea Peoples associated with the PHILISTINES. This group probably remained a strong element in the population throughout successive changes of overlord. In all likelihood the grants of the port to Baal of Tyre by Assyria in the C7 BC and to Eshmunazar of Sidon by Ptolemy I of Egypt in the late C4 BC simply confirmed de facto possession. Thus in the C1 AD it was believed that the Phoenicians had founded the city, and that it was named after Doros, the son of Poseidon, the sea-god.

After a century of Ptolemaic control the Seleucids of Syria acquired possession in 201 BC. Taken by Alexander Jannaeus (103–76 BC), Dor was liberated by Pompey in 63 BC and attached to the Roman province of Syria (*Antiquities* 14: 76). Since Josephus describes Dor as an unsatisfactory port where goods had to be transshipped by lighters from ships at sea (*Antiquities* 15: 333), it must have suffered from the development of CAESAREA, which is only 15 km away. Dor is not mentioned by the geographer Strabo (c.AD 25), and Pliny the Elder (c.AD 70) describes it as a

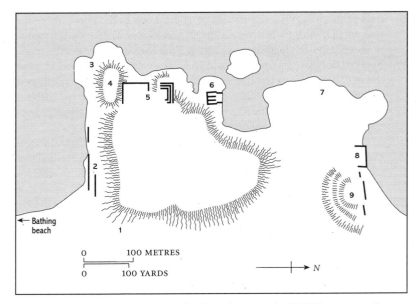

▲ **Fig. 60.** Dor. Excavated areas. 1. Byzantine church; 2. C11 BC quay; 3. Breakwater; 4. Acropolis; 5. Podium; 6. Boat slips; 7. Dye factory; 8. Roman warehouse; 9. Roman theatre.

'mere memory'. Yet in the reign of Agrippa I (AD 37–44) it had a Jewish synagogue and a sizeable pagan population (*Antiquities* 19: 300), and had its own mint from AD 64 to 222.

The same ambiguity appears in later references. Jerome consistently describes Dor as deserted and in ruins, but later in the C5 the city appears as sufficiently important to justify a resident bishop. Either the city had a very curious history or certain authors did not check the facts. There is no mention of Dor in the early Arab period. The Crusader castle on the small cape was named after the fief-holders de Merle. It was in the possession of the Templars, however, when captured by Saladin in 1187. In May 1799, during his retreat from AKKO, Napoleon dumped his cannon in the sea here; it was then the Arab fishing village of Tantura.

Visit (Fig. 60). Exit from the Tel Aviv–Haifa highway (route 2) at Mehlaf Zikhron Yaakov Interchange (if coming from the south) or at Mehlaf Atlit Interchange (if coming from the north). From route 4 take the turn-off signposted Nahsholim-Dor. From the bathing beach it is possible to walk north to the tel. Excavations are still in progress and some of what is here reported necessarily has a provisional character.

The Ancient Harbour

It takes a great imaginative effort to see the harbour of Dor as it was in the days of its glory. Visualize the sea-level dropping to the point where the four small islands formed a continuous breakwater. The sandy spit which now separates the lagoon thus created from the bay to the north (south bay) did not exist; its tip in fact continued the natural breakwater as far as the tel. The waters of the harbour curved round the tel to the north-east and filled the area now occupied by fish ponds. It was a narrow harbour 1 km in length open to the south. The inner basin offered excellent protection against the prevailing north-west wind.

The principal landing area was at the foot of the tel [**2**] where traces of the **quay** are clearly visible. Three or four rows of cut stones are so laid that their narrow ends face the sea. It was some 35 m long and 12 m wide. At each end was a rectangular building. A retaining wall marks the inner side of the quay. When originally constructed in the C13 BC the level of the sea was half a metre lower. In subsequent centuries it rose gradually and the quay had to be raised to match it. In the mid-C11 the trend was reversed and the dropping sea-level made the harbour unusable.

At the seaward end of the quay is a stone-lined rectangular **well** of the C13 BC which was maintained in use for some 300 years. It does not go far into the ground. From as early as the Neolithic period it was known that along the coast a shallow level of fresh water was to be found above the seawater level in the ground.

Continuing around the edge of the tel on the rocks one encounters a vertical cut through the tip of the promontory which was made to serve as a 'wave catcher'. The highest abrasion notch (caused by the lapping of waves) shows the sea-level c.AD 600; the one below is dated to the C3 AD.

The Byzantine Church

A fenced area due east of the southern side of the tel and just north of the houses of the kibbutz [**1**] enshrines the remains of an early C4 church built on the ruins of a temple of the Hellenistic period (332–152 BC). Destroyed at the end of that century it was rebuilt on the same plan. Its lay-out is unique in the Holy Land. Not only is the colonnaded atrium longer than the monoapsidal church, but there is an external aisle running along both sides of the church and atrium. That on the north is the best preserved, and is interpreted as reflecting the rite of Christian initiation. After having been baptized in the pool with two steps on each side, the neophyte would have been anointed in the first mosaic-paved room and admitted to the eucharist in the second mosaic-floored room which contained a chancel and altar.

Little remains of the south external aisle which may have housed the sick who came there in hope of healing. This interpretation is based on a unique feature of the tomb at the east end of the south internal aisle. It is closed with five slabs but there is a hole in the middle. Oil poured through this hole was sanctified by the holy remains inside and ran through to a plastered basin outside to the north. Such need for quantity hints at a considerable number of suppliants. These may also have been attracted by a precious relic, part of the rock of Golgotha. A grey marble column was found with a Greek inscription 'A stone of the Holy Golgotha'.

Fire destroyed the church in the late C7. In the following century Arabs used the church as a cemetery and continued to do so until the C14.

Tel Dor

This mound is the area where excavation is still in progress, and only the most generic information is unlikely to be quickly dated. Until the end of the last century a **tower** stood on the south-west corner of the mound [4]. It was the site of the Crusader castle of Merle, and much earlier most probably was the acropolis of the Phoenician city. Just to the north is the podium [5] of a large public building, probably a **temple**. Looking down to the edge of the beach it is easy to discern the outline of a great rectangular building parallel to the slope. That part should be in the sea highlights the tremendous erosion which has taken place in this sector.

Each of the three rock-cut **slips** [6] could take a 20 m boat with a beam of 3–4 m. The holes drilled in the partitions were to support a roof. On either side are basins in which wood destined for the ribs was soaked to make it pliable. At present the slips are stratigraphically undatable, but they were just at the northern limit of the Phoenician city because not far to the east the traces of what were once a monumental building constructed of fine cut stones are dated to the C13–C11 BC.

The large excavation areas on the east side of the mound near the Byzantine church [1] contain elements of the city's **fortifications** of the pre- and post-Exilic periods with corresponding residential areas.

The Purple Dye Factory

On the other side of what is locally called Love Bay is the best-preserved purple dye factory in the eastern Mediterranean [7]. There are three shallow rock-cut tanks south of a rectangular paved courtyard. There are two others on the west side. These could be filled with fresh water by the channel coming from the north, whose connection to the aqueduct coming from the east is unclear. They could also be filled with sea water by the channel on the west. The channel to the south drained both tanks. At a later stage two additional tanks were constructed in front of these two. In the centre of the complex are large plastered basins, which were remodelled at least four times. From these run channels on all sides save the south, on which storage facilities were constructed. The installation appears to have been in use from the C1 to the C6 AD.

Roman Installations in North Bay

The large building [8] north of the dye factory is thought to be a storage facility of the C2–C3 AD. Stretching north from it along the shore are

Purple

In antiquity purple was the symbol of authority and the colour of religion; purple garments were the prerogative of rulers and those to whom they granted the privilege. Pliny, who gives a detailed description of the collection and fabrication process, speaks of 'robes of scarlet and purple, which the same mother, luxury, has made almost as costly as pearls' (*Natural History* 9: 124). Martial mentions a purple robe costing $10,000! The dye was derived from the hypobrachial gland of the murex sea snail, the best species of which inhabited the coastal waters south of Tyre. Collected in the spring in a baited trap like a lobster pot, it took 12,000 murex to produce 1.5 grams of dye which, in today's terms, would have been worth about $200. According to Diocletian's *Edict on Maximum Prices*, which was promulgated in AD 301, wool died with Tyrian purple was literally worth its weight in gold.

the remains of an ancient quay. After some 50 m it turns west underwater towards the centre of the bay. The inner basin thus created was kept clear of silt by a series of three rock-cut scouring channels corresponding to different sea levels. To the east of the building are the remains of a Roman theatre [**9**].

Museum

Housed in what used to be a glass factory, the **Centre for Nautical and Regional Archaeology** in Kibbutz Nasholim displays finds from the excavations and discoveries made by underwater archaeologists in the harbour and along the coast. Open: 8 a.m.–2 p.m.; Saturday 10.30 a.m.–3 p.m.

Druze

The eighteen Druze villages in northern Israel, with a combined population of some 55,000, represent only a small proportion of a religious movement which has over a million adherents, most of whom live in the Shuf and Matan districts of southern Lebanon, on the slopes of Mount Hermon, and in the Jebel Druze in southern Syria.

The movement originated in Egypt when the Fatimid caliph al-Hakim (AD 996–1021) permitted some of his entourage to consider him a divine being. This doctrine was first formulated by al-Darasi who presented al-Hakim as the incarnation of the cosmic intelligence in 1017. His teaching that the faithful were obliged by no moral precepts forced al-

Hakim to disown him, and the use of his name to describe the movement was originally intended as abusive. In 1019 the mantle passed to Hamza ben Ali who gave the cult of al-Hakim its definitive form. He took over the classic Ismailite doctrine that all proceeds from the One and returns to the One through knowledge, but modified it by insisting on the immediate presence of the cosmic One incarnated in al-Hakim. The Druze, therefore, call themselves Muwahhadun, 'unitarians'. Knowledge of the One was the only way of salvation, the symbolism and practices of the revealed religions no longer had any meaning.

After the unexplained disappearance of al-Hakim during a nocturnal excursion in Cairo in 1021, Hamza also withdrew after delegating his powers to al-Muktana. The latter encouraged the missionary expansion of the movement by numerous letters written between 1021 and 1042. Although he himself objected to the importance given to his work, later Druze tradition considers him responsible for the collection of 111 letters (mostly his own but some from al-Hakim and Hamza) which became their canonical scripture, 'The Letters of Wisdom'.

After the withdrawal of al-Muktana all missionary activity ceased, and the Druze became a closed community permitting neither conversion nor defection. Those who believed in the time of Hamza are continually reincarnated as Druze, this long-drawn-out process of purification will make them capable of ruling the human race when al-Hakim and Hamza returned to establish justice.

At least since the C15 Druze have been divided into 'the wise' and 'the ignorant', the latter are not initiated into the secret doctrines of the community. Any adult Druze, male or female, can ask to be initiated. Those who pass the severe test become 'wise', those who fail have another chance in their next reincarnation. The 'wise' wear a distinguishing garment and a white turban. Their privileged position is also one of greater responsibility, for they are obliged to participate in the cult ceremonies on Thursday evenings, to say the daily prayers, to abstain from drink, lying, theft, and vengeance. The 'ignorant' enjoy greater freedom. The more pious or learned among the 'wise' are accorded the authority of sheikhs. They receive instruction in a special school and are expected to spend some time in contemplation in retreat-houses located in remote areas. In addition to copying their sacred scriptures, the sheikhs offer spiritual direction to the 'ignorant' and preside at marriages and funerals. In each Druze district one sheikh, normally from a particular family, is recognized as the supreme religious authority. In Israel the honour is enjoyed by the Tarif family of Julis.

The political history of the Druze is one of internal and external struggle. While different dynasties vied for internal power, the community had to fight for its identity against Christians and Muslims. They are in consequence a hardy, vigorous people who do not ask for friendship but who demand respect. Their most remarkable leader was Fakhr-a-Din II

(1591–1635) who, to the ire of the Turks, carved out an independent kingdom in central Lebanon, which he extended as far south as NABLUS, and ruled from 1595 to his death, with the exception of the six years (1613–18) he prudently spent at the court of the Medicis in Florence. He fostered the development of religious minorities, building churches, mosques, and synagogues.

The Druze hold Jethro, Moses' father-in-law and adviser, in special reverence. They call him Nabi Shueib, and his tomb (erected in 1930) below the HORNS OF HATTIN is one of their holiest sites. On 25 April each year thousands gather there for a great festival.

Emmaus: *see* ABU GHOSH, LATRUN, QUBEIBA

En Afeq (J5)

The mill was one of the significant medieval institutions. While waiting to grind his own grain or that of his lord, the peasant's small world expanded as he heard the news from far and near. If in Palestine he was subject to the draconian laws protecting the seigneurial monopoly of milling, which the Crusaders brought with them from Europe, they in turn had to adapt themselves to his techniques. This combination of European construction and Arab technology is portrayed in the perfectly preserved C12 mill, which is the centre-piece of the nature reserve at En Afeq on the Naaman river.

After Jerusalem the most important Crusader city was St Jean d'Acre (AKKO). The only stream in the vicinity capable of driving a water mill to meet its need for flour was 'the river Pacida or Belus, which covers its narrow bank with sand of a kind used for making glass; the river itself flows out of the marsh of Cendebia at the foot of Mount Carmel' (Pliny, *Natural History* 5: 75). It runs parallel to the coast for some 6 km before entering the sea just south of Akko. In 1154 a Casale Recordance (whence the modern name Kurdani) with its mills is listed as a property of the Hospitallers. The flow of the river was not suited to the large vertical water-wheel, which was the standard in Europe, and the Crusaders were forced to adopt the horizontal wheel of the East. Flour was conveyed to Akko by ship. The mill was fortified when the Crusaders retook Akko from Saladin in 1191, but it could not resist the Mamluk sultan Baybars in 1263. He did not destroy it, and the mill was still in use in 1925.

Visit. Open: 8 a.m.–4 p.m. in winter; to 5 p.m. in summer; to 3 p.m. on Fridays. Toilets. The 325 m dam both raised the level of the sluggish river and directed its flow to the four V-shaped openings. The compression and the drop produced high-pressure jets which drove the horizontal wheels in the four milling units. These were located in parallel tunnels whose barrel vaults are visible on the other side of the building; through them the water flowed back into the stream. A vertical axle transmitted power from the wheel to the runner millstone in the room above and caused it to move on the nether millstone. The milling room is now used for a slide show on the nature reserve. From the roof of the two-storey tower, which was the defensive element of the mill, there is a fine view over the reserve and the rich plain of Akko.

En Avdat* (E28)

The plain between Kibbutz Sede Boker and the ancient city of AVDAT is slashed by a deep canyon which is the nature reserve of En Avdat. There are two entrance roads from route 40, one leading into the bottom of the canyon from Midreshet Ben Gurion (open: 9 a.m.), the other, further south, leading to the observation point on the rim of the canyon. Ladders link the top of the cliffs to the bottom, but only ascent is permitted. To the right on the way up is a cave used by Byzantine monks.

The canyon with its long deep pool is beautiful, but the area on the top of the cliffs is more interesting because prehistoric tribes camped there for over 100,000 years. They dwelt, not in caves, but in huts made of branches. The sections of the plain in which they lived can be detected by observing the **concentrations of flint tools**: their darker colour makes them stand out from the brown soil.

The easiest section to find is on the north rim of the canyon west of the **Byzantine watch-tower** where there is a big Middle Palaeolithic Site (1,200,000–45,000 BC). It is traversed by the C1 AD NABATAEAN trade route linking Petra via Avdat with the port of Gaza. The road is recognized by the line of untrimmed kerbstones. It would have been a two-day march from here to the coast.

The density of prehistoric occupation is shown by the fact that flint tools here cover an area of 1 km², and in addition are found up to 1 m beneath the present surface. Other sites appear on the crest of the line of low hills to the north; these yield small tools of the Upper Palaeolithic and Mesolithic periods (45,000–15,000 BC).

Exactly 2 km on the road to Avdat (route 40) from the turn-off to Midreshet Ben Gurion an orange sign points the way to Bor Hawwarim. This great **Nabataean cistern** is located in a little gully to the left (north) approximately 150 m from the road. The rock roof is supported by a central pillar in which a miniature standing stone (now badly eroded) was carved in relief. It was the Nabataean symbol of the divinity who protected the water without which life in the desert would have been impossible.

En el-Mamoudiyeh (H20)

According to Byzantine tradition, Elizabeth brought her infant son, John the Baptist, to a cave in EN KEREM in order to save him from the murderous wrath of Herod (Matt. 2: 16–18). Medieval pilgrims believed that thence she travelled underground to HEBRON, and that it was in the desert to the west that John grew up and began his ministry. This tradition is centred on En el-Mamoudiyeh (= the Baptism Spring), over which is built a unique baptistry protected by a small fort.

Visit. The tarmac road from Hebron to Taffuh passes on the right a Russian church where a late tradition placed MAMRE. At the dispensary in Taffuh go between the houses to the south. From the edge of a deep wadi the ruins of the fort are visible on the opposite hill. The baptistry is at the narrowest point in the bottom of the wadi.

The Baptistery

The building is very small (6.6 × 3.15 m), and is the only baptistery in Palestine that is not associated with a church. It is dated to the time of Justinian (527–65). At ground level in front of the apse is a circular baptismal font with a flight of steps. It was fed by a spring, which is at the far end of the 8 m tunnel in the south wall. The vaulting of the tunnel leading to the main spring, some 10 m downstream, is medieval, and betrays Crusader interest in the site.

Why a Byzantine baptistery should have been located here remains obscure. Its existence goes a long way to explaining the origin of the medieval tradition.

The Fort

The easiest way to reach the fort (today called Khirbet ed-Deir) is to follow the path up to the left (looking downstream) for some 70 m and then go left again across country to the top of the hill.

A single entrance gives access to a corridor with rooms on either side. The locking system of the door is worthy of note. A vertical bar was first inserted in the slot on the right side of the lintel. The base was then pushed into place following the curved groove in the sill. Finally, a traverse bar was slid into the holes in the door posts. The hole drilled through the centre of the lintel meets the top of the closed door; water poured through it would have kept the wood damp in case of an attempt to fire it. Further protection for the door was provided by a round stone set on a stone rail, which could be rolled to seal the doorway. This type of closure is a common feature of small forts constructed in North Africa during the reign of Justinian, but in Palestine it is attested only for tombs, and the MONASTERY

OF ST MARTYRIUS. What happened to the poor devil assigned to move the stone into place, and how the occupants expected to get out, remain unsolved mysteries.

En Farah (En Perat) (K17)

The steep walls of a mountain valley close in abruptly as if to shelter the perennial spring which still creates a little oasis whose fertility shames the barren hillsides. The story of the MONASTERIES IN THE JUDAEAN DESERT is long and complex, but it began here about AD 330 when Chariton, a pilgrim from Iconium in Turkey, was brought here by bandits. After they were miraculously removed, he found himself in possession of their cave hide-out and the treasures it contained. Little did he know that in the C1 AD it had been one of a complex of caves fitted out by the Jewish rebel leader Simon Bar-Giora as his base (*War* 4: 512).

His desire for solitude was frustrated by growing numbers of disciples who settled in nearby caves, and Chariton against his will became the founder of the first laura in Judaea. It was known as Pharan. Subsequently he established the lauras of Douka (MOUNT OF TEMPTATION) and of Souka (WADI KHAREITUN). The second great figure of Judaean monasticism, Euthymius of Lesser Armenia (377–473), spent his formative years as a monk at En Farah (406–11).

Visit. From route 457 turn east towards the Israeli settlement of Almon. Although there are erosion gullies in the dirt road, with great care it is possible to drive to the old British pumping station in the bottom of the valley. From there go upstream for 100 m and the monastery is visible on the left. Alternatively, leave the vehicle at the ruined upper booster pumping station near Almon, and descend by the **Byzantine monastic path** which lies to the north of the pipeline; the path is rough but has been levelled by a retaining wall on the downhill side. It goes directly to the monastery. A network of such paths links the desert monasteries. They made guides unnecessary, and travel more secure.

The most obvious feature of the site is the enclosure wall erected when Russian Orthodox monks established a monastery here in the early C20; it was abandoned for lack of support and subsequently vandalized in the 1970s. The oldest part of the complex is probably the **cave church**, which has two windows and an emplacement for the altar near the east wall. It is 12 m above ground-level at the foot of the cliff, and is reached by three flights of steps and a vertical chimney. The latter cannot be climbed without a ladder; Simon Bar-Giora's security precaution also protected the monks from bedouin raids. To the east of the church three caves on the same level were adapted as **cells**.

Almost directly below the cave church are the remains of a small stone-built Byzantine chapel. Some 25 m west (upstream) of this church are a **reservoir** (with an estimated capacity of 600 m³) and traces of a building paved with white mosaics, which may have been a bakery and store-rooms. From this point the nine hermit caves on the other side of the wadi are clearly visible; they average 4 × 6 m, and are 35 m from each other.

Downstream from the spring one can see the **aqueduct** constructed by Herod the Great (37–4 BC). It supplemented the flow from En Fawwar (p. 293), whence another aqueduct brought water to En Qilt, and there fed into the four aqueducts in the Wadi Qilt which supplied the fortress of KYPROS and the winter palace at TULUL ABU EL-ALAIQ.

En Gedi (L21)

Date-palms, vineyards, aromatic and medicinal plants made En Gedi in biblical times a symbol of beauty. 'My love is a cluster of henna flowers among the vines of En Gedi' (S. of S. 1: 14; cf. Sir. 24: 14). It is still a vivid slash of green on the barren coast of the DEAD SEA and one can even swim beneath the waterfall in Nahal David (Fig. 61). Tribes just emerging from the Stone Age came to the plateau above the waterfall to worship in a little temple from which there is a spectacular view over the oasis and the southern part of the Dead Sea.

The area is a nature reserve. Both Nahal David and Nahal Arugot are open Sunday–Thursday and Saturday 8 a.m.–4 p.m.; Fridays to 3 p.m. In summer visiting times are progressively extended, so check with the reserve office (tel.: 057–84285). The gate at Nahal Arugot is shut to incoming visitors two hours before closing time.

Tel Goren

The amusingly vulgar encounter between David and Saul (1 Sam. 24) suggests that there was no permanent occupation here in the C10 BC. The tel is not worth a visit; the excavation showed that the first Israelite town was established at the end of the C7 BC.

Occupation continued after the exile, but intensive economic development began only in the early C2 BC when En Gedi became a royal Hasmonean estate and the administrative centre of Idumaea. The wealth derived from agriculture was supplemented by the sale of salt and of bitumen extracted from the Dead Sea. For some unknown reason the population declined in the Herodian period and was wiped out during the First Revolt (AD 66–70) when the defenders of MASADA slaughtered over 700 women and children (*War* 4: 401–4).

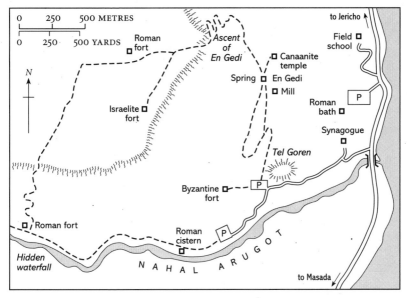

▲ **Fig. 61.** En Gedi.

Canaanite Temple

From the parking lot at the foot of Tel Goren a dirt road leads up to a tiny oasis; a long detour can be avoided by taking the short cut from the ruined Byzantine building. The ruined building to the right at the top of the short cut is a **flour mill** of the Ottoman period (1517–1918). Water from the spring was carried on an aqueduct to the 9 m shaft down which it plummeted to exit via the 15 cm nozzle with sufficient force to turn the millstone.

Surrounded by luxuriant growth, the **spring** gives the area its name. En Gedi means the 'Spring of the Kid'. Ibex, a type of mountain goat, and the Syrian hyrax, a timid herbivorous animal about the size of a terrier, can often be surprised by a quiet approach. 'For the ibex there are the mountains, in the crags the hyrax find refuge' (Psalm 104: 18). From the other side of the oasis the wall of the temple is visible at the edge of the first plateau in front and to the right. The square building east of the spring is the C7 BC **tower**. The round structure on the other side of the path is a C2–C5 AD limekiln. Since limestone was everywhere, it was easier to burn it wherever fuel could be found, particularly the intensely burning thorn.

The **temple** was in use about 3000 BC and, since no trace of habitation was found in the surrounding area, it must have served as a central sanctuary for the region. Why it was abandoned no one really knows, but some sort of threat is suspected, because it seems likely that the hoard of

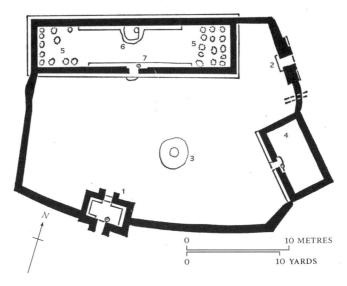

▲ **Fig. 62.** En Gedi. Chalcolithic Temple (after Ussishkin). 1. Main entrance; 2. Secondary entrance; 3. Plastered basin; 4. Store-room or residence; 5. Buried offerings; 6. Altar; 7. Door recess.

416 copper objects, found in the Cave of the Treasure in Nahal Mishmar (6 km south), belonged to the temple. The copper crowns and the wands tipped with figures of birds and animals suggest cult objects. Carbon dating of the straw mats in which they were wrapped shows that the dates coincide.

The mud-brick walls have eroded to nothing but their stone foundations remain to reveal the complete plan (Fig. 62). Each of the two entrances faces a spring further down the hill. The elaborate main entrance lacks part of the bench; the door was designed to open flush with the wall. Beside the other entrance a small opening in the bottom of the wall was the exit for the drain of the once plastered basin. One of the two buildings may have been a store-room, or even the home of a resident priest. The other was certainly used for cultic purposes. At either end offerings were buried in small pits. Sacrifice was offered in the centre where a thick ash layer contained animal bones, beads, and broken figurines. A neat recess received the opened door.

Ascent of En Gedi

From the Chalcolithic temple black trailmarkers go to the left of the protruding rock and up to a white saddle. The **trail** from there zigzags up a wide cleft to the top of the cliffs; it may be the Ascent of Ziz mentioned in 2 Chr. 20: 16. The route was first constructed in the C7 BC by piling stones on both sides in order to permit pack animals to ply between En Gedi and Jerusalem. The gradient respects the loads they had to carry. The Romans improved the route in the C2 AD by building retaining walls where necessary. They had learned its value during the siege of MASADA, when it was their link with Jerusalem.

On top of the cliff are military positions. On the edge of the cliff south of the Nature Reserve sign is the **Israelite fort** (Mizpe En Gedi). A polygonal wall surrounds a small rectangular building; it is dated to the C7 BC. Some 200 m west of the sign and 75 m north of the trail is a **Roman fort**. The four or five room building is dated to the C2 AD. The basic function of both forts was the same, to protect the road, but their siting suggests that they feared different dangers!

Synagogue

The tent-like roof with several apexes protects a **mosaic floor** dated to the mid- or late C5 AD, a time when the 'very large Jewish village' (Eusebius) of En Gedi was peaceful and prosperous. The modern wooden walkway runs the length of the porch (*narthex*) from which three doors gave access to the prayer hall. Piers parallel to the three sides supported the roof. The central area contains two mosaics. A small rectangular carpet with a bird lies before the platform (*bema*) on which stood the ark of the law. It is flanked on the far side by a stepped seat ('the Seat of Moses'). The central circle contains four small birds; pairs of peacocks nibble grapes in the corners of the square.

The western aisle contains a large **inscription** whose content is most unusual. The first eight lines are in Hebrew, the rest in Aramaic. (The following numbers identify the lines and the words in square brackets are my commentary.) '(1) [The Patriarchs] Adam, Seth, Enosh, Kenan, Mahalalel, Jared; (2) Enoch, Methuselah, Lamech, Noah, Shem, Ham, and Japeth. (3) [The Signs of the Zodiac] Aries, Taurus, Gemini, Cancer, Leo, Virgo; (4) Libra, Scorpio, Sagittarius, Capricorn, Aquarius, and Pisces. (5) [The Months of the Year] Nisan, Iyar, Sivan, Tammuz, Av Elul; (6) Tishrei, Narheshvan, Kislev, Tevet, Shevar; (7) and Adar. [The Pillars of the World] Abraham, Isaac, Jacob. Peace; (8) Hananiah, Mishael, and Azariah. Peace unto Israel. (9) [Recognition] May they be remembered for good; Yose and Ezron and Hizziqiyu, the sons of Hilfi. [Warning] Anyone causing a controversy between a man and his friend or whoever (11) slanders his friend before the Gentiles, or whoever steals (12) the property of his friend, or whoever reveals the secret of the town (13) to the Gentiles—He whose eyes range through the whole earth (14) and Who sees hidden things, he will set his face on that (15) man and on his seed and will uproot him from under the heavens. (16) And all the people said: Amen and Amen Selah. (17) [Recognition] Rabbi Yose the son of Hilfi, Hizziqiyu the son of Hilfi, may they be remembered for good (18) for they did a great deal in the name of the Merciful Peace.' (trans. L. I. Levine)

This beautiful building was destroyed in the first part of the C6, thus bringing to an end a tradition of prayer and study that went back to the foundation of the first synagogue here in the late C2 or early C3 AD.

Excavations to the north of the synagogue have brought to light the **Byzantine street** leading to it. There were houses on both sides, but the doors of those on only one side opened on to the street. The doors on the other side gave on to a different street. Basins and channels in the houses suggest a form of interior plumbing fed by the spring at the top of the cliff. Such water supplies were necessary to enable the inhabitants to survive the torrid heat of summer.

Roman Bath-house

The later strata of Tel Goren show that the centre of the settlement had moved to the north-east by the Herodian period. It is precisely here that a long, narrow Roman bath (40 × 5 m) was discovered; the cleansing process began at the north end. At this stage (beginning of the C2 AD) En Gedi was a personal estate of the Roman emperor, and the highly unusual shape of the bath suggests that it might have been one side of the market-place. During the Second Revolt (AD 132–5) the bath was converted into temporary dwellings when the town served as one of the military and administrative centres of the rebel leader Bar Kokhba. As the Roman troops advanced on En Gedi rebel officers were forced to seek refuge in caves in the Nahal Hever which enters the Dead Sea 5 km south of En Gedi. When the correspondence they took with them is published new light will be thrown on En Gedi at this period.

Fortified Building

This small structure of the late Roman and Byzantine period is contemporary with the synagogue, but it is located at a considerable distance. Since its stones are taken from the same landscape it blends in so well that it is difficult to see. It lies some 400 m south-west of Tel Goren towards the entrance of Nahal Agurot. A fortified courtyard protected the entrance to a tower whose walls were reinforced by a sloping glacis. Within the glacis was slotted a round stone which could be rolled in front of the door. Inside is a long, narrow 2 m-deep plastered basin which is connected to one outside the wall. Some connection with the production of opobalsam has been suggested (see p. 469).

Nahal Arugot

This is a magnificent nature reserve resonant with the sound of water. It is also the route used by the Romans to establish and supply their camps on both sides of Nahal Hever. Each was sited on the cliff edge above a cave in which Jews had taken refuge at the end of the Second Revolt (132–5), both in order to prevent a break-out and to observe what was happening in the cave in the opposite cliff. The Cave of the Letters yielded the archives of a

Supplies Not Sent

'From Shimeon bar Kosiba to the men of En Gedi, to Masabala and to Yehonathan bar Beayan, peace. In comfort you sit, eat and drink from the property of the House of Israel, and care nothing for your brothers. . . .' (trans. Y. Yadin)

The Four Species required for Succoth

'Shimeon to Yehudah bar Menashe to Qiryath Aravaya. I have sent to you two donkeys that you shall send with them two men to Yehonathan bar Beayan and to Masabala in order that they shall pack and send to the camp, towards you, palm branches and citrons. And you from your place, send others who will bring you myrtles and willows. See that they are tithed and send them to the camp. [The request is made] because the army is numerous. Be well.' (trans. Y. Yadin)

litigious woman named Babata, and documents written by and to Bar Kohkba dealing with the administration of the revolt (see box).

The Romans built the **cistern** on the left some 200 m from the ticket office, but their most extraordinary achievement is the **cliff path** they constructed to climb to the southern rim of the canyon. Today called Maale Halssim 'Ascent of the Essenes', it is visible from the bluff just before the descent to the Hidden Waterfall. Look for the retaining wall of the path at the top and bottom of the vertical cliff, and the zigzags linking the two on the left side. Near the bottom of the modern hiking trail, Maale Benei HaMoshavim, the Romans built a little **fort** which permitted them to keep the whole route from the Dead Sea to the top of the cliff opposite under observation.

En Hemed* (J17)

Perhaps the most vivid image which anyone has of the CRUSADES is that of the thundering charge of the mailed and mounted knights of the Temple and the Hospital. But where did the old soldiers go as they faded away? To a quiet rest-home in a verdant valley. A fine example of such a building is found in the national park at En Hemed, whose medieval name of **Aqua Bella** ('Beautiful Waters') emphasizes the gentle tranquillity of the place.

It is located on the south side of the Jerusalem–Tel Aviv highway (route 1) at the Hemed Interchange.

Visit. Open: Sunday–Thursday and Saturday 8 a.m.–4 p.m.; in summer to 5 p.m.; Fridays to 2 p.m. Toilets and snacks.

The rectangular structure was slotted into the hillside below the spring sometime before 1163. It belonged to the Knights of St John of the Hospital. The main gate in the east wall gives access to a **courtyard** surrounded on three sides by two-storey buildings. A door beneath the half-arch on the left gives access to a large barrel-vaulted room which had an exit to the stream; it contains the circular stone base of an olive press. Over this was an airy groin-vaulted hall, reached by an outside staircase. An aumbry and the curve of an apse are visible in the partially destroyed eastern wall. This part of the room served as **the chapel of an infirmary** where terminally ill members of the Order had the consolation of the Real Presence. Beyond the foundations of the chancel screen there is space for twenty beds; the small turret-chamber could have been used for ablutions.

The functions of the other rooms have not been determined, but it is reasonable to assume that those on the ground floor served practical purposes (cooking, storage), and that the upper floor contained the dormitory and refectory of the serving brothers who ran the retirement community.

The small structure reached from the flat roof of the room at right angles to the chapel-infirmary was a **signal tower**. It is the only point in clear view of the Crusader castle of **Belmont**, whose distinctive silhouette crowns the hill to the south. It protected a section of the route from Jerusalem to Jaffa. It also served as the administrative centre of an extensive domain belonging to the Hospitallers, which included ABU GHOSH on the opposite slope of the valley. Little is known of the castle's history, and little remains to be seen; it was razed by Ibrahim Pasha in 1834, and thereafter absorbed by an Arab village. The castle cannot be reached from En Hemed. Access from the west is through Kibbutz Zova; exit the Jerusalem–Tel Aviv highway at the Harel Interchange and follow route 396.

En Yael (J18)

The C2 AD ROMAN ROAD from Jerusalem to BET GUVRIN parallels the railway line in the Rephaim valley. The valley narrows after it passes the village of Battir, the site of the Jews' last stand against the Romans in AD 135. Closer to Jerusalem it is wide and fertile, and was farmed from the third millennium BC. It became part of Jerusalem's agricultural supply area as the city expanded. The gentle spring at En Yael enticed a Roman officer to build a luxurious residence there. The villa and its 4.4 hectare property is being developed as a living museum.

Visit. From Teddy Stadium take the settlement by-pass road in Emek Rephaim. The site is directly across the valley from the Jerusalem Zoo, and is reached by the first paved road on the left.

The C2 AD Roman road (see ROMAN ROADS) opened up the valley to easy settlement, and the construction of the villa is dated towards the end of that century. The number of roof tiles stamped with the mark of the Tenth Legion suggests that the owner might have been a soldier, possibly one of those who availed of the permission to marry while in the army which was granted in AD 197. An earthquake destroyed the villa towards the end of the C3. The presence of a spring and the quality of the terraces ensured that the farm stayed in use up to the C20. Most of the visible remains are Roman.

The covered structure beside the spring protects a series of fine mosaic floors. As at SEPPHORIS, the T-shaped mosaic indicates that the largest room was a *triclinium* or **dining-room**. It was pointless to decorate the area beneath the couches lining three of the walls. Around the central fountain nereids sit on the tails of ichthyocentaurs who offer them gifts, and erotes ride dolphins. Just inside the door fish surround the sea goddess Tethys; on either side are square panels with Medusa heads.

The mosaic in the square room beside the triclinium has a bird in each corner and between them a lion, lioness, and panther. Only two of the four theatrical masks remain. The centre medallion probably represented Dionysos.

The **vestibule** of the triclinium contains an unusual representation of the four seasons, the figures are male and are not in the corners of a square. Winter (hood) and Spring are separated from Summer (hat) and Autumn by the centre panel in which someone carrying a basket approaches a satyr seated on a rock and weaving a garland.

On the next terrace down is a Roman **bath-house**, which was reused in the Byzantine and Early Arab period, and a wide arched entrance leading to a paved **courtyard** containing an olive press and oil vat. The present reservoir is modern. The pool on the third terrace is Roman, and beside it is a much more elaborate **bath-house** of the same period. The mosaic floor of the circular room represents a perfectly preserved double-twisted rope six-pointed star. This geometric design was in use by many civilizations from the third millennium BC.

At the edge of the excavated area note the sophisticated system for distributing water to the various terraces, some of which have been brought back into cultivation. A canal at the base of the wall permits water to be directed to specific plots, and the surplus flows into the channel of the terrace below.

Eshtemoa (Sammu) (H22)

After his campaign against the Amalekites David (1004–965 BC) divided the spoils among the towns and villages south of Hebron which had given him and his men hospitality when he badly needed it. Eshtemoa was one of these (1 Sam. 30: 28). In the C4 Eusebius classed it as 'a very large Jewish village'; this assessment is borne out by the monumental synagogue dated to that century.

The access road (route 356; signposted) from the main Hebron–Beer Sheva road (route 60) ends in a T-junction; take the right-hand branch and then turn left in the open space in the centre of the village. The synagogue is just beside the mosque; if the guard is not present, ask anyone to find him.

The disposition of the synagogue, which remained in use until the C7 AD, is identical with that at nearby KHIRBET SUSEYA, even to the triple entrance in the narrow east wall. The *bema* (raised platform), orienting the building towards Jerusalem, stands in the middle of the north wall; the unusual depression in the centre may have been for the chair of Moses. In the wall above are three niches; the centre one contained the Scrolls of the Law while those on either side housed ritual objects, such as the *menorah*. The niche built above the benches in the opposite wall is the *mihrab* added (by Saladin, according to legend) when the synagogue was converted into a mosque in the Middle Ages.

The walls rise to a considerable height (in one place 8 m) but it is clear that the façade has been badly restored. Vertical moulding betrays that there were originally two lateral doors, now blocked up. The centre door has been narrowed, which means that the lintel cannot be the original one; many such lintels can be seen in the older buildings of the village, particularly those near the T-junction.

Essenes

The discovery of the Dead Sea Scrolls in early 1947, and the subsequent excavation of QUMRAN, threw new light on the Essenes, already known from detailed accounts in the C1 AD writings of their Jewish contemporaries, Philo (*Quod Omnis* n. 75–91) and Josephus (*War* 2: 119–61; *Antiquities* 18: 18–22).

The sect originated in Babylon as a reaction against the religious laxity which, in their view, had provoked the divine punishment of the exile (586–538 BC) of the Jewish people from Jerusalem. The members of this

New Covenant dedicated themselves to perfect observance of the Law. Some returned to Judaea about 164 BC, and immediately found themselves at odds with the religious establishment. To their highly conservative eyes the Judaism of the Temple had irremediably compromised itself by assimilating foreign elements. A naïve attempt to convince Jews that the Essenes alone had the truth failed, and the morale of the returned exiles began to crumble. To escape from the hostile pressures of Jerusalem they settled in rural areas. This attempt to salvage their identity was not entirely successful, but only a small number accepted the leadership of the Teacher of Righteousness and moved to Qumran about 150 BC. The tension between the Teacher and the Man of Lies described in some of the scrolls reflects this split in the Essene movement.

The Teacher of Righteousness was the one significant convert made by the Essenes in Judaea. A member of the Sadok family, traditional holders of the High Priesthood until dispossessed in favour of others more amenable to the hellenizing policy of the Seleucid rulers of Syria, he was predisposed to radical religious reform. A power vacuum in the religious establishment (159–152 BC) gave him the chance to act as High Priest. His summary dismissal by Jonathan Maccabaeus, whom the scrolls called the Wicked Priest, brought him into the Essene camp. A powerful spiritual personality (some of his hymns are preserved), he not only introduced Saduccean elements but he gave his followers an even more radical orientation.

The rigorous austerity of life at Qumran attracted few adherents until persecution of the Pharisees towards the end of the reign of John Hyrcanus (134–103 BC) forced a number of them to seek refuge in this remote desert settlement. The grudging external obedience they offered in return for security provoked a period of spiritual difficulty attested in the scrolls. The community recovered its equilibrium in time to survive a major destruction in the second half of the C1 BC. When the members were dispersed by the Romans in AD 68 at least one member escaped to MASADA with a scroll, 'The Songs of the Sabbath Services'. What happened to the others no one knows.

At Qumran the food supply came from flocks of sheep and goats and from the farm run by the Essenes in the Buqei'a (the flat plain above the cliffs behind the settlement). It is still possible to trace the cliff-path they used. Subsidiary settlements around the brackish springs of En Feshkha and En el-Ghuweir, further south on the shore of the Dead Sea, also contributed their share. Some members devoted a considerable portion of each day to such work. Others laboured as potters or scribes, and the kitchen staff must have been large. Saturday was a day of absolute rest; they did not even relieve themselves because their regulations demanded that they dig a hole.

The Law was the *raison d'être* of the Essenes and it was studied twenty-four hours each day. During the day one in each group of ten took it in turns, and the whole community was divided into three to cover the three night watches. The need for copies of the books of the Old Testament is obvious, and the caves yielded copies of all the books of the Hebrew canon with the exception of Esther. Their study was also productive. The caves contained a series of commentaries (*pesharim*) on the prophets in which the Essenes read their own history into the inspired word. Books which now do not figure in the canon of sacred scripture had a place in their library (e.g. Henoch, Jubilees), and the needs of liturgy and discipline forced them to generate their own literature.

All the existing documents are easily available in a good English translation by Florentino García Martínez and W. E. Watson, *The Dead Sea Scrolls Translated: The Qumran Texts in English* (Leiden: Brill, 1994). The 'Rule of the Community', in particular, furnishes details on the testing of candidates, the procedure in public meetings, and the more common faults of members. Such legislation reveals the very human side of life at Qumran, and balances the rather idealized, but highly readable, description of their way of life given by Josephus in his *Jewish War* (pp. 125–9 in the Penguin Classics edition).

An Extraordinary People

'On the west side, but out of range of the poisonous vapours of the Dead Sea, live the Essenes. They are unique and admirable beyond all other peoples in that they have no women, no sexual desire, no money, and only palm trees for company. Owing to the influx of newcomers, they are daily reborn in equal numbers. Many are those who join them because they are weary of life and the arbitrary fluctuations of fortune. Thus, incredible as it may seem, a race in which no one is born has survived through thousands of ages, so profitable for them is the urge of others to do penance for their past lives.' (Pliny (C1), *Natural History* 5: 73; trans. H. Rackham)

Gamla (05)

Looking due east from the long straight stretch of road at the north end of the SEA OF GALILEE (Fig. 107) one can see far into a wild valley (Nahal Daliyyot) split by a steep-sided hill in the centre. The thought of a perfect natural fortress comes at once to mind. From the Golan the site (Khirbet es-Salam) is even more impressive; a narrow ridge links a ruin-encrusted rock island to the plateau. Under planing eagles the Sea of Galilee shimmers in the distance, waterfalls smoke in the valleys on either side.

The place grips the imagination; the temptation to identify it with Gamla is easily understood. According to Josephus (*War* 4: 1–83), Vespasian with three legions began the siege of Gamla (or Gamala) on 12 October AD 67. The Romans quickly broke through the wall, but suffered a defeat in the narrow confines of the town; 'the houses were built against the steep mountain flank and astonishingly huddled together, one on top of the other, and this perpendicular site gave the city the appearance of being suspended in air and falling headlong on itself' (*War* 4: 7). When the Romans had regrouped, the carelessness of the Jewish sentries permitted three legionaries to undermine a tower. This threw the population into panic but the Romans deferred their entry until the following day (10 November), permitting many to take refuge in the citadel. In the fierce battle next day, 4,000 fell before the legions, 5,000 committed suicide by flinging themselves over the cliff. The parallel with MASADA is obvious (in both cases two women escaped to tell the story), but to call Gamla 'the Masada of the North' is a poor compliment to its valiant defenders.

Khirbet es-Salam appears to fit Josephus's description of Gamla until one looks closely at the details. Then difficulties begin to emerge: for example, at Gamla the citadel is south of the city on the hump (*War* 4: 8), while here the citadel is west of the hump. Josephus's description is thought by some to apply much more accurately to Tel ed-Dra near the village of Jamle (P6) on the Syrian side of the armistice line. Be that as it may, Khirbet es-Salam was certainly a Jewish fortress-town taken by the Romans during the First Revolt (AD 66–70). In the houses were arrowheads bent from impact, and on the slopes hundreds of round stones fired from the legion catapults. After the Roman victory the site apparently was never reoccupied.

Visit. Open: Sunday–Thursday and Saturday 8 a.m.–4 p.m.; Friday to 3 p.m. From route 92 in the north-east corner of the Sea of Galilee turn up hill on route 869, and then left (north) on route 808 for 2 km. Note the dolmen beside the signposted access road.

The city needed a **wall** only on its vulnerable eastern side. It is built over, or on occasion reuses, earlier structures. A date in the Herodian period would seem appropriate. Juxtaposed to the city wall is a colonnaded rectangular building (13.4 × 9.3 m) with stepped benches on all sides. The three doors faced the city wall. Specifically Jewish features either in design or decoration are lacking. In all probability, however, it should be identified as a **synagogue** because on the far side of the little entrance courtyard is a Jewish **ritual bath** (*mikveh*), which was fed by a channel that collected rain-water from the roof of the synagogue. If this is correct, and its C1 BC date stands, it is the oldest synagogue in the Holy Land. Its only competitors are those at MASADA and at HERODIUM. During the First Revolt the building was requisitioned in order to provide living quarters for refugees; a round basin and a water channel running out through the city wall were installed in the north corner.

Beyond the *mikveh* is a C1 AD **olive oil press**. The restored arch shows that it was roofed with stone slabs, as in NABATAEAN buildings in the wood-poor NEGEV. Note the crushing mill and the weights for the two beam presses whose slots in the west wall are evident. The stepped bath on the north side can only be interpreted as a *mikveh*. Oil was so fundamental to all facets of Jewish life that those who produced it had to be ritually pure. There are other dwellings, baths and oil presses as one goes towards the summit.

Gezer (G16)

As seen from the Jerusalem–Tel Aviv highway, the low, undistinguished silhouette of Tel Gezer yields no hint of its importance. One has to stand on the top to appreciate its commanding position; there is an unimpeded view in all directions. The whole coastal plain from Ashqelon to north of Tel Aviv is spread out like a map; no force could move there without being seen from Gezer. In antiquity it was sited at the junction of two trade routes. The Way of the Sea, the main commercial link between Egypt and Mesopotamia, passed through the plain to the west; to the north was the road between Jerusalem and the coast. No general or merchant could ignore Gezer, for its ruler had the power to disrupt all communications; the name Gezer is in fact derived from the Semitic root 'to cut', 'to divide'.

The camp-sites of the 4th millennium BC had developed into a fortified city by about 1650 BC. It was destroyed by Thutmose III *c.*1466 BC and the record of his victory inscribed on the wall of the temple at Karnak is the first mention of the name Gezer. Thereafter, it remained under Egyptian domination, and the relationship during the C14 BC is well documented by letters in the archives of the Foreign Office at el-Amarna in Egypt. There are ten letters from various kings of Gezer and many references in letters from other city-states such as MEGIDDO and Shechem (TEL BALATA).

Egyptian control, lost sometime early in the C13 BC, had to be reimposed by Merneptah in 1230 BC; the strategic importance of the city is underlined by the title he gave himself, 'The Binder of Gezer'. Egypt did not hold it long. At the beginning of the C12 BC the PHILISTINES had to extend their authority to Gezer in order to secure their bridgehead on the coast. David skirmished in the region but never took the city (2 Sam. 5: 25; 1 Chr. 14: 16; 20: 4), perhaps because it might have drawn the wrath of Egypt upon the nascent Israelite kingdom.

At the death of David in 965 BC the Israelites had become a force to reckon with in the politics of the region. The succession was not without problems (1 Kgs. 1–2), and the pharaoh Siamun attempted to capitalize on Solomon's difficulties. He gravely underestimated the capacity of the new king and to extricate himself had to give his daughter in marriage to Solomon, her dowry was the city of Gezer (1 Kgs. 9: 16). No other foreigner ever married a pharaoh's daughter. When his request for one was denied, a Babylonian king cunningly suggested that any beautiful woman could be sent from Egypt since none of his subjects would know the difference!

The civil war, which followed Solomon's death in 928 BC, gave Egypt another chance; Gezer was

▲ **The Gezer Calendar.** A limestone tablet containing an agricultural calendar (see box).

abandoned for a while after its destruction during the pharaoh Shishak's murderous raid into Palestine (*c.*924 BC). This state could not have lasted for long; its strategic position, fertile fields, and abundant water were too attractive. Gezer must have been one of the first cities taken when the Assyrians under Tiglath-Pileser III undertook two campaigns against the Philistines in 734 and 733 BC. It definitely became part of the Assyrian

---

The Gezer Calendar

Around 925 BC a child inscribed in a stone exercise tablet this mnemonic ditty designed to help children remember the months of the year:

> 'His two months are olive harvest,
>   His two months are planting grain,
>   His two months are late planting;
>   His month is hoeing up of flax,
>   His month is harvest of barley,
>   His month is harvest and feasting;
>   His two months are vine-tending,
>   His month is summer fruit.'

(trans. W. F. Albright)

empire after the fall of the Northern Kingdom, Israel (to which it belonged), in 721 BC. Two business contracts of the mid-C7 BC suggest that Assyrian colonists maintained themselves there until the Babylonian invasion early the following century.

Though inhabited, Gezer seems to have lost all its importance during the C6–C3 BC. It comes to prominence again only during the Maccabean wars of the C2 BC. First fortified by the Syrians in 160 BC (1 Macc. 9: 52), it fell to Simon Maccabaeus in 142 BC. He strengthened the fortifications and built himself a residence (1 Macc. 13: 43–8). A Greek graffito signed by one of the citizens reveals the resentment caused by the change of regime; in frustration he wrote, 'To blazes with Simon's palace!' In 141 BC Simon gave his son John Hyrcanus command of the army with headquarters at Gezer (1 Macc. 13: 53).

Once the Hasmonean dynasty had been securely established in power, Gezer apparently became a private estate. Seven boundary stones have been found, six with identical Hebrew and Greek inscriptions; the Hebrew reads, 'the boundary of Gezer', and the Greek, 'belonging to Alkios'.

On the plain between the tel and RAMLA Baldwin IV defeated Saladin on 25 November 1177. The sultan narrowly escaped with his life. Fourteen years later Saladin camped there during his negotiations with Richard the Lion-Heart. A fortified village existed into the C15, but after that there is only silence.

Visit. There are three ways through the fertile fields to Tel Gezer. (1) The easiest is via Karmei Yosef. From the Ramla–Bet Shemesh road (route 44) follow Tamar Street to the roundabout, and then Gefen Street to the left, which circles down. At the bottom continue straight ahead, leaving Samadar Street on the right. From the rough parking-lot look north along the line of houses, Tel Gezer is to the left. A dirt road snakes up to the white

▼ **Fig. 63.** Tel Gezer (after Dever).

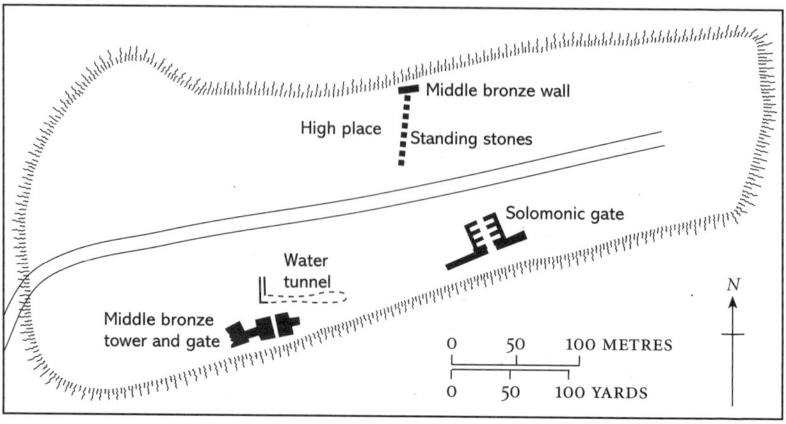

sign on the top, and there are four trees to the right. The jagged outline betrays the activity of archaeologists. Go through the gate and take the second dirt road to the left, and then the first right. (2) From the Ramla–Latrun road (route 424) go into Kibbutz Gezer and follow the signs. (3) At the first right-angled bend of the paved road leading into Kefar Bin Nun from route 424 continue straight ahead on the dirt road, which is not in good condition; it eventually joins up with (1).

Despite extensive excavations, erosion and undergrowth limit the areas worth visiting to four, three on the south side of the tel and one on the north. They are unmarked and the function of the sketch map (Fig. 63) is to indicate their relationship to one another.

Middle Bronze Age Gate and Water System

The dominant feature of this area is a great stone **tower** over 15 m in width. Built in the C17 BC, it is linked by a 4 m-wide wall to a **city gate** a little further east; orthostats line each side of the entrance and the mud-brick superstructure is beautifully defined. This wall was burnt by Thutmose III in 1468 BC, necessitating the erection of a new wall just outside at the end of the C15 BC; the gate of this period was probably outside the Solomonic gate further east.

A square pit inside the walls and between the tower and the gate is the entrance to the steeply sloping **water tunnel**. Less elaborate than similar installations at MEGIDDO and HAZOR it cannot be dated with certainty but must have been dug between the C15 and C10 BC.

Solomonic Gate

This magnificently preserved three-chambered gate dates from Solomon's reconstruction of Gezer in the C10 BC. Each of the chambers has a bench running around three sides; a plastered gutter at the western inner corner carried rain from the roof to the main drain running beneath the street. The large stone basin may have contained water to refresh the guards or the elders who sat at the gate. Traces of a casemate wall are visible on both sides of the gate.

High Place

This row of ten monoliths was set up about 1800 BC and functioned as a cultic centre, perhaps related to the renewal of a covenant between Gezer and other tribes or city-states. The stone block with a hollow cut in the centre may have been a basin or a socket for another monolith.

Near the edge of the mound are sections of two **city walls**. The inner one with a tower is contemporary with the High Place and with the South Gate [**1**]; the outer wall is dated to the C15 BC.

Finds made at Gezer complemented by illustrative displays are to be seen in the **Skirball Museum** at 13 King David Street, Jerusalem (see p. 147).

Golan (O and P 1–6)

The Golan is a high, basalt plateau to the east of the SEA OF GALILEE bounded on the north by Mount Hermon and on the south by the Yarmuk river. The fertile volcanic soil of the southern part gives way to wild pastureland in the north. The whole area is characterized by the small cones of extinct volcanoes.

Basalt hand axes and choppers attest human occupation in the Lower Palaeolithic Age (1,000,000–120,000 BC). Some twenty-five villages of the Chalcolithic period (4500–3300 BC) have been located. Typically they have five or six parallel rows of terrace houses and are sited near perennial streams. In the third millennium BC towns appear; their number and size reveal a flourishing and energetic civilization whose most extraordinary achievement is undoubtedly RUJM EL HIRI. This Early Bronze Age culture disintegrated towards the end of the third millennium, and nomads roamed the area. Their most enduring monuments are undoubtedly the dolmens or stone tables in which they buried their dead (*c.*2000 BC).

The southern part of the Golan appears in the Bible as the land of Geshur. Although within the tribal divisions it was not in fact occupied by the Israelites (Josh 13: 13). David married a daughter of the king of Geshur (2 Sam. 3: 3), which is why her son Absalom sought refuge there for three years when he rebelled against his father (2 Sam. 13: 39). At that stage it was under the control of the Arameans of Damascus, but occupation in the Iron Age does not appear to have been intensive.

In the C3 BC the Golan was an independent administrative unit (Gaulanitis) of the Ptolemaic empire. True development began when it was granted to Herod the Great by the emperor Augustus in 20 BC. After Herod's death in 4 BC this part of the divided kingdom fell to his son Philip who built his capital, Caesarea Philippi, at BANYAS. The strength of the Jewish population is attested by the part they played in the First Revolt against Rome (AD 66–70). The climax of the struggle for the Golan took place at GAMLA, a fortified town on a narrow rock promontory. Subsequently there was a drastic decline in Jewish presence on the Golan.

When Hadrian crushed the Second Revolt in AD 135 and forbade Jews to settle in Judaea, Galilee benefited by the movement of Jewish population to the north, but Jews returned to the Golan only in the C4. QASRIN is but one of some twenty-five sites in which synagogues have been found. These exhibit architectural and stylistic variations from Galilean synagogues, and a number are not oriented towards Jerusalem.

An unusual form of Christian presence is attested in the abandoned C19 Circassian village of Er Ramtaniyya (P3). A series of lintels offer an extraordinary combination of Christian and Jewish symbols. The cross and the fish appear with the palm branch (*lulav*) and the seven-branched candlestick (*menorah*). These are certainly the symbols of a marginalized Christian community of Jewish origins. Since the lintels are all in secondary use, their original context cannot be invoked to date them. The site was certainly occupied in the C1 AD, and continued to be so in the C2 and C3. The first church in the village was erected in the third quarter of the C4, at which point the religion of the village was drawn into the mainstream of orthodox Christianity.

A strong economy based on olive oil caused the Golan to flourish in the Byzantine period. 173 inhabited sites of the C5–C6 have been identified. Only the few large towns had mixed Jewish and Christian populations; in the villages it was one or the other.

The victory of Omar's bedouin over the Byzantine army at the battle of the Yarmuk on 20 August AD 636 was followed by massive depopulation of the Golan; pottery from the Early Arab period has been found at only 14 of the 173 Byzantine sites. The reasons must have been economic because the Arabs did not persecute Christians or Jews. The subsequent history of the region is shrouded in obscurity, until we reach the Mamluk period (1250–1517) when 139 sites were occupied, and the great castle of NIMRUD rebuilt. Caravanserais were built along the mail routes linking Egypt with Damascus.

The **Golan Archaeological Museum** in Qasrin houses finds from Gamla and ancient Qasrin in addition to documenting the human occupation of the Golan from prehistoric times to the end of the Byzantine period. Open: Sunday–Thursday 9 a.m.–4 p.m.; Friday 9 a.m.–1 p.m.; Saturday 10 a.m.–1 p.m.

Gush Halav (M3)

The name of this site, which means 'Fat Soil', was roughly transliterated into Greek as Gischala, the first syllable of which is preserved in the Arabic Jish; it is a Christian village located about half-way between Meron and Baram on route 89. In the wadi just east of the village are the remains of a fine synagogue.

According to the *Mishnah*, it was a walled city (Arachin 9: 6) at the time of Joshua, but occupation is attested only from the C10 BC, and the first written references appear in Josephus. It was the home of his rival, John of Gischala, 'the most unprincipled trickster that ever won ill fame by vicious habits' (*War* 2: 585–631), who slipped away when the town was besieged by Titus (*War* 4: 84–120), and became the leader of one of the factions that squabbled in Jerusalem as the Romans tightened their grip in AD 69–70. Much earlier the parents of the Apostle Paul had also suffered at

Paul's Galilean Ancestors

Commenting on Philemon vv. 23–4 Jerome of Bethlehem (342–420) wrote, 'They say that the parents of the Apostle Paul were from Gischala, a region of Judaea and that, when the whole province was devastated by the hand of Rome and the Jews scattered throughout the world, they were moved to Tarsus a town of Cilicia; the adolescent Paul inherited the personal status of his parents'.

'Judaea' is used here to mean the whole of Palestine (Luke 23: 5). The likelihood that Jerome, or any earlier Christian, invented the association of Paul's family with Gischala is remote. The town is not mentioned in the Bible. It had no connection with Benjamin, the tribe to which Paul belonged (Phil. 3: 5). It had no associations with the Galilean ministry of Jesus. And there is no evidence that it had Christian inhabitants in the Byzantine period. The Romans took control of Palestine in 63 BC, and subsequently there were a number of occasions (61, 55, 52, 4 BC, AD 6) when Jews from various parts of the country were enslaved and deported.

Roman hands (see box). Enjoying close commercial contacts with Tyre, and renowned for the quality of its olive oil, the town prospered greatly in the C3–C6 AD. Benjamin of Tudela, who passed through it in the C12, noted that only twenty of the inhabitants were Jewish.

Visit. The 800 m road to the synagogue starts from the four-way cross at the beginning of the hill in the village; when you come to an electricity transformer pylon turn right (east) on to a dirt road with green trail-markers which cuts across the slope to reach the bottom of the valley.

Erected about AD 250, the synagogue survived the earthquakes of 306, 362, and 447 without major repairs, before being finally thrown down by the great earthquake of 551. The builders must have recognized that the site was on the fault line of the Safed epicentre, and so gave the walls particularly strong foundations in the form of a trapezoid almost 2 m deep. The edifice is unusual in that the rectangular sanctuary with its two rows of four columns was bordered on three sides by long narrow rooms entered from the central hall. There is a carved eagle on the underside of the lintel of the principal entrance in the south wall, the position of this decoration is still without explanation. Just inside this door to the west a small podium (*bema*) is built on top of a larger one. That this provided the orientation to Jerusalem is confirmed by the quality of the south wall. It is built of finely trimmed ashlar blocks in contrast to the other three which are of rough-hewn field stones.

Haifa: *see* **MOUNT CARMEL**

Hammat Gader (07)

In the C4 AD the Roman baths here (Fig. 107) were reputed to be so magnificent that they bore comparison only with those at the imperial resort of Baiae on the Bay of Naples. Excavations have revealed this claim to be fully justified, and the recreational tradition of the site has been revived by the provision of hot natural pools, a wildlife park, and even an alligator farm.

Soundings indicate that the site was occupied in the Early Bronze Age (3150–2350 BC). In the C1 BC Strabo mentioned the waters, noting that 'when animals taste it they lose hair, hoofs, and horns' (*Geography* 16: 2. 45). None the less, in the C2 AD the inhabitants of Gadara (today Umm Qeis on the summit of the hill to the south) constructed baths over the hot springs. Origen commented on their fame a century later; their therapeutic qualities attracted clients from as far away as Athens. This was not their only interest, however, as we can gather from Epiphanius, who rather sourly comments, 'There the Devil sets his snares . . . since men and women bathe together' (*Pan. haer.* 30: 7).

The decisive battle of the Yarmuk on 20 August 636, which asserted Muslim control over Palestine, meant a renewed lease of life for the baths. They had been severely damaged by a series of earthquakes towards the end of the Byzantine period, but were repaired by the Umayyad caliph Muawiyah I (661–80) and reopened in 663. Decline set in about a century later, and the baths were no longer in use by the early C10. The surrounding town, which drew its sustenance from them, died the same slow death.

Visit. Open: 8.30 a.m.–4 p.m., Fridays 3 p.m. The road east from the south end of the SEA OF GALILEE is well marked (route 98). Just before the entrance to the parking-lot are the remains of a railway station; it was the last stop in Palestine on the Turkish line between Haifa and Damascus.

The Roman Baths

The installation (Fig. 64) is sited between two sets of springs. The hottest are those in the south, with temperatures ranging from 25 °C to 52 °C in what is known locally as the 'Frying Spring' [9]. The temperature of those in the north and west averages 20 °C. The bath erected in the C2 AD comprised the spring [8], a hot room [7], and a warm room [10], the two latter being constructed of limestone. The other elements [3, 5, 6, 12] built of basalt blocks were added in the early C3. In the C7 or C8 three pools [3, 5, 12] were transformed into passages and halls.

In the **entrance hall** [1], reached by a flight of steps from a basalt-paved courtyard, a double fountain [2] provided drinking water. The colonnade screen through which one entered [3] was erected in the C4. The massive piers supported a 14 m-high vaulted roof; through one set of

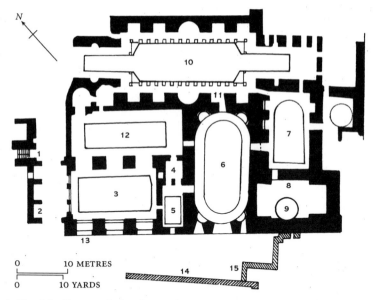

▲ **Fig. 64.** Hammat Gader. Roman Bath (after Solar). 1. Entrance; 2. Double fountain; 3. Hall; 4. Antechamber; 5. Pool; 6. Pool; 7. Pool; 8. Spring basin; 9. Hot spring; 10. Pool; 11. Inscription; 12. Pool; 13. Stone pipe; 14. Service area; 15. Overflow channel.

piers there was free access to [**12**], while between the other set, beneath the windows, tubs were built in at ground level. Beneath the three niches, which held statues (said to be erotic), two doors give access to a much smaller antechamber [**4**] and a pool [**5**]. The excavators' identification of this area as the **Lepers' Pool** was inspired by the discovery in the pool [**5**] of scores of C3–C4 lamps, and a description written over two centuries later (see box).

It is more likely, however, that the writer is referring to a special bath reserved for lepers alone; in the Byzantine period they were forbidden to enter public baths. Moreover, the description does not fit because the pool [**5**] is separated from the 'furnace of water' [**9**] by a large room [**6**].

Being closest to the spring [**9**], the two **oval pools** [**6** and **7**] received water at close to 50 °C. In order to control the temperature lead pipes brought cool water to the tubs in the semicircular niches of [**6**] and to the six fountains set on the rim of the pool. The other pool [**7**] was originally rectangular and received its oval shape and the five fountains in the C8. At this time changes were also made in the spring area [**8**], particularly to the circle of upright basalt slabs linked by butterfly-shaped lead clamps located over the spring [**9**]. This structure raised the water level, permitting it to flow to the various pools.

The Lepers' Pool

'In that area, three miles from the city [Gadara] are hot springs which are called the baths of Elijah, where lepers are cleansed [2 Kgs. 5: 10–14] and have their meals from the inn there at public expense. In the evening the baths are filled. In front of the furnace of water is a large tank. When it is filled, all the openings are closed, and they are sent inside through a small door with lights and incense, and sit in the tank all night. They fall asleep, and the one who is going to be cured sees a vision. When he has told it, the baths are not used for a week, and within seven days he is cleansed.' (Piacenza Pilgrim (C6), *Travels* 7; trans. J. Wilkinson)

Unlike the other areas, the **largest pool** [**10**] was open to the sky. There were ashlar vaults at either end over the narrowed extensions of the pool; with these its total length is 58 m. The twenty-six fountains were installed by the empress Eudokia (544–60), who also contributed a poem inscribed on a marble slab set into the floor [**11**]. It is a first-person impressionistic description of her visit to the baths some five years before her death.

The 1.3 m-high and 50 cm-wide conduit that brought water from the hot pool [**7**] to the middle pool [**12**] comes through the door between [**6**] and [**7**] around the top of [**6**], and under the wall to the pool. This hall was covered by a barrel vault. It ceased to be a bathing area in the Ummayad period.

Outside the baths proper was a **service area** [**14**] delimited by a wall running parallel to the façade; in the Ummayad period it became another bathing area. Note in particular the stone pipe [**13**], which is built over the main drain of the baths. It takes the flow from [**5**] and [**6**] before running in a curve to an opening in the wall through which the water flowed to the Yarmuk river [**15**]. The stones of this opening are connected by dovetail joints, as are those of the rectangular pool in the vicinity.

The Synagogue

The synagogue is located at the top of the tel. From this, the highest point on the site, there is a splendid view of the fast-flowing Yarmuk river, which here is the border between Israel and Jordan. The road climbing the hill leads to Umm Qeis (ancient Gadera).

The apse orientates the synagogue towards Jerusalem, but in synagogues of this type it is unusual to find rows of pillars parallel to the other three walls. Except for one panel with two lions the design of the mosaic floor is entirely geometrical. There are four inscriptions mentioning contributors. One lists 'Moniqah of Susita the Sepphorite, and Kyris Patriqios of Kefar Aqabyah, and Yoseh the son of Dositheus of

Capernaum', a significant indication of the wide area from which the baths drew Jewish clients. The synagogue is dated to the C5–C6 AD. It rests on the remains of an earlier synagogue which was oriented towards Jerusalem by a platform (*bema*) attached to the south wall.

The Roman Theatre

The top is visible from the parking-lot. The fifteen rows of basalt seats provided places for 5,000 spectators.

Hammat Tiberias* (N6)

At least as early as the C1 AD medicinal hot springs attracted visitors to a spot just south of TIBERIAS (Josephus, *Life* 85). It is still a health spa, and the 60 °C (140 °F) waters may be taken either in a picturesque Turkish bath or across the road in a much more modern establishment capable of handling 2,000 bathers per day (Fig. 107).

The priestly order of Maziah settled here after the destruction of the Temple in AD 70, Tiberias being forbidden to them because it was built over a cemetery. Hammat was later joined to Tiberias for halakhic purposes, and shared its fame when, in the C3, Tiberias became a great centre of Jewish learning. A faint reflection of these days of glory can be caught in the shrine of Rabbi Meir (= the Illuminator) Baal Haness (= the Miracle Worker). A famous teacher of the C2 AD, he died abroad but asked to be buried in the Holy Land. His tomb lies between the two white domes of the C19 Sephardi and Ashkenazi synagogues.

Visit. The national park containing the synagogue is located just across the road from the modern spa. Open: Sunday–Thursday and Saturday 8 a.m.–4 p.m., Fridays to 3 p.m. A plan is available at the ticket office, and the site is well signposted. The most notable feature is a marvellous mosaic floor. Its depiction of the zodiac is the earliest found in Palestine.

This mosaic belongs to a **synagogue** of the C4 AD which was an almost square room (15 × 13 m) divided into four by three rows of pillars. Destroyed in the C5, the synagogue was rebuilt in a different style in the following century. An apse oriented the building towards Jerusalem; a gallery ran round the three other sides. The wall across the mosaic was the foundation for a row of pillars. This edifice survived for only a century; its replacement was destroyed in the middle of the C8. Squatters dwelt in the ruins until the C15. One of the hot springs for which the area is famous is located near the road.

The **zodiac mosaic** is very different from that at BET ALPHA, and clearly betrays its classical origins despite the Hebrew script. It is

▲ **Fig. 65.** The figure of Virgo in the zodiac mosaics at Hammat Tiberias *(left)* and Bet Alpha *(right)*.

described facing the apse. In the corners are the four seasons (anticlockwise from the top left-hand corner): *Nisan*, Spring; *Tammuz*, Summer; *Tishri*, Autumn; *Tebeth*, Winter. The zodiac signs differ from those at Bet Alpha in several respects. Not only are the representations here more realistic (Fig. 65) but they face outwards, and are correctly placed with regard to the seasons (Bet Alpha is 90 degrees out). The twelve signs start at 12 o'clock and run anticlockwise; *Taleh*, Aries (ram); *Shor*, Taurus (bull); *Teomin*, Gemini (twins); *Sartan*, Cancer (crab); *Aryeh*, Leo (lion), *Betulah*, Virgo (virgin); *Meoznayim*, Libra (scales); *Aqrab*, Scorpio (scorpion); *Kashat*, Sagittarius (archer); *Gedi*, Capricornus (goat); *Deli*, Aquarius (water carrier); and *Dagim*, Pisces (fish).

The verve of the **upper panel** at Bet Alpha is lacking here where the symbolic objects are depicted with greater realism. The rather ridiculous knotted curtain distracts from the meaning of the Ark of the Law which, moreover, is overwhelmed by two great flaming *menorah*. Each *menorah* is flanked by a *lulav* (bundle of branches), *ethrog* (citrus fruit), *shofar* (ram's-horn trumpet), and incense shovel; their disposition is the same on both sides of the Ark.

In the **bottom panel** two lions flank a series of Greek inscriptions in a nine-box square, but so arranged that four are read facing the zodiac, and four in the opposite direction. They give the names of the principal donors. The most important, Severus, is also mentioned in another inscription just to the left of the zodiac: 'Severus, pupil of the most illustrious patriarchs, completed [the construction]. Praise be to him and to Iullus the supervisor.' Above it is an Aramaic inscription: 'May peace rest on each one who has given an offering to this holy place, or will give an offering. May he be blessed. Amen, amen sela, and to me, amen.' Another Greek inscription in the middle of the aisle nearest the lake reads: 'May he be remembered for good and for blessing, Profuturus the official who provided this gallery of the holy place. On him be a blessing. Amen. Shalom'. The inscriptions show the importance of Greek in the Jewish community at this period.

South of the synagogue a section of the C6 AD **city wall** of Tiberias has been preserved. Running perpendicular to the lake it is 2 m wide and stands to a height of 2.8 m.

In addition to artefacts of different periods, the **Lehman Museum** (open: 8 a.m.–4 p.m.; Friday 9 a.m.–1 p.m.; closed Saturday) uses excellent graphics to explain the geomorphology of the hot springs and traces the history of the baths.

Hazan (G20)

The gentle rounded hills and wide valleys of the Shephelah (Josh. 15: 33) are celebrated in the Bible for their fertility; grapes, olives, and figs grew in abundance (Judges 14: 5; 1 Kgs. 10: 27; 1 Chr. 27: 28). There are also treasures beneath the surface. Natural caves in the soft chalk and limestone revealed that it would be as easy to tunnel as to build, and the area around BET GUVRIN and LAKHISH is honeycombed by underground installations. One of the finest examples is to be found at Hazan, which is 2 km south of Moshav Amazya.

The first hint of how easy it was to work the rock came with the excavation of two bell-shaped cisterns sometime in the C2 BC. At the end of the C1 AD or the beginning of the C2 a large subterranean complex was developed for the production and storage of olive oil. On the surface at this stage was a two-storey square house with an entrance into the underground area near its south wall. The Jewish character of the settlement is clear from the presence of two ritual baths (*mikveh*), one 5 m north of the house, and the other in the north-east corner, where there are traces of an earlier building.

Early in the Second Revolt (AD 132–5) the underground area was adapted to the new political situation. According to Dio Cassius (160–234), 'Since the Jews did not dare confront the Romans in open field, they selected favourable positions in the country and strengthened them with subterranean passages and walls in order to have places of refuge when hard pressed, and might meet together unobserved underground' (*Roman History* 69: 12.3). The passages hewn at this stage were deliberately designed to make attack difficult; they inhibited movement by being both low and narrow. No soldier in armour could have reached those who took refuge there; they could only have been smothered or smoked out.

With other Jews the inhabitants were expelled from Judaea by the emperor Hadrian in 135. The site was again occupied only in the C4. The subterranean area was cleaned and the oil press brought back into use. A sloping revetment strengthened the repaired square house, and the other buildings were constructed. A Roman bath was installed beside the northern ritual bath. This little farm survived throughout the Byzantine period, but was abandoned sometime after the Arab conquest in the C7.

Visit. The turn from the Qiryat Gat–Bet Guvrin road (route 35) to route 3415 is signposted in English, but thereafter the signs are only in Hebrew. At a fraction over 9 km from the junction turn right on a sealed road; the parking-lot and ticket office are on the left after about 3 km. As the road circles around Tel Lakhish there is a fine view of the outer and inner walls of the C8–C7 BC city.

The entry fee includes a video presentation and a guided tour. In order to avoid the delay required to assemble a group, advance reservations are recommended (tel.: 051–880267 or 880623). Open: 9 a.m.–3 p.m.; Friday to 1 p.m.

There are three points of interest on the short walk to the main site. The triangular niches which transformed the **bell-cave** (see p. 000) into a *columbarium* must be dated to the early Arab period (C8–C10 AD); the roof subsequently collapsed. The nearby **wine press** is very crude. The liquid produced by treading was collected in the lower tank and then had to be transferred by hand to the plastered decantation basin beside the treading floor. The **ancient road** is simply the original entrance to the C1 farm. It came in on the south side; the modern entrance is from the west.

The square building on the right is the C1 AD **farmhouse** which is shored up by the sloping C4 revetment. The only other item of interest on the surface is diagonally across to the left. The relation of the hot room of a C4 AD **bath-house** shows that the adjacent C1 *mikveh* was then used as the cold pool.

The existence of a *mikveh* at the entrance to the **underground oil press** suggests that some oil must have been sent to the Temple in Jerusalem. The olives were first crushed on the circular mill. The pulp collected in woven baskets was then compressed to extract further oil in the beam press. The oil was kept in five **store-rooms.** Their rock floors had hollows to hold the jars upright. In order that nothing should be wasted in case of an oil spill the floors slope towards a collection basin in one corner and all the hollows are linked by channels. The total storage capacity is estimated at 10,000 litres.

It takes some agility to scramble through the C2 AD passages; those who cannot walk crouched small have to go on hands and knees in parts. The main rooms are nearly 2 m high and one can rest on the stone benches on which Jewish rebels sat. There were much smaller chambers in which dried foods could be preserved. The major problem, however, was the water supply. The **central cistern** had adequate capacity (it is 20 m deep and has an internal rock-cut stairway), but its surface entry made it a liability. The solution of the Jewish rebels was to cut a 9 m **vertical shaft** with footholds in one of the secret passages. From its base a horizontal tunnel ran to the cistern, permitting water to rise up the vertical shaft as the cistern filled. Unless the cistern ran dry no one could detect the existence of the parallel system.

Hazeva (K28)

The leaders of the great camel caravans that criss-crossed the desert in the Roman period must have experienced a lift of the heart when they came in sight of En Hazeva. It offered not only abundant water, but security and shade. Bedouin raiding parties stayed a prudent distance from the forts of the Roman frontier police.

The fort erected in the C2 AD controlled a major road junction. The north–south route linking the DEAD SEA with Elat had a commercial importance comparable to that of the modern highway (route 90). At En Hazeva it was joined by a road (parallel to route 227) coming from the Mediterranean coast via MAMSHIT and MAALE AQRABIM. The site is probably to be identified with Tamara which, according to Eusebius, was a day's march from Mamshit (*Onomasticon* 8: 8). The name echoes the biblical Tamar, which is mentioned in 1 Kgs. 9: 17–18; Ezek. 47: 19; 48: 28. In fact the earliest remains on the site go back to the Iron Age (C10–C6 BC), when kings of Judah built desert fortresses to defend their southern borders, and to protect the lucrative trade in luxury goods from Africa and the Arabian peninsula.

Visit. Open Monday–Thursday 8 a.m.–4 p.m. Take the road to Ovot from route 227. The **Roman fort** measured 46 × 46 m, and is the largest of its kind known in the Arava. None the less it occupies only the eastern quarter of the much greater (100 × 100 m) C8 BC **Israelite fortress**. This was roughly the size of the regional administrative centre at BEER SHEVA, and four times bigger than its contemporary at ARAD. Projecting towers protected the corners, while the casemate wall was constructed in an inset/offset pattern to permit enfilading fire. The majestic proportions of the gate just north of the eastern corner reflected the grandeur of the fortress. On each side three piers creating two chambers flanked a 4 m-wide entrance. The fate of this fortress is uncertain, but in the C7–C6 BC a new fort was built on the site. Two of its square towers are visible in the southern quarter of the C8 fortress. Outside this corner is a **Roman bath**.

Hazor* (N4)

Commanding a well-watered pass at the point where trade routes from the north, east, and west joined to enter northern Canaan, the strategic and commercial importance of Hazor is underlined by its sheer size. In its heyday, between the C18 and C13 BC, the city covered over 200 acres.

A settlement had existed on the mound for over 1,000 years when in the C18 BC it suddenly expanded into a great city. Texts of the C18 BC from Mari on the river Euphrates show that Hazor had close political and

▼ **Fig. 66.** Tel Hazor.

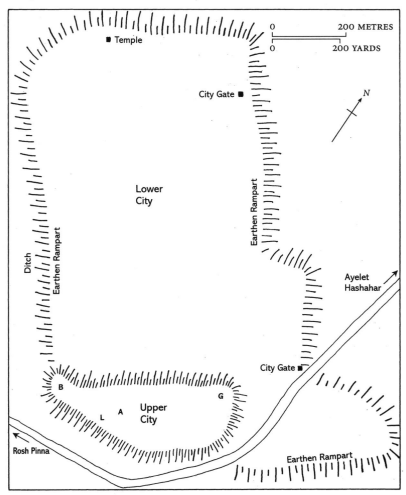

economic ties with Mesopotamia; one refers to the export of tin and another to Hammurabi's ambassadors resident in Hazor.

Egyptian dominion began in the C15 BC, but in the following century Hazor was unique among the Canaanite city-states, according to the Amarna letters (MEGIDDO) its ruler bore the title 'king' and was responsible for other cities. Throughout these centuries the city was periodically washed in blood, but the memory of its grandeur was still vivid at the time of Joshua when it is described as 'the head of . . . kingdoms' (Josh. 11: 10).

The destruction of the city by fire in the second half of the C13 BC harmonizes with the note that Hazor was the only city burnt by the invading Israelites (Josh. 11: 13). How they did it remains a mystery (contrast Megiddo) because the first Israelite settlement reveals a much inferior culture. The Lower City was then abandoned, and the Upper City regained something of its former glory only when Solomon (965–928 BC) rebuilt part of it. A thick ash layer covering this city betrays the passage of the Aramaeans in 885 BC. The Omrid reconstruction in the same century doubled the size of the Solomonic city, but it endured only 100 years. No sooner had the damage caused by an earthquake been repaired than the Assyrians razed it to the ground in 732 BC. Hazor never recovered from this mortal blow. In succeeding centuries travellers would see only a lonely police fort.

Visit. Across the road from the tel, at the entrance to Kibbutz Ayelet Hashahar (on route 90), is the **Hazor Museum** (open: 8 a.m.–4 p.m.; Friday to 3 p.m.; closed Saturday). A visit is recommended because Hazor's fourteen excavation areas revealed twenty-one occupation levels; only the more accessible are treated here.

The Lower City

This vast area is defended by a great earthen rampart with a brick core. Since no one could conceive of a city ten to fifteen times larger than contemporary cities in Canaan, it was first thought to be merely an enclosed chariot park. Excavations at selected points, however, revealed that stone buildings filled the whole space. At each point there was evidence of the same four occupation levels ranging from the mid-C18 BC to the mid-C13 BC. The city, therefore, had a sudden beginning and an equally sudden end. A migration of some 30,000 people is the simplest explanation of the abrupt appearance of buildings throughout such an extensive area, but it raises the unanswered questions of who they were and where they came from. That they were a pious lot is suggested by the cultic installations found in each probe. At the northern edge of the city, for example, four superimposed temples were unearthed. Such consistency of use is also evident in the city gates; in each of the two sites excavated there were five superimposed gates.

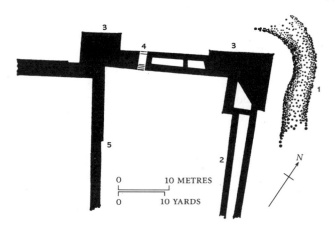

▲ **Fig. 67.** Hazor. Area G (after Yadin). 1. Ditch; 2. Casemate wall; 3. Tower; 4. Postern gate; 5. Wall.

Area G (Fig. 67)

With the exception of the C18 BC glacis and its stone-faced ditch [**1**], all the visible remains are from the C9–C8 BC. The filled **double-wall** [**2**] reinforced by towers [**3**] was built by Omri or Ahab to defend their extension of the Solomonic city. A small **postern gate** [**4**], protected by screen walls, gave access to what used to be the Lower City. When news came of the Assyrian advance in 733 BC the defenders filled in the gate with mudbrick, carefully camouflaging the outside with stones to match the wall. Just inside was a large stone-lined grain silo. Another **massive wall** [**5**], providing a second line of defence, ran parallel to the older casemate wall found in Area A.

Area A

This area is again being excavated, and it is not yet clear what remains will be preserved, apart from the **Solomonic gate**. In the C10 BC Solomon installed here a magnificent gate with three chambers on each side. It had two towers on its external face, and formed part of a double (casemate) wall. As at GEZER and MEGIDDO, only the foundations remain. The line of the casemate wall can be prolonged across the gate to Area M where it turns towards the citadel; at this point the slightly narrower Omrid wall coming from Area G joins it.

In order to permit excavation of the Canaanite levels, two Iron Age structures were dismantled and reconstructed on the north side of the track. The **columned building** is of the C9 BC and contemporary with the Omrid wall which, by extending the city, reduced the casemates to the status of store-rooms. The structure of the columned building is identical with that of the so-called 'stables' at Megiddo, but here the contents show indisputably that it served for storage.

When the area was rebuilt in the C8 BC after a great conflagration, the public buildings of previous periods gave way to **private dwellings**. The house with the pillared corner court is the finest known example of its kind. Its opulence is in vivid contrast to the cramped two-rooms-and-a-courtyard of Mrs Makhbiram's next door; her name is known from an inscription and the rooms have yielded all the household furniture of an Iron Age home.

Area L

Just inside the Solomonic casemate wall the Omrids, with expert geo-logical advice, dug a 19 m-deep **rectangular shaft** through solid rock and from it a 25 m stepped tunnel to find the water level within the hill; the same technique was employed at GEZER. The menace of Assyria made such preparations to withstand a long siege imperative. The beautifully engineered entrance was controlled from a four-roomed building.

Area B (Fig. 68)

Its position relative to the Solomonic gate (Area A) marks this as the **citadel** of Hazor. There is no trace of whatever building Solomon placed there, but his casemate walls [1] are evident on both sides of the bottle-neck. These were filled in to make solid walls when the Omrids

▼ **Fig. 68.** Hazor. Area B (after Yadin). 1. Casemate wall; 2. Fortress; 3. Monumental entrance; 4–5. C9 BC buildings; 6. Tower.

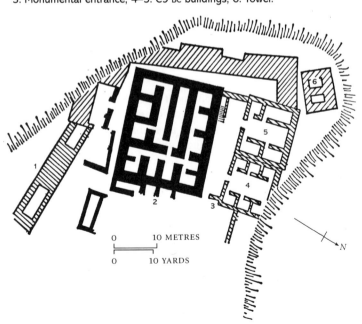

constructed their square **fortress** [2] which was flanked on both sides by ancillary buildings whose outer walls constituted all the rampart necessary. Two of these buildings remain visible [**4** and **5**]. The street separating them from the fortress had a monumental entrance [3] with proto-Aeolic capitals, and at the far end a staircase led to the first floor. As in Area G, the threat from Assyria prompted a strengthening of the fortifications in the C8 BC by the building of a **tower** [6] and a massive offset/inset **wall** over the outer part of [4] and [5].

Hebron (H2O) ★

Sacred to Jews, Christians, and Muslims as the burial-place of Abraham, Isaac, and Jacob, Hebron is notable for the superb wall that Herod the Great (37–4 BC) built around the Cave of Machpelah (Haram el-Khalil). It is perfectly preserved and the refinement of the construction technique has to be seen to be believed.

The ancient city was on Jebel er-Rumeideh, across the valley from the Haram. Excavations (not worth a visit) show occupation from about 2000 BC. There Abraham bargained for the cave (Gen. 23) in which he, his sons, and their wives were to be buried; there David reigned for seven and a half years before moving to Jerusalem; and there his son Absalom raised the standard of rebellion (2 Sam. 5 and 15). Even though a city of refuge (Josh. 21: 13), it suffered the same fate as others in wars throughout the centuries until Herod built the Haram, today its sole glory.

The size of the stone blocks (the largest 7.5 × 1.4 m) inspires wonder. The largest appear near the corners, imparting tremendous strength to the structure. A series of clever visual deceptions avoids the impression of heaviness. Each course is set back 1.5 cm on the one below, and the upper margin is wider than the others. The surface of the wall is broken up by calculated irregularity of the joints and by the finely trimmed bosses whose hint of shadow enhances the lustrous patina of the stone. This effect is intensified by the pilasters; their single-block bases each have seven faces. Attention is directed to this element by a series of projecting knobs which highlight the depth of the bevel. All the blocks originally had such knobs to protect them when coming from the quarry and while they were being set in position. The paved area within the wall is also Herodian. This courtyard originally must have contained a cenotaph (or several), and was reached by a staircase from an entrance at the base of the wall.

By the C6 porticoes had been built around the four sides; a screen partitioned the uncovered central area between Christians and Jews. In the early C10 the original entrance was blocked by a building housing a

Fourteenth-Century Hebron

'The Haram at Hebron is built of hewn stone, and one stone is 37 spans in length. The Haram is said to have been built by Solomon aided by Jinns. Within is the holy cave, where are the tombs of Abraham, Isaac and Jacob; opposite lie the tombs of their wives. To the right of the pulpit, and close to the southern outer wall, is a place where you may descend by solidly built marble steps, leading to a narrow passage, and this opens into a chamber paved with marble. Here are the cenotaphs of the three tombs. They say that the bodies lie immediately adjacent beneath, and hereby was originally the passage down to the blessed cave. At the present time, however, this passage is closed. To the first chamber I myself descended many times.' (Ibn Batutah (C14); trans. G. Le Strange)

cenotaph of Joseph; the present entrance was then cut in the east wall. The description of the Haram by Mukaddasi in 985 shows that a mosque existed in the southern half of the enclosure, and that the disposition of the six cenotaphs was the same as today.

The most likely date of the existing building is the reign of Baldwin II (1118–31). The construction may have been stimulated by the discovery of the Cave of Machpelah beneath the Herodian paving by the Augustinian Canons in 1119. Jews, Christians, and Muslims visited the underground area until the middle of the C13 (see box). The exclusion of Christians and Jews from the Haram promulgated by the Mamluk sultan Baybars in 1266 was not seriously enforced until the middle of the C14. By 1490 not even Muslims were permitted to enter the underground area.

Saladin added four minarets, of which only two remain. The Mamluks contributed a number of other features to be noted in the course of the visit. The careful measurements of the Haram made by Mujir ad-Din in 1496, when coupled with his detailed description, show that no substantial alterations have taken place subsequently.

Visit (Fig. 69). Open: Sunday–Saturday 7–11 a.m.; noon–2.30 p.m.; 3.30–5 p.m. On Friday the Muslim section of the Haram is closed to visitors, as is the Jewish section on Saturday. The tensions between the Muslims and Jews who share the building can build to explosive levels, and visitors should ascertain whether it is safe to go to Hebron.

The polychrome **entrance-gate** to the Muslim section [1] betrays the Mamluk origin of the stairway, which permits close inspection of all levels of wall and leads to the Djaouliyeh mosque [2] built in 1318–20.

▶ **The Pulpit of the Haram al-Khalil at Hebron.** The inscription over the doors dates its construction to 1091 in Ashqelon. It was sent to Hebron by Saladin when he destroyed Ashqelon in 1191.

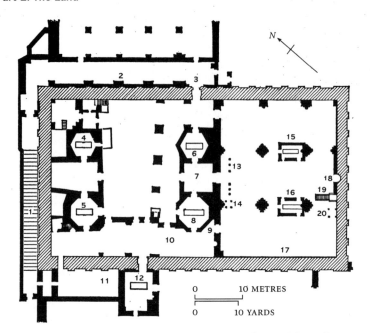

▲ **Fig. 69.** Hebron. Haram el-Khalil (Tomb of the Patriarchs). 1. Entrance; 2. Djaouliyeh mosque; 3. Cut in Herodian wall; 4. Tomb of Leah; 5. Tomb of Jacob; 6. Tomb of Sarah; 7. Synagogue; 8. Tomb of Abraham; 9. Adam's footprint; 10. Women's mosque; 11. Mosque; 12. Tomb of Joseph; 13. Tribune; 14. Shaft to tomb chamber; 15. Tomb of Rebecca; 16. Tomb of Isaac; 17. Herodian gutter; 18. *Mihrab*; 19. Minbar; 20. Medieval entrance to underground area.

The passage through the Herodian wall [**3**] is dated to 918. The six-sided C9 **tomb of Sarah** is straight ahead. Enter the mosque by a door of uncertain date.

Medieval visitors entered **the underground area** by a flight of steps beneath the C12 baldacchino [**20**]. They found themselves in a straight corridor (15.35 × 1.06 × 0.59 m) whose walls, ceiling, and floor are constructed of massive Herodian cut stones. At the end is a rectangular room (3.65 × 2.97 m) with a 4 m-high corbelled roof pierced by the hole beneath the small cupola [**14**]. There is a *mihrab* in the south corner, and beside it an entrance to a double natural cave below.

The **tribune** [**13**] reuses elements of the medieval choir. On the right of the *mihrab* [**18**] stands the glory of the mosque, the magnificent *minbar* or **pulpit** [**19**], a mosaic of exquisitely carved wood made in 1091 for a mosque in Ashqelon and donated by Saladin in 1191 when he burnt the port city. Tankiz, Mamluk viceroy of Syria, in 1332 gave the **cenotaphs** of Isaac [**16**] and Rebecca [**15**] their present form, and adorned the walls with geometric sheets of marble. The marble frieze in decorative script is also his; its horizontal line accentuates the slope of the pavement towards the Herodian rain **gutter** [**17**], which shows that the space was originally unroofed.

A door gives access to the **mosque of the women** [**10**], from which one can see the C9 octagonal **tomb of Abraham** [**8**]. According to Arab legend Adam prayed so frequently in the corner [**9**] that his foot left a mark in the stone (now part of a small shrine).

The entrance to the Jewish section is through the mosque [**11**]. Both it and the **tomb of Joseph** [**12**] with their entrances in the Herodian wall date from the C14. The courtyard owes its shape to the Mamluks who gave the **cenotaphs** of Jacob [**5**] and Leah [**4**] their present form in the C14.

Heptapegon (N5)

It was perhaps inevitable that this well-watered area with its shade trees on the shore of the SEA OF GALILEE (Fig. 107), where Byzantine pilgrims ate their picnics, should have been identified as the location of two gospel episodes involving the consumption of food, the multiplication of the loaves and fishes (Mark 6: 30–44) and the conferral on Peter of the responsibility of leadership after a fish breakfast (John 21). Then it became convenient to localize the Sermon on the Mount (Matt. 5–7) on the small hill nearby. The Greek word Heptapegon means 'the place of seven springs'. Until relatively recently they powered mills, and the name was corrupted in Arabic into Tabgha.

A Byzantine Pilgrim

'Not far away from there [Capernaum] are some stone steps where the Lord stood. And in the same place by the sea is a grassy field with plenty of hay and many palm trees. By them are seven springs, each flowing strongly. And this is the field where the Lord fed the people with the five loaves and the two fishes. In fact the stone on which the Lord placed the bread has now been made into an altar. People who go there take away small pieces of the stone to bring them prosperity, and they are very effective. Past the walls of this church goes the public highway on which the Apostle Matthew had his place of custom. Near there on a mountain is the cave to which the Saviour climbed and spoke the Beatitudes.' (Egeria (C4), trans. J. Wilkinson)

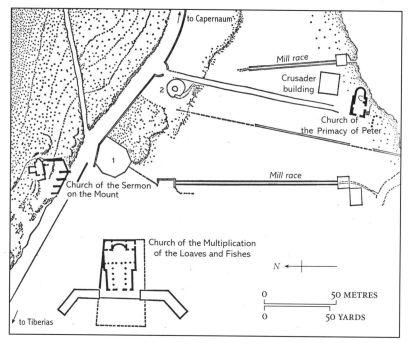

▲ **Fig. 70.** Heptapegon. 1. Birket Ali ed-Daher; 2. Tannur Ayyub.

The Church of the Multiplication of the Loaves and Fishes

Open: 8.30 a.m. (Sunday 10 a.m.)–5 p.m. The present church, dedicated in 1982, is a reproduction of the mid-C5 edifice, which an inscription attributes to the patriarch Matryrios (478–86). The sill of the left entrance to the atrium, some of the basalt paving stones of the atrium, and part of the frieze in the apse, all belong to the Byzantine church, as does one of the most beautiful mosaic floors in the country; it is also the earliest known example of a **figured pavement** in Palestinian church art. It does not cover the whole floor area but is limited to the two transepts and the intervals between the pillars.

The artist, indisputably a great master, had enough confidence in his skill to avoid any repetitious pattern and covered the area with a free-flowing design of birds and plants (Fig. 71). The prominence of the bell-like lotus flower (not found in this area) betrays the influence of the Nilotic landscapes popular in Hellenistic and Roman art, but the other motifs are drawn from the flora and fauna of the lakeside. Despite the detail which permits the identification of each species, the whole is infused with unique verve and humour. The round tower in the right transept is to measure the water level in the lake; the Greek letters are the numbers 6 to 10.

▲ **Fig. 71.** Heptapegon. Mosaic floor in the Church of the Multiplication of the Loaves and Fishes.

Immediately in front of the altar is the celebrated **mosaic of two fish** flanking a basket of loaves. Below the altar table is a block of undressed limestone (1 × 0.6 × 0.14 m). It is unlikely that this is the stone altar mentioned by Egeria, though Christians of the C5 undeniably considered it the table of the Lord.

The **C4 church** lies beneath the present floor. It was much smaller (15.5 × 9.5 m) and the two sections left exposed show that the orientation was slightly different. During the restoration of the mosaics in 1936 the complete outline was established (plan in narthex).

Church of the Sermon on the Mount

Above the road the ruins of a small church dated to the end of the C4 are still visible. Beneath it is a rock-cut cistern. On the south and south-east are the remains of a little monastery. The remnants of the mosaic floor are on display at CAPERNAUM.

To replace this chapel, put out of commission in the C7, a new church was built in 1938 further up the hill, on what is today called the **Mount of Beatitudes**. The entrance is not from the lake road but from the main road going up to Rosh Pinna (route 90). Although devoid of archaeological interest, it is worth a visit (open: 8.30 a.m.–noon; 2.30–5 p.m.). The octagonal shape of the church commemorates the eight beatitudes (Matt. 5: 3–10) and conveys an impression of immense tranquillity. Its shady gallery is the best place from which to contemplate the spiritual dimension of the lake; one can see virtually all the places in which Jesus lived and worked.

Church of the Primacy of Peter

Open 8 a.m.– noon; 2–5 p.m. The modest Franciscan chapel was built in 1933, but at the base of its walls, at the end furthest from the altar, the walls of a late C4 AD building are clearly visible on three sides. The eastern end of this edifice has completely disappeared, but cuts in the rock and the proportions of the comparable C4 Church of the Multiplication suggest that its length was twice its width. It thus enclosed the flat rock projecting in front of the present altar. This is probably the one mentioned by Egeria. In the early Byzantine period it would have been venerated as the table on which Jesus offered breakfast to the disciples: 'As soon as they came ashore they saw that there was some bread there, and a charcoal fire with fish cooking on it' (John 21: 9). This text probably explains why, in the C9, the site was known as the Place of the Coals. The church survived longer than any others in the area, and was finally destroyed only in the C13.

On the lake side of the church are the **rock-cut steps** of which Egeria speaks. How old they are no one knows. They may have been cut in the C2 or C3 AD when this area was quarried for limestone; the characteristic cuts to liberate the blocks on three sides prior to the insertion of metal wedges (two were found) are visible in the vicinity.

Below the steps, sometimes under water if the lake level is high, are six heart-shaped stones. They are double-column blocks designed for the angle of a colonnade, and never served any practical purpose in their present position. Known as the **Twelve Thrones**, and first mentioned in a text of AD 808, they were probably taken from disused buildings and placed there to commemorate the Twelve Apostles. It takes little insight to appreciate the mental jump from John 21: 9 (cited above) to 'You will eat and drink at my table in my kingdom, and you will sit on thrones to judge the twelve tribes of Israel' (Luke 22: 30).

Just beside the church is a small **Crusader building**. The other structures are **water towers** called Birket Ali ed-Daher and Tannur Ayyub. These date back to the Byzantine period and were designed to raise the water level of the powerful springs so that they flowed into a series of irrigation canals and mill-streams. The existing mills are of recent date.

Herodion (Har Hordos)* (K19) ★

The landscape south of Jerusalem is dominated by a peak whose shape suggests a volcano. It is in fact the citadel of a palace complex built by Herod the Great between 24 and 15 BC to commemorate a victorious rear-guard action on his flight to MASADA in 40 BC (*Antiquities* 14: 352–60). From the top there is a magnificent view over the Judaean desert, and of the deep WADI KHAREITUN with its monastery and prehistoric caves immediately to the south.

Set in open rolling landscape improved by well-watered gardens, and within easy reach of Jerusalem, Herodion would have been an admirable summer palace; there the king entertained Agrippa, son-in-law of the emperor Augustus, in 15 BC (*Antiquities* 16: 13). On a much more mundane level it was the administrative centre of a district (*War* 3: 54–6). Perhaps because it was a place of pleasant memories, or because he had once thought of suicide there, Herod chose Herodion as his burial place. No tomb has been found so far. There is even some doubt that his body was brought there, because Josephus's two accounts do not agree. They can be reconciled if we assume that the dignitaries walked for only a symbolic eight stadia (*Antiquities* 17: 199) from JERICHO, whereas servants bore the coffin the remaining 192 stadia (*War* 1: 673) to Herodion.

Its insignificant role in the First Revolt parallels that of MASADA, and it was the first conquest of Lucilius Bassus in AD 71 (*War* 7: 163). During the Second Revolt (AD 132–5) it served as an administrative centre for the rebels, and may even have been the headquarters of the leader, Bar Kokhba. In anticipation of an assault the defenders integrated the three large Herodian cisterns dug into the north-eastern slope in the vicinity of the stairway into a complex tunnel system, which would have given them both a place of refuge and the opportunity to make a surprise attack. It availed them little. The next occupation was more peaceful. Byzantine monks turned the fortress into a monastery in the C5–C7, and built churches around its base.

Visit. The access road from the Bethlehem–Tekoa road (route 356) is signposted. There is a parking-lot with toilets and drinking water. There are two distinct parts to this complex, Upper Herodion, the fortress, and Lower Herodion, the palace. The former, on top of the hill, is open

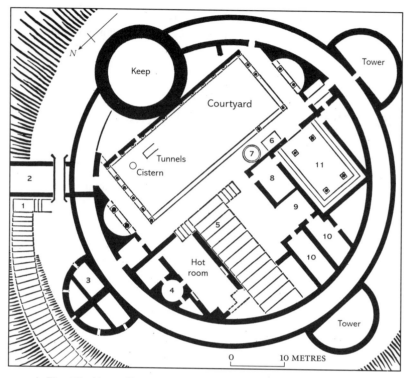

▲ **Fig. 72.** Upper Herodion. The Fortress (after Corbo). 1. Modern entrance; 2. Original entrance; 3. Tower; 4. Warm room; 5. Modern steps; 6. Ritual bath; 7. Furnace; 8. Pantry; 9. Stones; 10. Living quarters; 11. Dining-room/synagogue.

Sunday–Thursday and Saturday 8 a.m.–4 p.m.; Fridays to 3 p.m. The latter, near the main road, is accessible at any time.

The Fortress (Fig. 72)

The fill on the slopes, which now hides the remains of the building, has been supplemented by archaeological dumping, but it dates from the time of Herod. By design his circular edifice rose above a smooth slope, which both enhanced its beauty and guaranteed its security.

Although none of Herod's guests would have done it, it is best to enter the fortress through the **underground area**. Ask at the ticket office for the key, and take the down path angling left from the path to the summit. The lighting system in the tunnels is a little erratic; it is best to come prepared with flashlights.

The **vaulted corridor** inside the grille shows how Herod protected the cistern entrance from the fill with which he covered the slopes. The great **narrow-waisted** cistern is paralleled by an even bigger one to the left, and a smaller one on the other side of the original entrance staircase [**2**]. Their combined capacity was some 2,500 m³. The only access to these cisterns was from outside. Fearing a Roman siege during the First Revolt (AD 66–70) the Zealots cut a **narrow steep tunnel** to link the two waisted cisterns with the courtyard cistern of the fortress, thereby guaranteeing their water supply. This tunnel was obliterated to a great extent by the **wide-stepped tunnel** cut during the Second Revolt (AD 132–5) which we take to ascend to the **courtyard cistern**. Originally it was filled by water drawn from the lower cisterns, which was brought up the entrance staircase, and poured into a funnel whose rectangular pipe can be seen in the far right-hand corner of the cistern. A bucket could be lowered down a **vertical shaft** from the courtyard. In order not to betray their tunnelling operations to the Romans, Bar Kochba's followers dumped the debris behind the retaining walls in this cistern. Follow the Second Revolt tunnel to the courtyard. The same key opens the grille. Do not forget to return it to the ticket-office.

The rectangular colonnaded **courtyard** is tangent to the circular **keep**. Only its solid base has been preserved. The original must have been some 25 m higher; it certainly dominated the lower semicircular towers [**3**], as did the south-east tower of the ANTONIA. Beyond the shaft to the cistern is the **original entrance** from the monumental staircase of white marble, whose remains can be traced down the slope from the modern bridge above.

The crude steps left by the archaeologists [**5**] divide the living area into two. To the left the Zealots of the First Revolt transformed the beautifully proportioned chamber, which Herod designed as a **dining-room** [**11**], into a synagogue by the addition of tiered benches. At the entrance they dug a stepped **ritual bath** [**6**]. The nearby **furnace** [**7**] also stems from one of the revolts against Rome; it would have been needed for the manufacture and repair of arrow- and spear-heads. The **round stones** [**9**] originally stacked on the roofs would have been deadly weapons against attackers coming up the steep slope. Many are found at the base of the hill on the eastern side. When the fortress went up in flames they cascaded into the interior. The other rooms were living or servants' quarters.

No Herodian establishment would have been complete without a **Roman bath** Here it is located on the other side of the modern steps. Since this was the only section with stone roofs (on account of the humidity), the Byzantine monks installed themselves here, setting up cells and a bakery in the hot room. The domed roof of the warm room is noteworthy; the small triangular space behind the grille was the cold pool. On the other side was the dressing-room [**4**]. The monks also built a chapel in what was originally an open area. It is now partially blocked by the modern stairway.

The Palace (Fig. 73)

Having made a circuit of the summit in order to appreciate the stunning views over the desert, from the bridge one can look down on 'the other palaces which Herod erected around the base for the accommodation of his furniture and his friends' (*War* 1: 421). The unified vision behind the plan is evident.

The dominant feature is the great colonnaded **pool** (70 × 46 × 3 m) supplied by the aqueduct (6 km) from Artas, near SOLOMON'S POOLS. The circular **pavilion** in the centre indicates, however, that the pool was no mere reservoir. It was the architectural focal point of the palace area, and must have served as a swimming pool (as in the palace at JERICHO, p. 288) and as a miniature marina. The double walls [2] were both a retaining wall for the artificially levelled **formal garden** and the foundation of a long hall (110 × 9 m), the counterpart of that at the other end. The **elevated colonnade** on two and a half sides facilitated appreciation of the garden.

Behind the south end of the western hall is the colonnaded courtyard of the **bath-house**. Steps give access to the dressing room from which one entered the first warm room. To the right is the large hot room with niches in all four walls; they would have contained tubs of water. The left exit from the first warm room leads to two others serving the circular sweat-room and the rectangular cold room.

The **large palace**, presumably for the entertainment of guests, dominated the 350 × 25 m **stadium**, and had a projecting observation gallery

▼ **Fig. 73.** Lower Herodion. The Palace (after Netzer). 1. North church; 2. Retaining walls; 3. West church; 4. East church.

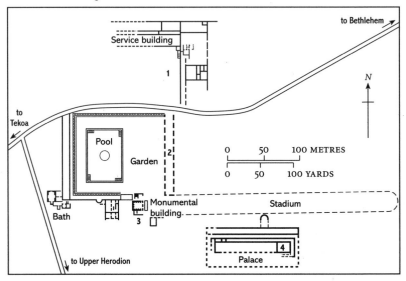

at the mid-point. At its eastern end fragments of an elaborate mosaic floor betray the position of a C5 **church** [4]; only the baptistry is relatively well preserved.

The function of the **monumental building** is still unclear. The central room with niches in three walls communicated with two rooms on both north and south. The thickness of the walls (3 m) suggests a pyramid roof. The long narrow pool in front of the building may have been a reflection pool. The grooves cut into the half columns were a later adaptation to carry pipes. In the Byzantine period this building was subdivided to accommodate squatters.

A C5 date for the nearby **church** [3] is recommended by the fact that it has only one apse bracketed by two square rooms. One contains a monolithic cruciform **baptismal font**. Its magnificent stones were certainly robbed from an Herodian building. The fact that the hillside had to be cut away to achieve a level floor explains why the main entrance is in the south wall.

The structures on the far (north) side of route 356 are not at all as well defined, but it is clear that they were at least as extensive as those around the pool. In the C5 many of the stones were used to erect a **church** [1]. Unusually it has no apse; the sanctuary is square. The bench running along three walls is also unusual. The holes for the four legs of the altar straddle a hollow for a reliquary. The small room in the south-east corner is a **baptistry**.

The large **inscription** in the nave lists a number of families, who donated the church to 'Lord the Son Christ and holy Michael', an exceptional formula suggesting perhaps that the donors were not entirely orthodox. If so, they had company, because the door-like inscription in the narthex reads 'This is the gate of the Lord; the righteous shall enter into it. O Lord, the Son, Christ, remember your servant Anael and Saprica'. These two (with a certain Mamas) also donated the room along the north side of the church as their dedicatory inscription to St Michael testifies.

Hippos: *see* SUSITA

Hisham's Palace: *see* KHIRBET AL-MAFJAR

Horns of Hattin (Qarne Hittin) (M6)

The skyline west of the SEA OF GALILEE is dominated by a long low hill with a little peak at either end (Fig. 107). It owes its name to this distinctive horned shape. Here Saladin defeated the Crusaders on 4 July 1187 in a battle which changed the course of history. A sign-posted tarmac turn-off to the north on the Tiberias–Nazareth road, roughly 2 km from both Kibbutz Lavi and Zomet Poriyya, leads to a dirt road which goes all the way to the southern summit.

By the summer of 1187, after seventeen years of inconclusive skirmishes, Saladin was determined to bring the Crusaders to a decisive battle. On 27 June his 12,000 mounted archers streamed down from the GOLAN to camp at the southern end of the Sea of Galilee. Leaving his heavy equipment there, three days later he moved up the Yavneel valley to create a forward base at En Sabt (2390/1920) some 2 km east of Sede Ilan. Until 2 July his troops rampaged throughout the countryside and Saladin battered his way into Tiberias.

The Crusader forces assembled at the spring of SEPPHORIS (Zippori). Despite intense heat and the fact that prisoners could be ransomed, and villages and churches rebuilt, the king, Guy de Lusignan, decided on confrontation. From the moment they set out before dawn on 3 July, the tightly disciplined Crusader column—1,200 knights surrounded by 16,000 infantry—came under fire from the Kurdish archers. As the column fought its way east along the ROMAN ROAD (parallel to route 77 on the north) the need for water made itself ever more urgently felt. The spring at Turan proved insufficient for the numbers. Instead of driving fast for the lake, the fatigue of the rearguard, which had borne the brunt of Saladin's attacks, induced the king to order the army to camp at the village of Marescalcia (today Horvat Mishkena some 300 m north-north-east of the Golani Junction) in the vicinity of which there was a pool. The pool is beside route 65 about 100 metres north of the Golani Junction.

Next morning Saladin attacked only when the brazen summer sun was shining into the Crusaders' eyes as they moved slowly east. Accounts of the order of subsequent events vary to the point of making an accurate reconstruction impossible. One critical moment came when Raymond of Tripoli led the vanguard in a desperate downhill charge for the spring against Saladin's right wing led by Taqi ed-Din; at a signal the latter's troopers wheeled their fast ponies to either side and the charge went through without making contact. As the barrier on the crest closed again, Raymond and his men rode miserably away to the north.

This broke the morale of the Crusader foot soldiers who began to swarm to the Horns of Hattin. It was a more defensible position than would appear today. Remains of a C14 BC wall surrounded the southern peak, and a broken C9 BC rampart enclosed both horns. Sustained fire by Crusader archers from the protection of these walls permitted the knights to regroup in the hollow between the horns. The red tent of the king was erected on the southern peak.

Twice the knights charged downhill through the western gap at Saladin's centre in the hope of capturing the sultan. Twice they were driven back. The surviving knights dismounted to form a wall around the southern horn. They were overwhelmed by a fierce Muslim charge. The reliquary of the True Cross, the battle-standard, was wrenched from the dead hands of the Bishop of Acre. Some moments later the king was taken. Saladin was master of the field and commemorated his success by erecting a victory dome; it is identified with the meagre remains of a two-roomed building (8.6 × 10 m) in the south-west section of the southern peak.

Hunin (N1)

Built on the edge of the steep escarpment overlooking Qiryat Shemona, the Crusader fortress of Chateauneuf offers a magnificent panorama of the Hulah valley, to the east DAN, BAMYAS, and NIMRUD lie beneath Mount Hermon.

The first castle was built in 1107 by Hugh of St Omer to command the ascent which carried the important commercial route from Damascus to Tyre. It thus took its place in the line of castles defending the eastern border of the Latin Kingdom. Destroyed by Nur ed-Din in 1167, it was rebuilt in 1178. That same year it successfully resisted a siege by Saladin. After the latter's victory at the HORNS OF HATTIN, the garrison held out for five months before finally surrendering to the sultan's brother, al-Adil, in December 1187. Fearing that it might be recaptured by the Franks, al-Muazzam had it demolished in 1222. It was reconstructed by the Mamluk sultan Baybars in 1267. Its subsequent history is obscure.

Visit. Going north from Qiryat Shemona on route 90, turn left to Kefar Giladi, and then left again on route 9977 following the signs to Margaliyyot.

The wide, dry moat was cut by the Crusaders. It served a dual purpose. While being cut it provided construction material for the castle. When finished it became a defensive barrier. Unlike BELVOIR there were no corner towers. Apart from some Crusader stones in the western wall, all the visible remains, in particular the great entrance gate, are of the Mamluk period.

Hyrcania: *see* KHIRBET MIRD

Jacob's Well (K12)

A deep well (22.5 m), located on the eastern edge of NABLUS (Fig. 100), is venerated as the spot where Jesus encountered the Samaritan woman (John 4). Open 8 a.m.–4 p.m. (winter); to 5 p.m. (summer). Ring bell.

The existence of a well in the immediate vicinity of so many springs tends to confirm the traditional attribution to Jacob. When he bought land to settle down (Gen. 33: 18–20) the water rights to the springs would have long been assigned; the only alternative to perpetual disputes was to find his own source of water. The same, of course, is true of any other latecomer.

About AD 380 a cruciform church was built, incorporating a baptistery associated with the exposed well-head. After destruction in the SAMARITAN uprising of 484 or 529, the church was rebuilt and survived until the C9. Early Crusader pilgrims speak of the well but not the church, which is first mentioned in 1175 as belonging to the Benedictine sisters of BETHANY. Its construction may have been made possible by the patronage of Queen Melisande, founder of the abbey at Bethany, who was exiled to Nablus in 1152 and lived there until her death in 1161.

The Greek Orthodox Church acquired the ruined site in 1860, and restored the crypt with the well to Christian use in 1893. The half-built church, like that on the MOUNT OF TEMPTATION, was a victim of the troubles that beset Greece and Russia during and after the 1914–18 war. It reflects the general lines of the Crusader church. The T-shape of the crypt and the steps leading down to it are medieval.

Jericho (Yeriho) (M16)

The lowest (258 m below sea-level) and the oldest town on earth, strategically located on the border between the desert and the sown, lush green against the surrounding dust-brown, Jericho opens many windows on the past (Fig. 74).

Tropical in summer but beautifully mild in winter, the climate attracted prehistoric nomads to the area. They settled at TEL ES-SULTAN near a powerful perennial spring (En es-Sultan; 4,500 litres per minute) whose water is still distributed throughout the oasis by a complex system of gravity-flow irrigation, producing abundant fruit, flowers, and spices. The first massive defence wall was erected around the settlement c.8000 BC, the inhabitants having passed from the status of wandering food-gatherers to settled food-producers. The town beside the spring had fallen to many waves of invaders from the desert before it was captured by Joshua and the Israelites c.1200 BC. Occupation of the tel ends at the time of the Babylonian exile (586 BC).

In the late C6 BC Jericho became a Persian administrative centre, and there must have been some sort of settlement elsewhere in the area to house those who worked the rich plantations. From the time of Alexander

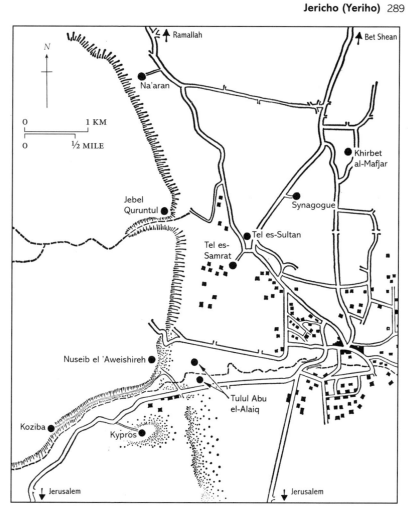

▲ **Fig. 74.** The Jericho area.

the Great (336–323 BC) the oasis was considered the private estate of the ruling sovereign, and this blocked any true urban development. Shortly before the middle of the C2 BC Baccides, a Syrian general at war with the Maccabees, strengthened the defences of the area by building forts on Jebel Quruntul (MOUNT OF TEMPTATION), on Nuseib el-Aweishireh and on its companion peak at the other side of the entrance to the Wadi Qilt, which was later refortified by Herod the Great (37–4 BC) and named KYPROS after his mother.

Herod the Great first leased the oasis from Cleopatra, who had been given it by her paramour Mark Antony. After their joint suicide in 30 BC

A Roman View of Jericho

'Jericho is a plain surrounded by a kind of mountainous country, which, in a way, slopes toward it like a theatre. Here is the Phoenicon [i.e. palm-grove], which is mixed also with other kinds of cultivated and fruitful trees, though it consists mostly of palm trees. It is 100 stadia in length and is everywhere watered with streams. Here also are the Palace, and the Balsam Park. The balsam is of the shrub kind, resembling cytisus and terebinth, and has a spicy flavour. The people make incisions in the bark and catch the juice in vessels. This juice is a glutinous, milk-white substance. When it is put up in small quantities it solidifies. It is remarkable for its cure of headache and of incipient cataracts and of dimness of sight. Accordingly, it is costly; and also for the reason that it is produced nowhere else.' (Strabo (C1), *Geography* 16: 2. 41; trans. H. L. Jones)

Octavian, the new master of the Roman world, rewarded Herod's adroit diplomacy by handing it over to him. Herod laid out new aqueducts to irrigate the area below the cliffs and to supply his fabulous winter palace at TULUL EL-ALAIQ. To divert himself and his guests he also built a hippodrome-cum-theatre (TEL ES-SAMRAT). In Judaea he was succeeded by his son Archelaus (4 BC–AD 6) who built the village of Archelais to house the workers in his date-palm plantation (KHIRBET EL-BEIYUDAT).

The cemetery of Hasmonean and Herodian Jericho is cut into the lowest part of the cliffs between Nuseib el-Aweishireh and Jebel Quruntul. Rock-cut tombs containing wooden coffins and stone ossuaries show it to have been in use from 100 BC until AD 68.

Jericho suffered from the depredations of the Roman army in AD 68–9 as Vespasian waited for the Jewish factions in Jerusalem to weaken each other and for the engineers of the Tenth Legion to complete the road necessary to get their heavy siege equipment up to the Holy City.

The area was heavily populated in the Byzantine period. In addition to a C6 synagogue at En Duk (biblical Naaran, Josh. 16: 7) and another near Tel es-Sultan, there were many monasteries of which only two survive, the MONASTERY OF ST GEORGE OF KOZIBA clinging to the cliff of the Wadi Qilt, and DEIR HAJLA near the Jordan river. The most remarkable monument of the Arab period is the magnificent hunting palace at KHIRBET AL-MAFJAR which reflects the vast resources of the Umayyad empire in the C8 AD. In the Middle Ages sugar-cane was intensively cultivated, and there are very ruined remains of Crusader sugar-mills. At this period churches commemorating the temptations of Christ were erected on Jebel Quruntul (MOUNT OF TEMPTATION).

The departure of the Crusaders from the area after their defeat by Saladin in 1187 left Jericho without protection against bedouin raids from the desert, and a thriving town degenerated into a miserable village. The canals fell into disuse and the desert reclaimed what had been its own. Only with the establishment of effective police control after the First World War did Jericho begin to recover something of its former glory by developing into a great fruit-producing area. The most evident traces of the impact of the C20 on the oldest of towns are the two great Palestinian refugee camps. From 1948 to 1967 these mud huts housed over 70,000 displaced persons, many of whom again fled during the Six-Day War.

Jib (J17)

A picturesque Arab village on a rocky island in the midst of a small intensively cultivated plain (10 km north of Jerusalem), Jib has the most interesting ancient water system in the country.

Jib retains the first syllable of the biblical Gibeon; identification has been confirmed by discovery of inscribed jar-handles on the site. Already a great city (the earliest remains are Ancient Bronze) when the Israelites entered Palestine (c.1200 BC), the old clothes and stale bread of the Gibeonites deceived Joshua into signing a peace treaty (the full story is told in Josh. 9). He none the less kept his word and went to their defence when the five kings attacked; in order to prolong the slaughter he prayed, 'sun, stand still at Gibeon' (Josh. 10: 12).

Apart from Solomon's visit (1 Kgs. 3: 4–15), the site is notable only for a series of gory episodes (2 Sam. 2, 20, 21). In the C8–C7 BC the production and exportation of wine made it a prosperous city but this glory never returned after the city's destruction by the Babylonians in 587 BC.

Visit (Fig. 75). Jib lies on route 437, which can be reached from either the Bet Horon road (route 436) or the Nablus road (route 60). On reaching the village turn on to the old Biddu road and then immediately up the hill with houses on the left and rock threshing-floors on the right. From the corner of the parking-lot (courtesy term!) a rough path leads to the two key areas which are all that remain of a much larger excavation. Bring flashlights.

The round holes cut in the rock are the entrances to C8–C7 BC **wine-cellars**; sixty-three were discovered, each one capable of storing forty-two 36-litre jars. The total storage capacity was 95,000 litres. When sealed by a fitted capstone these cellars maintain a constant temperature of 18 °C. The wine was sold in smaller jars with the name of the city and the producer stamped on the handles.

The great **rock-cut pool** (2 Sam. 2: 13) with its spiral staircase is dated to the C12–C11 BC. The steps continue beneath the rock floor to the water chamber. It could be that the water-table dropped, but it seems more likely that a new administration in the city found a cheaper way of continuing a ridiculously expensive project. At any rate the steps got little use (note the straight edges) because in the C10 BC two new **tunnels** were cut. One brings water from the spring in the centre of the hill to a pool just inside its edge. The other descends from just inside the ancient city wall to the pool. This system denied water to attackers while still making it available to inhabitants under siege. In time of peace they simply walked down the side of the hill and entered the pool from the outside; slots in the walls and floor near the entrance show that it could be sealed quickly in an emergency.

Without knowing it, the archaeologists put their dump over the original entrance to the tunnel. This error has now been rectified. Just inside one can see how the tunnel was constructed. They first cut a vertical trench 4 m deep outside the city wall and then ran one tunnel under the wall and the other down to the pool. The corbelled roof of this section is

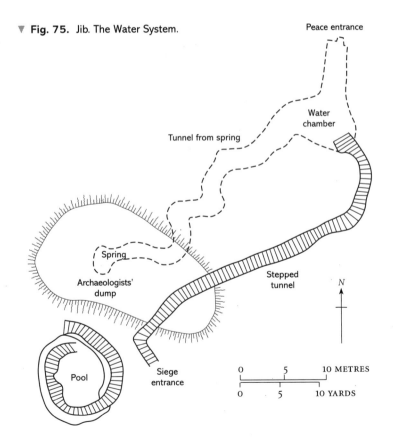

▼ Fig. 75. Jib. The Water System.

Peace entrance

Water chamber

Tunnel from spring

Spring

Archaeologists' dump

Stepped tunnel

N

Pool

Siege entrance

0   5   10 METRES

0   5   10 YARDS

still visible; outside it was camouflaged with earth. The worn steps and polished sides bear witness to frequent passage; note the smoke-darkened niches where oil-lamps stood.

Kebara Cave: *see* RAMAT HANADIV

Kedesh: *see* TEL QEDESH

Khallat ed-Danabiya (L16)

To call a MONASTERY IN THE JUDAEAN DESERT the Machu Picchu of Palestine might appear an exaggeration, but Khallat ed-Danabiya exhibits the dominant physical feature of the great Inca city in Peru; a huddle of structures linked by stairways clings precariously to a narrow ridge jutting out into a deep canyon. Admittedly, the dry Wadi Makkuk is nothing like the valley of the thunderous Urubamba river.

Its forty cells make this one of the largest lauras in the Judaean desert, but it cannot be identified with any of the forty-one monastic establishments known from the literary sources. Its history, therefore, has to be deduced from the remains. Sometime in the C4 AD a monk seeking solitude settled in a cave on the east side of the ridge. His choice had a double justification. The cave contained a cistern of the C1 AD which could provide him with water in summer when the nearest spring, 600 m away, dried up, as it still does. In addition the east end of the cave curved to make a natural apse. For the desert monks this was the sign of 'a church made by God'. The cave was in fact consecrated as a church when the hermit's reputation for sanctity drew other monks who settled in the nearby caves. As their numbers grew the monks were forced to develop the top of the ridge. In the absence of caves they were obliged to build. The typical unit consists of a cell with a store-room and a cistern adjacent to an agricultural terrace. The fate of the laura is unknown, but its end appears to have been as quiet and unremarkable as its beginning.

Visit. The site is just to the east of the Allon Road (route 458) which begins half-way between Jerusalem and Jericho (route 1). At 4.5 km from the junction a paved road on the right (north) descends steeply to **En Fawwar** in the Wadi Qilt (Nahal Perat). A ruined British pumping station spoils the beauty of the powerful intermittent spring. It once fed a Herodian **aqueduct** (now repaired and again in use) which can be followed all the way to En Qilt, the start of the three aqueducts going to Herod the Great's winter palace at TULUL ABU EL-ALAIQ. Across the wadi from the spring are twelve monastic cells. They have been identified with the **Laura of the Spring** whose superior attended the Council of Constantinople in AD 553.

Very shortly after the descent to En Fawwar the Allon Road crosses the wadi. It is worthwhile parking there and going up stream for some 500 m. The wadi coming in from the left is a spectacular gorge on whose left (south) bank is the Herodian aqueduct from EN FARAH.

At 14.5 km from the Jericho road junction, route 458 is joined by route 457 (coming from the Jerusalem–Ramallah road) in the middle of a large S-bend. At the highest point of the southern end of the bend two dirt roads lead east. The northern one has red trailmarkers, which lead directly to the cave church, which is the centre of the laura.

The rock spur has a hump in the centre surmounted by a square **medieval building** about which nothing is known. On the saddle and climbing the hump are the ruins of small rectangular buildings, the cells of the monks. Nearby are cisterns with vaulted roofs. They are built in pairs connected by a channel in such a way that one serves as a decantation basin for the other.

Just before reaching the saddle the red trailmarkers turn down to the right and follow a series of **flights of steps** cutting diagonally across the cliff face. These were cut by the monks, who also carved the **water channels** which conveyed run-off rain-water to the cisterns. This path runs across the face of a number of caves which were the **cells** of the first monks. They carved benches as beds, hewed niches for storage, gouged grooves for shelves, and broke open windows for extra light.

The **cave church** is essentially a rock shelter (25 × 9 m) whose open side would have been closed by a wall. It is reached by a double flight of steps, to whose left is the stepped entrance to a tomb and beside it the main cistern. Just inside the rock shelter is a mosaic-floored cave high in the eastern wall; presumably it was here the founding saint first settled. The round hole in the floor of the church is the C1 cistern. Beneath the middle of the church is a burial area. Flanking the apse at the far end are the hewn niche of the sacristy and a small square pool identified as a **baptistery**. A flight of steps around the corner from the baptistery (the first part is only toe-holds cut in the rock) follow a water channel to the gentle slope above the church on which the communal buildings of the laura, e.g. the bakehouse, may have been sited.

Khan el-Ahmar (L17)

Surrounded by graceless factories, the forlorn ruin of Khan el-Ahmar bravely continues to bear witness to a spirit which is the antithesis of the crass political materialism behind the establishment of an industrial zone

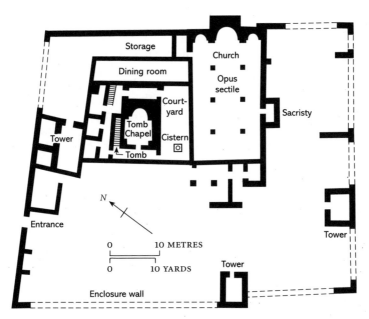

▲ **Fig. 76.** Khan el-Ahmar. Monastery of St Euthymius (after Hirschfeld).

in one of the most beautiful valleys in the Judaean desert. This was the laura (a cluster of solitary cells around a church) of St Euthymius, once the most important monastic centre in the Holy Land (MONASTERIES IN THE JUDAEAN DESERT).

Born in AD 377 in Lesser Armenia, Euthymius came to Palestine and became a disciple of St Chariton at EN FARAH in 406. Five years later he and Theoctistus founded a new laura in a remote part of the desert, Wadi Mukellik. The Arab tribe which pastured its flocks in that region became Christians and Euthymius eventually ordained as bishop the sheikh, Peter Aspebet (a Persian title meaning 'master of horse') who later played a significant role at the Council of Ephesus (431) as Bishop of the Arab Camps.

After moving round the desert in a vain attempt to escape the disciples who flocked to him, Euthymius finally capitulated. In 428 the church of the laura at Khan el-Ahmar was consecrated. He insisted, however, that those who desired to participate in the organized hermit life of the laura should first be trained in the monastery (*coenobium*) of Theoctistus in the Wadi Mukellik. In the next century this prudent innovation was made the normal pattern by Sabas, the greatest of Euthymius' disciples (MAR SABA).

Euthymius himself recognized that the site at Khan el-Ahmar was too central to provide the solitude necessary for a laura and left orders that after his death it was to be transformed into a monastery. He died on 20

January 473, and reconstruction began immediately. According to the historian Cyril of Scythopolis, who lived here from 544 to 555, 'taking an engineer, a quantity of skilled workmen, and many assistants, Fidus went down to the laura and built the coenobium, which he surrounded with walls and made secure. The old church he made into a refectory, and built the new church above it. Within the coenobium he constructed a tower that was at the same time entirely secure and extremely beautiful, and he also contrived that the burial vault should lie in the middle of the coenobium' (*Life of Euthymius* 64; trans. R. M. Price). The construction took three years (478–81). Though ruined by an earthquake in 660, the complex was rebuilt on the same lines. Extensive restoration and construction took place in the C12, but the monastery was abandoned a century later. Subsequently it may have been used as a caravanserai by those on the pilgrimage route from Jerusalem to Mecca via NABI MUSA.

Visit (Fig. 76). From the Jerusalem–Jericho road (route 1) take the turn to Mishor Adummim; go straight through the settlement; the ruin is on the left about 1.5 km from the turn-off.

The **church**, and the three vaults on which it rests, date from the post-earthquake (660) reconstruction, to which the mosaics of the aisles also belong. The *opus sectile* decoration of the nave stems from the C12 refurbishing. The **tomb** of Euthymius and his companions is north of the church. Above it was a mortuary chapel. A stone table is still in place in the **dining-room**, which adjoins a storage area. A strong **tower** provided a place of refuge in case of attack. Outside the walls of the monastery to the east is a vast underground **cistern** of the C5; known to the Arabs as the 'Well of Seven Mouths', it collected run-off rain-water from the surrounding area.

A Desert Father

'It is related of Euthymius that his expression was angelic, his character unaffected and his behaviour most gentle. As for his body, the appearance of his face was round, bright, fair and with fine eyes. He was dwarf-like in build, with hair completely grey and a great beard that reached his stomach. All his limbs were unimpaired; neither his eyes nor his teeth had suffered any damage at all, and he died with full physical and mental vigour. . . . Born following a revelation, he was consecrated to God at the age of three at the beginning of the reign of Theodosius the Great; on progressing through all the ecclesiastical grades, he came to Jerusalem in the twenty-ninth year of his life. He spent sixty-eight years in the desert and died at the age of ninety-seven in the fifth consulship of the emperor Leo and the sixteenth year of his reign.' (Cyril of Scythopolis (C6), *Life of Euthymius* 40/59–60; trans. R. M. Price)

Khirbet ed-Deir (K20)

The Arabic name accurately describes the site; it is 'the ruin of a monastery'. No name could evoke the beauty of the location. The monastery nestles in the elbow of a small wadi whose rock walls shelter rather than confine; energetic devotion built a dam at the foot of the winter waterfall and turned the bed of the wadi into a verdant garden. Apart from its foundation in the early C6 AD, nothing certain is known of its brief history. It is simply one of the seventy-three Byzantine MONAS-TERIES IN THE JUDAEAN DESERT, but here perhaps better than anywhere else one can experience the remote stillness that drew men closer to God.

Route 3698 to the monastery (located at map reference 1739/1038) begins at Tuqa (K19; Fig. 59), from among whose shepherds the prophet Amos was called (Amos 1: 1). The modern tarmac road follows approximately the line of the Israelite and Roman trail to EN GEDI; in a car with exceptional clearance it is possible to cross the shallow wadis at the southern end and descend the cliffs to the DEAD SEA at Metzoke Dragot.

Just 0.5 km from the new settlement of Maale Amos, on the left side of the road, is the ruin of a little **Roman fort**, Khirbet Sabha. If one walks across the road and down to a point where the bed of the Wadi Arugot becomes visible one can see the great wave-curve of the **prehistoric cave** of Sabha, which was occupied between 100,000 and 45,000 BC. Five km from Maale Amos the road makes a sharp bend; profiled on the skyline to the right are the ruins of a small **Israelite fort**; it is the highest point on the ancient trail and offers a magnificent view over the desert.

The trail to the monastery (marked in blue) begins at 9.5 km from Maale Amos just where the road, dipping into a small plain, begins to make a big curve to the left. The dirt road runs down a narrow wadi to the right. With care a car can be brought to the top of the cliff. From there it is a 40-minute hike to the monastery. Follow the rough road to the bed of the wadi. Go up the wadi bed to the right and turn into the second tributary coming in from the left; projecting out from it is a heavy drystone wall built by the monks to protect their fields, which are still tilled by the bedouin.

Once in the tributary, called Shaab ed-Deir, 'the ravine of the monastery', one is conscious of constructive activity. On the left a circular rock-cut cistern is fed by a channel which collected run-off rainwater. Thick walls cross the wadi bed to create terraces on which the monks grew vegetables and cultivated fruit trees.

The monastery (Fig. 77) is built against and into the cliff to the right. The purpose of the rock-cut room is unclear; it may have been a burial cave. The rectangular building with a mosaic floor and a rectangular basin in one corner is probably a **baptistery** [1]. Sanctity not only attracted

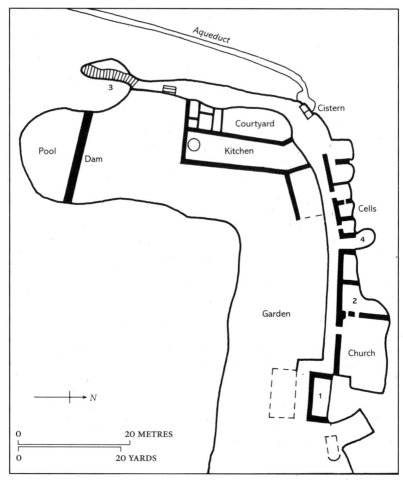

▲ **Fig. 77.** Khirbet ed-Deir (after Hirschfeld). 1. Baptistery; 2. Sacristy; 3. Steps to clifftop; 4. Founder's Cave.

followers but also inspired conversions. The large cave served as the main **church**. The mosaic floor is covered with earth to protect it; if this is removed for inspection it should be replaced. The floral pattern is framed by medallions depicting baskets of fruit, a sickle, etc. The holes for the pillars and the slots for the marble chancel screen mark off the **sanctuary** area. At the base of the well-cut rock niche to the right are traces of a reliquary; immediately in front is a well-preserved mosaic floor with a particularly striking design of radiating arc-like rays. One of the rooms at the west end of the church must have been the **sacristy** [2].

From outside the church a **stone-flagged path** runs through the monastery; it is bordered by a rain gutter. The mosaic pavement with a Greek inscription mentioning the resurrection from the dead gives special importance to a **cave** with a bench cut into one wall [**4**]. This may have been the cell of a hermit, whose sanctity attracted disciples, and thus gave birth to the monastery. After his death it must have been transformed into a shrine.

The row of rooms built against the cliff began as the **cells** of the first monks and later served as storage rooms. An **aqueduct** coming over the top of the cliff and fed by flash floods in the wadi supplied water to the central **cistern**. A covered channel cut in the rock carried the overflow to the gardens below. The small **courtyard**, with a pantry and store-rooms at the end, was on the same level as the no longer extant refectory, which was built over the **kitchen**; the brick-lined circular structure at one end was a bake-oven.

A heavy plastered wall closed off the end of the wadi to create a **reservoir**; it also served to break the force of winter floods which without some control would have endangered the gardens further downstream.

Very rough steps [**3**] bring one to the top of the cliff. It is worthwhile backtracking along the **aqueduct** to see how it diverted part of the water when the wadi flooded. From this point it is possible to perceive another aqueduct on the far side of the reservoir.

The path leads up to the top of the ridge where there are traces of long **rectangular structures**, one built above a plastered and vaulted cistern fed by its own catchment aqueduct coming along the side of the hill to the west. It is suggested that these structures were rows of cells but the evidence is far from clear. A **tower** stood over the cave-church and served as a place of refuge in case of attacks by the bedouin.

Khirbet el-Beiyudat (M15)

According to Pliny, JERICHO was celebrated for its dates (see box). Archelaus (4 BC–AD 6), a son of Herod the Great, created a new date plantation north of the city, which was watered by an aqueduct fed by the powerful spring today known as En Auja. To house the workers he founded a village called Archelais (*Antiquities* 17: 340). It survived into the Byzantine period and is illustrated in the C6 Madaba map. By that time at least part of the population had become Christian and worshipped in the church which has been excavated here.

Visit. Ten km north of Tel es-Sultan is the village of El Auja et-Tahta. The road to the west goes past Yitav into the steep-sided valley sheltering the spring. The ancient **aqueducts** are as obvious as the ruins of Khirbet el-Auja el-Fauqa on the ridge to the south. It is identified as the town of **Senaa** (Ezra 2: 35), whose inhabitants rebuilt the Fish Gate in Jerusalem in the C5 BC (Neh. 3: 3); in the C4 AD it was known as Magdalsenna.

Two km north of the crossroads in El Auja et-Tahta a wire fence just off the road to the east is the site of the **church**. West of the road lie the channels leading from the main aqueduct to the date plantation of Archelais. The church is of the typical early Byzantine type with a single apse. Five inscriptions complement the architectural analysis of the structure which reveals several building phases.

The earliest inscription (mentioning two priests Apheleos and Lukas) is that in the middle of the **south aisle** and dates the foundation of the church to the second half of the C5. The same Lukas, who presumably stayed on as the resident priest, is named in another inscription as having added the **eastern room** attached to the south wall of the church. Around the middle of the C6 the **mosaic floor** of the entire church, with the exception of the southern aisle, was renewed. The inscription in front of the sanctuary reads, 'In the time of our most holy and pious bishop Porphyrius, this church was paved, owing to the zeal of the priest Eglon and for the salvation of the benefactors'. At this stage apparently the two small square rooms on either side of the apse were added, but (abnormally for this church) no one claimed the credit; normally such rooms housed reliquaries. The inscription in the **western room** attached to the south wall is dated to the 60s of the C6 and reads, 'O Lord Jesus Christ, receive the offering of thy servants, John the priest and Abbosobos, for they erected this room with their own hands'. The latter was subsequently ordained and, with other benefactors, is credited with having given a new mosaic floor to the **sanctuary** by the inscription in front of the altar, which contains the date 12 November 570.

Dates

'The "pig-headed" date supplies a great deal of food but also of juice, and from them the principal wines of the East are made. These strongly affect the head. Hence the name of the date! Not only are these trees abundant and bear largely in Judaea, but also the most famous are found there, and not in the whole of that country but specially in Jericho, although those growing in the valleys of Archelais and Phaselis and Livias are also highly spoken of. Their outstanding property is the unctuous juice which they exude and an extremely sweet sort of wine-flavour like that of honey.' (Pliny (C1), *Natural History* 13: 44–5; trans. H. Rackham)

Khirbet el-Mafjar (M16)   ★★

Located just north of JERICHO (Fig. 74) and commonly called 'Hisham's Palace' because it was at first thought to have been built by the Umayyad caliph Hisham ibn Abd el-Malik (AD 724–443) who ruled an empire stretching from India to the Pyrenees. Many of the Umayyad dynasty had such hunting lodges which enabled them to recover the freedom and independence of the desert which was their birthright, but the extravagance and unorthodox decoration of Khirbet el-Mafjar is incompatible

▼ **Fig. 78.** Khirbet al-Mafjar. Umayyad Palace (after Hamilton). 1. Modern entrance; 2. Forecourt; 3. Monumental gate; 4. Central courtyard; 5. Mosque; 6. Bath; 7. Dining-room; 8. Path; 9. Reception room; 10. Pool; 11. Bath hall; 12. Hot rooms; 13. Furnaces; 14. Dressing-room; 15. Wine bath; 16. Toilets.

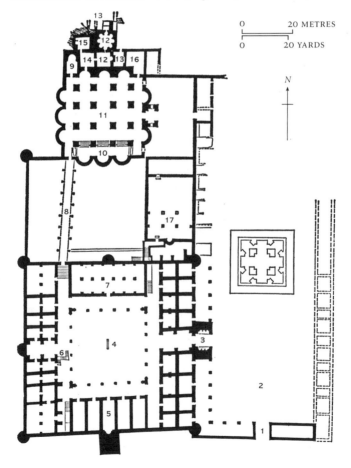

with the character of the austere, righteous Hisham. It harmonizes best with what we know of his nephew and successor al Walid ibn Yazid (743–4).

'Banished from the court for wild living and scurrility, passionate aesthete and drinker, habitual companion of singers, himself the best poet and marksman of the Umayyads' (R. W. Hamilton, *Levant* 1 (1969) 65), Walid first built the bath which shows signs of having been in use for a number of years. It and the great walled hunting park were his main interests. Walid was assassinated a year after coming to power so the palace was never completed and, despite an attempted restoration in the C12 (possibly by Saladin's troops), thereafter served as a quarry of cut stones for the people of Jericho. The architecture and the motifs of the stucco decoration (used here for the first time in Palestine) betray strong Persian influence. Much of the ornate plasterwork is well displayed in the Rockefeller Museum in Jerusalem.

Visit (Fig. 78). Open: 8 a.m.–5 p.m. Toilets are located to the left of the present entrance [1].

On both sides of the **forecourt** [2] architectural elements scattered by the earthquake of 747 have been arranged in their proper relative positions. The **entrance-gate** [3] was originally vaulted in brick, showing that master builders from Iraq were employed in the construction. The monument in the middle of the central court [4] was erected by the excavators. Intended as a **window**, it illustrates the way in which the Umayyads transformed the motifs (in this case Roman) which they found in the lands they conquered.

A small **mosque** abutting on the minaret [5] was probably intended for the personal use of the caliph. A flight of steps [6] leads down to a **subterranean bathing-hall** floored with mosaic. The big hall [7] must have served as a **banqueting-room**. Since few of the rooms round the central court communicate with one another the royal apartments must have been located on the upper floor reached by stairways in the north-east and south-west corners.

The paved path [8] leading from the palace to the **bath** was probably reserved to the caliph because when Walid was in residence a curtain closed off the area between his reception room [9] and the **swimming-pool** [10] which he had filled with rosewater mixed with musk and turmeric. The floor of the raised area in the **reception room** is one of the most beautiful mosaics in the Holy Land; the tassels round the edge suggest it was modelled on a carpet. Stucco floral patterns carved in high relief covered the walls.

The floor of the **bath-hall** [11] is completely covered by a mosaic in geometric patterns. Only part is exposed because the projected protective roof was never completed. The two **hot rooms** [12] were heated to different temperatures by separate furnaces [13]. They were entered from

A Very Unusual Bath

'Utarrad speaks, "I was brought into Walid, and he was sitting in his palace on the edge of a small pool, just large enough for a man to turn round in when immersed. It was lined with lead and filled with wine. I had hardly time to give him the greeting when he said, 'Are you Utarrad?' 'Yes, Commander of the Faithful,' said I. 'I have been longing to hear you,' said he. 'Now sing to me [three lines of a poem are quoted].' So I sang it to him. I had barely finished when, by God, he tore apart an embroidered robe that was on him, worth I know not what, flung it down in two pieces, and plunged naked as his mother bore him into that pool; whence he drank, I swear, until the level was distinctly lowered. Then he was pulled out, laid down dead to the world, and covered up. So I got up and took the robe; and no one, by God, said to me 'take it' or 'leave it'. So I went off to my lodging, amazed to see the liveliness of his mind and the violence of his emotion." ' (Abu al-Faraj al-Isfahani, *Kitab al-Aghani* 3: 303; trans. R. W. Hamilton)

an unheated room [**14**] which may have been used for massage or depilation. It links with another room [**15**] containing two small **square tanks** in which Walid bathed in wine (see box).

The **latrine** [**16**] was flushed by waste water from the hot rooms. The step shows that the users followed the oriental practice of squatting on foot-rests. The **public mosque** [**17**] was open to the sky except for a covered area in front of the *mihrab* and the door leading to the royal apartments.

Khirbet Mird (Hyrcania) (L·18)

The peak stands out from the mass of the Judaean hills, dominating the great plain of the Buqei'a which stretches to the cliffs behind QUMRAN with NABI MUSA at its northern entrance. First fortified by John Hyrcanus (134–103 BC), whence its original name Hyrcania, Khirbet Mird served as one of the treasure-houses of the Hasmonean queen Alexandra (76–67 BC) before being pulled down by the Romans under Gabinius in 57 BC. Herod the Great (37–4 BC) rebuilt the fortress very soon after coming to power, and used it to dispose of those who displeased him (imprisonment or execution). None the less, he brought Marcus Agrippa, son-in-law of the emperor Augustus, to admire its magnificence in 15 BC. Strategically of no importance, it fell into ruin once the security-mad king died. Only five days before his own death he had sent his last victim, his son Antipater, to be buried here.

The pain and sorrow which penetrated the stones may account for the atmosphere that St Sabas encountered among the ruins during his solitary sojourn in Lent 492 (see box). Having chased away the demons, he worked all summer to confirm his victory by constructing a monastery which was dedicated on 23 November 492. Occupation in the C8–C10 AD is attested by the discovery of manuscripts in Arabic, Greek, and Christo-Palestinian Aramaic, which demonstrate the integration of the monks into their new Muslim environment. The monastery was abandoned only in the C14 AD. An attempt to restore the monastery in 1923 by monks of MAR SABA was defeated by the bedouin.

Visit. Between the end of the suburb of Bethany and Maale Adumim turn south. On reaching route 398 from Abu Dis turn left, and at the top of the hill again left on to the desert road (7104) with red trailmarkers. From that point it is 6 km on a fairly good dirt road to the parking-lot on the south shoulder of **Jebel Muntar**, at 524 m the highest point in the area.

The Trail

The 360-degree panorama of the desert makes the ten-minute walk to the summit of Jebel Muntar well worth while. The sparse remains, including a cistern, belong to the **tower** built by the empress Eudokia in 455 to receive St Euthymius (KHAN EL-AHMAR). Monks squatted there subsequently. In 509 St Sabas regularized the situation by appointing as abbot a certain John known as 'Scholarius' (d. 544) because he had been a member of the

---

Sabas at Castellion

'Sabas went to the hill of Castellion, which is about 20 stades northeast from the laura [Mar Saba]. This hill was terrifying and unfrequented because of the large number of demons who lurked there, so that none of the shepherds in the desert dared to go near the place. The revered old man, however, making the Most High his refuge and sprinkling the place with oil from the most Holy Cross, stayed during the season of Lent; and by his ceaseless prayers and divine praises the place was tamed. . . . Since the demons were thwarted by his perseverant prayer, they departed from the place, shouting in human speech, "What a brute you are, Sabas! The gorge you colonized does not satisfy you, but you force yourself into our place as well. See, we withdraw from our own territory. We cannot resist you since you have God as your defender." With these and similar words, they withdrew from the mountain with one accord at the very hour of midnight, with a certain beating sound and confused tumult, like a flock of crows.' (Cyril of Scythopolis (C6), *Life of Sabas* 27/110; trans. R. M. Price)

imperial bodyguard in Constantinople before becoming a monk. He expanded the tower into one of the largest coenobia in the desert, which was known subsequently as the **monastery of the Scholarius**.

From the parking-lot the walk to Khirbet Mird takes about ninety minutes. Hiking boots and canteens of water are essential. A good road leads down the side of Jebel Muntar. When it levels off, follow the steep road down to the cistern (surrounded by drinking troughs) of Bir el-Amarah. From there go down the bed of the wadi, and eventually, at the second (dry) waterfall, along its right side following the line of the Herodian **aqueduct** (fed by run-off rain-water) which once supplied the fortress, and later the monastery.

As the wadi deepens, the ruins of the **monastery of Spelaion** (= the Cave), founded by St Sabas in AD 508, become visible on the far side of the wadi. The Byzantine path to the monastery begins on the left before the remains of the dam which fed the Herodian aqueduct. In the next wadi to the north the path runs parallel to the aqueduct which fed the main cistern of the monastery. Today it serves the shepherds, who know it as Bir el-Qattar 'the Well of Drops'. The church (12 × 5 m) was built in the middle level below the cave of Sabas. Cells and service area were scattered about the area within a wall defended by two towers.

▼ **Fig. 79.** Khirbet Mird (after Wright). 1. Modern wall; 2. Church; 3. Sacristy; 4. Courtyard; 5. Rooms; 6. Modern cells; 7. Entrance to cistern; 8. Tomb chamber.

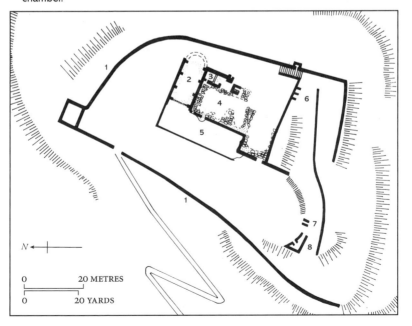

The aqueduct trail eventually rejoins a dirt road, which is an alternative route (green trailmarkers) back to Jebel Muntar. The ruins beside it are those of an aqueduct bridge. At the far end the trail diverges from the road and curves left around the hill.

The Monastery

The next **aqueduct bridge**, immediately below the monastery, is preserved to a much greater height. The bottom four courses laid headers above stretchers is Hasmonean. Above it the masonry is Herodian, but the existing channel on the bridge is Byzantine. It could have supplied water only to the four lowest **cisterns** on the southern slope. The other ten cisterns demand an Herodian channel 6.3 m higher. The cisterns had a total capacity of 16,000 m³. There are two open **reservoirs** north of the bridge and one to the south. These began life as quarries for building stone.

The drystone surround wall [**1**] is modern. The masonry of the two parallel vaulted cisterns supporting the sloped floor of the **courtyard** [**4**] is Herodian and so, therefore, are the rooms on three sides. One of these was turned into a **chapel** [**2**] in the C6 by the addition of an apse. The **sacristy** [**3**] had a fine mosaic floor. The row of monastic cells [**6**] dates from 1923. A low opening is the entrance to a rectangular plastered chamber [**7**]. The hole in the wall opposite opens into a large **cistern** in which manuscripts dated C6–C10 AD were discovered in 1952. A very small door in a triangular rock-lined depression is the entrance to the **cave** in which Byzantine monks were buried [**8**]. It was transformed into a chapel in 1925, when the original frescos representing anchorites of the Judaean desert were repainted. The faces have been obliterated by bedouin.

The rubble structure crowning a crag 300 m south-west of the fortress was probably a **funerary monument**, perhaps to be related to the Herodian **graves** (stone circles in a square enclosure) in the plain below. Are they the resting places of some of Herod's victims, including his son? At the bottom of the narrow section of the Wadi Abu Shale due north of the fortress two **stepped tunnels** descend into the rock. Their date and function are unknown.

Khirbet Shema (M4)

The impressive assemblage of crude massive blocks, traditionally venerated as the tomb of Shammai the great Jewish teacher (active *c.*30 BC), has always drawn visitors to one of the eastern spurs of Mount Meron, the highest mountain in Israel (1,208 m). Recent excavations have enhanced the interest of the site by restoring an unusual ancient synagogue.

Separated from the settlement of Meron by a wadi of the same name, the site is reached by a 15-minute walk up the steep slope from the hairpin bend in route 866 which links routes 85 and 89. Of particular interest are (1) the synagogue, (2) the mausoleum, (3) the wine press, and (4) the ritual bath.

The history of the site is a simple one; it was originally only a farming village in an area famous for the quality of its olive oil. In the C2 AD it was a remote extension of Meron, but as the population of Galilee increased owing to the expulsion of Jews from Judaea, it eventually became an independent village in the second part of the C3. This new identity was marked by the construction of the first synagogue. Destroyed by the earthquake of 306, this edifice was rebuilt only to be again levelled by an earthquake in 419. It was never reconstructed, even though the site continued to be occupied into the Arab period.

Synagogue (Fig. 80)

The synagogue complex is made up of two buildings, a study hall-cum-guesthouse and the synagogue proper. The former is entered from the **paved street** to the east via a short flight of steps; the western side is higher and a rock bench runs along the walls; when in use the whole room was plastered.

The unique architectural structure of the synagogue was imposed by the nature of the terrain. The western end is higher than the body of the building, part being solid bedrock [1]. A wooden floor laid on top of the rock extended to the south, covering the room below and creating a **gallery** with an entrance at each end. The room beneath [2] was decorated with frescos, and probably served for the storage of liturgical objects. From it there is an entrance to a **small cave** under the steps [4] from the western entrance; it is suggested that this was the treasury and/or *genizah* (storage place for deteriorating sacred objects).

The broad-house prayer hall is oriented towards Jerusalem by a **bema**, a raised platform from which scripture was read; note that the pedestals of the columns on this side of the building are more elaborate. This *bema* belongs to the second synagogue because it covers a bench of the original building which had a carved stone torah-shrine at this point. In the corner is a **ritual bath** (*mikveh*) [3] antedating the first synagogue whose construction put it out of commission.

Mausoleum

This unique structure lies some 100 m south-south-west of the synagogue. No certain date can be assigned to it. It is assumed to be contemporary with the settlement (C3–C5 AD). The association with Shammai began only in the Middle Ages. The floor of the main level is cut to receive

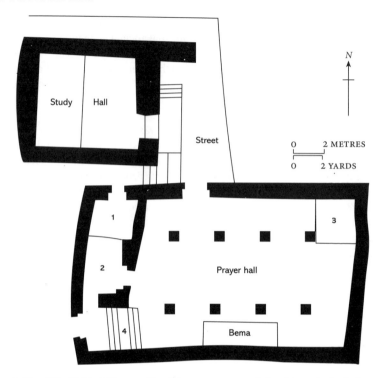

▲ **Fig. 80.** Khirbet Shema. The C4 AD synagogue (after Meyers). 1. Gallery; 2. Room (below); 3. Ritual bath; 4. Entrance.

two corpses, a lower level was intended for secondary burial of the bones once the flesh had disappeared. There are many underground tombs in the immediate vicinity, all contemporary with the settlement.

Wine Press

The installation is cut into bedrock in the immediate vicinity of the mausoleum. The grapes were pressed in the area surrounded by a circular groove; the juice flowed automatically into a series of settling basins, becoming progressively purer. No precise dating is possible.

Ritual Bath

About 110 m due east of the mausoleum is a ritual bath (*mikveh*). A flight of steps leads down to an antechamber with a small opening on the right leading to a small bath in which the hair was cleansed prior to ritual immersion. An interior chamber contains the steps leading down to the bath proper; it was supplied with rain-water from overhead via a channel coming from a sump which collected rain flowing down the entrance steps. This installation was in use during the C4 AD.

Khirbet Suseya (H21) ★

In the springtime Khirbet Suseya ('the Ruin of the Liquorice Plant') rises above a sea of green when the intense cultivation in the shallow wadis south of HEBRON begins to produce its fruit. It is crowned by one of the finest and best-preserved synagogues in the country.

Nothing is known of the history of the Jewish settlement whose ruins cover the adjoining hill. It has to be deduced from the remains and the general history of the region. After the Second Revolt (AD 132–5) the Romans put a garrison in nearby Khirbet el-Karmil (biblical Carmel; 1 Sam. 25). Feeling uncomfortable in the presence of pagan symbols, religious Jews moved their residences some 2 km south-west to an area which perhaps they already farmed. They settled on the tip of the eastern arm of a U-shaped ridge open to the north. It would have been folly to attempt to build fortifications, but they achieved the same result by juxtaposing the outermost houses to one another and leaving the outer walls without windows or doors.

The town gradually expanded around the southern end and up the western arm of the ridge. Naturally the inhabitants still thought of their new community as Carmel, but the name disappeared from history when the village declined in the early Arab period. The garrisons who had been their best customers had departed, and the new Muslim overlords would have had little tolerance for an economy based on wine. Still it survived for several centuries because the synagogue remained in use until the C9 AD. In the C12–C13 the Crusaders established garrisons at nearby Chermala and Esthemoa, and some families moved into the deserted ruins in order to exploit the rich agricultural land.

Visit. Open: Sunday–Thursday: 8 a.m.–4 p.m.; Friday: to 1.30 p.m.; closed Saturday. At the ticket office ask about the explanatory video in English, French, German, Spanish, and Hebrew. The 4 km dirt road from the Yatta–Sammu road (route 356) is not really suitable for the average car. It is better to go around three sides of a square from Sammu. Take the first sealed road (route 3178) on the right on entering the village; where it divides, go uphill to the left through the houses and out into open country.

Shortly after the junction of route 3178 (from Sammu) with route 316 (linking the Beer Sheva–Arad road with Suseya) the ruins of **Horvat Anim** lie just beside the road. The biblical name Anim (Josh. 15: 50) survived into the Byzantine period as Anaia, which Eusebius described as a 'very large Jewish village'. The walls of its C4 **synagogue** (14 × 8 m) survive to a height of 3.5 m. A platform (*bema*) running the width of the north end oriented the building towards Jerusalem. The doorways in the east wall have not been restored. A colonnaded porch with a coloured mosaic floor separated the prayer hall from the paved courtyard (7 × 4 m). The synagogue went out of use in the C7.

The Town

The parking-lot is at the bottom of the U-shaped ridge, and the visit focuses on the western arm. The **cisterns** on the right after leaving the parking-lot are typical of some 150 similar installations which made life here possible; note the grooves that caught run-off rain-water. The **burial cave** closed by a circular stone and preceded by a square rock-cut courtyard was outside the Jewish town, which ended at the nearby **curving wall**. It represents the backs of a row of houses, whose doors opened towards the interior of the town. Menorahs are inscribed on lintels and door jambs have slots for a tiny scroll (*mezuzah*). The **ritual bath** (*mikveh*) has seven plastered steps. The **caves** in which the area abounds were used for accommodation as well as for work-rooms. They were sited below **courtyards** shared by five or six families living in one-storey houses.

The **Wine-Cellar Cave** is much more elaborate. It owes its name to the suggestion that, while the outer large chamber served as a dwelling, the inner part faced with cut stone was used as a wine-cellar; the small opening could be sealed to ensure a constant temperature during the fermentation period. Throughout the cave are a number of small baths; one contained a number of hard stones for heating the water. The utilization of this cave antedates the Crusaders whose presence is attested only in the eastern extension of the cave which has its own entrance. The original entrance was at the other end via a sloping ramp covered by a barrel vault.

The **Menorah Cave** is directly across from the courtyard of the synagogue. It got its name because of the inscribed lintel over the entrance, which is reached by a right-angled flight of rock-cut steps. The wall inside to the left is the western wall of a large cistern. An elaborate water-collection system was hewn in the rock above. The well-mouth and trough are carved from a single block. The semicircular room at the far end was secured by a door with four bolts. Subsequent to Byzantine Jewish occupation intensive use was made of the cave in the C12–C13. A Crusader family must have found it worthwhile to exploit the good soil in this area.

The press in the cave behind the synagogue devoted to the **production of olive oil** is of the screw type, as opposed to the beam type found elsewhere, e.g. BET GUVRIN, TEL MIQNE. After being crushed in the mill, the olives were piled in bags between the uprights. When the screw had been tightened to the point that the uprights began to lift, their weight constituted the pressure.

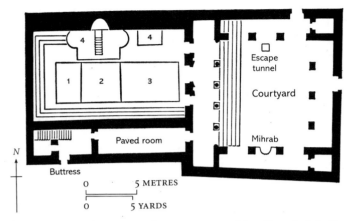

▲ **Fig. 81.** Khirbet Suseya. The C5 AD synagogue (after Netzer). 1–3. Mosaic floor; 4. *Berna*.

The Synagogue (Fig. 81)

The first synagogue was constructed in the late C3 or early C4 AD, and continued in use until the C9, when a mosque was erected in the southern part of the courtyard. All masonry above a black line has been restored.

The two entrances to the courtyard could be sealed by rolling great **circular stones** into position. The crude steps in the hole in the courtyard lead down to a lighted **escape tunnel** through which one can pass to the open ground to the north. In order not to betray the tunnel's existence by debris scattered outside, crushed rock was piled behind walls of cut stones underground, as in similar tunnels beneath the HERO-DION. The small apse built between the columns on the opposite side of the courtyard is the *mihrab* by which the C9 mosque was oriented to Mecca.

As with its contemporaries at ESHTEMOA and ANIM, the doors of the prayer hall are in the east wall. The synagogue is oriented to Jerusalem by a raised platform (*bema*) in the north wall. Even to the untrained eye it is clear that the **principal *bema*** is the result of a series of additions. Originally a flight of steps leading up to the niche containing the scrolls cut across the plastered **benches** which run round three sides of the building. Later a ledge was built in front; the square sockets were for the marble posts of the chancel screen, now lying on the benches opposite. Still later, circular steps were added at each end and the whole was faced with marble, traces of which are still visible low down on the left. To the right the **second *bema*** is a curious and unique feature; it may have served for the reading of the Scriptures because its importance is underlined by the mosaic in front. Two rams and menorahs flank the gabled Ark of the Law.

A **three-panel mosaic** covers the floor. Nearest the entrance [**3**] squares, lozenges and octagons enclose (damaged) pictures of birds. In the centre [**2**] a geometric pattern is laid over an earlier zodiac, of which only part of the rope surround and the beginning of a divider remain (see Fig. 49 BET ALPHA). The final panel [**1**] appears to have depicted Daniel in the lions' den. A window links the prayer hall to the **paved long room** with a bench. At some stage the west and south walls were strengthened by the addition of a sloping **buttress** which, on the west, was subsequently incorporated into a much thicker wall.

Korazim: *see* CHOROZAIN

Kurdani: *see* EN APHEK

Kurnub: *see* MAMSHIT

Kursi* (06)

The largest Byzantine monastic complex in Galilee is located 5 km north of En Gev where route 789 makes a right-angled turn from route 92 into Nahal Samakh to mount the GOLAN (Fig. 107).

It has been a place of pilgrimage since the C5 AD, presumably because of Jesus' dramatic exorcism where swine cast themselves into the lake. According to the gospels this took place 'in the land of the Gerasenes/Gadarenes/Gergesenes' (Mark 5: 1), 'which is opposite Galilee' (Luke 8: 26). The fact that there are three different names for the same place is suspicious. Jerash and Gadara (= Umm Qeis) are in Transjordan far from the lake. Gergesa has never been identified; it may have been invented to designate this site when local scholars became aware that neither of the two other places fitted the circumstances of the gospel narrative. St Jerome confused Gergesa with CHOROZAIN but his personal knowledge of Palestinian topography was limited. This site thus became known by the name of the town which is in fact located 3.5 km north of Capernaum. Kursi is possibly a dialectical deformation of Chorozain (Korazim).

The monastic area is enclosed by a great rectangular plastered wall (145 × 123 m); decorative paintings can be found on parts of its interior face. In the original C5 plan each side had a gate, but at a later stage, prob-

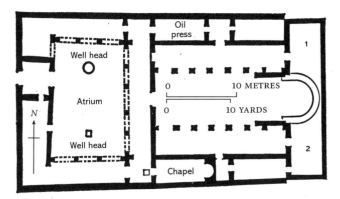

▲ **Fig. 82.** Kursi. The C5 church (after Tsaferis). 1. Sacristy; 2. Baptistery.

ably after the Persian invasion of 614, only the strongly fortified western gate was retained. From it a paved way leads to the church located in the middle of the compound. It is most unusual to find a church and the main gate on the same axis. The monastery was destroyed by the earthquake of 741.

Visit (Fig. 82). Open: Sunday–Thursday and Saturday 8 a.m.–5 p.m.; Fridays to 4 p.m. The church, which has been greatly restored, is a classical late C5 AD type. Mosaics cover the entire floor area. Most are simple geometric designs, but the medallions of the lateral aisles contain representations of the flora and fauna of the area; with a few rare exceptions all the living things have been systematically destroyed. Presumably this was done by Muslims in order to adapt the church to their prayer requirements. One small room [**2**] was turned into a **baptistery** in the C6; an inscription at the entrance dates the pavement to 585. The function of the rooms along the north side is not clear, one contained an **olive press.** A grille at the entrance to an external chapel on the south side is the entrance to a **crypt** which was the burial place of the monastery. There was a cistern beneath the courtyard. The living quarters of the monks were in the area north of the church.

From the church a small ruined structure is visible on the hill to the south. A retaining wall, possibly the base of a tower, enshrines a **huge boulder.** To the east is a mosaic floor and an apse. The Byzantine date of the material suggests that this was identified as the precise site of the gospel miracle.

Between the enclosure and the lake there are traces of a village of the Roman period with a small port and breakwater 100 m north of the little tel.

Kypros (M17)

Dominating the entrance of the ancient road from Jerusalem to the rich plain of JERICHO (Fig. 74), this strategic peak (Tel el-Aqaba) is a miniature MASADA in terms both of its surprising buildings and of its isolation from the land mass to the west. Two roads lead to a parking-lot just below the summit (15 m above sea-level). It is less nerve-wracking to walk up.

This is one of the two fortresses, Thrax and Taurus, built by the Syrian general Bacchides during the Maccabean wars, and destroyed by Pompey as his legions tramped down the valley to inaugurate Roman dominion in 63 BC (Strabo, *Geography* 16: 2. 40). The other (Nuseib el-Aweishireh) is clearly evident on the opposite side of the Wadi Qilt; its history is identical with that of Kypros.

Herod fortified this site, which he named after his mother Kypros, before building his palace at TULUL ABU EL-ALAIQ just below. His manic fear of revolt demanded a secure citadel in which he could take refuge. His equally strong concern with his comfort is the best explanation of the rather elaborate **bath** (the room with two niches) on the very summit. The nearby cisterns were filled by hand (as at Masada) from reservoirs on the north and east slopes. The debris on the slopes below show that there must have been other rooms in the summit building.

The buildings on the plateau belong to three different periods. The **round structure** in the southern corner is dated to the C2–C1 BC and served for the raising of pigeons, whose flesh and droppings were valuable, the former as food and the latter as fertilizer. Virtually all the other buildings are Herodian. Note in particular the mosaic-floored **bath** on the side overlooking the winter palace. Reading from the summit side are the cold room (one wall missing), the dressing room (both have access to stepped cold pools), the rectangular tepid room, which has doors to the circular vapour bath and to the square hot room. The last room is the furnace. The **square building** in the centre of the plateau was erected by Byzantine monks. They took over all the Herodian structures in the desert, because their cisterns and cut stones facilitated the construction of monasteries.

The water supply of the C2 BC fortress was secured by a **collecting channel** dug around the hill some 300 m to the south-west at the level of the saddle linking the two hills. The channel continued round the north side of Kypros to four cisterns in the eastern slope. Their capacity is 2,000 m³, but despite the fact that Jericho gets an average of only 140 mm of rain per year 3,500 m³ could be harvested yearly from the 100,000 m² catchment area. Herod considered this arrangement insufficient and constructed a 20 km **aqueduct** involving ten bridges (the longest near En

Qilt is 135 m) and five tunnels to bring spring-water from EN FARAH and EN FAWAR.

After the emperor removed Herod's son, Archelaus, from the throne in AD 6, a Roman garrison manned the fortress. Some of its members were admonished by John the Baptist (Luke 3: 14). In AD 66 the Zealots slaughtered the Roman garrison and threw down the fortifications.

Lakhish (F20)

Lakhish is a very deceptive site. From a distance it is lost among the rolling hills of the Shephelah but its height is impressive as one turns into the rough unpaved access road. It is only when one stands on top that the authority of its situation becomes apparent. From the great palace-fort there is a magnificent view to the west (coastal plain), north (the outline of Mareshah near BET GUVRIN is clear in the middle foreground), and east (the Hebron hills with the underground area at HAZAN).

Canaanite cities had existed on the mound for almost 2,000 years before it was taken by Joshua. The king of Lakhish had joined the coalition of the five kings defeated by the Israelites at Gibeon (JIB); this prompted an Israelite swing to the south-west during which his city fell in two days (Josh. 10: 1–32). Such a speedy end to the siege of a city with the natural advantages of Lakhish would be incredible had the archaeologists not shown that it was not fortified at this period (c.1220 BC). The city was left in ruins until it was fortified by Rehoboam (928–911 BC) as the southernmost of the line of forts protecting the western flank of the kingdom of Judah (2 Chr. 11: 5–12). One of his successors remade the city on a grandiose scale, erecting a great palace-fort on a raised podium and ringing the mound with a double line of walls. At this period Lakhish was probably the most important city in Judah after Jerusalem, king Amaziah (798–769 BC) fled there when a rebellion broke out in Jerusalem, 'but they sent after him to Lakhish and slew him there' (2 Kgs. 14: 19).

An earthquake occurred about 760 BC which necessitated the rebuilding of parts of the city (Amos 1: 1; Zech. 14: 5). In 701 BC Sennacherib invaded Judah and made Lakhish his base (2 Kgs. 18: 13–17, 19: 8). The importance he attached to his successful siege of the city is attested by the carved reliefs of the battle which he installed in the central room of his new palace in Nineveh (Fig. 84): archers, supported by infantry, protect mobile picks digging at the double wall defended by bowmen and slingers. The passage of the Assyrians is marked by the evidence of fierce fires throughout the city.

The city-gate and wall were rebuilt, but not the palace. It is not clear by whom. An inscription of Sennacherib says that he gave the captured towns of Judah to the PHILISTINE kings of Ashdod, Ekron, and Gaza. Lakhish was again in Jewish hands when the Babylonians under Nebuchadnezzar invaded in 587 BC. This was known, and the identity of the site confirmed, by the discovery of eighteen Hebrew ostraca in a guardroom. One reads, 'Let my lord know that we are watching over the beacon of Lahkish, according to the signals which my lord gave, for Azekah is not to be seen.' It was part of the rough draft of an anxious letter to be sent to Jerusalem; if Azekah had fallen, Lakhish would be next. According to the prophet Jeremiah (34: 7) Azekah and Lakhish were the last cities to be captured before Jerusalem.

After the Exile (586–538 BC) the area around Lakhish formed part of Idumaea, but the city was resettled by Jews (Neh. 11: 30). A representative of the ruling Persians presumably occupied the palatial residence built on the platform of the Israelite palace-fort (*c.*450–350 BC). Occupation continued in the succeeding Hellenistic period and then ceased abruptly in the C2 BC.

Visit (Fig. 83). From the Bet Shemesh–Qiryat Gat road (route 35) turn south on to route 3415. Where the road divides keep to the right. The tel

▼ **Fig. 83.** *(Left)* Lakhish. Fortifications and excavated areas. 1. Siege ramp; 2. Outer gate; 3. Inner gate; 4. Outer wall; 5. Inner wall; 6. Palace area; 7. Moat temples; 8. Buttresses; 9. Well; 10. Sacred area; 11. Great shaft.

Fig. 84. *(Right)* Relief from Nineveh showing Sennacherib's siege of Lakhish.

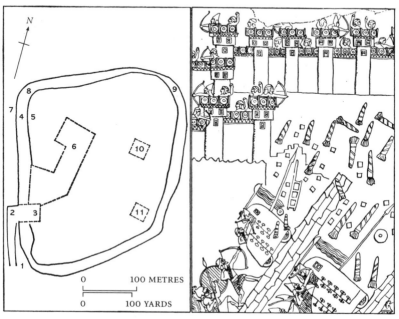

rises sharply on the left. It is possible to drive up the rough dirt road running across the slope, but it is better to use the parking-lot.

The loose stones [1] piled against the side of the mound just north of the crude car park were part of the Assyrian **siege ramp**. Thus notified of the point of attack, the defenders heightened and strengthened the defences by building a counter-ramp against the inner face of the city wall in the south-west corner. The Israelite access road [2] forced attackers to expose their unprotected right side to the defenders on the walls above, the shield being carried on the left arm.

From the turn at the head of the ramp one can look down into the **Canaanite moat** in which successive temples [7] were built between the C15 and C13 BC; nothing visible remains. On the slope of the mound are the outer [4] and inner [5] **Israelite walls** represented in the Assyrian relief; these walls are best seen in the section between the buttresses [8] and the 44 m-deep **well** [9]. Both it and the **great shaft** (22 × 25 and 22.5 m deep) [11] are assigned to the C10 BC. The shaft has been interpreted as an abortive alternative water system, but others consider it a quarry.

There are three excavation areas, the Gate Area [3], the Palace Area [6], and the Sacred Area [10].

The Gate Area

When the gate complex was reconstructed in the C9–C8 BC it comprised two elements. Having passed through an **outer gate** at the top of the access ramp, one had to turn right in an open court to reach the three-chambered **inner gate** which is the largest known in Israel. Similar structures of the same period appear at BEER SHEVA, GEZER, and MEGIDDO. This gate served until its total destruction by Sennacherib; mobile picks brought down the western wall of the outer gate. It has been restored using the original stones; everything above a cement line has been rebuilt.

When the defences were rebuilt after the Exile the inner gate was simply a gap in the stone city wall; a new outer gate was erected on the ruins of the old one. The south side of this gate is still visible on the right looking in; the important ostraca (inscribed pottery fragments) were found in 1935 in the little guardroom which has also been restored.

The Palace Area (Fig. 85)

The most noticeable feature is a **huge platform** (35 × 75 m) which served as the foundation for a series of great buildings. It was not built all at once. Rehoboam in the C10 BC constructed a square fort; one of his successors doubled the area by extending the platform to the south, the joint is evident. Some time later (early C8 BC?) additions were made on the north [1] and the width of the east wall was doubled. The intermediate walls in the platform give some indication of the disposition of rooms in the buildings above. Nothing of the superstructures (probably built of

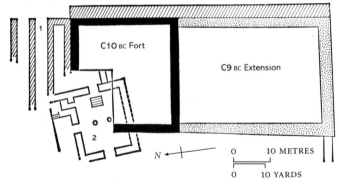

▲ **Fig. 85.** Lakhish. The Palace Area (after Ussishkin). 1. C8 BC structures; 2. Canaanite temples.

brick) survives; the ruins left by Sennacherib were cleared in order to level the platform for the Persian residence of which only two column bases and a door-sill remain. Prior to 701 BC there were storehouses at the south-east corner and a heavy wall linked the platform to the city wall on the west. Between this wall and the city gate there were houses of the Israelite period (C10–C6 BC).

Beneath the north-west corner of the platform is a **Canaanite temple** [2] of the city destroyed by Joshua. Entered via a paved antechamber on the west, the main chamber had a brick floor and cedar of Lebanon roof beams, with a flight of stone steps (still in place) leading up to the most sacred chamber (the cella) on the east. An earlier three-unit temple appears at TEL BALATA. Such religious edifices were the prototypes of the three-unit temple erected by Solomon in Jerusalem.

▼ **Fig. 86.** Lakhish. The Sacred Area (after Aharoni).

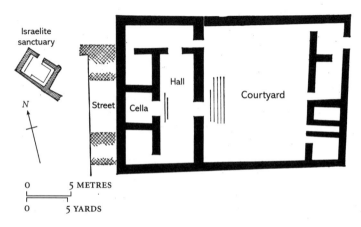

The Sacred Area (Fig. 86)

The first **Israelite sanctuary** was a small room with a low bench and a slightly raised 'altar' in the western corner; it dates from the time of Rehoboam. Subsequently it was covered by a terrace whose retaining wall is visible at the edge of a cobbled **street**. Traces of a similar street of the same period, which remained in use for several centuries, have been found further down the slope, suggesting that Israelite Lakhish had another gate on the east.

Excavations have disturbed the floor levels of the **C2 BC temple** (solid black) but the plan is still perfectly clear. Its orientation is the reverse of that of the Canaanite temple but the basic plan is the same. Two small chambers with benches inside the door gave access to the courtyard from which a flight of steps led up to the main room paved with stone slabs. Two further steps mark the entrance to the cella. The cult vessels found *in situ* furnish some basis for the belief that the temple was used for Jewish worship.

It has been suggested that the badly overgrown building between the Sacred Area and the great shaft was a temple of the C4–C3 BC; the row of pillars would have divided the main chamber into two.

Latrun (G17) ★

Until 1967, when the inhabitants were deported and their homes levelled, the Arab village of Imwas preserved the biblical name Emmaus; today the site is called Aijalon Park. Families picnic where the famous scholar Julius Africanus once walked the streets of a Roman city.

Emmaus is first mentioned to locate the Syrian camp taken by Judas Maccabaeus in 161 BC (1 Macc. 3: 38–4: 15); a year later it was again in Syrian possession and Baccides fortified it because it controlled the three routes to Jerusalem from the plain (1 Macc. 9: 50). Josephus records its misfortunes. In 43 BC Cassius, the assassin of Julius Caesar, sold the inhabitants into slavery for non-payment of taxes (*War* 1: 218–22); in the anarchy following the death of Herod in 4 BC Emmaus became the centre of an insurrection which Varus quelled by burning the town (*War* 2: 60–5, 71). The Fifth Legion camped there for two years before moving up to the final attack on Jerusalem in AD 70 (*War* 4: 444). After the Sanhedrin moved to Jamnia many famous rabbis came to Emmaus on business, e.g. 'Rabbi Akiba [d. AD 135] said "I asked Rabban Gamaliel [*c.* AD 90) and Rabbi Joshua in the market of Emmaus, where they went to buy a beast for the wedding-feast of the son of Rabban Gamaliel..."' (*Mishnah*, Kerithoth 3: 7); the text seems to suggest that Rabbi Akiba lived there.

Christians may have lived in Emmaus from a very early date, but the first we know of is the soldier-diplomat turned scholar, Julius Africanus. In 221, because of his contacts in the imperial court, the city sent him with a delegation to the emperor Elagabalus to request the reconstruction of Emmaus with the rights of a Roman city and a new name, Nicopolis. All requests were granted. The change of name is noted by Jerome (in 386) who adds, 'where the Lord made himself known to Cleophas in the breaking of bread, thus consecrating his house as a church' (*Letter* 108). The localization here of the gospel event (Luke 24: 13–31) goes back at least as far as the *Onomasticon* of Eusebius (330): it was never questioned during the Byzantine period, but seems to have been forgotten after a plague wiped out Emmaus in 639. According to Arab writers (who all revert to the original name, abandoning Nicopolis) the plague started there and spread throughout the Middle East.

The Crusaders built a church where there had been one before, but were attracted to this area for other than religious reasons. A fortress here was imperative to guard the southern route to Jerusalem from Jaffa. Some time between 1150 and 1170 the Templars built Toron of the Knights on the hill behind the present Cistercian Abbey of Latrun.

Though Emmaus-Nicopolis has in its favour the oldest Palestinian tradition identifying it with the Emmaus of Luke 24: 13–31, it is not likely that the identification is correct. It fits with the distance of 160 stadia (31 km) from Jerusalem given by some manuscripts of the gospels, but it is more probable that the alternative reading of 60 stadia (11.5 km) is the original. This latter distance suits both ABU GHOSH and QUBEIBA, but these two sites were identified with New Testament Emmaus only during and after the Crusader period.

There is, however, a fourth possibility. In the C1 AD there was another Emmaus closer to Jerusalem. After crushing the First Revolt (AD 66–70) Vespasian assigned to '800 veterans discharged from the army a place for habitation called Emmaus, distant 30 stadia from Jerusalem' (*War* 7: 217). The new military colony completely eclipsed the little town, and the site

▼ **Fig. 87.** The Latrun area.

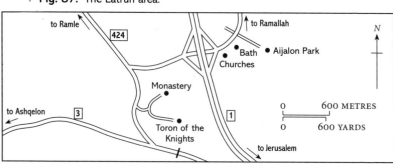

acquired a new name, conserved until recently by the Arab village of Qoloniya. Abandoned in 1948, it was located on the rocky ridge which forces the Jerusalem highway to make a right-angle turn below Motza (J17). C1 AD material has been found on the surface.

The name of this Emmaus having disappeared, it is not surprising that Byzantine Christians should have selected Emmaus-Nicopolis as the place of Jesus' meal with his disciples. The figure of 60 stadia (which originally covered the round trip) was then transformed into 160 stadia.

Visit (Fig. 87). Access to the Templar fortress, **Toron of the Knights**, is through the grounds of the **Cistercian monastery** of Latrun, famous for the variety of its alcoholic products. The remains of the fortress are badly overgrown, and are not really worth a visit. Other sites do merit close inspection, namely, the Byzantine and Crusader churches, the Roman bath, and the wide variety of remains in Canada Park.

The Churches of Emmaus-Nicopolis (Fig. 88)

The walled compound is just to the north of the bridge carrying route 1 over route 3. The metal gates carry the words 'Communauté des Beatitutes' and 'Emmaus-Nicopolis'.

The **Crusader church** is built within the much bigger C5–C6 AD **Byzantine church**. It reuses only the central of its three apses. Presumably the two lateral apses were retained in order not to weaken the structure. The northern apse would have been blocked from view had the original plan to construct an absidal building in front of it been carried through. Excavations have created the present surface, which is 0.40 m below the medieval floor. The **baptistery**, fed by its own reservoir, is also Byzantine—probably C5. It seems likely that the rectangular building running out from the baptistry was also a church; it may have been erected after the destruction of the larger church in the SAMARITAN revolt of 529. Some walls, and the **mosaic** with the panther and birds, come from a C4 villa; the other mosaic floor may belong to the same building.

The Roman Bath

The half-buried building is hidden from the road by trees and Arab graves. Enter the only gate in the wire fence and follow the path to the right.

First erected as part of the intensive building programme that followed the grant of the imperial charter in AD 221, the disposition of the three rooms was modified in the reconstruction necessitated by the earthquake of 498. Between the C8 and C12 it was used as a storehouse for wine, oil, and foodstuffs. During the C13 it was transformed into the shrine of Abu Ubaida, the commander of the Arab armies who conquered Palestine in the time of the caliph Omar (629–38). Abu Ubaida died in Emmaus in the plague of 639, and the Mamluks may have espoused his

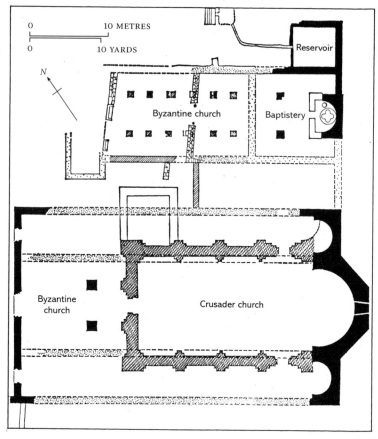

▲ **Fig. 88.** Latrun. Churches of Emmaus-Nicopolis.

cause in order to give them a religious claim to this strategic crossroads, particularly since there was nearby a site venerated by Christians.

Aijalon Park (Fig. 89)

This newly developed recreational area contains a fascinating series of wine presses, a sophisticated Roman aqueduct system, a Crusader castle, a Hellenistic city, and some rather unusual tombs. Picnic tables, drinking-water, and toilets are provided.

After the entrance take the first road to the left. A small grove of date palms locates a Roman-Byzantine **tunnel spring** whence water flowed along a 17 m channel to a square stepped catchment pool.

From the parking-lot steps lead down to the bottom of the valley in which the double aqueduct system that served Nicopolis is located. The

upper aqueduct was fed by a horizontal 25 m-long vaulted tunnel similar to that in the Wadi Bijar (SOLOMON'S POOLS); its location is marked by the square masonry inspection shaft [**1**] above the modern pool. Below the pool a perfectly preserved round masonry shaft is part of the sophisticated hydraulic installation [**2**] that fed the **lower aqueduct**. The footholds in the side of the shaft permitted access to a vaulted chamber (1.5 × 2 m) in which the spring flowed from the bottom of an almost square pool. Erosion has buried the channels, but there is an excavated section about 100 m downstream just before a square **stepped pool**. On the left some 350 m further down is a **Roman tomb** in a pyramid-shaped rock freed by erosion; there is an identical tomb of the same period 115 m further along the path. Stay to the left of this tomb and after 50 m bear left slightly uphill to reach a C2 BC **Hasmonean grave complex**. Steps lead down to a square rock-cut courtyard; inside the burial chamber are eight horizontal shaft tombs. Just alongside is a **Byzantine wine press**. Below a small storage area is the treading floor; remains in one corner show it to have had a mosaic floor. The liquid flowed into a lower basin with a mosaic floor.

From the parking-lot continue east along the road. At the first junction go left, then through the cattle-gate, and finally left again at the next junction. From the viewpoint on the left there is a splendid vista embracing the whole of the Valley of Aijalon. One would have thought this the natural place to site the **Crusader fortress**, Castellum Arnaldi, built in 1133 to command the northern (the Ascent of Bet Horon) and the central (via Beit Liqya, Beit Inan, QUBEIBA, and NABI SAMWIL) routes to Jerusalem. Its clear, if unimpressive, remains in fact appear at the bottom

▼ **Fig. 89.** Aijalon Park. 1. Aqueduct shaft; 2. Water chamber; 3. Cave; 4. Khirbet el-Aqed Gate.

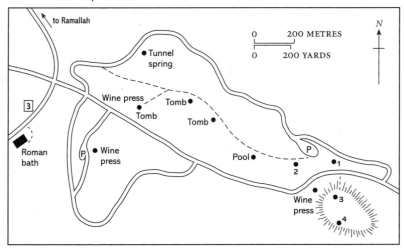

of the hill. It was from here that Richard the Lion-Heart unsuccessfully threatened Jerusalem in the summer of 1192. It is possible to drive down to the fortress, but the ruins are more impressive at a distance. Return through the park.

A pedestrian gate in the barbed-wire fence is the entrance to **Khirbet el-Aqed** (Horvat Eqed), the modern name given to the ruins of an early C1 BC administrative centre for the royal estates in this fertile area. The place was destroyed either by Varrus as he quelled the uprising that followed the death of Herod the Great in 4 BC (*War* 2: 63), or by Vespasian as he moved to put down the First Revolt in 68 BC (*War* 4: 444). Partisans of Bar Kokhba in AD 132 developed burial caves and cisterns into underground bunkers. It did them little good. After the Romans stormed the site it remained unoccupied.

One **underground complex** [3] is just at the point where the path reaches the summit. It consists of an enlarged natural cave, a square artificial chamber (8 × 8 × 3 m) and low narrow tunnels linking two bell-shaped cisterns. Their openings ensured ventilation and could be emergency exits. The tunnel entrances are 2 m above the bottom of the cisterns, which must have continued to serve their original function. Traces of quarrying are everywhere manifest, but the most notable feature is a fine **gate** [4] which is preserved to a height of 2 m. The original vaulting has collapsed, but the slab-roofed guardrooms on either side are intact. The gate belonged to a 1 km defensive wall with towers, which enclosed an area 400 × 150 m.

Some way down the hill is another **Byzantine wine press**. The arrangement is the same as the one mentioned in the next paragraph, but here the trodden grapes were further processed in a beam press. They were piled, separated by mats, on the centre basin. One end of the beam fitted into the recess in the wall and the other was loaded with stone weights.

The **most elaborate wine press** in the park marked the eastern border of Nicopolis; it is dated to the Byzantine period. From the entrance to the parking-lot go about 40 m uphill bearing right. On two sides of the treading area are three square holding areas, each with its own circular plastered basin, which caught the liquid generated by the pressure of piled grapes. Each holding area was allotted to a different vineyard. From each area in turn the grapes were shovelled on to the treading floor; at this point the pipe at the bottom of the small corresponding basin would be unblocked. The square stone with a hole in the centre fitted into the socket cut in the treading floor, and supported an upright pole carved with screw ridges. Trodden grapes were placed on mats at the base and pressure was exercised by rotation of a wooden nut. Though demanding greater technological skill and a larger investment, this screw press was both easier to operate and more efficient than the beam press as on the slope of Khirbet el-Aqed.

Makhtesh Ramon (G30)

From the edge of the observation point in Mizpe Ramon the rock plunges vertically to the floor of the crater 300 m below. Over 2,000 years ago aggressive merchants exploited a crack in this apparently insurmountable barrier in order to transport frankincense and myrrh from Arabia to Gaza whence they were shipped to Europe.

These fragrant gum-resins are produced by trees that grow only in modern Yemen and Oman and across the Gulf of Aden in Somalia. Limited production and infinite demand made frankincense and myrrh worth their weight in gold in the ancient world. An indispensable part of the ritual of all religions, they were integral to the manufacture of cosmetics and perfumes, and were essential ingredients of medical remedies for everything from broken heads to haemorrhoids.

Of the carefully organized distribution network, which utilized every known form of transport to many regions, we are concerned only with the route across the middle of the Arabian peninsula to the north. The collecting point for this caravan was Thomna/Timna. From at least the C3 BC once it set out on its two-month journey (see box), it was under the control of the NABATAEANS. At their capital, Petra, there was a division. Loads of frankincense and myrrh were sent to Egypt and Syria, but the bulk crossed the Arava valley into the NEGEV *en route* to Gaza.

The Makhtesh Ramon contains one of the best preserved sections of this great road. Nomads may have used the route from time immemorial, but the Nabataeans gave the road its present from in the late C1 BC. They graded and cleared the terrain, and built forts and caravanserais.

Pay, and Pay, and Pay

'Thomna is 1487.5 miles distant from the town of Gaza in Judaea on the Mediterranean coast. The journey is divided into 65 stages with halts for camels. Fixed portions of the frankincense are given to the priests and the king's secretaries, but besides these the guards and their attendants and the gate-keepers and servants also have their pickings. Indeed all along the route they keep on paying, at one place for water, at another for fodder, or the charges for loading at the halts, and the various octrois; so that expenses mount up to 688 denarii per camel before the Mediterranean coast is reached, where again payment is made to the customs officers of our empire. Consequently the price of the best frankincense is 6, or the second best 5, and of the third best 3 denarii a pound.' (Pliny (C1 AD), *Natural History* 12: 64–5).

Anything that promoted speedy and secure passage made excellent commercial sense. The road lost its importance when Rome annexed the Nabataean empire in AD 106, and made passage to the coast much easier by constructing the cliff road at Maale Aqrabbim (ROMAN ROADS, p. 400), which gave MAMSHIT an importance that AVDAT once had.

Visit. In order to understand the formation of the crater, and to become aware of its flora and fauna, a visit to the **Visitors' Centre** in Mizpe Ramon is indispensable (open: Sunday–Thursday, Saturday 9 a.m.–4.30 p.m.; Friday and eves of holy days 9 a.m.–3 p.m.).

Going south from Mizpe Ramon, at 8 km from the lowest hairpin bend on route 40, turn left (east) on to an unsealed road, which is signposted 'Saharonim Plateau/Ein Saharonim'. Just beyond the Be'erot camp-site turn right on the red trail. Immediately after the rather rough crossing of the wadi bed the road divides. The black trail to the left leads to a parking-lot on the plateau from which there is a splendid view. The red trail to the right overlies the incense route and leads to the Nabataean caravanserai of Shaar Ramon. It is 35.5 km (24.5 Roman miles) from Avdat by the ancient road, just a little over the average day's journey of 22.8 Roman miles according to Pliny's figures (see box).

Sited at the crossroads of four wadis, the **caravanserai** sits on a low ridge above the spring of Ein Saharonim, whose moist greenery must have delighted both camels and drivers. Rooms surround the open space for camels and baggage in the middle of the square structure (42 × 42 m). Guard-towers flank the entrance in the north wall. Travellers used the building between C1 and C3 AD.

In order to see something of the ancient road return to the point where the red and black trails separate, and follow the unmarked jeep trail directly ahead, leaving the wadi on the left. It is suitable for an ordinary car at the beginning, but subsequently deteriorates. After 100 m or so you will notice to your right two parallel lines of stones some 5 m apart. These are the **kerbstones** of the Nabataean trade route. As you walk along the road to the north it will become obvious that the road has been cleared of stones. Camels made much better time when they did not have to pick their way carefully on stony ground.

Return to the vehicle and continue along the jeep trail to the north. At 2.5 km from the junction of the red and black trails there is a group of **milestones** on the left. Another group appears on the right 1.5 m further on after crossing the blue trail (route 8563). Although inspired by the Roman practice these milestones are much simpler than their Roman counterparts. The square base may be very slight and sometimes completely independent. Each milestone was composed of two drums, very rarely three, and averaged 1.6 m in height.

At the junction with the green trail (route 8561) go left, and when it joins the black trail (route 8552) turn right following the sign to **Maale**

Mahmal. Driving towards the escarpment (on terrain that now requires four-wheel drive) the question that must have preoccupied neophyte Nabataean camel drivers becomes ever more imperative: how are we going to get up that cliff? As one angles north-east a fissure begins to open up. Through it went the trade route. The camels had to go in single file on a zigzag track barely a metre wide. The ancient road at the base of the pass was destroyed by the installation of a pipeline, but the work done by the Nabataeans to improve the upper part is still visible. They cleared the path and constructed retaining walls on the down-slope side. A **small fort** (6.90 × 7.20 m) protected the top of the pass. Its water supply came from a stone-roofed **reservoir** some 550 m further north. Little dams across the wadi bed created ponding areas in which the soldiers grew vegetables. The fort can be reached in a four-wheel-drive vehicle by taking the red trail (route 8545) up Maale Noah or by following the rim of the crater on route 8546 from Mizpe Ramon.

Mamre (Ramat el-Khalil) (J20)

Camped beside a great oak, Abraham here received the three mysterious visitors and bargained with the Lord for the salvation of Sodom (Gen. 18). Some 2,000 years later in a great stone enclosure the emperor Hadrian sold the children of Abraham into slavery after crushing the Second Revolt (AD 132–5).

Long a place of popular Jewish devotion because of a great tree, the site became the focal point of local superstitious practices for pagans, Jews, and Christians, culminating in an annual festival. Constantine's mother-in-law, Eutropia, did her best to discourage such practices by requesting the emperor to build a church there (325). Its magnificence merited representation on the C6 Madaba Map. Her gesture was as ineffective as that of the editors of Genesis who, for much the same reasons (Hos. 4: 13; Ezek. 6: 13), tried to lose the site completely by identifying Mamre with Hebron (Gen. 23: 19; 35: 27). Her architects were forced to cram the church into one end of the enclosure to avoid the site of the pagan altar, and the festival continued into the C7. After the Persian invasion (614) monks built cells in the ruined church.

Visit (Fig. 90). Roughly half-way between Halhul and HEBRON turn east on route 3507. The great wall appears just beside the road after some 500 m. The monumental blocks of the **enclosure wall** (50 × 60 m) make one think of Herod, but the technique (no boss) is quite different. Characteristic Herodian masonry does appear here and there—e.g. the pilaster base—suggesting that he may have begun a structure that was

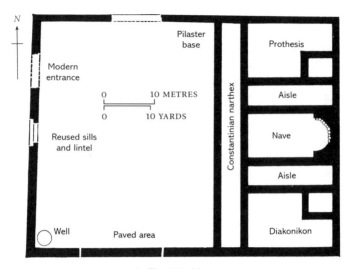

▲ **Fig. 90.** Mamre.

never completed. The reused stone door-sills and lintel were possibly intended for this edifice. The break in the wall is modern: the original entrance is unknown. According to local tradition, Abraham dug the **well** with his own hands: the adjoining basin is admittedly modern. The **pavement** was laid down in the Byzantine period and subsequently repaired. Though unusually cramped, the church has the classic disposition of a **Constantinian basilica**, a narthex, the central nave with two lateral aisles, having outside them the small square prothesis and the diakonikon.

Mamshit (Kurnub)* (H26) ★

Brilliant engineering explains the importance of Mamshit. Older trade routes from Gaza to Elat were forced to pass through difficult dry country in order to use natural passages through the high escarpment of the Araba, the valley joining the Dead Sea and the Gulf of Aqaba. Near Mamshit Roman engineers cut a stepped road in the steep cliff (ROMAN ROADS: SOUTH; *Mamshit–Arava*) which enabled the pack trains to travel the rest of the route on both sides in flat terrain with perennial water supplies every 25–30 km. The trade which used to pass through AVDAT began to flow through Mamshit, which in consequence never needed to develop the agriculture which characterized the other desert cities.

The NABATAEANS founded Mamshit in the C1 AD, and the plan of the city was fixed within a couple of generations. The buildings were of such

▲ **Fig. 91.** Mamshit (after Negev). 1. View-point; 2–3. House of Frescos; 4. Reservoir; 5. Bath; 6. Main gate; 7. Caravanserai; 8. Gate; 9. House; 10. Tower; 11. West church; 12. House; 13. East church.

quality that they were still in use in the C4 AD. The Romans assumed control in the C2 AD; the presence of a garrison to protect the trade route is attested by a military cemetery with tombstones inscribed in Latin. The growing wealth of the city necessitated the construction of a city wall at the beginning of the C4 which encloses an area of 4 hectares. Sporadic raids heightened the inhabitants' awareness of nomadic envy, and the Byzantines doubled the width of the wall. Their major contribution to the architecture of Mamshit, however, was the erection of two churches. The absence of any church of the triapsidal C6 type, and the rarity of coins dated after 500, suggest that the life of Mamshit ceased at the end of the C5. Its end was, indeed, violent when riders from the desert tasted the fruits of a victory long denied. The memory of its importance explains its appearance in the early C6 Madaba mosaic map; the name given there is Mampsis (Mamshit is the supposed Semitic original).

Visit (Fig. 91). Open: 8 a.m.–5 p.m., Fridays to 4 p.m. The former British police post [1] now houses toilets and a café. From the roof there is a fine general view of the site. Mamshit has good explanatory signs identifying the purpose of buildings and the function of the rooms within; the periods noted on these signs correspond to the following dates: Middle Nabataean = AD 1–50; Late Nabataean = 70–150; Late Roman = 180–324; Byzantine = 324–640. Everything above the blue line has been restored.

It is natural to enter the city by the **main gate** [6], outside which was a large **caravanserai** [7] where the Nabataean drivers rested while the caravan masters and merchants were entertained in the city. The only other gate [8] faces the wadi in which a Nabataean **dam** is still visible; three watch-towers ensured the protection of the precious water supply.

A very big **house** [9] is typically Nabataean in its general plan but much more elaborate than usual; it may have been the residence of the governor. Two features are noteworthy. The **staircase tower** is preserved to a considerable height and the care expended on the underside of the steps is remarkable. One room has two sets of arches, one running north–south, the other east–west; they could not have been in use together and show that the room was reconstructed. The arches supported stone beams; the brittle stone meant that they could not be more than 2 m in length. The **cistern** outside the single entrance collected rain-water from the street.

Beside the governor's house is a **tower** [10] which may have served as an administrative centre; store-rooms were built around the courtyard in which a cistern was sunk. Rain-water from the roofs was carried to the cistern by a gutter running along the outside of the building. The upper part of the tower has been reconstructed as an observation point.

A Greek inscription in the middle of the magnificent mosaic floor of the **West Church** [11] shows it to have been erected by Nilus; no date is given but it must have been in the latter part of the C4. The square rooms on either side of the apse probably contained reliquaries. In addition to storing rain-water from the roofs, the cistern in the courtyard of the church was served by a channel under the city wall which collected run-off from the slope outside.

The West Church was built over part of a fine Nabataean **house** [12]. The eastern end of the church virtually blocks the doorways of the southern portion of the house, and destroys the proportions of the courtyard. The roof of the cistern is almost intact and is a perfect illustration of the way the Nabataeans overcame the lack of trees for rafters: arches set closely together supported stone slabs which were then covered with plaster. The same roofing technique is found throughout the city.

The **East Church** [13] is the oldest church in the central NEGEV. The excavator dates it to the second half of the C4; it was certainly built before 427 because there are two crosses in the mosaic floor and such decoration was forbidden after this date. In the square rooms on either side of the apse one can see the marks of the legs of the stone tables which stood above the reliquaries built into the floors. At a later stage a second reliquary was added in each room; the purpose of the hole in the covering slab was to permit objects to touch the bone and become imbued with its virtue. The **baptismal font** in a room on the south had steps on three sides; the depression in the surface of the font was to hold a pouring vessel. The circular plastered basin in the adjoining room may have served for the disposal of water used in baptism. The **staircase** in the little courtyard beside the bathroom suggests that there was a gallery on top of the colonnade round the atrium; the drain-pipes in each corner of the atrium lead to the central cistern.

A large complex is called the **House of Frescos** [2–3]. Off the courtyard with four Nabataean columns [2] is a room labelled 'stables'; the troughs do in fact suggest mangers but the animals must have been exceedingly small! Similar structures of a much older period at BEER SHEVA, MEGIDDO, and HAZOR were **storehouses.** Beside it is a typically Nabataean **house** [3] built around an open court; note the decantation basin beside the cistern in the courtyard; water from the roofs was collected there and the overflow passed through a channel in the wall to another cistern in an adjoining room.

The **great pool** [4] was probably roofed over with wooden beams since the space between the arches is too great for stone slabs. The expense was justified as an alternative to loss through evaporation. The pool cuts through the foundations of an earlier edifice which projected beyond the line of the Roman city wall. Note the small **decantation basin** at one end of the pool. It cleansed the run-off rain-water from the slope outside which came through the channel at the base of the city wall.

From the other end of the pool a conduit brought water to the **bathhouse** [5], also built on top of earlier structures. This is a good place to examine the structure of the raised floor of the caldarium; the furnace room is obviously a secondary addition since the much inferior masonry is not integrated into the other walls.

Maon (B22)

To date this is the only known synagogue in the NEGEV. Dated to the C6 by coins found in the excavation, it rests on the remains of a C4 village. Very little was left of the walls, but it is clear that the synagogue was of the basilica type. It was oriented to Jerusalem by an apse in front of which stood a small *bema*. Outside the east wall are water channels, a cistern, and a ritual bath.

The site is worth a visit because of a **spectacular C6 mosaic** in the centre aisle, which is protected by a modern roof. The circular medallions are created by a vine growing from an amphora, which is almost totally destroyed. Above it in the centre of the mosaic are: an eagle, two baskets, four containers, a bird in a cage, and a *menorah*. On each side of the seven-branch candelabra is a lion. Reading down from the right-hand lion and from left to right are: palm tree and swan; two doves and dog with a lead; tame elephant and duck; pheasant and deer; hare and guinea-fowl; bustard and sheep; bullock and two birds; flamingo and antelope; panther and two partridges; a peacock.

If the site is not open, the key is available from the offices of the Regional Council during normal working hours, otherwise (e.g. Sabbath and holy days) from the office of the secretary of Kibbutz Nir Oz. In order to bring out the colours of the mosaic, bring water with which to wet it.

Maresha: *see* BET GUVRIN

Mar Saba (L18)

From the last turn in the road only two towers are visible. The buildings pour over the side of the deep Kidron Valley almost to the bottom. The stark landscape and the colourful airiness of the structures combine to leave an indelible memory of the greatest of the MONASTERIES IN THE JUDAEAN DESERT.

Born in 439 in central Turkey, Sabas came to Palestine at the age of 18 with the intention of becoming a desert monk. He served a 12-year apprenticeship in the monastery of Theoctistus before being permitted to live in a cave in the Wadi Mukellik (469–73). Then followed five years of wandering in the most remote parts of the desert living on whatever wild plants he could harvest. Finally he settled down in a cave in the Wadi Kidron. After five years of solitude (478–83) he began to encourage visitors attracted by his sanctity to settle near him. This was the beginning of the Great Laura, which grew progressively.

Sabas first built a tower, in order to claim land on both sides of the wadi, and a small church (483). The initial group of seventy monks soon doubled, and in 490 Sabas dedicated a spacious cave as a church. A bequest from his mother in 491 enabled him to erect a hospice. The arrival in 494 of two monks who had been professional architects paved the way for the construction of a bakery, a hospital, water reservoirs, and a large church, which was dedicated in 501. It served as the centre for between 250 and 300 hermits.

Despite the number martyred by the savage Persian attack in 614, the monastery enjoyed its golden age in the C8–C9. Of all the celebrated figures who then lived there (historians, poets, musicians) St John

Damascene (675–749), who came here in 716, deserves special mention; without his classic defence of the legitimacy of images the culture of Western Europe would be very different and our heritage immeasurably poorer. Surrounded by hostility which periodically erupted into murderous violence, even as late as the C19, the monastery none the less survived. Severe damage in the earthquake of 1834 necessitated almost complete reconstruction.

Visit. In Bethlehem follow the signs to the HERODION, and at the bottom of the hill, at the limit of Bet Sahur, branch left on the road going past the Latin SHEPHERDS' FIELD. The road (route 398) offers a magnificent panorama of the Kidron Valley and Jerusalem.

At the highest point of the road, St Theodosius (423–529), after a monastic apprenticeship of 28 years, founded a monastery in 479. The 1893 restoration, known as **Deir Dosi** (open: 8 a.m.–1 p.m.) is only a pale shadow of its mighty predecessor. In the early C6 it housed 400 monks. They ran a hostel for pilgrims, operated celebrated hospitals for the physically and mentally ill, slaved in two workshops, and served four churches.

Just beyond the monastery route 398 descends to the bed of the Kidron. Continue straight ahead through the village of Ubeidiya and along the ridge. After 5 km the road terminates at Mar Saba. Open 8 a.m.–4 p.m. throughout the year; no women admitted. Pull bell-cord in the lower door.

The Monastery (Fig. 92)

The stepped open corridor from the entrance gives access to the central courtyard. The building in the middle commemorates the **tomb of St Sabas**; it was built in 1929 in place of a much smaller structure. Sabas had originally been buried in the cemetery beneath the courtyard; his body is now in the main church.

▼ **Fig. 92.** Mar Saba. The Churches (after Patrich).

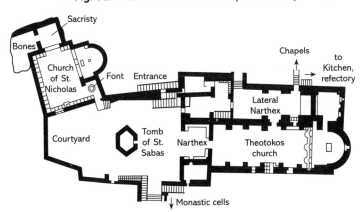

The **church of St Nicholas** admirably fits the description of the first cave church given by Cyril of Scythopolis (see box). The natural apse is now screened by the iconostasis, whose royal doors are C15, as are the set of five icons above the painted wooden band on the wall facing it. The stone basin is a baptismal font. The skulls of deceased monks are displayed in the sacristy, while their bones are collected in the room behind the grille. The 'secret passage like a spiral staircase within the holy cave, leading up from the sacristy to the tower' in which Sabas had his cell, has been blocked. Traces are evident in the ceiling.

The present **principal church** is certainly on the site of the large church of 501, which was dedicated to the Mother of God, but it is unclear exactly what elements go back to the C6. The major relic is the embalmed body of St Sabas, which is displayed on the right before the iconostasis. It was restored to the monastery on 26 October 1965 after spending many centuries in Venice. There are several contradictory versions as to how it got there. Most of the icons and frescos are modern; the two lateral doors in the iconostasis are said to be medieval.

The **lateral narthex** is now divided into a chapel and a sacristy. It may originally have been a single room. From it are stairs to the refectory, kitchen, and bakery, and to the gallery overlooking the wadi. Another stairway leads to a series of small post-Byzantine **chapels** of uncertain date. One sanctifies the cave in which St John Damascene did much of his writing. His tomb is there, but the Crusaders removed the body and its present whereabouts is uncertain.

Fourteen large Byzantine **cisterns** are still in use. Two aqueducts, which catch run-off from the slopes outside, supplement the rain-water collected from the roofs and passageways.

The Other Side of the Wadi Kidron

Below the isolated C17 **Tower of St Simeon**—the only tower outside the monastery—a good trail descends into the bed of the wadi and up the other side, whence there is a splendid view into the monastery. On the way up note a cave opening blocked by a metal grille with a cross between the letters A and C. This was the **cave of Sabas**, in which he spent five years as a solitary. The entrance is at a lower level. Inside two ladders climb a narrow 6 m-high shaft. The cave contains only a rock-cut bench along one wall and a prayer niche high in the east wall.

Such utter simplicity is not paralleled in the forty-five other **hermitages**, which were constructed in a 2 km section of the wadi. They were relatively spacious dwellings constructed by professionals. The vast majority were designed for a single individual, but six certainly accommodated two or three, probably an elderly monk and his disciple/attendant. Most are constructed on a narrow ledge parallel to the rock wall with an artificially levelled ledge outside. If a cave lacked such a ledge, a tower was erected on a lower level, both to facilitate access and to create living space in front of the cave. Care was taken to provide an efficient run-off water collection system linked to an internal or external cistern.

The dome of the main church dominates the **wide-angle view of the monastery** from the far side of the wadi. The three great buttresses retain the wall of the refectory, kitchen, store-room, and bakery. Beneath them in the walled space at the bottom of the wadi is the tiny 'sacred spring'. Between the church and highest point of the monastery, the so-called Tower of Justininian, are the residences of the monks, not all of which are occupied. There are other monks' dwellings to the left of the main church. On the far left the defensive outer wall is anchored by the Chapel of Anna and Joachim, the parents of the Blessed Virgin.

A Church built by God

'Persevering in prayer at this spot till daybreak, Sabas rose in fear and great joy to see the spot where the pillar of fire had appeared, and found a large and marvellous cave that had the shape of a church of God. On the eastern side there is an apse made by God, while he found on the north side a large chamber with the lay-out of a sacristy, and to the south a wide entrance that admitted sufficient illumination from the rays of the sun. After setting this cave in order with divine assistance, he gave instructions for the office to take place here on Saturdays and Sundays.' (Cyril of Scythopolis (C6), *Life of Sabas* 18/101–2; trans. R. M. Price)

Masada* (L22)   ★★

A great rock curiously like an aircraft-carrier moored to the western cliffs of the DEAD SEA, Masada is the 'most spectacular site in the country and the scene of one of the most dramatic episodes in its history (Fig. 59).

All our information on the history of Masada comes from Josephus's *Jewish War* to which the bracketed numbers refer. First fortified by Alexander Jannaeus (103–76 BC) to protect his south-eastern border (7: 285), it was taken by Herod the Great (1: 237) in the power struggle which followed the murder of his father Antipater in 43 BC. Forced to flee Jerusalem in 40 BC when the invading Parthians made Antigonus king, he put his womenfolk (mother, sisters, Mariamne his fiancée, and her mother) for security in Masada with a guard of 800 (1: 267) while he escaped across the desert to Rome. In his absence Antigonus besieged Masada. Shortage of water forced the defenders to begin girding themselves for a break-out, but a sudden cloudburst replenished the cisterns (1: 286–7). Shortly afterwards Herod relieved the garrison (1: 293–4).

This experience showed Herod the value of Masada, and he replanned it as a last refuge in case the Jews should turn against him, or Cleopatra should persuade Mark Antony to have him killed (7: 300). This must have taken place between 39 and 31 BC. From AD 6 the Romans controlled Masada, but in the summer of AD 66 Jewish rebels took it over by a trick (2: 408). Menachem was the first to see that Herod's stores would provide the weapons the rising against Rome needed (2: 433–4). This gave him the edge on his rivals, but he was quickly assassinated because of his brutality and arrogance, and some of his supporters, including his relative Eleazar ben Jair, barely escaped to Masada (2: 442–7). Thereafter they took no further part in the war against Rome, occupying themselves with raids on the surrounding villages (4: 400). The worst episode occurred at EN GEDI where, during Passover, they slaughtered over 700 women and children (4: 401–5). When Simon ben Giora tried to persuade them to carve out their own territory in the south they refused, preferring to stay close to their base (4: 503–7).

Masada, therefore, posed no threat to the Romans, and they were in no hurry to move against it. Some time after the fall of Jerusalem in AD 70 Lucilius Bassus was appointed legate in Judaea and saw the capture of HERODION and Machaerus as his first priorities (7: 163–4). Having taken Herodion first, it would have been natural to continue south to Masada, but instead he swung round the north end of the Dead Sea to deal with Machaerus which was a real danger. The site offered the defenders the same advantages as Masada, and an energetic defence prolonged the siege. Bassus followed his victory there with a foray into the forest of Jardes (7: 210), and it was left to his successor, Flavius Silva, to turn his attention to Masada (7: 252), probably in the winter of AD 73.

He set up his command camp just beside the present parking-lot at the end of route 3199 from Arad (7: 277). His first step was to surround Masada with eight fortified camps linked by a wall (7: 276); any visitor will see the futility of this rigid adherence to the military textbook. To reach the defence wall on the summit 150 m above he built a huge ramp to facilitate the construction on a rock spur directly beneath the wall of a 25 m-high platform of great stones on which he built an iron-sheathed tower equipped with quick-firing *ballistae* on top and a battering-ram below (7: 304–10). The Zealots had time to prepare their defences, and when the Romans made a breach they found a new wood-faced wall in front of them. The defenders had a moment of hope as the torches thrown against this wall flamed back against the tower, but the wind changed and the wall began to burn (7: 311–19).

Confident that the next day would see the end, the Romans withdrew and rested for the night (7: 319). The respite gave Eleazar the chance to make a long speech (7: 322–88), whose central point was that their defeat was the merited condemnation by God of the Jewish nation (7: 327, 359). Hence, 'let us not receive this punishment from the Romans, but from God himself, as executed by our own hands' (7: 333). His followers resolved on collective suicide. Having gathered all their possessions into one place and set them on fire (7: 394), each father killed his immediate family. Ten were then selected by lot to execute the men; one, again chosen by lot, slew the other nine, and finally stabbed himself (7: 394–7); 960 died that night. It was Passover AD 74 (7: 400–1).

An awful silence greeted the Roman vanguard next morning (7: 403). Their shouts brought out two women and five children (7: 399), who had hidden in a cistern; they recounted all that had happened (7: 404). The scepticism of the troops evaporated when they broke into the blazing palace and found the bodies of the dead (7: 406).

Although Josephus was not at Masada, he had access to official reports from the field, and may even have consulted Flavius Silva, who was in Rome in AD 81, just when Josephus was writing this account. Josephus is thus most reliable on questions of topography and the conduct of the siege. In questions of detail, however, the second-hand character of his knowledge becomes evident, e.g. he errs in the heights of walls and the number of towers, in his description of the Northern Palace, and in his assumption that there was only one palace. In place of the one great conflagration there were many small fires.

Josephus's account becomes utterly incredible from the moment he has the Romans retire once they have breached the wall. Even though night had fallen, it was Passover and there was a full moon. In any case they would have driven home the attack, as Vespasian did at Jotapata (*War* 3: 235, 323). This means that there was no time for Josephus's scenario of heroic suicide. In its place we must assume that some of the defenders killed their families, burnt their possessions, and finally committed suicide, while others fought to the death, and still others tried to hide and escape, but were dispatched out of hand when they were discovered. Josephus the Jewish apologist invented the speech of Eleazar to lay the blame for the war, not on the Jewish people as such, but on a minority of violent revolutionaries, the Sicarii. Josephus the rhetorical historian elaborated the suicide of some into the dramatic mass suicide of all, using motifs from the Graeco-Roman historiographical tradition. Josephus himself would have failed to recognize the radically distorted version of his story which became an important foundation myth of Israeli Zionists.

Silva left a small garrison in the corner of his command camp (near the base of the ramp), where they remained for some 30 years. His brief and standard textbook operation merited no mention in Roman records. The inexperienced Sicarii had posed no significant resistance.

As with most of the Herodian fortresses, which provided a ready-made supply of cut stones and well-designed water cisterns, Masada was occupied by Byzantine monks in the C5.

▼ **Fig. 93.** Masada (after Yadin).

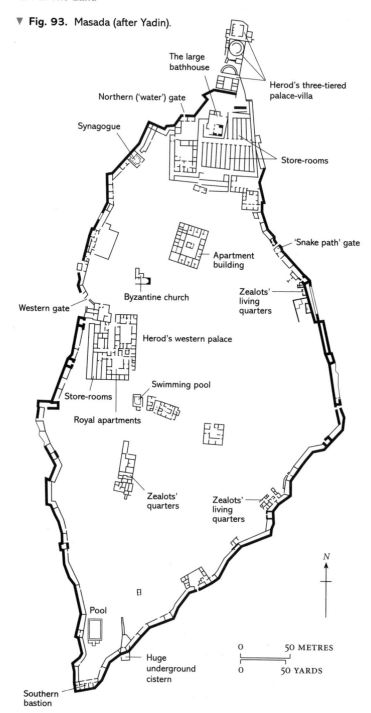

The large bathhouse

Herod's three-tiered palace-villa

Northern ('water') gate

Synagogue

Store-rooms

'Snake path' gate

Apartment building

Byzantine church

Western gate

Zealots' living quarters

Herod's western palace

Swimming pool

Store-rooms

Royal apartments

Zealots' quarters

Zealots' living quarters

N

Pool

0   50 METRES

0   50 YARDS

Huge underground cistern

Southern bastion

Visit (Fig. 93). There are two ways to the summit. Fom the Dead Sea there is a choice between the cable car (starts 8 a.m.; last car down 4 p.m.) and a very steep path which, according to Josephus, 'they call the Snake, seeing a resemblance to that reptile in its narrowness and continual windings' (*War* 7: 282); minimum forty minutes for the very fit. On the west a sealed road from Arad (route 3199) leads to the base of the Roman ramp which must then be climbed on foot (fifteen minutes). Open: 6.30 a.m.–3.30 p.m. At least two hours should be allowed for the visit, not counting the ascent and descent. Shaded areas, toilets, and drinking water are provided on the summit. All the buildings with the exception of the church are of the Herodian period. Everything above a black line has been restored.

On the Roman ramp side from April to October a 50-minute sound and light show is presented on Tuesday and Thursday at 9 p.m. Translations into English, German, French, Spanish, and Russian are available on request. For details and reservations telephone 057–958–8993 or fax 057–955–052.

Even if one comes up from the Dead Sea, it is best to cross to the west side and look down on the **siege ramp**. Nothing could illustrate more graphically the inexorable will of Rome. The ramp has a 20 degree slope. Working behind screens to protect them from fire from the summit, prisoners of war laid down interlocking wooden beams to hold in place the stones deposited by others. The ramp cut across aqueducts fed by winter flash-floods in the wadis on either side of the modern road from Arad. They led to **cisterns**, which can be reached by a path to the north at the base of the ramp. On the cliff face it rejoins the original channel serving eight cisterns; there are four more on a lower level. Each of the great square chambers held roughly 3,200 m³ of water (total capacity 38,000 m³) which from here had to be hauled up a dangerous path to the Water Gate (see below).

From the ramp we go round the summit clockwise. The **double-wall** (casemate) running along the edge is 1,400 m long. When danger threatened, the rooms were filled to create a thick wall, but otherwise they served as living space. An Essene from QUMRAN occupied a room in the wall near the synagogue where a fragmentary copy of the *Songs of the Sabbath Services* was found. From it there is a splendid view of Silva's **command camp** with a gate in each of the four walls. To the right the pointless circumvallation wall descends the cliff, as does the path by which the soldiers drew water from En Gedi. In its present form the **synagogue** dates from the First Revolt. The Zealots cut off a corner to create a small square room in which fragments of Deuteronomy and Ezekiel were found.

The **Water Gate** underlines the major problem of life on Masada. Water had to be manhandled to the summit. Below this point are two sets of cisterns, from which water was systematically carried up a path via this gate to the surface cisterns. The arrangement of the **bath-house** is typical. The door from the courtyard opens into a tiled and decorated dress-ing room. From it one had access to the stepped cold bath, and the warm room, beyond which is the hot room. The furnace was straight ahead, and hot-water baths stood in the apses in the two narrow walls. Small pillars supported the floor, beneath which hot air circulated, and was carried up the walls by flues. The present exit was cut to permit one-way traffic.

The **sloping white wall** isolated the **Northern Palace** from the rest of the summit. Herod designed it for his personal use; at the hottest time of the day it gets more shade than any other part of Masada. The only entrance was the present one on the east side. Square **staircase towers** linked the three levels. Today they have been replaced by metal steps on the western cliff. Some of the original steps move around a square central pillar at the entrance to the **lowest terrace**. This was a colonnaded square (17.6 × 17.6 m) off which at a lower level was a small **bath-house**. Three skeletons were found in the cold room beneath a thick layer of ash; a child of 11 or 12, a young woman aged 17 or 18, whose plaited hair and sandals were perfectly preserved, and a man in his early 20s with scales of silvered armour. The interpretation of the excavator that this individual was an important commander, who killed his family before setting the palace ablaze and falling on his sword (*War* 7: 397), is mani-festly impossible.

The building of the **middle terrace** was founded on concentric circular walls with an outer diameter of 15.3 m. Two rows of columns supported a pointed roof. Note the base of the staircase tower that once ascended 20 m to the **upper terrace**, where a small open courtyard sep-arated the semicircular balcony from mosaic-floored rooms. Monks sub-divided them into cells in the C5.

Pass to the left of the bath-house into the long, narrow **store-rooms**. Two blocks are divided by a corridor at right angles. The northern block has five rooms measuring 20 × 3.8 m. There are eleven rooms (27 × 4 m) in the southern block. The immense capacity (and these are not the only ones) shows that these were less for the permanent inhabitants than for the new army that Herod might need to recruit (see box). Note the column drums in one of the rooms of the southern block near the corridor. A Hebrew letter and one or more strokes are incised in each. This was done at the quarry. The letter indicated the column and the stroke the position of the drum.

Beyond the store-rooms go left to the casemate wall. From this point one can see how it circles the summit, and also look down on the **Snake Path** zigzagging along the steep slope to a **series of Roman camps** (one partially restored) linked by the circumvallation wall on the plain. The steps from the cable-car come through the wall at the original Snake Path Gate.

From this point it is best to cut diagonally across the summit to the southern end. Pigeons roosted in the **round tower**; their flesh made good

---

Preserved Supplies

'The stores laid up within would have excited still more amazement, alike for their lavish splendour and their durability. For here had been stored a mass of corn, amply sufficient to last for years, abundance of wine and oil, besides every variety of pulse and piles of dates. All these Eleazar, when he with his Sicarii became through treachery master of the fortress, found in perfect condition and no whit inferior to goods recently laid in; although from the date of storage to the capture of the place by the Romans well-nigh a century had elapsed. Indeed the Romans found what remained of the fruits undecayed. It would not be erroneous to attribute such durability to the atmosphere, which at the altitude of the citadel is untainted by all earthborn and foul alloy. There was also found a mass of arms of every description, hoarded up by the king and sufficient for 10,000 men, besides unwrought iron, brass, and lead.' (Josephus, *Jewish War* 7: 295–9)

---

eating and their droppings excellent fertilizer. The **underground cistern** was filled by means of a funnel from the summit which entered the hole high in the south wall which today illuminates the vast space. It could hold something like 8,000 m³ of water. From the **southern citadel** one can perceive the walls of a Roman camp on the top of the cliff opposite. Reports sent from there kept the Roman general Silva fully informed of everything that happened on Masada. Note the keyhole-shaped camp on the slope to the right. The large **open pool** must have been roofed in some way because evaporation in summer can be as much as 25 mm per day.

Coming back towards the Western Palace the first recognizable feature is a small, deep, stepped pool with a triangular balcony. The niches for clothes led to its identification as a **swimming-pool**. There are those who prefer to think of it as a ritual bath (*mikveh*); it may well have been used as such by the Zealots.

The 4,000 m² **Western Palace** was the main ceremonial and administrative building. The modern roof covers the **Roman bath** which formed part of the multistorey royal apartments built around an open courtyard. The quality of the geometric mosaic floors is remarkable. The lines on the cement are those drawn by the artists to guide them. The Zealots are responsible for the small intrusive structures. One of the storerooms on the west side measures 70 × 4 m.

The final building is also the only non-Herodian structure on the summit, It is a **small C5 church** with a narthex on the west side and dependencies on the north. It was the core of the laura of Marda, whose members lived in thirteen cells dispersed around the summit. The **arched gate** leading down to the Roman ramp is also Byzantine.

Mazor Mausoleum (G14)

Route 444 south from Midgal Aphek (see APHEK) passes through rough grazing country. It comes as a complete surprise to discover on the left, shortly after Nahshonim, a small building with a classical portico. It has survived virtually intact because for several centuries it has been a venerated Muslim holy place, Maqam en-Nabi Yahya. In fact it antedates Islam by several centuries.

Dated to the early C4 AD the structure contains two rooms. The unusual entrance is considered to resemble the open mouth of a dolphin. According to popular tradition, this animal accompanied the deceased to the netherworld. Inside is an ordinary burial chamber which once contained two sarcophagi. Beyond the fact that they were wealthy and prominent nothing is known of their inhabitants. The *mihrab* in the south wall is manifestly secondary; it indicates the direction of Mecca. The roofing technique betrays the scarcity of wood. The arches support stone slabs whose length could not exceed 2 m without cracking.

Such arches were not necessary in the narrow adjoining room whose original entrance was through a window at the top of the dividing wall. It is identified as a *columbarium* because of some sixty irregularly arranged niches. Those in the eastern wall have small projecting sills. Apparently the owner made provision for the deposit of the ashes of his slaves or employees.

North of the mausoleum and within the enclosure are three cisterns, two shaft tombs, and a small quarry.

Megiddo (J8) ★

Megiddo is the royal box in one of the great theatres of history. From time immemorial armies have surged from the surrounding valleys to play their parts on the flat stage of the Jezreel valley. Not surprisingly, Armageddon (= Har Megedon = Mountain of Megiddo) has become the symbol for the battle to end all wars (Rev. 16: 16).

Its position at the head of the most important pass through the Carmel range (Nahal Iron) gave Megiddo control of the Way of the Sea, the ancient trade route between Egypt and the east. Traders from all over the known world passed its gates, as did invading armies. It was a strongly fortified city before 3000 BC, but its name first appears on the walls of the Temple of Karnak where Thutmose III had carved a detailed record (the earliest known) of the victorious battle he fought at Megiddo in 1468 BC

The Battle of Megiddo 12 May 1468 BC

'His majesty [Thutmose III] set forth in a chariot of fine gold, adorned with his accoutrements of combat, like Horus, the Mighty of Arm, a lord of action like Montu, the Theban, while his father Amon made strong his arms. The southern wing of his majesty's army was at a hill south of the Qina brook, and the northern wing was to the northwest of Megiddo, while his majesty was in their centre, Amon being the protection of his person in the mêlée and the strength of Seth pervading his members.

Thereupon his majesty prevailed over them at the head of his army. Then they saw his majesty prevailing over them, and they fled headlong to Megiddo with faces of fear. They abandoned their horses and their chariots of gold and silver, so that someone might draw them up into this town by hoisting on their garments. Now the people had shut this town against them, but they let down garments to hoist them up into this town. Now, if only his majesty's army had not given up their hearts to capturing the possessions of the enemy, they would have captured Megiddo at this time. . . .

List of the booty which his majesty's army carried off from the town of Megiddo: 340 living prisoners and 83 hands; 2,041 horses, 191 foals, 6 stallions and [   ] colts; 1 chariot worked with gold, with a body of gold belonging to that enemy; 1 fine chariot worked with gold belonging to the Prince of Megiddo [   ], and 892 chariots of his wretched army—total; 924; 1 fine bronze coat of mail belonging to that enemy; 1 fine bronze coat of mail belonging to the Prince of Megiddo, and 200 leather coats of mail belonging to his wretched army; 502 bows; and 7 poles of meru-wood worked with silver of the tent of that enemy.' (*Annals of Thutmose III*, 85–95; trans. J. A. Wilson)

(see box). It remained a vassal city-state of Egypt for over a hundred years; six letters from its king, Biridiya, were found in the archives of the Egyptian foreign ministry at Amarna, one howling for aid against Shechem (TEL BALATA). The quality of the architecture and hoards of ivory, gold, and jewellery bear witness to the great prosperity of the city.

Too strong to be taken by the invading Israelites (Judg. 1: 27), it probably fell to David. Solomon (965–928 BC) surrounded the summit with a casemate wall and filled the surface with public buildings, as befitted one of the most important cities of his realm. Destroyed in pharaoh Shishak's campaign in 923 BC, it was rebuilt even more magnificently by Omri or Ahab in the mid-C9 BC. Megiddo fell in 733 BC to the Assyrians who made it the capital of the province of Galilee. They gave it spacious private dwellings and a new grid street system.

In the C7 BC Megiddo suddenly and inexplicably loses all importance,

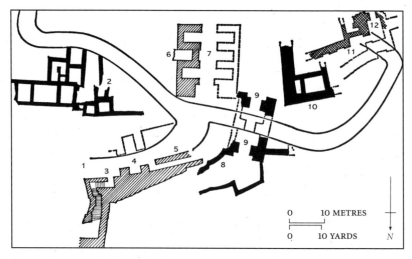

▲ **Fig. 94.** Megiddo. The Gate Area (after Loud). 1. Path from modern entrance;
2. Building; 3. Steps; 4. C10 BC outer gate; 5. Pre-Solomonic wall; 6. C7 BC
pier; 7. C10 BC inner gate; 8. C16 BC access ramp; 9. C16 BC gate; 10. Palace;
11. C18 BC access ramp; 12. C18 BC gate.

it became an open settlement with a small fortress. By the C4 BC it was
uninhabited, and was never resettled.

Visit. Open 8 a.m.–5 p.m.; Friday to 3 p.m. Megiddo is a complicated site;
there are twenty superimposed cities. The reception area has a highly
instructive exhibit with a model of the city as it looked in the time of Omri
or Ahab. A general plan of the site is available on request.

The Gate Area (Fig. 94)

The ruins visible here did not all exist at the same time; shading in the plan
shows elements that were contemporary. The path from the reception area
[**1**] leads up a ramp which formed part of the **entrance** to the city from
the time of Solomon. Earlier gates employed the same technique [**8** and
11], necessitating a right-angled turn to enter the city. Just in front of the
forward gate [**4**] a flight of steps [**3**] leads to a post-Solomonic **water
system**; the wall immediately inside [**5**] is pre-Solomonic. The **earliest
gate** [**12**] discovered at Megiddo is dated to the C18 BC. Only big enough
to accommodate pedestrians, it was built of mud-brick on stone foundations. A new **stone gate** [**9**], wide enough to take chariots, was built in
the C16 and served the city for some 400 years. Just beside it is the corner
of a large building [**10**] whose rooms surrounded a wide courtyard. The
rich collections of carved ivories and jewellery found therein justify calling it a **palace**. It was balanced, on the far side of the gate, by another
building [**2**] with thinner walls but the same room arrangement.

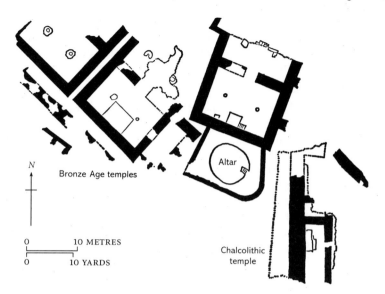

N

Bronze Age temples

Altar

0   10 METRES

0   10 YARDS

Chalcolithic
temple

▲ **Fig. 95.** Megiddo. The Sacred Area (after Loud).

The excavators left only one side of the **Solomonic gate** [**7**]. All that remains visible was below ground; the street level was at the top of the finely bonded piers. At a later stage the space between the piers was filled in to create the foundations for a C7 BC one-bay gate; its inner pier [**6**] is still in place.

The Palace Area

On the higher ground just to the east of building [**2**] is a palace (28 × 21 m) built by Solomon. The five rooms north of its courtyard formed part of the casemate wall with which he fortified the city. A 10 m-wide street separated the 2 m-thick south wall of this palace from another large Solomonic edifice.

The Sacred Area (Fig. 95)

The viewpoint on the south side of the deepest trench cut by the archaeologists is the best spot from which to appreciate the four temples. The city worshipped here for over a thousand years. The **oldest temple** was built about 3000 BC. The long room has an altar opposite the door which gives on to an open courtyard similar to its contemporary at EN GEDI. The round stone **altar** came into being some 500 years later. Originally an independent unit enclosed by a wall, it was shortly afterwards linked to a **two-room temple**. From the vestibule one entered a chamber with an altar at the far end; two pillars supported the roof. Within the same period (2650–2350 BC) **two further temples** were constructed to the same plan. What happened then is not clear, but the two eastern temples went out of use first, and the two-room temple some time later; by 1800 BC no traces remained. The ruins surrounding the viewpoint belong to a large building of the time of Omri-Ahab and to its protective offset/inset wall.

The Stable Area

Continuing clockwise around the tel, one passes a large **grain silo**. Just behind it is the entrance to a large square enclosure. Dated to the time of Omri and Ahab, it then contained no buildings since the palace built there by Solomon had been destroyed by Shishak in 923 BC. Adjoining it is another **large courtyard** with a series of long, narrow buildings along one side. Each was divided into three by two rows of pillars; the two outer aisles were cobbled, the centre one plastered. In some cases a stone trough was found between the pillars. Immediately, the excavators visualized two lines of horses facing the centre, and proclaimed the discovery of Solomon's stables, but it is now certain that they are not from the time of Solomon as the south-east corner lies over one of his ruined palaces. And if they were stables they must have housed very small, house-broken ponies. It is more probable that they were storehouses built by Omri or Ahab, as at HAZOR.

The Water System

Secure access to water was imperative for a city as often besieged as Megiddo. At the time of Solomon this was achieved by means of a **camouflaged 1 m-wide passage** still visible on the slope of the tel, outside the much more elaborate shaft-and-tunnel system installed by Omri or Ahab and perfectly paralleled at HAZOR.

The **shaft** is 30 m deep, and the **tunnel** 70 m long. Indentations in the right-hand wall going towards the spring show that the tunnellers worked simultaneously from both ends; at one point they realized they were going to miss each other, but did not make as many false starts as in the tunnel of Ezechias in Jerusalem (see p. 112). The present exit from the spring was the original Bronze Age entrance; a path on the right leads back to the Gate Area.

Meroth (M3)

According to Josephus, the village of Meroth marked the northern boundary of Upper Galilee, and thus of Jewish territory in the C1 AD (*War* 3: 40). Located in wild country between HAZOR and GUSH HALAV, the remains of its fine synagogue reveal something of the history of a remote community.

A wall and rock-cut ditch protected the village (*War* 2: 573), but the inhabitants also took the precaution of preparing thirty-five caves in the cliff above the south bank of Nahal Hazor; these were to serve as a last refuge if the Romans under Vespasian approached the village in force. What happened we shall never know, but at the end of the C4 or beginning of the C5 it was home to a Jewish community whose prosperity found expression in the construction of a magnificent synagogue.

This first **synagogue** was oriented to Jerusalem by its southern façade. Frescos covered the walls above the tiered benches which lined the walls. A portico sheltered the three entrances. Inside the main door on either side were the reader's platform and the raised Torah shrine. An unusual feature for this type of synagogue is a forecourt with a cistern in the centre. Sometime before AD 475 when it was covered by flagstones, the original floor was replaced by a mosaic (now in the Israel Museum), which in part depicted a young man surrounded by weapons and armour.

A natural disaster in the early C7 necessitated a complete rebuilding and the people of Meroth used the occasion to adapt the synagogue to the current convention. They blocked the apertures in the south wall and moved the entrances to the north wall. This meant that the original fore-court and portico lost their function. The space, however, was not wasted. The east side of the portico became a **children's schoolroom**, and a **house of study** (*bet midrash*) was built in the south-west corner of the courtyard, the first complete such institution to be found in Israel. A

▼ **Fig. 96.** Meroth. The C5 AD (left) and C7 AD (right) synagogues (after Ilan and Darnati).

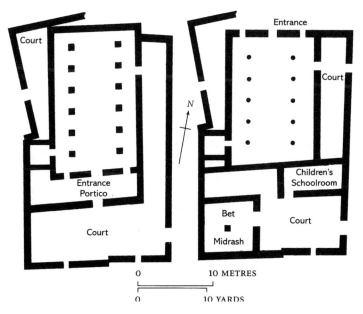

mosaic floor and brightly coloured plastered walls must have made it a cheerful place. The head of the school probably sat in the recess in the bench against the western wall.

This synagogue complêx continued to function until the C12. Hidden in the small room entered from a door in the south-west corner of the synagogue was a hoard of 485 coins; 245 were of gold, the oldest dating from the C1 BC and the latest from the year 1193. It seems that a peaceful and prosperous village fell victim to the intense struggle between the Crusaders and Saladin.

Visit (Fig. 96) The dirt road to the site is signposted south of HAZOR but, since it is in a military area, visits must be approved by the authorities on every day except Saturday. Guided tours can be arranged by the staff of the guest house at Kibbutz Ayelet Hashachar.

Monasteries in the Judaean Desert

D. J. Chitty called his book on Byzantine monasticism *The Desert a City* (Oxford: Blackwell, 1966), a title which perfectly characterizes an extraordinary phenomenon of life in the C4 to C6 AD. In all the provinces of the now Christian empire hundreds of thousands left the comforts of home to dwell in remote, desolate areas. Why?

In sharp contrast to the centuries of persecution, Christianity now offered security and respectability. However, the standard of Christian commitment had been set by the martyrs, and so the fervent, stifled by the mediocrity of an official, politicized religion, sought risk-situations elsewhere. If pagan officials no longer offered a challenge to survival they would find it in the wild places. In order to live fully they were drawn to the desert; they did not flee the world. In fact, the desert monks were intensely involved in all the major politico-religious movements of their time. From among them came poets, critical historians, and great theologians whose writings had incalculable influence.

Monasticism in the Judaean desert is indelibly associated with three saints, each of whom formed his successor: Chariton, who founded the first laura *c.*AD 330, Euthymius (376–473), who attracted thousands of recruits, and Sabas (439–532), the great organizer. The biographies of the two latter were written by a contemporary, Cyril of Scythopolis (525–58), whose *Lives of the Monks of Palestine* (trans. R. M. Price; Kalamazoo: Cistercian Publications, 1991) contains an abundance of vivid cameos. By the time of Sabas there were seventy-three monastic settlements in the desert east of Jerusalem. Literary sources name fifty, and surveys brought to light twenty-three more. These material remains are admirably described and interpreted by Y. Hirschfeld, *The Judean Desert Monasteries in the Byzantine Period* (New Haven: Yale, 1992).

Monks were normally formed in the regular life of an enclosed monastery (*coenobium*—fifty-four known) before being permitted, if they so wished, to live as hermits in a *laura* (nineteen known), i.e. a cluster of solitary cells around a common centre, consisting of a church and bakehouse, where they assembled on Saturdays and Sundays to worship together. Seven times each weekday they prayed alone.

While donations were always welcome, there was an effort to be self-sufficient. Monasteries made and sold oil and wine. Some cereals could be grown locally but the large monasteries needed to import wheat from Transjordan. Bread (baked once a week) was the staple element in the monastic diet, which was supplemented by cultivated fruit and vegetables (lupine, lentils, carobs, dates, and figs). In addition wild plants (caper, mallow, asphodel) were systematically collected. Wine and oil were permitted at the one meal at about 3 p.m. A favourite hot drink on cold evenings was an infusion of cinnamon and fennel flavoured with pepper. The typical cell contained a mattress, brazier, cooking utensils, a stool, and a lamp.

Life in a laura was significantly more austere. For five days each week the monks lived alone and subsisted on bread, water, and dates. Each could have but one each of the most basic necessities; even a lamp was considered a luxury. They occupied themselves by making baskets and ropes whose sale was organized by the laura (see box).

Today only MAR SABA can boast of continuous occupation since its foundation. A number of monasteries have been reconstructed but only the MONASTERY OF ST GEORGE OF KOZIBA, DEIR HAJLA, and that on the MOUNT OF TEMPTATION willingly accept visitors. Others have been excavated, namely, St Euthymius's laura at KHAN EL-AHMAR the converted Hasmonean-Herodian fortress at KHIRBET MIRD, the spectacular KHALLAT ED DANABIYA, the immense MONASTERY OF ST MARTYRIUS, and the lonely KHIRBET ED-DEIR. Neither the first laura of St Chariton at EN FARAH

A Hermit's Week

'Finally Longinus authorized Sabas to live as a solitary in a nearby cave for five days of the week. On obtaining the permission he so longed for, our father Sabas maintained for five years the following pattern of life. In the evening of Sunday he would leave the monastery taking palm-leaves, the labour of the week, last the five days without taking any food at all, and then on the morning of Saturday return to the monastery bringing with him as the handiwork of the five days, fifty completed baskets.' (Cyril of Scythopolis (C6), *Life of Sabas* 10/94; trans. R. M. Price)

nor his last in the WADI KHAREITUN have been excavated, but the wild crags of the gorges add an unforgettable dimension to their ruins.

Monastery of St George
of Koziba (L17) ★★

Clinging to the steep cliff of the Wadi Qilt above a small garden with olive trees and cypresses, this perfect example of a MONASTERY IN THE JUDAEAN DESERT has always been famous for its hospitality which, from the C6, has also been extended to women (see box).

A small oratory built by five hermits (AD 420–30) was transformed into a monastery by John of Thebes about 480. The numerous cave-dwelling hermits came there for the divine liturgy on Saturdays and Sundays. The direction of St George of Koziba gave the monastery its period of greatest renown in the second half of the C6 and led to its present name. Born in Cyprus *c*.550 he trained as a monk here, but lived at the laura of Calamon in the Jordan valley before an intense desire for the ascetic life drove him to take up residence in one of the caves in the Wadi Qilt. Although virtually abandoned after the destructive visit of the Persians (614), the legends which still influence its iconography came into being in the C8 and C10. The prophet Elijah stayed there on his way to Sinai; there St Joachim wept because of the sterility of his wife Anne and an angel announced to him the conception of the Virgin Mary. The monastery was restored in 1179 by the emperor Manuel I Comnenus (1143–80). In 1483 Felix Fabri saw only ruins. Reconstruction of the monastery began in 1878 and was completed in 1901.

Visit. Open: 9 a.m.–3 p.m. (winter), to 4 p.m. (summer); Saturday 9 a.m.–noon; closed on feast days. The monastery can be approached either from Jerusalem or from JERICHO (Fig. 74). Coming from Jerusalem make a hairpin turn left at the entrance to Mizpe Yericho, and right at the first T-junction on to route 7011. The ruins (Khan Saliba) to the left, at the top of the road (route 7012) down to the Herodian **aqueducts** at En Qilt, cover the C5 Byzantine **monastery** of St Adam, 'for there he stayed and wept at losing Paradise' (Epiphanius). About 3 km from the T-junction on the right side is a 10 m section of the **aqueduct** channel going to KYPROS. From the small hill on the other side of the road there is a magnificent view of the monastery at the bottom of the wadi. A free-standing arch marks the beginning of the path down to the monastery. The broken vaulted cistern in the Byzantine period was called **Pepingia** 'the drinking place'. Monks distributed water to pilgrims passing between Jerusalem and Jericho. It is inadvisable to leave cars unattended.

Access from Jericho begins at the police fort marking the southern limit of the built-up area. Turn west towards the escarpment dominated by Kypros. The ruined building (Bait Jubr at-Tahtani) where the road crosses the (repaired) Herodian aqueduct was a small **Crusader tower**. As the road curves up around the shoulder of the hill one can see hermitages below in the far side of the wadi.

Hikers (those who do not suffer from vertigo) can reach the monastery by a path which follows an Herodian aqueduct on the north side of the wadi in about forty minutes from TULUL ABU AL-ALAIQ. Below one 500 m section of the

▲ **The Monastery of St George.** Restored at the end of the C19, the oldest chapel goes back to the C6.

path are fifteen **hermit caves** which were occupied in the Byzantine period. The entrance to this complex is marked by what is now a free-standing gate beside the path about 1.5 km from the monastery. Three of the caves have mosaic floors, and there are mud-brick ovens outside many. The four caves in the south wall of the wadi were reached by a bridge whose piers are preserved on both sides.

From the balcony of the roofed inner court of the monastery **Herodian aqueducts** supported by massive walls are clearly visible on the far side of the wadi. The C6 mosaic floor of the **church of SS John and George** is the oldest part of the building. A long reliquary contains the skulls of the fourteen monks martyred by the Persians. A niche contains the tomb of St George. Linked with this church by a narthex is the **principal church** dedicated to the Blessed Virgin. The base of the walls is medieval, as is the mosaic lattice pattern laid on the floor by two unco-ordinated mosaicists. The double-headed Byzantine eagle in black, white, and red mosaic dates only from the late C19. The iconostasis was erected in 1942, but the royal doors in its centre are attributed to Alexios II Comnenus (1180–3). The vast majority of the paintings and icons date only from the last restoration.

The **cave-church of St Elijah** is reached by stairs from the inner court of the monastery. According to legend the prophet lived there for three years and six months, being fed by ravens (1 Kgs. 17: 3). This tradition has supplanted a medieval one according to which St Joachim hid for forty days bewailing the barrenness of his wife. From this cave a narrow tunnel forms an escape route to the top of the mountain.

Why Women can visit St George's Monastery

'A wealthy Byzantine noblewoman, suffering from an incurable disease, decided to go to Jerusalem to pray for a cure. Having visited the Holy City she went to the Jordan, and made a tour of the monasteries, offering gifts and asking the prayers of the monks for healing. As her litter was being carried up the Ascent of Saint Zachaeus, she had a vision of the Mother of God, who said to her, "Why, noble lady, do you go about everywhere and yet do not enter my house?" She replied, "Where is your house, my Lady, that I may enter it?" The Mother of God said, "When you reach the place called Pepingia, my house is below in the valley." "I have heard," replied the noblewoman, "that women may not enter there." "Go down," said the Blessed One, "I will introduce you." When the noblewoman arrived at the monastery, all the monks were at prayer, and the door was open. When the monks emerged, they were enraged to find a woman in the inner court. After she explained the circumstances, the superior took counsel with the senior monks, and concluded, "This is from the Mother of God. We can do nothing!" He had her litter placed in the sacristy. At the sound of the night office she rose, completely cured, and gave thanks to Our Lady.' (Anthony of Koziba, *Miracles of the Mother of God at Koziba* 1)

Monastery of St Martyrius (K17)

Today an elevated island of rock in the midst of graceless urban development, this was once a celebrated MONASTERY IN THE JUDAEAN DESERT. No structures remain, but the perfectly preserved floor-plan covered with mosaics provides a unique insight into the organization and life-style of a Byzantine monastery.

Born in Cappadocia Martyrius became a monk in Egypt but moved to Palestine in AD 457. After some time in the laura of Euthymius (KHAN EL-AHMAR) he settled in a cave on this site, which he eventually transformed into a monastery of which only the chapel has been identified. This was before 474 when he was ordained a priest of the Holy Sepulchre. Four years later he became the Patriarch of Jerusalem, a post he held until

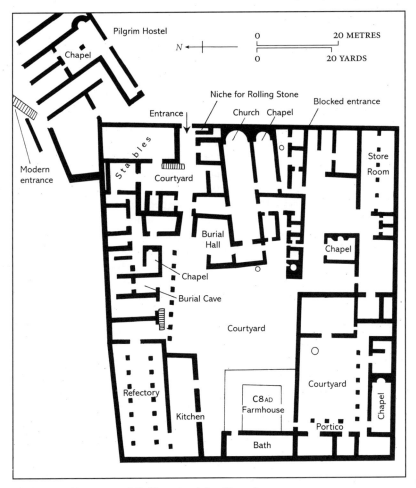

▲ **Fig. 97.** Monastery of St Martyrius (after Magen).

his death in 486. He used the resources of his office to develop his monastery, then under the direction of a certain Paul, to its present size. Literary sources mention a number of other superiors, but the most significant is Genesius who in the latter part of the C6 carried out a major reconstruction of the monastery. An earthquake destroyed his work. Not a building remained intact, and the family who brought the gardens back into cultivation in the C8 AD had to erect a farmhouse in what had been the western side of the central courtyard.

Visit (Fig. 97). Open: Sunday–Thursday 8 a.m.–4 p.m.; Friday to 1 p.m.; closed Saturday. Although in the middle of the settlement of Meale

Adummim the site is not difficult to find. Follow the orange signs around the peripheral road for just over 2 km.

The modern stepped entrance gives access to the **guest-house** of the monastery. In order to prevent disruption in the daily routine of the monks visitors, mostly pilgrims, were housed separately. In addition to stabling for their animals and a chapel for their devotions there would have been accommodation for some sixty visitors.

Originally the monastery had two **entrances** in the eastern wall. As the situation in Palestine deteriorated in the C7, one was blocked and the door of the other was reinforced by a rolling stone 2.5 m in diameter. Its position inside the door was much more intelligent than the siting of a similar defensive device at Khirbet ed-Deir above EN EL-MAMOUDIYEH. The rooms to the left inside must have been for the gate-keeper and drivers. Across the paved yard with a trough are well-drained **stables** complete with mangers and hitching rings. In addition to the transportation of crops grown in the vicinity, a monastery of this size would have needed to import food. The **flight of steps** here and near the refectory show that the buildings along the north wall were two-storeyed.

The orientation of Martyrius' first chapel proved more important in determining that of the **main church** than the symmetry of the complex. Most of its mosaic floor and that of the narthex has been destroyed, but one can still discern a tufted duck, a cock, a donkey, a rabbit, a hooked fish, an elephant, a partridge, a gazelle, and chickens. Outside the lateral chapel is a long narrow space with a **cistern**; it must have been a light well both for the chapel and the service rooms on the other side.

A square tombstone in the middle of the **burial hall** was inscribed 'Tomb of Paul, presbyter and archimandrite'. It contained ten skeletons, all presumably of superiors of the monastery. Beneath the centre of the north wing is a **cave** in which, according to an inscription, a number of priests were buried. Since it does not appear to have been cut as a tomb it may be the one in which Martyrius lived as a hermit. Ordinary monks must have been buried outside the monastic complex.

The monks reached the vestibule of the **refectory** via a covered gallery. The refectory could have seated fifty on the benches around the wall. The vivid colouring and bold design of the fourteen small mosaic panels between the columns distract attention from the serene dignity of the long central mosaic carpet. The large **inscription** at the east end framed by a *tabula ansata* reads, 'In the days of our pious father Genesius, priest and archimandrite, this work also was done for his salvation and that of his community in Christ. It was completed on the fourth day of the month of March of the first indiction'. There is some uncertainty as to which indiction, but the limit dates are AD 568 and 583. The inscription insinuates that Genesius was also responsible for other building activities, thus confirming the implication of an incomplete inscription in front of the sanctuary of the main church mentioning the same personage.

When the long room beside the refectory was excavated it was found to contain all the equipment of a **kitchen**, somewhat damaged by the collapse of the mosaic floor of the second storey. Just inside one of the doors leading to the courtyard is a beautiful little square mosaic representing a partridge standing on an amphora from which a vine grows. Note the **cellar** entered by a ladder; it functioned as a cool room.

Along the west wall is the first, and so far the only, **bath-house** found in a Byzantine monastery. It had only a hot room and cold pool, and lacked the spacious amenities found in more secular establishments.

The large complex filling the south-west corner gives the impression of a self-contained unit, but its function is unknown. A portico lines two sides of a courtyard which is in fact the roof of a **vast cistern** of the same dimensions and 16 m deep. It could hold 6,000 m³. It received the run-off rain-water from the rest of the monastery and distributed it to most of the other cisterns through sluices which could be opened and closed. The total storage capacity of the monastery in its six cisterns is estimated at 25,000 m³ of water, which had to serve its agricultural as well as its human needs.

The area just east of the courtyard was transformed in the Umayyad period into an irrigated **agricultural area**. Water from the cistern was poured into a plastered pool from which it flowed into stone channels. These C8 occupants built their **farmhouse**, which had a central court, adjacent to what had been the monastic bath-house.

Fortunately such changes did not affect the mosaic floor to the east which is all that remains of a **tiny chapel** built by three priests when they joined the community. The inscription in a *tabula ansata* reads, 'O Lord our God remember in your kingdom, the priests Elpidius, John, and George, and all their community in Christ'. The same names appear in a fragmentary inscription above the burial cave.

The last in the row of rooms separating this chapel is particularly interesting. It consists of a circular bowl with signs of burning. If its identification as an **incinerator** for rubbish is correct, it is another unique feature of this monastery.

The now-unblocked opening in the east wall must have served originally as a service entrance through which supplies were brought into the monastery. This has led to the identification of the pillared room as a **store-room**.

Montfort (K3)

When compared with the other Crusader castles of NIMRUD or BELVOIR Montfort is of limited interest. Though finely situated on a high wooded promontory jutting out into Nahal Keziv (which reaches the sea half-way between Nahariyya and Rosh Haniqra), it commands only a limited perspective to the north-west. The Galilee Countryside Park on the north side of the wadi provides a dominant view of the fortress; from the observation point a good path leads down to the castle. The sign-post on the road (route 899) east from Shelomi is marked 'Goren Natural Forest'.

In the C12 AD the area was a fief of the Courtenays. Only in recent times did the village of Miilya spill over the confines of their fortress, **Castrum Regis**. The Teutonic Knights bought this fortress in 1220. The north wall with its corner towers is perfectly preserved; the east and west walls are easily traced. Crusader structures within the rectangular enclosure have been absorbed into later buildings. From Miilya a narrow **Crusader road** runs through the woods to Montfort; it is a walk that evokes another age.

Seeing that a Crusader presence could not much longer be maintained in the Holy Land, another member of the Courtenay family sold the small fort (which was to become Montfort) to the Teutonic Knights in 1226. These knights were the German equivalent of the older Frankish military orders, the Templars and the Hospitallers. Originally the branch of the Hospitallers which administered the hospital/hospice of St Mary in Jerusalem (see p. 76), they had become an independent order in 1190 and were in quest of a site to serve as their central treasury and archives. The construction of the keep and central building of Montfort or, as they called it, Starkenberg, was completed by 1229. The castle was subsequently expanded. It had no strategic value, being far from any of the main routes which traversed Galilee, and functioned as an administrative centre.

A valiant defence repulsed Baybars who laid siege to the fortress in 1266. When he returned in June 1271 his troops, protected by mantlets, worked their way up the steep slope at the western end, and succeeded in undermining the southern wall after a week. For a short while the knights held out in the keep, but eventually surrendered and marched out to Acre (AKKO). On Baybars's orders the fortress was demolished.

Visit (Fig. 98). The state of the ruins does not permit a complete plan, and the one offered here is deliberately schematic. The site is entered beside a semicircular retaining wall which dominates the outer wall further down the hill. The three-storey **tower** straight ahead is preserved to its original height. Once the main entrance of the castle, it was transformed into an inner gate by the construction of the outer wall, which had two gates. The two **vaulted chambers** support a 20 m-square hall with an octagonal central column. In it the knights met on ceremonial occasions. This hall is a secondary addition to the **central building** on a higher terrace to the east; its west wall originally had firing slits. Four construction stages can be detected in this building, in one of which the three rows of seven gothic

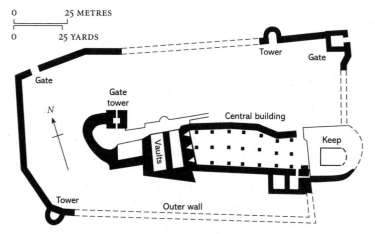

▲ **Fig. 98.** Montfort. Castle of the Teutonic Knights (after Frankel).

columns were added. The ground floor contained a chapel, and service rooms: one has a wine press, another may have been a kitchen, another was certainly the armourer's workshop.

The ruins of the **keep** look out over the 20 m-wide **moat** which cuts across the saddle linking the fortress to the adjoining land mass. Its massive stones underline that it was the last resort of the defenders. Beneath the roofed central chamber is a large cistern.

Below the castle in the wadi bed (Nahal Keziv) is a 50 m-long **two-storey building** of the C13 AD. The ground floor was originally a mill, whose grinding stones were powered by water stored behind the **dam** spanning the wadi. Its centre has been washed away, but the two extremities are visible. When the castle was constructed, the building was transformed into a guest-house for important visitors by the erection of a beautifully **vaulted hall** above the mill.

Mount Carmel (G6–J9)

The majestic promontory of Mount Carmel, which creates the Bay of Haifa, is known in Egyptian texts of the C15 BC as the 'Holy Headland'. This tradition of sanctity, inaugurated by the Phoenicians, is its dominant characteristic. An author of the C4 BC calls it 'the holy mountain of Zeus'. The Roman general Vespasian came there to make a sacrifice at the end of the C1 AD, enabling the historian Tacitus to comment 'Carmel lies between

Judaea and Syria; the same name is given to the mountain and a god. This god has neither statue nor temple; so willed the ancients; there is only an altar and worship' (*Hist.* 2: 78). In the C4 AD Jamblicus, the biographer of Pythagoras, thought it appropriate to have his hero visit Carmel, 'a mountain holy above all and regarded as inaccessible to the vulgar' (*Life* 3: 14); the fact that he wrote 800 years later makes the accuracy of his information suspect, but it underlines the reputation of Mount Carmel.

The promontory dominating Haifa is in fact the tip of a ridge widening to the south-east for some 25 km until it merges with the mountains of Samaria. There are two passes, Nahal Yoqneam and the more important Nahal Iron, which in antiquity was guarded by MEGIDDO because of the great trade route, the Way of the Sea, which passed through it.

There is much evidence of Stone Age occupation in the little wadis which reach the sea on the west; the most accessible group of caves are those in Nahal Mearot (CARMEL CAVES). At the mouth of the river Qishon the Egyptians had a port (now Tel Abu Hawam) which served as a naval base and the point of entry for imports from Mycenae and Cyprus. This settlement flourished during the C14–C13 BC, but did not survive the onslaughts of the PHILISTINES a century later. The site was occupied sporadically down to the Byzantine period, but from the C10 BC onwards the most important town was at Tel Shiqmona on the other side of the cape. Destroyed time and time again, it was always rebuilt, and the Byzantine town covered an area of some 20 hectares, spreading up the side of the hill where hundreds of tombs were cut into the rock; some of these can be seen in Histadrut Park.

First attested in the form Hefa in the C4 BC, the name Haifa was applied to Shiqmona by Eusebius in the C4 AD. Jewish sources of a century earlier, however, seem to distinguish two villages; perhaps through expansion they became one. Though taken by the Crusaders in 1100, Haifa played but an insignificant role in the life of the Latin Kingdom, and subsequently suffered the cycle of destruction and reconstruction which was the fate of the coastal cities. Razed by the Mamluk sultan Baybars in 1265, it was refortified only in 1761 by the rebel Arab chieftain Daher el-Omar. His walls were used as a quarry to provide stones for houses for the expanding Jewish population at the end of the C19.

Haifa

Just at the traffic lights marking the turn from the coast road into Allenby Road, a flight of steps gives access to a public garden. A winding path leads to the **Cave of el-Khader**, also known as the School of the Prophets, to the left of a modern building. From remote antiquity Baal-Adonis was worshipped here, but from the C3 AD he began to be replaced by the prophet Elijah; graffiti scratched on the walls in the C5–C6 attest the veneration of both Christians and Jews. Islam shares the same respect, and the site was a mosque until taken over as a synagogue in 1948.

Beneath the church of the Carmelite Monastery further up the hill behind the lighthouse (from Allenby Road turn right into Stella Maris Road) is another cave associated with Elijah; every 19–20 July it becomes the focal point of a great assembly of Christians, Muslim, and DRUZE who come to beg the intercession of the prophet.

The fortress-like **monastery** (completed in 1867) is the latest in a succession of buildings which began with a Crusader castle. It belongs to a Roman Catholic religious order which developed from a C13 group of hermits who came together in the Wadi Siyah, the valley between the western suburbs of Kababir and Karmeliya, where archaeologists have discovered a small medieval monastery.

More recent religious movements are no less worthy of notice. Kababir is the centre of a Muslim sect founded in India in 1889 by Ahmed al-Kadiani; inspired by Hindu principles, it has the unique distinction of believing in a pacifist holy war. The cluster of classical buildings in magnificent gardens (open: 8 a.m.–5 p.m.) on the hill above Sederot HaZionut is the **central institution of the Baha'i faith**. On the down-hill side the square structure with the golden dome (open: 9 a.m.–noon) enshrines the body of Siyyid Al Muhammad (1819–50), known as the Bab (the 'Gate'), who proclaimed the imminent arrival of the Promised One expected by Shiah Muslims in Persia. In April 1863 his chief follower, Mizra Hussein Ali, had a revelation in Baghdad that he was the one foretold by the Bab, and became known as Baha'u'llah ('Glory of God'). He fostered a movement committed to the unity of humanity and the fundamental oneness of all religions. His insistence that diversity of religion should cease and differences of race be annulled inevitably provoked violent opposition, and in 1868 Akko became his final place of exile. He died in 1892 and is buried in the grounds of his house at Bahji in the north-eastern suburbs of AKKO (open: Friday–Monday 9 a.m.–noon).

Haifa is exceptionally well endowed with museums that repay a visit by those interested in archaeology. The **Haifa Museum** at 26 Shabbetay Levi Street (open: Sunday–Thursday and Saturday 10 a.m.–1 p.m.; Tuesday, Thursday, and Saturday also 6–9 p.m.; closed Friday) has a fine section devoted to ancient art up to the C7 AD. The main building of the University of Haifa, which is located on the road to Dalyiat el-Karmil on the top of Mount Carmel, contains the **Hecht Museum** (open: Sunday–Thursday 10 a.m.–5 p.m.; Saturday 10 a.m.–1 p.m.; closed Friday), presenting archaeological materials illustrating the theme 'The People of Israel in the Land of Israel'.

Other museums cater to more specific interests. The **Stekelis Museum of Prehistory** (open: Sunday–Thursday 8 a.m.–2 p.m.; Saturday 10 a.m.–2 p.m.; closed Friday), in Gan HaEm at the top of the Carmelite Subway, uses finds, dioramas, and reconstructions to depict the life of prehistoric humanity in this area. The **National Maritime**

Museum (open: Sunday–Thursday 10 a.m.–4 p.m.; Saturday 10 a.m.–
1 p.m.; closed Friday) is located at 198 Allenby Road and uses models to
illustrate the development of sailing craft throughout history. In antiquity
Galilee was famous for its olive oil; ancient presses are on display in the
Edible Oil Museum (open: 9 a.m.–12 noon; closed Friday and Saturday)
located in the 'Shemen' Oil Factory on Jaffa Road. Just one street over
towards the harbour is the unmistakable silhouette of a grain silo. It
houses the **Dagon Museum** (guided tours daily, except Saturday, from
10.30 a.m. or by appointment (tel.: 04–664221)), devoted to the history of
the cultivation, storage, and distribution of grain from the beginnings of
the domestication of wheat.

Along the Ridge

The 'Majesty of Carmel' (Isa. 35: 2) had a great impact on the Old
Testament prophets, they used it as a symbol for strength, beauty, and
fertility (Isa. 33: 9; Jer. 46: 18; 50: 19; Amos 1: 2; Nahum 1: 4; S. of S. 7: 5). It
was often visited by Elisha, who had inherited the mantle of Elijah (2 Kgs.
2: 25; 4: 25), but the episode that has fired the imagination of all succeeding generations is the epic trial of strength between Elijah and the 450
prophets of Baal (1 Kgs. 18).

The region is best appreciated by a drive along the scenic road (route
672) on top of the ridge. From Rum Carmel (546 m), the highest point
of the Carmel range, the road descends to two DRUZE villages, **Isfiya** and
Daliyat el-Karmil. The former is identified with Husifah, a Jewish village
of the Roman-Byzantine period. A hoard of 4,560 silver coins, the latest
dated AD 53, was found there; it may have been the annual collection
for the Temple. No traces now remain of the excavated C6 synagogue,
which had a zodiac mosaic floor. Daliyat el-Karmil is famous for its
basket-work.

Shortly after leaving the village take the first road to the left (east) to
Muhraqa (2.5 km). Meaning 'the Sacrifice', this is the traditional site of
Elijah's contest with the prophets of Baal (1 Kgs. 18: 20–46), and offers a
splendid view of the Jezreel valley. The reliability of the identification is of
course open to doubt, but site and text in fact harmonize perfectly. From
the platform in front of the little Carmelite monastery (built 1868) one
can see the sea (1 Kgs. 18: 43), and there is a spring, Bir el-Mansoura, just
below (18: 33). The Qishon brook runs at the bottom of the hill (18: 40) in
the Jezreel valley (18: 45–6). The colourful narrative comes to vivid life
when read in this setting.

Some 2 km on route 672 from the Muhraqa turn-off there is a dirt
road to the right (west) which leads to **Sumaq** (2 km). This was a large
Jewish village in the Late Roman and Byzantine periods. The C3 synagogue was destroyed in the early C5. Dwellings were built as *insulae* as at
CAPERNAUM. There are many workshops, wine and oil presses, and decorated burial caves.

Mount Gerizim (K13)

From the top of the sacred mountain of the SAMARITANS, dominating NABLUS (Fig. 100), there is a panoramic view of central Samaria. The ancient trade route from the great highway on the coast, the Way of the Sea, came through the pass (whence the importance of TEL BALATA) and continued down the deep cut of the Wadi Farah (Nahal Tirza) to the Jordan Valley. A north–south route, never as important, passed through the fertile plain to the east. The view to the north is blocked by the slightly higher Mount Ebal. It is considered accursed by the Samaritans, and one can see the reason why if one compares the sterility of its grey rocks with the luxuriant trees surrounding TEL ER-RAS (Fig. 100) in the foreground.

The modern houses on the plateau below the summit belong to the Samaritans who live there during the forty days of the feast of Passover; the lambs are sacrificed in a fenced area south of the road, just before the dirt track leading to Tel er-Ras. Previously the sacrifice took place in a fenced area of flat rock on the very summit.

Even though their temple on Mount Gerizim had been destroyed in the late C2 BC, the Samaritans managed to maintain a continuity of worship on the summit. They came there to pray in the early part of the Byzantine period. In the C5 Christians began to agitate for a church on the mountain. The words of Jesus in John 4: 21 were distorted into a promise that 'in the time to come the Samaritans will not worship there, but the true worshippers will worship there' (Procopius of Caesarea, *Buildings*). The only effect that the bitter anger of the Samaritans had on the determination of the emperor Zeno (474–91) was to cause him to surround the church with a 7 m-high defensive wall. It was dedicated to Mary the Mother of God in 484. The presence of a church on their holy site was a permanent affront to the Samaritans, and was one of the causes of the great Samaritan revolt in 529. After its suppression the emperor Justinian strengthened the fortifications of the church by building two irregularly shaped wards on the north side to protect the gate. He also guaranteed the water supply by providing a large reservoir.

The Muslims destroyed the church in the C8, and the fortress was dismantled in the C9. The modern edifice built on the north-east tower is the tomb (*weli*) of Abu Ghanem, a Muslim holy man.

Visit (Fig. 99). Those who prefer to avoid Nablus may reach the summit via Berakha, which lies just south of Mount Gerizim. At the entrance to the settlement take the sealed road to the right. Beneath the building on stilts in the Samaritan village three houses of the C2 BC are ranged around a courtyard containing an oil press. Turn right at the T-junction. The road leads to the parking-lot on the summit.

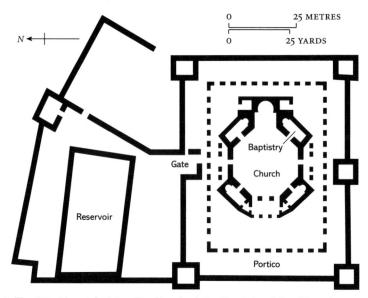

▲ **Fig. 99.** Mount Gerizim. The Church of the Theotokos (after Magen).

Given the history of the site, it is understandable that the church should be the dominant structure on the summit; other features are best grasped in relation to it. The **church** consists of two parallel octagons. The apse on the east is flanked by two square chambers. Normally these contained relics. Four chapels separated by three narthexes at the cardinal points filled the other seven spaces between the inner and outer octagons. In the apse of the south-eastern chapel is a hexagonal shaped unit which may be a baptismal font. Piers and columns supported the high octagonal centre surmounted by a segmented pitched roof. The entrance to the enclosure was in the north side of the five-towered defensive wall against whose inner face was a cloister. The gate gives access to the **outer ward** erected by Justinian. The **reservoir** takes up most of the centre.

The east wall of the church complex stands just inside **the wall and gate of the Samaritan temple area**. Between the south wall and the parking-lot is an excavated area in which seven well-preserved steps lead down from a flagged **square** to a large flat area of beaten earth on which were found numerous **hearths** containing traces of bones, perhaps the remains of paschal sacrifices. These structures date to the C2 BC, as does the side of a building outside the west wall of the church enclosure. Apparently its components are venerated by the Samaritans as the **Twelve Stones**, taken by Joshua from the bed of the Jordan and set up in the camp at Gilgal (Josh. 4: 1–24). The building north of the church complex began life in the C2 BC as a private house, but subsequently was transformed into an **oil press**, in which a weighted beam compressed crushed olives. The other excavated areas contain houses of the same type and date. In the early C2 BC the mountain city was encircled by a wall, traces of which are to be found to the south of the access road, and to the north about half-way between the church and Tel er-Ras. Many of the houses revealed traces of destruction. Presumably they suffered the fate of the temple, which John Hyrcanus destroyed in 128 BC.

A Temple for Love

In the late C4 BC Manasseh was a priest of the Temple in Jerusalem, the brother of the high priest. He accepted as his wife, Nicaso, the daughter of Sanballat, the leader of the Samaritans, who hoped thereby to forge an alliance between his people and the Jews. The authorities in Jerusalem were scandalized, and demanded that Manasseh choose between his foreign wife and his priestly office. If he retained her as his wife, he could no longer officiate at the altar. Although deeply in love, Manasseh seriously considered divorce. Emotionally he could not surrender the priestly office that was the hereditary dignity of his family. When Sanballat became aware that his daughter might be repudiated, he promised Manasseh that, if he followed his heart, he would make him high priest of the Samaritans, and would build for him on Mount Gerizim a temple like that in Jerusalem. Many of the priests in Jerusalem whose marital situations paralleled that of Manasseh followed him to Samaria. (Josephus (C1), *Antiquities* 11: 302–12)

Mount of Temptation (Jebel Quruntul) (M16)

A thirty-minute climb on a good path, passing through the monastery (open: 9 a.m.–1 p.m., 3–4 p.m. (winter); to 5 p.m. (summer); closed Sunday; no shorts or sleeveless blouses allowed), permits a magnificent panorama of the entire JERICHO area (Fig. 74) with the DEAD SEA to the south and the towers of the MOUNT OF OLIVES on the western skyline. The monastery is open to women. On payment of a small fee permission to go to the summit is granted by the superior; one must return within an hour.

The Monastery
Byzantine pilgrims visiting Jericho had much to entertain and uplift them

▲ **The Monastery of the Mount of Temptation.** Below is the plain of Jericho.

(the walls which fell to Joshua's trumpets, the house of Rahab, the sycamore tree of Zacchaeus) but they never thought of locating here, or anywhere else, the temptations of Christ (Matt. 4: 1–11). None the less, very early in the C12 the invitation of Satan to turn a stone into a loaf of bread was localized in a cave half-way up the mountain, and his offer of all the kingdoms of the world in return for worship was considered to have been made on the summit. The extent to which this development is related to the occupation of caves in the mountain by Latin hermits must remain conjectural.

Hermits were still there in the C14, but none are mentioned from the beginning of the C15. The Greek Orthodox Church acquired the site in 1874, and most of the present monastery had been reconstructed by 1895. The northern half is cut into the cliff, while the southern half is cantilevered out into space. The first large cave serves as a kitchen and dining-room. The **medieval cave-church** is on two levels, and is of masonry built in front of a cave.

The medieval chapel of St Mary, now known as the **cave of St Elijah** (40 m below the monastery) was rebuilt in 1949–65. It is kept locked and contains no datable remains.

The Fortress of Doq

A new church on the summit was begun in 1874 but only the surrounding wall was completed. The area it circumscribes is within the fortress of Doq built by the Syrian general Baccides just before the middle of the C2 BC. There Ptolemy, the governor of Jericho, assassinated his father-in-law Simon Maccabaeus in 134 BC (1 Macc. 16). Some 70 m west of the enclosure a **rock-cut ditch** betrays the western limit of the fortress. Beneath the eastern side of the enclosure wall are traces of much older **retaining walls** on the cliff edge. The base of a **tower** can be discerned in the centre, and both north and south corners are evident. According to the Copper Scroll from QUMRAN, a treasure of twenty-two talents is buried under the east angle of the fortress at a depth of 3.5 m!

About 70 m due north of the enclosure wall is an **aqueduct** coming from the west. A weir some 500 m to the west in the wadi diverted run-off water into a channel, which is particularly well preserved at the point where it disappears over the cliff edge and swings south to terminate at nine big **cisterns** with a total capacity of 2,000 m³. From them water had to be drawn by hand to the fortress. In 1172 Theoderic noted that 'The crest of Mount Quarantana and its subterranean caves are full of victuals and arms belonging to the Templars, who can have no stronger fortress or one better suited for the annoyance of the infidels'.

As with many other MONASTERIES IN THE JUDAEAN DESERT, the Hasmonean ruins served as construction material for the central buildings of the **laura of Douka** founded by St Chariton in AD 340. He had come from EN FARAH, and was to stay here only five years before confiding the direction to Elphidius and going on to found the laura of Souka in the WADI KHAREITUN. According to Palladius, who lived there around AD 386, there were so many monks that the mountain resembled a city. The monks abandoned the site after the Persian invasion of 614.

The **ancient road** to the fortress starts about 1.5 km further north. From the parking-lot below the monastery follow the aqueduct coming from En Duk, which once served Herod's winter palace at TULUL ABU EL-ALAIQ. The trail begins behind a group of houses and climbs southwards at a very easy gradient to the wadi in which the aqueduct for the fortress begins. Originally this was an Iron Age road linking Bethel with Jericho.

A bridge across the wadi just before En Duk carried an aqueduct to KHIRBET AL-MAFJAR. On the eastern bank of the wadi a tin roof marks the site of the C6 AD **synagogue of Naaran** (Fig. 74). The rectangular building was entered from the north; there is no orientation to Jerusalem. At the far end of the mosaic floor (now removed) two *menorahs* flanked an Ark of the Law; in the middle of the floor was a zodiac. Scattered around are remains of the village whose intensely Jewish character is noted in the literary sources. Its tradition went back to Josh. 16: 7 and 1 Chr. 7: 28.

Mount Tabor (Har Tavor) (L7)

The perfect breast shape of Mount Tabor excites awe and wonder; it has the aura of a sacred mountain. From the dawn of history it was a place where humanity found contact with the numinous and it is hardly surprising that Christian tradition eventually located there the transfiguration of Jesus (Matt. 17: 1–8).

Neanderthal people came there from 80,000 to 15,000 BC to make flint tools: because of the lack of water, it served only as a factory site. The mountain is first mentioned in the Bible in connection with the defeat of the army of the king of HAZOR at the hands of Deborah and Barak in 1125 BC. The 900 Canaanite chariots swept across the plain of Jezreel from near MEGIDDO, but a sudden downpour bogged them near the foot of Tabor, holding them for the Israelite charge from the mountain (Judg. 4–5). Heterodox Jewish worship on Tabor is condemned by Hosea (5: 1); for Jeremiah it symbolized the might of Nebuchadnezzar (46: 18). In 218 BC Antiochus III of Syria, by feigning retreat, enticed the Egyptian garrison from their position on the summit and slaughtered them in the plain. The same stratagem enabled the Roman general Placidus to defeat the Jews who, under Josephus, had built a wall around the summit in forty days (AD 67). This latter text (*War* 4: 54–61) incidentally suggests that a village existed on the summit in the C1 AD, possibly inhabited by the descendants of a garrison left behind by Alexander Jannaeus (103–76 BC) when he consolidated Jewish control over the centre and north of the country.

The localization of the Transfiguration fluctuated at the beginning of the Byzantine period. Eusebius (d. 340) hesitates between Tabor and Mount Hermon, while the Pilgrim of Bordeaux (333) places it on the Mount of Olives. In 348 Cyril of Jerusalem decided on Tabor, and the support of Epiphanius and Jerome established the tradition firmly. The date of the first religious constructions is uncertain. The anonymous pilgrim of Piacenza saw three basilicas in 570. Willibaldus (723), on the contrary, mentions only one church dedicated to Jesus, Moses, and Elijah. The contradiction disappears if we assume three chapels architecturally linked, as in the present building.

A Crusader text suggests that the Byzantine edifice was still standing when Tancred installed Benedictine monks on Tabor in 1099. They were massacred and their buildings destroyed by a Turkish attack in 1113. When the Benedictines returned they defended the new church and monastery with a stout wall which successfully resisted Saladin's attack in 1183: the nearby Greek church of St Elijah was destroyed. The fortress-monastery capitulated after the defeat of the Latin Kingdom at the HORNS OF HATTIN in July 1187.

The threat of the Fourth Crusade (1202–4) inspired Melek el-Adel, ruler of Damascus, to fortify the mountain; this was in fact done by his son Melek el-Mouadzam between 1212 and 1214. The presence of a Muslim fortress on the site of the Transfiguration was made the occasion of the Fifth Crusade. A seventeen-day Crusader siege in 1217 failed, but a year later Melek el-Adel ordered the fortress to be dismantled because he recognized that it would be a continuous provocation. A series of truces permitted Christians to return to Tabor later in the C13 but they were expelled by Baybars in 1263.

Visit. After leaving the village of Dabburiya (where Byzantine tradition located the cure of the epileptic boy (Luke 9: 37–43), the miracle immediately subsequent to the Transfiguration) the road runs above the ancient Way of the Sea before turning to climb the mountain. The summit is divided equally between Greek Orthodox and Latin Catholics; a wall highlights the character of the relationship.

The first turn-off leads to the Greek sector. Just inside the medieval Arab wall an iron door, flanked by two small windows in a broken wall, is the entrance to the **Cave of Melchisedek**; according to a bizarre medieval tradition this was the dwelling where he received Abraham (Gen. 14: 17–20). The key is kept in the **Church of St Elijah** (at the end of the drive) which is built on Crusader foundations. All the ruins visible throughout the area are medieval.

The entrance to the Latin sector is through the main gate of Melek el-Adel's fortress, today called the **Gate of the Wind**; it was restored in 1897. The defence wall of which it formed part can be traced all round the summit; there are twelve towers. About 150 m from the gate on the right (south) is a **small chapel** built on Byzantine foundations; unmentioned in any ancient document, it today commemorates the conversation between Jesus and the disciples after the Transfiguration (Mark 9: 9–13). It is bracketed by two cemeteries, that on the north is medieval while the southern one contains tombs of the C1 AD.

The drive ends in the piazza in front of the **basilica** (open: 8 a.m.– noon, 2–5 p.m.; closed Saturday) constructed in 1924. The new building to the right (south) is the Franciscan monastery and hospice, to the left are the ruins of the **medieval Benedictine monastery**. A small oratory, the chapter room, and the refectory are easily discernible. Two rooms between the oratory and the chapter room contain entrances to an Arab bath.

The towers of the basilica cover the Byzantine-medieval chapels of Moses and Elijah; in the crypt traces of the earlier main church are still visible.

The ruins of Mount Tabor are less interesting than the panorama its altitude provides. A flight of steps in the medieval refectory to the north of the basilica leads to the top of the fortress wall of the monastery. The line of Melek el-Adel's wall with its two towers leads the eye to the north and the mountains of Upper Galilee. Slightly to the east is the great mass of Mount Hermon with the HORNS OF HATTIN in the foreground above the depression (further east) containing the Sea of Galilee. NAZARETH crowns the crest to the west.

There is a similar viewpoint south of the basilica on the medieval walls near the Tower of the King's Daughters, but it is not as good as the balcony of the Franciscan hospice. This offers an uninterrupted panorama of the plain of Jezreel bounded by the south-eastern part of the Carmel range and the northern extremity of the mountains of Samaria. This vast arena resounded to the tramp of the armies of all the great generals who campaigned in the Middle East, from Thutmose III (MEGIDDO) to Allenby, and including Alexander the Great and Napoleon. The BET SHEAN valley is clearly a natural highway connecting the Jordan valley with the route across the plain to the coast at Haifa. It has carried trade since the beginning of commerce, but was less important than the Way of the Sea, the trade route linking Damascus and Egypt, which swung round the Nazareth side of Tabor. From Afula the highway followed the modern road across the plain to the pass of the Nahal Iron guarded by Megiddo.

Muhraqa: *see* MOUNT CARMEL

Nabataeans

In pre-Christian centuries trade ships from the east could not sail against the strong winds in the north of the Red Sea. They had to land their goods in the Arabian peninsula whence they were carried overland to the Mediterranean coast. The Nabataeans were an Arab tribe who had the wit to see the possibilities of this trade route crossing their territory. Through the systematic exploitation of cisterns they developed trade routes across Arabia to the Persian Gulf. Their name derives from a root 'NBTW' meaning 'to dig for water'.

The first historical reference to the Nabataeans is in 312 BC, 'they surpass all other Arabian tribes in wealth, although they are not more than 10,000 in number'. At this time they were already involved in the exportation of bitumen from the DEAD SEA to Egypt. The collapse of the Ptolemaic (Egypt) and Seleucid (Syria) empires towards the end of the C2 BC permitted them to develop into an independent state. Immense revenues were generated by taxes levied on the caravans; the cost of incense from Dhofar, pearls from the Persian Gulf, silk from China, spice and cotton from India doubled during transit through Nabataean controls.

The NEGEV was always a critical area in the Nabataean route system because it gave them access to the Mediterranean coast. At AVDAT the route from Petra divided, one section going to the port of Gaza, the other joining the ancient Way of the Sea at el-Arish for Egypt. The loss of Gaza to the Jews under Alexander Jannaeus *c.*100 BC cost the Nabataeans dearly; there is a break in their occupation of Avdat, Haluza, and NIZZANA. When the Romans marched into Syria-Palestine in 63 BC an arrangement with the Nabataeans was worked out by Antipater, father of Herod the Great; his wife, Kypros, was a Nabataean. The civil wars in Rome, which led to the end of the Republic, made this arrangement irrelevant and the Nabataeans had effective control of Transjordan until the advent of Augustus (27 BC–AD 14). He confirmed their lack of real authority in the north by giving the area to Herod the Great (BANYAS), and sapped the commercial basis of their power by having ships land their goods for Europe on the Egyptian side of the Red Sea. The effect of this measure was not immediately apparent.

The defeat by Aretas IV (9 BC–AD 40) of Herod Antipas, who had thrown aside the former's daughter to marry Herodias (Mark 6: 14–29), was interpreted as divine vengeance for the murder of John the Baptist (*Antiquities* 18: 116). Such a private war angered the Romans and Petra came under threat. None the less the Nabataeans had control of Damascus in the time of St Paul (2 Cor. 11: 32), probably as a gift of the emperor Gaius Caligula (AD 37–41). In this period Nabataean cities in the Negev flourished again. As the century progressed, however, the consequences of the Roman economic squeeze became more manifest; in AD 106 Trajan was able to annex the kingdom of Nabataea without a struggle. Thereafter the Nabataeans settled down as farmers and assimilated more and more into other elements of the local population.

Nabi Musa (M17)

To the south of the Jerusalem–Jericho road (route 1), just before the final descent into the Jordan valley, the numerous domes of a great building stand out from the humps of the low barren hills which hide the entrance to the Buqeia. A new tarmac road leads to the site venerated by the Muslims as the tomb of Moses. Entrance to the building depends on the availability and humour of the guardian.

In AD 1269 the Mamluk sultan Baybars built a small shrine here. It was a point on one of the old roads from Jerusalem, used particularly by pilgrims to Mecca, where Muslims were accustomed to venerate Moses whose tomb on Mount Nebo was visible on the other side of the Jordan Valley. This act of piety inspired others to build rooms for travellers adjacent to the shrine. Between 1470 and 1480 the hospice grew to its present spacious dimensions. Not only did it mark the end of the first day's march to Mecca, but in the minds of simple people the place from which the tomb of Moses was venerated inevitably became the tomb itself.

About 1820 the Turks completely restored the buildings which had fallen into total disrepair, and actively encouraged a seven-day pilgrimage for the Muslims of the area. Their purpose was to provide a counter-balance to the Easter ceremonies, and the date was fixed according to the Christian calendar. Accordingly, on Friday of Holy Week a tumultuous procession of thousands of pilgrims left the el-Aksa Mosque in Jerusalem for the day-long march to Nabi Musa and five full days of prayer, feasting, and games. It became one of the most popular and colourful Palestinian institutions. As tensions in the area grew it acquired political overtones which led to tight controls by the British authorities and ultimately to suppression by the Jordanian Government in 1948.

Muslim legend identifies the double-domed structure covering an immense tomb some 2 km south of Nabi Musa as the resting place of Hasan er-Rai, the shepherd of Moses. The dirt road running due west from Nabi Musa follows the line of the ancient Islamic route, which it has almost totally destroyed. It follows a ridge all the way to KHAN EL-AHMAR.

Nabi Samwil (J17)

The skyline north of Jerusalem is dominated by a peak with a large mosque whose stark lines are softened by one great tree. From it there is a magnificent panorama of the territory of the tribe of Benjamin with JIB in the foreground. On a clear day one can see both the Mediterranean and the mountains of Jordan.

This is the scene of the defining event of Solomon's reign, his prayer for wisdom (see box). In the C6 AD the hill was identified as Rama, the burial place of the prophet Samuel (1 Sam. 25: 1). In his honour the emperor Justinian (527–65) built here a fortified monastery; the name of Samuel dominates the subsequent history of the site.

From the ruins at dawn on 7 July 1099 the Crusaders first saw the city that had preoccupied them for three years. Their explosion of joy was echoed by many pilgrims, and the popular name of the place became Mountjoy. The church built in 1157 by the Premonstratenians was abandoned when the canons retreated to AKKO after the defeat of the Crusaders at the HORNS OF HATTIN in 1187. Richard the Lion-Heart spent a few hours there in 1192. It was his one glimpse of the city he had come so far to liberate; he was forced to abandon his plan to attack Jerusalem when expected support did not arrive. The defences of the monastery gave it the

The Prayer of Solomon

'Solomon, and the whole assembly with him went to the high place at Gibeon, where God's Tent of Meeting was, which Moses, servant of God, had made in the desert. . . . There Solomon presented 1,000 burnt offerings before the Lord on the bronze altar of the Tent of Meeting. That night God appeared to Solomon and said, "Ask what you would like me to give you." Solomon replied to God, "You showed most faithful love to David my father, and you have made me king in succession to him. Lord God, the promise you made to David my father has now been fulfilled, since you have made me king over a people as numerous as the dust of the earth. Therefore give me wisdom and knowledge to act as leader of this people, for how could one otherwise govern such a great people as yours?" "Since that is what you want," God said to Solomon, "since you have asked, not for riches, treasure, honour, the lives of your enemies, or even for a long life, but for wisdom and knowledge to govern my people of whom I have made you king, therefore wisdom and knowledge are granted you. I give you riches too, and treasure and honour such as no king had before you and none will have after you." ' (2 Chr. 1: 3–12).

aspect of a fortress, and as such it was torn down by Ayyubid sultan al-Muazzam in 1219. He excepted the church, which was demolished in the early C18 and a mosque erected on its foundations. Jews and Muslims came here on pilgrimage in the late Middle Ages. Begun in 1911, the present building was severely damaged in the battle for Jerusalem in 1917, and was subsequently restored during the British Mandate.

Visit. The access road from the straight, level section of the road linking the suburb Ramot with the settlement of Givat Zeev (route 443) is signposted.

The ruins closest to the parking-lot in line with the mosque date from the C2 BC and represent a **Hasmonean public building**. The way the rock-cut walls are shaped in the rectangular building to the right of the access ramp indicate that the structure was vaulted. The adjoining area began as a quarry from which stone was extracted for the medieval monastery; then it was beautifully levelled to create a courtyard with service buildings.

The mosque stands in the centre of a **rectangular C12 AD enclosure** (100 × 50 m). The interrelation of the remains is best grasped from the roof of the mosque before attempting detailed examination. Going anticlockwise from the minaret one looks down on a once-vaulted building juxtaposed to a square tower. Below the inner edge of the excavation is a **Byzantine wine press** (left) and a domed **Mamluk smelter** (right). The raised part in the middle of the **levelled quarry** contained caves, which were cleverly preserved as storage space. In the left corner rock-cut troughs betray a **stable**; note the cistern outside to the left. The single large medieval wall between the mosque and the levelled quarry leads to a vaulted area on the west from which projects a square tower. Just outside the tower is another **quarry** in which one can see three enormous blocks ready to be detached, and the beds of four others already removed. Outside the south–west corner this quarry has become a 5 m-wide **defensive ditch**. Two **vaulted halls** extend along the south side. A square tower projects from the centre.

Nablus (Shechem) (K12)

Whereas a political decision made Jerusalem the capital, nature itself gave this status to Shechem, 'the uncrowned queen of Palestine'. In the mouth of the only east–west pass, surrounded by springs, the centre of an ancient road system, it is the natural capital of the mountain region (Fig. 100).

The site first settled by Chalcolithic people (c.4500–3100 BC), TEL BALATA, was just in the process of becoming an imposing city when Abraham arrived (c.1850 BC). Having crossed the Jordan by a ford, he would have come up the beautiful Wadi Farah (Nahal Tirza; route 57) to Shechem where he received the promise of the land (Gen. 12: 6–7).

The political significance of the city decreased in the C9 BC when the capital of the dissident northern kingdom was moved to SAMARIA (Shomeron). In succeeding centuries historical forces conspired to give the SAMARITANS their distinctive identity. In opposition to Jerusalem, they built their own temple in the early C2 BC on MOUNT GERIZIM. John Hyrcanus destroyed this edifice some 80 years later, but the memory of it was still vivid (John 4: 20) when Jesus stopped to drink at JACOB'S WELL. John Hyrcanus sacked Shechem in 107 BC and the site was never reoccupied.

The name of the present town, Nablus, derives from Flavia Neapolis, a Roman colony built further east in the pass for the veterans of Titus in AD 72. One of these settlers became the father of the great Christian apologist Justin Martyr, who was born there c.AD 100. Not long afterwards the temple of Zeus was erected on TEL ER-RAS. The same century saw the construction of the theatre shown in the Madaba Map at the foot of Mount Gerizim. Excavations show that it had a diameter of 110 m and could seat between 6,000 and 7,000. Despite the intense pressures highlighted by this symbol of an alien culture the Samaritans prospered; witness a grandiose monumental tomb (dated c.AD 200; now reconstructed) at Khirbet Askar. A visit to their synagogue in the city highlights the disastrous difference in their present condition.

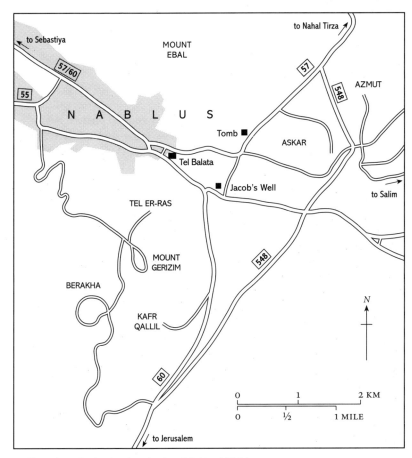

▲ **Fig. 100.** Antiquity sites in the vicinity of Nablus.

According to John 3: 23, John the Baptist 'was baptizing at Aenon near Salim'. Salim still exists, 5 km east of Nablus. Aenon simply means 'springs'; and the five springs in a 1 km line on the eastern face of Mount Gerizim is the most probable candidate. Jesus' ministry paved the way (John 4: 38) for the successful mission of Philip, followed by Peter and John (Acts 8: 4–25). This early Christian presence intensified in the Byzantine period, leaving traces in churches at Jacob's Well and on Mount Gerizim. The dominant view from this point underlines the strategic importance of the city; the natural trade routes are immediately evident.

Queen Melisande lived here from 1152 to 1161, but the rapacity of the inhabitants removed the cut stones of all Crusader buildings. Virtually wiped out by the earthquake of 1927, the town has nothing to offer visitors, and the uncertain temper of the populace counsels speedy transit.

Nahal Teqoa: *see* WADI KHAREITUN

Nazareth (K7)

The evangelists do not agree as to where Mary and Joseph lived before the birth of Jesus. Matthew implies that it was BETHLEHEM (Matt. 2), but Luke says that it was Nazareth (Luke 2: 4–5). It is more probable that Matthew is correct. Joseph belonged to a Judaean family. Were Nazareth their home it would have been more natural to return there when Herod menaced the family than to go to Egypt. Judaeans, on the other hand, automatically thought of Egypt as a place of refuge (1 Kgs. 11: 40; 2 Kgs. 25: 26; Jer. 26: 21). When Archelaus (4 BC–AD 6) showed that he had inherited the murderous unpredictability of his father, Herod the Great, Joseph decided to move his family to the north. Just at that moment Herod Antipas, who had become tetrarch of Galilee, was recruiting artisans for the construction of his capital SEPPHORIS (today Zippori). Joseph settled at Nazareth 6 km to the south-east on the Roman road from Sepphoris to SAMARIA and Jerusalem. All that Luke knew was that the family had lived in Nazareth for so long that it was considered Jesus' 'home town' (Matt. 13: 54; Luke 4: 16) and that Jesus had relatives there (Matt. 13: 55–6). He therefore assumed that Joseph and Mary had been born there.

Slender evidence suggests that a Judaeo-Christian community survived in Nazareth during the C2 and C3 AD. According to Julius Africanus (AD 160–240), the village was a centre of Jewish Christian missionary activity. Conon, martyred in Asia Minor during the reign of Decius (AD 249–51), affirmed in court, 'I am of Nazareth in Galilee, I am of the family of Christ to whom I offer a cult from the time of my ancestors.'

The early Byzantine pilgrims do not seem to have paid much attention to Nazareth. In 384 Egeria was shown 'a big and very splendid cave' in which Mary had lived. Then silence descends for almost two centuries, a period in which many legends were born (see box). At the end of the C7 Arculf saw two 'very large churches', one in the centre of the city on the site of the house where Jesus was brought up, the other on the site of the house where Mary received the angel Gabriel.

One of Tancred's first concerns on becoming Prince of Galilee in 1099 was to erect a church above the cave in the centre of the city. Dedicated to the Annunciation, it was visited by the Russian pilgrim Daniel in 1106; every corner of the cave is related to something in the daily life of the Holy Family. He also mentions a second church built above a well and dedicated to the angel Gabriel.

The Beauty of the Women of Nazareth

'We travelled on to the city of Nazareth, where many miracles take place. In the synagogue there is kept the book in which the Lord wrote his ABC, and in this synagogue is the bench on which he sat with other children. Christians can lift the bench and move it about, but the Jews are completely unable to move it, and cannot drag it outside. The house of Saint Mary is now a basilica, and her clothes are the cause of frequent miracles. The Jewesses of that city are better looking than any other Jewesses in the whole country. They declare that this is Saint Mary's gift to them, for they also say that she was a relation of theirs.' (Piacenza Pilgrim (C6), *Travels* 5; trans. J. Wilkinson)

After the collapse of the Latin Kingdom at the HORNS OF HATTIN in 1187, a series of truces permitted pilgrims to get to Nazareth for just over a hundred years. Thereafter it became too dangerous, and only the very brave attempted to visit the city of ruins and murderous Moors (to paraphrase a traveller in 1598). In 1620 the Franciscans were permitted to buy back the ruins of the church of the Annunciation thanks to the benevolence of the DRUZE emir Fakhr-a-Din II (1591–1635), and thereafter managed to maintain a Christian presence despite incredible difficulties. With the approbation of another Muslim rebel, Daher el-Omar, they built a church in 1730 which was demolished in 1955 to make room for the new basilica.

Visit. Modern Nazareth is dominated by the massive basilica of the Annunciation; visible from anywhere in the town, it serves as a perfect orientation point.

The Basilica of the Annunciation

Open: 8.30–11.45 a.m. and 2–5 p.m.; 6 p.m. in summer; closed Sunday morning except for those who wish to attend mass. No shorts or sleeveless shirts are permitted. The building has been designed to enclose and protect the discoveries made in the exhaustive archaeological excavations. These can be seen in the lower church.

The present basilica (dedicated in 1968) preserves the outline of the C12 **Crusader church**, minus one bay at the west end. The main entrance facing Casa Nova Street gives access to the lower church. On the left, the north wall of the Crusader church is visible. The north-east corner with its spiral staircase is completely Crusader, as are significant portions of the three apses. The **six capitals** displayed in the museum were made for the Crusader church by artists from northern France. They had not yet been put in place when the news of Saladin's victory at Hattin arrived; they were hidden for safety and only came to light during the excavations. They represent episodes in the lives of the twelve Apostles drawn from the Bible and legend.

The **Byzantine remains** are conserved in an octagon whose floor level is lower than that of the Crusader church. The apse belonged to a small 18 m-long church of the mid-C5, which was built over what might have been a synagogue. Juxtaposed to the south nave was a monastery. On the west an atrium went as far as the present façade. The floor of this Byzantine church covered a small square basin into which one descended by seven steps. Very ambiguous graffiti incised into its plaster covering have persuaded the excavators that it was a pre-Constantinian baptistry. Just beside it is a mosaic panel whose north–south orientation suggests that it antedates the Byzantine church; the motif—a victory crown with trailing ribbons surrounding a monogram cross—is certainly Christian and could be dated to the C4. This mosaic is in line with a flight of steps leading down to a square mosaic of the same period whose inscription reads, 'Gift of Conon, deacon of Jerusalem'. The **small cave** behind is considered to have been dedicated, before the C4, to the martyr of the same name. The larger cave must have been venerated at the same time; the steps leading out on the far side have not been dated.

Stairways in the tower at either side of the main entrance lead to the upper church. An exit in the north wall leads into a courtyard from which one can look down into the **excavated area** and see silos, oil presses, storage areas, even traces of the foundations of houses; all belong to C1 AD Nazareth. The **museum** is on the lower level.

To reach the Church of St Joseph continue across the courtyard leaving the large Franciscan monastery on the right.

Church of St Joseph

Open: 8.30–11.45 a.m. and 2–5 p.m.; 6 p.m. in summer.

This church, built in 1914, follows the trace of a triapsidal medieval church. In the **crypt** a square basin (2×2 m) cut in the rock has a white mosaic floor carefully arranged to fit with a piece of black basalt let into the floor; six rectangles are outlined in black. Seven steps lead down into the basin. The arrangement is evocative of what has been identified as a pre-Constantinian baptistry in the Basilica of the Annunciation. The pieces of pottery in the plaster of the basin could be late Roman or early Byzantine.

Beside the basin a flight of rough steps lead down to a narrow passage which, after a 180 degree curve, opens into a 2 m-high **underground chamber**; it has been artificially enlarged and openings betray a number of bell-shaped silos at a still lower level. At the end furthest from the entrance there were four such silos, one above the other; the enlargement of the cave cut into the second from the top. It is not certain whether the extension of the cave was in any way related to the baptismal basin.

From the C17 the cave has been identified as the workshop of Joseph, a pious tradition that has no foundation. The gospels identify Joseph simply as a 'worker' (Matt. 13: 55), not specifically as a 'worker in wood' or carpenter; he might have been a smith or a stonecutter. It would perhaps be more realistic to think in terms of an all-purpose village builder.

Convent of the Sisters of Nazareth

Open only by previous appointment. Beneath the convent lies a **Jewish necropolis** containing a tomb sealed by a rolled stone. The masonry structures are medieval, and probably belonged to a Crusader monastery or convent. After the expulsion of the Franks, the site was used by the Muslims as a place of worship.

Negev

The Negev is best conceived as an isosceles triangle expanding north from Elat. The two long sides are the Egyptian border and the Jordan Valley. The short side is a line drawn from the south end of the DEAD SEA to Gaza. Deep sand inwards from the coast gradually gives way to a loess plain as the land rises. It was forced up in the Miocene period to create a range of mountains running east-north-east to west-south-west whose highest point is Har Ramon (1,033 m). At certain points the dome cracked. After water penetration had worn an opening to the east, erosion intensified ultimately creating a series of spectacular craters, Makhtesh Qatan (p. 401), Makhtesh Gadol, and MAKHTESH RAMON. The latter is 40 km long, 8 km wide, and 500 m deep. High on its rim at Mizpe Ramon is the **Makhtesh Ramon Visitors' Centre** whose displays illustrate the geology and natural history of the area (open: Sunday–Thursday and Saturday 9 a.m.–4.30 p.m.; Friday 9 a.m.–2.30 p.m.). East of the mountain range there are some wide plains as the land drops into the Jordan Valley.

The habitable areas of the Negev are the loess plain west of the mountains and the eastern edge of the mountains north of Elat. Traces of prehistoric tribes are everywhere in the loess plain. The beautiful gorge of EN AVDAT is the most accessible concentration of palaeolithic sites. According to the Bible, TEL BEER SHEVA was a centre of the activity of Abraham, Isaac, and Jacob. ARAD flourished in the third millennium, but had been desolate for 1,500 years when the Israelites fortified it and Beer Sheva.

In the C13 BC the Egyptians came to mine copper at TIMNA. The NABATAEANS appeared on the scene in the Hellenistic period, and developed a network of trade routes marked by cities such as AVDAT, MAMSHIT, NIZZANA, and SHIVTA. These were fed by desert farms, whose system of water management excites as much awe as admiration. Mamshit is linked to the Jordan Valley by the most spectacular ROMAN ROAD in the country at MAALE AQRABIM. Lonely forts, such as HAZEVA, protected the trade routes. In the Byzantine period the old Nabataean cities filled with churches, and pilgrims crossed the desert to Sinai. The synagogue at MAON attests Jewish presence.

Nimrud (01)   ★

The keep towering above a long, narrow-waisted enclosure gives the great fortress the air of an alert guard-dog ready to spring. Its raised head faces Damascus; behind and below is BANYAS. From the battlements one can see other great castles, Beaufort (1139) on the cliffs of the Litani river (north-west), and Chateauneuf at HUNIN on the heights beyond Qiryat Shemona (south-west). The wide sweep of the Huleh valley, with its ordered agriculture, gives no hint of the sacrifices required to drain its malarial swamps.

Any attempt to write the history of the fortress is complicated by uncertainty regarding medieval allusions to 'the fortress of Banyas'. They could refer to the fortifications of the town or to Nimrud. If in the past the latter was assumed, it now appears that the former should be preferred. It is certainly wrong to think of Nimrud as the bulwark of Banyas. As the crow flies they are 2.5 km apart. Were Banyas besieged, the garrison of Nimrud could help only by a counter-attack in the open, which would leave the fortress undefended!

In the light of the available evidence Nimrud is an entirely Muslim fortification designed to defend the road to Damascus from a possible Crusader attack from the coast. Inscriptions commemorate Ayyubid construction in 1228–30, and again in 1239–40. The name Qalaat Subeiba ('Cliff Fortress') is first attested in 1253. Arab tradition subsequently associated it with the mighty hunter Nimrud (Gen. 10: 8–9), around whom many legends accumulated. As part of his comprehensive campaign against the Crusaders the Mamluk sultan Baybars I (1260–77) extensively remodelled the fortress. After the final defeat of the Crusaders in the Holy Land at AKKO in 1291 Nimrud lost its strategic value. It became the seat of a regional governor, and in the C14–C16 served as a prison. Thereafter it was completely abandoned.

Visit (Fig. 101). The medieval route between Banyas and Subeibe is paralleled by a marked hiking trail (1151); it is a 2.5 km walk with an average gradient of between 30 and 40 degrees. The access road from the

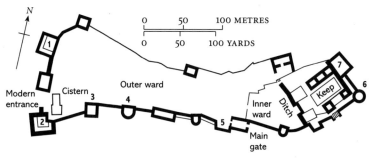

▲ **Fig. 101.** Nimrud (after Solar).

Banyas–Neve Ativ road (route 989) leads to a parking-lot. Open: 8 a.m.–4 p.m.; Fridays to 2 p.m. (toilets and drinking water).

The two **towers** [1 and 2], which dominate the parking-lot, perfectly illustrate the changes that the Mamluks made to Ayyubid structures. In each case small square towers were doubled in size by the addition of rooms on the western and southern sides. In [2] the original tower became the central chamber, and five of its eight firing slits were enlarged into doorways leading into a series of small rooms with thirteen firing slits. Baybars thus almost doubled the number of archers who could be deployed at this point.

Two building phases are also discernible in the great **cistern**. The northern part, with the original access steps, has barrel vaulting, whereas the southern part (with the modern entrance) has cross vaulting. Rain was the only source of water, and its conservation was a high priority. There is another cistern to the north in the courtyard, and still others in a series of towers [1, 5, 7].

The location of the **kitchen** just inside suggests that the entrance at the base of the tower [3] was for provisions. The central pier of the **circular tower** [4] supports a pointed annular vault, to which there are no parallels. The **principal entrance** of the fortress was in the eastern face of a massive tower with a levelled ward outside.

The nerve centre of any fortress was **the keep**, the most strongly fortified part of the complex. Here attackers who broke through into the outer ward had to surmount the wall protecting the inner ward, and cross a ditch before arriving at another wall, which formed the third line of defence. There is a postern gate at the base of the **circular tower** [6]. The **north-eastern tower** [7] is the best built of all the towers. Two massive piers create six cross-vaulted bays.

The steep slope outside explains why the **north wall** had far fewer towers than the south wall; no serious attack could be mounted from this side. A staircase within the walls of the **north-western tower** [1] leads to a postern gate in the ditch, from which there is a path to the parking-lot.

Nizzana (B27)

Once a NABATAEAN frontier post, Nizzana today is 3.5 km from the Israel–Egyptian border. The remains do not bear comparison with those of nearby SHIVTA, but it is the starting point of a road (route 10) that runs south along the border for some 45 km when there is a turn to the east on to route 171 which joins the Beer Sheva–Elat road just north of Mizpe Ramon. From the observation areas there are spectacular views over the desert, particularly of the region around Qadesh Barnea, which was fortified by the Israelites in the C10 BC and became an important site in the Deuteronomic history of the exodus from Egypt.

The Nabataeans founded Nizzana in the C3 BC as a trading post at a point where the route from Elat to Gaza crossed a desert road from Palestine to Egypt. In the C1 BC a large building (a temple?) was reached by a monumental staircase. The traffic on the east–west route enabled it to survive when in the early C2 AD the Roman emperor Trajan (AD 98–117) diverted the trade from Elat to Damascus. The Byzantine period saw a significant growth in prosperity. In the late C3 or early C4 AD the fort was extended to house a cavalry regiment; graffiti show them to have used both horses and camels. Not long afterwards the North Church was built. Gifts of land to this frontier militia expanded the town at the foot of the hill; tax registers from the years 587–9 show that it had 1,500 inhabitants distributed among 116 houses. This was the period of Nizzana's greatest importance, because about 600 the Gaza–Elat route was opened again for trade, and pilgrims began to come through here on their way to Sinai. The life of the town is documented in great detail by a find of late-Byzantine papyri.

The transition to Arab rule in the C7 was peaceful, but the land that fed the city fell progressively into disuse as the Muslims gradually assumed direct control, and Nizzana passed away quietly in the C8.

Visit (Fig. 102). Little remains of the Byzantine buildings because the stones were removed to build various structures throughout the area, notably the Turkish military hospital which dominates the site today. The ground-plans, however, are perfectly clear. The steps leading up from the main road must approximate the line of access in the Nabataean and Byzantine period. At the top turn left for the fortress and right for the North Church.

The Fortress

This late C4 AD structure [2] is nothing more than a great enclosed space (85 × 35 m) with small rooms on both long sides and an enormous **cistern** [1] fed by run-off rain-water from the courtyard. Unlike the

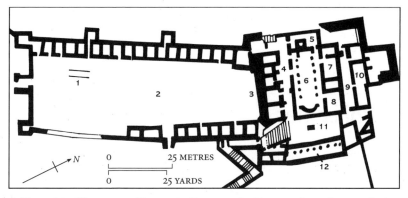

▲ **Fig. 102.** Nizzana. 1. Cistern; 2. Fortress; 3. C2 BC wall; 4. Courtyard; 5. Narthex/baptistery; 6. Church of SS Sergius and Bacchus; 7. Chapel; 8. Sacristy; 9. Courtyard; 10. Covered gallery; 11. Courtyard; 12. Covered gallery.

Crusader castles, it was not built to withstand a siege, but to house the garrison and to serve as a place of refuge for the population of the town during bedouin raids of short duration, as at AVDAT. The wide **north wall** of the fortress [**3**] is all that remains of the C2 BC structure, which covered the area now occupied by the North Church.

The North Church

This complex is dated to the C4 AD. The **courtyard** [**11**] at the top of the steps communicates with two other courtyards [**4** and **9**] which isolated the church from the surrounding buildings. The **church** is dedicated to SS Sergius and Bacchus, and had a single free-standing apse. The two doors in the north wall led to a side chapel [**7**] and a sacristy [**8**]; these were added in the C7, at the same time as the transformation of the original narthex [**5**] into a **baptistery**.

The function of the two long covered galleries [**10** and **12**] is not clear; they may have served the monastic community as refectory and dormitory. Two of the small rooms opening on to the south courtyard [**4**] were originally a **martyrium** dedicated to SS Stephen and Sergius; the others were added in the C7.

The South Church

This free-standing edifice is some 60 m south-east of the fortress, whose south gate provides the easiest means of access. The wall linking the two structures is not original. The two doors are in the north wall, one leading into the church, the other into a **narthex** flanked by a small atrium. The fact that this church has three apses shows it to be later than the North Church. Dedicated to the Virgin Mary, it is dated to the early C7. The

chapel along the south side has only a single apse but three aisles. The sacristy in the south-west corner has entrances to both the chapel and the church.

Philistines

According to the Bible, the Philistines first appear in the Patriarchal period (Gen. 20–6). These references are certainly anachronistic, because the earliest traces of their distinctive material culture appear only in the C11 BC. They were then the opponents of the nascent Israelite state, and a later writer thought it appropriate to give their name to the enemies of Abraham many centuries before.

The Philistines are first mentioned by name as a subgroup of the Sea Peoples whose land and sea assault on Egypt was defeated by Rameses III c.1190 BC. Some fifty years later they and others of the Sea Peoples had firmly established themselves on the coastal plain. The Sherden appear north of MOUNT CARMEL. The Sekels/Sikuli (once known as the Tjekker) were centred on DOR, and the Philistines occupied the south. Their northernmost city was APHEK, but their power was concentrated in the five cities, ASHQELON, Ashdod, Gaza, Gath, and Ekron (TEL MIQNE) (Josh. 13: 3).

The Aegean origins of the Philistines (Amos 9: 7) are confirmed by their earliest pottery and cult objects; the closest parallels come from Crete, Cyprus, and the Peloponnese. They also brought with them the newly discovered technique of producing carbonized iron (steel). This gave them an advantage over the Israelites in the mountains, to whom they sold agricultural implements but not offensive weapons (see box). The story of Samson amusingly illustrates the quality of the relationship between the two peoples (Judges 14–16). The expansionist ambitions of both gradually increased the tension, which eventually exploded into open conflict.

Matters came to a head towards the end of the C11 BC, when the Israelites elected first Saul and then David to combat the better-organized Philistine forces (1 Sam.). Just at this point, however, when Israel was finally achieving her social and political identity, the Philistines were losing theirs. Though the armour of Goliath (1 Sam. 17: 5–7) still reflected Aegean models, a distinctively Philistine material culture had disappeared by the time of David (c.1000 BC). This makes it difficult to continue to speak of the Philistines as an ethnic group from the C10 BC onwards. The Bible continues to use the name in succeeding centuries, but it should be understood to mean the non-Jewish inhabitants of the coastal plain without the specific connotation it had earlier.

The Steel Monopoly

'There was not a single blacksmith throughout the territory of Israel, the Philistines' reasoning being, "We do not want the Hebrews making swords or spears." Hence, the Israelites were in the habit of going down individually to the Philistines to sharpen their ploughshares, axes, mattocks, and scythes. The price was two-thirds of a shekel for ploughshares and axes, and one-third for sharpening mattocks and straightening goads. So it was that on the day of battle, no one in the army with Saul and Jonathan had either sword or spear; only Saul and his son Jonathan were so equipped.' (1 Sam. 13: 19–22).

The original territory of the Philistines was known as Philistia (Exod. 15: 14; Isa. 14: 29), which by the C5 BC had been Graecized into Palestine (Herodotus 7: 89). Gradually the term acquired a wider extension, and by the C1 AD was commonly applied to the whole country between the Jordan and the sea (Josephus, Philo). Only in AD 135, however, did Syria-Palestina become the official name of what had been the Roman province of Judaea.

Qasrin (O4)   ★

A vivid picture of life on the GOLAN in a Jewish village of the Byzantine period has been created at Ancient Qasrin Park where a synagogue and part of the village has been excavated and reconstructed.

Jewish occupation of the site began in the late C4 AD. The first roughly square synagogue was dismantled in the early C6 and transformed into a rectangular building by moving out the north wall which contained the principal entrance. The building was orientated towards Jerusalem by a platform (*bema*) supporting the Torah shrine in the centre of the south wall. A century later subsidence necessitated substantial repairs. A significant decrease in the quality of the workmanship points to a deteriorating economic situation. The earthquake of 746 which destroyed the synagogue also devastated the village, which is estimated to have sheltered some 300 people in seventy-five houses. After a brief attempt at resettlement the site was abandoned until the C13–C15 when new occupants moved into the ruins, repaired the houses, and transformed the northern part of the synagogue into a mosque. At the beginning of this century Syrian villagers in search of arable land reused the buildings. They fled in 1967.

Visit (Fig. 103). The park is located a kilometre east of the town of Qasrin

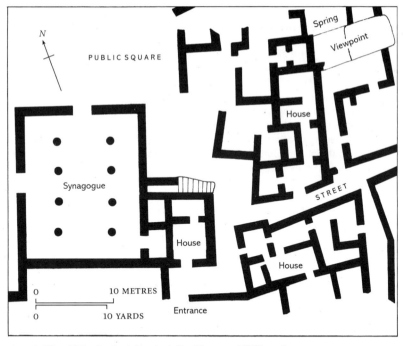

▲ **Fig. 103.** Ancient Qasrin (after Maoz and Killibrew).

on route 9088. Open: 8 a.m.–4 p.m.; Friday to 3 p.m. Directly in front on entering the ancient village is a two-room **house** dated to the mid-C5, but which was used in all the periods of occupation. To the right is a larger house with an identical history. It has been restored to create a **typical Byzantine dwelling with all its furnishings.** The main door opens into the kitchen, whose rough stone floor would originally have been finished in smooth plaster as elsewhere in the house. A small oven is set within a mud-brick chimney running up through a bedroom above, which it heated in the cold Golan winter. One door leads into a store-room containing farming implements. The other communicates with the living-room which has a food storage area at one end. The table is set with local and imported ware. The ladder gives access to a second bedroom in which a wool blanket covers a rope-webbing bed. Outside to the east is the courtyard in which domestic animals and fowl were housed. It was the centre of household activity for most of the year. Small hand mills and two ovens symbolize the never-ending task of food preparation. Large jars stored water.

On the east side of the excavated area is an **observation platform** on the roof of a stone house. In addition to providing an overview of the site which easily distinguishes streets from buildings, it conveys an impression of the original extent of the village and the land use (olives, cereals, and grazing) from which it lived. Even more important to survival was the little **spring** (below to the right) which tranquilly fills the bedrock basin.

The **synagogue** is the best preserved in the Golan. The restrained dignity of the carving of the lintel and jambs of the C6 main entrance is complemented by the sober proportions of the interior. There was a secondary door in the west wall, and worshippers were accommodated on two rows of benches along the walls. The *bema* projected from the pilasters in the south wall as far as the first two pillars. The foundation of the first synagogue is visible in the trench in the north-east corner.

Qubeiba (J17)

Venerated since 1500 as the site of Emmaus where Jesus, in the breaking of bread, revealed himself to Cleophas and another disciple (Luke 24: 13–35); a wall of the very house of Cleophas is shown within the Franciscan church.

The truth is rather more prosaic. The site lies on a Roman road leading down to the plain. Along its edge Arabs built houses in the C8–C9 AD. Some time between 1114 and 1164 the Canons of the Holy Sepulchre founded a village here which they called Parva Mahomeria, possibly because of a small Muslim shrine (el-Qubeiba = 'a little cupola'). Their purpose was to intensify the agriculture of the vast domain from which they drew their substance. They may also have had the charitable thought of providing a resting-place for pilgrims *en route* to Jerusalem. The complex included a church and a small castle in addition to the usual buildings of a farming village. At a later period Christians assumed that the foundation commemorated an event in the life of Christ. What could it be? The distance from Jerusalem given by Luke (according to certain manuscripts) suggested Emmaus. And so it was. The Crusaders themselves located Emmaus at ABU GHOSH.

Visit. After NABI SAMWIL on route 436 take the road to Biddu. Go straight through the village towards Bet Inan. The Franciscan property is on the right just over a kilometre from the Biddu crossroads. Open: 8–11.30 a.m. and 2–5 p.m.; in summer to 6 p.m.

The Crusader castle was to the left of the present entrance. The **church** was reconstructed in 1902, but the lower part of the three apses is medieval. The **wall preserved in the floor** is not parallel to those of the church. At one time thought to be part of a Jewish house which the Crusaders preserved by incorporating it in their church, it is more likely to be a later edifice built in its ruins. The **Roman road** is bordered by the

houses of the medieval village; the basins for the preparation of olive oil or wine and the millstones underline its agricultural character.

Qumran* (M18)   ★★

Community centre of the ESSENES who produced the famous Dead Sea Scrolls. They lived in natural caves in the adjoining cliffs, in tents, and in underground chambers cut in the soft marl. They gathered here for all the religious and economic activities of the sect. The well-preserved ruins, situated on a little plateau on the north-west shore of the DEAD SEA, make it easy to visualize the daily life of these people whose austere dedication excited the admiration of the Roman statesman Pliny the Elder and the Greek orator and philosopher Dio Chrysostom.

The Essenes were not the first to occupy this site. In the C8 BC the Israelites established here a small fort (A in Fig. 104); it may have served as the centre of a farming settlement, the 'City of Salt' mentioned in Josh. 15: 61–2. The fort had been long abandoned when the Teacher of Righteousness and some fifty Essenes settled there about 150 BC. They took over the earlier building with its round cistern, and modified the plan only to the extent of adding two rectangular stepped cisterns beside the round one, and two kilns in the south-east corner (B in Fig. 104).

At the end of the reign of John Hyrcanus (134–103 BC) an influx of new members necessitated an extensive rebuilding programme (C in Fig. 104). These buildings (which we visit) were damaged by an earthquake in 31 BC, after the Essenes had been forced to abandon the site as the result of military action in the days when Herod the Great fought for his kingdom (40–37 BC). They returned after some years to continue their monastic form of life until the Romans expelled them in AD 68. They were no threat to the Romans, but the fortress-like building would have been visible when Vespasian came to the north end of the Dead Sea to test its reputed properties by throwing in a number of bound non-swimmers to see if they would float (*War* 4: 477). A small Roman garrison remained on the site to control the traffic on the Dead Sea until the fall of MASADA in AD 74.

Visit (C in Fig. 104). Open: Sunday–Thursday and Saturday 8 a.m.– 5 p.m.; Friday to 4 p.m. Toilets and refreshments available.

A platform on the **tower** [4] permits a good general view of the whole complex. In particular one can see the double line of the **aqueduct** going towards the cliffs. The Essenes had constructed a dam (no longer visible) in the Wadi Qumran; water was directed through a rock-cut tunnel (still extant) into the aqueduct and so into the large **decantation pool** [3]. Sand sank to the bottom and clear water flowed from the top of

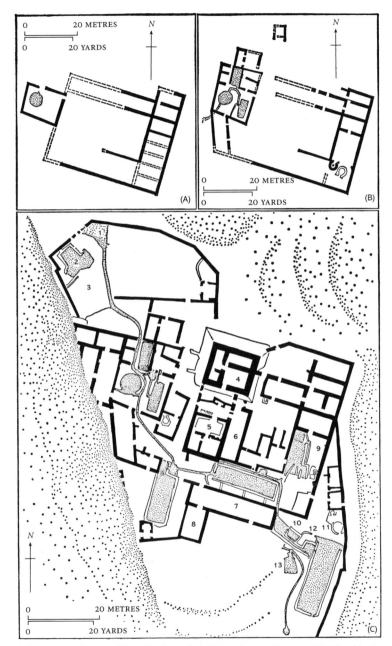

▲ **Fig. 104.** Qumran (after Couäsnon). 1. C1 AD decantation pool; 2. Ritual bath; 3. Original decantation pool; 4. Tower with viewpoint; 5. Council chamber; 6. Room below scriptorium; 7. Refectory; 8. Pantry; 9. Earthquake crack; 10. Ritual bath; 11. Kilns; 12. Potter's wheel emplacement; 13. Clay preparation.

the pool into the channel system and thence to the cisterns (shaded). This area naturally silted up when the site was abandoned in the late C1 BC. Rather than dig it out when they returned, the Essenes simply extended the channel to a new smaller decantation pool [1].

As gravity moved the water through the system, each of the **cisterns** (shaded) filled in turn; some have their own decantation basins. Associated with the water system, but not part of it, are two **ritual baths** [2 and 10]; the Essenes had to purify themselves by bathing in cold water before entering the 'holy temple' of the refectory.

This **refectory** [7] was easy to identify. The adjoining room [8] contained over 700 bowls arranged in piles of a dozen, 210 plates, 75 beakers, and assorted other vessels for food and drink. In addition, the floor sloped from a water inlet to the external door at the far end; this ingenious cleansing system shows the room to have been a place where dirt was inevitable and cleanliness essential. Here the community expected to receive the Priestly and Royal Messiahs (see box). The members of the community received bread, wine, and a single bowl of one kind of food; this was sometimes meat (mutton, beef, goat), usually boiled but sometimes roasted. At least some of these meals had a religious significance (at present not fully understood) because the meat bones, carefully covered with broken potsherds, were found buried in most of the open areas.

The community was run on strictly democratic lines; debates took place in a **council chamber** [5]. Just inside the door is a water-basin which could be filled from the outside. Perhaps they worked on a conclave system; no exit without a decision! The stairs outside the door led to the **scriptorium** [6] on the first floor, a 5 m-long plastered table and two inkwells were recovered from the debris in the room below. Here, presumably, many of the scrolls found in the cave were copied.

Near the cistern [9] cracked by the earthquake in 31 BC is a complete **pottery workshop**. The clay was first washed in a plastered basin [13] with a small cistern fed from the main channel. It was then left to mature in a storage pit, before the final mix was made in a shallow tank beside the

The Messianic Banquet

'When they shall gather for the common table, to eat and to drink new wine, when the common table shall be set for eating and the new wine poured for drinking, let no man extend his hand over the first-fruits of bread and wine before the Priest; for it is he who shall bless the first-fruits of bread and wine, and shall be the first to extend his hand over the bread. Thereafter, the Messiah of Israel shall extend his hand over the bread, and all the Congregation of the Community shall utter a blessing each man in the order of his dignity.' (*The Messianic Rule* 2: 17–21; trans. Vermes)

circular pit [**12**] in which the wheel was set. The kilns [**11**] were nearby, one for domestic objects, the other for the large jars in which some of the scrolls were found.

The **cemetery,** 50 m east of the buildings towards the Dead Sea, contains about 1,100 tombs marked by an oval outline and arranged in orderly rows. Very few of the thirty-two men and seven women (plus two children) in the forty-one excavated tombs had passed their fortieth year.

A marker south of the buildings points to the openings of **Cave 4** on the far side of a deeply eroded cut. Originally a bell-shaped underground dwelling, this artificial cave contained 40,000 fragments of documents. None of the ten other caves in which manuscripts were found is marked. Caves 1–3 and 11 are in the cliffs between 1 and 3 km north of the buildings. A number (caves 5 and 7–10) have completely disappeared through erosion.

Cave 6 is the most accessible cave in which manuscripts were found. Follow the path beside the double line of the aqueduct going towards the cliffs. The triangular cave is visible (below and to the left) from the point where the double line of the aqueduct has been obliterated by a rockfall. The path running above Cave 6 is much safer than it looks. Very quickly traces of cement on the rock to the right betray the presence of the **aqueduct**. Once around the outcrop the channel of the aqueduct leading to the 20 m-long **tunnel** is visible about 3 m above the path on the right. It is possible to go through the tunnel on hands and knees to discover other channels coming from where the dam used to be.

If one climbs straight ahead instead of turning left over Cave 6 it is relatively easy to detect the **cliff path** used by the Essenes to reach their farms in the plain above. Not only does it follow what is obviously the easiest line, but the rock underfoot is worn smooth, and parts have been levelled by small retaining walls on the downslope side.

Ramat Hanadiv (G9)

Ramat Hanadiv is the site of Baron de Rothschild's mausoleum whose grounds have been developed into beautiful gardens and a great park containing a number of important archaeological sites; there are walks to a prehistoric cave, a C1–C5 AD farm unit, a Roman theatre, aqueduct, and bath-house. The entrance is signposted on route 652 between Zikhron Ya'aqov and Binyamina. Open: Sunday–Thursday and Saturday 8 a.m.– 4 p.m.; Friday to 2 p.m. Excellent explanatory leaflets for the different trails and sites are available in English.

The Cave

The Kebara cave is one of the most celebrated prehistoric caves in Israel and has given its name to the first part of the Mesolithic period (18,000–12,000 BC). Like its successor, the Natufian period (12,000–9000 BC), the Kebaran is characterized by artistically worked bone instruments and small flints which were set into handles to produce composite tools such as sickles; one sickle handle was carved in the form of a young gazelle. Occupation of the cave began about 60,000 BC, and is thus parallel to the latter part of the occupation of the CARMEL CAVES. Excavations are still in progress and the cave is off-limits to the public for the present.

Visit. Following the blue trail from the parking-lot it takes fifteen minutes fast walking to reach the edge of the wadi; the trail down to the cave is clayey and rough. The opening of the cave is 15 m wide and gives access to a roughly rectangular hall some 25 m deep.

The Farm (Mansur el-Aqqab)

The first farm was set up in the early C1 AD and remained in operation for a century. Its establishment may be related to the development of CAESAREA; as the population of the city grew the demand for agricultural produces increased. A wall enclosed a 2,800 m² area containing a threshing floor in addition to oil and wine presses. Why the farm was abandoned is unclear. The date coincides with the suppression of the Second Revolt (AD 132–5), but there are no signs of violent destruction. In the C5 AD an L-shaped two-storey villa was built on the ruins. Vaulted stables constituted the eastern wing. As the family increased, dwellings and animal pens were built in the internal courtyard. At both periods the economic base of the estate was the production of wine for Caesarea. When teetotal Muslims occupied the city in the C7, this market dried up, and the estate slowly declined.

Visit. A twenty-five-minute stroll on the red trail from the parking-lot brings one to the ruins which occupy the best viewpoint in the park. The narrow coastal strip inside DOR broadens out dramatically into the majestic **plain of Sharon** (Isa. 35: 2). Two *kurkar* ridges (water-hardened sandstone) 1 and 4 km inside the present shore represent ancient coastlines. The plain between the innermost ridge and the foothills is ideal for agriculture and has been farmed since at least 3000 BC.

The **farm unit** has been restored and has excellent signs. The enclosure is entered from the east as in the C1. The highest walls are those of the C5 building, whose entrance was in the west wall. They rest on the remains of the C1 farmhouse within its much larger enclosure wall. The Jewish identity of its inhabitants is indicated by a **ritual bath** (*mikveh*) in what became the Byzantine courtyard; a massive **tower** underlines their need for a place of refuge in such an isolated area. There was another residential block in the south-west corner of the C1 enclosure. Structures in the south-east corner provided storage areas and stabling for animals.

The two **wine presses** with a square treading floor are C1, whereas the circular mosaic-floored press to the south is Byzantine; all three have decantation basins to catch the liquid. The **oil press** had a rotating upper millstone which cracked the olives in preparation for the final pressing.

The Village, Aqueduct, and Bath

En Tzur is very reminiscent of EN YAEL near Jerusalem. Houses of the Roman period dominated a tunnel spring, which fed a bathhouse and irrigated the terraces below. En Yael looks out into a narrow valley, whereas En Tzur has a splendid view over the intensely cultivated Biqat Hannadiv, in which rise the springs that fed the high-level aqueduct of CAESAREA.

Visit. Follow the green trail from the entrance to the parking-lot, and make a sharp right turn beside the **ancient quarry** at the first intersection. The ruins of the Arab village of Umm el-Aleq overlie **a farming village** founded at the end of the C4 BC. The small houses were dwarfed by their C1 AD protective **fortress**. A 3.1 m-wide *proteichisma* defends the base of the 1.3 m wall on all sides. There is a central-pillared stairwell in the north-east corner of the three-storey tower, and a neat bath-tub in the north-eastern room. This perfect example of a fortified village (e.g. Josephus, *Antiquities* 17: 290) appears to have been abandoned by its inhabitants in AD 66. Caesarea was very close and 20,000 Jews were massacred there at the beginning of the first Jewish revolt against Rome (*War* 2: 457).

The trail continues downhill to **three shafts**, which were cut into the bedrock to facilitate construction of the water tunnel which runs into the hill for 57 m (bring a flashlight). It is cut through a level where porous limestone rests on darker impermeable volcanic tuff. The **round structure** above the exit from the cliff is the base of a tower for the raising of pigeons; their flesh was eaten and their droppings were prized as fertilizer. Still common in Egypt, the care and management of pigeons is documented for the Roman period by Marcus Terentius Varro (116–27 BC), *Rerum rusticarum* 3: 7.1–7, 11.

The roofed channel with an inspection hole carries water to a large reservoir. It served a late C1 BC **Roman bath** whose remains are now protected by a roof. Steps gave access to the cold room, the warm room adjoined it. Note the positioning of the doors to avoid loss of heat from the hot room. The lowest room contained the furnace which heated the air beneath the floor of the hot room. Warm water could have been fed to the rectangular bath from a boiler above the furnace.

In the C3 AD the water from the spring fed an **aqueduct**, which runs off at an angle on the west side of the large square reservoir, and terminates in the pools at Shuni (see below). The water was celebrated for its magical powers. In AD 333 the Bordeaux pilgrim (AD 333) wrote that 'At the third milestone from Caesarea is Mount Syna, where there is a spring and women who wash in it become pregnant.' This explains the 2,000 Byzantine coins and many pieces of jewellery found in the tunnel beneath one of the shafts. They were offered as a bribe or in gratitude.

The Roman Theatre

For those who like exercise it is possible to walk to Shuni by following the mauve trail from the parking-lot. It is easier, however, to drive down to the bottom of the hill on route 652 and enter Jabotinsky Park. Open: Sunday–Thursday and Saturday 9 a.m.–6 p.m.; Friday 8 a.m.–1 p.m.

The little **theatre** is within the building, and has been partially restored. The diameter of the orchestra suggests that it could have seated between 1,000 and 1,500. Constructed at the end of the C2 or the beginning of the C3 AD, the theatre was in part rebuilt after suffering during the SAMARITAN revolt of 484, but a century later, in response to the anti-pagan edicts of the emperor Justinian (527–65), it was transformed into an industrial area. There is an **oil press** just to the right on entering the theatre. It served until the C8.

The existence of this theatre is surprising when one remembers that the great theatre of Caesarea was less than 5 km away. The reason is given by the Byzantine name of the site, Maiumas. Found in various spellings thoughout the region, this word indicates the scene of an orgiastic pagan feast in which water games played an important part, and which also involved plays in honour of Dionysos and Aphrodite. A **great pool** has been brought to light between the theatre and route 652. It was fed from the **aqueduct** mentioned above. The overflow continued along a channel which is visible beside the road between the pool and the entrance to the park.

On the far side of the road there is a perfectly preserved section of a **Roman street** designed for quick drainage. The Hadrianic aqueduct from Ammikam, which fed the high-level aqueduct of Caesarea, runs along one side of the street (p. 215). Further west it was joined by the overflow of the Shuni aqueduct. The function of the **octagonal structure** on the other side of the street is debated. It may be a small market or a temple dedicated to the healing god, Asclepios.

Ramla (F16)

The only city in the region founded by the Arabs, Ramla was for several centuries the capital and biggest city of Palestine. Its extraordinary cisterns make it unique.

The city was planned and built in AD 715–17 by Suliman, one of the sons of Abd al-Malik, in an effort to emulate his father, who had built the DOME OF THE ROCK, and his brother al-Walid, who had erected the Great Mosque in Damascus and the EL-AKSA MOSQUE in Jerusalem. The very name of the city, 'The Sandy Place', explains why there had been no previous occupation; there were no springs. Wells produced only tainted water. Hence the extraordinary development of cisterns to collect rain-water.

Severely damaged by an earthquake in 1034, Ramla fell to the Crusaders without a battle in 1099. It became a vital link on their supply route from Jaffa to Jerusalem, and its possession was fiercely disputed by the Fatamid army based in ASHQELON between 1100 and 1110; the Egyptians succeeded in occupying it for two short months in 1102. Saladin failed to take it in 1177, but found the gates open when he arrived after his decisive victory at the HORNS OF HATTIN in 1187. In 1191, during the Third Crusade, he tore down the fortifications. When Richard the Lion-Heart arrived in November of that year he found the place empty; it became his headquarters during the two abortive attempts to penetrate as far as Jerusalem. In the peace treaty of 1192 the city returned to Muslim hands, but it reverted to the Crusaders in 1205 and remained in their control until it was taken by the Mamluk sultan Baybars in 1268. Though greatly reduced in size, Ramla enjoyed a certain renaissance under the Mamluks in the C14, but thereafter declined into a small market town, which served as a centre for European commerce until the restoration of Jaffa at the end of the C17.

Visit. The three sites worth visiting are within fifteen minutes' walk of each other. There is a parking-lot beside the Great Mosque. Both it and the tower of the White Mosque are visible from the main street, Rehov Herzl. All sites have the same opening hours: Sunday–Thursday 8 a.m.–2 p.m.; Fridays and eves of holy days 8 a.m.–noon; Saturdays and holy days 8.30 a.m.–3.30 p.m.

The Great Mosque

Open when the guardian can be found; closed during the times of prayer. Its function as a mosque dates only from 1268, according to an inscription of Baybars. In the C12 it had served as the **Crusader cathedral** of Ramla, and was dedicated to St John. In curious opposition to its sister church, St George in Lod, which was destroyed and rebuilt several times during the Crusades, it has remained intact, even to the roof. Traces of foundations would suggest that there was once a belfry beside the main door in the west wall; it may have been considered a strong point by Saladin in 1191 and thus demolished. An inscription dates the present minaret to 1314. The construction date of the church is not known.

The Cistern of Saint Helena

It is signposted from Rehov Herzl. At the junction of Herzl and Weizmann

▲ **The Tower of the Forty at Ramla.** Firing slits in the 30 m-high tower constructed by the Mamluk sultan Muhammad ibn Qalaun in 1318 indicate that it was intended to be more than a mere minaret.

Streets turn north into HaHagana Street; the cistern is located in a small fenced area some 70 m down on the right-hand side oppposite a public park. The roof of the cistern looks like a row of concrete furrows.

The origin of the present name is obscure, and the attribution erroneous. The **cistern** was constructed during the reign of the Abbasid Caliph Harun ar-Rashid, and an inscription dates its completion to May 789. It is best visited in the boat provided. Originally it was six bays long (25 m), but the southernmost collapsed at the beginning of the C20. The side walls converge towards the south, but this is compensated for by the diminishing projection of the wall-piers in this direction. Special attention should be paid to the **pointed arches**. They represent the earliest dated instance of the systematic and exclusive use of this technique, which may have been invented by Armenian architects working for the

Umayyads. The square holes in the roof of each of the twenty-four bays permitted a number of people to draw water simultaneously by means of buckets and ropes.

The White Mosque

The site is marked by the tall square tower visible from Herzl Street; it can be reached by taking either Weizmann or Dani Mass Streets.

The 30 m-high **tower**, according to an inscription over the entrance, was constructed in 1318 by the Mamluk sultan Muhammad ibn Qalaun. The careful provision for access to firing slits indicates that it was intended to be more than a mere minaret, even though it contains no rooms. The smaller topmost level is of modern construction; all that is known of the original is that its interior was circular and higher than at present. The local name, 'The Tower of the Forty', is given different explanations: for Muslims the reference is to the companions of the Prophet, whereas for Christians (who took the tower to be a belfry) it is to a group of unidentified martyrs.

The tower stands in the middle of the north wall of a **great square** (95 × 95 m). The two-aisle **mosque** runs along the entire length of the south wall with the *mihrab* in the centre. There is a perceptible shift in orientation after the fourth central pillar from the east end. The eastern portion is dated to the C7–C8; the rest to the C13. The same two periods of construction are also reflected in the **porticoes** along the east and west walls. At least one of the three vast **cisterns** beneath the esplanade between the mosque and the tower must date from the Umayyad period. The one parallel to the façade of the mosque is two bays wide and eleven bays long; the other two are each three bays wide and six bays long. An underground **aqueduct** fed the south and west cisterns, whereas the east cistern took the run-off from inside the north wall.

The Capital of Palestine

'Ramla possesses magnificent hostelries and pleasant baths, dainty food and various condiments, spacious houses, fine mosques, and broad roads. As a capital it has many advantages. It is situated on the plain, and yet is near both to the mountains and to the sea. There grow both fig-trees and palms; its fields need no irrigation, and are by nature fruitful and rich. The disadvantages, on the other hand, are that in winter the place is a slough of mud, while in summer it is a powder-box of sand where no water flows, neither is anything green, nor is the soil humid, nor does snow ever fall. Fleas here abound. The wells are deep and salt, and the rain-water is hoarded in closed cisterns. Hence the poor go thirsty, and strangers seek water in vain.' (Mukaddasi (C10), *Description of Syria* 164; trans. G. Le Strange)

Roman Roads

The function of this entry is to introduce the curious to an aspect of archaeological exploration which they might not have considered previously. Thus it focuses on roads which have unique features or which are relatively well preserved over a considerable distance.

In the South

Jerusalem – Bet Guvrin (J18, H18, G19)

The new road running along the valley below EN YAEL follows the line of a Roman road. All the features mentioned here can be reached by car. Some 2.5 km to the west of En Yael on the road to Battir is a fountain, **En Hanniyeh**, whose deep niche is flanked by Corinthian pilasters. It was constructed as a service to travellers when the Roman road was built by the emperor Hadrian in the C2 AD. In the C14–C15 it was identified as the place on the road from Jerusalem to Gaza where the deacon Philip baptized the eunuch of the queen of Ethiopia (Acts 8: 26–40). Roman kerbstones are clearly visible to the west of the spring above the modern road. To find the continuation of the Roman road take the road up through the village of **Battir**, which has two noteworthy features.

The first is the extraordinary **late Roman/Byzantine terraces** that fill the theatre-like depression in the centre of the village. Note the technique by which water is transferred from each terrace to the one below. The second is located on the ridge that creates the skyline to the west as one drives up the main street. It can be reached from a path to the right at the point where the street makes a hairpin bend.

This is Khirbet el-Yahud 'the Jewish ruins', the site of **Bethar** where Bar Kokhba was defeated by the Roman legions in AD 135. A hastily built wall around the summit protected the remnants of his weary fighters. The most vulnerable point was the saddle linking the hilltop to the main ridge to the south. The Jews cut a ditch 5 m deep and 15 m wide through the rock. After a long siege, however, the Romans succeeded in building an assault ramp across the ditch (both are still visible). Then the end came quickly. The road to the south-east from Battir runs through two large legion camps, which can be seen only from the air. At the junction with route 375 turn right.

From route 375 one can look down into the valley just west of Matta. Nestling beside the stream at the bottom of the valley are the ruins of the **medieval Cistercian abbey** of *Salutatio* (Allar as-Sufla; Horvat Tannur). As the road enters the forest a dirt road (route 6346) branches off to the right. To the left is a large rock-cut cistern. Just beyond the first turn and to the right is **Horvat Hanot** (Khirbet el-Khan: 1545/1244). The buildings date to the late Middle Ages when a Byzantine church was transformed into an inn. The floor of the central building preserves the colourful mosaic floor of the nave. The protective sand cover is easily removed but should be replaced. About 12 m north of the church is the white mosaic-paved treading floor and collecting basin of a winepress. The hollow in the centre was for a screw-press. A building with a white mosaic floor some 7 m east of the church may have been a bath.

After the road dips into the forest there are two lay-bys to permit access to those parts of the Roman road which survived the construction of the modern road. The first is on the right and marked by a wooden bridge leading to a **rock-cut cistern** whose roof is supported by a beautifully carved central column. Some 100 m up the road from the cistern a flight of steps is clearly visible on the left. A much longer and better-preserved **flight of steps** is visible from the other lay-by (a km or so further down on the left). When the road went out of use a wine press was cut in the top step. The wide valley of Emek HaEla is the traditional site of the contest between David and Goliath (1 Sam. 17). At the junction with route 38 turn left.

A **group of Roman milestones** has been re-erected at 1.5 km south of HaEla Junction on route 38. More are visible, as well as part of the roadbed, at 9.2 km from same point on the east side of the road beside the circular water trough. The detachments of the Tenth Legion who repaired the road commemorated their achievement by adding a new milestone to the nearest marker.

Between these two traces of the Roman road, at 4.2 km from the HaEla Junction, a dirt road runs east across the valley. It leads to a **monumental tomb** of the C1–C2 AD (Horvat Midras). It is 80 m to the right as the up-slope begins to level off. A circular stone moving in a built-up track sealed the tomb from the courtyard. The first chamber contains six slots (*kokhim*) for primary burial. The inner chamber has three *arcosolia* (burial benches) in which ossuaries with the collected bones were placed. Some 15 m to the south is a **Byzantine burial cave** with three *arcosolia*. It also was blocked by a circular rolling stone. The tunnel linking the two has nothing to do with either. It was part of an underground refuge system in the Second Revolt (AD 132–5), as at HAZAN.

Jerusalem–Jericho (K–L17)

Two long sections of this route are worth retracing, but they have to be done on foot. The scenery on both is spectacular. The first section should take about two hours, and the second section half that. The Roman road could have been constructed during the first Jewish revolt (66–70), but a date in the C2 AD is perhaps more likely. It was the most important route to Jericho for Byzantine and Crusader pilgrims.

There is a long straight stretch on route 1 on the eastern side of the Mount of Olives. At the only four-way cross go east through a group of

Arab houses. From the point where the road crosses the wadi bed take the dirt road running along the south side of the Wadi Umm esh-Shid. This is the Roman road, even though it soon narrows to a track. Before that happens a 2 m-high **retaining wall** of large rough stones will be seen on the downhill side. It is not always as prominent, but can be detected with some regularity. There are occasional **flights of steps** cut in the rock.

The ruins (known as Qasr Ali) on top of an open shoulder belong to the **Byzantine monastery of St Peter**, which the empress Eudocia erected in 459. The Roman road first makes a sharp turn to the right to avoid a tower, and then to the left to pass along the south side of a double reservoir. The rectangular church with a large cistern and the square living quarters lie north of the reservoir. Byzantine monks built **trails** to join their MONASTERIES IN THE JUDAEAN DESERT. One of the best preserved zigzags down the precipitous slope north of St Peter's and crosses two steep stream-beds before arriving at the monastery of Gabriel. The retaining wall is preserved at times to a height of 2 m.

After the monastery traces of the Roman road become sparser. Continue due east along the ridge. When the land begins to rise swing to the right into an unusual erosion break. After making almost a complete half-circle to the right, the trail makes a similar half-circle to the left, and descends a small wadi to join route 437. The remains of the **Roman roadbed** as it crosses the main wadi shows it to have been 5 m wide.

Follow route 437 to the main Jericho road (route 1). In the olive grove to the left near the bridge is a U-shaped **Roman way station** beside a large cistern. Sited approximately half-way between Jerusalem and Jericho it served as a changing post (*mutatio*) for imperial dispatch riders. At this point it is best to abandon the Roman road and to follow route 1 to the turn off to Wadi Qilt (Nahal Perat).

On account of the red rocks on the left just after passing the turn to the Alon Road (route 458) the ancient Israelite road at this point was called the Red Ascent (Josh. 15: 7). The Hebrew name, Maale Adumim, is preserved in Maldoim, the name of the **Crusader fort** on the hilltop, which was staffed by the Templars. The rock-cut ditch 4.5–6 m wide and 6 m deep delimits an area 90 × 110 × 95 × 120 m. A tower (9.3 × 8.5 m) stands roughly in the middle. To the west is an L-shaped barrel-vaulted structure. The medieval structures obliterated all traces of the Byzantine fort of Maledomni mentioned by Eusebius. The presence of a protective garrison led to the establishment of a caravanserai (now on the other side of the road, and in its present form dated to 1903), but its identification as the Inn of the Good Samaritan (Luke 10: 33) has little to recommend it. To Byzantine and medieval pilgrims the red colour of the rocks suggested rather the place where the traveller in Jesus' parable was attacked by robbers.

The turn-off from route 1 towards the Wadi Qilt hits the Turkish road (route 7011) at right angles. The ruins (Khan Saliba) to the left, at the top of the road (route 7012) down to the **Herodian aqueducts** at En Qilt, cover the C5 **Byzantine monastery of St Adam**, 'for there he stayed and wept at losing Paradise' (Epiphanius).

To regain the Roman road go up the path at the T-junction. From the crest there is a magnificent view over the deep gorge of the Wadi Qilt with its Herodian aqueduct (repaired in the 1920s) and the undulating desert beyond. The trail running east just below the ridge is the Roman road, which winds in and out among the little peaks while maintaining a very gradual descent. It is recognized in this section by departures from the normal erosion patterns in the desert, notably horizontal levels notched into the slope. There are no steps or retaining walls. The Roman road joins the surfaced route 7011 just west of a large cross from which one can look down on to the MONASTERY OF ST GEORGE. Just beside the modern road is a section of the **Herodian aqueduct** which brought water from En Fawwar to the fortress of KYPROS.

Jerusalem – Lod (H–J17)

On this route down to the coastal plain the Romans simply improved the trace of a much older Israelite road. After defeating the coalition of five Amorite kings at Gibeon (JIB), Joshua followed the retreating army down the **Descent of Bet Horon** (Josh. 10: 10–11). The name of the route is preserved in those of the two Arab villages, Upper Bet Horon (Beit Ur et-Fauqa) and Lower Bet Horon (Beit Ur et-Tahta) linked by the old road, which is parallel to the new settlement highway (route 443). There is a **flight of steps** between the old road and the Muslim cemetery in Beit Ur et-Tahta.

A **paved section** of the Roman road with kerbstones can be seen just as it comes out of the hills into the plain. From route 443 turn north on to route 455 (signposted Kharbata). At roughly 500 m from the junction a dirt road leads off to the left. Opposite it a narrow path runs to the east between the stone outcroppings. After about 100 m the parallel lines of the kerbstones begin to stand out clearly. Note how rough the paving is!

Jerusalem – Nicopolis (H–J17)

At the beginning of the main Jerusalem–Tel Aviv highway (route 1) turn left on to Givat Shaul Street, which becomes Ketav Sofer Street. Just 1 km before the great Jewish cemetery of Har Menukhot a road to the left descends the steep slope in a series of zigzags. Its name, Maale Romaim 'Ascent of the Romans', evokes the origins of an important road linking Jerusalem and the coast. Virtually all can be done by car, but in places the the dirt roads are very rough.

Traces of the **built-up edges and paving** are visible in the dirt road, which after a kilometre becomes Steinberg Street in Moza. It is unusual for a Roman road to follow the bottom of a valley where troops could be trapped. In this case, however, there was no danger. Roman forces were based in the immediate vicinity. Across from Moza, on the slopes below Mevasseret Ziyyon/Yerushalayim, the emperor Vespasian in AD 72 created a **Roman colony** in which he settled 800 veteran soldiers (*War* 7: 217). Originally called Emmaus, the village was probably the place mentioned in Luke 24: 13 (see LATRUN). Subsequently it became known as Colonia, a name retained by an Arab village which survived here until 1948.

The Roman road must have paralleled the highway on the north before angling towards ABU GHOSH, where a detachment of the Tenth Legion constructed a **reservoir**, both for their own needs and to supply water to travellers. From Abu Ghosh drive through the settlement of Neve Ilan. Two excellent dirt roads (6142 and 6143) lead to Horvat Mezad, but the Roman road ran on the ridge between them, where a new forestry road has been cut. Occasional sections of kerbing are the only visible remains.

On leaving the wood, cross the bare saddle, and up the road running through the pillars of 'Het Nederland Israel Woud'. From the top of the hill there is a splendid view over the Shephela and the coastal plain. A fort (today **Horvat Mezad**) was built here in the C2 BC. On part of its ruins Herod erected a smaller **tower**, which was repaired in the C5 AD. Across the road is a large rock-roofed cistern.

Traces of the Roman retaining wall are easily detected on the left side of the dirt road running west from the ruins. Follow the red trail-markers through the wood. About 100 m after leaving the trees a number of **Roman milestones** have been re-erected on the right; one is dated by an inscription to the reign of the emperor Maximian I (235–38). These are exactly one Roman mile from Horvat Mezad. Continue down the dirt road and go right on route 6148 at the T-junction. Just beyond the brow of the hill the Roman road bore off to the left, but from this point it becomes difficult to trace in the maze of roads in what used to be the Arab village of Yalu, whose inhabitants were deported in 1967. It is better to start at the other end.

From the car park in Aijalon Park just beyond the tunnel spring (fig. 89) go across the paved road, up the rudimentary track, and through the park fence. Just over the brow of the hill is a large water tank. The terrace running east from the tank is created by the **retaining wall** of the Roman road. The logic of the terrain makes the line of the road unambiguous. **Curb stones** are visible at certain points.

Mamshit–Arava (J27)

The prosperity of MAMSHIT was due in great part to the Gaza–Elat trade route which crossed the escarpment of the Araba (the valley linking the Dead Sea and Elat) at Maale Aqrahim (Ascent of the Scorpions). The name is biblical (Num. 34: 4 = Josh. 15: 3; Judg. 1: 36), but the reality is Roman. The average slope of the escarpment at this point is 34 degrees, an impossible incline for laden pack animals. In a brilliant engineering operation the Romans created a cliff road with an average

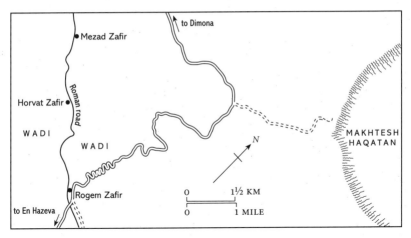

▲ **Fig. 105.** Roman Road at Maale Aqrabim.

gradient of only 16 degrees by making sharp curves and by cutting steps in the really bad portions.

At Zomet En Hazeva, which is 23.5 km south of the Dimona turn-off (Zomet HaArava) on the Elat road (route 90), turn right (west) on to route 277. To the left is HAZEVA. After a km the paved road makes a right-angle turn; continue straight on on the dirt road. Park at the foot of the escarpment where a small fort, **Rogem Zafir**, has been excavated. The hike should not be attempted without adequate water supplies.

Rogem Zafir cannot be dated independently but is identical with Horvat Zafir. The Roman road is indicated by blue trailmarkers in the wadi to the left. It angles up the ridge between two wadis for some 600 m before one encounters the first **flight of steps**; shortly afterwards there is a retaining wall on the left. In parts the road is given a level surface by being notched into the slope. There are five flights of steps between the wadi and **Horvat Zafir** which is effectively the top of the ascent. The amount of debris and the remains of a staircase indicate that this square fort originally had two storeys. The pottery is typical of the C3–C4 AD, but probes nearby brought to light Nabataean pottery of the C1 AD. From this fort **Mezad Zafir** is visible on the skyline to the north. A rectangular building consisting of two rows of rooms and dated to the C2–C3 AD was demolished a century later in order to provide the material for the construction of another square two-storey fort. Three forts in close proximity to each other highlights the importance of the Roman road.

The road to the top of the escarpment is sealed but becomes a dirt road once the ground levels out. From this a very rough track leads to the top of the rim of the **Makhtesh HaQatan** (J26). The bottom can be reached by a sealed road from the Jordan Valley–Dimona road (route 25).

This roughly circular depression looks as if it had been formed by the impact of a huge meteor. It is in fact the result of severe erosion. The Makhtesh Qatan is the smallest of three such geological phenomena in the NEGEV. The other two, MAKHTESH RAMON (E31–G30) and ha-Makhtesh ha-Gadol (G27–H26), can be inspected much more easily because they have been cut by scenic sealed roads. These depressions began as cracks in the sedimentary surface caused by movements in the Miocene period. After water penetration had worn an outlet to the south-east, erosion intensified, eventually exposing the volcanic basalt of the Precambrian period in certain areas.

In the North

Haifa–Tiberias (K3–L3)

This road, one of the two east–west Roman roads in Galilee, parallels route 77 in the Tiran Valley. It was the route along which the Crusaders fought on 3 July 1187 in their abortive attempt to relieve the siege of Tiberias. All that broiling day Saladin's mounted archers poured arrows into the tightly bunched armoured column from the slopes on both sides. The end came the next day at the HORNS OF HATTIN. Three sections of the road are well preserved.

From route 77 just north of SEPPHORIS take the side road to Rumat Heib and Uzeir. Just beyond the second right-angle bend the wide Roman road is visible on both sides. The stone roadbed is easily traced for some 600 m to the west. It then swings to the south-west towards Sepphoris. The next section of the road appears immediately to the west of Turan. Drive 1 km from route 77, and turn left on to an inferior road at the base of the hill. It overlies the Roman road. Continue to the edge of the built-up area where the ancient road becomes visible.

The final section of the road is to be found some 700 m north of the Golani Junction. To the right lie the ruins of the village Marescalcia (today Horvat Mishkena) where the Crusaders were forced to camp in the late afternoon of 3 July 1187. It had taken them over twelve hours to fight the 17 km from the Spring of Sepphoris. At the point on route 65 where the power-lines cross the modern road go due east for between 600 and 700 m. This is perhaps the best-preserved section of the Roman road.

Rosh Zayit (K5)

Solomon gave Hiram, king of Tyre, twenty towns in Galilee as payment for the wood and gold that the latter provided for the building of the Temple in Jerusalem. According to the Bible the area was known as 'the land of Kabul' (1 Kgs. 9: 13). A town of that name is listed on the boundary of the tribe of Asher (Josh. 19: 27). The Arab village of Kabul in western Galilee (K5) preserves the name, but nothing in the village can be dated before the C3 BC. Only 1.5 km to the north-west, however, is a site which was certainly in existence at the time of Solomon. It is known as Horvat Rosh Zayit in Hebrew and Khirbet Ras ez-Zetun in Arabic.

Located on an intermediate ridge between the hills and the plain, the town was founded in the C12 BC. After its destruction in the C10 BC a fortress was erected in the centre of the site. It survived for a century until it was destroyed in a conflagration whose intensity was enhanced by quantities of burning olive oil. Other agricultural produce was stored in great amounts. In the cellar sickles, axes, plough points, and a saw, were found. These hints that the structure functioned as a tax-collection centre are confirmed by the institutional quality of the stonework. The presence of a remarkable quantity of Phoenician pottery indicates that the site had passed out of Israelite hands. It was a Phoenician administrative centre for 'the land of Kabul'. During the First Revolt (AD 66–70) it served as the temporary headquarters of Josephus (*Life* 213).

Visit. At 1 km east of the turn-off to Shaab on route 805 the forest on the right side of the road ceases. Continue up the hill for 400 m. Signs in Hebrew on the left indicate the dirt road to the site on the top of the ridge. It is a five-minute walk.

On entering the site an **C8 house** is visible on the right. A 2 m-thick wall protected a single two-storey building consisting of a central hall surrounded by rooms. The entrance was in the north-west corner. On the far side of the **fort** is another house of the C8 BC with a row of five monolithic pillars. Nearby is a **beam press** for producing olive oil. Crushed olives in woven baskets were placed on a round stone base with a groove around the rim. One end of the beam was notched into the wall, while the pierced stones were attached by ropes to the other. The piled olive baskets acted as the fulcrum and took the weight.

Rujm el-Hiri (Rogem Hiri) (P5)

Its Arabic name 'the stone heap of the wild cat' conveys something of the mystery of this unique megalithic monument. A **central cairn**, an oval stone heap some 5 m high and 25 m in diameter, is surrounded by **four concentric walls**, which get more substantial the further they are from the centre. The innermost (*c*.1.5 m wide) is a semicircle on the north-west. Radial walls link it to the next (*c*.2 m), which would be a perfect circle were it not for a pronounced bulge on the south side. The third wall (*c*.2.6 m) is linked to the second by eight radials, and is pierced by several openings. The outermost wall (*c.*3.2 m), which is preserved to a height of 2 m, gives the structure its majestic dimensions. The circle is 145 m from east to west, and 155 m from north to south. It has entrances on the north-east (29 m wide) and in the south-east (26 m wide). The monument is surrounded by straight low stone walls and by hundreds of **dolmens**.

All agree that the monument must be dated to the Bronze Age, but differ as to whether it should be ascribed to the earliest (3150–2200 BC) or to the latest (1550–1220 BC) periods.

As to the function of the monument one can only speculate. The best suggestion is that the grave of a tribal ancestor so revered as to be accorded mythical status developed into a central gathering-place for pastoral nomads. The central cairn here is in fact a burial chamber. Veneration was progressively ritualized (were the circles to direct cir-cumambulation as today at Mecca?), and the participants used the occa-sion to arbitrate disputes, arrange marriages, and exchange goods.

Visit. Rujm el-Hiri is 3 km from any sealed road in rather wild country. It is not easy to find. The visitor should be equipped with number 1 of the 1 : 50,000 Israel hiking map series. Coming up from the Sea of Galilee on route 869, turn left on to route 808 at the Daliyyot Junction. Go north for almost a kilometre to just beyond the water-catchment area. Then turn right on to the first dirt road. At 1.2 km the track makes a dog-leg to the south for roughly 200 m. At the T-junction turn left. After 1.5 km there is a track leading to the site some 250 m further south.

Samaria (Shomeron) (J12)

At a distance the site appears insignificant. Only the view from the steps of the great temple on the acropolis reveals its dominating position. The surrounding hills stand at a respectful distance; on a clear day one can see the Mediterranean coast.

This opening to the west gives the city a character quite different from that of the two earlier capitals of Israel, Shechem (TEL BALATA) and Tirza (TEL EL-FARAH). In founding Samaria in 876 BC Omri broke free of the confining hills and turned his face to the great world of the eastern Mediterranean. This new orientation was sealed by the marriage of his son Ahab to Jezebel, princess of Tyre. The influence of Phoenicia on Israel was not limited to trade and material culture; alien religious importations aroused the ire of the prophet Elijah (1 Kgs. 16: 29–34). The quality of their buildings highlights the energy and initiative of Omri and Ahab, but it was Jeroboam II (784–748 BC) who gave Samaria its greatest days.

His long reign saw the development of a powerful aristocracy who became the symbols of decadent arrogance for the prophets Hosea and

A Prophet condemns Samaria

'Lying on ivory beds, and sprawling on their divans, they dine on lambs from the flock, and stall-fattened veal. They bawl to the sound of the lyre and, like David, they invent musical instruments. They drink wine by the bowlful, and lard themselves with the finest oils, but for the ruins of Joseph [the kingdom of Israel] they care nothing. That is why they will go into captivity, heading the column of captives. The sprawlers' revelry is over.' (Amos 6: 4–7)

Amos. The latter contrasts the miserable lot of the poor with the luxury of aristocratic houses with their couches of ivory (see box). Many of these plaques of carved ivory (produced in Damascus or Tyre but with Egyptian motifs) which were used to decorate furniture are on display in the Rockefeller Museum, Jerusalem.

After the Assyrian invasion (724–722 BC) 30,000 citizens were deported and their places taken by foreigners (2 Kgs. 17: 24); a significant contribution to the origins of the SAMARITANS. Under the Persians Samaria became the capital of a province, and with the fall of that empire it passed to Alexander the Great. He may have come there in person in 333 BC to punish the rebels who had burnt his representative alive. Some of the leaders escaped, but were betrayed and died, with their documents, in the cave of Abu Sinjeh in the Wadi Daliyeh. Alexander installed some of his veteran Macedonians in Samaria. The more religious among the Samaritans eventually moved out and established a new city on MOUNT GERIZIM.

Razed by John Hyrcanus (108 BC), but restored by the Roman general Gabinius (57 BC), Samaria was granted to Herod the Great by Augustus in 30 BC. He did his usual first-class building job and to honour his patron renamed the new city Sebaste (the Greek for Augustus). He further intensified the non-Jewish character of the population by installing foreign mercenaries. At Sebaste he celebrated one of his many marriages and executed two of his sons. In an effort to live up to its new status when Septimius Severus made it a Roman colony with full privileges in AD 200, the Herodian structures (weakened by age and earthquakes) were restored. The vitality thus injected did not last long, and the city steadily lost population to NABLUS. The legend that John the Baptist was buried there attracted Christians in the Byzantine and Crusader periods.

Visit (Fig. 106). Open 8 a.m.–5 p.m. A new road entering through the West Gate avoids the twisty narrow streets of the village of Sebastiya, an Arabic corruption of Herod's Sebaste. Toilets and refreshments available.

The **West Gate** served the city at least from the time of Alexander the Great. A Hellenistic square tower [2], but not its wall [3], was incorpor-

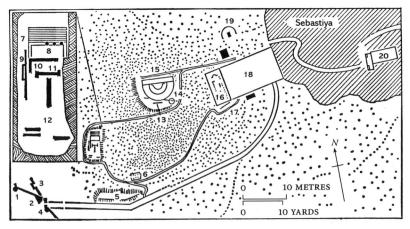

▲ **Fig. 106.** Excavated areas at Samaria. Enlarged inset: the Temple of Augustus. 1. Tower; 2. Tower; 3. Wall; 4. Tower; 5. Byzantine street; 6. Church; 7. C2 AD steps; 8. C2 AD stylobate; 9. Israelite wall; 10–11. Herodian stylobates; 12. Israelite and Hellenistic elements; 13. Hellenistic wall; 14. Hellenistic round tower; 15. Roman theatre; 16. Basilica; 17. Israelite wall; 18. Forum; 19. Viewpoint; 20. Crusader cathedral.

ated into the reconstruction of the gate under Septimius Severus when the three towers [**1, 2, 4**] were built. At this stage the city wall was over 3 km in circumference.

The **colonnaded street** ran through the business section below the acropolis. A series of small one-room shops of the Roman period opened on to covered pavements 4 m wide. The width of the street between the columns averaged 12 m, but this spaciousness was lost in the Byzantine period when the covered area was used as a second room and shops were built in the street [**5**].

The great open area [**18**] corresponds to the **Roman forum** (128 × 73 m) which is artificially levelled. The row of columns nearest the parking level are all that remain of the porticoes that once surrounded it. These are at a lower level than the other two rows which were part of the **basilica** [**16**] and may have belonged to the original Herodian basilica; in AD 200 the level of the north end was dropped 1.5 m and a small semicircular tribune added. The curve of a much wider semicircle can be seen just alongside. Beyond the toilets a viewpoint [**19**] overlooks the rectangular **stadium** (230 × 60 m), similar to the one which Herod built in CAESAREA and in Jericho (TEL ES-SAMRAT).

Just behind the C3 AD **Roman theatre** [**15**], which may rest on an older Herodian one, is a late C4 BC **round tower** [**14**] described as the finest monument of the Hellenistic period in Palestine. It sits astride an Israelite wall breached for insertion, and links with a Hellenistic wall [**13**] forming part of the defences of the acropolis in the time of Alexander the Great. The way the stones in the tower are laid is unique, as is the bevel cut on the outer face.

The summit of the acropolis was crowned by the **temple** Herod dedicated to Augustus. To prepare the site he had to level and fill in ruins of the Israelite and Hellenistic periods [**12**]. One beautiful wall [**19**], with bossed foundations (see [**17**]) and perfectly smooth header and stretcher upper courses, shows the skill of the C9 BC builders employed by Omri or Ahab. Two walls [**10** and **11**] supported the columns framing the porch of Herod's temple. In the time of Septimius Severus the front of the building was moved forward some 5 m; the present steps [**7**] are from this period as is the wall supporting the column bases [**8**].

Christian tradition very quickly (before 361) identified Samaria as the site of the infamous birthday party at which Herod Antipas had John the Baptist executed (Mark 6: 17–29). With greater probability Josephus locates the murder at Machaerus in Jordan (*Antiquities* 18: 119). This information, however, was not available to all Christians, and Samaria was both associated with the name of Herod and much more accessible. Two churches were built in John's honour, one near Herod's temple and the other in the modern village.

A **small church** [**6**] commemorates the finding of the Baptist's head. A C6 three-aisled monastic chapel was radically transformed at the end of the C11. The original apse was retained but the other three walls and narthex were rebuilt; four granite columns were introduced into the nave to support a central dome. In the second half of the C12 Greeks reconstructed the west door, and encased the four columns in masonry in order to support a heavier dome. In the north-east corner they built a chapel of St John and beneath it a crypt in which, according to John Phocas (1185), the head of the Baptist had been found. The bases of the four pillars of the C11 narthex are still visible on the inner face of the crude wall outside the main door.

Just to the south of the basilica [**16**] three courses of an **Israelite wall** of the C9 BC are still visible [**17**].

The great **cathedral** [**20**], enshrining the reputed tomb of John the Baptist, is built in the Burgundian style of the mid-C12. The lower courses visible on the outside of the north wall are all that remain of a C5 church which was already in ruins at the beginning of the C9. Saladin transformed the Crusader building into a mosque whose subsequent history is unclear. The present mosque, and the other buildings inside, were erected in the latter part of the C19 when the triple apse was pulled down to make a straight wall. The **tomb-chamber** is entered via a staircase from a small domed building in the north side of the nave. The stone door and the six burial niches reveal it to be a Roman tomb of the C2 or C3 AD. Another **tomb** of the same period can be seen at the bottom of a deep hole some 50 m south of the cathedral among the houses; the rise in ground level (due to the accumulation of rubbish) around the cathedral explains why this tomb is now buried. One hopes it will be made accessible because it contains possibly the earliest instance of the use of pendentives (triangular segments of a sphere) to impose a dome on a square chamber.

Samaritans

A tiny dissident Jewish sect (300–400 members) with one community in NABLUS and a smaller one in Holon. In opposition to other Jews, they recognize only the five books of Moses as inspired scripture. Their origin goes back to the split between the northern (Israel) and southern (Judah) kingdoms which followed the death of Solomon (1 Kgs. 12–13).

In the north religious differences, introduced to make the political separation effective, were intensified when the Assyrians settled great numbers of foreigners there in 721 BC. Thereafter, for Jerusalem, the Judaism of Samaria was suspect. However, when the Jews of the south returned from sixty years' exile in Babylon, they found the Samaritans claiming to be the guardians of the pure faith of Moses. They refused the Samaritans' offer of help in rebuilding the Temple. In return the Samaritans made things as difficult as possible, resorting to every dirty trick in a large repertory. In the C5 BC Nehemiah persuaded the Persians to withdraw Judah from the political control of Samaria. The resentment this provoked was exacerbated by the religious reforms of Esdras, and the Samaritans built their own temple on MOUNT GERIZIM (2 Macc. 6: 2). This serious breach in the unity of Judaism became definitive only in the late C2 BC when John Hyrcanus, anticipating the tactics of the Spanish Inquisition, destroyed the temple and brutally imposed the Jerusalem version of Judaism on the Samaritans (*War* 1: 62–6).

When Pompey freed them from the political control of the south in 64 BC they would have nothing more to do with Jews. The Samaritans prospered under direct Roman rule, and enjoyed sufficient credit to procure the dismissal of Pontius Pilate in AD 36. With the ineptitude that characterized his tenure as Prefect of Judaea he had massacred a crowd assembled because a visionary had promised to find the sacred vessels hidden by Moses on Mount Gerizim.

The golden age of the Samaritans came in the C4 AD when Baba Rabba secured a high degree of political autonomy for Samaria and inspired a great revival in worship, literature, and language, to which Markah and Amram Darah made major contributions. Influential in trade and learning, their communities were established in the most important cities of the empire. Synagogues of this period have been excavated on both sides of the Nablus–Tulkarm road (route 57), namely, at el-Khirbe (1671/1846;

in the great bend just west of the turn to Sabastiye on route 60), and at Khirbet Samara (1609/1872; south-west of Enav). The latter is a paved hall of the C4 AD, which was oriented to Mount Gerizim a century later by the addition of an apse. It is set in a unique semicircular atrium paved with a patterned mosaic.

The greatly increased Christian presence in the Byzantine period inevitably provoked incidents which led to repressive measures. The response was a revolt in NABLUS in 484. In order to make it clear who was master the emperor Zeno removed Mount Gerizim from Samaritan jurisdiction and built a church on the summit. The resentment thus engendered simmered for a generation before bursting out with even greater violence in 529. The Samaritans swept across the country venting their frustration on churches and monasteries. Justinian's response was savage. The Samaritans were effectively exterminated, and new legislation made the existence of the survivors as a religious body virtually impossible.

The advent of the Arabs in the C7 did not relieve the pressure and the Samaritans lost many converts to Islam. They retained some sort of identity at the price of keeping an extremely low profile. Denial of access to Mount Gerizim forced them to elaborate a secondary liturgy celebrated in their city quarters. Apart from this there has been no development in the last 1,500 years. In the C18 they were able to purchase a piece of land on Mount Gerizim for their sacred rites. This was soon annulled, but they reacquired the right to celebrate there in the C19. Each year the whole community moves to houses below the summit for the six weeks of Passover, one lamb is sacrificed for each family according to the ancient tradition. Unfortunately crowds of tourists tend to turn a dignified ceremony into a rather vulgar circus.

Sammu: *see* ESHTEMOA

Sea of Galilee (N5–7)

In the Old Testament the Sea of Galilee (Fig. 107) is known as the Sea of Kinnereth (Num. 34: 11; Josh. 12: 3; 13: 27), a name that is imaginatively associated with the Hebrew word *kinnor* meaning a harp. For some the lake is shaped like a harp, for others the music of its waters resembles the sound of a harp. Matthew and Mark call it the Sea of Galilee (Matt. 4: 18; 15: 29; Mark 1: 16; 7: 31) or simply the Sea (Mark 2: 13 etc.) to which John adds the Sea of Tiberias (6: 1; 21: 1). Luke pedantically calls it the Lake (8: 22) or the Lake of Gennesaret (5: 1), a name which reflects the usage of Josephus who calls it the Lake of Gennesar because of the remarkable qualities of the region north of Tiberias (see box).

The Fertility of Ginnosar

'There is not a plant which its fertile soil refused to produce, and its cultivators in fact grow every species. The air is so well tempered that it suits the most opposite varieties. The walnut, a tree which delights in the most wintry climate, here grows luxuriantly, beside palm-trees, which thrive on heat, and figs and olives, which require a milder atmosphere. One might say that nature had taken pride in thus assembling, by a *tour de force*, the most discordant species in a single spot, and that, by a happy rivalry, each of the seasons wished to claim this region for her own.' (Josephus, *War* 3: 516–18)

The lake is 21 km from north to south and 12 km wide at its broadest point. The water-level fluctuates considerably, depending on the rainfall each year and on the quantity pumped from the lake which serves as the reservoir for the National Water Carrier; the mean level is 210 m below sea-level. The water is sweet, and in summer (when the temperature averages 33 °C) too warm for a really refreshing swim. Twenty-two species of fish are found in the lake; fishing is again the important industry it was in the time of Jesus, and the small boats have still to watch for the sudden gusts from the surrounding wadis which can whip the normally tranquil surface to turmoil in a matter of minutes (Matt. 8: 23–7; 14: 24–33). The waves driven against one shore bounce back to collide with those coming in.

The physical charm of the lake is enhanced by its historical associations. Prehistory is represented by the AMUD CAVES and Sha'ar HaGolan. Bet Yerah was an important Canaanite city in the third millennium BC. Some thirty years after the Roman general Pompey made SUSITA part of the Decapolis, one of the most brutal episodes in Herod the Great's rise to power took place in the caves of ARBEL. His son, Herod Antipas, founded TIBERIAS in AD 20. A little later Jesus made the fishing village of CAPERNAUM the centre of his ministry in Galilee. His most prominent disciples came from BETHSAIDA. In the First Revolt (AD 66–70) GAMLA was the scene of a famous battle between Jews and Romans.

After the transformation of Jerusalem into Aelia Capitolina in AD 135 Galilee became the centre of Jewish life in Palestine. Great schools of learning developed, and magnificent synagogues were built at CHOROZAIN, CAPERNAUM, HAMMAT TIBERIAS, and HAMMAT GADER. Because of its connections with the ministry of Jesus, Christians flocked to the area in the Byzantine period, and the glory of the synagogues was rivalled by splendid churches at HEPTAPEGON, CAPERNAUM, KURSI, and SUSITA. The next attempt to establish a Christian kingdom in Palestine occurred in the Middle Ages, but eighty-eight years of effort came to

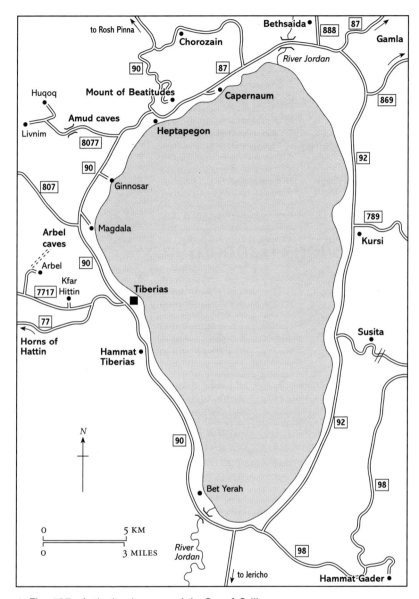

▲ **Fig. 107.** Antiquity sites around the Sea of Galilee.

nothing when Saladin defeated the Crusaders at the HORNS OF HATTIN on 4 July 1187.

'Humanity in the Galilee' is the theme of the **Yigal Allon Centre** in Kibbutz Ginnosar on the lake roughly half-way between Tiberias and

Heptapegon. In addition to providing an excellent introduction to the history and ecology of the area, it also houses the C1 boat discovered in 1986 when the lake-level dropped. Open: Sunday–Thursday 8 a.m.–5 p.m.; Friday 8 a.m.–1 p.m.; Saturday 9 a.m.–5 p.m.

The history of human settlement in Galilee is also depicted in the displays of **Beit Gordon** in Kibbutz Deganya Alef at the south end of the lake. Special attention is given to the development of writing and of the techniques of sailing and fishing in antiquity. Open: 9 a.m.–4 p.m.; Friday and Saturday 9 a.m.–noon.

Sebastiya: *see* SAMARIA

Sepphoris (Zippori)* (K7)　　★★

For the Babylonian Talmud (*Meg.* 6a) Zippori got its name because it sits on a mountain top like a bird (*zippor*). Rising only 115 m above the Bet Netofah Valley the mound is no eyrie, but it does permit a bird's-eye view over the surrounding countryside. This hint of its strategic importance is confirmed by its primary role in the history of Galilee.

Sepphoris was already a strongly fortified city in 100 BC when alone among the cities of Galilee it held out against Ptolemy VIII of Egypt. In the reorganization (57–55 BC) which followed the Roman conquest of Palestine Gabinus made it the seat of the council which governed Galilee (*War* 1: 170). This suggests that it was already recognized as the most important city in the region. It crystallized the opposition of the old Hasmonean nobility to the upstart who became Herod the Great (37–4 BC). He took it during a snowstorm in 38 BC, and stockpiled weapons there. At his death the son of his old enemy used them to arm his followers and rose in rebellion (*War* 2: 56). Varus, the Roman legate in Syria, immediately intervened. 'He took the city of Sepphoris and burnt it and made slaves of its inhabitants' (*War* 2: 68).

Herod Antipas, who inherited Galilee under his father's will, thus found his capital a deserted ruin. His decision to rebuild in 3 BC probably drew the artisan Joseph and his family to settle in nearby NAZARETH (Matt. 2: 21–3); the project would provide work for many years. Antipas made Sepphoris 'the ornament of all Galilee' (*Antiquities* 18: 27), which is probably an allusion to its defensive strength rather than to its beauty. The founding of TIBERIAS between AD 17 and 20 pushed Sepphoris into second place. It recovered the primacy only when the emperor Nero (54–68) made a gift of it to Agrippa II (53–?100). Probably on this occasion it received the name Eirenopolis Neronias ('Nero's City of Peace'), which appears on its coins from 67–8. Despite its predominantly Jewish population, Sepphoris took no part in the First Revolt (66–70), and thereafter it maintained very intimate relations with Rome to the point of changing its name to Diocaesarea in the reign of Hadrian (117–39). Despite its pro-Roman stance Sepphoris was the home of leading Jewish scholars before Rabbi Judah Ha-Nasi (c.135–217) took up residence there c.200. For seventeen years he directed the affairs of the Sanhedrin and completed the codification of Jewish law known as the *Mishnah*. A Christian presence in Sepphoris is not attested until the early C4 when a certain Joseph of Tiberias, a convert from Judaism, was authorized by the emperor Constantine (306–37) to build a church. In 351 a brief and abortive revolt against Rome resulted in Gallus Caesar burning Sepphoris. The city, however, recovered quickly, and was considered by Theodoret the church historian (c.450) to be entirely Jewish in the reign of Valens (364–78). None the less, it slowly found a place on the Christian pilgrim route from the coast, and the Piacenza Pilgrim visited there in 570.

In the early Arab period Sepphoris appears to have been a large township. Its location at an important crossroads on the pilgrimage route from Acre (AKKO) to Nazareth led to the erection of a Crusader fort, but the town appears to have been of no real significance. The few Franks who lived there never finished the church they had begun. In 1177 John Phocas described Sepphoris as having 'almost no houses and displays no trace of its original prosperity' (*Description of the Holy Places* 10: 1). It was from the spring south of Sepphoris (En Zippori) that the Crusader army set out on 3 July 1187 for the relief of Tiberias and were defeated the next day at the HORNS OF HATTIN. Taken by Saladin that summer, it was restored to the Crusaders by treaty in 1240 and was held by the Templars until captured by the Mamluk sultan Baybars in 1263.

Visit. From the main Nazareth–Akko road (route 79) turn north on route 7926. The springs, where the Crusaders camped on 2 July 1187, are on the right about 300 m from the junction. Drive through the modern settlement of Zippori for some 3 km to the parking-lot beyond the ticket office. Open: Sunday–Thursday and Saturday 8 a.m.–4 p.m.; Friday to 2 p.m. Access is also possible from the north via route 2870 from the Tiberias road (route 77). The Citadel on the summit of the mound has been transformed into a visitors' centre with an exhibition of finds from the site and interactive computer displays. In order to reach the Crusader church take the side road to the 'Instituto Educativo Assistenziale S. Anna'.

The Upper Town

From the parking-lot take the path up through the trees to the acropolis. The tent-like structure protects a **mosaic floor** representing birds, flowers, and fruit. The border takes into account the pilasters supporting a now-fallen arch. The **theatre** is notched into the slope. Constructed wings framed a centre cut into bedrock. The seating capacity is estimated at 4,500. While it is difficult to think of an Herodian city without a theatre, it appears that this one was built only at the end of the C1 AD or the beginning of the C2. Sometime in the Byzantine period all the seats were ripped out, and the stage area demolished.

Continue to the viewpoint. Below is the roof of the 'Instituto Educativo Assistenziale S. Anna', from which the key to the church enclosure is available. The C12 **Crusader church** is hidden by trees to the left. The three apses have survived and are now integrated into a modern monastery. It was dedicated to SS Anne and Joachim, the parents of Mary. The Piacenza pilgrim reported, 'we venerated what they said was the flagon and bread-basket of Saint Mary. The chair also was there on which she was sitting when the angel came to her.' By the Middle Ages the whiff of scepticism had evaporated, and some (but not all) were convinced that both Anne and her daughter Mary were born here. In the distance one can see a single-storey rectangular building with a domed tower over the door. Since the Middle Ages it has been known as the **Tomb of Rabbi Judah Nessiah**, the grandson of Rabbi Judah Ha-Nasi. It is in fact a Roman mausoleum. Opposite the entrance is a vaulted burial bench (*arcosolium*).

The number of ritual baths in the excavated area *en route* to the citadel indicates that the **houses bordering the paved street** belonged to Jews. Built around small courtyards, these two-storey dwellings had underground rock-cut storehouses and cisterns. After the earthquake of AD 363 the area was rebuilt.

The **'Citadel'** dominates the summit, and from its roof there is a splendid 360 degree view. Its walls clearly betray different construction periods. In the C12 the Templars reused Roman sarcophagi to strengthen the corners of a small fort, which was destroyed after the Crusader defeat at the Horns of Hattin in 1187. In the C18 it was rebuilt as a fortress to consolidate the rule of Dahar al-Omar, the bedouin sheikh who defied the Turks and ran Galilee as a·private fiefdom until 1775. The top floor was added at the end of the C19 to provide a school for the Arab town of Saffuriya which had 12,000 inhabitants in 1947.

The modern building enshrines roughly half of a **luxurious mansion** erected at the beginning of the C3 AD. In the centre facing a colonnaded court was a dining room (*triclinium*). As at EN YAEL, the identification is based on the fact that a U-shaped portion of the periphery is undecorated; it was covered by the couches on which the diners reclined. An atypical feature, however, is the number of doors giving on to the courtyard and to the narrow corridors on either side. The other wall was pierced for a window. The building was destroyed by the earthquake of 363.

The dining room floor is a **magnificent mosaic** containing twenty-three different colours. Most are cut from local limestone, but glass cubes had to be used for colours like blue and green. The fifteen centre panels

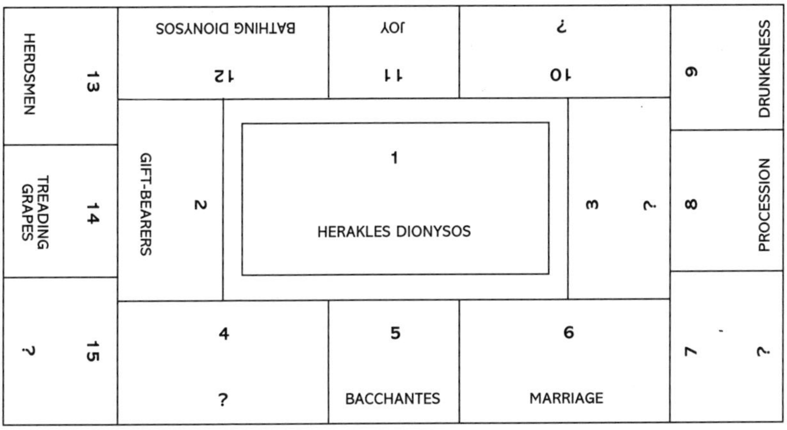

HERDSMEN 13	BATHING DIONYSOS 12	JOY 11	? 10	9	DRUNKENNESS
	GIFT-BEARERS 2	1 HERAKLES DIONYSOS		3	8 PROCESSION
				?	
TREADING GRAPES 14					
? 15	4 ?	5 BACCHANTES	6 MARRIAGE	7 ?	

▲ **Fig. 108.** Sepphoris. The Dionysos Mosaic.

focus on Dionysos, the god of revelry and the generative forces of nature. Each has an explanatory Greek word, and they are designed to be seen from the direction indicated by the numbers in Fig. 108.

[1] 'Herakles (and) Dionysos'. The two gods are locked in a drinking contest, between them a satyr (a male follower of Dionysos) plays the double flute. Dionysos raises his goblet high in victory. [2] 'Gift-bearers'. Three carry different gifts to a tune played by a centaur (half-horse, half-human) on the double flute. [3] Damaged. [4] Damaged. [5] 'Bacchantes', i.e. maenads, female followers of Dionysos. As a child on Mount Nysa the god is taught to ride a goat. One woman supports him while the other leads the animal. [6] 'Marriage'. The reclining god is being crowned by a small Eros, while a seated Ariadne holds a basket of fruit. A satyr at left holds a torch, while his companions on the right carry grapes and wine. [7] Damaged. [8] 'Procession'. Dionysos in a chariot celebrates his conquest of India. [9] 'Drunkenness'. A male and female assistant attempt to aid a completely inebriated Herakles, whose famous club is seen to the left. [10] Damaged. [11] 'Joy'. A maenad with a double flute and a satyr with a staff flank a maenad holding a basket of grapes. [12] 'Bathing of Dionysos'. The child god is bathed by the nymphs who raised him on Mount Nysa. A satyr stands on the right. [13] 'Herdsmen'. A maenad holding the sacred staff of the god and a man in animal skins bracket a seated figure milking a goat. [14] 'Treading the grapes'. Three satyrs hold on to vine branches in order not to fall. [15] Damaged.

The Dionysos panels are framed by twenty-two medallions created by acanthus leaves. Each has a hunting scene. An extraordinarily beautiful female face has been perfectly preserved directly below where the host/hostess would have reclined. Her companion on the far side was less lucky. The U-shaped outermost section depicts a procession in which each person carries a gift or offering, presumably country people on their way to a Dionysiac shrine. The luminosity of this peaceful day out is enhanced by the deep colours of its wide border whose geometric patterns frame human faces and groups of birds and fish. At some stage the base of this U-shaped procession was replaced by a Nilotic scene in which naked youths hunt a bird and a very nervous long-eared crocodile.

The Synagogue

Just on the far side of the parking-lot is a C6 synagogue. Unusually it is oriented to the west, not to Jerusalem. The long narrow hall (16 × 6.5 m) is divided into two unequal areas by a single row of five columns. There is space for a platform (*bema*) at the west end opposite the two doors.

Those who entered by the left door into the wide aisle were faced by a **colourful mosaic containing seven panels**. The first (nearest the entrance) is badly damaged, but can be reconstructed on the basis of a wall mosaic in the church of San Vitale in Ravenna, Italy. Sarah stands in a doorway while Abraham offers food to the three visitors beneath a tree at MAMBRE (Gen. 18: 1–8). The second represents the **Sacrifice of Isaac** (Gen. 22: 1–19) and is divided into two parts. In the left panel the two servants wait, while in the right panel the ram's head looks down at the two pairs of shoes, one large, the other small, which Abraham and Isaac have removed because of the holiness of the place.

The third panel is a **zodiac**. Figures representing Winter (well bundled-up) and Autumn (right) stand in the top two corners, whereas the bottom corners are occupied by Spring (left) and Summer (right). The zodiac signs are named in Hebrew beginning with *Aries* at 9 o'clock, and continuing clockwise with *Taurus, Gemini, Cancer, Leo, Virgo, Libra, Scorpio, Sagittarius, Capricorn, Aquarius,* and *Pisces*. Most unusually a Greek inscription surrounds the four-horse chariot driven, not by the figure of Helios, but by the radiant sun.

The fourth panel contains three segments. The Table of the Shewbread is bracketed by the Daily Offering (left) and the First Fruits (right). In the latter note the pigeons tied to the basket lest their droppings soil the contents. The fifth is dedicated to the **Consecration of Aaron**. To the left are the sacrificial bull and ram (Exod. 29: 10–15). In the centre is the damaged figure of Aaron, whose garment had bells on the hem (Exod. 28: 33–34). On his right is the bronze basin for washing (Exod. 30: 18) decorated with the oxen heads of a later era (1 Kings 7: 25).

The sixth panel depicts the ark, in which the scrolls of the Law were stored, flanked by seven-branched candlesticks (*menorah*). The seventh and last panel contains a garlanded inscription between two lions, each with the head of a bull under its forepaw.

As at BET ALPHA, the pagan zodiac is bracketed by specifically Jewish religious personalities and symbols. The implication is clear: the fate of the descendants of Abraham and Sarah is determined, not by the stars, but by God, the all-powerful ruler of his creation. Curiously, however, the zodiac signs are labelled in Hebrew, as are the specifically religious components of the daily offering and the figure of Aaron.

The inscriptions in the floor tell us something about the socio-linguistic mix of the Jewish community that frequented the synagogue. All the donor inscriptions in the plain geometric floor of the narrow aisle are in Aramaic, whereas those in each picture panel in the main aisle are in Greek. It would appear that Greek-speaking Jews were wealthier than those who spoke only Aramaic.

The Lower Town

Since the archaeologists are still working in this area, and will be for a number of years, what follows is necessarily provisional.

The dominant feature of the lower town is its **grid pattern of streets**. The two principal streets, the *cardo maximus* and, crossing it at right angles, the *decumanus*, are identified by their colonnades, which covered sidewalks paved with mosaics. The slabs of the street are laid diagonally. A circular Greek inscription at the junction of the main streets reads, 'Under our most saintly father Eutropius the Bishop, the whole work of the mosaic [pavement] was done by the provision of the most learned Marianus, the chief physician and father of the city in the time of the four-teenth indication.' The precise date cannot be established, but is certainly post-C4 AD.

The buildings in the *insulae* created by the streets underwent contin-uous changes in the Roman and Byzantine period. Only major structures are worthy of mention. A **church** and a **Roman bath** with an octagonal hot room graced the west side of the *cardo maximus*. A significant portion of the east side was taken up by a large mansion that has become known as the **House of the Nile Festival**.

The identification is based on a **magnificent intact mosaic** covering the entire floor of a square room (6.7 × 6.2 m). Dated to the C6, it uses 18 different colours. The picture is divided into upper and lower panels by the Nile pouring from the mouth of a hippopotamus, on which sits the male personification of the river. Opposite him is a reclining female iden-tified as AIGU[PTOS] 'Egypt'. At her feet a fisherman with a small trian-gular fishnet stands in the river, near a stork in the process of devouring a snake. In the centre a man standing on the back of a woman incises IZ (=17 cubits or 8 m) on a nilometer. This instrument recorded the height of the Nile. The bigger the flood, the more silt deposited, the better the crop, and the higher the taxes. The three animals (sheep and a goat) on the Egypt side of the nilometer are balanced by three male figures on the Nile side.

Two registers can be distinguished in the lower panel. Immediately beneath the river two horsemen, watched by a boy, gallop towards a city. The identification of the city gate flanked by two towers is made certain both by the name inscribed above (ALESAN[DRI]A 'Alexandria') and by the higher tower to the right with flame coming from the top. This can only be the Pharos, the celebrated lighthouse, which was one of the seven wonders of the ancient world. The riders leave behind a column on which is the statue of a man holding a torch and a spear. Perhaps it was a real monument in Alexandria. The horsemen are bracketed by the number IZ, which also appears on the nilometer in the upper panel. Were they hastening to announce the good news of a record flood?

The lower register depicts 'nature red in tooth and claw'. A lion attacks a bull. A panther leaps on a gazelle. A boar fares badly in an encounter with a bear. The verve of the drawing is infused with humour. Note the Cheshire mouse just below the city gate. One of two mice evades a pursuing leopard by escaping out of the picture! Only his hind legs and tail remain.

Other figurative mosaics are found among the geometric carpets in corridors of the same building. One shows a rearing centaur holding in his hands a vessel bearing the word 'God the helper'. Another shows two Amazons hunting from horseback. A third depicts three Amazons dancing, apparently before a female figure seated beneath a canopy. Throughout antiquity artists found the piquant combination of feminine beauty and virile accomplishments irresistible (see box).

Water Supply

Originally the inhabitants relied on rain-water collected in cisterns, but as the city expanded a more reliable and voluminous supply became imperative. Aqueducts were constructed from springs some 5 km to the east in the present villages of Reina and Mashad, which lie on the road (route 754) between Nazareth and Kafr Kanna. The two channels merge into a single conduit until near Sepphoris where they again separate. The northern branch terminates in a pool, whereas the southern one ends in a **great subterranean reservoir**. To reach it continue through the excavation area and along the sealed road for 1.4 km from the parking-lot. Stairs make everything accessible. The numbers below refer to those in the reservoir.

The size of the **aqueduct channel** [1] is surprisingly small. The water flowed into a deep square **decantation basin** [2]. Silt drifted to the bottom, and clean water poured down a slope into the 260 m-long narrow reservoir. The height and width vary; the capacity is estimated at 10,000 m³. The north wall [3] is of hard limestone, whereas the south wall [4] is of soft permeable limestone. The modern **floor** hides the original five layers of plaster and one of asphalt [5], which made the base of the reservoir waterproof. **Arches** [6] were inserted at points where the walls showed a tendency to bulge inward. Rock-cut **steps** [7] from the surface were for maintenance. At one place [8] the roof has collapsed. Water left the reservoir through a lead pipe which enabled the flow to be controlled.

Amazons

'They say that Amazons spend ten months of the year by themselves, ploughing, planting, pasturing cattle, and particularly in training horses, though the bravest engage mostly in hunting on horseback and practise warlike exercises; that the right breasts of all are seared when they are infants so that they can easily use their right arm for every needed purpose, and especially that of throwing the javelin; that they also use bows and sagaris, and light shields, and make the skins of wild animals serve as helmets, clothing, and girdles; but that they have two special months in the spring in which they go up into the neighbouring mountain which separates them and the Gargarians. The Gargarians also, in accordance with an ancient custom, go up thither to offer sacrifice with the Amazons, and also to have intercourse with them for the sake of begetting children, doing this in secrecy and darkness, any Gargarian at random with any Amazon; and after making them pregnant they send them away; and the females that are born are retained by the Amazons themselves, but the males are taken to the Gargarians to be brought up.' (Strabo (C1), *Geography* 11: 5. 1; trans. H. L. Jones)

Shepherds' Fields (K18)

The dramatic circumstances of the first public proclamation of the birth of the Messiah (Luke 2: 8–14) could not have failed to impress the pilgrims who came to the Holy Land in the C4. They were anxious to see the spot where the angels appeared to the shepherds. In 384 in a valley near BETH-LEHEM Egeria was shown the church called 'At the Shepherds'; she reported 'a big garden is there now, protected by a neat wall all around, and also there is a very splendid cave with an altar'. Arculf (670) adds that it was 'about a mile to the east of Bethlehem'.

Today two sites near Bethlehem are pointed out as the Shepherds' Field, one belonging to the Greek Orthodox, the other to the Roman Catholics. Both have been excavated. The former corresponds better to the clues given by Egeria and Arculf but, of course, it is unlikely that the tradition has any historical value. From Bethlehem follow the signs to the HERODION; on the outskirts of the town other signs point the way to the two sites.

Kenisat er-Ruwat (Greek Orthodox)

The site in the middle of the valley east of Bet Sahur is marked by a fence and protective roof beside a new church. Open: 8–11.30 a.m. and 2–5 p.m.; 6 p.m. in summer. This at least is the principle, but all depends on the availability of the local priest.

In the second half of the C4 AD a natural **cave** was given a mosaic floor. The crosses on this floor show that it must have been laid before 427, when this type of decoration was forbidden as offensive to genuine piety. Soon afterwards the rock was cut away to permit the erection of a **church** within the cave; the barrel-vault ceiling is still intact, and this church served the Greek Orthodox community of Beit Sahour from the beginning of the C14 until 1955. It is the only C5 church outside Jerusalem to have survived intact. A **chapel** was built on the roof of this Cave Church; its mosaic floor (set on an axis different from that of the later buildings) is perfectly preserved together with the two holes which permitted visitors to look through to the cave below.

By the C6 these facilities had proved inadequate to cope with the number of pilgrims; Bethlehem was a major religious site and the cave lay on the main road to the MONASTERIES IN THE JUDAEAN DESERT. The Roof Chapel was removed to make way for a much **larger church** which was destroyed by the Persians in 614; the collapse of the burning roof ruined the colourful mosaic pavement. The church was rebuilt in the C7 as the centre of a monastic community which survived until the C10.

Khirbet Siyar el-Ghanem (Roman Catholic)

The Franciscans consecrated this site by the erection of a tent-like chapel in 1954. Open: 8 a.m.–noon, 2–5.30 p.m. (winter); to 6 p.m. (summer).

The ruins on the other side of the parking-lot from the chapel are from the Byzantine period. The first monastery was founded at the end of the C4 AD on a site occupied during the C1 AD by nomadic shepherds. The monastery was enlarged during the C6, the apse of the church being reconstructed with stones from the original polygonal apse of the Church of the Nativity at BETHLEHEM.

Since the excavations did not bring to light a venerated cave it is impossible to reconcile this site with the description given by Egeria. It was simply one of the many MONASTERIES IN THE JUDAEAN DESERT during the centuries when Byzantine monasticism was at its zenith. It may have been where Palladius began his monastic life with the miracle-worker Poseidonius in 419. Its lack of special significance is shown by the fact that it was not reoccupied after having been destroyed by the Persians in 614.

Shiloh (Shillo) (K14)

Loose stones without plan or structure on a small mound are all that remain of the first temple of the God of Israel. At some time in the C12 BC it became the permanent resting place of the Ark of the Covenant. 1 Sam. 1–3 gives a vivid picture of life in this remote sanctuary.

The earliest evidence of occupation and destruction is in the Middle Bronze Age (1750–1550 BC). The sloping glacis stretching 25 m out from a massive wall still contributes much to the characteristic shape of the tel. Why and to whom the city fell is still a mystery, but less intriguing than the nature of the site. A series of excavations revealed no dwellings of this period. Shiloh appears to have been essentially a cultic site serving the region. During the C15–C13 BC this pattern is maintained; nomadic groups came here to make offerings.

A sacral tradition of great antiquity coupled with the sparse and mobile Canaanite population in the surrounding area explains why the Israelites chose Shiloh as their major sanctuary (Josh. 18: 1). They constructed a temple to house the Ark of the Covenant (1 Sam. 3: 2–15), which became the focal point of a great annual pilgrimage (Judg. 21: 19; 1 Sam. 1: 3), which came to an end c.1050 BC when the PHILISTINES swept in to destroy Shiloh after their capture of the Ark of the Covenant at Ebenezer (Izbet Sartah) (1 Sam. 4: 1–18).

Inevitably there has been speculation as to the exact spot on which the Ark was housed, but intense occupation and extensive building on the summit in the Roman and Byzantine periods has destroyed all evidence. Persistence of a religious tradition is perhaps the best explanation of such interest, even though Shiloh drops out of Israelite history once the Ark was removed to Jerusalem (2 Sam. 6: 12).

The site was correctly identified by Eusebius in the C4 AD, but Egeria is the only pilgrim recorded as having visited the sanctuary.

Visit. From the Jerusalem–Nablus road (route 60) turn right and then immediately left into the modern settlement of Shiloh. At the first turn within the settlement continue straight ahead. There is a wine press on the left and on the right a Byzantine church, which has been absorbed into a modern building.

Beside the parking-lot is another **Byzantine church** of the C5 or C6, which has been walled and roofed to protect the mosaics. From the paved courtyard one passes into a narthex. The inscription before the main door into the church reads, 'O Lord, remember Zachary, and him who laid this floor'. Only sections of the geometrically patterned mosaic floor have survived. A fire consumed the church sometime in the C7–C8.

Nearby a sturdy trapezoid building shelters beneath a venerable tere-binth. It is called the **Jame Yetim**, 'the Mosque of the Orphans'; nothing of its history is known.

An **observation tower** marks the summit of the mound. From it there is a fine view of the surrounding area, but no patterns among the ruins leap to the eye. The one relatively intelligible excavated area is on the west, the side facing route 60, inside the modern railed retaining wall.

Sometime between C12 and C10 BC **two houses** were cut into the glacis that protected the base of the C16 BC **rampart**, which became the east wall of the split-level houses. The difficulty of this operation suggests that it was part of a more general plan, which can no longer be grasped because of the disruption caused by later occupation. The conflagration which destroyed these buildings is plausibly attributed to the destruction of Shiloh by the Philistines.

Shivta* (D27)   ★

Although much deeper in the NEGEV (40 km south-west of Beer Sheva) than either AVDAT or MAMSHIT, Shivta (the Hebrew version of the original Sobata) offers something unique. In order to survive in an area where the rainfall averages only 86 mm per year, the city was planned to catch and store every drop that fell.

The NABATAEANS first settled here in the C1 AD; their town occupied the southern third of the present city, and the double reservoir on its northern edge collected run-off from the slope to the east. Little is known of Shivta in the C2 and C3, but in the C4 it began a period of expansion which continued into the next century. Christianity made its presence felt in the construction of two churches. One was squeezed in next to the double reservoir, the other was erected some distance outside the city to the north so that it would not interfere with the catchment area.

In the C5 the population increased. More land had to be brought under cultivation. New quarters had to be built. Buildings now filled the area between the double reservoir and the North Church, but the 4 m-wide streets were laid out to respect the Nabataean catchment channels. The paved areas of the unusually wide streets and frequent open spaces acted as highly efficient water collectors. The upkeep of the water system was a public duty; citizens who participated presumably got a tax rebate because receipts for service were provided.

The city was not walled, but the exterior buildings formed a continuous line save for nine openings which were simply the ends of major streets and these were secured by gates. The Arab take-over in the C7 was extraordinarily peaceful; in building their mosque the Muslims took great care not to damage the adjoining South Church. The city survived for a further two centuries, gradually dying as the quality of water management decreased.

Visit (Fig. 109). From BEER SHEVA take the NIZZANA road (route 211); the turn south to Shivta is 15 km west of the turn-off to Sede Boqer; the tarmac road ends at the parking-lot on the west of the city. The area

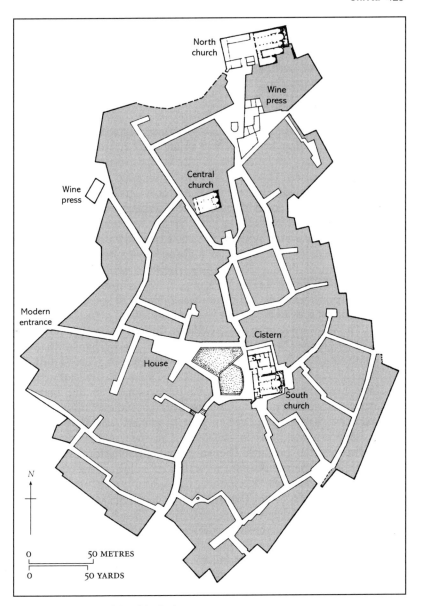

▲ **Fig. 109.** Shivta (after Woolley).

is used for military exercises. Only on Saturday is a bullet-free visit guaranteed.

At 3.2 km from the junction, where the road makes two right-angled turns, **Mizpe Shivta** (422 m) to the south is crowned with ruins. They are the remains of a Byzantine monastery, whose monoapsidal church is easily recognizable. It may be 'the fort and guest-house of St George', which the Piacenza pilgrim visited *en route* to Sinai in 570. There is a magnificent view of the way stones were cleared from the water-catchment areas for the desert farms.

The City

The gate left of the excavators' house leads into a typical street lined with houses. The average **house** is built around a courtyard which provided light and air, very few houses have windows on the street side. Each house has its own cistern to which clay pipes in the walls led water from the roof. In a land without trees for beams, roofs were made of stone slabs laid on arches set closely together: rubble walling levelled up the spandrels.

The **public water system** is well illustrated in the road on the north edge of the double reservoir. Parallel channels collected the run-off from the street. One filled a cistern whose overflow was carried to another cistern under the narthex of the South Church; its overflow went into the other channel which brought street water directly to the south reservoir. The total capacity of the double reservoir is 1,550 m³.

The awkward entrance to the **South Church** shows the builders to have been limited by existing structures. There is no atrium; the narthex is entered from the street. Originally there were two square rooms on either side of the central apse; at a later stage these were transformed into smaller apses each containing a built-in receptacle for the bones of martyrs. According to one inscription, the floor of the southern aisle was laid in 640. Another, engraved on a lintel, commemorates the building of an addition to the church in 415/430; this may refer to the rooms around the little court to the north. The cruciform **baptismal font** is cut from a single block. The *mihrab* of the mosque is cut in the outside of the north wall of the baptistery.

The three apses of the **Central Church** are original. In the Negev this feature is paralleled only in the early C7 South Church at Nizzana. It is the latest of the three churches in Shivta; the adjacent buildings may have been a monastery.

The monastic (?) complex adjoining the North Church contains a fine **wine press**. The grapes were trodden in a square stone-lined pit from which an underground pipe carried the liquid to a square basin where most of the skins could be trapped, thence it flowed into a round settling tank. In the similar wine press near the parking-lot separate chambers were provided around the treading floor so that farmers could store their grapes while waiting their turn. Such separation was alien to the monks who worked their land in common.

The **North Church** is the most elaborate of the three ecclesiastical buildings, showing that space was not a factor in its construction. The whole complex is girdled by a retaining wall suggesting that the structure had been weakened by an earthquake in the C5. A single entrance led from the square to the atrium with its large cistern and stylite column. The original mid-C4 church was monoapsidal; the two early C6 lateral apses with their reliquary niches are secondary, as are the **chapel and baptistery** to the south. The beautiful mosaic floor of the chapel can be seen by anyone prepared to take the trouble of scraping away the protective covering of sand which, of course, should then be immediately replaced. Above the monolithic baptismal font a pipe comes through the wall; to fill the font, water was poured by hand from a cistern outside. Water from the catchment area on the slope flowed through the wall into a division box, thence part went to the baptistery cistern and part out into the square where it was integrated into the public system.

Members of the clergy were interred in the baptistery, the dates on the tombstones run from 614 to 679. Graves in the church and atrium date from 506 to 646.

Byzantine Farm

Just 1 km from the parking-lot the exit road crosses a shallow wadi; 200 m up the wadi bed to the right (east) is a Byzantine farm which Israeli botanists have brought back into use. Here one can see all the features mentioned in the description of desert agriculture appended to the description of AVDAT. Fine crops of carobs, figs, grapes, pomegranates, olives, almonds, peaches, and apricots have been produced here using ancient techniques. The reconstruction of the farm and its catchment area gave the researchers an idea of how long it would take to set up a complex of this size; a family with three or four children could have done it in two years.

Shuni: *see* RAMAT HANADIV

Solomon's Pools (Berekhot Shelomo) (J18)

Even if it is only a legend that Solomon frequently came here to disport himself among the waters and gardens (*Antiquities* 8: 186), one can easily see why he might have. The leafy shade around the three great reservoirs (until very recently crucial to Jerusalem's water supply) with their attendant Turkish fort, makes it a perfect picnic spot. Just to the south the well-preserved remains of the ancient aqueduct system are definitely worth a visit.

This area contains the closest large springs to Jerusalem at a higher altitude than the city. As the city's need for water grew an aqueduct was built terminating in the Temple; traces can still be seen on both sides of Birket es-Sultan, the great pool outside Jaffa Gate and along the south wall of Jerusalem (p. 20). It was certainly in existence at the time of Herod the Great (37–4 BC), and may go back to the C2 BC. In AD 195 the engineers of the Tenth Legion built a second aqueduct at a higher level to bring water to the Upper City, the western side of Aelia Capitolina. Part of the **great stone pipe**, which acted as a syphon, is still in place 400 m south of Rachel's tomb on the Hebron road below a row of cottages on the east side; examples of the carved blocks are displayed in the courtyard of the American Colony Hotel in Jerusalem and at the entrance of the Notre Dame Centre opposite New Gate.

The supply to the pools was augmented by two aqueducts from the south. The lower aqueduct comes 45 km from the great pool at 'Arrub. It was built to a tolerance of one in a thousand, i.e. it drops only one metre per kilometre. Constructed by Herod the Great (37–4 BC), it was extensively repaired by the Mamluks. The upper aqueduct begins at Bir el-

▼ **Fig. 110.** Aqueducts at Solomon's Pools (after Schick).

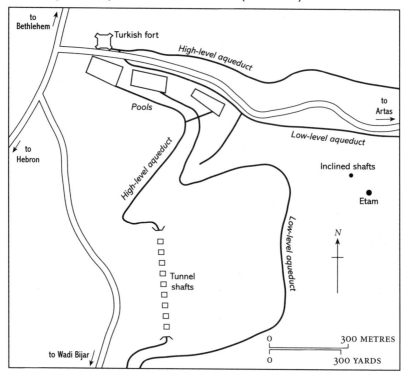

▲ **Fig. 111.** Cap-stones cover aqueduct to prevent evaporation.

Daraj, 5 km south of the pools; the construction technique shows it to be Roman.

Visit (Fig. 110). Strong rubber-soled shoes are essential; the complete circuit takes two hours. A crude channel of uncertain date leads to the **upper aqueduct** from the south-west corner of the lowest pool. Follow it to your left (south), around the head of a small wadi, until it disappears into a tunnel; impress on your mind the configuration of the rough cap-stones (Fig. 111) for at a later stage they will be the only guide to the line of the lower aqueduct.

Nine square vertical shafts permit you to follow the line of the **tunnel** over the hill. On emerging from the tunnel the upper aqueduct continues up the Wadi Bijar, disappearing where the road crosses the bottom of the valley. This is the beginning of a 3 km tunnel leading to the spring. It is pierced by about fifty **square shafts** (some visible in the fields), which are used by the farmers and give the wadi its name, 'wadi of the wells'. The purpose of the tunnel is to gather extra water from aquifers; it is modelled on the *qanat* system in Persia which the Romans copied throughout their empire.

To find the **lower aqueduct**, descend the slope southwards from the south end of the tunnel for some 50–70 m going directly towards the ruins of the large Byzantine building on the far side of the wadi; it is called **Deir el-Banat**, 'the Convent of the Maidens', but nothing is known of its history. A small cairn directs attention to the line of cap-stones (see Fig. 111). Following these to the east you will soon see traces of the masonry substructure and of the plaster lining of the water channel.

Eventually the aqueduct crosses a small saddle in a deep rock-cut channel. At this point it is worthwhile leaving the aqueduct to cross to the ruins on the small hill. This is **Etam**; fortified by Rehoboam (2 Chr. 11: 5–6) but never excavated. From the summit there is a magnificent view of Artas which, since the C16 AD, has been identified with the 'enclosed garden' of the Song of Songs. The spring in the village once supplied the aqueduct built by Herod in 23 BC to bring water to the HERODION. Just

Constructing an Aqueduct

'The first stage is to fix levels. The more accurate method is by the chorobates because the dioptrae and the water levels mislead. The chorobates is a straight plank about 20 feet long . . . having a channel on the top side of the plank, 5 feet long, an inch wide and an inch and a half deep. Let water be poured in. If the water evenly touches the lips of the channel, we shall know that the levelling is successful. Further, when we have levelled with the chorobates, we shall know the amount of the fall. . . . In the case of channels, the structure must be on a very solid foundation, and the slope of the channel must not be less than 6 inches in 100 feet. The channels are to be covered to protect the water from the sun. . . . If there are hills between the city and the fountain head, we must dig tunnels underground which are levelled to the fall described . . . and having air shafts 120 feet apart.' (Vitruvius (C1), *On Architecture* 8: 5. 1–6. 3; trans. F. Granger)

above the level of the saddle, facing the road to Artas, a **stepped tunnel** with an elaborately carved entrance descends deep into the rock. Parallels at GEZER, HAZOR, MEGIDDO, and JIB date it to the Israelite period; it was designed to provide safe access to water in time of siege. An easy path leads back to the base of the lower pool. Just below the metal pipe another aqueduct is visible, coming from En Atan; it fed the lower aqueduct to Jerusalem.

Subeibe: *see* NIMRUD

Susita (O6)

Behind En Gev on the eastern side of the SEA OF GALILEE a high promontory juts out between two wadis (Fig. 107). The flat top (2 km in length, averaging 500 m in width) is joined to the GOLAN by a narrow neck of land. If a little imagination suffices to see a camel in the hump of GAMLA, a much wilder flight of fancy is required to find the shape of a horse here. Yet, from the time of its foundation in the Hellenistic period (332–152 BC), the town was known as *Hippos* in Greek and as *Susita* in Aramaic, both meaning 'horse'.

The Seleucids of Syria were the first to recognize the natural advantages of the site in the mid-C3 BC. It became the administrative centre of an area extending from the Wadi Samakh to the Yarmuk river. The Roman general Pompey in 64 BC removed it from the Jewish control imposed by Alexander Jannaeus (103–76 BC) some twenty years earlier, and made it part of the Decapolis, the league of ten cities which he hoped would disseminate Graeco-Roman culture throughout the region. The emperor Augustus granted the city to Herod the Great in 30 BC, but after the latter's death in 4 BC it was returned to the Province of Syria to the great satisfaction of the inhabitants.

Susita was given a new look in the C2–C3 AD, when new buildings were erected according to a grid street plan. The great prosperity of Susita in the Roman and Byzantine periods was due to its location on the Roman road linking Scythopolis (BET SHEAN) with Damascus; it controlled the one steep ascent and provided a convenient staging-point. The inhabitants were careful to protect their wealth by a massive wall ringing the summit. No resistance, however, was offered to the Arabs after their victory over the Byzantine army at the battle of the Yarmuk in 636. The slow decline which followed the peaceful occupation was brought to an abrupt end by the earthquake of 746.

Visit. There are two approaches. The 300 m climb up the zigzag track at the west end from behind En Gev takes about forty minutes. For those with less energy the new road in Wadi Jamusiyeh, following more or less the trace of the Roman road, makes it possible to drive to the east end of the ridge linking the city to the Golan plateau. The road is not signposted but begins 300 m south of the main entrance to kibbutz En Gev on route 92. At 3.5 km from this point the kerbstones of a section of the Roman road can be seen on the far side of the wadi. At 3.7 km the black-marked trail to the summit begins on the left.

The vertical face on the lake side of the ridge reveals that it was artificially narrowed to make it more defensible. Two **milestones** (square base, rounded top) lie end to end beside the path. The Roman road passed in the immediate vicinity. A little further on are portions of the water pipe cut from basalt stones. A complete section of this **stone pipe**, which carried water from the Golan, is evident on the left just inside the East Gate. Two of the hollowed-out blocks have vent holes to relieve the pressure on the plastered joints. Only part of the moulding of the southern pier of the **East Gate** survives. First erected by the Romans, this gate was rebuilt in the Byzantine period. The **city wall** is best preserved on the south side of the city, but significant traces can also be found on the west where there was a smaller gate.

The track crossing the city from east to west follows the line of the Roman **main street** (*cardo maximus*). Another portion of the stone pipe and the diagonal basalt paving of the street are visible in the trenches to the right of the track. An excavated area just south of the middle of this street is the site of the C5 **cathedral**. A beautiful well-head decorates the atrium, whose black basalt slabs contrast with the geometric designs of the tiling within the church. The building was destroyed by an earthquake; all the granite columns lie pointing in the same direction. The apse has a mosaic floor with the sockets for a marble chancel screen. The **baptistery** built along the north side of the church in 591 has two features which make it unique: it is triapsidal and dedicated to special patron saints (the framed inscription in the south aisle mentions SS Cosmas and Damian). There was another church to the east. Three further churches are located on the other side (north) of the main street; the floor plans can be traced among the ruins. As was customary, all the churches are oriented to the east.

Tabgha: *see* HEPTAPEGON

Tel Arad* (J23)   ★★

Some 2 km north of the highway (route 31) and 8 km to the west of the new city of Arad a square fortress squats on the highest of a group of low hills. Known as Tel Arad, this site offers the best example in the country of an Early Bronze Age city. The excavated area covers several hectares and the street plan is perfectly clear. Excellent restorations (everything above a heavy line of plaster), signs identifying the purpose of each building, and an explanatory leaflet facilitate a visit. Open: 9 a.m.–4 p.m.; Fridays to 2 p.m.

Lower City

In contrast to the surrounding area the rock formation here is impervious to water. This feature explains why the first squatters settled here, and why, when they built their city, it was not limited to the ridge. The horseshoe shape acted as a natural catchment area during the winter rains; the bottom of the little valley caught and held the run-off from the surrounding slopes. In the C9–C8 BC Israelites dug the 21 m-deep **well** which reaches the aquifer. Water was carried up to the citadel and poured into the channel under the west wall whence it flowed into the cistern within the fortress. The well remained in use until the C6 BC. The upper limestone lining belongs to a restoration in the C1 BC. The wide **city wall**, strengthened by frequent semicircular towers, is sited on bedrock and follows the exact line of the crest; it is 1,200 m long and encloses an area of some 10 hectares. The population is estimated at between two and three thousand.

The city flourished between 2900 and 2700 BC. The inhabitants cultivated the plain and pastured their flocks there; quantities of cattle, sheep, and goat bones were found. The city was also a trade centre. Some of the local pottery is made of sand found only in the Araba (the valley linking the Dead Sea with the Gulf of Aqaba) and in the mountains of southern Sinai. This was only one import; Egyptian vessels attest contact with more distant lands. The city was destroyed twice. The first time it recovered, but after the second its life came to an abrupt halt, and the site lay desolate for 1,500 years.

The layout of the city shows evidence of deliberate planning. Streets following the contour lines are cut by radial streets leading to the reservoir. They both directed run-off rain-water to it, and facilitated water carriers. Public buildings are located in the centre with private dwellings on the periphery.

From the well follow the street parallel to the city wall uphill. It quickly becomes apparent that all the private **houses** were built to the same basic design; one large living-room, a kitchen or store-room, and a courtyard. The living-room is characterized by a stone bench running round all four walls. All the doors open to the left, as the position of the hollowed stone door socket shows. The level of the street or courtyard is normally higher than the room floor, a curious feature in an area which gets an average of 170 mm of rain a year. The houses had no windows, and the light roof was supported by a wooden pillar resting on a stone base. One of these, together with a carved stone mortar, appears in most houses.

Just inside the postern gate in the city wall the archaeologists have cleverly preserved two levels. The corner of a later room overlaps part of an earlier one. Both are of the same type, showing ethnic continuity, but the overlap reveals that the earlier building had been destroyed.

Continue north along the ridge to the reconstructed **Western Gate**. There appears to have been a market just inside. Further down the street on the right is a large closed complex, identified perhaps a little romantically as 'the palace'. Across the road from it lies the sacred precinct. The most striking feature is the **large double temple**. Each is entered from a courtyard on the east. The northern courtyard contains a square altar, and beside it a beautifully constructed pit (for libations?). Parallel to these temples on the east side of the street, but not accessible from it, is a **smaller double temple**, to which a large ceremonial building is juxtaposed on the south. Like their fellow Canaanites, the inhabitants of Arad worshipped the forces of nature.

Citadel

When the site was resettled in the early C11 BC occupation was concentrated in the highest part of the ancient city, because for the Israelites its importance was primarily strategic. A fortress there commanded the frontier road to Edom and Elath. A series of fortresses was built on the ruins of those destroyed by enemy attacks; the last is dated to the end of the C1 AD.

The visible remains are virtually all from the Israelite period. There is a splendid view from the walkway on top of the reconstructed C8–C7 BC wall. To the north one can see very clearly where the Judaean mountains stop and the Negev begins. The most interesting building within the citadel is an Israelite temple with a small **Holy of Holies** and a brick and rubble **altar of sacrifice** (Exod. 20: 25). The altar was taken out of use in the religious reforms of king Hezekiah (2 Kgs. 18: 4, 22), but the temple itself was not suppressed until the more radical reforms of king Josiah (2 Kgs. 23).

Finds from the site are displayed in the **Arad Museum and Visitors' Centre** (28 Ben Yair Street, Arad). Open: Monday and Wednesday 6–9 p.m. (summer); 5–7 p.m. (winter); Saturday 11 a.m.–1 p.m. and 6–8 p.m.

Tel Aviv–Jaffa (Yafo) (E14)

The confused urban sprawl of Tel Aviv belies the fact that the city was founded in this century. In 1909 a group of sixty Jewish families moved out of Jaffa to settle in the sand dunes to the north. At first a suburb of Jaffa, it became independent in 1921 and thereafter grew uncontrollably as new immigrants poured in. In May 1948, on the eve of the declaration of the State of Israel, Jewish forces took control of Jaffa.

The first settlements in the area between Jaffa and the Yarkon river date from the end of the Stone Age (*c.*5000 BC), and evidence for continued occupation during the subsequent Copper and Bronze Ages has also been found. The name Jaffa appears for the first time in the list of cities captured by Thutmose III in his campaign of 1468 BC. The trick used by his general Djehuty to take the city became a favourite Egyptian folk-tale (see box). Letters conserved in the archives at Amarna show Jaffa to have been under Egyptian control in the C14 BC, and they retained it until the PHILISTINES established themselves in the area *c.*1200 BC.

According to 2 Chr. 2: 16, cedar-wood for Solomon's temple came from Lebanon in great rafts which were brought ashore at Jaffa, but after Solomon's death the Philistines reassumed control of the port. It reverted to the Israelites during the reign of king Uzziah of Judah (769–733 BC), but later in that century it fell victim to Assyrian expansionism. Seeing the threat to his mountain kingdom, king Hezekiah of Judah (727–698 BC) took the death of Sargon II in 705 BC as the signal to organize a revolt in Palestine. One of his allies was Sidqia king of ASHQELON who occupied Jaffa and its hinterland. What happened thereafter is succinctly described on the famous Prism of Sennacherib: 'In the continuation of my campaign I besieged Beth-Dagon, Jaffa, Bene-Berak, Asor, cities belonging to Sidqia who did not bow to my feet quickly enough; I conquered them and carried their spoils away' (701 BC).

The collapse of the Assyrian empire came very quickly, and in subsequent centuries Jaffa passed from hand to hand, being occupied in turn by

Jaffa Baskets Prove to be a Trojan Horse

'Djehuty ordered the 200 baskets, which he had made, to be brought, and then caused 200 soldiers to get into them; then one filled their arms with fetters and manacles and then the baskets were closed with seals . . . The one appointed good heavy infantrymen to carry them, 500 in all. Then it was said to them, "When you enter the town, release your companions, seize all the people who are in the town and put them in fetters at once!" Then a servant went out to say to the charioteer of the Rebel of Jaffa, "Your master says this: Go and say to your mistress that God has given us Djehuty along with his wife and children. Behold this is the advance of their tribute, she should tell herself, concerning these 200 baskets." Which actually were full of people, manacles, and fetters. And then the charioteer went at the head of them to give good report to his mistress, saying, "We have taken Djehuty!" Then the fortifications of the town were opened before the heavy infantrymen. When they had entered the town they released their companions, and then they seized the town, the small person as well as the great and they put them in fetters and manacles at once. And so the valiant arm of the Pharaoh took the town.' (*Harris Papyrus* 2: 4–3: 4; trans. H. Goedicke, adapted)

Egypt, Babylon, Persia, and Sidon. Under Alexander the Great, who campaigned in Palestine in 332–331 BC, it became a Greek colony. The book of Jonah was written about this time; the hero tried to escape God's command to go to Nineveh by taking ship from Jaffa (1: 3). The port remained under the control of the Ptolemies of Egypt until they were pushed out of Palestine by Antiochus III of Syria (223–187 BC).

When the Maccabees revolted against Syria, two hundred Jaffa Jews were treacherously drowned. In reprisal (163 BC) Judas Maccabeus burnt the port (2 Macc. 12: 3–7). The city was conquered by his brother Jonathan, and annexed to Judaea by his other brother Simon (1 Macc. 12: 34). In 63 BC Pompey restored its independence, but in 47 BC Julius Caesar returned the city to Jewish control. A besotted Mark Antony gave it to Cleopatra; on her death in 30 BC Augustus added it to Herod's realm.

Jaffa lost much of its importance when Herod built a new port at CAESAREA. After raising a woman from the dead, Peter stayed in the house of Simon the Tanner in Jaffa where he received the vision which showed him that pagans should be admitted into the church (Acts 9: 36–10: 23). After having suffered badly during the First Revolt (*War* 3: 414–31), the city was rebuilt by Vespasian and given an independent charter. Economically it could not compete with Caesarea and remained a small place. When Jerome translated the *Onomasticon* of Eusebius in 390 he felt obliged to substitute 'town' for 'city'; he is also the last to mention the legend of Andromeda bound to the rock which was first associated with Jaffa by Strabo (c.AD 19).

As the harbour at Caesarea deteriorated, Jaffa regained its position as a port, and remained the principal Mediterranean point of entry into Palestine until this century. The Crusaders took it without a battle in June 1099 and immediately began to fortify it. The lower town was enclosed by a wall and a castle built on the hill by the harbour. The city changed hands several times in the struggle between Saladin and Richard the Lion-Heart at the end of the C12. Crusader possession in the following century was marked by continuous refortification, but it availed little. The Mamluk sultan Baybars took the city on 8 March 1268, and stripped it of timber and marble for his new mosque in Cairo. In 1344–6 his successors systematically razed the buildings and filled in the harbour in order to deny the European powers a base. This is why there are virtually no remains from the post-Byzantine period.

Visit. There are two archaeological sites in Tel Aviv–Jaffa, both associated with museums.

Jaffa

Part of the archaeological history of Jaffa can be seen in an excavation (with excellent explanatory signs) across from St Peter's Church on the high ground above the port. Finds from the dig and the area are displayed in the **Antiquities Museum of Tel Aviv–Yafo**, which is housed in a refurbished Turkish bath-house at 10 Mifratz Shlomo Street. Open: Sunday–Friday (Tuesday excepted) 9 a.m.–1 p.m.; Tuesday 4–7 p.m.; Saturday 10 a.m.–2 p.m.

Tel Qasile

This mound, located on the north side of the Yarkon river just east of Derech Haifa, was apparently first settled by the PHILISTINES in the C12 BC. It has not been identified with any site known from written sources, even though it was occupied until the C15 AD. The most significant discovery was a series of **Philistine temples** of the C12–C11 BC. In its most developed phase the complex included two courtyards, a central temple with a smaller secondary temple, and an altar. Some of the reconstructed **Iron Age houses** can be visited, and a number of the artefacts are housed nearby.

It is easier to appreciate the historical and cultural context of Tel Qasile than any other site because it is located within one of the best museums in the country. The **Eretz Israel Museum** (2 University Street, Ramat Aviv) has notable collections of coins and glassware. Of equal interest to those concerned with archaeology are the displays showing the development of, and the techniques employed in, ancient mining, fishing, farming, construction, transportation, and ceramics. Various types of mills and presses are scattered throughout the grounds. Open: 9 a.m.–1 p.m.; Tuesday 9 a.m.–1 p.m. and 4–7 p.m.; Saturday 10 a.m.–1 p.m.

Tel Balata (K12)

Site of the biblical city of Shechem, the natural capital of the mountain region (Fig. 100), it offers a unique opportunity to visualize the complex of buildings around a city gate of the Bronze Age.

Settled in the Chalcolithic period, the first city was founded in the C19 BC; its name appears in Egyptian texts. Abraham camped in its vicinity on his arrival in Canaan and received the promise of the land (Gen. 12: 6–7); there Jacob bought land to settle down and his son Joseph was later buried there (Gen. 33: 18–20; Josh. 24: 32). The small city the patriarchs knew saw a great expansion in the C17–C16 BC, when its only rivals in Palestine were MEGIDDO and GEZER; it was a powerful city-state whose borders embraced the entire hill country. In the late C14 BC it was strong enough to threaten Megiddo, but the king, Lab'ayu—with great realism but almost certainly with his tongue firmly in his cheek—bowed humbly before his overlord the Pharaoh of Egypt (see box).

After the arrival of the Israelites in the Promised Land (*c.*1200 BC) Joshua held a great assembly of all the tribes (not all Israelites were at

All I have is Yours

'To the king, my lord, and my Sun-god: Thus Lab'ayu, your servant, and the dirt on which you tread. At the feet of the king, my lord, and my Sun-god, seven times and seven times I fall. I have heard the words which the king wrote to me, and who am I that the king should lose his land because of me? Behold, I am a faithful servant of the king, and I have not rebelled, and I have not sinned, and I do not withhold my tribute, and I do not refuse the requests of my commissioner. Now they wickedly slander me, but let the king, my lord, not impute rebellion to me! Further, my crime is namely that I entered Gezer and said publicly, "Shall the king take my property, and not likewise the property of Milkilu [king of Gezer]?" I know the deeds which Milkilu has done against me. Further, the king wrote concerning my son. I did not know that my son associates with the Apiru, and I have verily delivered him into the hand of Addaya. Further, if the king should write for my wife, how could I withhold her? If the king should write to me, "Plunge a bronze dagger into your heart and die!" How could I refuse to carry out the command of the king?' (*Amarna Letter* n. 254; trans. W. F. Albright)

Sinai) to swear allegiance to the new faith (Josh. 24). The abortive attempt of Abimelech to make himself king (Judg. 9) gives a vivid picture of life in the city during the C12 BC, and explains the violent destruction at the end of the Bronze Age.

When Rehoboam refused to grant tax concessions, the Shechemites would not recognize his right to succeed his father Solomon as king (1 Kgs. 12). Shechem thus became the first capital of the dissident northern kingdom. This privilege it lost first to Tirza (TEL EL-FARAH), then to SAMARIA in 876 BC. The Assyrian invasion (724–722 BC) wrought terrible damage, and the city did not recover until the end of the C4 BC. In order to control a vital crossroads Alexander the Great built here a fortified military and commercial centre (c.330 BC). Its tormented history came to an end in 107 BC when John Hyrcanus reduced it to rubble. No one ever settled there again because, in AD 72, Titus founded a new city (NABLUS) a little to the west in the centre of the pass.

Visit (Fig. 112). The unmarked entrance is a path between two buildings on the road just north of the tel (Fig. 100).

All the walls visible around the gate [**7**] are dated to between 1650 and 1550 BC, permitting the imagination to recreate the bustling life of the

▼ **Fig. 112.** Tel Balata. Area around the North-west Gate (after Wright and Dever). 1. Cyclopean wall; 2. Pillared reception hall; 3. Stairs; 4. Antechamber; 5. Cella; 6. Secondary wall; 7. City gate; 8. Spyhole; 9. Guardroom; 10. Fortress temple; 11. Sacred area; 12. Retaining wall.

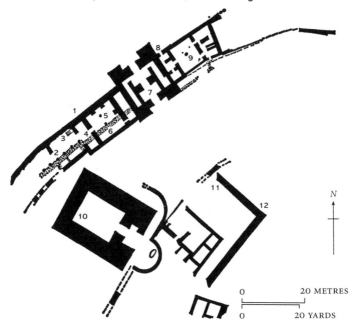

most important quarter of the city. The great **cyclopean wall** [1], filled on the inner side, raised the city 10 m above the land outside. A ramp led up the **main gate** [7] in which sat the tax collectors and senior citizens; here the news was fresh, visitors could be inspected, business was transacted and judicial decisions given (Gen. 23: 10; Deut. 21: 18–21; Prov. 31: 23). The guards who occupied the adjoining **barracks** [9] had a peephole [8], permitting them to anticipate problems such as might be created by the arrival of a notorious trouble-maker or a group too heavily armed.

The complex on the other side of the gate had a different function; it was the **private temple** of the ruler. The arrangement is not immediately obvious because, late in this period, a new wall [6] was inserted in order to create a new defence line. With the inner wall of the existing building it made a casemate, i.e. a double wall designed to be filled with earth in times of danger. If we ignore this intrusion the plan becomes clear. A reception hall [2] had a line of columns in the centre, supporting an upper floor (royal apartments?) reached by a staircase [3]. The temple comprised three halls (a model later adopted by Solomon for his temple in Jerusalem); an antechamber [4], a square room [5] whose roof pillars rested on squared bases (one now in the middle, the other in the base of the casemate wall) with an altar facing the entrance, and a small rectangular chamber.

This temple must have been for private use because just nearby was a large **fortress-temple** [10] to serve the general public. The width of the stone foundations shows that the brick walls must have risen to a considerable height. The **standing stone** before the entrance was restored by the archaeologists to its original position. To do so they had to rebuild the **courtyard**. It is no less artificial than the original one, because in order to build the fortress-temple the Bronze Age occupants of the city had to cover a huge area [11] which had been the temple domain since the C19 BC. The wall [12] which had served to separate the sacred area from the rest of the city was reused to retain the fill. The buildings in the bottom of the trench belonged to this earlier temple complex.

At the far side of the tel there is another **city gate** dated some 75 years after [7], the single bay is constructed of four pairs of great flat stones. In order to explain why some are worn on the inside, it has been suggested that they functioned as sliding doors.

Tel Beer Sheva* (F23) ★★

In the Old Testament, 'from Dan to Beer Sheva' is a stereotyped expression for the limits of the land of Israel (Judg. 20: 1; 1 Sam. 3: 20; 2 Sam. 3: 10; 17: 11; 24: 2; etc.). Although located in the NEGEV just beyond the southern edge of the mountainous region where the Israelites were able to maintain effective control, Beer Sheva was important because of its association with the Patriarchs. The name is explained as 'the well of the seven' or 'the well of the oath' in the narrative of Abraham's treaty with Abimelek the Philistine (Gen. 21: 25–33). The dispute centred on the possession of a well (extremely important for pastoral nomads) and flared up again after the death of Abraham. It was settled in the same amicable way, and Isaac built an altar there in memory of the promise of Yahweh (Gen. 26: 15–33). It was at Beer Sheva that Jacob received the vision encouraging him to take his family to Egypt (Gen. 46: 1–7).

The allusions to PHILISTINES in the Patriarchal narratives are anachronistic, and reflect the situation at the time of the Judges (C12 BC), when the area was settled again. Excavations at various sites scattered around the modern town show that the area was occupied during the fourth millennium BC. These people, who had introduced domesticated sheep to the Negev, moved away about 3000 BC; thereafter nomads wandered through the area in seasonal patterns.

After the return from Egypt, Beer Sheva is listed as part of the territory of Simeon which was eventually absorbed by Judah (Josh. 15: 28; 19: 2); the corrupt sons of Samuel judged there (1 Sam. 8: 2). A frontier settlement, with the Philistines and Amalekites as threatening neighbours, Beer Sheva cannot have had a very tranquil existence until David (1004–965) strengthened Israelite control over the area.

Excavations at Tel Beer Sheva contribute most to our knowledge of the region from that time on. Late in his reign David built a fortified town on this mound where Saul, his predecessor, had erected a small fort during his campaign against the Amalekites from the south (1 Sam. 14: 48; 15: 2–9). It was destroyed in a tremendous conflagration at the end of the C10, which is plausibly related to the invasion of Israel by the pharaoh Shishak in 925 BC. In the list of the captured cities which the pharaoh had inscribed on the wall of the temple at Karnak in Egypt the town is called 'Fort Abram', a hint that the tradition claiming Abraham as the town's founder should not be dismissed too easily. Beer Sheva rose from the ashes, and there is clear evidence of growing prosperity in the C9–C8 BC.

The most significant artefact from this period is a great horned altar (now exhibited in the Israel Museum, Jerusalem). The cut stones of this altar do not conform to biblical law which lays down that an altar should be 'of unhewn stones upon which no man has lifted an iron tool' (Deut. 27: 5; Josh. 8: 31). The hint of irregularity in the cult practised at Beer Sheva is confirmed by the condemnation of the C8 prophet Amos (5: 5; 8: 14). The altar was broken up and used as building material during the religious reforms of king Hezekiah (2 Kgs. 18: 4). In 701 BC Sennacherib destroyed the city utterly. Some of the survivors made a feeble attempt to rebuild, but soon gave up and moved to the area of the present town. Thereafter the

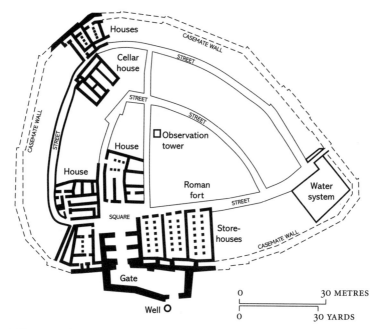

▲ **Fig. 113.** Tel Beer Sheva. Excavated area (after Aharoni).

mound was the site of a series of fortresses starting with a Persian one of the C4 BC and ending with an Islamic fort of the C7–C8 AD.

Visit (Fig. 113). The tel is located east of modern Beer Sheva, and the turn-off from the main Beer Sheva–Jerusalem road (route 60) is signposted. Open: Sunday–Thursday 8 a.m.–4 p.m.; Friday 8 a.m.–3 p.m.; Eve of Feasts 8 a.m.–2 p.m. In addition to toilets, the attractive picnic area contains the **Museum of the Negev**, which displays artefacts found in the area. Open: Sunday–Thursday 10 a.m.–4 p.m.; Friday to 1 p.m.; closed Saturday. On the right just beyond the ticket-office is a replica of the C8 BC horned altar.

With a few exceptions the visible remains are from the second half of the C8 BC. Extensive restoration makes it very easy to visualize streets and houses, but everything below a white plaster line is original. The 1.13 hectare town was planned as an administrative centre, with housing only for civil servants and military officers. They numbered about 300 and were distributed among seventy houses. The lower orders lived outside the walls in villages and farms.

The **wall and glacis** to the right on the track to the gate date from the C10 BC. Electric light reflecting on the water over 80 m below accentuates the extraordinary achievement represented by the C10 **well**. Originally the sole source of water, it became a reservoir in the C8 city. Rain-water from roofs and courtyards was collected by channels beneath the streets and eventually flowed into the main channel whose route through the gate area is marked by the cobble-stones. An **outer gate** forced those entering to make two right turns before passing through the **main gate**. The two bays on either side served as guardrooms.

Inside the gate is a **small square**, which anchored the two circular streets. Follow the first road to the left. On the right is a large structure whose cut stones led to its identification as **the governor's residence**. The road then has to make a dog-leg to avoid an excavation to deeper levels. Just beyond it on the right is **the cellar building**. Its foundations do not rest on earlier levels but go down to bedrock. Fill was then necessary to bring the floors up to street level; two unfilled rooms became cellars. The existence of such a pit is best explained by the thoroughness with which king Hezekiah destroyed the illegal temple to which the horned altar belonged (2 Kgs. 18: 4). Opposite is a group of **four-room houses**. All exhibit the same plan: a room parallel to the street with an oven and stairs to the roof, two storage rooms separated by pillars, and a living-room in the casemate wall. A turn to the right brings one to the **observation tower**. From the top the the systematic nature of the planning of the city becomes evident. The eye is also caught by the three **storehouses** similar to those at HAZOR and MEGIDDO. They can be reached by taking the first road to the left. The section of smooth paving belongs to the **Roman fort** (C2–C3 AD). Another section is visible at eye level near the storehouses. Beyond them steps descend into the great pit of the **water system**, which is reminiscent of that at HAZOR. Dividers separated those descending from those coming back up with water jars.

Tel Dan (01)   ★★

Today the ancient city is the centre of an extensive nature reserve whose luxuriant vegetation is watered by one of the headstreams of the River Jordan. The spring pours out 250 million m³ of water per year.

In the division of the land following the conquest by Joshua, the tribe of Dan received territory in the coastal plain inside Jaffa (Josh. 19: 40–6). When they found that they could not hold it against the chariots of the PHILISTINES they moved to the north, and occupied a Canaanite city-state called variously Leshem (Josh. 19: 47) or Laish (Judg. 18: 27) whose name was then changed to Dan. Laish is mentioned in Egyptian Execration Texts of the C19 BC and in the mid-C15 BC list of cities conquered by Thutmose III; it also appears in documents from Mari across the desert on the Euphrates.

The Danite invasion took place about the middle of the C11 BC, but the city came into prominence only as a result of the political schism which followed the death of Solomon in 928 BC. In order to give his new kingdom a distinctive identity and to prevent his subjects from being propagandized when on pilgrimage to Jerusalem, Jeroboam (928–907 BC) 'made two calves of gold. And he said to the people, "You have gone up to Jerusalem long enough. Behold your gods, O Israel, who brought you up out of the land of Egypt." And he set one in Bethel and the other he put in Dan' (1 Kgs. 12: 28–9). These two towns were respectively the southern and northern limits of his kingdom. To mark the new importance of Dan, Jeroboam erected a second line of fortifications outside the great C18 BC wall which ringed the summit of the mound; its monumental gate was on the south slope. The destruction of this gate is dated to the Syrian invasion of the north (1 Kgs. 15: 20) inspired by king Asa of Judah (908–867 BC).

The city was rebuilt during the reigns of Omri (882–871 BC) and Ahab (871–852 BC); the last phases of the gate and of the huge podium on the northern part of the tel are dated to this restoration. Dan is not mentioned explicitly in the account of the Assyrian invasion of the north under Tiglath-Pileser III in 732 BC (2 Kgs. 15: 29), but it is highly probable that its inhabitants were deported with all others of the region.

The subsequent story of the site is shrouded in obscurity. An inscription from the C4–C2 BC confirms the identification of the site (see below). In the C1 AD Josephus shows that he knew the history of the place. In describing Lake Semechonitis (= Lake Huleh), he says, 'its marshes extend as far as Daphne, a delightful spot with springs which feed the so-called Little Jordan, beneath the Temple of the Golden Calf, and speed it on its way to the greater river' (*War* 4: 3). Occupation continued until the C4 AD, but left no mark on history.

Visit (Fig. 114). The archaeological site is part of the Nature Reserve, which is signposted from the Qiryat Shemona–BANYAS road (route 99). Open: Sunday–Saturday 8 a.m.–5. p.m.

▼ **Fig. 114.** Tel Dan. Excavation areas (after Biran).

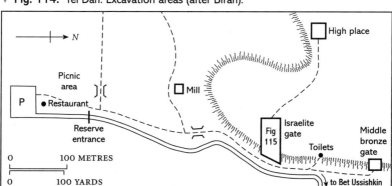

Finds made during the excavations, and replicas of the unique objects, are on display in two museums: **Beit Ussishkin**, the museum of nearby Kibbutz Dan, which also has an excellent natural history section (open: Sunday–Thursday 9 a.m.–3 p.m.; Friday 9 a.m.–noon; Saturday 10 a.m.–2 p.m.) and the **Skirball Museum** (13 King David Street, Jerusalem; open: 10 a.m.–4 p.m.; Friday and Saturday 10 a.m.–2 p.m.).

The lay-out of the paths in the reserve facilitate a chronological visit of the site. From the restaurant go through the picnic area and follow the path parallel to the entrance road. Leaving the magnificent Israelite gate for a moment, take the path below the toilets to the Middle Bronze Age Gate (covered by a white roof). Return and pass through the Israelite Gate to the High Place.

The Middle Bronze Age Gate

The modern roof hints at the importance of what lies below, the only **mud-brick arched gate** in the Near East to have survived intact (compare ASHQELON). It is dated to the middle of the C18 BC. Plaster originally covered the fragile construction material. Created by three radial courses, the 2.4 m-wide arch is the outermost of three such arches; the gate contains two guardrooms on either side. From the plain, then some 12 m below, **stone stairs** climb to the gate. Inside the city a similar flight of steps leads down to a street. The gate is recessed between two **towers.** A distinct bulge outward in the northern one necessitated a buttress, which is strengthened by a sloping stone revetment. The danger of collapse probably explains why the gate was taken out of commission after only a couple of generations. Then it was completely filled with earth, which was also poured over it.

The abandoned gate thus became an indistinguishable part of a huge **earthen rampart** that circled the top of the mound. Soil was deposited around a core of stone (6.5 m thick and at least 11 m high) to create a triangular rampart whose base is 60 m wide and whose plastered sides slope at 38 degrees. It is estimated that the 1.7 km rampart contains a million m³ of material; steady work for 1,000 labourers for three years. The disadvantage of this gigantic construction was to severely restrict the habitable area inside. Were growth not to be strangled, it would have to be abandoned, as it was when the Israelites arrived in the C10 BC and began construction outside.

The Israelite Gate Area (Fig. 115)

The main gate was the social, juridical, and economic centre of an Iron Age city. There the king sat in audience (2 Sam. 19: 9). There the respected elders assembled to witness oral contracts (Gen. 23: 17–19) or to act in judgement (Deut. 20: 19). There minors (Job 5: 4) and the poor (Amos 5: 12) came to plead, prompting the demand of the prophet, 'Let justice reign at the city gate' (Amos 5: 15; cf. Zech. 8: 16). There people gathered to

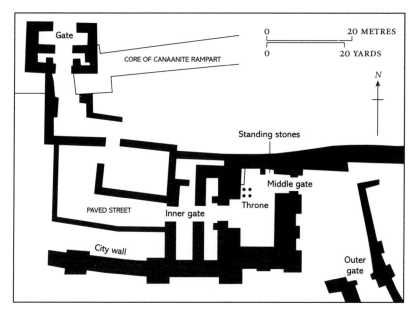

▲ **Fig. 115.** Tel Dan. The Israelite Gate Area (after Biran).

gossip (Ps. 69: 13). There news brought by travellers was as fresh as the produce from the countryside. In the C9 BC in order to provide a suitable setting for these varied activities king Ahab abandoned the security of the C18 rampart, and created an elaborate gate complex at the foot of the slope. Three doorways were separated by two paved areas.

The doorposts of the **outer gate** fitted into hemispherical stones which pivoted in concave sockets. The plaza inside covers some 475 m². Fill in its eastern wall contained the broken C9 BC inscription containing the words 'king of Israel' and 'house of David'. Either this or the 200 m² inner plaza could be 'the square at the gate of the city' (e.g. Judg. 19: 15; 2 Chr. 32: 6). On the right just inside the **middle gate** five small flat stones (*massebot*) stand in a niche; they vary between 50 and 30 cm in height and width. The long narrow stone table in front of them confirms their cultic connotations, and so illustrates 'the high places of the gates' (2 Kgs. 23: 8), which Josiah (640–609) condemned. The elders no doubt sat on the 4.5 m-long **bench** of dressed stones directly ahead (Prov. 31: 23). At one end is a small hollow square preceded by a step; decorated stone bases at its corners supported the pillars of a canopy, which has now been reconstructed. This is the sort of **throne** that the king might have used when 'he sat in the gate' (2 Sam. 19: 9).

The paving of the two plazas continues through the **inner gate** and then opens into a **10 m-wide street**. The stones are polished by thousands of feet. Originally it must have ascended to the cult centre on the

> ## Job Recalls His Former Happiness
>
> 'When I went out to the gate of the city,
> when I took my seat in the square,
> as soon as I appeared, the young men stepped aside,
> and the old men rose to their feet.
> Men of note broke off their speeches,
> and put their hands over their mouths;
> the voices of rulers were silenced,
> and their tongues stayed still in their mouths.'
>
> (Job 29: 7–9)

summit. In the C8 a wall built across the road forced pedestrians to make two 90 degree turns into a paved square outside the western entrance of a **new gate complex** which reused the stone core of the Canaanite rampart. The threat from Assyria necessitated strengthening the defences of the city. The convenience of the century-old gate at the bottom of the slope had to give way to other imperatives.

The modern path leads directly to the High Place.

The Cult Centre

The cult centre at Dan, founded by Jeroboam I in the C10 BC, served the religious needs of the inhabitants of the city until the C4 AD. The gods worshipped changed with the cultures. Inevitably some petitioners were not sure who precisely was in charge, and preferred vagueness in their prayers (cf. Amos 8: 14). A bilingual C2 BC inscription reads in Greek, 'To the god who is in Dan, Zoilos vowed a vow' and in Aramaic (reconstructed), 'In Dan, Zilas made a vow to the god'. The surround wall with the entrance and the circular reservoir are dated to the period of the inscription. The other remains have been restored as they were in the time of Jeroboam II (784–48). Holographic viewers depict the ritual of sacrifice in biblical times.

The **horned altar** (symbolized by a metal outline) stood in a walled square with doors on the east and south. On the assumption that the proportion of the height of the one horn recovered to that of the altar was 1 : 6, the altar stood 3 m high. Stairs at two corners gave access to the top.

Perfectly aligned with the centre of the altar steps led up to the **sanctuary** (*bamah*). Its walls have been partially restored using the header and stretcher technique of the original, and a wooden beam has been inserted into the slot in the eastern wall. Similar slots are visible on the southern and western faces. Rectangular dowels held the wood in place. The wood they contained was burnt out in the Assyrian destruction. It is not quite the 'three courses of stone and one of wood' of the temple in Jerusalem

(Ezra 6: 4; 1 Kgs. 6: 36; 7: 12), but the same principle is at work; wood stabilizes drystone buildings shaken by earthquakes.

Three **small altars** were found in the room with two entrances west of the main altar. All showed traces of fire. This room also yielded the only two C8 BC **incense shovels** in the country.

Tel el-Farah (L12)

One of the most scenic drives on the West Bank is the road from NABLUS to Jiftlik in the Jordan valley. It runs in the beautiful Wadi Farah (Nahal Tirza) which was probably the route by which Abraham (Gen. 12: 5–6) entered the land of Canaan and came to Shechem (TEL BALATA); the present route follows the line of a Roman road. The intense cultivation is made possible by two powerful springs En Duleib and En Faria, which flow the length of the valley. Between them rises Tel el-Farah, once Tirza, the first capital of the Northern Kingdom (Israel).

Neolithic hunters were the first to settle by the springs about 7000 BC. This occupation was very small and poor, and the one which followed in the Copper Age was not much better. A sudden change took place c.3100 BC when a new people moved in; they knew how to build with stone and had experience of urban life. They fortified the site for the first time and built houses of mud-brick on foundation courses of stone. This civilization came to an end c.2500 BC, in a period which shows a marked decline in urbanism throughout Canaan, and the site lay abandoned for nearly 600 years.

The new settlers were few in number, but c.1700 BC there was an increase in population, but still not sufficient to occupy the whole area of the earlier town. They built a new wall which excluded the eastern section of the mound and, in the process, modified the position of the western gate. The most interesting building of this period is an underground sanctuary in which young pigs were sacrificed; in the ancient Orient such sacrifices were essentially related to magic and exorcisms.

Tirza is mentioned as one of the Canaanite cities captured by Joshua (Josh. 12: 24). In the early Israelite period (C10–C9 BC) houses of uniform quality lined well-marked streets; the city had the dignity befitting the capital it became when Israel seceded from Judah after the death of Solomon (1 Kgs. 14: 17). This city was brutally destroyed in the early part of the C9 BC. The timing fits perfectly with a series of events dated to 882 BC when Zimri assassinated king Elah and reigned for seven days in Tirza. When the news reached the army the troops proclaimed Omri king, 'So Omri went up from Gibbethon, and all Israel with him, and they besieged Tirza. And when Zimri saw that the city was taken, he went into the citadel of the king's house, and burned the king's house over him with fire and died' (1 Kgs. 16: 17–18).

Omri reigned for six years in Tirza (1 Kgs. 16: 23) but the first four were taken up with the struggle against his rival Tibni. The delay this caused in the reconstruction of the city is betrayed by a hiatus in the archaeological levels. New buildings do appear, but the most important one was abandoned when only half finished; a dressed stone, almost ready to be put into position, was found as the stonecutter left it. It is impossible not to relate this to Omri's decision to move the capital to SAMARIA (1 Kgs. 16: 24), taking, it seems, most of the population with him, because the site lay uninhabited for a short period.

Intensive occupation in the C8 BC is clearly attested. Israel enjoyed great prosperity under Jehoash (800–784 BC) and Jeroboam II (784–748 BC), and this flourishing period is represented here by rich private houses whose opulence contrasts vividly with the miserable hovels of the poor. Such social inequality, with the development of an urban proletariat, evoked the condemnation of the prophets (Amos 5: 10–13). The fire predicted by Hosea (8: 14) arrived in the form of the Assyrians who devastated the city in 723 BC (2 Kgs. 17: 5). Tirza became an open city and continued to decline until the site was finally abandoned c.600 BC, possibly as the result of an epidemic of malaria which was endemic in the area until this century.

Visit. From the Nablus–Damieh Bridge (Gesher Adam) road (Route 57) take the turn to Tubas (Route 58). Located 4.5 or 3.5 km from the main road (depending on which turn-off is used), the site is not marked in any way but is easy to recognize (Fig. 116). Where the tarmac road bears sharply right after crossing a small stream in the bottom of a steep-sided valley, go left on to a dirt road which circles behind the mound. It is possible to drive right to the edge of the excavated area. Parts of the site have been excavated to a greater depth than others; fine lines show the edges of the different levels which can be used as orientation points.

The C8 BC level is the most natural one at which to start since it is nearest the end of the access road. The miserable **houses of the poor** [1] are separated by a long straight wall from two **upper-class houses** [2] whose plan is perfectly preserved. The single door gives access to a courtyard with rooms on three sides, some of the floors are cobbled. Around these houses are other buildings [3] of the Iron Age.

In the C9 BC a **large building** [4] was started but never rose above the foundation levels; no trace of a floor was found. Three rooms are disposed around a central courtyard entered from the north; on the west is a long hall with a wide entrance. Just beside the north-east corner is a dressed stone designed for the superstructure, now lying flat; it was discovered tilted at the stonecutter's angle as if the mason had been summoned abruptly to another job.

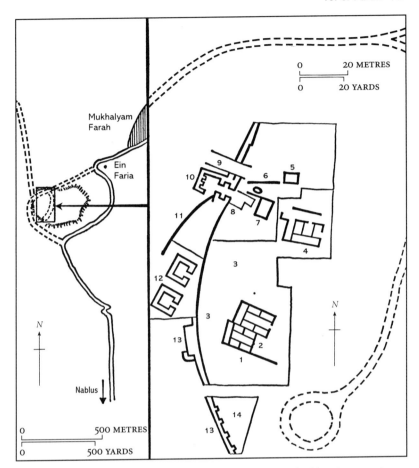

▲ **Fig. 116.** Location of Tel el-Farah on Nablus–Tubas road with enlargement of excavated area (after de Vaux). Fine lines indicate different levels. 1–2. C8 BC houses; 3. Iron Age buildings; 4. C9 BC Unfinished building; 5. Underground sanctuary; 6–7. Early Bronze Age houses; 8. Collapsed mud-brick; 9. Section through city wall; 10. Middle Bronze Age gate; 11. Middle Bronze Age glacis; 12. Early Bronze Age gate; 13. Middle Bronze Age city wall; 14. Early Bronze Age houses.

From the unfinished building go along the edge of the deep trench to the north-east corner where it is easy to get down. The wide stone walls of the **underground sanctuary** [5] stand out clearly; for some two hundred years (1750–1550 BC) pigs were here sacrificed to the gods of the underworld. The walls [6] nearby are the foundations of a house of the Early Bronze Age (3100–2500 BC), the upper courses were of mud-brick.

In the centre a shallow circular pit about 2 m in diameter is all that rem
ains of a **hut of the Copper Age** (4500–3100 BC); the walls were of mud
mixed with rubble. Just beside is another **Early Bronze Age house [7]**,
the two rows of stones in the centre were the foundations of wooden
pillars supporting the roof. A similar house to the west was buried when
the **mud-brick city wall** collapsed on top of it. The tumbled bricks can
still be seen in the side of the baulk [8], and a cut in the side of the 2 m-
thick wall clearly reveals the method of construction.

One can leave the Early and Middle Bronze Age level by the section
[9] cut through the city wall; note that the original mud-brick wall was
reinforced on the outside by stone facing. The structure of the **city gate**
[10] is well preserved; it was of the indirect entrance type and was rebuilt
many times, for it served the city for over 1,000 years (1700–600 BC).
Running south from the gate is the curved line of the **Middle Bronze
Age glacis [11]**. When complete, this covered the original Early Bronze
Age gate [12]; its hollow square towers of mud-brick protected the city
during the first part of the third millennium BC.

Continuing to the south the **city wall [13]**, which was in use from
1700 to 600 BC, is clearly visible. The structures at the bottom of the triangular trench [14] are the foundations of **Early Bronze Age houses**.

Tel er-Ras (K13)

The northern peak of MOUNT GERIZIM towers above NABLUS (Fig. 100).
Coins minted in the reign of Antoninus Pius (AD 139–61), with the
inscription 'Flavia Neapolis of Palestinian Syria', show a temple on the
summit linked to the city by a long flight of steps (Fig. 117).

With this clue archaeologists brought to light a 10 m-high **platform**
(65 × 44 m) on which stood a small **temple** (14 × 21 m). Dated to the
middle of the C2 AD, it was dedicated to Zeus Hypsistos. At the end of
that century the temple collapsed or was destroyed. A new temple some
2.5 m higher was erected at the beginning of the C3 AD, perhaps under
the emperor Caracalla (211–17). It does not appear to have survived
the C4.

The temple is not mentioned by the Pilgrim of Bordeaux, but he
asserts that **1,300 steps** led to the summit. This feature is mentioned by
two other Byzantine authors (Epiphanius and Procopius), and 65 steps
have been found cut into the rock of the mountain. The building depicted
at the bottom of the stairway lies beneath the present mosque of Rijal
el-Amud.

▲ **Fig. 117.** C2 AD coin showing temple on Tel er-Ras.

Tel es-Samrat (M16)

From the road which leads to its base it is only a small dusty mound (Fig. 74), but from the top one looks down into the semicircle of Herod's **theatre** with the long rectangle (315 × 84 m) of the **hippodrome** stretching out in front.

This site is intimately associated with three events which took place in the tense days surrounding the death of Herod the Great in 4 BC. There, lying on a couch because too ill to stand, he reproached the leaders of the Jews for an abortive uprising in Jerusalem, which he interpreted as base ingratitude. This hint of the temper of his people worked on his diseased mind and he had eminent Jews from throughout Judaea interned in the hippodrome with orders that they be killed at the moment of his death. This manic plan, to ensure that tears would accompany his departure, was ignored by the king's sister Salome, who instead used the hippodrome to win the mercenaries' loyalty to her nephew Archelaus (*War* 1: 647–73).

Visit. On leaving the parking lot at TEL ES-SULTAN turn left and immediately right. Bear left and continue out of the built-up area on a very rough road. After crossing the wadi the tel is directly ahead.

The tel is in fact an artificial platform of mud-brick projecting out from the back of the theatre. It supported a **building** (70 × 70 m) erected round a courtyard, probably a reception area. JERICHO was a private royal estate, and those who attended the shows here would have been members of the court. They would have been comfortably accommodated in the 3,000–4,000-seat theatre with their backs protected against the cold north wind of winter; no benches have been found in the walled hippodrome.

The rigidly horizontal line on the nearby cliffs is the **aqueduct** which brought water from the springs near Naaran to the palace at TULUL ABU EL-ALAIQ. Just below the aqueduct, piles of excavation debris reveal the openings of a number of **rock-cut tombs**. These were part of the great cemetery, stretching for some 10 km along the cliffs, which served Jericho between 100 BC and AD 68. The tombs are of a very common type: burial recesses are cut into three walls above a bench. In some of the recesses were remains of wooden coffins. Made of planks mortised to the four corner-posts, these generally had gabled covers and painted decoration.

Tel es-Sultan* (M16)

The jagged outline beside the main road leading out of JERICHO to the north suggests a badly kept rubbish dump, but the climb to the top is worth while (Fig. 74). In a deep trench stands a **great stone tower** (diameter 8.5 m; height 7.75 m) with a perfectly preserved stairway running up the centre. Constructed about 8000 BC, this supreme achievement of a Stone Age people is without parallel elsewhere in the world. Open: 7.30 a.m.–5 p.m. (winter); to 7 p.m. (summer).

The mound grew to its present height of 15 m as town after town was built on the same site. Hunters probably visited the spring (En es-Sultan) from time immemorial. In the Mesolithic period (15,000–8300 BC) their camp included a small sanctuary. They lived in flimsy shelters which later evolved into mud-brick huts with domed roofs. Their tools were of flint, bone, and wood, and in place of pottery they used limestone utensils. Their construction of the tower and its associated defence wall in the first part of the Neolithic period attests a very high degree of communal organization, which must have been reflected also in the agricultural and irrigation systems needed to support a town of some 2,000 inhabitants. Jericho was one of the places which saw human society move from its food-gathering to its food-producing phase.

Around 6800 BC the original settlers at Jericho were displaced by another Neolithic people who brought with them a much more sophisticated form of architecture; courtyards were surrounded by large airy rooms. It seems that they practised a form of ancestor worship because ten skulls were found whose **features were restored in plaster** (these are to be seen in the Rockefeller Museum, Jerusalem). The delicate individualized modelling of ears, noses, and eyebrows, and the flesh-coloured tinting make them extraordinarily lifelike. A head sculpted in unbaked clay with shell eyes and hair marked by lines of paint is probably also from this period.

Having survived for some 2,000 years, these people disappeared as suddenly as their predecessors. Around 4500 BC they were succeeded by others whose architecture was inferior (they lived in pits or semi-subterranean huts) but who had discovered pottery. However, neither they nor any of the subsequent waves of immigrants ever produced anything as extraordinary (for their time) as the tower or the plastered skulls. Succeeding periods in the archaeological history of Tel es-Sultan are parallel to what has been discovered at many other sites. What was discovered in the careful stratigraphic cuts, and in the many undisturbed rock-cut tombs, augmented existing knowledge and made it more precise but without contributing anything unique.

Two elements from these later periods are still visible. At the north end of the tel, facing the refugee camp, the Middle Bronze Age (2200–1550 BC) **glacis**, which steepened the angle of the slope to 35 degrees, is clearly evident in the side of the trench. Those with trained eyes can follow, around the summit of the tel, the **mud-brick wall** which defended the Early Bronze Age (3150–2200 BC) town. At one time this was thought to be the wall blown down by the trumpets of Joshua (Josh. 6), but now it is known to have been in ruins for 1,000 years before the exodus took place around 1250 BC. Nothing subsequent to the end of the Late Bronze Age was found on the surface of the tel, but evidence for reoccupation in the C7 BC appeared on the sides. After the Babylonian exile the site was abandoned.

Tel Miqne (F17)

It should be called 'the Invisible Tel'. The mound barely protrudes above the surface and from any distance is easily taken for one of the gentle undulations of the great plain. Yet it was once Ekron, one of the five great cities of the PHILISTINES (Josh. 13: 3).

Occupation of the site began in the Chalcolithic period (4500–3100 BC) and continued, though not without trials and tribulations, throughout the succeeding Bronze Age (3100–1200 BC). It really enters history, however, only with the advent of the Philistines in the C12 BC. Their chariots of iron gave them control of the coastal plain and assertions of Israelite possession reflect a much later situation (Judg. 1: 18–19). After its capture at Ebenezer (1 Sam. 4: 11), today IZBET SARTAH, the Ark of the Covenant was placed in the temple of Dagon in Ashdod. Having caused a plague there and in Gath it was brought to Ekron whence it was returned to the Israelites (1 Sam. 5). They pursued the Philistines to 'the gates of

Ekron' after David killed Goliath (1 Sam. 17: 52). The non-Jewish character of the city in subsequent centuries is underlined by the facts that its
god was Baal-zebub (2 Kgs. 1: 2) and that it was cursed as Philistine by the
prophet Amos (1: 8).

In the C10 BC the aggressiveness of Israelite kings cut the economic
prosperity of Ekron and it shrank from 20 hectares to 4 hectares.
Occupation was limited to the upper city. Ekron got a new lease of life
when it came under Assyrian dominion in the C8 BC. Sennacherib
(704–681 BC) restored Padi to his throne (see box). According to an
inscription found here in 1996 (which makes the identification of the site
certain), Achish, son of Padi, dedicated a temple at Ekron to an Assyrian
goddess. In the C6 BC Ekron with other towns had to provide and transport timber to Nineveh for the palace of king Esarhaddon (680–669 BC).
None the less the city prospered and grew again to the limits of the
mound. At least 20 per cent of the space within the city was concerned
with the production of olive oil. The presence of large numbers of loom
weights in the same rooms suggests that textile-making occupied the time
between olive harvests.

Ekron never really recovered from its destruction by Nebuchadnezzar
in 603 BC, and is not mentioned again until 147 BC when Alexander Balas
of Syria granted it to Jonathan Maccabaeus (1 Macc. 10: 89). Ekron benefited by the emperor Hadrian's expulsion of Jews from Aelia Capitolina
and its territory in AD 135. In the C4 AD Eusebius describes it as 'a very
large Jewish village'. It was important enough in the C6 to merit a place in
the Madaba map, but thereafter it fades into insignificance.

Visit. The white sign on route 3 for Revadim is supplemented by an
orange one reading Eqron. Drive straight through the kibbutz; the excellent dirt road through the intensely cultivated fields is signposted wher-

---

Sennacherib Captures Ekron

'The officials, the patricians and the (common) people of Ekron, who
had thrown Padi, their king, into fetters (because he was) loyal to (his)
solemn oath (sworn) by the god Ashur, and had handed him over to
Hezekiah, the Jew, who held him in prison, unlawfully as if he had been
an enemy. . . . I assaulted Ekron and killed the officials and patricians
who had committed the crime and hung their bodies on poles
surrounding the city. The (common) citizens who were guilty of minor
crimes, I considered prisoners of war. The rest of them who were not
accused of crimes and misbehaviour, I released. I made Padi, their king,
come from Jerusalem and set him as their lord on the throne, imposing upon him the tribute (due) to me (as) overlord.' (*Prism of
Sennacherib*, trans. A. L. Oppenheim)

ever a doubt might arise. The meandering line of high reeds indicates the course of the Wadi Timnah.

The 20-hectare tel (twice the size of LAKHISH) falls naturally into two parts; the 16-hectare square **lower city** and the 4-hectare **upper city** projecting from the north-east corner. A **double wall**, one on the top and the other at the bottom of the slope, encircled the C7 BC city. The **city gate** was in the middle of the south wall. Flanked by towers, it has two guardrooms on both sides.

Immediately inside the upper wall on all four sides, but most extensively on the south, was the **industrial area**. To date 105 oil-production units have been found. Together they would have produced 1,000 tons or 1,322,400 litres of olive oil per year, which makes Ekron the largest known olive-oil industrial centre in the ancient Near East. The city took full advantage of its position between the hills in which the olive trees grow and the harbours on the coast. Much of its production must have been for export; it could not have been absorbed locally. The residential area was in the centre of the city.

The **typical production unit** comprised three rooms. The innermost contained the press, the middle was for storage, and the third opened on to the street. The pressing involved two procedures. The olives were first crushed with a stone hand roller in a shallow rectangular basin. The pulp thus produced was packed into woven baskets which were placed on the vats on either side of the crushing basin; a pierced board resting on the ledge ensured that the baskets did not sag. One end of a wooden beam fitted into a niche in the wall behind, and pressure was applied by roping pierced stone weights to the outer end. The oil was removed from the vats by dipper juglets, but it is also possible that the vats were lined with skin bags which could be lifted out when full. In either case the vats were then emptied into the sort of large krater found in the storage rooms. Such vessels had holes a little more than half-way down so that the water could be drained away once the oil had risen to the surface.

An oil press has been reconstructed in the **Revadim Archaeological Museum** in the kibbutz (open by appointment; tel.: 08–591063). Models and maps explain the history of Ekron. For the complete history of oil production the place to visit is the **Edible Oil Museum** located in the 'Shemen' Oil Factory on Jaffa Road in Haifa.

Tel Qedesh (M3)

The majority of sites in Galilee contain either a synagogue or a church. A Roman temple dedicated to the God of the Sky makes Qedesh unique. It is the southernmost example of Roman temples in Syria and Phoenicia, and may have influenced the architectural style of synagogues at Kefar Baram, GUSH HALAV and others in the vicinity of Qedesh.

The site, which is easily identified (Tobit 1: 2), had a long history before the Romans arrived. It was already strongly fortified in the Early Bronze period (2850–2650 BC), but the earliest attestations of the name appear in Egypt in the battle records of Thutmose III (1468 BC) and Seti I (1303 BC) inscribed on the walls of the temple of Amon in Karnak. Once the Israelites arrived it was attributed to the tribe of Naphtali (Judg. 4: 6), and was designated both a city of refuge (Josh. 20: 7) and a levitical city (Josh. 21: 32). Tiglath-Pileser III of Assyria deported the leading inhabitants in 734 BC (2 Kgs. 15: 29). Six centuries later Jonathan Maccabaeus defeated the Syrians there in 145 BC (1 Macc. 11: 63–74). At that stage the city belonged to Tyre, and was noted for its hostility towards Jews (*War* 4: 105). In AD 66 Jews burnt it in reprisal for the massacre of their co-religionists in CAESAREA (*War* 2: 459). The city recovered in the C2 AD and, although it suffered in the earthquake of 363, it remained a modestly prosperous village throughout all subsequent changes of power until this century.

Visit. The only remains of any significance are those of a C2 AD temple. It is located to the north of route 899 at approximately 1.5 km west of its junction with route 866, which runs north to HUNIN. Once the ruin comes into sight continue until a path running past the tombs becomes visible.

The complex consists of a sacred area (*temenos*) with a monumental temple in the centre. Enough of the **enclosure wall** has survived, especially on the west and south, to indicate that it measured 80 × 55 m. The single entrance must have been in the east wall as in other temples of this type.

The **temple** consisted of a rectangular *cella* and a portico with six columns, but only part of the façade survives. There are three ornamentally carved entrances. The square sockets cut into the threshold of the central door and the vertical groove in the jamb suggest that a screen of some sort blocked access when the door was opened. Worshippers could look in but not enter; they had to be content with a glimpse of the statue of the god in the apse at the far end. According to a Greek inscription of the early C2 AD the temple was dedicated to the 'Holy God of the Sky', i.e. Baal-Shamin, one of the principal divinities of the Syro-Phoenician pantheon in the Roman period.

Between each lateral entrance and the corner are **reliefs of volute kraters** with ribbed bodies surmounted by small apsidal niches. An inclined groove runs through the wall to a larger niche on its internal face. These are unparalleled elsewhere, and their interpretation is necessarily hypothetical. The most obvious possibility is that libations—sacrificial blood, wine, or oil—were poured into the outer niche and collected in a basin placed at the bottom of the internal niche. The fact that there are tombs on three sides of the sacred enclosure has led to the hypothesis that this ceremony was part of a rite designed to link the world of the living with that of the dead. The figure carved in sunken relief in the recess above the left-hand krater is clothed in a toga and holds a spear and a libation vessel.

The temple was in use in the C2–C3 AD, and appears to have been destroyed by the earthquake of AD 363.

Tiberias (N6) ★

Founded between AD 17 and 20 by Herod Antipas (4 BC–AD 39), the son of Herod the Great, and mentioned in the gospels (John 6: 1, 23; 12: 1), Tiberias' spiritual authority is enhanced by a rich variety of archaeological remains.

The west side of the SEA OF GALILEE (Fig. 107) was lined with villages in the C1 AD, and Herod Antipas's choice of a virgin site betrays his desire to emulate his famous father. He wanted to create a showplace that would be entirely his own. He named it after his patron, the emperor Tiberius (AD 14–37), and made it the capital of Galilee in place of SEPPHORIS. Its unfortunate location on the site of an ancient cemetery created difficulties in finding inhabitants, and compulsion became necessary (*Antiquities* 18: 36–8). By the middle of the C1 AD Jews, however, were in the majority as well as being the ruling class. The city did not resist Vespasian in AD 67, and played an insignificant role in the Second Revolt (132–5), whose failure reduced the Jewish population of Judaea to virtually nothing. Galilee thus became the Jewish sector of Palestine, and it was in Tiberias that great scholars completed the labour of learning that preserved the identity of Judaism after the destruction of the Temple (AD 70).

Rabbi Johanan ben Nappaha (180–279) founded the great rabbinic school of Tiberias *c.* AD 235. He had been one of the last disciples of Rabbi Judah ha-Nasi (*c.*135–217), the compiler of the *Mishnah* (the organization of the oral code of law), and set himself to test the logical consistency of the *Mishnah*. He thus laid the foundations of the *Gemara* which was completed by his disciples in Tiberias *c.*400. The *Mishnah* and the *Gemara* together constitute the Palestinian (or Jerusalem) *Talmud*. Owing to Christian pressure the school of Tiberias began to break up in the middle of the C5. It came to life again in the C8–C10 when the five generations of the family of Ben Asher established the pointed text of the Hebrew Bible which won universal acceptance. To Tiberias therefore we owe the classic forms of the written and oral Law.

The great earthquake of 1033 destroyed Tiberias. In 1099 Tancred

A Tenth Century Riddle

'Of the people of Tiberias it is said, "For two months they dance, and for two more they gorge; that for two months they beat about, and for two more they go naked; that for two months they play the reed, and for two more they wallow." The explanation of this is they dance from the number of fleas, then gorge off the Nabak fruit. They beat about with fly-whisks to chase away the wasps from the meat and the fruits, then they go naked from the heat. They suck the sugar-canes and then have to wallow through their muddy streets.' (Mukaddasi (C10), *Description of Syria* 161; trans. G. Le Strange)

conquered Galilee for the Crusaders and rebuilt the city slightly further north of its original site. Its capture by Saladin in July 1187 provoked the battle at the HORNS OF HATTIN in which he destroyed the Latin Kingdom of Jerusalem. In 1562 Suliman the Magnificent granted Tiberias to Joseph Nasi, a Marrano Jew from Portugal. Aided by his mother-in-law, Donna Gracia, he rewalled the town and tried to develop a silk industry with a view to establishing an independent Jewish enclave. The project failed, and the city became prominent again only in the C18 when a bedouin sheikh, Daher el-Omar (1694–1775), rewalled the city and built the citadel from which he controlled all of Galilee to the frustration of the Turks. He was assassinated in 1775, and his fortress (today the 'Donna Gracia' restaurant) was ruined by the earthquake of 1837. The city received the Jews of the First Aliyah at the end of the C19 and since then has not ceased to prosper, expanding from the lake-front up the slopes to the west.

A serene park-like enclosure between Elhadeff Street (route 77) and Hakkam Rabbi Street houses the **tombs of the great Jewish sages**: Rabbi Yohanan ben Zakkai (C1 AD), Rabbi Eliezer ben Hyrcanus (C2 AD), and Rabbi Moses ben Maimon (C12 AD), better known as the Rambam (from the initial letters of his name) or Maimonides. On the hillside above, a white dome covers the cave-tomb of Rabbi Akiva (C2 AD) who acclaimed Bar Kokhba as the Messiah; he was executed by the Romans.

There are Crusader foundations to the many visible portions of the C18 walls. Erected around 1100 the **church of St Peter** has had a chequered history, becoming a mosque and later a caravanserai before being rebuilt in 1870 as a church; it was given its present form in 1944. The remains of the **Crusader cathedral** are visible in the archaeological park below the Jordan River Hotel and in front of the Plaza Hotel, together with the ruins of a **Byzantine synagogue** and a **Mamluk caravanserai**.

The **Municipal Antiquities Museum** is housed in what used to be the Jami al Bahr mosque on the lakeshore near the Marina.

Ancient Tiberias

The original site of Tiberias was south of the present built-up area, in the open space between the Geullim and Ahawa quarters and the Ganei Hamat Hotel. The remains are widely scattered and in most cases overgrown. There are plans to transform the area into an archaeological park.

Visit (Fig. 118). At the south end of the parking-lot across from Sironit Beach is a square complex (38 × 38 m) whose most distinctive feature is the apse of a **basilica**. It was built in the C2 AD to serve the administrative needs of Roman Tiberias. Four centuries later the fact that the apse was oriented to the east inspired the conversion of the building into a church. From the courtyard to the west of the colonnaded room follow the path

▼ **Fig. 118.** Ancient Tiberias (after Hirschfeld).

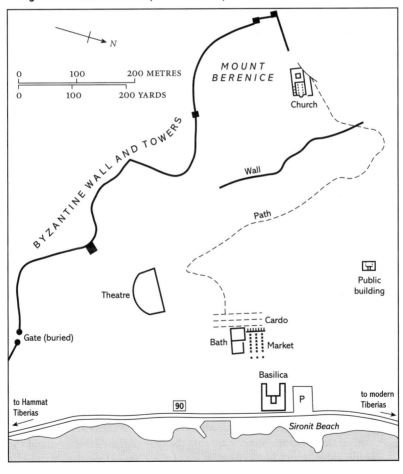

going slightly south-west for some 80 m to an excavated area marked by a protective roof.

The roof covers a **large bath-house**, which remained in use for 800 years after its construction in the C4 AD. The entrance was on the east. A large vestibule gave access to two halls to the south. All three have colourful **mosaic floors** in which animals, birds, and fish predominate. The organization of the bathing area proper is not as clear as in other baths, apart from the small pillars supporting the floor of the hot room.

The bath was bordered on the west by the *Cardo Maximus*, the main street running north–south through the centre of ancient Tiberias. Only part of the east side has been excavated. The covered 4 m-wide sidewalk separated the diagonally paved street from a **row of shops** (3 × 6.3 m). These were lit only by their doors.

Behind the shops are a series of column bases, each row terminating in a 2 m-square pier, which is in line with the façade of the bath. Similar piers appear to the west. Hence the inference that we have to do with a covered **market-place** divided by a 5 m-wide street. If the same length is assumed for the continuation of the market on the eastern side, there is just room for a street of similar width before the courtyard of the basilica.

Some 130 m to the south of the baths a quarry mars the slope of the hill. A little further to the south a curved wall has been brought to light. It implies a circle with a diameter of 70 m, and is plausibly identified as the outer wall of the **theatre**. It was in use in the Roman and Byzantine periods.

From here it is best to return to the parking-lot. The city gate at the south end of the *Cardo Maximus* is covered in silt washed down by the winter flooding of the wadi. Originally a free-standing arch flanked by two magnificent basalt towers (each 7 m in diameter), it was incorporated into the defensive system when the city was walled in the C6 AD.

Below the caves in Mt Berenice, in the immediate vicinity of the sewage purification plant, are the remains of part of a **large public building**. A covered porch runs around three sides of rectangular courtyard paved with white mosaic. Three square outlines in black filled with red triangles are the only decoration. Opposite the double entrance is a pool with rounded steps in two corners. Occupied from C3 AD to C8 the building has been tentatively identified as the Great Study House of Rabbi Johanan ben Nappaha. If correct, it would have been the scene of the intense debates of the sages which preceded the formulation of the Gemara.

Mount Berenice

The modern name of the peak which dominates ancient Tiberias originated in the romantic suggestion that the lady of the Arabic name of the place, *Qasr Bint el-Malik* 'The Palace of the King's Daughter', should be identified with the scandalous queen Berenice, daughter of king Agrippa I and a great-granddaughter of Herod the Great. After the death of her second husband, she lived with her brother, Agrippa II (Acts 25: 13), to whose domain Tiberias belonged (*War* 2: 252), and which may have been used as a winter residence. The expectations that the ruins on the summit would prove to be those of the gold-roofed palace built by Herod Antipas (*Life* 65–6) were not realized. They proved to belong to a Christian church!

Visit. An excellent unsealed road winds up the slope from the edge of the built-up area (the Geullim and Ahawa quarters) to the saddle linking Mount Berenice to the tree-covered higher ridge to the west. Originally a paved ascent from the area of the Roman bath angled across the steep face of the cliff to a point some 200 m north of the church where it made a dog-leg to the south-west.

The **wall with towers** on the right as one walks from the parking-lot to the edge is part of the city wall erected by the emperor Justinian (527–65). Its original height is estimated at 15 m. Unfortunately most of its facing stones have been robbed out and only the cement-bonded rubble core remains.

The **church** on the cliff edge exhibits the typical features of its Byzantine contemporaries. An atrium built over a large cistern (300 m³) lies to the west of a basilica, which is entered by three doors. The geometric tile patterns (*opus sectile*) of the nave contrast with the birds and fruit of mosaic floors of the two aisles. The three apses date the building to the C6. The stone bench circling the central apse was for the clergy who assisted the bishop. Beneath the altar was a marble slab with a circular hole through which one could reach to touch the relic below. In this case, however, the 'relic' proved to be a pierced stone weighing half a ton! It is in fact a **pagan cult stone** of the first half of the third millennium BC, but its resemblance to an anchor stone must have inspired some Byzantine Christians to see its gigantic size (ten times the weight of a normal anchor) as a symbol of the great quantities of fish caught at the direction of Jesus (Luke 5: 1–11; John 21: 1–8).

The earthquake of 749 completely destroyed the church, but within the next fifty years it had been rebuilt on its original foundations. The height of the columns, however, was halved. Byzantine columns average 3–4 m, but those here (including base and capital) are only 1.3 m. Such low arches (2.1 m) may betray Muslim influence because they are found in mosques of this period in Persia and in Mesopotamia. As the number of Christians decreased, part of the nave nearest the altar was walled off to create a small chapel in the centre of the church. The Crusaders, who used the edifice until their expulsion in 1187, added a square bell tower to the southern part of the original façade.

On the lower part of the slope is a **theatre** of the C2–C3 AD and the **aqueduct** which brought water from springs in Nahal Yavniel (9 km to the south) to a large reservoir in the centre of the city.

Timna (G40) ★

Patches of black on the red, brown, and white of the Arava cliffs betray the presence of heat even more intense than that furnished by nature. The ancient Egyptians came to smelt copper in this vast erosion basin; their mines, furnaces, and temples offer a unique insight into the exploitation of an important metal.

The earliest efforts to extract copper in this area go back to the third millennium BC. The Egyptians began systematic development of the site in the C13 BC. If at first the Egyptians were rather unwelcome guests, they soon worked in harmony with the local Midianite population, who maintained production for some time in the C11 BC after the Egyptian expeditions had ceased. The resources were exploited again only in the C2 AD by units of the Third Legion Cyrenaica. There followed another long interval until the late C20, when the Israelis began large-scale production.

Visit (Fig. 119). Open: 8.30 a.m.–4 p.m.; Fridays 3 p.m. The entrance road is about 26 km north of Eilat on route 90, and exactly 3 km north of the access road to the modern mining operation. Toilets and drinking-water are available at the gatehouse, which also has a small covered auditorium with displays illustrating the geological formations and the mining techniques. A similar exhibit is to be found at the **Yotvata Museum and Visitors' Centre** (across the road from Kibbutz Yotvata) which also displays discoveries made at Kuntillet Ajrud in Sinai. Open: 9 a.m.–2.30 p.m.; Friday to 1 p.m.; Saturday 10 a.m.–2 p.m.

The Temple of Hathor

The parking-lot at the end of the paved road is opposite a rock formation of Nubian sandstone known as **'Solomon's Pillars'**. The temple is

---

Rameses III (1184–1153 BC) reports:

'I sent forth my messengers to the country of Atika [= the Arava?], to the great copper mines which are in this place. Their galleys carried them, others on the land journey were upon their donkeys. Their mines were found abounding in copper; it was loaded by tens of thousands [of bars] into their galleys. They were sent forward to Egypt and arrived safely.' (*Papyrus Harris* 1: 78, 2)

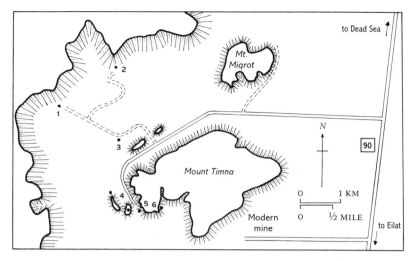

▲ **Fig. 119.** Timna (after Rothenberg). 1. Mines; 2. Rock carvings; 3. Mushroom camp; 4. Defended smelting sites; 5. Solomon's Pillars; 6. Hathor Temple.

located around the corner of the bluff to the right. It is a simple **square enclosure** with the entrance opposite the *naos*, a low rectangle of stones built around a **niche** carved in the cliff. At one stage two square pillars with Hathor heads flanked the niche. Hathor, the divine cow who gave birth each day to Horus the sun-god, was also the 'Lady of Turquoise' and as such was patron of the turquoise mines at Serabit el-Khadem in central Sinai. It was this association that led to her being venerated here. The temple was in Egyptian use from *c*.1300 to 1150 BC. When they left the Midianites took it over. They added an offering bench inside the entrance to the left, and a small chamber (for a priest?) outside the east wall. They defaced the Hathor pillars, and reused one (standing on its head) as part of a row of standing stones inside the west wall. The excavations brought to light along the east and west walls rolls of heavy red and yellow cloth with beads woven into it; in the Midianite period this was the tent that covered the sanctuary (compare the 'Tent of Meeting' in Exod. 33: 7–11).

From the temple a modern flight of steps leads up to a point where, with the aid of the sighting tube, one can see the **hieroglyphic inscription** showing Rameses III offering sacrifice to Hathor. It is worthwhile continuing up the steps in the cliff to a natural arch from which there is a splendid view. The path straight ahead leads down to the parking-lot.

Defended Smelting Sites

The presence of defensive installations at both these sites suggests that they date from the very early part of the Egyptian mining operation, when the intruders were viewed with suspicion by the local population.

Both the ancient and the modern footpaths to the southern summit are on the west side; the ancient route passed through the rudimentary wall of rough stones at a **gate defended by a tower**. The most interesting feature is at the extreme north-east end of the plateau, where a flight of natural rock steps leads up to the artificially flattened top of the rock (3 × 3 m). The presence of a series of cup marks (conical artificial depressions in the rock) at its foot suggests that the platform served as an **altar**. The remainder of the plateau is covered with broken-up slag, probably the work of a later people who came to scavenge copper pellets in the old slag-heaps.

From the altar one can see the semicircular **defensive wall** of the northern summit anchored to the base of the northern tip of the hill to the west. The single entrance in the north-west segment was defended by two towers. The eastern half of the enclosure contains rudimentary **shelters** for the workers, whereas the western half is the **work area**.

Two types of smelting furnace are visible. Though not separated by any great interval of time, they betray a significant advance in metallurgical technique. The **earlier, smaller furnaces** (35 cm in diameter and 50 cm deep) used small bellows and had no tapping pit, the slag being permitted to run on the ground before being crushed to extract the copper pellets. The **later furnaces** were larger; the coating of their walls with slag-tempered clay and the use of bellows almost twice as big permitted much higher temperatures; they also had tapping pits.

The Mushroom Camp

After passing over the low ridge between two dark hills the natural phenomenon from which this site takes its name is immediately visible; it is a 6 m-high free-standing sandstone mass scoured into the shape of a mushroom by the wind. East of the mushroom excavations have laid bare an undefended smelting site of the period when the Egyptians had established good relations with the local Midianites.

The first fenced-in area contains a small **Midianite temple**, a simple rectangular enclosure with an offering bench inside the entrance to the right, a flat-topped stone that served as an altar in the centre, and a line of standing stones; the arrangement is identical with the last phase of the Hathor temple.

West of the temple three dark slag-heaps draw attention to the **smelting furnaces**, of which little is now to be seen. Much more interesting is the fenced work area to the north. The central feature here is a courtyard. It contains a deep **stone-lined pit** in which the ores brought from the mines were stored. The adjacent **stone platform** served for the preparation of the smelting charge. The ores were crushed and mixed with the equally finely ground fluxes; a slight amount of water bound the powder into pellets ready to be dropped through the open top of the smelting furnaces. The two rooms on the west contained cisterns and more storage pits.

The two-roomed structure on the east appears to have served as **living quarters**, a small stone-built hearth was found outside the wall on the side furthest from the crushing platform. In the northern part of the courtyard were **casting furnaces** whose crucibles transformed the copper globules brought from the smelting furnaces into the ingots that were shipped to Egypt.

The Mines

From the parking-lot go towards the natural sandstone arches from which a signposted trail (500 m) leads to one of the many mining areas. **Shafts**, some 20 m deep, with niches for hand- and footholds, were driven down into the copper-bearing white sandstone. From them branch out **galleries** roughly a metre square. It takes little imagination to visualize the hellish working conditions, an aspect that is emphasized by the numerous **cisterns** used for the collection of run-off rain-water; the thirst of those working underground must have been terrible.

Rock Carvings

About 50 m west of the parking-lot a narrow canyon opens into the mountainside. On the left side, protected by an overhang, is a 9 m-long rock engraving dated to the C13–C12 BC. All the figures did not belong to the **original composition**, which represented a procession of chariots, each drawn by two animals and containing two figures. These wear a triangular loincloth with a dagger at the waist, and carry a battleaxe and/or a shield. The reins are tied to the charioteer's waist in order to leave his arms free. All these elements are paralleled in Egyptian temple reliefs of the New Kingdom. Offerings placed at the foot of the drawing underline its votive character.

The original theme is interrupted by a **secondary insertion**; a group of figures in the upper centre. Their bodies are drawn with double outline in order to give them greater stature than the Egyptians. With the aid of dogs they are hunting animals identified as ibex and the straight-horned oryx; there is also an ostrich. The addition of these figures, presumably representing the local Midianites, probably reflects the same type of take-over as noted with reference to the Hathor temple.

Toron of the Knights: *see* LATRUN

Tulul Abu el-Alaiq (M16) ★★

From even a short distance nothing is visible save two brown mounds separated by the Wadi Qilt/Nahal Perat (Fig. 74). None the less, for over a century this was the winter playground of Jewish kings. 'The air is so mild

that the inhabitants dress in linen when the rest of Judaea is under snow'
(*War* 4: 473). Most of the structures were of mud-brick, which has eroded
to nothing, but the stone foundation courses and mosaic or tiled floors
give a vivid impression of what the quality of life must have been when
Herod brought his court to JERICHO.

The site was occupied in the last part of the Chalcolithic Age
(*c*.4500–3100 BC), a period that is missing at TEL ES-SULTAN. There is no
trace of any subsequent occupation until the Hasmoneans developed the
site in the C1 BC. Three building phases have been discerned, the first two
attributed to the reign of Alexander Jannaeus (103–76 BC), and the third
to that of his widow and successor, Alexandra (76–67 BC).

During the years 34–30 BC, when he rented the immensely profitable
balsam plantations (see box) from Cleopatra (*War* 1: 361), Herod the
Great built a winter residence just west of the mound on the south side of
the wadi. More a house than a palace, these ruins are no longer visible.
Sometime after Octavian (Augustus) had granted Jericho to Herod (*War*
1: 396), the latter took over the Hasmonean palace on the north bank of
the wadi and remodelled it completely. It was probably at this stage that he
built the theatre and hippodrome (TEL ES-SAMRAT). Despite its magnificence the restored palace failed to satisfy his lust for ostentatious display,
and perhaps ten years later he constructed a new group of buildings on
both sides of the wadi (*War* 1: 407). The sentinel guarding this complex
was the fortress of KYPROS on a cliff-top to the west.

It was to this verdant spot that Herod came in his last terrible illness,
and it was here that he died, five days after killing his eldest son and heir,
Antipater. The king's body was borne to HERODION for burial (*War* 1:
656–73). According to Josephus, Herod's ex-slave Simeon, who claimed
the crown, burnt the palace (*War* 2: 57), which was rebuilt by Archelaus
when his right of succession had been confirmed (*Antiquities* 17: 340).

The Value of Balsam

'Every other scent ranks below balsam. The only country to which this
plant has been granted is Judaea, where formerly it grew in only two
gardens, both belonging to the king; one measured not more than
2.6 km² and the other less. This variety of shrub was exhibited to the
capital [Rome] by the emperors Vespasian and Titus; and it is a remarkable fact that ever since the time of Pompey the Great even trees have
figured among the captives in our triumphal processions. The balsam-
tree is now a subject of Rome, and pays tribute together with the race
to which it belongs. . . . It is now cultivated by the tax authorities, and
was never before more plentiful.' (Pliny (C1), *Natural History* 12:
111–12; trans. H. Rackham)

Evidence for these events has been found only in the great hall of the Wadi Palace. After the dismissal of Archelaus in AD 6 the situation becomes unclear. A Roman garrison occupied Kypros (*War* 2: 484) and, presumably, those who could afford it continued to return each winter in order to avoid the bitter cold of Jerusalem. Traces of their villas have been found among the plantations south of the palaces. These were the people who went out to hear John the Baptist (Mark 1: 5). It was in this resort that Jesus cured a blind man, encountered Zachaeus, and told a parable alluding to Archelaus (Luke 18: 35–19: 27).

Visit. The two routes to the site are indicated in Fig. 74; both are paved. The southern route starts at the police fort at the entrance to Jericho. Drive 1.5 km to the first mound beside the road (Fig. 120). Climb it for an overview of the Wadi Palace. The northern route begins in the little street between a café and the Franciscan church. Drive through the houses to the T-junction. There turn left and take the first road to the right. Just over 1 km from that point, a dirt road leads to the structures numbered 1–9 in Fig. 120.

▼ **Fig. 120.** Tulul Abu el-Alaiq. Buildings on both sides of Wadi Qilt (after Netzer). 1. Reception room; 2. Courtyard; 3. Cool room; 4. Dressing-room; 5. Warm room; 6. Hot room; 7. Courtyard; 8. Service area; 9. Dining-room.

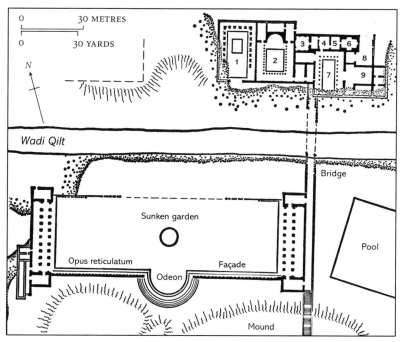

The Wadi Palace (Fig. 120)

The **artificial mound** dominating the sunken garden raised a square building containing a round hall above the mosquito-laden vegetation. The columned porches stood 2 m above each end of the **sunken garden**, and were linked by a monumental façade with alternating semicircular and rectangular niches in Roman *opus reticulatum* (square bricks laid at 45 degrees to create a net effect). Flowerpots were found on the steps of the central semicircle, which may have originally been an **odeon**. The bridge crossing the wadi must have been between this garden and the **great pool**, whose function was to cool the atmosphere. An entrance in the complex north of the wadi is in the line of the steps descending from the raised building.

The varied negative impressions of the floor tiles hint at the sumptuous decoration of the roofed **main reception hall** [1]; the shallow square holes indicate the position of the pillars; the roof beams were 15 m long. Throughout the complex there is evidence of frescos and stucco moulding. The columns of the two open **courtyards** [2 and 7] were of small segments of stone encased in plaster, producing the effect of marble

▼ **Fig. 121.** Tulul Abu el-Alaiq. The Hasmonean Palace area (after Netzer).

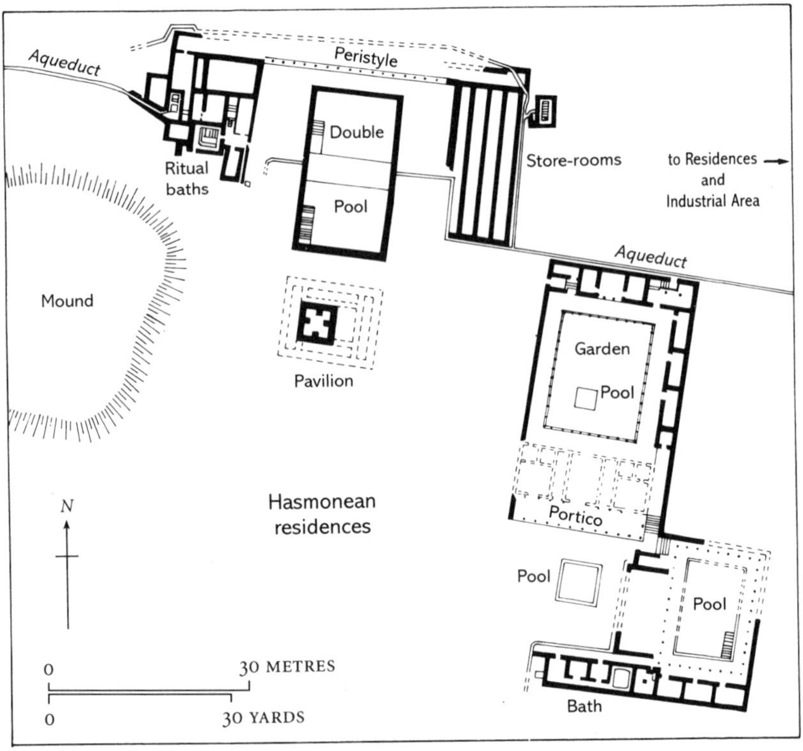

but without the expense! Inevitably, there was a **bath** with its hot room [**6**], warm room [**5**], dressing-room [**4**], and cool room [**3**], whose original floor was of plaster laid on wooden beams. The big room [**9**] may have been a **dining chamber** adjoining a service area [**8**].

The Hasmonean Palace Area (Fig. 121)

The Wadi Palace is easy to appreciate because all the structures are of one period and form a unified whole. Here all the elements exposed by the excavations were not all in existence at the same time, and a much greater imaginative effort is required to correlate the structures belonging to a given period.

The centre-piece of the Hasmonean Palace was a great **double pool**. It saw the end of Hasmonean aspirations in an episode typical of Herod's brutal career, for in it in 35 BC the king drowned the young high priest, Aristobulus III, the last Hasmonean and an increasingly dangerous rival (see box). At this period the **Hasmonean buildings** comprised an edifice of mud-brick around a central court, now beneath the mound, a number of **ritual baths** built on what had originally been a garden, a **peristyle** beyond which was a 62 × 48 m pleasure garden or orchard, a series of long store-rooms replacing an earlier garden, and a **pavilion** in the style of a Doric temple. On the slope of the wadi were two residential buildings flanked by courts with pools. The two residences were mirror images of each other. Each had a central courtyard, around which were disposed various rooms including a kitchen, a bathroom, and a double ritual bath; the remains of a square staircase pillar suggest that there were two storeys. Between the mound and the cliffs is another complex with two square swimming-pools which antedate the large double pool.

Murderous Sport

'When Herod was feasting at Jericho with Alexandra, who entertained them there, he was very pleasant with the young man [Aristobulus III]. He encouraged him to drink without restraint, and at the same time played and sported with him in an agreeable manner. Now it was hotter than usual, so they went out and stood by the fish ponds of which there were large ones near the house. In a moment of madness, Herod's friends and acquaintances decided to cool themselves by jumping in, because of the heat of the day. The king and Aristobulus at first were only spectators, but after a while Herod induced the young man to participate. As he swam those designated by Herod pretended to duck him, but in the dark of the evening held him under until he drowned. Thus was Aristobulus murdered, having lived less than eighteen years, and having held the high priesthood for only one year.' (Josephus, *Antiquities* 15: 53–6)

Herodian additions modified this ensemble considerably. He inserted stone foundation walls into the mud-brick building, whose rooms he packed with fill from the wadi, thus creating an artificial **mound** on which he erected a building (40 × 45 m), which may have served as living quarters. Raised above the surrounding vegetation, it caught every fresh breeze. Demolishing the ritual baths and store-rooms, he covered the area around the large **double pool** with earth, transforming it into a garden in which he constructed a new pavilion smaller than its predecessor. The residences on the south having been felled by the earthquake of 31 BC, he developed a series of terraces on the wadi slope.

East of the garden Herod constructed a two-level leisure area. The upper level consisted of a large **peristyle court**, whose porticoes surrounded a slightly raised garden; the earth was retained by an 80 cm-high wall between the columns. Just at this point one can see a 1 m-square plastered pool for irrigating the garden; a clay-pipe siphon system brought water from the wall to the west. The pool in the middle dates from the Hasmonean period and was covered over. The central room on the south is identified as a **dining-room**. A **portico** overlooked the lower area reached by a flight of steps. The large **swimming-pool** was surrounded by porticoes. The nearby Hasmonean pool remained in use, and the area was bounded on the south by an elaborate **Roman bath**, the stone pillars supporting the floor of the hot room are easily remarked.

Housing Area

Going east along the line of the **aqueduct** (Fig. 121) one comes to a row of seven or eight buildings (20 × 20 m). Since each one contains a twin-pool ritual bath they must have been **residences**, presumably for minor members of the royal family or senior officials. Constructed during the Hasmonean period, they remained in use under Herod. Further to the east is a much bigger house (at least 28 × 20 m) marked by an unusually large ritual bath.

Industrial Area

This extensive section of the site is located east of the housing area between 250 and 350 m from the Hasmonean Palace. At the centre is a large courtyard (20 × 25 m). It is surrounded by installations whose ultimate role is not yet clear. The complexity of the remains is due to the fact that four strata must be distinguished; the earliest is Hasmonean, the second Herodian, and the last two subsequent to the death of Herod. One might surmise that at least part of this facility served for the **exploitation of the balsam plant** 'the most precious drug there is and which grows only there' (*Antiquities* 15: 96). Pliny gives the most complete description of its cultivation, harvesting, preparation, and the tests for adulteration (see box).

Harvesting Balsam

'An incision is made in the branch with a piece of glass or a stone, or with knives made with bone. The plant strongly dislikes having its vital parts wounded with steel, and dies off at once, though it can stand having superfluous branches pruned with a steel knife. The hand of the operator making the incision has to be poised under skilful control, to avoid inflicting a wound going below the bark. The juice that oozes out of the incision is called opobalsamum. It is extremely sweet in taste, but exudes in tiny drops, the trickle being collected by means of tufts of wool in small horns and poured out of them into a new earthenware vessel to store. It is rather like thick olive-oil, and in the unfermented state it is white in colour. Later on it turns red and at the same time hardens, having previously been transparent. When Alexander the Great was campaigning in that country, it was considered a fair whole day's work in summer to fill a single shell [0.005 or 0.15 litre], and for the entire produce of a rather large garden to be 17 litres and of a smaller 2.8 litres, at a time moreover when its price was twice its weight in silver; whereas at the present day even a single tree produces a larger flow. The incision is made three times in every summer, and afterward the tree is lopped. There is a market even for the twigs. Within five years of the conquest of Judaea the actual loppings and the shoots fetched 800,000 sesterces.' (Pliny (C1), *Natural History* 12: 115–18; trans. H. Rackham)

Outlying Areas

Looking towards the cliffs from the mound in the Hasmonean Palace (Fig. 121) a double line of masonry is visible beside the electricity pylon. This is the **aqueduct** which supplied all parts of the palace with water; at the foot of the cliffs it turns right (north) and can be traced about half-way up the slope all the way to the springs near Naaran (Fig. 74). Looking in the same direction (west), a second aqueduct is also visible as a straight line at the base of the cliff; it comes from the springs in the Wadi Qilt, and sections can be seen all along the cliff path to the MONASTERY OF ST GEORGE OF KOZIBA.

For a closer look at the aqueducts continue on the paved road to the first hairpin bend at the foot of the cliff. Just beside the bend is a **round structure**, identical with that on KYPROS. In it pigeons were raised for food and as a source of fertilizer. Follow the trail into the little wadi.

From the lowest waterfall in the small wadi the Wadi Qilt aqueduct is below to the east and the Naaran aqueduct above to the west. Some 100 m to the south the **two aqueducts meet** in an arrangement strongly evocative of a modern highway interchange. This permitted water from the Wadi Qilt aqueduct to be diverted to the Herodian palace. Originally it served the Hasmonean farm to the north; it continues under the modern road and can be traced along the foot of the slope.

One of the installations of this farm, a magnificent **wine press**, can be seen just beside the road running into the electricity transformer station. There are three large treading or crushing floors, each with a channel leading to a settling basin. The three basins are in turn connected to a collecting vat with a flight of steps. This installation may have been used to process the renowned date wine which was produced for export in the Hasmonean and Herodian periods, and which graced imperial tables in Rome. The plastered channel between the collecting vat and the road belongs to the aqueduct coming from the Wadi Qilt.

If one continues along the dirt road to the north beyond the little wadi in which the transformer is located the Wadi Qilt aqueduct is again visible and with it the western wall of the 100-hectare **Hasmonean farm**. Further along the Naaran aqueduct can be seen much higher on the slope.

Cemetery

This point on the dirt road is roughly the beginning of a great cemetery stretching north along the slope for some 10 km. To date over 120 tomb-caves have been recorded. Those that have been excavated are all of the same type; a low square chamber with a bench running below the burial recesses (*kokhim*) cut into three walls. The burial customs are not as consistent. In the C2 and C1 BC the dead were interred in wooden coffins with a gable lid. From about AD 6 the bones are found collected in ossuaries.

Wadi Khareitun (Nahal Teqoa) (K19) ★

About 2 km past the entrance to the HERODION the road from Bethlehem (route 356) crosses the beginning of a deep wadi. A good path on the right-hand side remains fairly level as the wadi deepens, permitting a perfect view of three great prehistoric caves on the far side. After about 3 km the path ends at the ruins of a Byzantine monastery.

Prehistoric Caves

The first cave, **Erq el-Ahma**r, under a huge wave curve in the wadi wall, is occupied by bedouin who have walled up the entrance. Prehistoric families lived there between 100,000 and 10,000 BC. The second cave, **Umm Qalaa**, has never been excavated and projects the classical image of a prehistoric cave, a high triangular opening well above the wadi bed. Surface finds suggest occupation from about 8000 BC. The third, **Umm Qatafa**, is located just across from the ruins of the monastery and is by far the most important. The original shape has been distorted by excavation.

First occupied in the Lower Palaeolithic period (1,000,000–120,000 BC) it provides the earliest evidence of the use of fire in Palestine. Large stones were arranged in a circle around a hearth, creating the conditions which fostered the development of language. On a flat ledge below the cave is a series of rock-cut basins whose function is unclear.

When these caves were occupied the area looked very different. Europe was still in the Ice Ages, and this region enjoyed a climate similar to that of southern Europe today. The undulating hills on both sides were green and full of animals; the wadi was a river.

Byzantine Monastery

This superb example of the MONASTERIES IN THE JUDAEAN DESERT is known in Byzantine sources as the Old Laura. It was founded c.345 AD by St Chariton, who had established the first desert monastery at EN FARAH. Most, if not all of the visible ruins date from the Byzantine and/or the period immediately following the Arab conquest of 638.

The tall ruined tower was the southern corner of the fortified **triangular centre of the laura**. It provided security in case of a bedouin raid. A massive retaining wall on the south increased the space within the walls. From the tower go around the corner into the tributary wadi where there is a magnificent intact **reservoir** known to the bedouin as the 'Well of the Goats'. The elaborate crosses moulded in the plaster of the interior of the east wall betray its Byzantine origin, and perhaps imperial munificence. An aqueduct brought water from it to two **smaller reservoirs**, one rectangular (note the channel at its upper end), the other beside it circular. They are located about half-way back to the tower and on the same level.

A guaranteed supply of water was necessary for the **gardens** in which the monks grew wheat and vegetables. Retaining walls created communal gardens on both sides of the tributary wadi. The one on the north was some 3,000 m², whereas its companion on the south covered only 600 m². The private gardens associated with the thirty-five individual **cells** (some built over cisterns) account for a further 14,000 m² of cultivated land.

To reach the famous **'hanging cave'**—where Chariton went into seclusion until shortly before his death—take the lowest trail from the Well of the Goats. It is 1 km to the spring En en-Natuf and a further 500 m to the cave which owes its name to the fact that the upper portion seems to hang in the air. It is identified by two large holes side by side. From the large ground-level chamber beside the path a hole in the ceiling gives access to the chapel. Another ladder is necessary to exit from the chapel on to a dangerously narrow ledge which leads to the cell.

After Chariton the most notable occupant of the cave was Cyriac of Corinth (449–557). A monk from the age of 16 he had known Euthymius and Sabas, and was consulted here on at least two occasions (544 and 556) by Cyril of Scythopolis, the great historian of Palestinian monasticism.

An Ascetic Life

'Our father Sabas gave Aphrodisius a cell with the words, "Be content with your cell, do not visit any other cell or go outside the laura, exercise control over your tongue and belly, and you will be saved." Accepting this command and not infringing it in any respect, Aphrodisius for thirty years neither went outside the laura nor visited a cell, never possessed an earthen or copper pot, an oven or mattress, drank no wine or mixed drink, and did not possess two tunics. Instead, he slept in straw on a rush mat and patchwork cloak, and getting palms from the steward, supplied the guest-master with 90 completed baskets each month. Taking the leftovers of the cooked food, whether greens or pulses or roughage, he would put them in a single bowl and take a little from the bowl each day, and was satisfied with this.' (Cyril of Scythopolis (C6), *Life of Sabas* 44/134; trans. R. M. Price)

Yehiam* (K4) ★

Yehiam has nothing of the beauty and authority of the great castles such as BELVOIR and NIMRUD. Its rather chaotic jumble of ruins evokes MONFORT. But whereas Monfort has only a narrow field of vision down the Nahal Keziv, Yehiam is sited on a rocky ridge 405 m above sea-level and offers a sweeping view over the entire coastal plain from Mount Carmel to the border of Lebanon.

In 1283 Burchard of Mount Sion mentioned 'a castle called Judin, which belonged to the Teutonic House, but is now destroyed'. The name is preserved in the Arabic name of the valley to the south of Yehiam, Wadi Jiddin, and the approximate distances from other Crusader sites given by Burchard fit. The Teutonic Knights—founded in 1190 as a German-speaking offshoot of the Hospitallers—began to acquire property in western Galilee in 1220, and must have built the fortress sometime after that date. It would have been staffed by twenty to thirty knights under a castellan, who was also the religious superior.

Judin fell to the Mamluk sultan Baybars (1260–77) during the series of campaigns in which he swept the Crusaders from the coast. The fortifications that he tore down were restored and expanded in the middle of the C18, principally by Daher el-Omar, who in 1749 ousted the Ottoman governor of Akko and reigned supreme in Galilee until his murder in 1775. The following year the castle was in the control of his son, but he was quickly brought to heel by Ahmad al-Jazzar ('the Butcher'), whom Istanbul in 1775 charged with restoring Ottoman authority in Galilee. He made the fortress unusable.

Visit (Fig. 122). Open: Sunday–Thursday and Saturday 8 a.m.–4 p.m.; Friday to 3 p.m. From the Naharayyia–Maalot road (route 89) turn south-east on route 8833 which is signposted 'Gaton' and 'Yehiam'. Drive straight through the modern settlement. From the ticket office all the visible masonry at ground level dates from the C18. The site is less confusing if the buildings are visited in the order suggested here. Climb the steps beyond the toilets, pass the vaulted room used for functions, and enter at the ruined corner of a large building.

The **great hall** (28 × 36 m) with three rows of five tall piers was constructed by Daher el-Omar in order to extend the available space on higher ground above by supporting the large platform. Al-Jazzar made this part of the fortress useless by knocking off the two corners. At the south end of the platform is a small two-room **bath** with water tanks above a furnace on the east side. The original functions of the adjacent long narrow room and the juxtaposed vaulted area are unknown. They are now a café. The east wall of this latter structure (through which one passes to the toilets) is Crusader and probably adjoined the gate by which the knights entered their enclosure. A central pier supported the roof of the C18 **mosque**. The niche beside the window in each bay was for books.

From the eastern door of the mosque follow the path to the modern **observation point** in the south-east corner of the Ottoman enclosure. The ruins to the left belonged to the south wall of the Crusader keep area. One look down into the steep-sided Wadi Jiddin reveals that the fortress

▼ **Fig. 122.** Yehiam. The Crusader and Ottoman Castles (after Wilson).

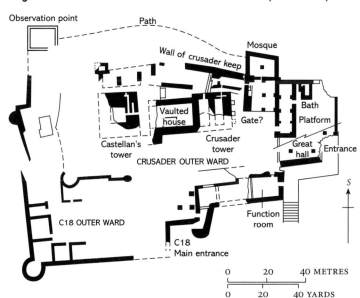

was impregnable from this side. Conditions along the east wall were very different. Two curious dog-legs were introduced to permit more effective covering fire. Only the first and a round tower are visible from the observation point.

The mass of masonry in the middle of the high ground is essentially Crusader. The two towers built by the knights are distinguished by their square plan, immensely thick walls, and the use of large stones. Smaller stones above them betray Ottoman rebuilding.

The complete collapse of the north-eastern part makes an exact plan of the **Castellan's tower** impossible, but it must have been approximately the same dimensions as its fellow, i.e. 16 × 16 m. The walls, however, are thicker (between 3 and 5 m) and there were only two storeys. The original door on the west side gives access to a square barrel-vaulted basement. The first opening to the right is a staircase to the upper levels. A grille unfortunately denies access to the second passage. It leads to a **latrine**. The dog-leg was designed to give privacy to anyone using the facility; its chute passed through the wall to the wadi outside.

The staircase makes two right-angled bends to reach the **principal room** of the tower. Debris from the collapsed roof has raised its floor by 1.3 m; hence the need for the modern steps, beside which is the entrance to another dog-legged passage to a **latrine**. The staircase to the second floor was constructed during the recent consolidation of the tower. The original must have started some 2.75 m further north. The small room (4 × 2.5 m) off the second landing may have been the **cell of the castellan**.

The view from the top of the tower offers the best chance of making visual sense of the jumble of ruins. The Teutonic knights occupied only the highest part of the site. They erected the massive tower on which we are standing, the vaulted area now supporting a C19 one-room domed house, and the second great tower just beyond it, and now inaccessible. This tower may have served as the refectory and dormitory of the soldier monks. The keep wall surrounded these buildings rather closely. The intermediate **round tower**—almost hidden by shrubbery—dates from the C18, but probably marks the north-east corner of the Crusader outer ward. The position of the C18 north-east tower highlights the extent to which Daher el-Omar expanded the Crusader fortress.

The exit from the outer ward is via the **main gate** of the C18 fortress. Two right-angle turns bring one to the door from which the problems facing any attacker become apparent. Those coming from the west were forced to circle the projecting rounded tower, and to enter an enclosed space controlled by firing-slits on three sides, before approaching the door.

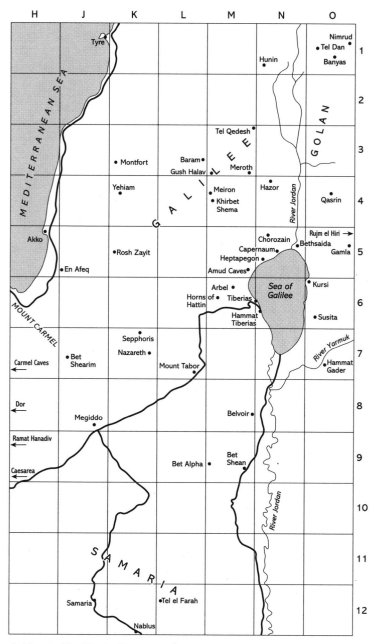

▲ **Map 2.** The North. (The side of each square is 10 km.)

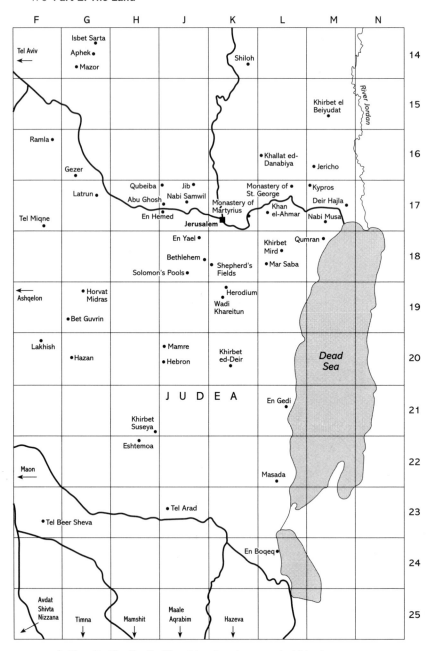

▲ **Map 3.** The South. (The side of each square is 10 km.)

Index

References in italic are to illustrations